PIMLICO

527

THE MONEY AND THE POWER

Sally Denton, an award-winning investigative reporter in both print and television, has written for the *New York Times*, the *Washington Post*, and the *Chicago Tribune*. She is the author of *The Bluegrass Conspiracy: An Inside Story of Power, Greed, Drugs, and Murder*. She lives in America with her husband, who is her coauthor, and her three sons.

Roger Morris served on the senior staff of the National Security Council under Presidents Johnson and Nixon, until he resigned over the invasion of Cambodia. He has won several national journalism prizes, including the Investigative Reporters and Editors Award for the finest investigative journalism in all media nationwide. He is the author of several books on history and politics, including *Richard Milhous Nixon: The Rise of an American Politician*, which was short-listed for both a National Book Award and a National Book Critics Circle Award.

THE MONEY AND THE POWER

The Making of Las Vegas and its Hold on America, 1947–2000

SALLY DENTON and
ROGER MORRIS

PIMLICO

Published by Pimlico 2002

2 4 6 8 10 9 7 5 3 1

First published in the United States of America by Alfred A. Knopf 2001
First published in Great Britain by Pimlico 2002

Pimlico
Random House, 20 Vauxhall Bridge Road,
London SW1V 2SA

Random House Australia (Pty) Limited
20 Alfred Street, Milsons Point, Sydney,
New South Wales 2061, Australia

Random House New Zealand Limited
18 Poland Road, Glenfield,
Auckland 10, New Zealand

Random House (Pty) Limited
Endulini, 5A Jubilee Road, Parktown 2193, South Africa

The Random House Group Limited Reg. No. 954009
www.randomhouse.co.uk

A CIP catalogue record for this book
is available from the British Library

ISBN 0-7126-6855-1

Papers used by Random House are natural,
recyclable products made from wood grown in sustainable forests.
The manufacturing processes conform to the environmental
regulations of the country of origin

Printed and bound in Great Britain by
Biddles Ltd, Guildford

For Gloria Loomis and Maya Miller,
true angels of this book

and for those of the Sweet Promised Land,
"humbled by long neglect"

There has never been another place like it for connecting the unconnectable.

—Michael Herr, "The Big Room"

Contents

Two photo inserts of 8 pages each will be found
following pages 182 and 310, respectively

The Money and the Power

Prologue

First City of the Twenty-first Century

The city is as up front as it ever was, for it can deny neither its purpose nor its psychology.

—Michael Ventura, "Literary Las Vegas"

I t is a soft, starlit night in mid-May 1998, the high desert bathed in a temperate spring darkness.

Dressed in polo shirts and tailored slacks, the men stream out of the CasaBlanca casino and spa at Mesquite, Nevada, on the Utah border, one of them telling his usual lewd jokes, the others laughing, as they clamber into the three stretch limousines idling at the entrance. The group has spent the weekend as they expected, flying to the resort in chartered jets, relaxing around the pool, enjoying massages and facials, trying their luck at the tables. Over a lengthy dinner one of their hosts secretly calls the "Last Supper," they avidly discussed how to handle the latest half-billion dollars in drug proceeds already on hand. Waiters heard them cheering and shouting excitedly behind the closed doors of the private banquet room.

To celebrate agreement on dividing the money, they plan to finish the evening with the special attraction promised for the weekend—Nevada's Chicken Ranch brothel some miles away, renowned for its beautiful women and rustic setting. Chauffeurs drive them in caravan, eight to a car, along Interstate 15 southwest of Mesquite. The highway follows the original Mormon Trail by which America first came to the Las Vegas Valley 143 years before. Further west, the road will begin to parallel another, later migrant path, old Highway 91 from California, whose approach to the city would be known to the world as the Strip. The routes are historic if little-known passageways of people, money, and power, and this midnight these men are part of an unbroken tradition.

The unmistakable glow of Las Vegas already fills the horizon when the cars suddenly slow and pull onto the shoulder surrounded by flashing lights. "Sorry, I guess I was speeding," one of the chauffeurs explains to his passengers. But they see there are too many police cruisers for a traffic stop.

U.S. Customs officers now encircle the limousines and take into custody twelve prominent Mexican bankers along with their lawyers and associates. Others riding with them are undercover American agents, posing as the suspects' partners and chauffeurs. What the Customs men call their "takedown" here in the southern Nevada desert climaxes an unprecedented covert operation, part of more than 140 arrests at six locales across three continents. "The largest, most comprehensive drug-money laundering case in the history of United States law enforcement," Treasury Secretary Robert Rubin calls it in the later public announcement in Washington. The investigation has uncovered crimes in the hundreds of billions of dollars amid international corruption at the highest levels of business and government. And now, as over the past half century, Las Vegas is a nexus of it all.

From the outset, the Mexican criminals insisted on meeting in Las Vegas for regular exchanges with their supposed American partners. The city seemed to both sides a natural, traditional setting, like a summit of governments in Geneva or winter Olympics in the Alps. "All of them felt comfortable in Vegas, knew they could talk freely there," a U.S. official says in recalling the meetings. They stayed in plush suites at Steve Wynn's famous Mirage resort, their undercover American hosts spending freely to entertain them. Casino executives up and down the Strip treated the well-known, Armani-suited traffickers and bankers as high rollers, gave them a lavish welcome of special privileges. At century's end, as always, the city is a fount of cash legal and illegal for criminals, businessmen, and politicians from every continent, though by the mid-1990s there was relatively little of the comparatively crude processing done so commonly over the decades at Nevada tables. Scarcely three years before this undercover investigation, other Customs agents in Las Vegas had come upon signs of an intricate and far-flung financial conspiracy involving Japan and Korea and the suspected investment by American and international organized crime of hundreds of millions in some of the city's most famous new casinos. But the mere five agents posted to Las Vegas, long one of the world centers of money laundering and criminal finance, were no match for a network that controlled fortunes, deployed a fleet of private jets, and marshaled an array of bankers, lawyers, politicians, and corporate giants. Like Mexican drug lords, the Strip commands its own governments and financial systems, its own sophisticated means in the world at large.

Reviewing some of the 3,000 hours of audio and video recordings of their dealings in the sting—repeating, "Play it again, play it again"—Customs agents code-named their case "Operation Casablanca," after the motion picture's supposedly familiar line, "Play it again, Sam." After one of them mentioned driving by a casino named the CasaBlanca in Mesquite, not far from Las Vegas, they decided to stage some of the climactic arrests there, an apt touch as well as a more secure setting. "In Vegas everybody's watching everybody else," a U.S. agent recalls. "The casinos knew these people were high-level Mexican Mafia, and you never know who might have noticed something and tipped them off." While the proprietors of the CasaBlanca knew nothing of the operation, Customs men posed as new owners of the casino, inviting the Mexicans for another enjoyable interlude in Nevada, a meeting to parcel more profits and a memorable visit to the Chicken Ranch. Like the gatherings at the Mirage, it was all credible enough—that American drug-money brokers would own a casino, and that the resort was a place to do business, and to celebrate. "The key to being successful undercover," one U.S. agent said afterward, "is to blend a lot of reality with the mask."

"Why wouldn't they want Vegas?" a Customs agent says of the traffickers and bankers. "They know the town. These people know their history."

It is a heritage less familiar to most Americans, though it is theirs as well Drug money founded modern Las Vegas. When World War II interrupted narcotics shipments to the United States from Asia and Europe, the gangster Meyer Lansky opened a new route south of the border. Managing the traffic in Mexico City was a formidable, if less-known, peer of Lansky in the leadership of American organized crime, Harold "Happy" Meltzer, a pivotal figure in gambling, prostitution, and union corruption as well as drugs, and later an operative for the U.S. government involved in the assassination of heads of state. At the frontier, their flamboyant partner Bugsy Siegel oversaw a brisk traffic of planes, speedboats, and cars smuggling opium into Southern California, some of it in hidden compartments in his own Chrysler Royal convertible, the polished black roadster a familiar sight to friendly Mexican and American border guards at the Tijuana crossing. The Mexican drug trade flourished throughout the 1940s with the collusion of corrupt officials in both Mexico and the United States, especially in the postwar years with the complicity of Mexico's newly organized federal intelligence service and secret police, modeled after, and in close liaison with, America's Central Intelligence Agency.

Lansky's Mexican drug profits capitalized in part Siegel's legendary Flamingo, the extravagant casino that launched the modern Las Vegas Strip in 1947. Laundered at the Flamingo and the many resorts that soon followed it along the desert highway southwest of Las Vegas was a constant outpouring of cash from narcotics and other vice throughout the United States, from Miami to Seattle, Boston to Los Angeles, Minneapolis to Dallas. That criminal money built much of the Strip after 1948. Over the rest of the twentieth century, the city's casinos thrived as centers for the laundering and investment of billions in drug profits, which had a historic impact on the course and control of American politics and business during the closing decades of the millennium. Meanwhile, the main routes of the narcotics traffic into the United States went full circle, first from Mexico, then the Middle East and France in the fifties, Southeast Asia in the later sixties, South America over the next twenty years, and then Mexico again in the nineties.

Yet proceeds from the drug traffic and other corruption were only one of many sources of the money that made for a Las Vegas so largely operated by and for organized crime. American capitalism was also a founding if silent partner in financing the Strip. In 1946, Phoenix and Salt Lake City banks quietly joined Lansky and his partners to back the Flamingo. By 1954, international drug money, national vice profits, and the incessant skim of casino earnings all began to mingle in organized crime's deepening pool of capital—often interchangeably through the same intermediaries—with the furtive investments of prominent American banks, the Mormon Church, union pension funds, an eminent Wall Street brokerage, the Princeton University endowment, a leading defense and aerospace contractor, a major construction combine, an owner of the New York Yankees, a Manhattan real estate consortium, a respected Texas insurance company, a Caribbean bank run covertly by the CIA, and other, similarly representative and powerful interests.

The national underwriting of Las Vegas casinos from the 1950s capitalized much of American corruption nationwide in the second half of the century. The added finance enabled criminal forces and their collaborators in business to magnify their investment and control far beyond the Strip or holdings elsewhere to other major sectors of the national economy, particularly along the booming southern tier of the postwar United States. They expanded into entertainment, public service contracting, hotels, food and restaurant chains, agribusiness, manufacturing, electronics, shopping malls, real estate development, and eventually into banking, insurance, securities, and other fields. This burgeoning wealth and influence enlarged their hold over still wider and deeper reaches of American politics and governance. By the 1990s, the undercover operation's Mexican guests at the Mirage—crime lords in partnership with prominent financiers, businessmen, and politicians—were part of a venerable tradition on *both* sides of the border. As the Customs agent said: "These people know their history."

There is no place like it. It is literally a beacon of civilization. Peering from space at their cloud-speckled blue and blood-rust planet, astronauts make out the lights of Las Vegas before anything else, a first sign of life on earth. The sighting is apt. The city's luminance draws a world. More than 50 million people journey to it every year. Only Mecca inspires as many pilgrims.

Las Vegas knows its visitors, caters to them. Though strangers, they are familiar. Nearly half of America has been there, more than to any other locale in the nation. Most of the country recognizes the remarkable silhouette of the city. From its suburban approaches it might seem like any other squat, sprawling western metropolis of subdivisions and freeways. A cluster of taller buildings marks the older downtown. But then suddenly, not far to the southwest, there rises a great corridor of massive structures, marching across the valley as if in phalanx. It is a skyline like no other, not for offices or apartments but for the visitors themselves. The glow visible from space ignites here, in the city's colossal hotels, among them the ten largest in the nation. There are more guestrooms in Las Vegas than anywhere else in America, twice as many as in New York, Chicago, or Los Angeles—and plans for more.

To the delight of the throngs, the huge resorts take as their themes some of the most popular tourist attractions around the world. Off a sham Piazza San Marco, gondolas glide on simulated Venetian canals carved onto the face of the Great American Desert. Not far away rise grand imitations: an Eiffel Tower, a Roman palace, a medieval castle, an Empire State Building, a volcano erupting on cue in growling flame. Upward from a dark glass pyramid beams a searchlight of 40 billion candlepower, said to be the brightest ray in the solar system, save for the sun or a nuclear blast. At a massive copy of a Belle Epoque grand hotel in the Alps, its eight-acre lake sunk in a lot once dotted with scrub and cactus, two hundred gardeners tend a solarium with thousands of flowers changed several times a year. Nearby, the publicly subsidized private collection of the casino's founder comprises one of the more impressive galleries in North America, featuring works by Renoir, Van Gogh,

Cézanne, Picasso, and de Kooning, masterpieces together worth hundreds of millions of dollars.

Still, for all the recent attractions and refinements, the essence of the city remains its original commerce, and the might of a single business whose customers spend six times more than is spent on all other spectator sports and entertainment combined in the United States. With 30 to 50 percent profits, double the average of even the most successful business, the global gambling empire of Las Vegas is a force like few others in the history of human affairs. By its contributions to politicians, its tax revenue to reliant public treasuries, its hold over collateral enterprise, and not least its millions spent for ceaseless lobbying that leaves nothing to chance, the industry gains and wields unique influence throughout the nation and world.

Its extraordinary and dominant business has also made Las Vegas the fastest-growing metropolitan area in the United States, its population expected to double over the next decade, another million residents in a few years. Fifteen hundred people migrate to the city each week. Tracts of their pale, tile-roofed houses flow over the valley and up the sloping foothills of the bare, jagged mountains at its edge. Their children need a new school every month. Their cars choke hundreds of miles of new roads and soil a once crystalline blue desert sky with a grimy pall. They are part of a pounding, audacious, unrelenting growth not seen in most of America since the postwar boom a half century ago, though then, too, this uncontainable city was leading the nation in the pace of its rise. Once only a callow town where the young or rootless came to make their way, Las Vegas is now also a place where the old come to live out their days, sanctuary as well as frontier. Once a secluded watering hole, haven of horse thieves, and lonesome stop on a rail line across a wasteland, the valley now is filling with humanity.

The metropolis seems insatiable. More resorts rise. New lights blaze. Old wonders reincarnate. Customers keep coming. Money and power accumulate. Celebrated for its prosperity and matchless appeal, the city is seen as a panacea for much of the rest of the country, a prime Wall Street investment, a shrine to which the most famous politicians of both governing parties make their own obligatory pilgrimage for anointing and finance, a realization of the American dream. "Las Vegas now melds fun, work, and wealth, showing a path toward the brightest vistas of the post-industrial world," two scholars wrote in 1999. "It is the first city of the twenty-first century."

None of it was here only decades ago. The cities whose classics it copies—Cairo, Rome, Paris, Venice, New York—measure provenance in centuries. Not this place. Sixty years ago, Las Vegas was a gritty, wind-whipped crossroads of faded whorehouses and honky-tonks with stuttering neon. If it vanished tomorrow—the millions of visitors and residents, the huge structures, even the astronomically bright lights—what might posterity make of the traces? It would be a ruin of what had been at once so artificial and so authentic, mimicking other monuments while a memorial to itself.

It is a city in the middle of nowhere that is the world's most popular destination. It is a fount of enormous wealth that produces nothing. Far from traditional centers of commerce, it is a model for much of the nation's economy. It is a provincial outpost become an arbiter of national power. Once thought the society's most aberrant city, it is not just newly respectable but proves to have been an archetype all along.

What made Las Vegas so unique, so derivative, in the end so exemplary? What was its true purpose and context, this facade of fantasy for harsh fact, a dominion of unyielding reality fed by indomitable illusion?

As nowhere else, people come to Las Vegas seeking something with a self-consciousness and intensity, if not desperation, that has always set the city apart—diversion, entertainment, money, sex, escape, deliverance, another chance, a last chance, another life for a few hours, days, forever. As nowhere else, they come in search of what they and their world might yet be. In one way or another, they come for power. More than ever, the city attracts its customers from among the nation's increasing numbers of near-poor and elderly, America's dismal if discreetly unnamed proletariat of marginal jobs and paltry pensions. They bring with them, like carry-on baggage—offerings for an altar—numberless small dramas. Their stories make Las Vegas a literary or cinematic backdrop for the climax of tales and destinies plotted elsewhere, though rarely a subject in itself. For most, this is a place of acceptance and of faith, exempt from quibbling and from banality. If America is still about wanting and believing despite the odds, as so many of its chroniclers portray, fabulous Las Vegas is about both too, what social critic Robert Goodman calls the "pathology of hope."

Not that the city lacks either the dramatic or the banal. As social phenomenon it enthralls designers, academics, journalists. They ponder the subtle order of its riotous architectural allure, the pumped-in oxygen ambiance of its clanging, cavernous casinos that never close, the lengths and expense to which it will go to create its world unashamedly *manqué*—"catering cynically to whatever the tourist want[s]," writes historian John Findlay, "keeping up the appearance of casual and harmless fun at all costs." Decade after decade, reporters sketch portraits of an ever-changing scene ever extraordinary, predictably seductive and repellent. Some think it vulgar, others "deliciously deranged," as *New York Times* columnist Maureen Dowd found it in the last summer of the twentieth century. In any case there seems no quarreling with success, the social significance in the sheer presence of 50 million pilgrims and the billions they spend. "An overpowering cultural arti-fact . . . ," urban historian Mike Davis calls the city, "the brightest star in the neon firmament of post-modernism."

A few, like Davis, notice too that the spectacular lights of the Strip wash back here and there on close-by, incongruous blight, America's most famous and extravagant street bordered by barren lots or blocks of near–skid row, dreary sockets of another essence beyond the gleam and expansion of the perennial boomtown. Seen from behind, the palatial replicas and resorts are a kind of Potemkin village, screening from view an inner squalor of local politics where wealth and power are in the hands of only a few, a parody of rich and poor. Compared to what it takes, the ruling industry gives back crumbs. Its rule is purchased, not won, though no less complete for the usurpation. It evades all but a minor fraction of taxes, recompense that might create public assets in Nevada to match the mountains of private profit. Instead, as from the beginning, it plunders the city, state, and nation, poisoning air, disfiguring land, stealing water, ransoming the future for rav-enous gain seized by fix and favor. It masks only thinly its habitual racism and sexism. If its prosperity is legend, many of its jobs are menial, and its coveted payroll is mocked by enormous inequity, the gap between millions taken by owners and the few thousand in shiftwork subsistence paid most workers.

Not surprisingly, in a city that exists to take money, the utter force of profit is the commanding, ultimately coercive order of business and society, and of politics and government, where the corruption of institutions at every level is all but functionally complete. Las Vegas, America's most public place, has no public in the sense of authentic democracy—no genuine polit-ical opposition, no candid history, no available recourse. The effect is a com-munity suborned. Even churches and charities are complicit, a tradition of relatively petty philanthropy exalting the most naked predator. Apart from the more presentable but powerless figureheads extolled in ritual pioneer myths, the city's real heroes, repeatedly voted "man of the year" by its hearty clubs, worshipped by emulation, obedience, and enrichment, have been overwhelmingly thugs and corrupters, often murderers, and more lately their legatees in spirit if not body—finely tailored, densely coiffed corporate touts. They have in common no genius save grasping, and their stature in a society that has long honored greed as preeminent civic virtue. Figures of conscience here are lonely—over a half century, only a tiny band of uncompromised reporters, officials, and labor leaders. The city absorbs, dismisses, drowns out dissent; if necessary, extinguishes it. Critics are spoilers for not letting Las Vegas define itself, and thus for threatening everyone's money. The city's rulers brand them as fanatics or naïfs shocked at its fetching frontier liberties, ignorant of its native integrity, not to say innocence, amid such forthright worldliness. Meanwhile, the regime runs nicely, politics confined to minor differences of personality or method on the margins of power. Management and labor are united to protect the gambling industry lest owners lose privilege and workers be made to pay the price. The media are often mouthpieces for profiteering. Law enforcement has become the less prosperous twin of private security. Elected officials stand as the open beneficiaries if not business partners of special interests. The corruption is so profound, so inherent in the social and economic order, that most citizens are cynically accepting of it or simply oblivious. And in a good deal of that too, some observe, Las Vegas is America's first city of the twenty-first century.

Yet there is always more here than the glorification of mass taste and tastelessness, aspiration, delusion, despair, a glossy if coarse mercenary despotism. In much written about Las Vegas, there is a deceptive sense of putting the crass, tawdry, *déclassé* city in its place, not taking it so seriously after all—a gamble the house always wins. Whatever else, this is an utterly, unsparingly serious place. And here, ironically, in the planet's most brightly lit display, visible so far away, the greatest wonder is mostly unseen. Of the questing hordes, almost no one comes for what may be Las Vegas's most important winning—the truth about its past and the meaning of its present. The city, a spectacle of lights, has always depended on darkness.

This book is an account of the rise of Las Vegas, and its significance today, and what that incomparable yet emblematic place reveals about the reality of America over the last half of the twentieth century.

Beginning as a remote oasis of legal vice, a criminal city-state grew as a colony, then clearinghouse, then international center of a pervasive and swelling American corruption. By the late 1980s, the city's original regime of organized crime had evolved and transfigured itself, at least in part, into a more refined and outwardly legitimate corporate oligarchy, though governing with largely the same purpose and oppressions, and even more open and blatant collusion with local, state, and national government. Its longtime tyranny over the people of Nevada spread across the nation with the expansion of legalized gambling to forty-seven other states as well as Native American reservations. Cast in the oligarchs' more respectable image, the city continues to flourish amid, and as a result of, rampant drug trafficking, gunrunning, money laundering, political corruption, and illicit national intelligence operations by the United States and other countries—those entangled, often indivisible forces epitomized in 1998–99 by the Casablanca episode, and integral to Las Vegas for fifty years.

Headquarters of a trillion-dollar industry commanding unparalleled influence, the end-of-century city is more than ever the wellspring of a corrupt, corrupting political economy, if not the seat of some postmodern Syndicate itself. In an America so widely dominated by corporate and individual wealth, the Strip's once disreputable Mob ethic of exploitation and greed has become in large measure a national ethic. In a new millennium, radiant Las Vegas stands at the zenith of its power, in many ways an unacknowledged shadow capital.

That emergence traces the often secret annals not only of a city in the desert but of the nation whose innermost politics it sometimes silhouettes so uniquely, so starkly. In his small masterwork *Hidden History*, the eminent scholar and Librarian of Congress Daniel Boorstin warned his countrymen about what they had not yet confronted about the forces shaping America. "How much still remains to be discovered about our past," he wrote in 1988, "and how uncertain is our grip on the future." Las Vegas and its relation to the nation at large is a vivid example of the history Boorstin found buried by common ignorance or preference, as well as by the intent of perpetrators.

The city has been the quintessential crossroads and end result of the now furtive, now open collusion of government, business, and criminal commerce that has become—on so much unpalatable but undeniable evidence—a governing force in the American system. In that, of course, Las Vegas was never the exception it seemed. Ever brazen, the city was simply less covert than the country it mirrored too well. For all its apparent uniqueness, all the hype, the garish town in the southern Nevada desert has always been more representative of America than either wants to admit. It was founded and grew as an open reflection of what the rest of the nation had long been doing in the shadows, and would continue to do. To chart its rise is far less a walk on the dark and aberrant side of American life than a way to see the larger history of the nation more completely, and without illusion. To look closely at this remarkable place—at those who built it, at its unchecked, steadily mounting influence, at the frequently decisive and concealed role it plays in national and international events—is to see more clearly what has happened to America over the last half century, and why.

The story that unfolds here is no civic history in a conventional sense, nor a study of gambling and America's historic penchant for it, nor another painting of the cultural colors of Las Vegas entertainment and the city's end-less cast of remarkable characters on and off stage. With debts to that already rich literature, this book sets the city in a different perspective, as a Rosetta stone for deciphering significant but still entombed or encoded chapters of our national past. Read through the rise of Las Vegas, the seemingly familiar story of organized crime and corruption in America takes on new implica-tions. The compromising of politics and government is earlier, wider, more decisive, and more often the play of rival factions beyond the visible parties and personalities, the penetration of business and finance deeper and more permanent, the dominance of society more insidious and enduring. In the tradition of the underlying economic and political culture glimpsed by Operation Casablanca, the vast money from drug trafficking in the last half of the century and beyond plays an even larger role in politics and the national economy than most of the country has ever imagined. Recent American history seen in terms of the Strip becomes at once plainer yet subtler, less mysterious though often more ominous, than from any other perspective.

The record is richly documented. Out of Prohibition emerged a loosely bound collection of criminal factions taking political and economic power not only in the larger metropolitan areas but also in smaller cities and towns across the nation. With Repeal, some in this world invested their consider-able fortunes in whole or in part in legitimate businesses or industries such as entertainment, liquor, construction, and transportation, fields where they may already have had a role as enforcers or extortionists for both sides in the bitter, poisonous struggle between management and labor, and where their money and methods were widely welcome, especially during the Depression. Most also continued to build their holdings in the most lucrative national vices—gambling and drugs. Unchecked and even unheeded by law enforce-ment, increasingly protected by political patrons and compromised officials at all levels, these elements expanded in the thirties beyond their original bases. Despite inherent rivalries, deep-seated clan distrust, and a shared sav-agery, they formed a more integrated network of expedient partnerships and alliances, apportioning profits, and control, throughout the nation.

During World War II, they prospered still more from black markets and unprecedented if traditional war profiteering, further widening their cor-ruption of elected officials. At the same moment, in covert action while the war was being fought, and then in rivalry with the Soviet Union afterward, increasingly powerful intelligence agencies of the U.S. government came to rely upon, and joined forces with, leaders of this criminal combine. The alliance was not novel. Federal law enforcement agencies, particularly the

Federal Bureau of Narcotics, had already grown increasingly reliant on organized crime figures as informers and double agents even before Pearl Harbor. The collaboration commonly gave the criminals de facto immunity from government prosecution in return for informing or, especially, for aid in suppressing leftists at home and abroad, and in supporting American corporate interests and friendly foreign regimes. By a similar rationale, U.S. authorities allied themselves with organized crime abroad—most notably the Italian Mafia, but criminal elements as well in Latin America, the Philippines, and elsewhere—forming coalitions that curled back over the ensuing decades to further the spectral alliances in the Western Hemisphere. In the same era, following much the same pattern of their own practices at home and abroad in the twenties and thirties, American corporations operating overseas after the war, particularly in Latin America, enlisted some of the same figures and forces, entered the same collusion. It comprised a triad of the nation's most powerful institutions.

By 1947, though nomenclature was becoming part of the politics of bureaucratic self-protection and deception that would suffuse the larger system, law enforcement reports began to identify the American criminal network by what would become over the decades a series of names—Top Hoodlums, the Mafia, organized crime, La Cosa Nostra, and, finally, the Syndicate, the most accurate reflection of the truly multiethnic, integrated national scope of the phenomenon. Under any of its names, the Syndicate by the later forties was an authentic empire. Its several branches and baronies commanded millions of dollars from a substratum economy of vice deeply enmeshed with both legitimate business and the political world, altogether one of the largest segments of the economy and rapidly to become the nation's most formidable source of political patronage. With the opening of the Flamingo in 1947 and the Desert Inn two years later, that power began to concentrate in Las Vegas, where it has become historic.

At midcentury there were voices in national politics warning about the extent and danger of this evolution in American life, among them Tennessee senator Estes Kefauver and Attorney General Robert Kennedy. What happened to those fleeting challenges and why—pivotal points in the larger hidden history—is told in the pages that follow. By the end of the sixties, the emergent Las Vegas was uncontested. The decades beyond chart the further rise of the city, through the national political crises and drug pandemic of the seventies, the succession to power of the corporate regime in both Las Vegas and Washington in the eighties, and the triumph of the Strip ethic full-blown in both city and nation in the nineties.

Other forces obviously shaped America as well over these years. The last half of the century is also the story, among much else, of the Cold War, of the freedoms and tyrannies of technology, of clashes of culture, class, gender, and race, of the country's dazzling wealth haunted by widening disparities of income, influence, security, and power. But the history of seemingly peripheral Las Vegas casts new light on all that and more, at least beginning to suggest for future historians why America's course on those powerful currents so perpetuated and enlarged the values of the Strip. If the city has become a shadow capital at the beginning of a new millennium, that is less because it somehow conquered the rest of the nation than that the nation came round more openly to what it represented, and ignored or denied its own emerging reality, much as it remained blind to the larger meaning of Las Vegas.

Part One

The Juice

Vegas was never a town to begrudge a man his past.

—Alan Richman, "Lost Vegas"

They call it juice. "He's got juice," they say. "He's a juice peddler. A juice merchant. He's juiced in."

It is more than power or influence, money or social standing, though it is all these. Beyond cash and chips, juice is the real currency of Las Vegas. It is a way of life, a culture. Juice is how things work, what it takes to succeed, or sometimes just to survive. But the term also has an even more exclusive meaning—the name for a handful of figures whose power and example are decisive in the course of the city. In the ultimate sense, they *are* the juice.

Every town claims its founders—pioneers and patriarchs, rogues and romantics. Las Vegas memorializes its conventional ancestry as much as any city, and perhaps more than most, always conscious of respectability, of the need to show that behind its gaudy reputation the town is a real community of real people. In 1999, the *Las Vegas Review-Journal* with some fanfare published profiles of what the paper called "The First One Hundred," predictable doctors, lawyers, judges, politicians, businessmen, entertainers, and bankers, along with a colorful if minimum number of wealthy casino owners and three acknowledged gangsters, suitably deceased. But the city has never admitted its authentic paternity, the reality of the men that made it and the larger forces behind them, though Las Vegas today reflects more than ever the character and legacy of its true fathers.

The meaning of the place begins with some of these figures. In a society that has never given power to women, they are, of course, all men. They are very different, though similar in telling ways. Some live in Las Vegas, others only visit it. Some are partners or collaborators, others archenemies. They are all simple yet complex, vivid portraits from disparate corners of America over the early years of the century. In any case, the lives of these emblematic figures are entwined. Each is symbolic in what the city, and the nation, have become. They are not city fathers or founders in a sense Las Vegas would ever officially recognize, at least not in their candid biographies as apart from the cosmetic booster myths, the civic kitsch. There are obviously others of historic importance as well. But these men begin to tell the essence of the story: the most significant organized crime figure in American history, who makes Las Vegas what it was and is; an illiterate thug epitomizing the backroom oppression that is always the city's ethos; a legendary, epic-scale local politician embodying the tragedy of Nevada; a charming psychopath whose portfolio of drug money, bank loans, and civic pride pioneers the most famous street in the world; a publicist signifying the sale as well as surrender of the city's soul; an ambitious southern senator whose glimpse of Las Vegas and of a shrouded America, and whose reckoning as a result, are prophetic of the city and nation to come.

If, as the Roman maxim put it, character is the arbiter of everyone's fortune, the character of these men is very much the biography, the fate, of the city. Their lives illuminate a history seemingly familiar yet largely hidden, connecting the unconnectable.

1. Meyer Lansky

The Racketeer as Chairman of the Board

He was born Maier Suchowljansky in 1902 at Grodno, in a
Poland possessed by Tsarist Russia. As a child he envisioned
the United States as a place of angels, "somewhat like heaven," he would say
much later. When he was ten, his family fled the pogroms directed at Jews for
the land of his dreams. In the Grand Street tenements of the Lower East Side
of Manhattan he found not angels but what he called his "overpowering
memory"—poverty, and still more savage prejudice.

In school, where he excelled, his name was Americanized. Meyer Lansky
was a slight child, smaller than his peers. But he soon acquired a reputation
as a fierce, courageous fighter. One day, as he walked home with a dish of
food for his family, he was stopped by a gang of older Irish toughs whose
leader wielded a knife and ordered him to take down his pants to show if he
was circumcised. Suddenly, the little boy lunged at his tormentor, shattering
the plate into a weapon, then nearly killing the bigger boy with the jagged
china, though he was almost beaten to death himself by the rest of the gang
before the fight was broken up. Eventually, he would become renowned for
his intelligence rather than his physical strength. Yet no one who knew him
ever doubted that beneath the calm cunning was a reserve of brutality.

He left school after the eighth grade, to find in the streets and back alleys
of New York his philosophy, his view of America, ultimately his vocation. He
lived in a world dominated by pimps and prostitutes, protection and extor-

tion, alcohol and narcotics, legitimate businesses as fronts, corrupt police, and ultimately, always, the rich and powerful who owned it all but kept their distance. There was gambling everywhere, fed by the lure of easy money in a country where the prospects of so many, despite the promise, remained bleak and uncertain.

A gifted mathematician with an intuitive sense of numbers, he was naturally drawn to craps games. He was able to calculate the odds in his head. Lore would have it that he lost only once before he drew an indelible lesson about gambling and life. "There's no such thing as a lucky gambler, there are just the winners and losers. The winners are those who control the game . . . all the rest are suckers," he would say. "The only man who wins is the boss." He decided that he would be the boss. He adopted another, grander axiom as well: that crime and corruption were no mere by-products of the economics and politics of his adopted country, but rather a cornerstone. That understanding, too, tilted the odds in his favor.

By 1918, at the close of World War I, Lansky, sixteen, already commanded his own gang. His main cohort was the most charming and wildly violent of his childhood friends, another son of immigrants, Benjamin Siegel, called "Bugsy"—though not to his face—for being "crazy as a bedbug." Specializing in murder and kidnapping, the Bugs and Meyer Mob, as they came to be known, provided their services to the masters of New York vice and crime, and were soon notorious throughout the city as "the most efficient arm in the business." Like other criminals then and later, and with epic consequences in the corruption of both labor and corporate management, they also hired out their thuggery first to companies, and then to unions—most decisively the Longshoremen and Teamsters—in the bloody war between capitalists and workers. Some employers "gave their hoodlums carte blanche," as one account put it, which they took with "such enthusiasm that many union organizers were murdered or crippled for life." Lansky and Siegel would be partners and close, even affectionate friends for more than a quarter century, and in the end Lansky would have "no choice," as one journalist quoted him, but to join in ordering Bugsy's murder.

At a bar mitzvah, Lansky met Arnold Rothstein, the flamboyant gambler involved in fixing the 1919 World Series, and he soon became Rothstein's protégé. During Prohibition they made a fortune in bootlegging while dealing in heroin as well. Their collaborators, competitors, and customers in the criminal traffic, as Lansky later reminisced, were "the most important people in the country." On a rainy night in 1927 in southern New England, a gang working for Lansky hijacked with wanton violence a convoy of Irish whiskey being smuggled by one of their rival bootleggers, an ambitious Boston businessman named Joseph P. Kennedy. The theft cost Kennedy "a fortune," one of the hijackers recalled, as well as the lives of eleven of his own men, whose widows and relatives then pestered or blackmailed a seething Kennedy for compensation.

Ruthless with enemies, Lansky was careful, even punctilious, with his partners and allies. One of his closest and most pivotal associates was yet another boyhood acquaintance and fellow bootlegger, an astute, pock-marked Sicilian named Charles "Lucky" Luciano. Their rapport baffled those who witnessed it, bridging as it did bitter old divisions between Italians and Jews. "They were more than brothers, they were like lovers," thought Bugsy Siegel. "They would just look at each other and you would know that a few minutes later one of them would say what the other was thinking."

Lansky's share of the enormous criminal wealth and influence to come out of Prohibition in the early thirties would be deployed shrewdly. He branched out into prostitution, narcotics, and other vice and corruption nationwide. But his hallmark was always gambling. "Carpet joints," as the ubiquitous illegal casinos of the era were called, run by his profit-sharing partners—proconsuls like the English killer Owney Madden, who controlled organized crime's provincial capital of Hot Springs, Arkansas—were discreetly tucked away and protected by bribed officials in dozens of towns and cities all over the United States. Still, Lansky's American roadhouses were almost trivial compared to the lavish casinos he would build in Cuba in league with a dictatorial regime.

For Luciano and other gangsters, Lansky was the preeminent investment banker and broker, a classic manager and financier of a growing multiethnic confederation of legal and illegal enterprises throughout the nation. He organized crime along corporate hierarchical lines, delineated authority and responsibility, holdings and subsidiaries, and, most important, meticulously distributed shares of profits and proceeds, bonuses and perquisites. There would always be separate and distinct provinces of what came to be called most accurately the Syndicate—feudal baronies defined by ethnic group, specialty, assets, or geography, that ruled their own territorial bases and colonies, coexisting warily with the others, distrusting, jockeying, waiting, always conscious of power. It was part of Lansky's clarity of vision to see how they might be arrayed to mutual advantage despite their unsurrendered sovereignty and mutual suspicion. He recognized how much the country—in the grip of Wall Street financial houses and powerful local banks, industrial giants in steel, automobiles, mining, and manufacturing, the growing power of labor unions, the entrenched political machines from rural courthouses to city halls of the largest urban centers—was already ruled by the interaction of de facto gangs in business and politics, as in crime. A faction unto himself, after all, he would never subdue or eliminate the boundaries and barons. Over the rest of the century their domains would only grow. In business, he preferred to own men more than property, especially public officials whose complicity was essential. He did not, like most of his associates, merely bribe politicians or policemen, but worked a more subtle, lasting venality, bringing them in as partners.

Americanizing corruption as never before, Lansky extended it into a truly national network and ethic of government and business, a shadow system. His Syndicate came to bribe or otherwise compromise, and thus to possess, their own politicians, to corrupt and control their own labor unions and companies, to hire their own intelligence services and lawyers, to influence banks with their massive deposits. But it was Lansky who gave their expedient alliance a historic cohesion, wealth, and power. Already by the thirties their shared apportioned profits were in the tens of millions of dollars, equivalent to the nation's largest industries.

The wiry adolescent Lansky had grown into a small, unprepossessing man. He was barely five feet four inches tall, weighing less than 140 pounds. By his late thirties, he was the father of three in a colorless and arranged first marriage. With a pleasant open face, limpid brown eyes, and neatly combed dark hair, he resembled nothing so much as the earnest accountant or banker that in a sense he had become. Save for white-on-white silk shirts and the largest collection of bow ties in the country, he exhibited none of the coarse ostentation or pretensions of his colleagues. His private life was discreetly modest. At home he spent most of his time in a wood-paneled den and library lined with popular encyclopedias. Able to recite from memory the Gettysburg Address and long passages from *The Merchant of Venice,* he was an avid reader, a regular subscriber to the Book-of-the-Month Club, ever conscious of his lack of formal education. His personal hero, he confided to a few friends, was another figure of similar physical size and historic imprint, Napoleon Bonaparte.

Above all, he was a *political* man. Like most denizens of his world, he was insistently patriotic, and generally conservative if not reactionary in the usual political terms, with an understandable distaste even for reformers, let alone social revolutionaries—though he always seemed to understand, long before more educated men, that ideology and conviction in American politics commonly have a price. Like his successors over the rest of the twentieth century who learned the lesson well, he would be an inveterate contributor to Democratic politicians at all levels. Lansky paid "handsomely"—legal scholar and sociologist William Chambliss recorded his secret cash contributions—into the presidential campaigns of Al Smith in 1928, Franklin Roosevelt in 1932, Harry Truman in 1948, Lyndon Johnson in 1960 and 1964, and Hubert Humphrey in 1968, as well as the races of senators, congressmen, governors, mayors, and councilmen. At a Democratic National Convention in the 1930s he met the amply corrupt Louisiana senator Huey Long, whose partnership opened the South to the alliance, and for whom Lansky opened what would be one of the first foreign bank accounts for corrupt American politicians. Covering his bets, he also passed cash through an intermediary to the 1944 Republican presidential campaign of onetime New York "gangbuster" Thomas Dewey, and backed a few GOP candidates over the years, though generally preferring, and thus flourishing under, Democrats. Beneath the surface, Lansky knew, Dewey was a classic example of the American prosecutor and politician who exploited the public fear of criminals but in the end did remarkably little about crime, a prosecutor who convicted a few big names while imprisoning mostly street-level small fry, leaving the Syndicate and the system that fed it undiminished. "You can't help liking Mr. Dewey," a shrewd New York socialite would say of the man in an epigram that captured his real record as well, "until you get to know him."

Lansky's practical politics were plain. Applying the wisdom acquired on the Lower East Side and in the national underworld he came to dominate, he was unyielding and merciless with those who challenged or cheated him. But he would be very different from many of his predecessors and successors, in legitimate business as in crime, who overreached. Monopolistic greed, he believed, led to blood or headlines, rupturing society's usual apathy, arousing if only for a moment a spasm of reform that was bad for everyone's profits. He welcomed his competitors—the more corruption the better; the more people compromised, the more collusion, acceptance, and resignation, the less danger of change. Nowhere was this strategy more decisive than in his convoluted relations with his supposed enemy but often de facto ally, the government of the United States.

Those closest to Lansky would claim that he accomplished the supreme blackmail in the thirties, obtaining photographs of homosexual acts by J. Edgar Hoover, the increasingly powerful and celebrated director of the Federal Bureau of Investigation. The pictures were said to hold at bay this most formidable of potential adversaries. But the racketeer and the bureaucrat also had mutual friends, backers, and associates, among them prominent businessmen like Lewis Rosenstiel of Schenley Industries or developer Del Webb, or groups, like the American Jewish League Against Communism, that shared the right-wing politics the gangster and G-man had in common. Whether by crude blackmail or the more subtle influence of their common circle, over the decades Lansky enjoyed almost singular immunity from serious FBI pursuit; "Lansky and the Bureau chief in a symbiotic relationship, each protecting the other," University of California scholar Peter Dale Scott would write of the suborning.

But sexual compromising, mutual friendships, or ideology only began the collusion. In 1937, Lansky arranged for the FBI and the Federal Bureau of Narcotics (FBN) to make the highly publicized arrest of one of his associates, drug trafficker Louis "Lepke" Buchalter. The betrayal at once removed a Lansky rival, gratified Hoover and FBN director Harry Anslinger in their mutual obsession with popular image, and further compromised federal law enforcement, which was growing ever more dependent on informers and double agents for its successes.

Then, at the outset of World War II, U.S. Naval Intelligence and the nation's new espionage agency, the Office of Strategic Services (OSS), enlisted Lansky and the Syndicate in a historic collaboration, the top-secret Operation Underworld, in which government agents employed mobsters and their labor goons in a campaign of coercion and bribery ostensibly to prevent sabotage and quell uncontrolled leftist unions on New York docks. The "dirty little secret of Operation Underworld," as a former White House official put it, "was that the United States Government *needed* Meyer Lansky and organized crime to force an industrial peace and a policing of sabotage on the wharves and in the warehouses. The government turned to him because hiring thugs was what government and business had been doing for a long time to control workers, and because it could conceive little other choice in the system at hand."

Working conditions on the docks, as in much of the economy, remained harsh, and the struggle between management and labor violent and unpredictable. Industrial amity was one of the many myths of World War II. The early 1940s would see more than 14,000 strikes involving nearly 7 million workers nationwide, far more than any comparable period in the country's history. The secret little war on the waterfront was a major step beyond the Buchalter betrayal, which had redounded to the advantage of both criminals and bureaucrats, and was another mark of the self-reinforcing, almost complementary accommodation and exploitation emerging so widely out of the nineteen-twenties and -thirties. Beyond public relations or displays like Hoover's or Dewey's, federal and state law enforcement at this time remained widely inept, if not corrupt.

For Washington, it was only the start of what would be a growing covert alliance with organized crime, beginning during the war and becoming all but institutionalized afterward, a "continuing mode of operation," as one scholar called it later, that included the sharing and protection of hundreds of double agents, and the Syndicate's complicity in the invasion of Sicily. Many of the American troops landing on the island in 1943 carried small handkerchiefs specially embroidered with the initial "L" to identify them with Lucky Luciano; the American invasion restored the Mafia to its pre-Fascist-era power and left it the de facto government of much of Italy. After the war there was U.S. government enlistment of the Mafia in the suppression and even murder of leftists in postwar France, Italy, and elsewhere, not unlike what they had done on the banks of the Hudson and East rivers. As it was, Lansky's successful intervention on the New York waterfront "secured" the port, and also, inevitably, left it ruled by shipping combines and corrupt, Syndicate-controlled labor, and a government entwined with both. Through it all Lansky acquired even more official collaborators, more implicit immunity.

Not long afterward, in 1944, at the behest of FDR, Naval Intelligence agents implored Lansky to arrange the resignation of Cuban dictator Fulgencio Batista, who was a partner with Lansky and organized crime in Caribbean casinos, but whose wartime coalition with Cuban Communists made Washington, with an eye toward the future, nervous. When Lansky paid Batista a quarter-million-dollar bribe, the Cuban tyrant quietly left office, destined for a comfortable exile in Florida, at least for a time. Batista would later return to Havana with America's blessing and covert support to win a rigged reelection and subsequently crush his old Communist allies. But for now Lansky succeeded again as a government agent, his mutual interests and ties with Washington deepening. An ardent Zionist, he also soon forged ties with Israeli intelligence, to which he was introduced, as he later told Israeli journalists, by a "prominent American Jew." When the military of the would-be Jewish state asked him to help smuggle arms to Palestine in the forties, he told them simply: "What's the problem? I am at your service."

The corruption, the intrigue, the ruthless reading and exploitation of upperworld as well as underworld America—it all seemed a fitting prelude to Lansky's greatest, most far-reaching venture. In the early 1940s, while scheming with the government and presiding over booming wartime profits in a number of black market enterprises involving gasoline, sugar, and other rationed commodities and consumer goods as well as in their standard gambling, prostitution, and drugs, he drove with Bugsy Siegel across the desert highway from Los Angeles to a gritty crossroads in southern Nevada. It was a harrowing journey. The temperature rose to 120 degrees, the wires in their Cadillac melting. "There were times when I thought I would die in that desert," Lansky said. "Vegas was a horrible place, really just a small oasis town." But through the swelter and sand and backwardness, he envisioned, as so often in his career, what no one else yet saw.

He had been watching Nevada since the twenties, earlier than most outsiders. Soon after the state's most recent legalization of gambling, in 1931, he had acquired hidden interests in Reno in both the Golden Casino and the famous Bank Club, then the largest single legal gambling establishment in the country, where he entered into an early agreement as well with the local political boss, a professional poker player become banking magnate, George Wingfield. Lansky had first dispatched Siegel to Las Vegas in 1942 to capture control of betting on racing results coming in by wire, and to scout possible casino investments. Bugsy, his tailored suit and $300 gabardine topcoat whipping in the desert gale, was unimpressed with the place. Contrary to legend, it was Lansky, not his hot-eyed hit man, who imagined the future of the almost vacant windswept valley.

"What I had in mind was to build the greatest, most luxurious hotel casino in the world and invite people from all over America—maybe the high rollers from all over the world—to come and spend their money there," Lansky would say. He saw even the barrenness of the desert as an asset. "Once you got tourists there, after they had eaten and drunk all they could," he told a friend, "there was only one thing left—to go gambling."

Before he was finished, he would not only build their luxury casino but receive the profits from more than a half-dozen others as well. Lansky was never licensed in the state of Nevada, never officially acknowledged as the owner and operator of so much of the Strip. There would be no statue or monument to this genuine father of the city, which he would rule from afar as an international capital of narcotics and gambling, money laundering and political corruption. "Meyer owns more in Vegas than anybody—than all of ours put together," an envious Italian gangster would be overheard saying on an FBI wiretap. "He's got a piece of every joint in Vegas." "No matter where you went, the Mob had its finger in the pie," another mobster later wrote of their growing portfolio of legal as well as illegal businesses, "and usually it was Meyer Lansky's finger." By the 1950s, the boy from Grodno would be known as "the Chairman of the Board."

As in any great success, any legend, there was always exaggeration, among friends, rivals, imitators, and by the officials and journalists who watched Lansky, though government and the press rarely acknowledged the man, and still less what he signified. He would come to represent a phenomenon far beyond himself, his actual holdings, his estate, his era. Even when he exercised no power in a given setting, took no cut, even when he was a frail old man in Florida or seeking haven in Israel, even long dead, Lansky would give his name to a culture he did so much to make dominant. The term "Lansky operation" came to be used by insiders—even when he himself was not involved at all—to denote a generic, classic blending of organized crime with the legal, surface world, even employing in many cases some of his purported official pursuers as well as his Syndicate associates. That evolution to a largely compromised, exploitative economy was his real legacy, and his real heirs much of a corporate and political elite—from the monopolistic owners of Las Vegas casinos to the masters of conglomerate mergers to presidential candidates taking in tens of millions of dollars from vested interests—governing the nation by Lansky principles at the turn of the next century.

Their capital in spirit would always be Las Vegas. What Lansky brought there in symbol and substance—the national power and organization of the Syndicate, the centrality of drugs and money-laundering as means of finance, the compromising of law enforcement and the corrupt collusion with government, the underlying principle that the only player who wins is the one who controls the game—would be constant elements in the rise and expansion of gambling and thus of the town itself. In what he had once called that "horrible place" in the Nevada desert, Lansky founded a city that would represent the essence of his vision of America. Far more than a string of carpet joints, it was to be an entire society dominated by the ethic he had adopted so long before—a boss's paradise of suckers.

2. Benny Binion

The Outlaw as Icon

He was the sickly son of horse and mule traders from the hard-scrabble plains south of the Red River, between the Oklahoma line and Dallas. Born in 1904, he suffered recurring bouts of pneumonia for years. Thinking fresh air would cure the little boy, his parents put him on horseback and took him on the road. He grew up in a world about to vanish: stockmen's wagons lurching over rutted prairie; card games and horse trades; guns and brawls; the last communal campfires in turn-of-the-century Texas.

At ten, he left the second grade to trade livestock—"interrupted by bad roads and sick a good deal of the time," he would say of his "education." At fourteen, Lester Binion, who would be known as Benny, had outgrown any childhood frailty. A taut young cowboy, he was just under six feet tall, with darting blue eyes and the sharp-edged look of his lineage. He had already become head of the household, his father having drunk and gambled away the family's meager livelihood.

During World War I, with only a wagon and two mules, he struck off for El Paso, where for a while he spread gravel on parking lots for Model Ts. He acquired a taste for smuggling and drifted through a series of shady jobs on the Mexican border. In the early twenties he made his way to Dallas, where as a "hip-pocket bootlegger," packing a .45 for each hand and a hidden .38 just in case, he soon became something of a local legend. Fearless and brazen, he once stole a truckload of liquor right out of a police evidence vault. By the time he was twenty, he had been to jail and he had made a lot of money. He could not read or write, add or subtract. But he *could* read people and figure odds, "especially," as one historian has said, "the odds that he could handle the people."

Binion apprenticed himself to the leading Dallas racketeer, Warren Diamond. He parked cars and ran errands in service of Diamond's famed no-limit craps games at the St. George Hotel in the shadow of the Dallas courthouse. At twenty-two, in 1926, he challenged his mentor, opening a permanent rival game in the nearby Southland Hotel, owned by the Galveston mob boss, drug smuggler, and future Lansky associate Sam Maceo. When the aging Diamond did nothing to stop him, Binion expanded into loansharking and the numbers rackets.

From the beginning, Binion was two men: the "square craps fader," the honest game boss who covered any bet, who might even give back money to hapless losers or remember loyal employees with turkeys at Christmas; and a barbaric outlaw of terrifying means, leaving the buckshot-mangled bodies of rivals or renegades beside railroad tracks or half-buried under quicklime all over North Texas, once poking a pencil through the eye of a numbers runner he thought had double-crossed him. "Do your enemies before they do you" would be his lifelong maxim.

By the early forties, there were twenty-seven illegal casinos operating in Dallas. The city had become a fount of vice for the region, and it was Binion's town. His business, as one observer said, was the community's secret pleasure, and vice versa. With his own well-known payoff men, he bribed and compromised local politicians, prosecutors, and police in a web of "fines" and kickbacks that constituted the real government of North Texas. He boasted of being the close friend and backer not only of local Dallas officials but also of Congressman Lyndon B. Johnson, still a relatively obscure if grandly ambitious politician. Binion was what one Texas journalist called the "king of the racketeers," though there was always a steady stream of competitors to be killed and new officials to be purchased. He would also make his peace and share the spoils with New Orleans crime boss Carlos Marcello, who ruled much of the rest of Texas. And he now attracted the attention of Lansky, who traveled to Texas to see for himself this infamous character whom insiders described as "a cross between Paul Bunyan and the Dalton Gang." Lansky, as the camps of both men would tell the story later, recognized Binion not only as a force of his own among the criminal factions but as a future partner and peer, who offered "to join the action" with Lansky in some later venture if mutually profitable.

During World War II, Binion bought a piece of the famous Top O'Hill Terrace in neighboring Fort Worth, where his high-stakes clientele was notably different from the blacks and poor whites who frequented his downtown Dallas club. His new customers included Texas millionaires and political powers H. L. Hunt, Sid Richardson, Clint Murchison, and the dashing young heir Howard Hughes. His casino manager was Louis McWillie, a figure with ties to Lansky's confederation, and the associate of a petty Chicago gangster and labor goon who soon moved to Dallas—Jack Ruby.

Suddenly, in 1946, Binion was driven from Dallas in a gang war sweeping the nation. In June, James Ragen, a Chicago tipster who ran the country's largest, most profitable racing wire, began talking to the FBI. His defection threatened people, said an official familiar with his statements, "in very high places." Ragen was said to know about Lansky's sexual blackmail of Hoover, as well as the penetration and control by organized crime of major elements of the American economy, including not only Nevada gambling casinos but the liquor and sugar industries, Hollywood studios and unions, major importers of tropical fruit, and owners of foreign holdings. In a pattern repeated again and again, as Ragen and others on the inside knew, the Syndicate had infiltrated legitimate businesses by various means—crucial investment of their Prohibition profits, serving as local and even international enforcers for companies like United Fruit, laundering their proceeds through movie studios, and extorting heavy payments from Hollywood executives. Most of all, he was reportedly ready to testify about the still little known magnitude and importance of drug trafficking for the Syndicate, the growing impact of what one newspaper account called "the narcotics racket." In any event, Hoover refused Ragen a bodyguard as the probe was getting underway, and the witness was gunned down from a panel truck on State Street, though only wounded. When news that Ragen had survived reached the Las Vegas Club, owner Gus Greenbaum and his hoodlum partners were furious, and immediately called Chicago.

"Solly, you didn't finish the job," Greenbaum screamed into the phone at one of the hit men hired to carry out the murder. "Either Ragen dies or you do," several witnesses heard him yell.

Not long afterward, the officially unidentified Solly and his accomplices found the would-be informer Ragen unguarded in his hospital room, and, according to one account, "shoved bichloride-of-mercury tablets (a metallic poison favored by the Mob in the forties) down Ragen's throat." Solly's call back to Las Vegas set off "cheers and applause," one insider remembered.

"Ragen's dead, they slipped him the salt," one of the owners, Joe "Bowser" Rosenberg, told his partners.

That evening, several Las Vegas gangsters gathered for a celebration dinner, "black chefs with high white hats" bringing silver trays piled with delicacies into the casino pit—the center of the floor surrounded by the gaming tables where pit bosses kept an eye on their customers and card dealers.

Ragen's murder had far-reaching consequences, fixing under mob control the enormously lucrative nationwide racing wire service. For Binion, meanwhile, the most immediate result was that the Chicago gangsters who eliminated Ragen now expanded to take over Dallas. By November 1946, the city was under a potent new regime. Ever the gambler, he knew when to fold. "My sheriff got beat in the election," Binion would say. He asked Lansky to help clear the way for him in southern Nevada.

The next month Binion packed his wife, five children, and several suitcases stuffed with cash into a chauffeur-driven Cadillac, and headed for Las Vegas. At forty-two, his greatest wealth and power lay ahead of him in the desert. His Texas casinos operated for the last time on New Year's Eve, 1946. The next day, he appeared in southern Nevada as a partner in the Las Vegas Club with some of the men who had ordered Ragen killed. Over the next four years he would buy in and out of two downtown gambling joints, before purchasing from Lansky men for $160,000 the lease for a casino, as well as an adjacent hotel closed as a tax loss on Fremont Street in the area of Las Vegas that was coming to be known as Glitter Gulch. In August 1951, he reopened the properties as Benny Binion's Horseshoe Club. From the first day of the Horseshoe, he was a national power. He already owned "a million dollars' worth of property," as an FBI report described it, in Nevada, Texas, Louisiana, and Mississippi, on top of the vast 200,000-acre Missouri Breaks Montana cattle ranch and a piece of the famous Log Cabin Club at Jackson Hole, Wyoming.

Appearing before the Nevada Tax Commission for licensing, he typically tried to bribe or bully his way through. Neither tactic worked with one earnest civil servant who served on the commission, a quiet bureaucrat named Robbins Cahill. But Binion won the decisive votes of the political appointees on the body, and in the process learned a lesson about his new home.

Commissioners questioned him about two Dallas murders. One victim was a numbers rival of Binion's named Ben Freiden. Binion admitted the killing but claimed self-defense. He proceeded to regale them with a cowboy-style tale: "Shot him three times in the heart . . . a bad man, a very bad man." As for the other killing: "Yeah, but he was just a nigger I caught stealing some whiskey." The officials thought it all very funny. When their laughter and smirking died down, he was given the license, despite Cahill's objections.

On another occasion the commission refused to approve him for a gambling license on the grounds of Benny's perjury in a "sworn affidavit" that he was not engaged in illegal activities, only to be overruled on a technicality by a Nevada governor to whom Binion had made large political contributions.

A few years later, Binion pled guilty to tax evasion charges in Texas. Thinking he had the judge fixed as was his wont, he drove to Dallas for sentencing with his black chauffeur, Gold Dollar, and a satchel containing $100,000 in cash. But police had gotten wind of the proposed payoff and intimidated the judge. To Binion's shock and fury, he was sentenced to prison in Leavenworth, where he served forty-two months.

A doughy, flaccid man of fifty-three upon release, he claimed to have been converted to Catholicism by a penitentiary priest. He would never be licensed again in Nevada. But the casino continued under his control even from prison, and he returned to manage it with no questions asked. "The state of Nevada was as anxious to keep this pudgy thug as he was eager to remain," said one account. "Their interests were mutual and so were their benefits."

He ran it like no other place in Las Vegas. Symbolized by a seven-foot horseshoe painted gold and encasing within its arch one hundred $10,000 bills, this house of the serious gambler was without shame or pretense—as with Binion himself, there was no mask. Ordinary people in dungarees and housedresses crowded the joint, trying to make the most of its looser slots, which offered the best odds in town. He deliberately provided no ersatz glamour or luxury, no fancy fountains or buffets, no flowers or flashy shows. His casino cuisine was greasy Texas chili made from a Dallas jailhouse recipe. "If you want to get rich," Binion said, "make little people feel big." He believed in "good food cheap, good whiskey cheap, and a good gamble. That's all there is to it, son."

The Horseshoe was "where the action is," said one visitor. "The thing itself." He was the first to put carpeting on the floor of a downtown joint. Wearing a white ten-gallon Stetson "cocked like a gunfighter," or sometimes a buffalo-hide coat or western outfits with three-dollar gold piece buttons and alligator boots, he was still prone to spit on the floor as if it were sawdust. His partner, an operator called Doby Doc Caudill from the northern Nevada ranching town of Elko, wore a diamond stickpin in his bib overalls and a pistol tucked in a holster. His other principal partner was organized-crime figure Eddie Levinson. And for decades a skim of the Horseshoe proceeds was paid, as from so many other Vegas casinos, to Lansky and his associates.

Binion's wife, Teddy Jane—a girl from Ardmore, Oklahoma, he had married in 1933—was now a tiny, chain-smoking woman with cheaply dyed hair, and a familiar sight along Fremont Street. Cigarette dangling from her lips or held between nicotine-stained fingers, pockets bulging with cash, she walked to the bank every day to make deposits she and Benny trusted no one else to make. "If I marry Benny Binion," she had once said, "I'll spend my life in a room above a two-bit crap game." In fact, she lived with him in a large stucco house until he came home one day and, suddenly tired of her smoking, kicked her out. She moved into a suite above the Horseshoe. Thirty years later, her clothes hung in the stucco house untouched, just as she had left them.

As Binion grew older, he became a devoted storyteller who held forth from a booth in the club's Sombrero Room. In Las Vegas, it constituted irresistible charm. The outrageous was now merely colorful, his bloody past a quaint caricature, another civic attraction. He became known as the "wily sage and grandfather of Glitter Gulch." At the end, he said of his life, "I would almost certainly be a gambler again, because there's nothing else an ignorant man can do."

Meanwhile, beneath the public confection, his present was, if anything, more brutal, brazen, and corrupt than his past. In Binion's Horseshoe, the police were rarely called for suspected cheats or security problems; instead, hired thugs mercilessly beat or even killed the accused. There were seven homicides and more than a hundred people assaulted in one six-year period at the casino. When homeless people wandered in off the streets in winter, they were hosed down and thrown into the alley. Unabashedly racist—to the point that some local black leaders respected his relative lack of hypocrisy among the bigoted casino owners of the city—Binion himself once threw out of the Horseshoe a paralyzed black veteran in a wheelchair. In the same year the club opened, Binion was still carrying on grudge wars with old rivals in Texas, trying to kill competitor Herbert "The Cat" Noble no less than eleven times before finally succeeding with a mailbox bomb on the twelfth attempt.

Meanwhile, Binion blatantly paid off U.S. senators, governors, judges, and other politicians and officials. He proudly boasted of delivering to President Jimmy Carter the vote of Nevada senator Howard Cannon on the Panama Canal Zone Treaty. Cannon's vote, as Binion told the story, was in exchange for a federal judgeship for Binion's friend and lawyer Harry Claiborne, who would later be the first federal judge since the Civil War to be impeached and convicted of a felony.

From the colorful casino, several murders were contracted for under the watchful and participating eye of Binion, including the fatal bombing of local lawyer William Coulthard, who had been the first FBI agent assigned to Vegas in 1946, and who had left law enforcement for a lucrative law practice. Through his marriage to the daughter of wealthy contractor and casino owner Pietro Orlando "P.O." Silvagni, who originally owned the property on which the Horseshoe casino was situated and who leased it to Binion, Coulthard had become Binion's landlord. Shortly before his Cadillac exploded in the Bank of Nevada parking garage in July 1972—the bomb so powerful it decapitated and severed the legs of the well-liked attorney— Coulthard had negotiated the sale of the property to one of Binion's competitors, according to FBI reports only recently revealed through the Freedom of Information Act. The killing shocked even jaded Las Vegas, where Coulthard's Silvagni in-laws were prominent socially as well as in gambling. Had the elder Silvagni still been alive, it was widely believed, he would have avenged the brutal slaying of his esteemed son-in-law. Though many suspected that Binion was involved, and the Horseshoe got a new hundred-year lease at low rent, Sheriff Ralph Lamb, to whom Binion had made "loans" that were never repaid, refused to bring charges against the bombing suspects. The FBI concluded that Binion was responsible for the murder, but had no jurisdiction in this local homicide. Federal agents pursuing the case would later say they had never seen such juice. Coulthard's assassination was still officially unsolved at the end of the century, "though everyone in town knows who did it," as one local lawyer said. The bomb itself—a "trimble trigger with a guitar pic"—was traced to a Las Vegas hit man whose "trademark" that was, according to one of the chief detectives on the case.

As it turned out, it was the same type of bomb used in the even more celebrated murder four years later of Arizona journalist Don Bolles. The Datsun driven by the newsman and father of seven was bombed in a Phoenix parking lot in June 1976. Bolles died eleven days later, after the amputation of both legs and one arm, but not before whispering to police the word "Emprise," which further connected his murder to Las Vegas. At the time of his death, the investigative reporter was in the middle of an exposé linking skimmed money from Las Vegas casinos to the racing monopoly in Arizona controlled by the local Funk family in a combine with the Jacobs family of Buffalo, New York, and their company called Emprise.

It was in Binion's Horseshoe in the 1970s that Texas narcotics dealer Jimmy Chagra laundered tens of millions of dollars in drug profits at the tables—money, as A. Alvarez put it, "as black as pitch." It was there too, in 1979, that a deal was cut for hit man Charles Harrelson to assassinate U.S.

District Judge John Wood as Wood prepared to preside over Chagra's drug trafficking trial in San Antonio.

That same year, a customer in the Horseshoe, having lost all his money, turned rowdy and claimed to have been cheated; he was hustled out of the casino and shot in the head point-blank with a 9mm revolver—a weapon found that night in the casino vault. When the FBI opened a bribery probe of city detectives on the scene and of officials in the office of Clark County district attorney Bob Miller, and ultimately a murder investigation of Binion, they could find no witness willing to testify. Miller, son of a Chicago mobster and strip-joint owner, would go on to become governor of Nevada in 1989.

Meanwhile, a larger-than-life bronze sculpture of Binion towered on a corner across the street from the Horseshoe. It was the first public statue in the nation honoring a gambler, and in otherwise gaudy, statue-laden Las Vegas, the only sculpture of a real-life character instead of mythological gods and monsters. But perhaps the ultimate tribute to Binion and the corrupt order he did so much to foster would be that after decades of the most outrageous violence and political bribery, from murder in broad daylight to assassinations in secrecy, the Las Vegas Metropolitan Police Department would report to the FBI in the 1990s that it had not a single investigative file on him.

Along the way, the unlettered son of a drunken horse trader had acquired an estate of more than $100 million. As with so many American fortunes of the century, the most conspicuous legacy would be a bitter, murderous struggle for the empire. One son, Jack, went on by the turn of the century to make the Forbes 500 list of the richest men in America. His brother, Ted— "even smarter than his father," a former federal judge said of him—died in a sleeping bag in May 1999, murdered by a lethal combined injection of heroin and a barbiturate, $4.5 million worth of silver missing from his underground vault. "This would never have happened if old Benny was still around," said one family friend.

For those who understood the real game being played in Las Vegas and America, Benny Binion was one of the most influential, and feared, men of his time; and in that enormous power, if not in his crude style, he set an example that would be followed into a new millennium.

3. Pat McCarran

The Democrat as Autocrat

He learned the law from books he carried in a saddlebag. He practiced debate standing alone on a rock, before a band of sheep in the silent foothills of the Sierra Nevada. He would rise to become one of the most influential U.S. senators in American history. As few others, and with a legacy often overlooked, he would sway foreign and domestic affairs far beyond his time and place. Near the end of his life, cartoonists portrayed him with his leonine mane and girth as a caricature of the Capitol Hill baron. But there was always much more to Patrick Anthony McCarran than the public image.

A major figure in the twentieth century, he was a child of the nineteenth. Born in 1876 in Reno to Irish immigrants, he was the only son of a pretty schoolteacher from County Cork with a gifted voice, and a hot-tempered sheepman who fled the potato famine and then deserted the U.S. Army for a ranch in a sageland river valley east of Reno. Patrick as a child was a freckle-faced redhead, a dog his only friend. He did not start school until he was ten, riding his horse several miles back and forth. He would be a loner, four years older than his classmates and often in schoolyard fights. At home, his mother raised him as a devout Catholic.

He was an indifferent, even poor student until inspired by an English teacher. At the age of twenty-one, he graduated first in a class of sixteen at Reno High. At the small University of Nevada his record was mediocre. Yet he excelled in debate, and once more acquired a mentor, his political science professor, the Nevada suffragette Anne Martin. His hero was the populist Democratic presidential candidate William Jennings Bryan.

When his father was injured, he left college to tend the ranch. He was soon studying the law on his own while herding sheep in the high meadows. A nephew of William Sharon, the political boss of the mining industry centered in camps and shafts of Virginia City's Comstock Lode outside Reno, drove out to find him there in 1902, a burly, good-looking young Irishman with dark, wavy hair and a two-weeks' growth of beard. At the urging of Martin and other politicians, the Sharon machine asked the ambitious and attractive young law student to run for the legislature on the Silver-Democrat ticket. McCarran jumped at the chance.

N evada is ten thousand tales of ugliness and beauty, viciousness and virtue," Richard G. Lillard wrote of the state. It was a place like no other, treated less as a land to settle than some alien fastness to be plundered, a colony valued only for what could be taken from it. Embedded beneath its lunar landscape was a fortune not even the most greedy could imagine. "The plaything of San Francisco nabobs," historian Gilman Ostrander called the silver and gold veins of northern Nevada, among the richest in the world. "A treasure house . . . robbed to build mansions on Nob Hill."

It was always a place to be used, one way or another. For three more votes in Congress during the Civil War, and its electoral count in a potentially close election in 1864, Abraham Lincoln and his fellow Republicans made a state of the lawless expanse of more than 100,000 square miles. It was christened Nevada—Spanish for "snow-covered"—with the motto "Battle Born." Its motley society and corrupt politics were remarkable even by the rawest frontier standards. "In Nevada the lawyer, the editor, the banker, the chief desperado, the chief gambler, and the saloon keeper occupied the same level of society, and it was the highest," wrote Mark Twain. "The cheapest and easiest way to become an influential man, and be looked up to by the community at large, was to stand behind a bar, wear a cluster-diamond stick pin, and sell whiskey . . . to be a saloon keeper and kill a man was to be illustrious."

Mine captains, railroad magnates, and cattle kings ruled successively and sometimes collaboratively in a ruthless oligarchy. "They all had the same agenda," one historian would write, "to keep the government from taxing or regulating them." To the extent the state acquired an electoral tradition, it was bribery and vote fraud fed by the raw greed for wealth, what Ostrander described as a "capitalistic authoritarianism." Still, the corrupters aspired to respectability, to a Nevada "aristocracy," as one writer depicted it, "consisting of the leading professional men, bankers, and brokers." It was the lawyers who made it all work, spending "hundreds of thousands of dollars of their clients' money to corrupt whoever stood in their way," recorded historian Hubert Howe Bancroft. The stakes were colossal. In the last years of the nineteenth century, dishonest officials granted 5 million Nevada acres to the railroads, leaving them the largest private landowners in the nation, rivals of any feudal lord in either hemisphere. In a nation and era of epic exploitation, the plunder of Nevada, as historians would sadly record, was remarkable: so much wealth taken from such a vast land at the expense of so few people; so much arbitrary power imposed so completely without restraint to stifle any civil society or authentic democratic tradition; such overwhelming corruption. "State history reads like a novel," Lillard noted typically in the next century about the color and popular mythology, if not the wantonness of it all. But fact or fiction, it was a tragedy.

Making the best of victimization, Nevadans developed a moral permissiveness scandalous for Gilded Age America. It was the easy license of the mining camp. Prostitution flourished in a legal limbo, neither criminal nor lawful, simply accepted. Nothing so symbolized the state's unique morality as its legalization of gambling. As early as 1869, with customary bribery, the legislature almost casually made lawful what would be outlawed in the rest of the nation. While the poker and fan-tan games went on, however, the price of silver plunged. During McCarran's childhood, once-teeming camptowns became ghostly debris, great cuts of the Comstock Lode left silent tombs of the old greed, bonanza now *borasca*, the Spanish term for "bust" used by locals. Cattle barons became the controlling political and economic force for a brief interval, but the worst blizzard in a hundred years wiped out their herds and San Francisco banks abandoned the ranches as swiftly as they had sealed the mines. "Poor, empty, used up Nevada," wrote one observer, "returning to its original state of nature."

Calamity motivated what a writer called Nevada's own "plutocratic populism." The state turned to the new Silver Party, which promised serious reform, uniting the grubstake prospector with the wrangler and sheepherder, high-country cattlemen with stolid farmers of the Midwest, all seeking a bigger money supply to pay their debts, and all united against the mammoth outside forces of Wall Street and the Washington it owned. Nevadans cheered in their streets when men read aloud the egalitarian speeches of Bryan in the 1896 presidential campaign. But Silverite politicians, as the eminent historian Richard Hofstadter and other chroniclers of the movement discovered, represented only a "shadow" of the authentic radicalism of other Populists. Soon merging with the Democrats in Nevada, the Silverites came to bear a striking resemblance to both their new allies and the GOP, devoted less to economic democracy, as Ostrander noted, than to "more money in the bank" for themselves.

As Nevada entered the twentieth century, fewer than a hundred corporations and wealthy individuals possessed more than three-quarters of the private land. Two-thirds of mining, cattle, and sheep ranches, railroads, and utilities were absentee-owned. Unlike most of the rest of the nation, or even the other heavily colonized regions of the West, desert and mountain Nevada had no sizable native class of capitalists or speculators. Given as well the large portion of the land owned by the federal government, the state itself turned out to be overwhelmingly the property of outsiders. Nevadans had become a people, an official history said in understatement, "humbled by long neglect."

McCarran won the assembly seat for the Washoe Valley between Reno and Carson City in 1902, backing unions and an eight-hour day. After one term he ran for the state Senate, lost, and returned to herding sheep and studying for the bar. Thus began a pattern of victory and defeat, advance and retreat, faithful loyalty and bitter enmity.

Newly married and with the first of five children, he moved to the boomtown of Tonopah, where he was elected district attorney but proved an indifferent prosecutor of drunks and petty miscreants. "His heart was with the sinner," a biographer concluded. When McCarran spoke out against the mine owners for using heavily armed mercenaries to break the 1907 miners' strike at Goldfield amid the most savage working conditions, he was labeled a "dangerous radical." It would be his first clash with Republican tycoon George Wingfield, "owner and operator of Nevada," as his biographer Elizabeth Raymond called him, who would rancorously oppose McCarran for years to come.

Having tried in vain to win a congressional seat in 1908, McCarran soon returned to Reno and became a leading criminal attorney. In 1912 he won a state Supreme Court judgeship. He was quickly bored, though some of his opinions from the bench were progressive and enduring. Restlessly, incessantly, he jockeyed for higher office.

In 1916 he ran for the U.S. Senate, supporting women's suffrage and losing decisively. He was branded a spoiler and an opportunist. When the state's other U.S. senator died a year later, McCarran scrambled for that seat too, but could not muster enough support. In what one of his biographers,

Jerome Edwards, called "desperation and embarrassment," he now pulled strings for a judicial appointment outside Nevada. By then he had antagonized most of the Democratic leadership, who accused him of "compulsive electioneering." The rivalries were raucous. One day on Virginia Street in the heart of Reno, a drunken Democratic U.S. senator, Key Pittman, stuffed McCarran's cigar down his throat, and these two distinguished denizens of Nevada lunged into a brawl.

McCarran lost reelection to the state Supreme Court in 1918, and seemed at a political dead end. He blamed enemies in his own ranks as well as Wingfield. The solitary, combative child was now all the more a lone wolf, harboring primal suspicions of malice if not conspiracy all around.

He returned to a lucrative Reno law practice for the next dozen years, specializing in divorce, about to be one of the state's growth industries. His cherubic handsomeness and deep, commanding voice held audiences spellbound. Championing the rights of defendants—mostly petty criminals—he saw sin, as one observer put it, as "a natural part of the human beast." Still, he was unforgiving of his old foe Wingfield. He detested the boss's rule, signified by Wingfield cronies Bill Graham and Jim McKay, Chicago gangsters whose bootlegging and illegal casinos propelled the "whirlpool of vice" that one reporter termed Reno in the twenties.

During the summer of 1927, McCarran defended two Nevada officials charged with embezzling state funds deposited at Wingfield banks. His clients were convicted, but he exploited the trial to expose Wingfield's stranglehold. "Can liberty of state go into bondage of gold and come out?" he asked the jury. "I want wealth in this state but I want liberty more—even if there is not a dollar in the state." Whatever the effect of McCarran's words on a generally apathetic public, Wingfield's grip seemed to loosen gradually, until broken at last by the Depression.

In 1932, McCarran achieved what many had thought would never happen. At fifty-six, he was finally a U.S. senator. He won by 1,700 votes, some said on Franklin Roosevelt's coattails. But he was intensely proud, owing his victory, he wrote one of his daughters, "to no faction and to no power" but to the "toilers and . . . men in the mediocre walks of life."

In Washington at last, he would thrive. He maneuvered himself onto the Capitol's most powerful committees—Judiciary for its patronage, Appropriations for pork-barrel millions. Gauging sentiment in Nevada, he opposed FDR's "packing" of the U.S. Supreme Court. He deplored some New Deal programs, his critique as harsh as any Republican's. But he was more liberal than the White House on labor, and supported even more spending on relief and public works.

His independence drew acclaim. To his delight, *Life* magazine saw him as an "unpredictable mustang," *Collier's* as "for the masses rather than the classes." In rare self-effacement, Huey Long touted McCarran as a future president. In his first Senate term, he was liked, respected, and feared, both a rebel and a conservative and on his way to prominence.

At home on the Potomac, he was ever nostalgic for Nevada. "Dear dear old desert," he called it in a letter, ". . . just dripping from the diadem of God." He was less sentimental in installing a political network that made him the most formidable politician in the state's history. He adopted not only the same weaponry of patronage and pressure once used to crush him but even some of the same people. He embraced ex-Wingfield men like Norman Biltz, who was married to Jacqueline Bouvier's aunt, and who picked up his tabs and bought him clothes and other gifts.

The senator, it turned out, lived rather well, usually beyond his means, with a stack of unpaid bills and creditors at bay all over the state. In its vast emptiness Nevada was still a small society, with fewer than 20,000 voters statewide and everyone in politics familiar with everyone else. "One square man for each square mile," was its jaunty slogan. By the mid-1930s, however, some thought that Nevada had, as usual, exchanged one boss for another: Wingfield for McCarran.

At sixty-four, before World War II and on the eve of his greatest influence, McCarran settled into a portly, white-haired, diamond stick-pinned archetype of Capitol Hill. He seemed to sense mortality. He long suffered from a bleeding ulcer, his diet confined to baby food for many years, and he now endured a near-lethal intestinal hemorrhage, as well as the first assault of the heart disease and sclerosis that would eventually kill him. He was passionate and emotional, his temperament and feelings playing across a wide spectrum. Patient, funny, and tender, he was also an earthy man and a ribald storyteller. His wife and children—a family many close to him suspected of a streak of hereditary madness from his wife's side—often treated him spitefully, though he was ever indulgent of them all.

He had an absorbent, confident mind, without depth of intellect or education, yet he was a man who knew what he thought, and especially the lessons a long, painful passage as lawyer and losing political infighter had taught. When insulted, he became now teary-eyed and melancholy, now blustering, enraged, and menacing. "There was nothing in this world he wouldn't do *for* or *against* you," remembered one aide. He was unyielding and rarely conciliatory; if he wasn't dominating, he was battling—with an unambiguous, unambivalent sense of being right. To McCarran, loyalty among his colleagues and friends was everything, and he demanded and offered it. Above all, he hated, feared, suspected, and ultimately expected the worst—ingratitude, treachery, betrayal.

To dozens of young Depression-generation Nevadans he was a doting, avuncular sponsor, giving them Capitol sinecures to pay their way through Washington law schools. "McCarran's Boys," as they were known, returned to Nevada to become its leading lawyers, judges, and political fixtures for decades. That patronage would be his finest legacy. Characteristically, he expected them to be personally loyal, and if not to adopt his increasingly polarized political views then at least not to undermine him publicly. When any turned on him out of pettiness or ambition, he was, he told one of them without guile, "heartbroken." He fought avidly for his constituents—"Nothing is too good for the fine people of Nevada," he declared emotionally and often—and took it personally when his efforts went unappreciated.

He outfoxed an effort by FDR to purge him in the 1938 election, and thereby inherited new power. He became chairman of the despotic District of Columbia Committee and in 1944 of Judiciary itself, where he controlled almost half of all Senate legislation, including his colleagues' precious private bills cloaking fix and favor. He would rule the Judiciary Committee as what one observer called a "patronage pigsty"; another would describe it as "the finest intelligence service on Capitol Hill." But there was also new hostility. A once-admiring national press condemned his prewar isolationism, and then a wartime filibuster to force needless stockpiling of silver, a windfall sluiced to Nevada mines. It was later said that the state's senators, in their provincial grasping on behalf of local patrons in mining and ranching, "made it their primary mission to keep the price of silver artificially high and the cost of leasing federal grazing lands inordinately cheap." More than 90 percent of the land in Nevada was owned by the federal government. McCarran was intent on getting as much money for the state out of Washington as the process would allow. During the forties, typically, thanks to his power and seniority, the people of Nevada paid scarcely $41 million in federal fees and taxes, while receiving more than $175 million in federal expenditures.

Then, in 1944, he was ambushed in a little-noticed yet venomous fight for reelection. Challenged by dissidents in the roiling politics of the Democratic Party, he was also up against what he saw as the radical Congress of Industrial Organizations (CIO), emerging in Nevada with the influx of new labor for war plants he had helped place in the state. He panicked at the robust new opposition, smearing his opponents with fabricated charges. Henchmen like Biltz paid to bus black "voters" from Los Angeles to Las Vegas, where they provided the margin that saved him. The race awakened

McCarran's hitherto dormant anti-Semitism; he railed at the outside "Jew money" spent against him.

Fatefully, he saw in his close call alien demons and plots rather than the reality of his precarious hold on the state party. He came out of the election convinced that Communists and left-wingers were out to get him personally, a conspiratorial menace deeper and darker than was obvious at the time. Thus, a little-noted campaign in Nevada in 1944 was a breeding ground of some of the worst of the Red Scare to follow.

By 1946, he had joined the drumroll of anti-Communist, anti-Soviet hysteria and hyperbole pounded out by leaders of industry, religion, and government. His motives, like theirs, were mixed—genuine ideological fear, ignorance, xenophobia, political opportunism, and vengeance. Not least, McCarran's Catholicism, deep if chiefly honored in the breach, fueled his fanaticism. Yet at one point he offended even the pope with the infamous McCarran-Walter Immigration Act severely restricting entry of Catholics from Communist-ruled Eastern European states. "I have just doomed myself to Purgatory," he confided after a visit to the Vatican, where he had refused to moderate the legislation. He was now on the phone several times every day with his close friend J. Edgar Hoover, who shared in the anti-Communist craze.

McCarran's instrument would be Judiciary's newly formed Senate Internal Security Subcommittee (SISS), infamous in the annals of American persecution. He appointed as SISS counsel his erstwhile personal aide and driver, a former Reno reporter turned lawyer named Julien "Jay" Sourwine. Sourwine, a compulsive gambler who played the numbers in Washington's ghetto, was known by casinos in Nevada as a welsher whose unpaid debts were discreetly covered by McCarran friends. He was also a rabid, half-educated zealot who denounced the Supreme Court as "an instrument of communist global conquest." He financed his gambling addiction in part by moonlighting scurrilous pseudonymous articles for the neo-fascist *Manion Report*. Sourwine's trademark as SISS interrogator, as Frank Donner wrote in 1980, would be "terrified witnesses" and "a scorn for legal niceties." Together with McCarran's eldest daughter, a reactionary nun named Sister Margaret, Sourwine played well to his suspicious, much-betrayed chairman. So wide was Sourwine's power that he became known as "the ninety-seventh Senator."

McCarran's stature lent weight to charges coming from more transparent demagogues like Senator Joseph McCarthy. SISS hounded scores of honest and gifted officials from government service and destroyed dozens of innocent people outside Washington, including some of the nation's most talented scientists, journalists, and educators. In a witch-hunt conducted against State Department specialists on the Far East, SISS looked for the men they thought had "lost China to communism." The inquisition drove out of government the very officials who knew Asia best. These men and their knowledge would be absent when, little more than a decade later, the decision was made to wage war in Southeast Asia.

Some of the most sardonic ironies went unseen: While McCarran pursued "crimes" of state, he enjoyed a regular supply of booze given by Washington liquor distributors in return for his cover-up of rackets in the D.C. committee. While he denounced witnesses for allegedly serving foreign powers, McCarran himself took payments, as some of his most intimate staff members would later reveal, from his own favorite right-wing dictators, Chiang Kai-shek of Nationalist China and Francisco Franco of Spain. Both shared McCarran's view of the value of silver bullion, and the stalwart senator even tried to negotiate a deal with Franco to trade silver for some Basque sheepherders for Nevada's ranches. The Spanish Fascist regime also awarded him the Order of Isabella the Catholic for generous arms deals and other subsidies the senator pushed through Congress. While he accused others of lax security and betraying secrets, McCarran routinely leaked classified defense information to crony newspaper publishers and businessmen back home in places like Lovelock and Winnemucca to alert them to upcoming investment opportunities.

In battle with one dubious threat, he failed to grasp the darker, more insidious—and far more palpable—form taking shape in his own beloved Nevada. As Meyer Lansky's Syndicate built its first luxury casino in Las Vegas in 1946, it was McCarran who intervened for them with a government agency to procure scarce postwar construction materials. That August, according to FBI agents in Los Angeles, Bugsy Siegel had paid cash to an intermediary "who, in turn, made money available to Senator PAT MC CARREN [sic]." Hoover slowed, and eventually killed, the field office's proposed bribery investigation involving his friend the senator.

As a notorious Lansky associate, Morris "Moe" Dalitz from Cleveland and Detroit, moved into another Las Vegas casino, the Desert Inn, in 1949, state officials hesitated to license him. McCarran, at his favorite table at the Riverside Hotel and Casino in Reno, met to discuss the problem with Texas crime boss Sam Maceo, Benny Binion's onetime landlord at the Southland Hotel in Dallas. When Dalitz's bootlegging routes across Lake Erie were temporarily interrupted by Canadian authorities, he had become a partner of Maceo's for a new route through the Gulf of Mexico and Galveston, and

since the thirties Maceo had become one of the nation's major narcotics traffickers as well, described in federal drug enforcement files as "very wealthy
and influential in politics." As it was, Maceo was only one of McCarran's
influential friends in Texas. Also among them was W. L. Moody, Jr., founder
of a business dynasty "with a history of dealings with criminal types," as
Kirkpatrick Sale wrote later, including furtive business partnerships with
Maceo and others in the Galveston branch of the Syndicate. In turn, Moody's
own American National Insurance Company (ANICO) would play an instrumental role in the financing of Las Vegas. Immediately after the Maceo-
McCarran meeting, Nevada officials granted the license they had refused
Dalitz just days before.

When fellow senator Estes Kefauver and others organized a national
investigation of organized criminal activity in 1950, including Las Vegas casinos, McCarran fought both the inquiry and the legislation coming out of it
"as far as the English language and Senatorial manipulation would permit,"
noted historian William Moore. It would be McCarran, ironically citing a
court precedent on witnesses' rights won by one of his own witch-hunt victims, who moved to quash Senate contempt citations against a list of organized crime figures "that stretches on," as one journalist reported, "for pages
in the *Congressional Record.*"

In the twilight of his long career, the worldly old criminal lawyer was
"not unduly shocked," his biographer Edwards concluded, at "the disturbing
aberrations of human character." Yet he remained relatively unsophisticated,
defensively provincial, even naive about the trap ensnaring his ever beleaguered Nevada.

He had studied the subject of gambling "earnestly," he wrote an old
friend in 1951, and found "one of the most difficult conditions of my whole
public career." He had seen it outlawed and legalized, watched it come and
go, but in recent years "the state has builded [sic] its economy on gambling."
Never before had it been so "woven . . . in its various forms into the warp
and woof of the State's economic structure." To purge or tax gambling, as
Kefauver threatened, would close the joints and devastate Nevada. Reno's
"Virginia Street would be in mourning," McCarran warned, "and the gleaming gulch of Las Vegas would be a glowing symbol of funereal distress."

Privately, McCarran called gamblers "tinhorns" and confided that he felt
"like a Nevada whore" defending them, while other senators, their own states
corrupted, were hypocritically "listening or laughing, condemning or ridiculing," as he wrote in a letter back home. "It isn't a very laudable position for
one to have to defend gambling. One doesn't feel very lofty when his feet are
resting on the argument that gambling must prevail in the state that he rep-

resents," said McCarran in confessing his personal embarrassment and misgivings. But like so many to come in a Nevada that felt so acutely the disdain of the rest of the nation, as well as its harrowing history of want and exploitation, he could be fierce in the face of outside pressure, even knowing the repugnance of all he was defending.

"You say you don't know who my advisers are here," he chided a Reno editor and old friend who had questioned him on the gambling issue. "I think you know me long enough to know that I'm my own adviser and I don't go off on a blind trail or a false road very often." But in this, he would be both blind and false. He held the fate of Nevada in his hands. In his time, he alone had the political power to confront the criminal forces of Las Vegas while they were still nascent and relatively vulnerable. In the climactic decision of his long and turbulent career, he characteristically chose to justify and defend his beloved Nevada rather than take it into one more battle with poverty and want. The man who toppled one machine and erected his own, fought a tyrant and became one, would now leave his cherished desert mountains to the most tyrannical machine of all.

Afterward, the harsh ironies of his career would be visible, if unintended, in his memorial statue in the Capitol rotunda, a seven-foot bronze figure, rigidly erect in flowing judicial robes, a faint smile on the face, standing above the legend: "Champion of the American way of life."

As a young man running for office and then as senator, McCarran always drew large, respectful crowds in his home state. Taking their dark Sunday-best suits and dresses out of mothball storage, the common people of Nevada—ranchhands and sheepherders, laborers and miners, storekeepers and clerks, Paiute, Mojave, and Washoe, farmwives and schoolteachers, prostitutes and dealers—came down from the hills and in from the country to see and hear him. For them, "humbled by long neglect," simply grateful someone cared, he was their hero no matter what anyone said, or what he did.

When McCarran dropped dead of a massive stroke at the close of a Red-baiting speech in Hawthorne in the winter of 1954, the same people crowded his funeral in solemn tribute and farewell. "The smell of mothballs," wrote one journalist, "was everywhere."

4. Bugsy Siegel

The Executioner as Entrepreneur

The murder made national headlines. Photographs and news-reels captured the gruesome scene in a living room of a palatial home in Beverly Hills: The corpse, like a discarded doll, crumpled at the end of a bloodstained chintz sofa, the left eye shot out with precision, its eyelid found intact ten feet away. Resting a .30-caliber army carbine outside the window on a rose-laced pergola a dozen feet from the target, the marksman had fired an additional eight copper jacketed shells for good measure. One left another dime-sized dark tunnel through the victim's forehead.

The killing was a brief sensation in the tabloid papers. Decades later, a movie version would reduce the story to cliché if not fiction. But at the time, America saw nothing more than another gangland slaying—which is what the murderers, and Las Vegas, counted on.

Born in 1905, Benjamin Siegel was another child of refugees, of hope. His family had fled the pogroms directed against Jews in Russian-ruled Kiev. In a Brooklyn ghetto, his mother wanted him to be an accountant. At nine, he was a fearless, cocky child of the streets. By thirteen, he had become odious. As a leader of the Bugs and Meyer Mob, he killed thirty men himself, more with other gunmen. "He had gotten away with so many gangland executions," said one associate, "that he felt murder was legal, as long as it was done by him." Detonating instantly into narrow-eyed furies that drove him to maim and kill, he could return just as suddenly to an eerie, grinning calm. He was and always would be chillingly unpredictable. Siegel, the FBI noted in one report, was "insane along certain lines."

The FBI later compiled at least a partial list of his prewar "business interests" with Lansky and their partners. It would be a first official glimpse of only a segment of the larger confederation: control of vice and other corruption in New York City, Philadelphia, and Baltimore; gambling in Newark and prostitution and other illicit businesses in the rest of New Jersey; illegal racing and gambling houses in Florida and a dozen other states; a dog track in Council Bluffs, Iowa; racketeering throughout the Midwest and Middle South; vice in Detroit; what the FBI called working "hand in glove" to share Chicago with the "Capone element" and its successors; narcotics nationwide. Bugsy was one of America's most successful entrepreneurs.

With the repeal of Prohibition, Lansky sent Siegel to Los Angeles to extort the film industry, to make book, and to run gambling on the side. In his mid-thirties in the years before World War II, he became mythic in his milieu. Despite his pathological savagery, he was a charmer and irrepressible social climber whose temper was part of his allure. "His rages were so pure and incandescent, so very much the essence of Benny," wrote Lansky's biographer, Robert Lacey, "that people who knew him did not take offense at them—not until he started to threaten them, at least."

He was an inveterate womanizer and dandy, and was soon a Hollywood celebrity. Known for expensive houndstooth jackets, he wore only the finest garments tailored by Pietro of Beverly Hills, along with silk shirts and alligator shoes.

He was called a "sportsman" in the euphemism of the time. Publicly, he appeared in the company of starlets and actors. Privately, he shook down studio executives for protection. By 1937, he had cornered the $500,000-a-day local bookmaking operation and ruled the ubiquitous gambling boats anchored off the coast, what prosecutor Burton Turkus and reporter Sid Feder in their famous book *Murder, Inc.* called "a beachhead of organized crime in California."

Yet the extortion and gambling for which Siegel was notorious were almost minor beside the drug trade that now became organized crime's major stake in the West. Though it was by no means generally known—and later histories would often fail to acknowledge it as well—by the late 1930s the heroin trade in the United States was already one of the nation's largest businesses, accounting for more than $1 billion annually, and almost entirely monopolized by the Lansky Syndicate. When the prevailing heroin routes from Europe and Japan were cut off by World War II, Lansky financed a new connection via Mexico, with Siegel overseeing the trafficking and often smuggling himself. In this period before Pearl Harbor, Bugsy became friendly with government officials on both sides of the border, among them a young assistant city attorney from Whittier, a would-be politician named Richard Nixon.

In the early forties, when the Nevada legislature voted to legalize betting on horse race results by wire, Siegel went to Las Vegas to take over bookmaking in the casinos, creating a monopoly for his new Trans America Wire Service. To achieve that status, Bugsy would brag to a friend, he had had to kill ten men. He was soon extorting from each subscribing casino more than $25,000 a week for the wire.

Meanwhile, the modern Strip was still a deserted road. Tom Hull, owner of the well-known Hollywood Roosevelt and other classic hotels, was driving from Southern California to Salt Lake City in 1940 when he got a flat tire on the outskirts of Las Vegas. While he was waiting for help, Hull began to count the out-of-state cars whizzing by. Amazed at the traffic and the potential for a new hotel, he paid $100 an acre for the land where his sixty-six-acre El Rancho would open the following year with a huge swimming pool next to the highway to entice the stream of motorists. It was soon joined by the newer, better-appointed Last Frontier. When Siegel first drove into Las Vegas in 1942 on the narrow Los Angeles highway, these were the sole sizable gambling establishments on the road. Both were squat, rambling motels with the only swimming pools and the first air-conditioned rooms in the often torrid valley, and a veneer of elegance over their dude-ranch essence. There were the first touches of what post-Depression America would later covet—or be persuaded to covet—in its own homes. "Stream-lined upholstered chairs in harmony with drapes and bedspreads," is how a newspaper reporter described the "luxurious" rooms. Unique in size and pretension, the two motels were always overbooked as wartime Las Vegas boomed.

Investing for Lansky and their partners as well as himself, Bugsy bought and sold interests in the downtown Golden Nugget, and in the Frontier, Las Vegas, and Boulder clubs. Despite gasoline rationing and the general decline in tourists traveling during the war, the casinos were flourishing. Hordes of servicemen stationed at the nearby gunnery range crowded the town, as well as busloads of soldiers and other personnel who drove down from remote army installations to the north. In 1943, Siegel tried to purchase the El Rancho. With scruple and candor rare for the town, its owner refused. "The people of Las Vegas have been too good to me," said Hull, "for me to repay them in that way." Two years later, Siegel bought the El Cortez, then sold it for a profit in early 1946, though leaving it in the hands of other Lansky associates. He looked back toward the Strip.

At this moment, too, the Syndicate's Mexican drug trade was already immense and growing—a fact altogether ignored in most conventional histories of the era, and even in accounts of organized crime. The drug trade through Mexico surpassed the combined narcotics traffic into the United States from the rest of the world. The web of heroin distribution included Havana, Mexico City, Miami, Los Angeles, New York, Philadelphia, and a score of other cities. It was all done with what scholar Peter Dale Scott documented as "high level corruption in the Mexican government," including the collusion not only of Mexican police and politicians, but also and especially of the notorious Dirección Federal de Seguridad (DFS), the intelligence service and secret police of Mexico's oligarchy.

From the beginning, America's OSS and successor CIA, on which the DFS patterned itself, were knowing and complicitous partners in the Mexican corruption and its flourishing narcotics traffic, shielding major drug dealers considered sources, and agents such as Harold "Happy" Meltzer, John Armento, Louis Tom Dragna, Nig Rosen—the same men and their associates hired as Cold War intelligence sources and agents, even as assassins. The founder of the DFS and a longtime intimate associate of the CIA, Captain Rafael Chavarri, would leave the intelligence agency to work directly and openly for Mexico's leading international drug trafficker, Jorge Moreno Chauvet, in turn a longtime partner of the Lansky-Luciano faction of the American Syndicate with its own European drug connections. Altogether, U.S. intelligence and law enforcement would be deeply "enmeshed," as Scott recorded, "in the drug intrigues and protection of the DFS," yet another nexus of crime and politics that extended Lansky's ties—now become Siegel's—to covert government. When Bugsy moved to Las Vegas in 1946, he was identified in FBN files as "one of the world's biggest dope ring operators," and by the FBI as "closely connected with narcotic smuggling and distribution."

The people of Nevada generally knew none of this. Nor did the state's officials or press wish to know, staying "abysmally ignorant of the machinations of organized crime," as native author Robert Laxalt said of them. The few Las Vegas gamblers familiar with Siegel's background in the rackets and as a drug trafficker were either "bought off or terrified into silence," one informer remembered. For most Nevadans, whispers about Siegel were easy to dismiss. "To the local gentry of Las Vegas," Laxalt wrote, "he was a handsome, wealthy, hard-driving man with a mind-dizzying vision. That he had chosen sun-baked and shabby Las Vegas was enough to quell those nasty rumors that such a man could be associated in any way with the underworld, whatever that was."

The vision they welcomed was imposing: a gambling palace unlike anything Nevada had seen before. Flush with drug profits, and under Lansky's direction, Bugsy began a bold new enterprise along a 1,000-foot frontage of the Strip at the site of a crumbling old motel on thirty acres of sand and scrub. He actually took over the project from a Hollywood society columnist who had begun a venture on the land in 1945 but had run out of money. The site he selected with shrewd foresight, around the first bend in the highway out of sight of the two existing Strip hotels or Glitter Gulch, was alone on the right side of the road, giving easier access to the incoming California traffic. It was to be an opulent resort—no dressed-up dude ranch or sawdust-covered floor, not another hot spot where the public crossed a state line or slipped into a backroom, but a showcase for star entertainers, celebrities, and customers from all over the world. It was to represent quality and taste, and to produce incredible profits and respectability, to marry criminal money to legal finance, famous names, and businesses, the throbbing new wealth and power of America. "A casino ambiance," one said, "that was Beverly Hills, rather than Nevada." Siegel invested more than $1 million. At one point "Dandy" Phil Kastel, a partner of New York racketeer Frank Costello, carried bundles of cash stuffed in two suitcases to Las Vegas. The hotel would be called the Flamingo.

Siegel, once a skeptic, was then a convert become a fanatic. "The goddamn biggest, fanciest gaming casino and hotel you bastards ever seen in your whole lives," was Bugsy's description to a reporter.

He built with the imperiousness and impatience of a pharaoh ordering his pyramid, which, in a sense, he was. He hired contractor Del Webb, frequent builder for the Syndicate and friend of J. Edgar Hoover, Howard Hughes, and other powerful figures. When even Webb met obstacles, Bugsy was implacable. He traded lavishly on the black market, often ransoming materials stolen from the site the night before. He flew in carpenters, plumbers, and electricians from California or Arizona, paying craftsmen triple time, insisting on only prime copper piping and other premium materials. He bribed the Teamsters to speed deliveries, and to loot other shipments. At one point he even traveled to the Middle East to find exotic desert landscaping, and tried as well to import live flamingos, watching two of them die in the heat before he canceled his order for a hundred more. "Pipe, palms, perfume, and parties alone came close to eating up the entire building budget," said Las Vegas reporter Dick Odessky.

The weekly *Las Vegas Tribune* protested the extravagance at a time when returning veterans could not get materials to build family homes. "The public will tolerate gambling only as long as gambling will subjugate itself to the welfare of the people of the community," it editorialized. The *Tribune* was wrong, and soon itself gone. Bugsy knew better.

He corrupted officials as a routine business cost, a portent of the city's next half century. In what the FBI called "Siegel's hook-up," he claimed to have paid off Senator McCarran and the Reno head of the federal Civilian Production Administration to lift a building freeze by falsifying records, affidavits, and permits. He bribed and bullied Clark County commissioners as they lagged in licensing. When one, a devout Mormon, held out, Bugsy met him in a steam bath. The commissioner emerged shaking, and promptly agreed to the Flamingo licenses.

According to an FBI report, Siegel told a friend in August 1946 that McCarran was "already cooperating with them." For that, Siegel said, the senator needed no more bribes. Bugsy went on to remark, the report continued, that if McCarran was questioned by lawmen, he "should play dumb and advise that he knows nothing about [deleted], SIEGEL, et al."

The chief FBI agent in Los Angeles recommended to Washington "an open and thorough investigation of this matter on both the Bribery and Fraud Against the Government theory." Five months later, FBI headquarters ordered that the agent "immediately discontinue" any investigation of the graft.

"We don't run for office," Bugsy later told an underling who wanted to go into local government. "We own the politicians."

Meanwhile, the casino took shape. Master stonemasons and woodworkers installed imported marble and rare woods. So well constructed was the casino's spiral staircase that thirty years later, when crews tore it down, it took them two full days of jackhammering. "His guiding principle was *class*," said one observer, "at least as conceived by a mobster."

Aptly, they had named their managing company the Nevada Project Corporation. "When he [Siegel] started building the luxurious Flamingo," one writer noted, "Las Vegans applauded the move as that of one of the community's most farseeing and public-spirited citizens." As so often in the state, the arrival of such obvious money and power was to be welcomed by the public as a reservoir of revenue and jobs. When Bugsy bought big ads in the town's *Evening Review-Journal,* the editor posted a note in the newsroom: "From this day forward Mr. Siegel of the Flamingo will never be referred to as 'Bugsy.' Make it Ben or Benjamin."

Siegel planned the Flamingo's grand opening for Christmas 1946, but his temper and extravagant demands brought nagging delays. Costs soared and he needed more money. His partners were uneasy not only about the expense and delay but now about his private life as well. He was obsessed both with the Flamingo and with a woman named Virginia Hill, whom the FBI would call a "fabulous woman of mystery." She was from backwoods Alabama, one of ten children of a poor marble polisher. At seventeen she had "turned some tricks," as an FBI agent put it, at the Chicago World's Fair. She was soon the girlfriend of hoodlums, serving as occasional courier and decoy. When Bugsy met her, she was nearly thirty, an auburn-haired beauty known for her stunning long legs—always one of his weaknesses.

He was instantly smitten. Their affair was tempestuous yet laced with innocent joyfulness. "They're like children," Lansky told his brother. An avuncular Lansky advised Siegel's wife, Esther, to file for divorce, thinking it would force Bugsy back from what one observer called "playing like a horse put out to stud." But Bugsy surprised them all when he agreed to a Reno divorce and to paying Esther $600-a-week alimony for life. In September 1946, the Flamingo a rising skeleton on the Strip, Virginia and Bugsy eloped to Mexico.

That autumn he flew east in need of still more capital from his partners, extracting $1 million after strained conversations. In November, Valley National Bank of Phoenix, known in Arizona for its longtime financial support of Webb and its close relationship with the wealthy Goldwater family, loaned the Flamingo $600,000. Bugsy had already secured another $500,000 bank loan outside Nevada and a crucial $600,000 from what the FBI identified only as "a Utah corporation." So began a long tradition of the financing of modern Las Vegas by Mormons, regional and local banks, unions and corporations, eventually by the nation's largest financial institutions and Wall Street itself.

But agreeable bankers, furtive corporations or fronts, and local boosters no longer controlled Bugsy's fate. Some in the Syndicate thought him insanely profligate and unaccountable to his investors. Others believed that Virginia, with or without him, was skimming cash. Lansky sent Moe Dalitz to spy on Bugsy. Early in December 1946, the Syndicate called a historic conference of its leaders in Havana. Pointedly, Siegel was absent. Every other major figure attended, all of whom would play prominent roles in the history of Las Vegas: Lansky, Luciano, Frank Costello, Marcello of New Orleans, Santo Trafficante from Florida and Cuba, Dalitz from the Midwest, even their fawning court entertainer, Frank Sinatra, who performed for the group but was not allowed into business discussions. Lansky brought up what he called "the matter of the Flamingo." The casino, he said, would cost $5 million more than planned. Following an outcry, he assured the others that it was "peanuts" compared to the money that would be made there. But then Dalitz reported from his Vegas spying that Bugsy had been stealing from them. Others confirmed from Swiss contacts that Hill had deposited half a million dollars in a Zurich bank.

Lansky pleaded with rare emotion, asking his colleagues to remember how much Bugsy had done for them. "They looked at him stony-faced without saying a word," said an eyewitness, "and Meyer realized that Bugsy's fate was sealed." Out of respect for Lansky, his colleagues let him make a quick trip to California to see Bugsy. "I can't do a thing with him," Lansky told a friend upon his return. "He's so much in that woman's power that he cannot see reason."

On the day after Christmas, the Flamingo opened as planned amid what one journalist called with unintended irony "the gaudy opulence of a top hoodlum's funeral." Siegel, who had bribed reporters to promote the opening, welcomed patrons in a swallow-tail coat and a white tie, with Virginia on his arm. Showman George Jessel was master of ceremonies. Xavier Cugat's Latin orchestra played in the showroom. But bad weather had grounded chartered planes in Los Angeles, and William Randolph Hearst, out of an old feud with Siegel over a woman, was said to have threatened celebrities with bad publicity if they attended the Las Vegas opening. The crowd was small, the rooms not yet ready. Guests drifted away early with heavy winnings before dealers hit their stride, leaving the brightly lit, half-finished Flamingo hauntingly isolated in the bare desert. "A lonely giant," was how journalist Hank Messick described it.

There were other omens. When Lena Horne sang at the Flamingo two weeks later, she refused to room in West Las Vegas, where blacks were segregated by city ordinance in neighborhoods without water lines or sewage. Bugsy relented and allowed her to stay near the casino in a cabana, though every morning the maids burned her bed linens.

Losing $300,000 in the first two weeks, forced to close by late January 1947, Bugsy scrambled again for capital. He coerced more out of Lansky. In February, Valley National in Phoenix shelled out another $300,000. By March, after a dress rehearsal attended by Lansky himself, the hotel reopened, rooms ready.

Bugsy's press agent, Herman "Hank" Greenspun, hatched new promotional schemes. With cheap buffets, bingo, and prize drawings, the Flamingo appealed to locals and a less affluent clientele. "Siegel's most desperate days," wrote one historian of the town, "gave birth to marketing techniques that have become mainstays of the industry ever since." Still, old methods endured. When a clerk at the El Rancho called the Flamingo a "gyp joint,"

Bugsy pistol-whipped him, threatening to kill the El Rancho's owner and burn the casino down.

There was also important collateral business. The Flamingo with its showgirls became, and remained, a major depot in what the FBI identified as the Syndicate's "white slave trade"—the FBI's term for prostitution and pornography. At the same time, the new resort and other casinos were becoming significant in money laundering of profits made elsewhere from narcotics and other vice. As William Chambliss would later record in his book *On the Take,* bagmen carrying the proceeds of Syndicate branches up and down the West Coast as well as from locales around the country—what Chambliss called "an inevitable outgrowth of the political economy of American cities"—converged on Las Vegas at regular intervals to "launder" and redistribute the cash. By May, the house showed a profit. But the partners were unappeased. And even apart from the tensions around the Flamingo, Siegel was locked in a major struggle for control of the lucrative off-track betting in California as well as Nevada. In the process he was defying the new Chicago owners of the Continental race wire, who the year before had killed James Ragen to silence his explosive testimony and take over the hugely profitable operation.

On the morning of June 20, 1947, Bugsy flew to Los Angeles. He went, as always, to Virginia's showy, Moorish-style bungalow at 810 North Linden Drive in Beverly Hills. Conveniently—some thought intentionally—she was in Paris. Late that evening, he relaxed on the sofa reading early editions of the morning papers. Latticed roses played at the windows. The heavy draperies, usually drawn, were open.

The bullet through his eye was a phenomenal shot. The sofa sat at an angle to the window, and "the killer almost had to shoot around the corner," concluded the FBI. The man who cradled the carbine on the pergola, and his partner beside him, were never charged or prosecuted, though their identities would be known by officials in Nevada and Washington. Like Binion's casino manager Louis McWillie, they were associates of Jack Ruby—the Chicago hoodlum who moved that year to Dallas.

Back in Las Vegas, the murder produced what state Tax Commission secretary Robbins Cahill called "the jitters." Sensational national stories about Siegel and his sordid past seemed sudden proof of what had only been whispered in the town. "When this thing began to scream in the papers . . . people began really finding out they'd probably gotten a little more than they'd bargained for," Cahill remembered. "They'd gotten a big beautiful palace, but also there were problems that probably were going to start . . . everywhere you would go, people were whispering in corners." Downtown in Glitter

Gulch, old hands thought the Siegel assassination would trigger a gang war. Soon after the killing, P. O. Silvagni, builder of the Apache Hotel in 1932, his thick Italian accent one of the town's amusements, announced to a crowd of customers, as one of them remembered, "Blood isa gonna run into the streets, blood isa gonna be runnin' in the streets."

Anxiety quickly gave way to new profits. Discreetly overlooked by bankers and boosters during his life, Bugsy's fame as a gangster became in death instant good business. The murder made Vegas "wickedly enticing," thought one historian, visitors swarming to the once desolate Strip, in a sense never to leave. For her part, Virginia was said to have attempted suicide when she heard of the shooting, and slipped into obscurity.

As Bugsy was buried, the town scarcely noticed. "A couple of gaming gents stopped casino action for five minutes during the funeral," a witness recalled. But the execution was a dividing line: Mania and larceny had sucked in too much money for the Syndicate, banks, or city to abandon. Within minutes of the bullet boring through Bugsy's eye, trusted men with "grifter sense," as one journalist put it, took over the Flamingo; "like generals mopping up after a coup," another reporter wrote of them. They and their more refined, businesslike successors, corporate executives with the hoodlum ethic, were to be the future of Las Vegas.

As a corpse dressed in a houndstooth jacket and clotted blood, the charming, volatile killer predictable at last, he would never be remembered as "Mr. Siegel of the Flamingo" or Ben—just Bugsy. But his final frenzy began a kingdom.

5. Hank Greenspun

The Hustler as Conscience

In Las Vegas, where concealment was a civic value, Herman Milton Greenspun hid in the open on the front page of his newspaper, for nearly forty years. Self-proclaimed conscience of the city of players, he was a player *extraordinaire.*

He was born in the late summer of 1909 in Flatbush when Brooklyn was still rural. He would remember his father as a small, "saintly" man, a Talmudic scholar of devout lineage, absorbed in books and ever improvident in his art shop. The force and example of the family was his dark-haired mother, Anna Bella, a fiery woman who supported them with her own small grocery, at one point bootlegging on the side while her unknowing husband pored over the Talmud.

Once, on Mother's orders, the little boy climbed through a window to collect from a tardy customer on his paper route, and was greeted with an anti-Semitic slur. Anna Bella marched him back to that house, where she was soon in a slapping fight with the man who had uttered the offensive remark while her son kicked his shins. Herman collected. "The episode taught me a lesson I would never forget," he would say.

The Greenspun family lived briefly in a house with chicken coops and a privy in a black section of New Haven, Connecticut, where Hymele, as he was known at home, fought with boys he called "niggers" and who called him "kike." Back in Brooklyn by the early twenties, he grew into a broad-shouldered six-footer, nicknamed "Dempsey" for the boxer he resembled.

He also bore what one historian called the family's "deep sense of its Jewish identity." He formed a child's vivid memory of the portrait of the founder of Zionism. "I knew every wrinkle on the painted face of Theodore Herzl," he wrote fifty years later, "before I could even identify a picture of George Washington."

Ever spurred by his mother, he went to college and on to law school at St. John's in Brooklyn. He worked his way through as a runner and tout for Leblang-Gray's Theater Ticket Agency. Tie pulled to one side and hat pushed back, shirtsleeves rolled up to the elbow, he was in the midst of a Runyonesque Broadway world of what its inhabitants called "lamisters," known for "making a fast buck and taking it on the lam." His early hero was a chronicler of the scene, Heywood Broun.

He received his law degree in 1934 and became active in Republican politics for New York mayor Fiorello La Guardia. He apprenticed as a clerk in the Harlem law offices of La Guardia's protégé, the GOP congressman and later renegade radical Vito Marcantonio. He also joined Tom Dewey's campaign for district attorney, and the future governor and presidential nominee offered to hire him full-time. But the job as gangbusting prosecutor paid less than he made hawking Broadway tickets, and by 1937, having just passed the bar, he was already bored with the law. "A lawyer," he would say of himself, "who liked the spirit, not the letter."

At the age of twenty-nine he began a run of larger-than-life, sometimes strangely implausible ventures. He would explain their success as fortuitous, the result of circumstance, pluck, and a gift for seizing opportunity. Some saw in it the man's daring, his dauntless brilliance and charm, his irrepressible energy and confidence. Others found a grandiosity, an often ugly hunger—and a labyrinth of coincidence and connections far beyond fortune or talent.

In 1938, he struck out on his own, founding Vulcan Steel, a jobber with twenty employees. Two years later, as he would tell the story, unidentified but obviously well-connected associates in upstate New York, whom he would call vaguely "some influential Republican allies in Buffalo," tipped him off about the Nagle Engine Works in Erie, Pennsylvania, on sale for half a million dollars, a fraction of its value. He optioned the plant for $1,000, and in 1940 promptly won from the Maritime Commission in Washington a $2.48 million contract, followed by a $12 million contract, to build Liberty Ship engines.

It was a market about to explode into the multimillions with the onset of World War II, and it was generally the preserve of only the most well connected if dubious giants of shipping and finance, such as Aristotle Onassis, Howard Hughes, or the furtive billionaire D. K. Ludwig—all of whom were to play shadowy, long-secret roles in the history of Las Vegas. In any case, the Maritime Commission with its fortune-making contracts was a well of prewar corruption, and the subject of later congressional inquiries. There would be allegations decades afterward that Greenspun had been tipped off about the Nagle Works earlier than he maintained, that he was involved even then in ties with Onassis and Hughes in what amounted to war profiteering, that he would keep these early anonymous contacts in Buffalo, Washington, and elsewhere throughout his life, the details locked away in his small office safe pregnant with secrets. But by the time any investigation of the Maritime Commission was underway, Greenspun would be long gone from the scene, never to be officially implicated with the suspect names or practices. Drafted by the army in the spring of 1941, he grudgingly ceded Nagle for $35,000 to a Texas partner later involved in war profiteering.

During the war he rose to the rank of captain, and found he had a flair for editing the camp newspaper. Trained in ordnance, he almost lost his feet to frostbite in Patton's Third Army, but won the Croix de Guerre as well as four battle stars and a commendation from Eisenhower. On the eve of Normandy, he had married an Irish Jewish beauty thirteen years younger, the daughter of a prominent Paramount Pictures distributor. At war's end he took her back to New York, where he planned, again, to practice law.

Then, only months later, he drove off across the country in his red Buick convertible with an equally colorful client who was a racetrack promoter. "Fast-talking Joe Smoot . . . who had already made and lost several fortunes," as Greenspun described his traveling companion, was yet another pivotal figure in his life, much like his Buffalo friends who had tipped him off to the Nagle deal. Smoot had long-standing ties to Buffalo's Jacobs family, whose Sportsystems combine of concessions and professional sports franchises would later be implicated in extensive dealings with organized crime. After saying he and Smoot were heading out west to build a racetrack, in September 1946, at thirty-seven, Greenspun turned up in Las Vegas.

"It was love at first sight," he said of the city Lansky had found a "horrible place" not long before. Greenspun was charmed, he wrote, by "a perfect paradise of majestic mountains, infinite skies, and balmy air," with the added color of "swinging door saloons, blanketed Indians, bearded prospectors, and burros." Yet what drew him most, he admitted later, was that "the whole town reminded me in the oddest way of Leblang's . . . a nesting place and sanctuary for lamisters . . . looking for elbow room and broadly tolerant freedom." It was a place he understood. "He quickly found people he could talk to," wrote one reporter.

He soon fell out with his partner in the racetrack scheme, both the track and Smoot effectively disappearing from the Las Vegas scene after a short interval. Greenspun launched a glossy, pocket-sized entertainment magazine called *Las Vegas Life,* a semimonthly for a nickel featuring his own column "Gleanings from Glitter Gulch." He claimed to have met Bugsy Siegel one evening in 1946, when Siegel bought the entire back page of the magazine to advertise the new Flamingo. When the casino reopened the following March, Hank, as he had now westernized his name, had taken what he called a "well paid position" as publicity agent for Bugsy's resort, writing a column called "Flamingo Chatter" for the *Review-Journal.* He was adept at luring the public. "Greenspun's pen," wrote one reporter, "captured the image Siegel wished to project." It was also, insiders knew, the image wanted by Lansky, who understood well that Bugsy and the Flamingo desperately needed someone like Greenspun.

A few months after Bugsy's death, Greenspun quit the Flamingo, scrapped his magazine, and for $6,666 bought a 15 percent interest in another Strip casino, the Desert Inn, going up on Bugsy's model. Its builder was a small, red-faced, prematurely gray gambler who had been a San Diego bellhop, a craps dealer at the Reno Bank Club of Graham and McKay, a manager of hoodlum gambling ships off the West Coast, and a part owner of El Rancho. For a generation the new casino's marquee would carry his name, Wilbur Clark, "a man I soon came to love as a brother," Greenspun said. The deal with Clark included a one-third share in a motel being built around the casino. He also became the Desert Inn's publicity director.

At about the same time, by the end of 1947, Greenspun invested in the start-up of the town's second radio station. On the day of the station's grand opening, with the governor of Nevada on hand, a phone call intervened. Greenspun's cousin Reynold Selk summoned him to meet at the Last Frontier with a friend who had just flown into town—Adolph "Al" Schwimmer. An American-born Zionist and former TWA flight engineer, Schwimmer was also a principal smuggler of weapons to the Jewish forces in Palestine then warring with Arabs, and destined to a certain eminence in the twilight world of espionage and big business in the last half of the century. Greenspun's "friend" would go on to become a ranking operative of the Israeli Mossad intelligence agency, one of the founders of the Israeli Air Force, a major international arms dealer, a special adviser to Israeli prime ministers, a

clandestine lobbyist in Washington with intimate contacts at the highest levels of U.S. intelligence, and a central figure in the Iran-Contra scandal some
forty years later. For now, however, he had come to Las Vegas on a plane
secretly chartered by the Jewish underground army to dispatch Greenspun
on a mission.

The new radio station owner dropped everything, left his wife and two
infants without saying good-bye, and boarded the chartered plane that day.
For most of the next year, by his own account, he forged, hijacked at pistol
point, and generally connived his way on an odyssey of gunrunning to
Hawaii, Mexico, the Dominican Republic, Panama, and New York. He would
claim credit for fifty-eight crates of machine guns and ammunition smuggled to the Middle East through the U.S. embargo. In the process he over-
came rebellious sailors and dishonest Mexican officials, feats he described in
some detail in his autobiography, *Where I Stand: The Biography of a Reckless
Man*. He was proud of getting to Palestine "anything that shoots," he wrote,
"whatever the consequences."

But the network he joined was also involved in what one historian called
"other covert operations," which the otherwise voluble Greenspun never
acknowledged, whatever his personal role might have been. Later disclosures
showed that Teddy Kollek, a future mayor of Jerusalem who was Greenspun's
close associate in the gunrunning, as well as other Jewish agents with whom
Greenspun was a "key operative," as Robert Friedman called him, performed
clandestine missions well beyond smuggling crates of weapons. Operating
out of Manhattan's McAlpin Hotel, they also carried briefcases of cash to
bribe Latin American presidents to recognize diplomatically or otherwise
aid the new state of Israel. They colluded with organized crime to move
waterfront contraband on the New York and New Jersey docks. They made
payoffs in that year's presidential campaign to the Democratic incumbent,
whose backing of a Jewish state would be crucial. "Two million dollars went
aboard the Truman train in a paper bag," said an eyewitness and White
House intimate, Steve Smith, "and that's what paid for the state of Israel."

Greenspun would be indicted twice for federal Neutrality Act violations,
his legal defense provided by Israeli interests. Acquitted in a first trial in the
fall of 1949, he pled guilty to a second set of charges in 1950. His lawyers managed an implicit arrangement with the judge about the sentence, and Senator
McCarran intervened "to keep Greenspun from going to jail," McCarran
would say later. Greenspun's crime was "most serious" because the arms were
"used to kill innocent people in a war," the judge pronounced at sentencing.
"Innocent people? *The Arabs?*" Greenspun blurted out. Still, he was given a
suspended sentence and ordered to pay a $10,000 fine, promptly taken care

of by people one reporter called "friends of Israel." An unrepentant and audacious Greenspun would later justify his actions, writing that a "man sometimes has to bend the law to travel the straight line of justice."

Meanwhile, he returned to Las Vegas in 1949 to find that Wilbur Clark had taken on new partners at the Desert Inn—Lansky associate Dalitz and some people he described as Cleveland "investors." As Syndicate millions poured in over the next few months to finish the casino, Clark withered to a figurehead. Greenspun's 15 percent dwindled to a single point.

But by this time, early in 1950, striking union printers from the *Review-Journal* had started their own *Free Press*. When they suffered an advertising boycott by anti-union casino owners like Dalitz, some of the printers approached Greenspun to take over the publication while McCarran cronies were also angling to buy it. He now quit the Desert Inn to acquire the small newspaper for $100,000. He paid the International Typographical Union (ITU) $1,000 down, borrowing the rest of the money from Nate Mack, a Las Vegas businessman who was "deeply sympathetic," as Greenspun put it, to the smuggling of arms for Israel. The new publisher signed a $99,000 chattel mortgage on his fledgling newspaper, but angry ITU members would charge its leadership with "draining $282,331 of pension funds" that was "slipped to Greenspun as a personal loan," according to later news accounts.

In town less than four years, he had tried to start a racetrack, published a nightlife magazine, flacked for Bugsy Siegel, worked for and owned part of a Strip casino, opened his own radio station, traveled widely for a year as a secret Israeli agent, and was now publisher and editor of what he would rechristen the *Las Vegas Sun*. It was only the beginning.

Greenspun published his credo in the first edition of the *Sun* on June 21, 1950: "I pledge that I will always fight for progress and reform; never tolerate injustice or corruption; never lack sympathy with the underprivileged; always remain devoted to the public welfare . . . always be drastically independent." The paper would be inseparable from the man, his passion and prejudices, and his ceaseless self-glorification.

At forty-one he had the boyish handsomeness of a muscular light-heavyweight, with steely blue eyes, black hair, a jutting angular jaw, and what *The New Yorker*'s A. J. Liebling saw as "two rows of square white and gold teeth frequently exposed in a menacing grin." His front-page column, "Where I Stand," in deliberate contrast to the *Review-Journal* editor's "From Where I Sit," led every edition with what he later called "primitive, pungent, and unpredictable prose." For the first three years, the *Sun* would have no full-time reporter, Greenspun himself a one-man show.

Notwithstanding McCarran's *ex parte* plea with the court on Greenspun's behalf, he quickly took on the senator. In part it reflected a loathing of political machines learned in the New York of Tammany Hall; in part it was simply good business to battle a politician who "had the rival *Review-Journal* in his hip-pocket," as one historian noted. "A large high-floating balloon," one reporter called McCarran at that moment, "held by frayed string." Another thought the choice of defending good government was simple: "Let's face it, it's easier to crusade for Jesus Christ than it is for Judas Iscariot." But Greenspun claimed to be driven even more by the naked anti-Semitism of the old Reno politician, who had chided New York senator Herbert Lehman about the "cloak-and-suit" crowd in Manhattan, and who referred to Greenspun as the "Israelite."

The publisher called him in return the "old buzzard," and attacked his "snorting" style, "cruel" immigration bill, and most of all corruption at home, including ties to criminals. ". . . The president might be interested," he wrote in an open column to Eisenhower in 1954, "that Sen. McCarran has been the protector of the criminal element of the country since 1938. And when I say 'criminal element' I do not mean isolated hoodlums in isolated places. The top crime syndicate in the country, the blackest names in criminal annals, have always looked to and received the protecting cloak thrown over them by the senior senator from Nevada." He saw a "political machine" behind McCarran, "bent on throttling all opposition, destroying democratic processes, dictating policy, and thriving on the proceeds." Wounded, the patriarch hit back in a reprisal that ended up only exalting his tormentor.

In March 1952, casino owners warned Greenspun to "back off" the senator. Within days most Las Vegas casinos canceled their *Sun* ads. The owners had met and agreed to "bust" Greenspun. "It was decided to clip his wings," a McCarran man remembered. In fact, the reprisal traced more to local political arbiter Norman Biltz than to McCarran himself. But when Greenspun asked Dalitz what was going on, the gangster answered, "You know as well as I do that we have to do what he [McCarran] tells us. You know he got us our licenses." Enraged, Greenspun sued McCarran and forty casino owners for their "conspiracy."

The legal clash was tangled, but in the end Greenspun uncovered a call from McCarran's office in Washington to hotel owners that coincided with the boycott. Attorneys for the gamblers quickly settled, giving Greenspun $80,500 and assuring the casinos' continued advertising in the *Sun*. He drove down Fremont Street and the Strip in a new convertible, top down, honking and flourishing the cash as he passed each joint. "He was harder than ever to handle after that," recalled a McCarran insider. The episode left him with unique strength as a civic voice and leader. As an editor, and in his heroic standing with the Israelis and the Jewish community, he already enjoyed national as well as local prominence greater than any other Las Vegan of the era. Behind all that were his powerful original backers in Buffalo, and now a growing friendship with the formidable Benny Binion, whom he had helped to obtain a gambling license and who would be the only owner not to join in the boycott. It all gave him his own juice, which adversaries like Dalitz clearly recognized and which Greenspun now began to flaunt.

He continued with attacks on an even more notorious demagogue, Senator Joe McCarthy. At a 1952 Las Vegas rally, McCarthy, who was in the habit of referring to the publisher as "Greenscum," charged him in a slip of the tongue with being an "ex-Communist" when he meant to say, more accurately, "ex-convict." Greenspun rushed the stage as McCarthy left, and won over the crowd with his fierce rebuttal. Most editors and politicians in the nation cowered before the Wisconsin Red-baiter, but Greenspun—now virtually libel-proof and often relying on documents provided by nationally syndicated columnist Drew Pearson and his protégé Jack Anderson—called him "the scabrous, slimy, loathsome thing," a "scheming swashbuckler," "sadistic pervert," and "the queer that made Milwaukee famous."

His brazenness, of course, earned him enemies among McCarthy and McCarran allies. Columnist Westbrook Pegler, a notorious reactionary but also a writer who exposed organized crime ties in baseball and other businesses, accused Greenspun of being Bugsy Siegel's henchman and of reaping a million dollars personally in the arms traffic to Israel—what fellow Jews called a *mamzer* for profiting from a noble cause. The IRS audited him. The Postal Service investigated the *Sun*'s mail status. Hoover's FBI produced what one historian called a "nasty report," opening a "Top Hoodlum investigation" of Greenspun that lasted until 1958, and identifying him as "unsavory" for "the fact that he was critical of the Director and the Bureau."

Meanwhile, the *Sun*'s circulation doubled, and Greenspun became a hero far beyond Las Vegas. "Chewing an expensive cigar, as he pounds out his columns on a 50s Underwood," as *The New Yorker* described him, he provided vivid copy for the national press. One magazine extolled him for the "*Sun* That Wouldn't Set," another for "fine, free-rolling frontier invective . . . an editor-publisher of a type popularly supposed to have gone out with Derringer pistols and the Gold Rush." Moments after exclaiming "Greenspunism must be defeated" in his final speech in Hawthorne, McCarran had dropped dead, leaving his nemesis to replace him as one of the more famous Nevadans.

Greenspun's courage, celebrity, and obvious flair for power now brought him friends much more important than his enemies. When the Justice

Department charged him with "tending to incite murder or assassination" with his anti-McCarthy editorials, the admiring Drew Pearson arranged for him to be defended by one of the most powerful and well-connected of Washington lawyers, Edward Pierpont Morgan, a former FBI agent who had been counsel to Senate committees, corporations, unions, and foreign governments. Though known for his advocacy of civil liberties, Morgan also had intimate, often covert, ties to law enforcement and intelligence agencies.

The attorney's defense at the 1955 Las Vegas trial was impassioned, winning Greenspun's acquittal. As they drove away from the courthouse, Morgan handed him a bill for more than $11,000 marked "Paid in Full." For this and more to come, Greenspun would emotionally refer to him as "my greatest benefactor," though the bond between them served the lawyer no less than the publisher. Like Greenspun's Zionism and his now public, now hidden relationship to Israel, the intimacy with Drew Pearson, Jack Anderson, and Ed Morgan would be pivotal for the rest of his life.

By the late 1950s, less than a decade after starting the *Sun,* Greenspun was what one observer called "widely heralded—and feared—as the most powerful man in Nevada." Having succeeded against enemies as formidable as McCarran and McCarthy, he told *Newsweek* with characteristic cockiness that he now planned to "watch for the next demagogue." His paper exposed local scandals, "unhorsing several corrupt leaders," said Las Vegas historian Michael Green, at one point forcing a Democratic National Committeeman to resign. His competition with the *Review-Journal* was acrid. "I prefer the sweet smell of independence a trifle more than the odor of a buck," he wrote of his chain-owned rival, whose longtime editor quietly held shares in a mob casino. He was "a powerful force for civil rights . . . working . . . to help desegregate the Las Vegas Strip," as Green put it. "He deplores discrimination in print and on the air," wrote his staunchest critic, Pegler, describing Greenspun as the "community's number one bleeding heart." He would spearhead the state's efforts against racial discrimination in Las Vegas casinos, to the disgust of the hoodlum owners. He was equally outspoken against local Mormon bigotry and the prejudiced white majority that ruled the town. There would be no question in those years of his commitment to the underdog, his genuine leadership in civil rights and as an inheritor of an intrepid Nevada populism. When the *Sun* burned to the ground in 1963, he and others suspected arson by any of a varied cast. Eventually he would even challenge the federal government's nuclear presence in southern Nevada, as well as the omniscient Internal Revenue Service—going so far as to offer free legal representation to anyone willing to take on the IRS.

"More feared than liked," Green described him, "he played the part of a tireless gadfly in Las Vegas civic life." Admired or hated for his public acts, he was in private often generous and tender. He doted on a daughter suffering from a rare illness. He quietly paid the medical bills of other children, even posted ransom for kidnap victims. He kept a "magic closet" of toys in his office for any visiting child. He kept needy relatives, in-laws, and friends employed for decades. "I saw him do wonderful things for people who needed help, and it usually went without notice," said Greenspun's attorney, and friend of forty years, John Squire Drendel. "If he liked you, he stood by you to the end." He lived well but in most respects unpretentiously in an elite downtown neighborhood, his only public ostentation his ubiquitous convertibles and eventual Rolls-Royce, as well as taking his famously well-dressed and beautiful wife to black-tie parties with casino owners.

After several petitions for a pardon of his old gunrunning conviction, he would finally receive one from President Kennedy in 1961. Rights restored, Greenspun promptly decided to run for governor in the 1962 Republican primary. Opposition was ferocious. Dalitz would brag that he and others spent an unprecedented half-million dollars to crush him. "Greenspun by comparison," said a typical ad, "would make Genghis Khan look like a Bible salesman." He was defeated two-to-one by a furniture dealer who was mayor of Las Vegas, Greenspun attributing his loss, not without reason, to his singular incorruptibility. His candidacy prompted a Carson City newspaper to liken him to Fidel Castro and write that "Nevada is not ready for another Huey Long." He would not try electoral politics again, preferring to manage events from the front page and, increasingly, from behind the scenes.

His celebrated crusades now began to seem more and more selective. He had flayed McCarran and his "hoodlum" friends. He had welcomed the Kefauver Committee, urging them to go after the "big boys" of organized crime. In the 1950s, the *Sun* ran a mug shot of Dalitz over an alias. When Dalitz branched out from the Strip to build a Las Vegas hospital in 1959, financed by his first of many millions in Teamster pension fund loans, the *Sun* uncovered safety code violations and editorialized with outrage. But only the city's insiders knew how much the attacks on Dalitz were vengeance for Greenspun's having been squeezed out of the Desert Inn, for the McCarran boycott, for the opposition to him in the 1962 race. In the casino backrooms, in a few law offices and banks, Greenspun's attacks were seen more as a factional grudge than as fastidiousness about criminal ties.

In fact, the first Teamster loan in Nevada had been made to Greenspun himself in 1955, according to an interview Greenspun gave the FBI in 1961. The $300,000 loan, though relatively minor compared to other Teamster financing in the city, remained hidden amid national revelations in the late fifties of the union's corruption and the *Sun*'s exposé of Dalitz's Teamster-financed hospital. Unknown, too, were Greenspun's close ties to Teamster president Jimmy Hoffa, with whom he traveled to Israel in 1956. He would even urge his friend Drew Pearson to "ease up" on Hoffa and the organized crime–dominated union, pressure that Pearson later said he found insulting. What even Pearson didn't know was "that the *Sun* was riding on the remains of a loan from a St. Louis bank which had been assumed or guaranteed by the Teamsters," according to later news accounts.

In the welter of later criminal investigations of the union and its plundered pension fund, there would be differing versions of exactly how much money Greenspun received from the Teamsters—whether a single loan or two, by one accounting of Teamster records $250,000, by another from the *New York Times* as much as $475,000, by FBI records even more. Whatever the exact figure, the sum was enormous for the time and went to his ceaseless promotion of a country club, golf course, and subdivision in the nearby suburb of Paradise Valley, later to be Green Valley. At the same moment he accused Dalitz of suborning inspectors at the new hospital, he was pressuring Governor Grant Sawyer to fire a state engineer who had denied Greenspun water rights for his development.

By the close of the fifties he had become a privateering and well-connected developer with so many financial interests, as he once told the FBI, that he could not recall "which of his several accountants" handled which account. On top of the Teamster money, according to newly released FBI records, Vice President Richard Nixon had introduced Greenspun to a wealthy Washington realtor, Leon Ackerman, who in turn brought the Las Vegas publisher into deals as far-flung as a chain of Arizona newspapers, a development in Florida called Indian Lakes, and the Alaska Oil and Mineral Company, which would provide stock to collateralize Greenspun's purchase of a Las Vegas television station. Greenspun in turn would introduce Ackerman to Ed Morgan, who helped secure for Ackerman some Teamster money. In a 1955 deposition, Greenspun "ticked off numerous ventures and holdings," according to the *Review-Journal,* including "1,500 hundred acres in Paradise Valley . . . 160 acres on the Boulder Highway, oil leases . . . stock in an oil exploration company . . . and a forty percent interest in Market Town," the city's first shopping center. In this same testimony, Greenspun adamantly denied ownership of two former military airplanes mysteriously parked at a private local landing strip. But clearly he was now a financial "player"—what CBS's *60 Minutes* would later describe as the second largest landowner in Las Vegas. As always, nothing would reflect so vividly both his hidden and visible interests as the pages of the *Sun.*

He would write fawningly about Benny Binion, always a Greenspun favorite and close personal friend. When the FBI later investigated Binion for the Coulthard murder and the myriad other crimes at the Horseshoe, the *Sun* would launch an all-out attack on the local FBI office, and Greenspun would try to ruin the career of the agent-in-charge, Joe Yablonsky. In time, he even reconciled with his bitter enemy Dalitz after the hoodlum pledged $400,000 for a new synagogue because Yablonsky, the FBI agent they both hated, attended the old one. When Dalitz donated money to Israel, Greenspun ran flattering stories—and a fresh photo in place of the mug shot.

In the early 1960s, when state officials caught Frank Sinatra harboring proscribed Chicago boss Sam Giancana at the Cal-Neva on Lake Tahoe, where the singer fronted for the hoodlum, Greenspun jumped to the defense of the notoriously mobbed-up celebrity, with whom he shared both political friends and enemies in Washington as well as Nevada. He would publicly champion Sinatra for years while concealing from his readers their convoluted and well-hidden financial ties with each other, including a takeover attempt of the Del E. Webb Real Estate Corporation, which owned a number of Nevada casinos. Like much else with Greenspun, the compromise was both grand and petty. Later, when an enraged Sinatra characteristically assaulted a casino pit boss in a brutal fistfight, the *Sun* reporter who wrote a straight story on the incident was summoned afterward to Greenspun's office. There he found "two guys in dark glasses" who "exchanged a few cryptic words" with Greenspun, as the journalist remembered, and the publisher quickly rewrote the story himself to absolve Sinatra. Greenspun would be one of the few who attended the wedding of Sinatra and Mia Farrow when the rest of the news media were shut out, and would later boast to a national reporter that he had traveled the world with "his buddy," from Tokyo to Egypt, and, especially, to Israel, where the two men went "many, many times."

When respected *Sun* reporter Ed Reid, whose work had brought the paper much of its early reputation, coauthored a 1963 exposé of the town, *The Green Felt Jungle,* Greenspun quickly derided the book on national television, touring the country to extol a "clean" Las Vegas "free of criminal domination." Publicly, he enjoyed the reputation of "fighting editor." But many Las Vegans knew that he had made his separate peace and side deals with the powers that ruled the city. His own fellow newsmen and staffers would be unsparing. "Hank isn't a liberal crusader. He is a very smart, very shrewd businessman who just happens to publish a newspaper," reported J. Anthony Lukas. "His crusades rarely have anything to do with abstract principle. They always begin with personal grievance . . . a way of settling scores," said another writer.

Meanwhile, his "benefactor" Morgan had introduced him to another associate from the world of covert intelligence, Robert Maheu. A former FBI counterespionage agent during World War II who many in intelligence circles believed had been in on the creation of the CIA, Maheu had known Morgan since the early forties. The Greenspun-Morgan-Maheu association created a unique triumvirate that would not only profit the three of them but have far-reaching consequences for the nation as well. Since the fifties, Maheu's private "security" agency had served as a front, or "cut-out operation," as Maheu called it, for some of the most repugnant covert actions by the CIA and multinational corporations. Maheu's firm was involved in providing prostitutes for CIA clients and making pornographic films to embarrass the agency's targets; it played a key role in what Jim Hougan, in his book *Spooks,* called "a bizarre intrigue" to ruin Greek tycoon Aristotle Onassis in behalf both of his shipping competitors and of an international oil consortium linked to then Vice President Richard Nixon.

By the mid-sixties, Maheu worked almost full-time for one client, the eccentric, obsessively reclusive Howard Hughes, whom Greenspun had known as far back as 1946, and during Hughes's furtive but extravagant sojourn in Las Vegas from 1966 to 1970, when he bought casinos and much else in Nevada, both Maheu and Greenspun acquired new wealth and power in the process. Greenspun's collusion in Hughes's takeover of Las Vegas was largely hidden from the *Sun*'s audience, shards of the story turning up only a decade or more later in court cases and subsequent investigative reporting. But the eventual exposure further tarnished the publisher's reputation. "The debate over Greenspun's motives increased after the arrival of Howard Hughes changed the face of Las Vegas—and expanded Greenspun's bank account," wrote one historian.

Beyond the Hughes millions, beyond the corporate facade erected for gambling, the grand cover given the enduring forces of the city, Greenspun, Maheu, and Morgan made other fateful history as well. Along with Drew Pearson and his successor, Jack Anderson, they would join in a series of maneuvers and manipulations in the dissemination of stories about the Kennedy assassination and other topics, to the advantage of all four. Their gambits would have the effect of masking the full ramifications of a plot by the CIA and organized crime to assassinate Fidel Castro, and thus effectively muddling as well vital evidence in the subsequent assassination of John F. Kennedy. They were also embroiled in concerted behind-the-scenes pressure on another president, Richard Nixon, to secure the release from prison of that other patron of Las Vegas, Jimmy Hoffa. Ultimately, they would all play a furtive, largely unseen role in the Watergate scandal that brought Nixon down. In the nation, as in Las Vegas, Greenspun was always more influential and important than he appeared on the public surface. But then his international intrigues were still more significant.

After he was dead, Israeli news accounts described "friends and former comrades in arms"—a group including foreign minister and future prime minister Shimon Peres, Jerusalem mayor Teddy Kollek, and several of the most senior figures of the Mossad—dedicating a square in 1993 in the Botanical Gardens of Jerusalem's Hebrew University to the memory of Herman Milton Greenspun. "He's like God in Israel," said Pulitzer Prize–winning journalist Seymour Hersh. "He's considered to be one of its founders."

Greenspun's "contribution to the establishment of the Jewish state," the *Jerusalem Post* said in an article at the time of the dedication, "is widely considered to be greater than any other American." The statement was stunning, given the thousands of American Jews who had risked their lives and given so generously, publicly as well as privately, for the founding of the Zionist nation. Greenspun, said Peres at the dedication, had been "a proud Jew and a defender of Israel" who was "always on the firing line." Among his exploits, the *Post* went on to say in startling but still vague revelations, Greenspun had "introduced the Israelis" to the notorious Saudi business magnate and international arms dealer Adnan Khashoggi—a client of Morgan's, and an arms merchant at the heart of the Iran-Contra debacle of the 1980s. Khashoggi was also a familiar figure on the Strip, "the biggest high roller to ever hit Las Vegas," according to his biographer, Ronald Kessler. Khashoggi's friendship with Greenspun linked the latter to a world—vividly described by Kessler in *The Richest Man in the World*—of international weapons sales, governmental intrigue across three continents, and multibillion-dollar financial dealings that wound their way back to the American West and the Mormon Church. In a plot worthy of Khashoggi himself, Greenspun had also been involved, the *Jerusalem Post* hinted, along with Prime Minister Menachem Begin, in a failed scheme to extract $100 billion from Saudi king Fahd in return for the Israelis allowing the Saudi flag to fly symbolically over the Temple Mount in Jerusalem.

Such exploits would have staggered many in Nevada who thought Greenspun quite famous enough as a local curmudgeon and wheeler-dealer. But his international escapades were rarely if ever publicized in his home city. It was clear that he was from the beginning far more than the comparatively naive, intrepid young arms smuggler he portrayed himself to be with such uncharacteristic understatement in *Where I Stand.* Not only in the 1940s but long afterward, he had obviously maintained deep ties to a foreign intelligence agency, his loyalties often divided. Compared to what Greenspun had done for Israel, the *Jerusalem Post* later wrote in reference to Israel's most notorious spy against America, "Jonathan Pollard's act was pure innocence." What services he had performed "always on the firing line" for Israel in a Las Vegas that was a hotbed of international money laundering and intelligence intrigues, what consequences his actions had for the security of the United States, for the people of Greenspun's adopted Nevada, would never be known.

Barely three decades after he published his credo, Greenspun's insider fortune would make his children multimillionaires, with interests from luxury real estate to cable television. Green Valley, the development initially fed by that first Teamster loan into Las Vegas, would become the heart of the suburb of Henderson, the second-fastest-growing city in the nation, surpassed only by Las Vegas itself. "Greenspun's substantial holdings . . . ," *Time* would report in 1975, "have made him so rich that he may be losing his maverick feistiness." By that time he was known more for "hobnobbing with the bigshots," as one longtime associate said, "than muckraking in Las Vegas." After "putting out his legendary paper," as *Harper's* magazine put it, "Greenspun would head for rollicking late nights on the Strip with Sinatra and the Rat Pack, occasionally joined by the odd Kennedy." He was known for his regular games of gin rummy in the executive offices of casino owners, and would tell *Time* that whenever he traveled, "Barron Hilton, a good friend of mine, makes the arrangements."

Greenspun would detonate at any suggestion, any innuendo, that he ever made an accommodation with the gangsters ruling his city. "He used the Italian definition of gangster," said one who knew him well. Asked by a national journalist about his ties to mobsters, Greenspun would exclaim: "That's the goddamnedest, most fabricated lie!" He would point to his decades of exposés in the *Sun,* to the fact that he had been sued more than a hundred times by his local and national targets, that he had challenged some of the state's most notorious characters—including McCarran, Dalitz, and Hughes—as evidence of his fearless, unbeholden journalism. His social and business ties with some of the same elements were simply life in Las Vegas, he said. "When you live in this town," he would tell *Time,* "you're rubbing shoulders with every facet of society."

Greenspun could be quite boastful about the size of his financial portfolio—"I've got more money than Sinatra . . . I own cable TV, I own half the gold and silver mines in Nevada," he once crowed to the *Washington Post.*

Meanwhile, his avowedly beloved *Sun* became more than ever a personal instrument rather than the objective chronicler it might have been. "A black-jack to advance his own personal ends," a critic called the once if briefly admired paper. Whatever Greenspun's early national reputation as the nemesis of McCarran and McCarthy, the *Sun* "never turned its investigative attention to the people who actually ran Las Vegas," as *Harper's* summed up the journalism of what became, in one of the most newsworthy towns on earth, "a very mediocre newspaper." To survive, the ghost of the *Sun* in the hands of his heirs eventually entered into a joint operating agreement with its hated conservative competitor, the *Review-Journal.* "Hank knew it had to be done," said one historian, "but he would never give them the satisfaction of making the deal while he was still alive."

When Greenspun died in 1989, he left a city hardly faithful to the ideals he had publicly espoused in the fifties. He had used his power for personal ends much more than as the public trust he had promised when he had begun the *Sun* with such ebullience forty years before. Like his old nemesis McCarran, he bore much of the responsibility for the city's fate. He had been its hope. He was one of the few, in his time, who had the juice and the courage to challenge its darker forces.

But the strutting, self-promoting publisher, charming and boisterous, who could be gallant in his defense of the community's ravaged virtue, ended up spending most of his time and talent in Las Vegas pursuing his own piece of the action. In a sense, the worst of his old foes, McCarran, McCarthy, and Pegler, had been right about him. For all his genuine acts of conscience, Hank Greenspun was just a hustler after all.

6. Estes Kefauver
The Opportunist as Prophet

Just turned eleven, he was a good swimmer. Once he saved Tucker Meek's granddaughter, pulling her by her long hair clear ashore of the Little Tennessee. He was just as big and a lot better in the water than his older brother Robert. "The smartest child that ever lived," Aunt Lottie would say of Robert, "the one the family pinned their hopes on." On this day the county had lifted the ban on swimming in the Tellico, a narrow tributary east of Madisonville, Tennessee, known for its swift flow. The boys couldn't wait to get there. "You watch out for Robert now, Estes," his mother had said. Hours later, Estes had just stroked to the far bank, strong and easy, when he heard the other boys scream. Robert was gone beneath the green water.

When Estes Kefauver grew up to be a national leader, he would feel he had a country to look after. And he would watch it slip away, too, in the unseen currents below.

He was born in 1903 in the lush, wavy foothills of southeastern Tennessee, to people expressive of the place. Cooke Kefauver, his father, was descended from Huguenots, son of a voluble Baptist preacher, and named for his mother's family, who had captured the land from the Cherokees. Cooke was a tall, spare, gentle man, with what a Kefauver friend called "a salty-tongued sense of humor." He sold hardware and farm implements in Madisonville, and made a modest but decent living. In Republican Monroe County, he took his Democratic politics seriously. He made sure his boys heard William Jennings Bryan at a Chautauqua speech in 1908, "the experience I best remember," Estes wrote later.

In 1912 they stumped the backcountry for Woodrow Wilson in a Ford touring car, "Mr. Cooke," as one recalled, bumping over the dirt roads in his "Panama hat and four-in-hand." Sitting up next to him were his well-scrubbed sons, dressed neatly in their churchgoing "round hats and flowing bow ties." At every stop the boys handed out pamphlets and tacked up posters. When Wilson carried the county, they reckoned it "a personal triumph," a friend remembered. Cooke went on to be a popular five-term mayor of Madisonville, and after building but losing his Kefauver Hotel, did well in real estate. Admiring and adoring, Estes always called his father "Popsy."

His mother was more formal. Though some suspected the genealogy, Phredonia Estes Kefauver claimed to be of Italian nobility in lineage back to a Roman senator. By the time Estes himself came along, the clan was decayed gentry. Still, her son, as a boy, often visited the ancestral Estes Hall and other relatives' mansions in the magnolia-and-cotton bottomland of West Tennessee, where "dreams of the Old South and its lost courtliness," biographer Charles Fontenay wrote, "permeated the Estes home."

Phredonia had carried across the state to Madisonville an Estes coat-of-arms and what one writer called "a concept of family worth." She was ever "a Southern lady," a friend said, "in the consciousness of her heritage, which would have put her perfectly at home directing the slaves in their chores on her grandfather's plantation." With her children she was firm but aloof. She instilled her inherited pretensions, albeit with a sense of *noblesse oblige,* as Fontenay put it, "tempering ambition with common kindness."

Estes himself was entombed by his brother's drowning. A freckle-faced, barefoot, laughing child running with friends, always paired with Robert before the accident, he was now "grave and withdrawn," a friend remembered, and usually alone. He would be what the family doctor called "a sort of by-himself boy," retreating into ponderous books his mother bought him, histories of the Civil War, biographies of Robert E. Lee, and Gibbon's *Decline and Fall of the Roman Empire,* which some thought Phredonia regarded as family history. "Knowing how bright had been his parents' hopes for Robert's future," a friend wrote, "Estes determined he would fulfill Robert's promise for them in his own life."

He had talked of being a lawyer since he was five or six. Now, in the years around World War I, country attorneys with cases at the Circuit and Chancery courts in Madisonville stayed over at the new Kefauver Hotel near the courthouse. At night Estes sat in the shadow of kerosene lamps, listening to the lawyers, judges, and politicians talk on the long porch about clients and politics, secrets and scandals, their cheroots smoldering, one observer recalled, "like resting fireflies."

In high school his principal thought him "a good average student," his classmates "a jolly good fellow in body, soul and mind." At six foot three, he augured the bony, even hulking, man he would become, a boyish clumsiness long part of his charm. At graduation, on the line after "Ambition" in a friend's autograph book, he scrawled: "To Be President." It was 1920. The Bugs and Meyer Mob was a force on the streets of New York. Benny Binion was a sixteen-year-old hip-pocket bootlegger in Dallas. Pat McCarran had quit a first political career in bitter defeat. Hank Greenspun was a child of eleven scrapping on the streets of New Haven.

Kefauver went on to the state university in nearby Knoxville, getting off at the depot with his boy's cap, a reddish green Sears, Roebuck suit bedecked with Sunday School attendance medals, and a straw satchel. In the years ahead he would often seem the bumpkin, bungling a prepared speech, slipping back into a drawling localism. It was usually deliberate, and cunning. His audiences loved him for it, while enemies fumed. "He was so adaptable, even opportunistic," a college friend would say of the countrified boy at the Knoxville station.

Though he had never played football, he became through sheer grit a solid guard in the Tennessee line, dubbed "Old Ironsides" for the hits he took without being knocked down. As a student politician he campaigned to "clean up" Prohibition-era campus dances, to ban drinking and what he called "immorality"; but with an early hypocrisy, he liked bootleg liquor on the sly as much as any of his contemporaries, and became what a friend called "popular with the girls," though he still blushed at their glances. Again his grades were only average. At one point he was implicated in a murky cheating scandal, but nothing went on his record. Early on he showed "an uncanny nose for promotional notoriety," as a friend put it. "He may have been a country boy when he got there," said a teammate, "but he was smooth as anybody when he left."

He began his legal studies as an undergraduate, and planned to go on to Tennessee Law. But in 1924 his mother was suffering from acute inflammatory rheumatism, and Estes took her to Hot Springs, Arkansas, for the healing waters. He stayed there for more than a year, teaching math and coaching football at the high school. It was a wide-open gambling town, in which he also became a regular in backroom poker games and at the betting windows of the racetrack.

The Springs, as the little city in the gorge of the Ouachitas was commonly called, had long been a center of illegal gambling, prostitution, and other vice, a traffic far larger than the bustling commerce of its Bathhouse Row. In the 1920s the Springs was gradually taken over from local hoodlums by New York's crime families. At the time Estes and his mother went there, it was already a favorite resort of celebrity gangsters. Al Capone would hold a permanent lease on a suite in the stately old Arlington Hotel. It was this provincial capital of organized crime—"you name it," said one of the town's newspaper editors, "and you could buy it here"—that was Kefauver's first exposure to the world outside his Baptist Tennessee. He acquired a lasting fascination, if not obsession, with some of its allure.

He decided to return to law school. Urged by a friend to apply to Yale, he did so and won a small scholarship. He would later tell reporters that he had fired furnaces and washed dishes to put himself through Yale. But in fact his father's sister, doting Aunt Lottie, paid much of his way, outfitting him with a raccoon coat, which he proudly sported down the main street of Madisonville while home during the 1926 Christmas holidays.

He was now a glib student, sleeping late, cutting classes, borrowing a friend's lecture notes at the last moment, passing exams with ease. In New Haven he would be remembered for poker games until dawn—"Kef was a very fine poker player," a roommate said—and for the "beer busts" he financed with winnings. He no longer blushed. In the Estes clan and elsewhere, he was known and whispered about as the "kissing cousin" for his lingering hugs and other attentions to women, the beginning of what would become a barely concealed lasciviousness.

He graduated *cum laude,* passing the Tennessee bar exam before finishing Yale. He planned to join the Washington firm of an Estes cousin, ex-Missouri governor Joe Folk, a Populist who ran for president trading on Lincoln Steffens's muckraking. But when Folk died, a resigned Kefauver returned to work in a cousin's Chattanooga law firm in 1927.

Over the next eleven years he led the life of a southern gentleman lawyer. After abruptly breaking off his engagement to one woman, he married a pretty Scottish girl who was visiting Chattanooga, though he would discreetly raid the family account to loan money to old girlfriends as well as needy clients. He was always cavalier with money; despite a respectable income, he found himself "constantly, vulnerably broke," as one friend noted, "perhaps because of his gambling," which remained a gentlemanly secret. Unlike most of the southern bar, he represented, even championed, poor black clients. But he was no rebel. He was an earnest Chattanooga booster who adhered to its racist laws and society; intent on being accepted and rising in the community, he would "join," as he once announced to a Yale classmate, "everything in town."

In his practice he ran afoul of a political boss, who then padded and destroyed ballots to beat Kefauver when in 1938 he ventured to run for the state Senate at the age of thirty-five. To him, it was a dreadful defeat—his first race, his last loss, in Tennessee at least. He made peace with the boss. The next year, nominated on the day Germany invaded Poland, he won a special election to Congress. He would be a man of one era come to office on the jagged edge of another. In the House for the next decade he proved a loyal Democrat, generally backing the New Deal, defending the Tennessee Valley Authority, pushing legislative reform, even writing a respected small book entitled *A Twentieth Century Congress*. Yet he was no ordinary southerner on the Hill.

"Shaymmme on youuu, Es-tees Key-fowver," Mississippi's arch-racist John Rankin yelled on the floor when Kefauver voted to abolish the poll tax. He had upheld segregation and opposed most civil rights bills; but the tax was something else. "Repugnant to democracy," he called it, the heart of a political feudalism that excluded and oppressed most Tennessee whites as much as blacks. The cause of wider economic freedom would be a haunting conviction in the man who had sat as a boy beside his father driving through the county for Woodrow Wilson. Like Wilson, Kefauver was seen as "too Southern for the liberals," as a colleague described him, and "too liberal for the Southerners."

Bored in the House, he ran for the Senate in 1948 against the divided but still formidable statewide machine of Memphis boss Ed Crump. "Reminds me of the pet coon that . . . will deceive any onlooker as to . . . what it is into," Crump dismissively said of him. "I may be a pet coon," he answered, "but I'm not Mr. Crump's pet coon." Donning what he invariably, endearingly mispronounced as his "skoonskin" cap, an advertising gimmick of a bank next to his old law office, he won the race handily. At forty-five, he was a U.S. senator. He looked forward, he told Popsy, to "a normal life." But his victory was intensely felt, enlivening his boyhood dream of still higher office.

He had won by "incredible stamina," as one observer put it. He had not employed the usual organization, much less machine; his method was sheer personal contact with masses of people. It was an ever-demanding, exhausting politics, a style he would carry into his future political career with historic consequences.

He ceaselessly cultivated reporters, often as their hard-drinking partner. Clipping several papers, he rushed off ingratiating notes to both subjects and writers. He was a quick study on the issues, deploying expertise, mastering detail. Confidently, brashly, he lobbied colleagues, though he loathed the old backslapping and -scratching. He rarely returned favor for favor, or appreciated disagreement. Flouting custom, he set the obliging press on his opponents. Still, he was highly regarded for his ability and independence. While he was still a freshman, *Time* magazine chose him as one of the ten best U.S. senators. Had the magazine somehow gauged ambition, Kefauver would have ranked even higher.

Only days after his election, some small Tennessee papers vaunted him for president. He began to discuss it privately back home. Even as he was sworn in, there was another hint of purpose long before the world saw it. A Kefauver crony wrote a friendly attorney in Chicago, asking confidentially if he might agree to be counsel in an interesting investigation quietly being planned by the new senator.

There would be many versions of how his famous committee came about: In part it was the national rediscovery of the "crime problem" in sensational news stories; in part Kefauver's disgust at judicial corruption in a House probe of bribery in Pennsylvania; in part lobbying by local crime commissions and others, including prominent media figures. "Jesus, Estes, don't you want to be vice-president?" *Washington Post* publisher Phil Graham asked him, goading a supposedly reluctant senator to chair an inquest on the paper's current enthusiasm. But no impetus would be stronger or earlier than Kefauver's own. From the beginning, he was shrewd, skillful, outwardly successful in getting his investigation off the ground and exploiting it for his own purposes. He was also tragically shallow, even naive, about what he would be confronting, and what it would cost.

He saw the subject as one more popular, opportune cause. On Capitol Hill, after all, the crusading committee was a time-honored means for advancement. To expose some wrongdoing was to gain almost ritually good publicity, recognition, and national support. Respect by political leaders might come grudgingly, but wasn't reform good politics for everyone? If an inquiry embarrassed the party, Kefauver told a worried colleague, all the better that Democrats "receive the public credit for cleaning their own house." Attractive as a border state moderate, he would be "available" for the ticket in 1956, or even 1952. If it took "talent and luck," as a friend put it, he counted on both. He plunged into the deeper, incomparable politics of American crime and corruption as if he could navigate anything, as if he were swimming the Tellico that first time.

After tentative starts, his committee found itself conducting a full-blown investigation of what was termed "Organized Crime in Interstate Commerce." It was to be the first—and last—of its kind, a sweeping, uncircumscribed mandate to look into the depths of the systematic, systemic vice and political corruption that had come to rule so much of the nation since Prohibition. By midcentury it was a subject Washington officially knew not at all, and privately too well. With few exceptions, as later biographies and memoirs disclosed, senators and congressmen from the rural South and growing West, as from the old population centers of the North and Midwest, knew full well and were frequently beholden to the underlying political power of the nationwide Syndicate.

In the Senate maneuvering in early 1950 to create the committee, Kefauver had to fend off Joe McCarthy, who was looking for an issue to exploit, and who then fatefully "lumbered off," as historian William Moore described him, "in the direction of the State Department." Behind the scenes, both Congress and the White House worked feverishly to emasculate the investigation. Arrayed against Kefauver were the most potent political forces "both in and out of government," as Moore noted. Not until a gangland double murder in Kansas City—part of a vote-fraud and bribery scandal amid the gangland rivalries around the Pendergast machine to which President Truman owed his political rise—could Kefauver break the impasse in authorizing the committee. Even then, as so often on Capitol Hill, politicians with their own individual scandals to keep hidden routinely chose "safe" members for the new committee, men who were suitably inane, compromised, or both, and thus could be relied upon not to dig too deep, or at least not to be taken seriously if they did.

Beyond Kefauver, the two Democrats were classics of their kind. Herbert O'Conor of Maryland was leader of a state party "in cahoots," as journalists Jack Lait and Lee Mortimer put it later, "with one of the tightest and biggest Mafia concentrations in the country." His colleague, Lester Hunt of Wyoming, was known to be "McCarran's man," a soldier in the Nevada senator's relentless war on the inquiry. Across the dais, the two Republicans, both absorbed by reelection campaigns, seemed burlesque. Charles Tobey, seventy years old, formerly a clerk, chicken farmer, insurance salesman, and shoe manufacturer from New Hampshire, had been a frothing foe of FDR. Wisconsin's Alexander Wiley, sixty-six, "a busy Babbitt from Chippewa Falls," as Moore called him, was a 220-pound, baby-kissing, polka-dancing dairy farmer, a Kiwanan, Mason, and Son of Norway, fond of carving busts of the famous in cheddar cheese.

The staff was also typical of congressional inquiries. Kefauver chose as counsel Rudolph Halley, a supposedly prodigal if conventional New York lawyer with an intermittent lisp, experience on a Senate committee chaired by Harry Truman investigating wartime profiteering, and a certainty that all trails led to what he referred to as Manhattan's "Mr. Big," Frank Costello. Halley also brought with him a controversial past as the protégé of a corrupt New York State Supreme Court justice and his own legal representation of the old Syndicate-dominated Hudson & Manhattan Railroad. Under Halley, the staff "investigators" were drawn from a time-honored pool, what one reporter described as "ex-cops, disappointed lawyers and the usual Washington hangers-on recommended for jobs by influential friends." In another capital tradition, FBN director Harry Anslinger generously "loaned" the committee some of his own agents, men who were to be the bureaucrat's eyes and ears in the investigation, ensuring that the committee's perspective and conclusions would be compatible with Anslinger's own, and thus enhance the FBN's position in its ceaseless rivalry with Hoover's FBI and other agencies. Together, politicians and lawyers, political parodies and bureaucratic spies, they were all solemnly charged to make what one reporter called "the most searching study of crime and politics ever conducted."

The committee began with "the old American proclivity," as Moore wrote, "to view organized crime as something set apart from the economic and social realities of American life." The politicians assumed a centralized, alien conspiracy imposing an aberrant corruption on the system, a simple notion of good versus evil, the latter usually identifiable by its Italian surname. Yet the evidence would reveal a far-flung phenomenon, inseparable from the nation's politics and economics, "American underworld and upperworld ultimately one," as the social and political historian Stephen Fox concluded.

But none of this was clear as Kefauver set his colleagues on their course in the summer of 1950. Over the next ten months his committee would hold sessions in 14 cities, travel 52,000 miles, hear 800 witnesses, and file 4 reports.

No one reckoned with the power of television, then in its novel, compelling infancy. The nation was transfixed by the broadcast hearings. "Like a countryboy looking at a painted woman for the first time," said a British observer. "People had suddenly gone indoors—into living rooms, taverns and clubrooms, auditoriums and back offices," *Life* reported. "There, in eerie half-light, looking at millions of small frosty screens, people sat as if charmed."

When Costello testified at climactic New York hearings—the cameras allowed to show only his "nervously writhing hands," as one reporter described them—theaters and stores were deserted, and power companies added generators to meet the demand. More than 30 million people watched, the largest audience ever exposed to such insider power and politics.

Soon the most familiar face on the glowing little tube, Kefauver became a national hero. "An oversize owl, benign and bland and forever genial," the writer Alan Barth portrayed him with typical affection. In the studied manner of what he was, both the southern lawyer and the ambitious politician, he could be cautious, impassive, yet persistent and severe. Meanwhile, he was ever the country boy from Madisonville and Chattanooga. He carried no house key. Returning from some faraway hearing to his Washington home late at night, he would "plough through the shrubbery," as a friend remembered, calling up to his sleeping wife behind an unlit second-story window, "Mom-meee . . . Mom-meee."

He was famous now. Applauding crowds greeted him. When it seemed the Senate might shut down the inquiry for lack of funds, small donations of a dollar or two poured into the Capitol to keep it going. Yet he and his family also received threats. Some accused him of suppressing and protecting. He allowed his ally, New Orleans mayor DeLesseps Morrison, to testify without challenge that he had cleaned up his city, while committee files brimmed with evidence that the mayor remained on the payroll of the ruling Syndicate. In Kansas City, home of the corrupt Democratic machine that had launched the sitting president, Kefauver clearly equivocated, prompting persistent rumors that he had been promised the vice-presidential nomination in 1952 in return for a "political whitewash." His investigation effectively ignored as well the spreading criminal, political, and financial grip of the Teamsters, a union strong in Tennessee and crucial to the senator's own reelection.

In each of the fourteen cities he visited, as local crime commissions as well as committee files would document, the Syndicate had bribed or otherwise compromised most of the ranking law enforcement officials and politicians. Despite stark and abundant evidence of that, he exposed only a few. Behind the vice was the inescapable corruption of the Democrats. "Organized crime had so penetrated the American upperworld by 1951," Stephen Fox later concluded, "that the Committee could not reveal all it knew." By his evasions, Kefauver tried in vain to stem the distrust, dread, and ultimate hostility engendered among his own party's leaders, the price of what columnist Jack Anderson called his "boldfaced political treason to Democratic bosses." Before it was over, he would do "everything short of tossing away his credibility," judged Moore, "to protect his own party prior to the elections" of 1950.

The popular chairman also had other "complications," as another scholar described it. Kefauver would later boast that he had turned down "six-figure" bribes for the Democratic National Committee. Throughout the inquiry he remained, as always, personally broke, often overdrawn at his Chattanooga bank by nearly $2,000. Then suddenly, in the midst of the hearings, he deposited an unaccountable $25,000, and paid off a $10,500 second mortgage on his Washington home, transactions never explained even in his voluminous papers, and that left his biographers puzzled. He was soon broke again, however, and overdrawn by more than $1,600.

During his rackets investigation, one of his closest friends and most prominent supporters was arrested in Tennessee. The man was revealed to be the numbers boss of Knoxville, who had given Kefauver thousands of dollars during the 1948 campaign, though only $100 had been reported—all of which became a great embarrassment to the vice-fighting chairman. Later, there were charges that a Mob lawyer named Sidney Korshak—who was to be intimately involved in Las Vegas in subsequent years—had blackmailed the chairman in Chicago hearings with an eight-by-ten glossy photograph taken of Kefauver *in flagrante delicto* with a Michigan Avenue call girl. His aides and even biographers would insist that no extortion took place, or at least that whatever happened had no effect on the inquiry. Still, the Chicago hearing would be notorious for ignoring a Democratic sheriff and party bosses who had become millionaires in government jobs paying a pittance a year.

When in Washington during the investigation, Kefauver attended, as usual, the races at Laurel and Pimlico, "making bets and expecting free passes and courtesy badges from the management," as one historian recounted. At one point he met privately with Meyer Lansky, whom he would name in a final report a year later as "one of the principal partners in the crime Syndicate dominating New York and the eastern half of the United States." The racketeer, who had kept track of the senator's own habits, asked him bluntly: "What's so bad about gambling? You like it yourself. I know you've gambled a lot."

"That's right," Kefauver answered. "But I don't want *you* people to control it."

In the end, his personal flaws or political compromises shaped his fate less than what his committee achieved: its revelation, often blurred and reluctant, of what one historian called "nationwide organized crime Syndicates" inextricably bound up with the "support and tolerance of public officials," in reality not two worlds, not two political or economic systems, but only one, indivisible. In the process, Kefauver glimpsed a deeper American reality; he "had lightning bolts in both hands," wrote a friend. Unlike his peers among the elite—presidents, senators, most of his fellow politicians of both parties—he chose to reveal at least part of the secret. For that he would be severely punished.

But that would come later. In the late summer and early fall of 1950, there was a growing sense on the committee staff that many of the lines from the disparate criminal dominion they were discovering seemed to converge on a still-small town in the Nevada desert. As an afterthought, the chairman scheduled a day of hearings there, though it was to be only a brief stopover on his way to more publicized sessions in California.

In November 1950, Las Vegas nervously awaited the visit of the famous Senator from Tennessee.

Part Two

City of Fronts

When I think of this artificial vividness plunked down in the midst of the most primitive part of the world, I have a curious sense of Las Vegas's history . . . the covered wagons so little a while ago, and now it's all air-conditioning and neon. I find a wonderful excess underfoot. Everything, you see, is arranged here. And yet, I suspect, there's a tragic side.

—Noël Coward, in "Mr. Coward Dissects Las Vegas,"
  New York Times Magazine, June 26, 1955

On a cool, cloudy, late autumn morning in 1950, community leaders subpoenaed to testify before a Senate committee investigating organized crime crowd the second-floor hallway of Las Vegas's federal courthouse and post office on Stewart Avenue. The Nevada press, with no apparent inconsistency or embarrassment, describes them as both "casino kingpins" and "prominent local citizens."

There are a dozen of them outside the courtroom where the hearing is to be held. Some sit in spare wooden chairs and benches, and some bury themselves self-consciously in newspapers. Others pace nervously. The pall of incessant smoking and the murmuring fill the dim corridor. Journalists and photographers from all over the country surge among the witnesses. "Reporters pelted them with questions to the popping of flash bulbs," remembers one writer. In time and place, the scene is remarkable—for those who are there and those who are not, for what it reveals and the much more left hidden.

7. "Beyond This Place There Be Dragons"

Behind the beckoning image was always another reality.

Ten to fifteen thousand years ago, the region was a paradise. Fed by the effusion of retreating glaciers, what an archeologist called "living rivers of ice," emerald grass and bright blue lakes covered much of the region. For a time there was abundant animal life. Mammoths and camels grazed peacefully until devoured by saber-toothed tigers and giant lions from the east. Some of the first humans of North America lived here as well, halfway between the Isthmus and the Arctic, their stone dart points embedded at nearby Tule Springs.

Then, without warning, long after the Ice Age, "nature played violent games," as one historian wrote of the mysterious events, and the land turned quickly into a sweltering hell. Water, animals, and people vanished, leaving to the mountains and desert only their chalky relics—barren lakebeds and scattered bones, all surrendering to what Hubert Howe Bancroft called a "bold and brazen-faced sun." Occasional cloudbursts broke over the landscape. But it was a strange pseudo-rain, swallowed up by an atmosphere "so light, elastic, and porous," a later visitor wrote, "that water seems never to satisfy it." On what was left, mesquite and creosote eked out a scraggly survival, along with "a collection of desert shrubs that have learned to kill their own offspring in competition for the little water." It became an emptiness cut only by gaunt mountain shadows at dusk. Not even the few streams went home to the sea, running instead into each other—"rivers to nowhere," one traveler called them. And everywhere wild sandstorms of furnace winds left the air heavy with saline, creating the mirage that would lure so many—a shimmering false promise, an illusion of life masking desolation.

In search of a trading route from Santa Fe to Los Angeles, the Spanish came early in the nineteenth century. When a young outrider, Rafael Rivera, separated from the main expedition around Christmas 1829, he rode unexpectedly onto a panoramic view of the seductive valley in the desert. He christened it "Las Vegas"—The Meadows—for the rare lush greenery thrown up by artesian wells. It would become a way station on the Old Spanish Trail, what traders called "the Diamond of the Desert." Yet the Spanish were under no illusions. "They were nearly fearless explorers," wrote Walter Van Tilburg Clark, "but this place made them afraid . . . they would have felt . . . an attraction of mystery; but they knew the desert too well to be misled."

From the beginning, the area held some special attraction for criminals, hypocrites, and political frauds, scoundrels whose methods were as extreme as the elements. Bill Williams, a Baptist minister become mountain man and cannibal, made Las Vegas the headquarters for his band of Indian horse thieves, who plundered California and Arizona ranches in the early 1840s. Williams also hired out as a guide for the U.S. government, and while taking one army detachment across the desert, introduced hungry troopers to "the long pig," the euphemism for eating one's own kind. "In starving times," said a man who knew the preacher, "don't walk ahead of Bill Williams."

The soldiers belonged to the command of John C. Frémont, credited as the official American explorer of the territory, and in May 1844 the first of many would-be presidents to visit Las Vegas. The event proved portentous. The weather was stifling. Some of the party's livestock died in the heat or were killed by marauding Indians. Frémont, whose name was given to the main street of the future city, was himself a kind of omen. Beneath his fame and charm, later biographers revealed, was a shallow creature of carefully confected image. His ambitious wife did most of the writing and thinking for him, while his feats of exploration belonged mainly to his scouts, especially Kit Carson. Like many others associated with Las Vegas, he was prone to grandiosity. As a politician and a general, he blithely watched corruption flourish in his ranks, and was wantonly promiscuous, even impregnating his chambermaid. Spared the reality, distracted by the fantasy, Frémont's public remained admiring.

Like some mythic trial to be endured, the desert stretching west from Mount Misery at the Nevada-Utah border became a lethal passage. "The quietude of death must indeed be present," a historian wrote of a large party that perished in 1848, their wagon tracks long afterward "as fresh and distinct now as the day they were made." Despite the odds the people kept coming, some out of indomitable optimism, others with a persistence fixed by sheer sacrifice. "Turn back! What a chill the words sent through one," wrote one woman entering what emigrants named the Valley of Death. "Turn back on a journey like that in which every mile had been gained by most earnest labor?" Still, there was often a sense of foreboding of what lay ahead. "Beyond this place," one of them warned, "there be dragons."

Sent out by Brigham Young, thirty Mormons established the Las Vegas Mission in 1855 with a small mud fort and farm, becoming the first white settlers in the valley. Their purpose was more military than spiritual, only incidentally to convert the local Paiute people whom they coveted as "scattered remnants of Israel," but principally to mine local metals for bullets and weapons needed for their growing resistance to U.S. rule. The Indians turned out to be unappreciative converts. They stole the mission's corn and gambled the hours away, as one account described them, "rolling bones and colored sticks in the brown sand, the true ancestors of the modern Vegans."

When the mining proved equally stubborn, Young's party gave up the outpost after only two years, ruefully calling it a land the "Lord had forgotten." But it was only the beginning of a colonial relationship between the Mormons and Las Vegas, this retreat hardly an indication of the ultimate profit and power the church would derive from the city. At the moment, however, the abandonment of the fort relinquished the site to its ancient bleakness. "It is easy to foresee," two French mapmakers noted at the time, that the importance of Las Vegas "will never become considerable." For most of the next century, it remained as insignificant as the Frenchmen predicted, a watering stop for an America going somewhere else.

By 1900, only thirty homesteaders dotted the valley, surviving on the prehistoric pools beneath the desert. That water now made the site a relay point for a new railroad built by Montana senator William Clark. In a hand-to-hand battle with shovels and pick handles, the copper magnate's company thugs fought to a standstill the matching gang of New York financial giant Edward Harriman's Union Pacific for a line through southern Nevada to Los Angeles. Clark became the town's first oligarch in what would be a lengthy tradition. By the time the inaugural locomotive pulled up in 1905, the senator had purchased and subdivided the choice lots beforehand, and proceeded to auction them off, making more than a quarter million dollars in two days—the first man to make a fortune in Las Vegas. But five years later, one of the desert's flash floods swept away a hundred miles of track in the Muddy Valley Wash to the east. Amid a nationwide economic decline, the break in rail service nearly emptied Las Vegas, leaving those who stayed to hard times. The town came back only slowly, numbering about 3,000 by 1921. "I guess we had more sheep than humans," said one Nevada resident. At the time the population of the entire state was only 77,000.

For years, Las Vegas was one more soon-forgotten name on timetables. The tracks repaired, passengers traveling from Chicago to Los Angeles peered out curiously at the country depot and ankle-high dust in the streets. The Union Pacific paused only minutes before it puffed on to California, though events elsewhere were already beginning to shape the town's destiny. America in the 1920s had begun to sample something of Nevada's mining-camp morality. The new worldliness of a disillusioned U.S. Army and society despite victory in World War I, and the breakdown of traditional ideals and optimism after the carnage of the western front, led many to leave their old moral restraints at the doors of speakeasies, bookie parlors, roadhouses, and "carpet joints." They began a fitful but lasting revolution in values and behavior that would make the way station between Salt Lake and Los Angeles an end in itself.

For Las Vegas, however, the twenties were more than a change in manners. The flourishing traffic in contraband alcohol, beginning with the advent of Prohibition in 1920, created immense fortunes that would found an unrivaled criminal ascendancy in the United States. Holdings legal and illegal, influence open and covert, figures respectable and notorious, all commingled to become a political and economic power as never before. In turn, that power pursued and depended upon an unparalleled, institutional public corruption, from municipal and county governments to the halls of Congress and the White House itself.

Even in hot, sleepy Las Vegas, so far from the tumult, the citizens heard on their first radios or read in the Chicago newspapers brought by the trains the saga of the gangsters who dominated America's great cities in the twenties. What was not printed or broadcast in Nevada, or anywhere else, was the sheer magnitude of the criminal force that would succeed the flamboyant outlaws and their relatively petty street-level or bank lobby crimes. Long after the crude caricatures of the era vanished—Dillinger, Capone, the corrupt or inept policemen—that force remained intact. Stronger and more dynamic than ever, its dominion grew with the official propaganda of Hoover's FBI that it posed no threat, that it was only an errant, alien strain in American life rather than the indigenous, dark essence it was becoming. Least of all was there any inkling that this new power would find a home in the Nevada desert, that it would come to hold hostage not only Las Vegas but the state and the nation.

Through its own roaring twenties, Nevada seemed "relaxed and wild," as one historian described it. In a rare and short-lived burst of reform, the state's small Progressive Movement managed to outlaw gambling in 1910. Over ensuing years, legislatures veered back and forth between loosening and tightening the ban, while gambling and bootlegging went on barely concealed, and quasi-legal houses of prostitution flourished as ever. Meanwhile, outside its speakeasies and boudoirs, chronically boom-and-bust Nevada—its mining again *borasca,* its ranches and railroads enriching only the few—plunged into ruin in the later twenties well before the rest of Depression America.

Characteristically, the natives fought gamely to maintain a semblance of civil society. Bankrupt counties gave schoolteachers vouchers which a few trusting merchants honored as scrip. In a state of less than 100,000 by 1930—Las Vegas the fourth-largest town behind Reno, Elko, and Ely—the agony of the unemployed and homeless could be felt and seen everywhere, only a small number of families untouched. For those who suffered, the sole advantage, if it could be called that, was an almost inbred stoicism born of having gone bust so often before. The Great Depression arrived in Nevada less as some shocking downturn than as one more cruel run of luck for people accustomed to losing. "They were proud of an exciting history," said one ghost-town child of the era, "even if that history was mostly being down and out."

The state's oligarchs had seen their own crash coming, and hatched what some thought a promising plan to preserve their stake. Once more the outside world was to be drawn to Nevada for something it wanted, though this time not the grimy hordes after gold or silver, but the already fortunate or famous in search of convenience. In 1927, the state legislature legalized a three-month divorce, hoping at least to fill Reno's vacant Wingfield hotels with escaping wives and husbands of sufficient means. Four years later, lawmakers further reduced the waiting period to six weeks, the fastest divorce in the nation. Less noted but equally significant, they also passed special fiscal measures to render the state an all-purpose shelter for private wealth. "Nevada made a deliberate choice to coddle rich people," remembered a prominent attorney, "the one place in America that had no sales, income, inheritance or corporate franchise taxes, and no bonded indebtedness."

Then, in 1931, Nevada's business leaders and their politicians took a final recourse. It was to be another major rigging of the economy in their favor, another way to pack their hotels and fatten state revenues—just as much of the nation would seek the same escape for the same reasons a half century later. For the first time, lawmakers discussed in public the issue of restoring gambling. A freshman assemblyman put in the hopper the bill that had been hotly argued and narrowly defeated in 1927. But it now passed with scant formal debate, and was quickly signed by the governor. On the streets of Reno, a handful of churchwomen had been protesting the furtive process, carrying small, hand-lettered signs warning of untold consequences. Nevada, one of them had said at a small rally not long before, "should not seek the riffraff of the world." When word of passage reached them, they disbanded and went home in dispirited, angry silence. Gambling was again legal in the state. This time it was here to stay.

At the same moment, in the worst of the Depression when Las Vegas needed it most, there was a boom with the building of nearby Boulder Dam. Outsiders came again to tear at Nevada's stubborn hardrock. Day and night, on the calm streets of the small town of Las Vegas, its citizens could hear the explosions twenty-five miles away in Black Canyon. For $48 million, the largest contract ever offered by the U.S. government, the soon-to-be-famous Six Companies consortium heaved uncounted tons of rock to raise the Colorado River toward its new palisade, pouring concrete twenty-four hours a day for more than two years, enough to pave a highway sixteen feet wide from coast to coast. Like the construction statistics, corporate profits were astronomical, with workers paying the price. Flooded gorges and an unsavory company town led to more than a hundred dead, violent labor unrest, and bloody racial bigotry.

In an almost frantic release from the enforced intensity and danger of their work, the men building the dam, high scalers and tunnelers, muckers and powder monkeys, swarmed into the two-block area of downtown Las Vegas, where bars and casinos began to prosper. "For most of these boys who had spent their lives in the countryside," a historian wrote of the moment, "Las Vegas was an unbelievably seductive place." It was now, in the early thirties, that local businessmen planned the first resort hotels for the area, and celebrities came not only for divorces or gambling but also to watch majestic Lake Mead claim the desert canyons. What they saw looming in the water and power of the caged Colorado would make possible not only the wartime production feats and vast growth and wealth of Southern California, but also the unimaginable sprawl and excess of Las Vegas itself sixty years later.

With the dam's completion in 1935, the men who built it returned home with what little they had left. For a time, the tourists would come and go to watch the reservoir lapping at Black Canyon and to sample the raucous two blocks of Las Vegas nightlife. But "Nevada was eighteen bumpy and unpressurized hours by plane from New York," as one author noted. To outsiders, the land still looked hostile, irreconcilable with any lasting civilization. "The people were not here yesterday," the English writer J. B. Priestley noted in 1937 of potential tourists, "and will not be here tomorrow." On the eve of World War II, the town fell stagnant again. The neon lights of the old Las Vegas, Apache, Boulder, and Northern clubs attracted few visitors, Fremont Street "as empty as could be found," reported one witness.

Once again, natives found customary solace—and self-deception. When local unemployed journalists and authors wrote their *WPA Guide to 1930s Nevada*, they were quick to point out that the state's legalized gambling had escaped the corruption synonymous with illegal betting everywhere else. Nevada's wheels, tables, and slots, they boasted, were "free of racketeers."

In fact, by any of its names, the organized crime growing out of Prohibition had been in and around Nevada gambling, illegal or legal, for years. Fitful tides of reform in other states after 1920 drove some hoodlums out of their carpet joints and into the desert, though established centers of vice like Hot Springs, Arkansas, continued to flourish well into the sixties. More often, gangsters moved in, especially after the 1931 legalization, simply because Nevada was wide open, with no real law enforcement, and offered a blithe official welcome to those who "knew the business," as one Carson City bureaucrat put it.

In the tourist-hungry state, unsophisticated if not merely corruptible, blinded by its parochial need and pride, it hardly mattered, then or later, that the "business" of gambling was a crime in the rest of the country, almost invariably controlled since the twenties by criminal figures like Luciano, Costello, Dalitz, Lansky, Trafficante, and Marcello, whose collective wealth and power would grow to match any other industry in the nation and rival government itself. It hardly mattered that the "businessmen" were not simply proprietors who might have suffered some minor brush with the law somewhere else, but rather full-fledged criminals whose profession was exploitation, men bound to their criminal origins and associations by money and power, and by the indelible kinship of complicity.

By the early thirties, organized crime controlled most of the lucrative gambling throughout the state. "Every town had its outfit," remembered an Elko prosecutor of the era. Collusion was classic, linking directly and indirectly gangsters, gamblers, politicians, and businessmen in a dynamic of exploitation and profit that became a prototype for Las Vegas and more. Lansky's man in northern Nevada in the thirties, Joseph "Doc" Stacher, "the fat boy that every gang needs," as one writer said of his origins in the Bugs and Meyer Mob, was a partner of the genial operator of Reno's Bank Club, Bill Graham. A bootlegger from the Midwest, Graham in turn was financed both by the banks of another accomplice, political boss George Wingfield, and by an underworld consortium led by Chicago mobster Charles "Trigger Happy" Fischetti. The relationships always went beyond party or politics. Then as afterward, corrupt ties passed from politician to politician, machine to machine, like a scepter of Nevada public office, frequently creating strange ironies. When Graham later faced federal charges, it would be Wingfield's mortal foe and successor, Senator Pat McCarran, who readily arranged a White House pardon for their old cohort.

The gangsters continued to frequent the Fremont Street casinos through the 1930s. Not long before Pearl Harbor, a new wave of hoodlum immigrants arrived from the West Coast in the wake of Los Angeles gang wars, and especially when vice boat operators, who once anchored their floating casinos and brothels off Santa Monica or Oakland, were run out in a 1941 Labor Day crackdown led by California's attorney general, an ambitious fifty-year-old politician and future chief justice of the Supreme Court named Earl Warren. Much as San Francisco banks once financed the mines of the Comstock or Great Basin ranches, California gambling capital, operators, and customers surged into southern Nevada at the beginning of the 1940s. The influx continued the singular interdependence of the two states—a unique, sometimes ominous reciprocity of wealth and resources, consumer trends and social mores, politics and crime, politicians and criminals that would shape the power of Las Vegas and its California hinterland over the rest of the century.

Typical of the migration was Captain Guy McAfee, a Los Angeles Police vice squad commander and secret owner of illegal casinos in Southern California, as well as husband of a Hollywood madam. Before Pearl Harbor, McAfee moved to Las Vegas to open his Pair-O-Dice Club on lonely Highway 91, a site later taken for the Last Frontier. McAfee liked to call the forsaken road outside his joint "the Strip," after the bustling Sunset Strip in Los Angeles, his optimism handing down one of the famous place names in American history. With friends like "Admiral" Tony Cornero, known as the "king of the western rumrunners"—who made his name in Catalina gambling boats and had run the Meadows Club, the fashionable casino and whorehouse on the Boulder Highway, and now ran the Apache for his partner Pietro Silvagni, who had been denied gambling licenses himself because of his association with "the Admiral"—McAfee and a retinue of corrupt Los Angeles policemen joined a growing colony of rogues in southern Nevada.

When Meyer Lansky sent Bugsy Siegel early in the war to take over the race wire, and then to build the Flamingo, those exiles and immigrants were already there in the dozens, giving Las Vegas "more socially prominent hoodlums per square foot," wrote an observer, "than any other community in the world." Mobsters major and petty, dirty cops, shady politicians and business-men, gamblers with the ultimate fix in the law itself, Hank Greenspun's "lamisters," almost everybody from somewhere else, were both emblems and exploiters of an America fleeing itself, all in an unbroken Las Vegas tradition. "A sunny place for shady people," one of its daughters would call the town. But nothing in the outlandish history of the place, from cataclysms of nature and man to the stolid acceptance of what the rest of America banned, antici-pated the city that took shape after Siegel's murder.

The silhouette of the town was only beginning to change in the autumn of 1950. Its prewar population had nearly tripled by 1947, to 23,000. With the first suburban settlement, the census of the valley overall rose to 48,000 by 1950. An influx of workers had come with new military installations nearby, as well as the wartime magnesium plant in neighboring Henderson, which employed more labor at one time than ever worked in the mining bonanza of the Comstock. Many of the servicemen stationed during the war at the old Las Vegas Gunnery School, later to be Nellis Air Force Base, returned to settle in the valley. Housing was scarce. The federal government on a lottery basis had allowed World War II veterans, many of whom lived elsewhere in the country, to buy federal land near the town for five dollars an acre. A few hung on to the parcels and eventually sold them at dizzying profit. But most undersold when local developers "turned their real estate agents loose," as one witness put it, and bought out five-acre parcels for $125 each. Developers and builders were just starting a half century of phenome-nal growth, their treeless tracts carved out of the desert like scars of some unexpected battle.

The place had not yet begun to spread. Only four roads led in and out of town, none with a stoplight. At a glance, it was still a narrow, flat oasis on the floor of a wasteland, still with a feeling of impermanence. In the old neigh-borhoods, discreetly distanced from what were called the "grind joints" downtown, sun-baked bungalows crouched row-on-row under cotton-woods and elms set down by the first settlers. The jagged, crevassed moun-tains framing the valley—"peach-colored cardboard," as an English visitor saw them—were still visible from almost any corner, looming larger and nearer than they would ever seem again.

During the day, the withering sun high in the sky, it could seem pale, col-orless, one-dimensional. But in the angular light of dawn or dusk, the land-scapes of nature and man came alive with a fiery then softening color, every shape and shade distinguished, bathed in a brash brilliance, light flinging darkness like a cape. For its beauty, as for its mystery, Las Vegas depended upon the shadows.

Night drivers coming from Reno or Tonopah in the north could see from miles away the familiar milky glow of casino lights reflected by the desert on the endless sky. Beneath the gleam of Fremont Street was the same "patchwork of gambling clubs," a reporter remembered. Side by side with tire stores and pawn shops were the ubiquitous wedding chapels. Open twenty-four hours a day, with names like "Gretna Green" and "Chapel in the Heather," the small, unconvincing facsimiles of the sacred provided their usual package weddings from $10 to $200, including license, witnesses, clergyman of preferred denomination, and flowers and music in the deluxe special. A few doors away would be a convenient one-story law office offering, for no more than $1,285 complete, to put asunder any mistake by quick divorce. There was always a cheap, stale, faded tawdriness about much of it, even when part of the city grew spectacularly rich.

The newer, more lush resorts were gathering beyond the city limits. Competing with mammoth neon signs that rose over their ranch-style buildings, the still sparse casinos of the Strip—the new Desert Inn and Thunderbird, along with the Flamingo and original El Rancho and Last Frontier—formed scattered islands of green and aquamarine along the stretch of highway winding south. Their grass, newly planted palm trees, and spacious, curving pools, all lavishly watered by wells pumped around the clock, seemed theatrically vivid against the desert just beyond the fence. Over it all, whether downtown or on the Strip, there was an air of incongruity and improvisation. The men building the new Las Vegas, as Jack Sheehan saw them, were "working without a script."

What had changed most were the crowds of visitors thronging the little city. "The most important development in Las Vegas history," said one native, "was the Carrier Air Conditioning company's ability to air condition large spaces, combined with direct flights from Los Angeles." Thousands now poured into the valley every day. Only a handful arrived by plane at the remote single-runway municipal airport built by a bond issue the year Bugsy was shot, well out on the Strip. Most drove in from California, as many as 20,000 a weekend from Los Angeles alone. Undeterred, they came even in the beastly heat of the summer, renting little "hydrofan" air conditioners to hang on the windows of their cars, having to "add a gallon of water to it every ten miles or so," one visitor remembered. They came for the two-minute marriages or six-week divorces, luxury hotels at four dollars a night, famous floor shows with free liquor and inexpensive prime rib, all-night drinking or prostitution or rubbing shoulders with celebrities—and above all, for the gambling. "If you can't do it at home," the state's advertising said without guile, "come to Nevada." In the flush of postwar prosperity, Americans were doing just that. "That's the promise of Vegas," a frequent visitor would say: "anything."

On the streets and in the casinos, the crowds saw a colorful if fleeting mixture of the town's cowboy past and thriving present. "Men with deep sunburns and sweaty underarms walked the streets in silver spurs," Susan Berman remembered, while "grizzled prospectors and tapped out gamblers" mingled with well-shaven men in wide-lapel silk suits from New York or Los Angeles. Despite the contrast, the new sociology of Las Vegas was plain around the casino tables and in the backrooms, where "alligator shoes," as one observer noted, "started to take the place of cowboy boots." With the change in clientele came a new reputation as well. If Reno had been the nation's "whirlpool of vice" in the 1920s, the place to get down the big bet and to launder stolen cash or drug profits, that distinction now passed to the boomtown in the south, the "modern amalgamation of Sodom, Gomorrah and Hell," as one observer described it. Yet even that notorious image was part of the facade. From this midcentury moment on, the *unseen* Las Vegas would always be more important than its glittering, slightly naughty surface.

It was a city of fronts. A casino public relations man voiced the town's governing adage. "Believe nothing of what you hear," he would say, "and only half of what you see." There were always the front men with their own shrouded histories, behind them still more front men, and behind them the *real* owners and the hidden world they represented. In 1950, visitors to Wilbur Clark's luxurious new Desert Inn—"the classiest resort for a generation," which boasted the first individual thermostats in guestrooms—might see Clark moving affably from table to table, or even one of his more famous and frequent guests, J. Edgar Hoover, crossing the lobby. What they could not see was that the controlling owner, Moe Dalitz—known as "the toughest Jewish mobster in Vegas"—had once killed a Cleveland city councilman who stood in his way, carried a long history of what one writer called "ruthless beatings, unsolved murders, and shakedowns," had bribed his way to "the big fix," as two reporters described it, in a half-dozen city halls around the nation, and now presided over the skim of millions a year for Lansky, the Cleveland mob, and his other secret partners.

Visitors to the two-year-old Thunderbird might see one of its frequent famous guests, Senator Pat McCarran or magnate Howard Hughes. With them would be the tall, lean Las Vegas lawyer and state lieutenant governor, Cliff Jones, a former Boulder Dam highscaler and McCarran protégé who wore expensive cowboy boots and calfskin vests, and owned 11 percent of the casino. The rest of the casino shares were held by former Long Beach vice boat operator Marion Hicks. And behind them both were what *New York Times* reporter Wallace Turner later called Hicks's "extensive mob ties." The $2 million that built the Thunderbird came from Lansky and his brother Jake, and Jones and Hicks played leading roles for the Lanskys and others in the casinos' expanding corruption of Nevada politicians with money and favors.

Customers at Bugsy's famous Flamingo might see his businesslike successor, a smiling, portly Gus Greenbaum, soon to be the unofficial mayor of Paradise, a new suburban township created as a tax shelter for Strip resorts, and quaintly named for Guy McAfee's old Pair-O-Dice Club. Usually at Greenbaum's side was a natty, visibly nervous little man named Moe Sedway, another would-be civic leader and recent chairman of the city's United Jewish Appeal. Behind them was Greenbaum's bloody past as one of Lansky's chief lieutenants; he was a drug addict and a killer, said to be "the second toughest Jewish mobster in Vegas," who had ordered the assassination of informer James Ragen, and who had been the Syndicate's principal bookie in Arizona, where he was an intimate of local businessman and Phoenix politician Barry Goldwater. Sedway had been one of Lansky's New York deputies, a ruthless dwarf who, "during periods of stress," as an FBI report put it, "wrings his hands, becomes wild-eyed, and resembles a small dog about to be subjected to the distasteful procedure of being bathed."

Then there was always the financial front, the visible money at play on the tables, the reported profits, losses, bank deposits, and taxes, the set of books for the government and the "clean" accountants. Behind that was a second or even a third set of books recording the millions being skimmed off the top for licensed or secret owners, and the tens of millions more in criminal money from around the country and world being laundered and redistributed. "Three for us, one for the government, two for Meyer," as someone present in the casino counting room recalled the routine formula for the skim and tax evasion performed three times a day, at the end of every shift. Since the war, deposits in Las Vegas's two banks had grown from $3.3 million to more than $30 million. In the hands of a few, that recorded money was only a fraction of the city's real cash flow, and had little impact on the rest of the town or state. But by 1950 even the acknowledged profits testified to some of the most rapid growth of wealth in a single community in the nation's history. "Sin and Sun Pay Off," headlined *Business Week*. "Las Vegas Strikes It Rich," *Life* said of "the biggest boom that has ever hit."

At the same moment, unrecorded in the pages of any journal, a succession of bagmen were converging on Las Vegas around the fifteenth of every month, each carrying hundreds of thousands of dollars in vice profits from locales across the country. The cash in their satchels would be duly laundered across the tables, converted to larger bills, added to the casino skim, and apportioned out to associates, investors, and client businessmen and politicians in Washington, Chicago, Cleveland, Detroit, New York, Los Angeles, San Francisco, and a dozen smaller places. It was only the beginning of profits in the hundreds of billions, of a thievery that would cost Nevada and the nation untold tax revenues, of Las Vegas as an international clearinghouse, and of a dominance and domain far beyond gambling.

In a sense, even the city's visible power was a cover. In 1950, there was its obvious success as a wide-open boomtown with growing influence in Nevada politics and business, though to all appearances it was still a provincial outpost in the desert, far removed from national or international events.

In 1950, however, the same year the Desert Inn opened and Kefauver came to town, Lansky used some of the millions skimmed from Nevada casinos to secure a new traffic in Turkish heroin through Marseilles, setting up laboratories, paying his new Mediterranean partners, and bribing officials in Europe and the Middle East. The trade was to feed a swelling, multibillion-dollar drug market in an America where demand for narcotics had grown rapidly after the end of the war. Just as Lansky's Mexican opium smuggling in the 1940s had financed the Flamingo and later in part the Thunderbird and Desert Inn, the Las Vegas boom now financed a vast new international network of narcotics and other contraband—and the profits from that drug traffic in turn would come back in various forms to build modern Las Vegas.

As so often in his career, Lansky in his new French connection enjoyed the U.S. government as a de facto silent partner. He trafficked with the secret sanction, protection, and sometime collaboration of the CIA, the FBN, and other Washington agencies. From its OSS roots during the war, the CIA was now in expedient alliance with organized crime against Communist influence around the world. CIA stations in Turkey and elsewhere in the Middle East discouraged or even suppressed investigations of opium-growing or -smuggling by local politicians, military, and other officials enlisted as allies or even intelligence assets against the Soviets. By the same rationale of national security, successive American administrations refused to confront the known collusion with drug traffickers of allied governments in France and North Africa. From the Mediterranean, the new heroin supply routes soon extended as well to Indochina, where U.S. intelligence and drug

enforcement agencies first clashed among themselves and ultimately colluded in what would become by the end of the sixties a vast new channel of
the Syndicate's narcotics trade, with momentous consequences.

Over the next half century, much of that history would wind back to the
pulsing casinos of the Strip, where it had already begun by 1950. In a very real
sense, the nation's covert government of Cold War intelligence would be one
more element in the making of Las Vegas. But that shadow was no more visible now than any other in the colorful desert town. Most visitors were gambling or being entertained in a casino tightly controlled, owned, or skimmed
by Lansky and his officially protected international confederation of narcotics, vice, and ever wider, ever deeper government corruption. Behind the
fronts—caricature cowboys and genial gangsters, the multiple sets of books
and hoodlum civic spirit—was the advent of America's criminal city-state.

8. "This Alliance of Gamblers, Gangsters, and Government"

Wednesday, November 15, 1950: The Kefauver Committee came to Las Vegas at a volatile moment in American politics. Five months earlier, the nation had gone to war in Korea. Victory parades were planned for Christmas, and U.S. troops were advancing toward the Yalu River, North Korea's border with China, where a massive Chinese intervention would beat them into icy retreat, fixing a bloody Korean stalemate for nearly three more years and the Cold War for a generation. Nine days before the Nevada hearing, in midterm elections marked by the worst smears of the era's Red-baiting, Republicans gained five seats in the Senate and twenty-eight in the House. Joe McCarthy was more feared than ever. With a venomous campaign that led to victory over Helen Gahagan Douglas in California, Senator-elect Richard Nixon would be launched toward national prominence.

Democratic leaders were already finding a scapegoat for their mounting defeats—however predictable for the president's party in midterm elections—in Kefauver himself, whose hearings, despite hedging, had bared his party's corruption and cost its candidates votes. "In Senate cloakrooms, Kefauver had the appeal of a 'skunk at a lawn party,' " wrote one observer. When he was asked about the impact of his inquiry on the election, Kefauver was somber. "I think it may have hurt," he admitted just before leaving for hearings in the West.

Headlines about the battles at home and abroad blared in the Las Vegas newspapers. But the uneasy men reading them in the courthouse the day of Kefauver's hearings faced their own siege, what an onlooker called "the heat in a usually cool November." Though the power of "the top brass of Las Vegas," as one reporter saw them, was enormous, they could not be completely sure in 1950 that their sanctuary in the desert would last. The lives and fortunes of many of them, after all, had been shaped by the random rhythm of reform elsewhere, the inevitable ebb and flow of civic outrage. "You might own 'em but you never really trust 'em," a gambler would say of the politicians of the twenties. Nevada, it was true, was unlike any venue they had known before. Yet if the fix seemed sure in state law and popular acceptance, in the patronage of McCarran and other politicos—they had already done much to curb or compromise the crime committee and would do more—Kefauver's national popularity and the unprecedented notoriety given organized crime by television coverage of the inquiry also posed a threat like no other. There was danger not only of federal taxation or authentic regulation but of a possible total shutdown.

"You just got to the point where you thought you didn't have to bribe everybody, or at least in Nevada not pay so much, and then along comes Kefauver," remembered an operator. That summer and fall of 1950, Las Vegas owners had already seen roadhouses in Kentucky and Louisiana fold under reverberating pressure from the hearings. Like fugitives from some lost battle streaming into the capital, the incoming refugees had an unnerving effect. "It was always part of their greed," a lawyer for the casinos thought afterward. "They were grabbing everything they could get their hands on because there was still the fear, justified or not, that it could end any time, that it was all too good to be true." Still, there were many who shrugged off the committee with the gangster's habitual contempt for politicians. "Privately my father and his friends joked that the Commission [sic] would never shut them down," remembered the daughter of one of the owners. "They had never had respect for politicians since they had made a career of bribing them." Whatever the mix of uncertainty or disdain at the moment, Las Vegans took the hearings seriously enough to lay odds on them. Even as the crowd gathered at the courthouse, bookies around town found almost no one willing to bet that Kefauver would "win," as one resident recalled. "The mobsters behind the casinos weren't cowed by the show," one author wrote later. "They'd seen him [Kefauver] too often around dames and racetracks to fear that he could truly hurt them."

The publicity around the courthouse hearings promised exposé if not sensation. "The crime committee knew what it was looking for long before it came to Las Vegas," Greenspun wrote, adding that "a sharp ten-year-old boy could have come to the conclusion that crime and politics in this state are on friendly terms." Kefauver and his colleagues—he had flown in that Wednesday morning, his fellow senators had arrived by train—held the customary press conference that preceded any hearing. "We are here," the chairman announced, "to find out whether Las Vegas casino operators have any connection with nationwide Syndicates." The committee was "in possession of information which would indicate ownership in Nevada enterprises by those who are carrying on illegal transactions in other states." A subpoena to appear did not necessarily convey a stigma of suspicion, he added. "But if there is any evidence turned up which warrants it," Senator Charles Tobey chimed in, "we will be happy to turn these birds over to the proper authorities for prosecution."

While the committee was to meet privately in executive session—the milling reporters outside were to be briefed on the testimony at intervals by Kefauver or counsel Rudolph Halley—the press was let into the hearing room for the opening. They found a truncated panel, the chairman accompanied only by GOP senators Wiley and Tobey, along with Halley and a few staff men. The two Democrats, O'Conor and McCarran's surrogate Lester Hunt, were notably absent. Lieutenant Governor Cliff Jones, subpoenaed as a witness to both state policy and his own casino partnership with mobsters, stepped forward to preen for cameras as he gave the committee the official welcome of Nevada. Kefauver then routinely expressed the committee's thanks to Nevada senators for their "assistance" in arranging a hearing in their home state though many in the room knew that both McCarran and his diffident Nevada colleague, Senator George Malone, had fought the committee from the beginning. Formalities and flashbulbs done, Jones and the press left the chamber.

In often sharp, sometimes wandering questions, the committee would now aim to confirm its preconceptions about what it saw as a disreputable desert town and its dubious industry. But in the testimony of a troop of witnesses involved in gambling and/or government, there were only flashes of the city's reality.

The first to testify was Bill Moore, an architect, promoter, and owner of the Last Frontier, who was also a state tax commissioner overseeing the casinos. Moore admitted that he made some $80,000 a year from his casino position while earning less than a tenth of that as a state officer, and confirmed under questioning that the Last Frontier had been given an unaccountably low rate on its race wire service from the same bookmakers he was charged to regulate. From Moore the committee would hear the first official rendition of what became the classic Nevada rationale.

Halley asked why Moore and the rest of the Tax Commission licensed Reno vicelords Graham and McKay when Nevada officials knew that both had federal felony convictions. Addressing Halley as "fella," Moore rambled on about what he called the "granddaddy clause" in the recent state law that required gambling licensing from the Tax Commission as well as counties or cities. The statute, he argued, "protected" established casino owners like Graham, McKay, Sedway, Binion, and many others, just as similar state or federal laws protected those already practicing in fields like architecture, engineering, or the law. Gambling, after all, was just another legal profession in Nevada. In any case, why should crime or criminal associations elsewhere matter out here?

"Is that any reason why you should put a man out of business if he is operating in the state of Nevada?" Moore asked the senators.

"Yes, I think it is," Tobey barked back before the exchange trailed off.

Is that any reason? Moore, an Oklahoman, had voiced what other Nevada officials were only beginning to say aloud. The rationale was born of a tangled mix of the state's profound sense of inferiority, its century-old economic desperation, its proud tradition of live and let live, and its weathered and tenacious insistence, despite a grim history to the contrary, that it could govern itself. Nevada was even to be credited for attempting to regulate and tax openly what in the rest of the nation was furtively managed by graft and bribery, "through the selling of protection by law enforcement officials," as one academic put it politely. The reasoning would become civic dogma, in effect justifying the acceptance of the Syndicate as the state's principal industry and ruling economic power. "The ugly skeleton of the American rackets," as one journalist recorded, "shows plainly through the pretense, as flimsy as Marlene Dietrich's show-stopping dress, that Nevada has built itself around its multi-million-dollar gambling." The conviction or pretext of authentic public control would underlie an ever stronger states' rights resistance to *any* federal reform or exposure of that criminal regime. In its opening minutes at the courthouse, the committee had already heard the credo of a half century of dissembling.

Even by 1950, the excuse required willful ignorance or complicity. "What percentage of income escapes federal taxation, in your judgment?" Tobey asked the tax commissioner–casino owner about the infamous skim. "Frankly," Moore replied in syntax as wayward as the answer, "I have no way of knowing, if any."

"You had to be deaf, dumb, and blind not to know about the skim," a Strip operator said of the era.

Moore's testimony set the tone for much of what followed. Next came the lieutenant governor, known as "Big Juice" for his deal-making, not only in Democratic politics or at the new mobbed-up Thunderbird, but for his points as well in the Golden Nugget and the Pioneer Club. "Jones was the man who got the machinery running," one casino insider would say. Like Moore, Lieutenant Governor Jones would testify that his government salary was only a small fraction of the $50,000 a year he made from his casino interests, as well as large legal retainers from gambling houses. But the lawyer, a former legislator and judge, professed to know almost nothing about his business partners in the casinos where he made the bulk of his income. When asked if he thought it "good policy" to allow men with criminal records to operate in Nevada, the state's second-ranking official responded, "I would say that I believe as long as they conduct themselves properly that I think there is probably no harm comes of it."

Halley wanted to know if Jake Lansky had any financial interest in the Thunderbird.

"I am certain that Lansky has none," Jones testified, though he admitted that Meyer's brother was a frequent guest at the hotel, where he spent "a lot of money."

Behind the exchange was a scandal that would break open a few years later, shattering the McCarran protégé's own political career, and exposing national connections to Senate majority leader and later president Lyndon Johnson, as well as his aide, Bobby Baker. For now, the barely disguised Syndicate backing and control of the Thunderbird remained in the shadows. After less than two hours with the two state officials, the publicity-conscious Kefauver was ready for lunch and another session with the waiting journalists. "I think we had better put the press off no longer," the chairman interrupted Jones in the testimony. The committee promptly recessed, opening the door to reporters in time for all of them to make the evening papers.

Giving Jones nearly three hours to think over his answer to any awkward questions, the senators made a hurried round-trip of fifty miles to tour the interior of Boulder Dam. When they reconvened at three o'clock that afternoon, the desert sun, as it sets so early in the Nevada autumn, was already sinking toward the western mountains. In the slanting light of the courthouse hallway, it was clear now that there would not be time to call all the subpoenaed witnesses before the senators left for California. The still edgy witnesses began to joke with one another about letting each other go first. "The corridor suddenly became alive with gentlemanly acts," one reporter remembered, "such as, 'you first, my dear Wilbur,' or 'no, I defer to you, my dear Gus.' "

Inside the hearing room, it was as if the senators no longer expected serious revelations. An underworld gambler, known for laying off large bets through crime channels around the nation, doggedly denied his interstate operation, despite being confronted with lengthy long-distance phone records showing hundreds of calls to dozens of cities. Jones's law partner, the executor of Bugsy Siegel's estate, cautiously kept to the public record in answers about the new management of the Flamingo. Reno police chief L. R. Greeson told the committee about Doc Stacher at the Bank Club boasting he would spend $250,000 to buy friendly Nevada politicians, though "that only come [sic] to us as hearsay."

"Perhaps you heard something about outside interests muscling in here?" Wiley asked him, referring to Las Vegas.

"You hear of it, yes," Greeson replied. "As to how much basis there is behind it, I don't know. I have enough in Reno that I don't have time to be worried too much about the other portions."

The Desert Inn's Wilbur Clark could hardly remember, or so he said, that he once owned the El Rancho Vegas, or who was now on the board of the hotel that bore his name. He had heard of gangsters only from the newspapers, he said. Looking for money to finish the casino, he had "approached everybody in the United States, almost," before "these fellows from Cleveland come in."

"Try to be a little more businesslike in explaining these transactions," Halley admonished him in vain. "You have the most nebulous idea of your business I ever saw," Tobey told the fatuous Clark.

"Before you got into bed with crooks, to finish this proposition, didn't you look into these birds at all?" Tobey asked Clark at another point about the Dalitz group who had taken over 74 percent of the Desert Inn. Wasn't he aware, Halley interjected, that "they were people who had operated illegal gambling enterprises throughout the country?"

"I have heard that, yes," Clark testified. "I have never saw them operate but I heard that."

By now it was almost dark outside. Lansky lieutenant Moe Sedway began by explaining for the record his many infirmities. "I have had three major coronary thromboses, and I have had diarrhea for six weeks, and I have an ulcer, hemorrhoids, and an abscess on my upper intestines," he told Kefauver. "I just got out of bed and I am loaded with drugs." He was also acquainted with prominent gangsters like Frank Costello and Lucky Luciano,

Sedway admitted, but had known them only in passing. He was now, he told the committee, just a fifty-seven-year-old businessman in Las Vegas real estate and gambling, with "these heart attacks and the other difficulty . . . making a living for my family, and not making a lot of money." He claimed to be unaware of any illegal activity in the casinos. Lansky had once owned "one hundred shares" of Flamingo stock while Bugsy Siegel was alive, Sedway acknowledged, but Lansky no longer held an interest in any Las Vegas casino.

Listening to the hoodlum recite his various sources of income from local land sales as well as gambling, Tobey, the former chicken farmer and shoemaker from New England, could no longer contain himself. "You don't contribute a thing in the way of production that makes real wealth . . . when decent men want to make a living, these men peel it off." He upbraided the witness for associating with the "scum of the earth" like Luciano. "What has come over the world?" asked Tobey. "Love of money and power . . . a cancer spot on the body politic."

In closing, Tobey asked Sedway how he would live his life differently if given the chance.

The little gambler and gunman was defiant, and sarcastic. "We don't get as rich as you think we do. This is hard work. I would not do it over again. I would not want my children to do it again," Sedway answered quickly. "No, Senator, the first thing I would do would be to get a good education like I am trying to give my children, and when I got real learned I would become a United States senator like you."

When it was over that evening, a subdued Kefauver was terse in a closing press conference. Nevada gambling had a "definite interstate character," he said. But he drew no more conclusions from the testimony, which he and Halley proceeded to summarize briefly for reporters before taking a plane for California.

As the briefing ended, Tobey and Wiley stepped in to lash out at "so-called legal gambling," and the setting that allowed it. "What I have seen here today leaves me with a sense of outrage and righteous indignation. I think it's about time somebody got damn mad and told these people where to get off," Tobey said of the gamblers. Then, reading sentences carefully written out on a small piece of paper, Wiley, the Wisconsin dairy farmer and cheese sculptor, talked about the obvious alliance between criminals and civic leaders in the city and state. As few others before or after, he spoke with an old-fashioned plainness. "The picture of legitimate gambling and its effect on the community in which it thrives shows that men in high places have lowered themselves," he said. "In my estimation, such activities are a sign that the public morality has sunk to a new low." The two Republicans then hurried off to catch the Los Angeles train. In the next day's newspaper stories in Nevada, Wiley's damning words were buried, or omitted.

In his five-month-old *Morning Sun,* Greenspun noted the "many interesting sidelights" of what he called approvingly "the crime probers." Unlike most in the city, the new publisher welcomed the Kefauver inquiry in general. He relished bad publicity for Dalitz, whose takeover at the Desert Inn had pushed out his close friend Clark, and he pored over committee findings for evidence against McCarran in his gathering crusade against the senator. The contrast was pointed at the *Review-Journal,* where senior editor Al Cahlan quietly owned his own interest in a casino, and his brother and assistant John was in turn Cliff Jones's brother-in-law, who thought Washington treated Nevada like a "bastard child" and deplored the committee. "We were perfectly happy with the way we were running things," John Cahlan would say later.

"Little New Light Is Shed On Casino Kingpins Here," the *Review-Journal* headlined that evening. "The United States senate's crime investigating committee blew into town yesterday like a desert whirlwind," the story began, "and after stirring up a lot of old dust, it vanished, leaving only the rustling among prominent local citizens as evidence that it had paid its much publicized visit here." Yet the digest of testimony that followed was scarcely "old dust," providing a first corroboration of what the state's citizens had only heard by rumor: Lansky was indeed behind the Flamingo; Dalitz and "the Cleveland boys" had seized the Desert Inn; Sedway was a mobster, and Reno Bank Club owner Doc Stacher a "member of a New York hoodlum combine." It was enough to belie later claims that Nevadans could not have known what was taking shape before them. But the *Review-Journal* was right in at least one sense. Even with those head-shaking shards, the committee uncovered "little" of the new Las Vegas.

Three months later, a sequel to the hearing played out when a dapper, ugly Dalitz with flaring, obsidian eyes sat before the committee at a session in California. He was one of those casino owners who avoided the committee "like the black plague," as Kefauver put it. Dalitz had evaded subpoenas in several jurisdictions, and appeared now only under threat of arrest. His recent takeover of the Desert Inn seemed further proof of the city's ties to the underworld. Yet the committee's interest in him was even more apt than they knew.

Dalitz was not only a Lansky intimate, with a central role in what author Rick Porello called "the complete corruption" practiced by the Syndicate in the Midwest and elsewhere, but also the harbinger of a growing fusion of criminal and legitimate business. The gangster was "clearly a man," a biographer wrote, "who knew how to invest ill-gotten gains wisely, and, equally important, to keep quiet about hidden partners." Expanding into a string of legal concerns and front corporations in California, Ohio, Kentucky, Arizona, and elsewhere, Dalitz would come to epitomize organized crime's capacity to adapt through the evolution of American capitalism. The pattern became classic: succeeding bootlegging with gambling, money laundering, drug trafficking, and union corruption; investing the newly laundered money into health care, insurance, service industries, entertainment, banking, real estate, and other major sectors; and through the well-oiled, surprisingly short passage from racketeer to capitalist, becoming one of Las Vegas's revered benefactors. To have revealed him for what he really was, even as early as 1950, would have shown much of what was in store for Nevada and the nation.

But the questioning now was anticlimax. Represented by one of Kefauver's old law school friends from Yale, Dalitz picked his way through questions about his interests in ice cream stores, bars, supper clubs, linen suppliers, and steel companies. The committee seemed more interested in some retroactive tax evasion than his penetration of the legitimate economy. Taking the Fifth Amendment and consulting his attorney, Dalitz kept them at bay.

Coming to the end, an exasperated Kefauver returned to the mobster's Prohibition bootlegging across Lake Erie in a region where he was so infamous that Erie was known to an era as the "Jewish lake" and Dalitz and his partners as the "Big Jewish Navy."

"Now, to get your investments started off, you did get yourself a pretty good little nest-egg out of rumrunning, didn't you?" the chairman asked.

"Well, I didn't inherit any money, Senator," the witness shot back, though even the sarcasm was a lie. Young Moe had indeed inherited lucrative family laundries in Detroit, including the famous Varsity that had a near monopoly on University of Michigan students.

Then, with a glare and undertone of menace some in the room remembered long afterward, he added a final sneer at Kefauver, whose fondness for scotch and betting Dalitz and his partners well knew—and in a larger sense at the collusion and hypocrisy of the system now putting him on display. "If you people wouldn't have drunk it," Dalitz said thickly, "I wouldn't have bootlegged it." Unique in both underworld and upperworld, the brutal, prickly Cleveland hoodlum was always more outspoken, more candid than anyone else, about the cynical interdependence of the two societies. He would later quip sardonically about his clubs in Kentucky and Ohio to a friend, "How was I to know those gambling joints were illegal? There were so many judges and politicians at them, I figured they had to be all right."

With that, the committee closed its books on the men of Las Vegas. In its final report in August 1951, based on what one author called "the largest single accumulation of data on organized crime in America," the committee gave barely four pages to the brazen little city in the distant desert. They duly recorded the "domination" of gambling everywhere in the country by "gangsters, racketeers, and hoodlums," and that "too many of the men running gambling operations in Nevada" were connected to the national Syndicate. As for Moore and Jones, the casino owners as state officials, "there is no question as to the character of these gentlemen," the report allowed, though the regulatory practices they represented were deplorable: "The licensing system which is in effect in the State has not resulted in excluding the undesirables from the State, but has merely served to give their activities a seeming cloak of respectability." The point was the sham of public control. "As a case history of legalized gambling," the senators concluded, "Nevada speaks eloquently in the negative."

The November hearing and Dalitz's coda were relatively minor in the larger inquiry, though what existed in southern Nevada already eclipsed any other single scandal. Following a criminal labyrinth in interstate commerce—a threat to the nation as serious as any danger visible in the rival headlines of the Cold War, a corrupting of democratic politics ultimately more subversive than any Communist conspiracy—the committee might have found much of what they were looking for at a single turn. But like other visitors to the town, Kefauver and his GOP colleagues had not seen beyond its fronts. Whether by ignorance or evasion, and despite broad subpoena power and access to police and crime commission files that pointed to the larger scope, they left no evidence of the already preeminent role of Las Vegas as a national clearinghouse for drug profits and the laundering of money from nationwide vice. "Whenever witnesses or informers got hot on narcotics, the spine of the Syndicate system, or began to talk about the huge investments of the underworld in legitimate business," wrote two journalists who trailed the committee, "they were brushed off."

Still, embedded in the passage on Las Vegas in Kefauver's final report was a strange premonition. It came only in the closing paragraphs. Whatever else the city showed, the report noted, there was the portent of a degradation of public life by the absolute power of money in politics. "The profits which have been taken from gambling operations are far greater than those which can be earned quickly in any other business," they explained. And with such exploitation and concentrated wealth went an inherent dynamic of political domination:

> The availability of huge sums of cash and the incentive to control political action result in gamblers and racketeers too often taking part in government. In states where gambling is illegal, this alliance of gamblers, gangsters, and government will yield to the spotlight of publicity and the pressure of public opinion, but where gambling receives a cloak of respectability through legalization, there is no weapon which can be used to keep the gamblers and their money out of politics.

It was a vision of the next fifty years: when "huge sums of cash" would become the essence of American politics, and Las Vegas with its "far greater profits" would be the epitome of "control"; of a time at the end of the century when casino conglomerates with departments of political affairs would deal with Washington and state capitals, foreign governments and Indian tribes, like a sovereign power; when their multimillion-dollar lobbying would dictate public policies and veritably rape the state of Nevada; when the city would anoint presidents and governors, congresses and legislatures; when the "alliance of gamblers, gangsters, and government," in a new likeness and legitimacy, would rule beyond even the report's grim forecast.

The prediction, only incidental, was soon forgotten in the brimming record. In 1950, Kefauver and his committee mistook a mythic city-in-the-making for a tawdry sideshow, leaving obscured much of the real America as well as the inner Las Vegas. Their hearing that November with the edgy gamblers in the smoke-filled courthouse had been another of the city's spectacles. In the end it was one more game won by the house. As usual, the fix was in, but only the insiders knew it.

The 1950 hearing had been an embarrassment and a warning to the outcast state. Long after the committee was gone, it represented the feared phantom of investigation, taxation, even shutdown. "It was the sword some really believed, some just used," said a lawyer for the Strip resorts, "but when you heard the name Kefauver it meant a lingering danger, an impetus to get things together." The threat would stir a generation of Nevada politicians and bureaucrats who struggled to establish some state regulation to reconcile their desperate, defensive *laissez-faire* with authentic control of the "undesirables" Kefauver exposed.

Ironically, the national impact of the committee only added to the Nevadans' dilemma. The crackdown it prompted in old centers of illegal gambling continued to spur a hoodlum exodus to Las Vegas, a burgeoning 1950s migration of those "schooled in the rackets," as one writer described it. Many walked away "from multi-million-dollar businesses" to "make a bee-line for Nevada." Ironically, the inquiry was also instrumental in Nevada remaining the sole, increasingly prosperous haven and headquarters for those men and their money. Many credited its stern conclusions with swaying voters in California, Arizona, Montana, and Massachusetts to defeat gambling legalization referenda in 1950, leaving Nevada operators, who quietly financed the anti-gambling campaigns, a monopoly on legal casinos for the next quarter century.

The aftermath of Kefauver in Las Vegas would be the turbulent politics and spectacular growth of the next decade and beyond, as the state confronted more openly if no more effectively the force forming within it. Yet before state officials would be the example of the rest of America. "Kefauver, one would think, must have been shouting to a nation of deaf mutes," as *The Nation* observed in 1960; "for nearly ten years later, nothing has changed—except, perhaps, for the worse." This became a telling legacy for both Nevada and the nation. In truth, of course, some had been listening all too well.

The fact that it was a supremely effective and magnificent show," William Moore, a scholar of the committee, reflected a quarter century later, "should not obscure its fundamental failure." Like any congressional inquiry, Kefauver's had crippling defects—the banality of committee members, the usual submission to politics and publicity, the trap of a predetermined perspective, the politician's shallow settling for a popularization of what was already known. Yet this was also a committee like no other. Whatever its ordinary Capitol Hill flaws, it carried a darker side, which made its result so grave, its hidden politics so insidious, and Kefauver himself its ultimate victim.

Beneath the drab celery-green cover of Senate Report #725 of the 82nd Congress lay an ugly and incomparable portrait of what had happened to the country. In the 11,500 pages of testimony, the committee had unearthed what Kefauver called "a government within a government," a criminal force making more than $20 billion a year, more than 10 percent of the gross national product, and already controlling the politics and much of the economies of several major cities and states from coast to coast.

Harsher than the very existence of such deep-seated, systemic corruption were the implications for American capitalism and democracy. Behind the gangsters and rackets loomed a national order in which once distinct lines between criminal exploitation and legal enterprise were vanishing. Hostage to its discovery, the committee could only hint at the ultimate meaning. At the height of the Cold War—with the nation invested in its own creed and myths as a fetish of national security to the point of a blanketing repression and conformity—the implicit message of the inquiry was all but seditious in what one historian of the period has called "a largely hysterical country, fearful of communism and afraid to find fault with itself." Yet that "fault" was primary. "Organized crime may not be something that exists outside law or government," William Chambliss later wrote in drawing the fateful inference, "but may be instead a creation of them—a hidden but nonetheless integral part of the governmental and economic structures of the society." Kefauver and his colleagues had found not something separate from the country but its dark essence, not some mutant corruption but the system itself.

Of that America, now cloaked by nationalism and ideology as well as the old fear and connivance, the committee found specimens everywhere. Whether Kansas City, Missouri, or Hot Springs, Boston or Dallas, Los Angeles or Miami, New York or New Orleans, the rural South, factory North, or rapidly growing West, corrupted politics were the lifeblood of exploitation in both the legal and illegal economy, and vice versa. The police chief of Hot Springs, boasting to a reporter at a moment in the fifties when the old spa's private clubs rivaled Nevada casinos in profits, said he had not made a gambling arrest in twenty-four years. "Without political and economic corruption," one journalist summed up what the senators saw but had not put so plainly or unreservedly, "there could be no organized crime Syndicate." When their mapping of the most pervasive and dominant collusion was done, it would include the South from Georgia to Arkansas and Texas; New England and California as well as New York; the political and financial crucibles of almost every American president for the rest of the century.

Still, at the heart of the Kefauver Committee's findings was a virulent and enduring distortion: It would put a single, simple name to the layer upon layer of corruption—*the Mafia*. "There is a sinister criminal organization known as the Mafia operating throughout the country with ties in other nations," the committee reported. It was "the binder," as Kefauver saw it, uniting the local camps, including Chicago and New York. The label was a historic misnomer and thus diversion. Whatever the authenticity of the

Mafia as an entity in the teeming variety of organized criminal enterprises, to identify the Syndicate and its inseparable political culture as an alien, Italian conspiracy was to contort beyond recognition—and with devastating implications—a complex, altogether homegrown product. The cliché of "The-Mafia-did-it," launched so prominently by the committee and carried forward for decades to come—used to explain everything from the assassination of a president and other political murders to embarrassing episodes of individual corruption and scandalous intelligence operations—would serve as yet another mask for the reality not only of Las Vegas but of the nation as well.

What the committee members had uncovered was rooted, after all, in the course of American capitalism and deep in the social history of the country, not in the factional feuds of faraway Sicily. Forced on the largely urban and ethnic working class by the ruling Anglo-Saxon elite in business and politics, the regime of Prohibition that produced so much of the criminal wealth and public corruption had been a device of industrial efficiency as well as small-town, middle-class Protestant moralism. Contrary to the perennial national myth and later historiography celebrating how much Americans had in common, divisions of origin, class, money, and power were enduring. "In the country's underlying racism and ethnocentrism, many Jews and Italians couldn't make it in white Anglo-Saxon Protestant America without turning to illegal means," said a historian of both Las Vegas and organized crime. "Moreover, it was then this dominant WASP society that patronized and paid for their illegal activities, ultimately making organized crime a seamless social web of supply and demand, as American as apple pie." What Kefauver also found decades after the great immigrations was an outgrowth of thoroughly native misrule begun well before the heavier tides of Italian immigration or the Roaring Twenties. "The spirit of graft and lawlessness," as Lincoln Steffens thought obvious in the nation's political machines and corporate venality growing out of the nineteenth century, "is the American spirit."

Just as Kefauver's persistent emphasis on gambling concealed the magnitude of drug money as the Syndicate's seed capital, Mafia and Italian stereotypes hid the enormity of a multiethnic crime confederation more profoundly *American* than any faction. Nothing might have illustrated so plainly the fallacy as a serious probing of Las Vegas. In 1950, it was a city where the infamous New York Mafia, whose tentacles the senators saw everywhere, still controlled relatively little—where Las Vegas operators of Italian descent like P. O. Silvagni from neighboring Utah, his partner, Californian Tony Cornero, and a handful of others, necessarily operated in alliances across ethnic and regional lines. Meanwhile, the drug proceeds and vice profits converging on the Strip were from communities and coalitions from all over the nation, money that came from, paid off, enriched, and empowered a spectrum as diverse in ethnic terms as the nation's society, business, and politics at every level.

The epic misconception was no accident. Much of the committee's blunder, and what would make it a prototype of coopted congressional inquiries, traced to a heavyset, balding Californian with darting eyes who embodied the unseen currents running beneath the postwar surface.

When FBN director Harry Anslinger offered his aide to the committee, Kefauver and his colleagues who were being spurned by Hoover and his FBI and other agencies in government readily accepted the offer. For Anslinger, in the time-honored tradition of shrewd Washington bureaucrats, an agent loaned to the committee staff was a de facto spy for the FBN, ensuring that the director would know the progress of the committee and thus be able to shape its outcome consistent with his bureaucratic interests. The plant was George White, destined years later to become infamous as an operative at the juncture of government and crime that one historian has aptly called America's "deep politics." A San Francisco reporter known for underworld contacts, White went to work for Anslinger in 1935 to help him compete for publicity with his despised rival, Hoover. He had risen rapidly, serving Anslinger's abuse of the still small drug agency as a fiefdom of personal power. Like other FBN agents, he joined the OSS during World War II, becoming a lieutenant colonel and close associate of future CIA counterespionage chief James Jesus Angleton. White would be a ranking officer in Operation Underworld, that founding collusion between U.S. intelligence and Meyer Lansky to control the New York docks. By war's end, he was known not only as a principal liaison between the bureaucracy and organized crime figures the government was widely enlisting as sources and operatives, but also as a brutal bully, "a stone cold alcoholic," as one account depicted him, who washed down lunch with a fifth of vodka.

Taking over the FBN's Chicago office in 1946, White promptly recruited and thus proceeded to protect as double agents several men—including Jack Ruby—in a circle implicated in the decisive murder that year of racewire boss James Ragen. By 1948, White was in Rome, working with the new CIA to arrange covert bribes in Italian politics. He was now a rabid Cold Warrior, crossing blurred bureaucratic lines in the convoluted world of covert action, "part of the 'inner circle,' " as Peter Dale Scott wrote, "who planned and carried out various lethal secret operations." With a reputation as a swashbuckling, cut-any-corner agent for whom the ends of national security justified the means, he would be a prototype himself for future perversions of federal drug policy, "a law enforcement official who regularly violated the law," as a historian put it. In the mounting Red Scare of the time, he would also be a discreet source and confidant to kindred spirits on Capitol Hill, like McCarran and his fanatical aide Julien Sourwine. White blamed Communist China for the growing heroin traffic into the United States, covering up the actual smuggling by Chiang Kai-shek's corrupt but U.S.-allied government—an eerie prototype for later justifications for the support of right-wing dictatorships and military regimes in other drug-producing countries. When the CIA later experimented with drugs on unwitting victims, it would be a zealous, sadistic White who provided the narcotics, hired prostitutes to lure subjects, then watched through a two-way mirror. "Where else could a red-blooded American boy lie, kill, cheat, steal, rape and pillage," White later wrote in reply to a writer's question, "with the sanction and blessing of the All-Highest?"

This was the man who came from Anslinger to the committee as a senior government authority. Though he in fact knew little more about the real shape of organized crime than anyone else in Washington, he would be presented to and accepted by the committee as what one member called "one of the great experts on the Mafia," a term the FBN seized as a catchall bogey to justify its own budgets. Thus it would be White, secretly compromised at so many levels bureaucratically and politically, who in the early months of the inquiry was "particularly influential" with the committee behind the scenes, as one writer recorded, giving the senators and their staff many of their initial briefings, suggesting leads and witnesses, deliberately shaping and manipulating their earnest but half-informed perspective. At one point in its New York investigation, the committee stumbled onto Operation Underworld, but White privately assured the members, according to his "secret record," that "OSS remained aloof" from any alliance with criminals. He gently but efficiently maneuvered to stop Kefauver from raising the curtain on the corrupt partnership between the government and criminals that was not only continuing but blossoming in the Cold War. White and his fellow FBN agents also steered the senators away from the massive drug-running that was the financial heart of the Syndicate, since exposure of that traffic threatened not only the FBN's double agents but the inept agency's bogus claims of enforcement results.

All the while, the FBN's self-serving subversion from within paralleled the obstruction of Kefauver and his colleagues by the FBI from without. Hoover had shunned them from the beginning because of his own corruption and his defensiveness about the bureau's near-complete neglect of organized crime. His hostility was all the greater when the inquiry—and its attendant popularity—seemed captured by his nemesis Anslinger. Added to all the other political obstacles in its path, the unwary, relatively unsophisticated committee was enveloped as well in a maelstrom of competing Washington bureaucracies. When it was over, the false history and narrow blame that lay in the term *Mafia* would hide the thriving connective tissue between politics, organized crime, government intelligence, and American labor and industry.

Kefauver would appear on the cover of *Time* in March 1951, and his ghostwritten book *Crime in America* would be a bestseller later that year. The sensation around the committee would inspire some seventy local crime commissions throughout the country. Under mounting public pressure, the Treasury Department set up a special rackets squad to investigate criminal fraud in income tax cases, though Hoover successfully blocked the creation of a federal crime commission that would have threatened his own power. Otherwise, on Capitol Hill or in the Truman White House, where the committee had always been anathema, if not an imminent danger, its legacy in legislation and policy was an unrelieved defeat. Of nineteen bills stemming directly from the hearings, and more than two hundred others that grew out of the report, none passed the Congress, and scores more like them failed in coming years.

On the last day of 1951, Kefauver opened his presidential campaign headquarters at Washington's majestic Willard Hotel on Pennsylvania Avenue. The fame of the committee had catapulted the forty-eight-year-old Tennessee lawyer farther and faster than even he had reckoned. "The boy has struck a wave of popularity from Maine to California," a privately rueful Senate colleague on the committee, Herbert O'Conor, confessed to Cooke Kefauver when he visited Washington that winter. "The road behind him was strewn with wrecked machines," an admiring Jack Anderson wrote. But despite the hatred of the Democratic bosses, the popular chairman of the crime investigation was a celebrity in the dawning media age, and to many the Democrats' best hope to keep the White House after a fierce, lavishly financed Republican resurgence following a twenty-year exile from the presidency. His appeal was made clear wittily in an epigram of the time meant to dismiss the Democratic field for 1952: House leader Sam Rayburn of Texas was too old, it was said, New York governor Averell Harriman too rich, Senator Robert Kerr of Oklahoma too oily, Georgia's Richard Russell too racist, and Estes Kefauver too honest.

Skirmishing in the early months, Kefauver tried in vain the traditional deference to party lords, paying a ritual visit to the White House in January 1952 to tell a still noncommittal Truman that he would not run if the president sought reelection himself. He had not made up his mind, Truman told him, but was friendly and encouraging about what he called "young Democrats" vying for national office. "Play up your victory over the Crump machine. The people will like that," the president said, cheerfully reminding him of his career-launching campaign against local corruption in Tennessee. It was a cutting charade. "Truman at that time seemed to have only one aim in life," *New York Post* publisher Dorothy Schiff wrote afterward. "That was to stop Kefauver at any cost." The president called the senator "Cowfever" and thought him a "peculiar person . . . ignorant of history, an amateur in politics and intellectually dishonest." Kefauver was "a man Truman instinctively disliked and distrusted, a feeling shared by most of the party regulars," presidential biographer David McCullough would write later, without elaborating the historic reasons for the enmity. It was not only that the equally willful, ambitious, and flawed Kefauver was unwilling to play the pliant politician that Truman expected in supporters and protégés. He had come far too close—with, in the end, too little compromise and hypocrisy of his own to make him dependable—to the inner core of power Truman not only understood but embodied.

A week later the senator formally announced his candidacy, making the usual pledges of a strong foreign policy and balanced budget, but adding an unmistakable priority: "We must first clean our own house." Donning his coonskin cap to the delight of crowds, he was soon in pitched battle in the party primaries, contests which a caustic Truman now dismissed as "eyewash." In New Hampshire that March, Kefauver was pitted against the president himself, who remained aloof while his minions in the party and labor "poured on the coal" for a Truman slate of delegates, as one writer remembered. Against those odds, the upset was electric, Kefauver defeating the sitting president decisively.

As an unpopular Truman eventually withdrew from the race, the Tennessee senator would go on to win fourteen of the sixteen Democratic primaries. By June, a national poll showed that Democratic voters backed Kefauver by more than three to one over his nearest rival for the nomination, and by nearly four to one against vacillating Illinois governor Adlai Stevenson, now being supported by the lame duck Truman. In some surveys Kefauver actually defeated or ran even with General Dwight Eisenhower, the GOP contender whose name eclipsed every other Democrat. Suddenly, Kefauver was a possible, even likely president, an alarming prospect for the Syndicate and its political allies all over America.

Then, later that summer, there were ominous signs. His campaign had been only weeks old when it began to run out of money, symbolized by a move out of the stately Willard to the shabby Raleigh Hotel around the corner. He had waged some of the final primary campaigns "on pennies," as he sadly told a friend, spending only $2,000 in California and little more than $600 in South Dakota. His organization remained weak and impoverished, the toll of his intensely personal style. His election victories nationwide and impressive strength in the polls only fired the hatred of Democratic politicians and machines, who remained supreme in a party still brazenly controlled in its backrooms. Their power was plain in the delegate count on the eve of the convention. Of the 482 floor votes from the states whose primaries he had swept, Kefauver would have only 226 on the first ballot. He seemed reconciled to the enmity, if not fully aware of its depth and potency. "I guess some of those opposed to me can't forget what the Senate Crime Committee dug up, showing some links with political circles," he told a columnist who asked about the bitter hostility of party regulars. "That's about it."

Still leading in delegates, clearly the popular favorite, he remained confident—and oblivious. In crucial days of maneuvering just before the convention, he startled backers by announcing he was heading home to relax and "for a few meals of black-eyed peas and Tennessee country ham."

From the opening gavel at the International Amphitheater, upwind from the Chicago stockyards, there would be a furtive, ferocious battle for the soul of the party, though largely unreported by the journalists and cameras attending the first fully televised national convention. In the chair, Rayburn was hostile to the Kefauver cause at every turn. Convention officials from the Chicago machine, run by Syndicate puppet Jake Arvey and an equally corrupt and power-hungry local politician named Richard J. Daley, routinely refused passes for Kefauver supporters, who were forced to pay off guards simply to get into the galleries. At one point, Kefauver managers appealed over national television for voters to wire their protests with regard to the convention tyrannies. The responses poured in, but were all intercepted. "Scores of bushel baskets of undelivered telegrams," as one witness recalled them, would be found hidden in a corner of the hall after the convention was over.

"We love him because of the enemies he has made," Tennessee governor Gordon Browning said in placing Kefauver's name in nomination, "and some of the enemies he has today are rather vocal here." In defiance, his delegates rose in a spontaneous demonstration, as they would numerous times in the hours ahead. But the grip on the party remained. On the first ballot, Kefauver stood at 340, still far short of the more than 600 needed for the nomination, though well ahead of Stevenson, who had finally emerged as an open contender after ceaseless behind-the-scenes jockeying. The trailing candidates, Russell and Harriman, now held the balance of power. The southerners still hated Kefauver for opposing the poll tax as well as exposing the region's endemic corruption. And though Harriman privately pledged his support to Kefauver on a later ballot, the millionaire governor was also dickering with Truman and the machine forces ostensibly behind Stevenson, who were secretly dangling the nomination before Harriman as well.

Like some nighttime ambush of a parading column, it would be for the Kefauver forces a battle fought by stealth and treachery against stubborn principle and enduring naïveté. During the second ballot, with everyone watching for either a surge or weakening of Kefauver's strength, Governor Alan Shivers of Texas, in machinations with Lyndon Johnson and their varied corporate and underworld patrons—later identified as Benny Binion and Carlos Marcello—secretly offered his state's 52 votes to Kefauver. The shift would have been the breakthrough that assured the nomination. The quid pro quo required Kefauver to issue a statement saying his "mind was open" on the explosive issue of Tidelands oil, giving the companies and their allies that dominated the Gulf states a monopoly on the billions in offshore petroleum.

"But my mind *isn't* open," the candidate said quietly, handing the draft back to an aide. "The whole thing is a steal. I can't sign it."

On the second ballot, as favorite sons fell out, Kefauver still led with 362 votes, but Stevenson had picked up more than 70. Now the final deals were being cut. Seen as an irony at the time, the fatal blow came from Kefauver's ostensible supporters among the party's northern liberals—future Democratic leaders like Senator Hubert Humphrey of Minnesota and Governor G. Mennen "Soapy" Williams of Michigan, as well as Harriman. As some of them made their way to his suite at the nearby Stockyards Inn, Kefauver seemed blind to the betrayal. "I think the Stevenson strength is about at its peak," he cheerfully told an aide after the second ballot, when the intrigues against him were rife. A faithful delegate from Tennessee remembered him "sitting there with a drink in his hand and a happy, bemused smile on his face, not even realizing that they had already cut his throat."

Stevenson was gaining momentum and Russell's southerners could not be allowed to shift their votes to him and take credit for the nomination, the liberals told Kefauver, though they well knew the diehard Dixie delegates would hold out until the end. Only afterward would it be known how much these men who now turned on Kefauver owed their own political fortunes to the same forces he had dared or happened to expose, and they officially deplored as well: how much campaign money and backing Williams had received from Dalitz and Hoffa, or that Humphrey, once a supposedly gang-busting mayor, would over his career accept generous campaign financing from Meyer Lansky and others like him. In January 1965, the widely admired Humphrey would take the oath as vice president of the United States with his old patron, Minneapolis vice lord Fred Gates, holding the Bible.

Deserted by his allies, his delegates being torn away, Kefauver headed for the floor to make his concession and urge his people to vote for Stevenson. On the way he picked up one of his oldest and still loyal supporters, Illinois senator Paul Douglas, a scholar and former marine who had stood up to the Chicago machine and the White House to back his friend Estes in both the committee and the quest for the presidency. "Exhausted and disconsolate," as a witness remembered him, the handsome, wavy-haired Douglas was in his room drenched in perspiration in the 100-degree heat when he rose to comfort the candidate. But it was Kefauver who wanted to help. "Paul," he said, "as far as I'm concerned the only thing that matters now is what I can do to pull you out of this."

On the convention rostrum, they were snubbed once again by Rayburn, who refused to recognize Kefauver for three sweltering hours during a tedious, still inconclusive third ballot. Meanwhile, in the backrooms, though the handpicked Stevenson himself was ready to accept Kefauver as a running mate, Truman and others scathingly vetoed him as a vice-presidential nominee, and the diffident Stevenson deferred. The president long gloated over his role in defeating Kefauver. "Had I not come to Chicago when I did," he wrote privately afterward, "the squirrel-headed coonskin cap man . . . who has no sense of honor would have been the nominee." Later furious at Stevenson for some slight to the Democratic machine, Truman could think of no greater insult than to compare him to the man they had crushed: "Cowfever could not have treated me any more shabbily than have you."

Recognized at last, Kefauver spoke "firmly and calmly," as one listener remembered, into the stilled, cavernous hall. "Ladies and gentlemen, I have fought the hard fight. We have done the very best we could."

In the gallery, a white-haired Cooke Kefauver bit back tears. He and the senator's wife, Nancy, made their way to the podium, and together they all walked out of the convention, as one supporter recalled, "without looking back." Sitting under the rostrum, Jake Arvey was "smiling happily," as columnist Anderson remembered him. A few instruments in the band struck up

"Happy Birthday," and some of the delegates began quietly singing the words of the song to the familiar, bespectacled man leaving the hall.

Forty-nine years old that morning, Kefauver had been briefly, if only in part and sometimes inadvertently, an unwanted truth-teller in American politics. Like an old graveyard convulsed by excavation, the truths about his country had pushed up around him whether he liked it or not, and the hard-drinking womanizer and opportunist who became an American hero was ultimately doomed by the reality he uncovered.

He would be a lingering presence on the edges of national power until his death from an apparent heart attack on the floor of the Senate in the summer of 1963. In 1956, he again ran for president, though his moment had passed. Defeated by Stevenson in most primaries, he was still popular enough to be nominated as his rival's running mate when, as a gesture to growing public disillusion, the party bosses threw open the choice for vice president on a ticket they knew was hopeless. He would go on to lead Senate inquiries into growing monopolization in pharmaceuticals, steel, and other industries—further concentrations of power growing out of the America he exposed in the Committee—but again his revelations were attacked or ignored by a political system beholden to those forces. Kefauver's historic role had already ended that hot summer of 1952. His reckoning in the Chicago stockyards marked the failure of even a frail chance to confront the forces that now made Las Vegas their capital, to turn them back before they became impregnable.

9. "Temple Town of the American Dream"

A river of wealth," one journalist called it, and on its sandy banks the gamblers erected their castles. It was a spree like no other.

In 1952, the Syndicate and its partners built the Sahara to imitate romantic North Africa, and then the sprawling Sands with one of its craps tables floating in the swimming pool, and its dancing Copa Girls whom they called the "classiest women in Vegas." In 1954, they launched the Showboat to mimic Mark Twain's Mississippi paddle-wheeler with a five-hundred-seat bingo room and a twenty-four-lane bowling alley. In 1955, they opened the New Frontier, the Royal Nevada, the high-rise Riviera—where patrons rode the town's first elevators amid what the hotel owners imagined as "European splendor"—and the Dunes, with its carpets and cocktail waitresses out of the *Arabian Nights*, its 30-foot turbaned sultan with arms akimbo standing guard over the entrance, and the first gourmet restaurant in Las Vegas. In 1956, the new downtown Fremont became the tallest building in the state, featuring up-and-coming acts like a plump twelve-year-old soprano named Wayne Newton singing "Danke Shein," and from its rooftop lounge while drinking an Atomic Cocktail—equal parts vodka, brandy, and champagne, with a splash of sherry—a much-coveted, unobstructed if sedated view of the blinding flash and great mushroom cloud of thermonuclear bomb tests at nearby Frenchman's Flat. In 1957, on the themes of "Old Havana" and

"Luxury First," they built the sleek Tropicana, with enough air conditioning to cool 1,000 homes in Death Valley, enough concrete to build 150 miles of freeway, and the Folies Bergère to amuse the crowds drawn by its wonders. Within months, they went on to open the largest hotel in the world, the legendary Stardust, with the sensational, topless Lido de Paris and the most opulent guestrooms in America. In only seven years, Las Vegas had become one of the most distinct and showy cities of its kind anywhere on the planet; yet its real monuments were still its secrets and its power.

To some it was, and always would be, a garish, vulgar place—either too greedy or too cheap, but in any case too much. "A disease, a nightmare, a paradise for the misbegotten," Nick Tosches called it. Another visitor dismissed the 1950s city as "a kind of mobster metropolis for well-to-do southern Californians." Las Vegas, concluded journalist Lucius Beebe with suitable contempt, "represents the ultimate achievement of the motor-court civilization." Some Las Vegans themselves, especially the older, native Nevada families, looked down on the tacky excess of it all. As a matter of taste and dignity, they held themselves and their families largely apart from the raucous scene on the Strip or in Glitter Gulch. In small acts of snobbery, if not jealousy, they kept the well-to-do gamblers and their wives out of private social clubs and away from their dinner or bridge tables. But these Nevadans' relatively conventional jobs and lives were inevitably entwined with the multiplying casinos, any one of which hosted every week the equivalent of the entire adult population of Nevada. "When the town was exploding like that," said a native, "it was as if there were two Las Vegases—one where you lived and the other you were a little ashamed or scared of."

Neither disdain nor aversion stopped the droves of customers. Americans now loved Las Vegas. By 1954, over 8 million visitors were flocking to the city every year. They left behind more than $200 million in what was now the gambling mecca of the world and the entertainment capital of the nation. They jammed the craps and blackjack tables, the roulette rails and Wheels of Fortune, leaving poker to the hard-core, high-stakes players, and the slots to the wives who now joined their men, the clanging machines put out on the casino floor in ever greater numbers "to keep the women busy while their husbands get trimmed," as a veteran gambler told a reporter.

After betting, the visitors could slip into the extravagant showrooms, where their sumptuous dinner and drinks would be "comped" by the house if they had won or lost enough, and in either case needed the enticement to keep playing. The show itself was free, and the ever-larger neon marquees of Las Vegas boasted an unparalleled presentation of artists and performers of the era, for every mass taste. There were the singers Elvis Presley, Bing Crosby, Perry Como, Ella Fitzgerald, Eddie Fisher, Nat King Cole, Rosemary Clooney, Harry Belafonte, the Mills Brothers, Andy Williams, Peggy Lee, Dick Haymes, the McGuire Sisters; famous vaudeville, film, and television comedians Jimmy Durante, Abbott and Costello, Milton Berle, Dean Martin and Jerry Lewis, Red Skelton, Edgar Bergen and Charlie McCarthy; world-famed dancers like the Flamenco master José Greco, and the celebrated stripper Lili St. Cyr; extravaganzas from Liberace's to Parisian showgirls, beloved big bands and orchestras, fashionable magicians and crowd-pleasing animal acts. Beginning in 1953, for what the house called "the highbrow money crowd," there were international opera luminaries Mimi Benzell, Lauritz Melchior, and Robert Merrill, Broadway stars like Carol Channing and Ezio Pinza, theater and cabaret legend Noël Coward and more like them, "class acts" who made as much as $30,000 for a two-week stand—more money, and often larger and more appreciative audiences, than they might enjoy on the most prestigious stages of the world.

The nation's major cities had theater, opera, dance, and nightclub acts. Throughout the country, people could see traveling circuses and roadshows, the flickering images of Hollywood stars and television celebrities on screens large and small. But now suddenly here, in this corner of the Mojave Desert, visitors could choose from the largest, brightest constellation of popular American entertainment—and for what seemed no more than the price of a drive-in dinner back home or a dingy motel on the way. To commemorate it all, the house thoughtfully provided shapely, fishnet-stockinged female photographers who roamed the showrooms capturing ordinary Americans in a fantasy moment. In the familiar black-and-white matte picture, smiling people, in evening clothes or often just the suits and dresses they wore to church or other special occasions, leaned together at an elaborately set, white linen table. It was a portrait that ended up on countless mantels and in family scrapbooks around the country, marking a time, place, and self, unique in their lives.

After the shows, visitors might gamble several hours more, before drifting away to the famous Vegas buffet suppers waiting for them between midnight and dawn. Again for a pittance, they found what one customer called "unrestricted vistas of Eastern lobster in aspic, terrines of Strasbourg *foie gras,* Shrimp Louis, cold birds, and all the delicatessen of the Super-Reuben's." At two or three in the morning, they might head back to their beds to snatch a few hours' sleep. Though many thought the new Las Vegas hotels the finest accommodations of their scale ever available, casino owners now estimated the average guest spent less than four hours in twenty-four in their attractive suites or cabanas. Like so much else, the lodging was incidental. During the day, if only briefly, they might leave the windowless, clockless casinos that never closed to spend a while under the startling blue sky of the valley, sipping free daiquiris and gin fizzes beside an azure pool, before returning to the addictive tables. But they always returned. That, after all, as the house understood far better than they did, was their purpose in being there—not for the spectacular lights or flashy hotels, or even the star-studded productions and pampered indulgence. The reason, the destination, the point, was still the gambling.

To the seductions of the city the crowds brought a long tradition of hope and escape. More than a half century before, the pioneering sociologist Thorstein Veblen had deplored the country's widespread "animistic belief" in sheer luck, in overcoming the odds. For all the history to the contrary by the mid-twentieth century, all the fixed games in the nation's life, America was still a place where the players at the table could think of themselves as equal, at least at the beginning—where there always seemed another hand to play, another roll of the dice full of possibility. From generations who filled in a nation and often took dreadful risks to find their fortunes and identities, most of them now shaped as well by depression, war, and an uncertain peace in the nuclear age, they remained indomitably what one historian called a "people of chance," still half-desperately looking for deliverance, quixotically expecting both to lose and to win, still seeking something for nothing, still thinking they could beat the house—"beset by an unnamed hunger," as a team of writers saw them, "ready to lay down their last dollar on a chance to break free."

In Las Vegas, as they might not acknowledge so candidly back home, they could concede that it was money that mattered most in this society after all. Here they could confront it, surrender to it, live by it, worship it without shame or pretense. "The satisfactions sold in Las Vegas are subtle and profound: They touch on the real lives, the real anxieties of the people who trek there from all over the United States," visiting screenwriter and novelist Julian Halevy recorded in 1958. "Las Vegas deals in the essence of the American Way, narcotizes the number-one preoccupation of daily reality and nightly dream, the Almighty Buck . . . the illusion is created that we are all rich, that money means nothing." As visitors swarmed around the tables in the 1950s—the *Saturday Evening Post* termed them "all the sad-faced people having fun at Vegas"—they presaged a time when the city and its then still singular ethos would be an unabashed hallmark of American values and civilization. Their hundreds of millions of dollars given over were proof of what it already had become—"a temple town," as one author described it, "of the American dream."

To the casino owners, of course, those who came and gambled were neither pilgrims nor bearers of tradition, but "victims to be plucked," as *New York Times* reporter Wallace Turner put it. With the succession of new hotels, the take was immense, declared income at the casinos collectively running in the tens of millions of dollars annually by the early fifties, and the skim many times the huge reported profits. In that decade, as the family of Chicago boss Sam Giancana would later confess, his "personal take" was "over three hundred thousand a month," and he was only one Syndicate figure among the literally dozens sharing in the Las Vegas skim. Just thinking about that money from the Strip, one of them remembered, made his heart skip. It was long rumored that after the Kefauver Hearings, the ever-discreet Lansky "never again set foot in Las Vegas," as one insider recalled. But up and down the Strip, as well as in Fremont's Glitter Gulch, the "Miami hotel men," the euphemism for Lansky's fronts, were skimming at least $3 million for every $1 million reported. Each month men and women couriers, often met along the way by intermediaries, carried satchels fat with cash by plane, train, or automobile to Miami, Lansky's eventual headquarters, from where he distributed the proceeds to his partners around the nation and abroad. "They all trusted Meyer to keep the books and divvy it up," a Las Vegas figure said later.

Much of the cash went directly to numbered accounts in Switzerland, where it would be relaundered back through banks and financial institutions in the Bahamas and then to the United States, often as construction loans to Las Vegas casinos and the other Syndicate-financed enterprises of hospitals, golf courses, shopping centers, housing subdivisions, and movie production companies. "When we borrowed money from the Swiss banks and other banks here," Lansky would say later, laughing, "it was our own money." Throughout the fifties, that secret, indirect, revolving traffic between the Strip and Switzerland was one of the heaviest flows of international capital of the era, making Las Vegas a world center of finance long before many knew its name.

From the inside, like an unseen shadow of the city's new skyline, the explosive growth of the decade had its own litany. In 1952, the Sahara was built with Oregon racewire money as well as West Coast bookie and extortion profits, was initially controlled by the Lanskys, and would eventually pass to the Chicago mobsters—the Fischetti brothers, Giancana, and their associates. Two months later, the Sands opened with the secret backing of two people infamous from the Kefauver inquiry, Joe Adonis and Frank Costello, and proceeds from Lansky vice around the country, including dealings with Hoover intimate and liquor magnate Lewis Rosenstiel, who in turn had made some of the capital and protected some of the operations with a half-million-dollar payoff to Senator Lyndon Johnson. Before the decade was over, the Sands would be infamous among insiders as "controlled by more mobs than any other casino in Nevada," including Syndicate branches in Houston, Galveston, St. Louis, Los Angeles, San Francisco, Minneapolis, Chicago, Detroit, Cleveland, New York, Newark, Jersey City, Brooklyn, Boston, Miami, and New Orleans.

In 1954, the Showboat was financed by Dalitz and his Desert Inn crowd, including now a more visible Ruby Kolod, a jowly, wrinkle-browed figure with thinning hair and a reputation as a killer and blackmailer. In 1955 the New Frontier, soon known in the backrooms as "the mob's amateur operation," at first yielded only marginal skim until Ross Miller, an experienced Syndicate manager, and father of a future Nevada governor, arrived from Chicago with his trademark pompadour and turtleneck sweaters to put things right. In the spring of 1955, the Riviera was built by the Chicago Outfit, as they were known, who soon brought over Gus Greenbaum from the Flamingo to oversee their investment when the skim slipped. Less than a month later, the Dunes began with mob-connected businessmen as fronts for the New England–based Patriarca crime family, the casino soon to be a "goldmine" for its Boston owners, as one of their chroniclers later wrote. Down the street that same year the new Royal Nevada, the only major casino of the era ever to go broke, was built by still other criminal interests, including among its backers a St. Louis attorney named Morris Shenker, whose ties to the Teamsters Union would play a role in the further development of the city far beyond the ill-fated Royal Nevada. In 1955, too, the Fremont rose to become the state's tallest skyscraper with loan-sharking money out of San Francisco, as well as the backing of Lansky associate Eddie Levinson from Kentucky and Florida, who now took most of the $16-million-a-year skim from the downtown landmark. Levinson was "a short man," in the description of one observer, "with a fringe of gray hair, and a pair of the sharpest, most opaque dark, dark brown eyes in Nevada." He gave off an air of "unspoken secrets . . . and cool courage" as he moved among the casino crowd in his white duck trousers, bright green shirt, and a trademark jockey cap. His intimates included both Hoffa and Bobby Baker, the ubiquitous chief aide to Lyndon Johnson, who by then was Senate majority leader and preparing to run for the presidency.

In 1957, with Lieutenant Governor Rex Bell of Nevada cutting the ribbon, the posh Tropicana opened, clearing over $650,000 in its first twenty-four days. The money and skim went not only to part-owner Frank Costello but also to Giancana and the Chicago Outfit, and to New Orleans crime boss Carlos Marcello. Marcello's points were represented at the casino by "Dandy" Phil Kastel, with his silk suits and gold-tipped walking stick, a one-time Manhattan murderer and proconsul for Hot Springs. Since Kastel was unable to obtain licensing himself, it was his avid showgirl wife Helen who was now Marcello's front, along with an Indiana insurance man named Ben Jaffe and a Las Vegan, J. Kell Houssels, Sr. In 1958, the Stardust was built initially by Tony Cornero, with gunrunning and hijacking profits out of California and elsewhere. When Cornero was refused a license by state officials, he expeditiously dropped dead on the casino floor of what one casino manager called "a supposed heart attack." The house was then taken over by Cornero's equally notorious successor, Jake "The Barber" Factor, and the Dalitz group. Dalitz and company had come in as secret partners in the Stardust not long before Cornero's timely death, and now financed the takeover with millions not only from the Teamsters but also from Louis Jacobs of Buffalo. Jacobs, known as the "Godfather of Sports," was repaying a favor to Dalitz, who had loaned him money in the thirties at a time when his Sportsystems baseball concessions firm—the corporate predecessor to Emprise—was in financial trouble.

Meanwhile, down from the Strip the connections ran no less densely or profitably along Fremont Street. Benny Binion's Horseshoe Club, whether its owner presided from prison or on the scene, was passing on its skim and part of the official profits to silent partner Eddie Levinson and inevitably on to Lansky—a fact unknown at the time and only recently revealed through interviews with associates. Nearby, the equally prosperous El Cortez belonged in large part to William Israel Alderman, a lumbering, laconic Lansky man from Minneapolis who was known as "Izzy Lump-Lump" for his girth, and more professionally as "Ice Pick Willie" for his reputation for settling disputes with that instrument through the ears. The new Mint Hotel, built to attract the low-end bus station crowd for bingo, keno, and slots—sucker games, as they're known in the trade—was an offshoot of the Sahara and its similar criminal finance.

It was these men and their money that produced the brightly lit spectacle of the new Las Vegas. In their unprecedented architecting and marketing of their product, they seemed to many extraordinarily gifted, applying the wisdom of decades in speakeasies and roadhouses satisfying illicit if ravenous tastes. Others thought them just as extraordinarily banal. "What occurred to me was that gangsters weren't smart at all," said a Nevada crime reporter after covering the lives and careers of many of them, "they just did things nobody else would do." For all their power and ruthlessness in the Las Vegas of the fifties, few were in reality the one-dimensional legends of the cold-blooded killer or racketeer. For every mythic Bugsy Siegel there was a host of nervous little Moe Sedways, or a figure like Charlie "Babe" Baron, an Arvey hit man from Chicago who was a greeter and front man at the casinos, but paraded his status as a brigadier general in the National Guard whenever he could. One gangster would tell the story of how George Raft, the movie star who played mobster roles in B movies of the forties, once visited a casino, and some thought he was there to study real-life gangsters to make his screen portrayals more authentic. But that mistook the frailty and contrivance in the criminals' own sense of themselves. "The reverse proved to be the case," said one account of the episode. "It was the gangsters who spent their time studying Raft."

From their early years in Vegas, the owners craved the social acceptance old Nevada society still denied them. "They sought respectability passionately," a local lawyer would say of Dalitz and the rest, and innately "saw themselves as second-class citizens." At the same time, most of them having lived on the outskirts of polite society since childhood, they were discreet, even self-deprecating, about their social standing. "They knew their place," said Las Vegas investigative reporter John L. Smith. "They didn't push to control the life of the community like the even more vulgar pirates who came after them," said another; "they just wanted to be accepted and, I guess, pretty much left alone." Even snubbed, they enjoyed a level of gentility and acceptance they had never known before.

Successive waves of often middle-aged hoodlums appeared on the scene with younger wives and new small children—"mostly older Jewish men with their shiksas," said a daughter of such a marriage, "the original wife left back home in New York or Chicago collecting large alimonies." Treated like royalty on the Strip, they longed instead for a middle-class existence in a small frame house with a white picket fence on 5th or 6th Street in the old downtown, and a coveted invitation to a women's auxiliary or private men's club. "Former outlaws could show up, shed their pasts like a desert reptile shedding its seasonal skins, and pick up anew as model citizens," wrote a member of one of their families.

Occasionally, a visitor found the whole scene bizarre if not sinister. "This is a fabulous, extraordinary madhouse," Noël Coward recorded in his diary in 1955 when he played the Desert Inn. "Beams of light shoot down from baroque ceilings on the masses of earnest morons flinging their money down the drain." He thought that "the gangsters who run the places are all urbane and charming . . . curious products of a most curious adolescent country." Yet their morals were "bizarre" in the extreme. "They are generous, mother-worshipers, sentimental, and capable of much kindness," the Englishman concluded. "They are also ruthless, cruel, violent, and devoid of scruples."

For all the facades, they were also brazen. In 1953, not long after the opening of the Sands, novice reporter Dick Odessky walked into the casino with columnist Walter Winchell, who promptly pointed out a gathering of "some of the most notorious gangland figures in the country," as the newcomer remembered. "This has got to be serious for these guys to get together out here," Winchell told the young journalist. "Vegas is supposed to be clean, and here you've got a Mafia council meeting right in the middle of the newest joint in town." Winchell added that in the next day or so, "some pretty important fish will be found dead." Within hours, there was a gangland murder on the East Coast; like so much else, the story of the casino meeting and the "coincidence" of the killing would go officially unreported in Nevada, though rumors would permeate the Strip.

Las Vegas in the fifties was more than ever a company town, and the company was the Syndicate. Like the casinos' true ownership, every dimension of the regime had hidden connections, a shadow side. Unknown to their adoring fans, many of the name entertainers came to the marquees of the Strip from pasts entwined with organized crime—some, like Joe E. Lewis, out of necessity since the Syndicate owned many of the best nightclubs or theaters in the country, others, like Frank Sinatra, blatantly engaged in business relationships with criminals. Las Vegas was to be a confluence of the empire's assets in men, money, chattels, and power across the broad range of American life it already ruled, in which the entertainment industry was an early and continuing possession.

The gathering of gangsters was in its way as colossal as the new record-breaking casinos and their profits. From a series of meetings in the late forties and early fifties, in New York, Havana, and Hot Springs, details of which would be revealed a decade later by government witness Joe Valachi, the affiliated hoodlums had decided that Las Vegas would be an "open city." The various urban and regional interests, who savagely guarded their economic and political cartels at home, would be free to invest unilaterally or in joint ventures in what scholar Robert Goodman called legal gambling's "monopoly export economy"—a Nevada, as one casino partner put it more simply, "with plenty to go around." They were all to observe a protocol against the kind of factional warfare that bloodied the sidewalks and backrooms of other cities—what they called a "purity code." When a notorious hit man, "Russian Louie" Strauss, drew unwanted attention with a crude execution at Lake Tahoe, and then tried to extort Binion for contracting him in yet another murder, a coalition of casino interests arranged for Strauss to be lured out of town, shot, and disposed of in the desert. For years, Strip insiders would joke about gamblers who supposedly put off paying their debts by telling their creditors: "You'll get your money as soon as Russian Louie gets back to town." Otherwise, they would come and go and profit from an increasingly sophisticated meshing of interests and investments, leaving Lansky, by his web of partnerships and shareholdings, still predominant, but in a thicket of disguised relationships and authority that made Las Vegas the parent and model of the corporate shell economy of the future. As *The Nation* reported of the true owners, they "obligingly faded a few steps farther into the background," their interests "hidden in the murky background of intricate finance."

If the Mafia itself had owned almost nothing in the town when the Kefauver Committee pronounced it all-inclusive of organized crime, by mid-decade Italian mobsters had begun to move into the city more aggressively with stakes in the Sahara, Riviera, Sands, and other hotels. Their presence, and the accompanying entanglement of so many other ethnic and regional confederates, began in earnest what was to be a preoccupation of the city's insiders for the rest of the century—"the big guessing game in Las Vegas," one author called it, "of 'who owns whom.' " In Nevada as nowhere else, Italian, Jewish, Irish, and other factions were allies and collaborators, associates and accessories, all bound together by what one writer called "an insatiable appetite for money." Yet here too, as in the rest of the nation, the stereotype Mafioso as the emblem of organized crime would continue to conceal and protect the depth and perpetuation of the all-American corruption the city embodied.

Of the many fictions blanketing the city, none was more insidious than the myth that the Mafia built Vegas. Looking back at the fifties, two historians documented that actual casino interests apportioned by ethnic origin had been roughly one-half Jewish and one-quarter Italian, with Irish and Polish shares as well. But such distinctions were truly academic. Before the decade was out, the profits and power that coursed from and to the city engulfed so much of the country at large, so much of its economy and politics, that ancestry and individuals scarcely mattered in terms of historical influence. Las Vegas was becoming a seat of power not for the Jewish Mob or Italian Mafia, or any single cabal, but for the multiethnic system of greed and political corruption that the different Vegas factions collectively embodied, and that was now seeping out into the nation at large.

In Washington, it was a cold January day in 1951 when Atomic Energy Commission chairman Gordon Dean paid a confidential "courtesy call" on the senior senator from Nevada. A preacher's son from Seattle, and a former Justice Department lawyer known for his anti-Communist zeal, Dean was so security-conscious that he was not sure he could fully trust even the notorious Red-hunting Pat McCarran. After all, a friend had told Dean, "a steady stream of ex-Communists were constantly parading through the senator's Capitol Hill office," and whether turncoat informers or persecuted witnesses, they were all "Commies" past or present, all security risks. Moreover, McCarran, the inveterate fixer, was known for passing on anything he learned, even classified information, that might provide some business advantage for his loyalists in Nevada.

But this time Dean saw no choice. His secret would be out soon, and not to tell McCarran in advance only invited the old pol's wrath. The AEC, Dean confided, was about to detonate the first nuclear tests in the continental United States since 1945, and the site was the Tonopah Bombing and Gunnery Range, sixty-five miles northwest of Las Vegas. The explosions would be "safe for the people," Dean assured McCarran, and were "necessary for national security," as an aide remembered. The senator, who really had little choice in the matter, simply nodded.

Plans to test nuclear weapons in Nevada, code-named Operation Ranger, had been secretly in the making for months. Officials had wanted a continental proving ground to replace costly, less manageable Pacific sites, and the outbreak of the Korean conflict in the summer of 1950 and other Cold War tensions made the decision more urgent. At a crucial classified meeting that August, eminent physicists like Enrico Fermi warned of the radiation hazards. Government scientists knew that repeated exposure to even low-level X rays, which resembled the anticipated atmospheric radiation, caused cancer and other fatal illnesses, "gardens of leukemia," as one writer described the effects, and fallout patterns were unpredictable, with the risk of "hotspots." While the general public was still largely unaware of these dangers, some officials thought the testing of the horrific weapon on American soil would be politically impossible. "The people of the United States," one of them told Dean, "will never stand for shooting off A-bombs in this country."

But Los Alamos Laboratory director Norris Bradbury—"a second-rate scientist who was a first-rate manager," as one colleague called the effective bureaucrat—insisted that there was at least one place in the country where the government, in effect, could get away with the blasts. Politically at least, empty Nevada, not yet nationally famous and where the federal government controlled more than 85 percent of the land, seemed ideal. "The population problem," Bradbury would say of the immediate area around the test site and in the path of its fallout, "was almost zero."

Before giving his final approval on January 10, 1951, Truman had asked Dean, "Can this be done in such a way that nobody will get hurt?" The reply was not quite an answer, though the AEC chairman seemed to appease the president as he had McCarran. "Every precaution will be taken," Truman remembered him saying. Later, with Nevada governor Charles Russell and state health officials in Carson City, AEC scientists were more categorical in their promises of safety. It all "marked the beginning," as former cabinet member and historian Stewart Udall noted, "of a decades-long policy of public deception," of "statements of reassurance," as another scholar recorded, that "were not only false but calculatedly so."

The AEC wasted no time. On January 27, the first bomb was detonated over a lunar terrain of Nye County once ominously called "Death Barren." It was, witnesses remembered, a typical, starkly beautiful winter day in the desert. The sharply etched landscape of snow-capped peaks and dry prehistoric lakebeds shimmered under a crystalline clear sky. Only later did those witnesses realize how the "perfect" winds out of the southwest had carried the fallout of the one-kiloton bomb. Two days later, the AEC received an extraordinary telegram from a forceful Washington lobby, the National Association of Photographic Manufacturers, acting on behalf of its most famous member: "Tests snowfall Rochester Monday by Eastman Kodak Company give 10,000 counts per minute, whereas equal volume snow falling previous Friday gave only 400 STOP. Situation serious STOP. Will report any further tests obtained STOP. *What are you doing?* STOP." To appease the giant Kodak firm and other corporations whose products were affected by fallout, AEC officials were soon secretly providing them advance warning of the tests—a privilege never extended to ordinary people in Nevada, Utah, or elsewhere in the path of the radioactivity.

In Las Vegas, the city nearest the blast, there would be some early trepidation. Characteristically, its residents seemed less worried about the effects of radiation on themselves than about the fallout for business: They feared that tourists would stay away or even that the explosions would bounce the dice and roulette balls off the tables—prompting some casinos to post signs warning that "in such an event the House's ruling, as always, will be final." Public fears were hardly alleviated when, after one of the early blasts, a team of Utah scientists and doctors mysteriously appeared and "went through the streets of Las Vegas in white coats sampling people," as one dismayed state official remembered. For the most part, though, city residents believed the government's assurances.

Over the following decade there would be more than a hundred nuclear weapons exploded in the air or on the ground at what was now called the Nevada Test Site, as many as four a month at the height of the experiments, making once ghostly Nevada place-names landmarks in the inner history of the arms race—Jackass Flat, Camp Desert Rock, Yucca Flat, Camp Mercury. The explosions became part of the lure and lore of the city. Almost immediately, the casinos celebrated the tests as local tourist attractions, still another way to wring money from the public. Serving their "Atomic Cocktails," advertising sky rooms and suites for their view of the mushroom clouds, managers instructed their pit bosses to go on with the games during the detonations for those who wished, but also sponsored special picnic lunches outside the city to view the blasts from an even closer vantage point. Al Freeman, the press agent at the Sands whom one colleague called "the uncrowned king of Las Vegas publicists," audaciously declared the casino the "official press headquarters for the bomb tests," and government agencies went along unquestioningly, bringing to the Sands hundreds of reporters, photographers, and film crews, as well as officials from around the country.

Days after the first test, the Chamber of Commerce printed publicity releases and what it called "cheesecake photos" showing the "Atomic Hairdo" featured by one local beauty parlor, or a voluptuous woman wearing a bathing suit and brandishing a Geiger counter as she checked the beard of a smiling old desert rat. "The angle," a chamber official told a *New Yorker* reporter, "was to get people to think the explosions wouldn't be anything more than a gag." The press did its part with no evident sense of irony. "I saw the big guy this morning, and he looks like a champ to me," the *Review-Journal*'s John Cahlan wrote of an early explosion as if it were one more Nevada prize fight. "Practically the whole town was on the way to ringside . . . the largest watching audience since Hiroshima." As casino publicists did with almost every other aspect of the town's attractions, they played up the sexuality of the artifacts at hand. Dancing girls were photographed with their nudity barely covered by a piece of cotton batting in the shape of a mushroom cloud rising from genitals to breasts. Scantily clad showgirls were posed on the Strip astride a gaily striped and smoking, unmistakably phallic rocket bomb.

Soon the casinos would be "packed" at the announced hours of explosions, as one observer remembered them, crowds driving up from Los Angeles especially for "dawn bomb parties" on the Strip. The resort crowds were now joined as well by a new wave of visitors, what one writer called "a different breed" from those who came to gamble or carouse, to marry or divorce. Americans thronged to the valley in old cars and trucks, cooking their own meals in trailer courts or modest motels on the edge of town, like the Atomic View Motel, advertising "unobstructed sight line to the bomb blast from the comfort of one's lounge chair." These visitors simply "wanted to be on hand for an explosion," as one person saw them. Many tried to get as close to the detonations as possible, and the AEC did nothing to stop even families with small children from driving or hiking as close to ground zero as possible, though preventing anyone from entering the closed government reservation. Clark County sheriff Ralph Lamb was one of the few who seemed concerned about the proximity, calling the onlookers "out of their minds."

At a typical detonation, the scene in various parts of the city was surreal. From the great windows of the Desert Inn's Sky Room, guests had a panoramic view beyond Mount Charleston toward the Test Site to the north. Throughout the night before the usual early morning blast, the standing-room-only crowd drank heavily—"like fish," one participant remembered—and commonly kept the pianist busy with incessant requests for old numbers they could chorus. "They sang as if they were on the *Queen Mary* and it was going down," one piano player recalled. "Loud, desperate voices." After a while, he "couldn't take it anymore," as he told a reporter, and improvised an "atomic" boogie-woogie just to drown out the raucous requiem. In the other windowless lounges around town, waitresses and bartenders were at pains to remind patrons when the hour for the shot approached so that they could "grab their drinks and dash out," one casino employee remembered.

At the same moment out in the streets, the bomb tourists would be steering their little silver Airstream trailers onto a rise near Railroad Pass or some other high point in Las Vegas Valley. Lights started going on at five-thirty in the morning in residential neighborhoods of the town. People wandered out on their porches in bathrobes holding steaming cups of coffee, or even climbed onto their roofs. Husbands backed cars out of garages into the street for a better view, leaving the motor running to warm the car before their families came out of the house to join them. Parents pinched small children or played games with them to keep them awake for the big event. Most were rewarded with an unforgettable memory: "Good bangs and so pretty coming at sunrise as they did," one Las Vegas native would recall. The incomparable flash, too bright to be photographed by the hundreds of primitive

Kodak cameras brought along for the moment, lit up Las Vegas in a spectral false midday, the light seen vividly several hundred miles away in Montana or by airline pilots flying from Hawaii to the mainland.

Not all the effects were so picturesque. The town's still large population of horses stopped eating. Dogs and cats refused to be touched for days afterward. Though the government would always minimize the impact of explosions, early blasts set burglar alarms ringing all over town, blew doors off their hinges, and even raised concerns about cracks in massive Boulder Dam.

Eventually, the city, if not the tourists in motor courts and resorts, grew jaded with the familiar explosions, which came to be "generally dismissed as having been something of a dud," as one writer put it, if the inevitable shock waves seven minutes later gave the town only "a mild tremor." "Bigger bombs, that's what we're waiting for," one casino proprietor told a reporter in 1952. "Americans have to have their kicks." Still, some never forgot the sense of apocalypse as well as the spectacle. "When I could see again after the blinding, terrifying flash, I was looking at the sun . . . just coming over the mountains," remembered one Las Vegas woman. "The sun, you know, isn't always kind to us here in the desert, but at that moment it seemed like an old friend. It made me feel safe."

Behind the paradoxical fanfare and secrecy that surrounded the early Nevada tests, the reality was grim enough. Within hours of an explosion, AEC monitors in their telltale protective suits would descend on nearby towns in Nevada and Utah, their Geiger counters clicking from fallout frequently so heavy that lawns, porches, and cars were blanketed in a thick layer of radioactive dust and debris. "Even the most ignorant citizen must have sensed that all was not well," two British reporters noted. Despite government assertions of safety, Sears and Montgomery Ward did a thriving trade in Geiger counters, the largest trade of its kind anywhere in the world, and for a time the sale of survival shelters in Las Vegas "zoomed," as one account put it. But for most, the official deception held lethally firm. Government and contract scientists periodically appeared in Las Vegas to mollify the public. "The dangers of radiation pollution have been unjustly overemphasized," Edward Teller, one such scientist, told a local audience typically, "and unless further nuclear testing for peaceful means is continued, man may revert to the Dark Ages." Teller would be constantly echoed by the local director of testing, Albert Graves, whose much-repeated phrase for the Nevada press was that "the tests would not be of the slightest danger." For years, no one noticed that Graves himself was going blind from the effects of radiation. It would be more than a quarter century before the breadth and depth of the federal government's brutal wantonness and cover-up would begin to be known. Following Truman, Eisenhower had authorized the testing of ever larger and more dangerous thermonuclear weapons at the site, telling an aide to keep Nevadans and others "confused" about the difference between fission and fusion.

In Carson City, though his mail expressed increasing public alarm on the part of local ranchers and even people out of state, Governor Russell remained satisfied with AEC briefings and in any case reconciled to his own impotence. "Since all the atomic tests in Nevada are carried out on federally owned property," he wrote in one representative reply, "there is nothing that I as governor . . . can do to halt such tests." For his part, Norris Bradbury continued to assure both the public and the rest of the government that the tests posed no danger, but at the same time secretly ordered his own daughter-in-law, who lived nearly 1,000 miles to the east, out of any possible path of fallout during her pregnancy. "Residents of Nevada, Utah, and Arizona had their bodies, their air, land, water, and livestock poisoned, while the AEC public relations staff made jokes to dispel fears of sickness and death from radioactivity," historian Mary Ellen Glass concluded, "and while the President of the United States joined in a plot to misinform and thus endanger the nation." Though some of the victims would be identified in later legal actions on behalf of the "downwinders," principally in southern Utah, the full toll would never be known, especially in Nevada. "Judging by the effects of the tests on people so much farther away," Michael Ventura wrote of the popular bomb-viewing outings organized by the casinos, "a lot of those picnickers probably died young." Only later would it be revealed that as part of its inducement to local officials to greet the tests with such approval and enthusiasm, the federal government had secretly agreed to shield the state from any radiation exposure–related legal actions.

In Las Vegas, whatever the moral and political considerations then or later, the tests only added to the city's ongoing bonanza. "We're in the throes of acute prosperity," one casino owner said to *The New Yorker*, summarizing the impact not only of the crowds but also the publicity gained for the city by the nuclear explosions. If Las Vegas and Nevada were in some disrepute at the beginning of the decade because of the Kefauver revelations and other unsavory publicity, their jaunty, patriotic welcome of the AEC now seemed to win a kind of absolution, if not respectability. But some came to see little difference between the impact of the scientists and that of the gamblers. "A study of which group damaged the state and its citizens more," wrote one historian, "could engage a generation of researchers and writers."

By the close of the decade, a permanent and growing nuclear weapons, military, and intelligence bureaucracy spawned by the Test Site had become a pillar of the southern Nevada economy, supplying thousands of jobs and a particularly plump national security payroll of both federal positions and allied contracting. In January 1951 alone, the population of the town had increased by some 10,000. Once again, as in the building of Boulder Dam, men rushed to Nevada for the well-paid jobs at the Test Site. Within a decade, some 12,000 would be commuting from Las Vegas to the site every day, the annual wages of all the workers totaling more than $100 million.

The installation included from the beginning what air force pilots called "Red Square" and insiders dubbed "the Ranch" or "Watertown"—the CIA's top-secret Area 51. Constructed in 1955, used in the development of the famous U-2 and SR-71 high-altitude spy planes, and later Stealth fighters and bombers, the clandestine base would eventually play a role in scandals— Iran-Contra and CIA-protected drug trafficking—and inevitably added to the already eccentric sociology of the city. "The subterranean spook culture," one local journalist would write in the 1970s, "thrives in Las Vegas."

In ways no one could have predicted, the U.S. government would be a mighty force in the rise of Las Vegas, principally in the shape of policies and practices based as much on secrecy and deception as anything on the Strip. But the blinding flashes and the mushroom clouds were only another manifestation of what would be the city's historic alliance of government, crime, and business.

Nuclear fallout and the accompanying government deception were hardly the only poisons of the time. Whatever else they were, the men who commanded the city were also, in a national cultural tradition beyond group or locale, classic American bigots, sexists, and exploiters.

Before 1930, though Ku Klux Klan crosses had burned briefly on Fremont Street in the twenties, Nevada's few black migrants had been relatively welcome in the area. But southern poor whites drawn to the workforces at Boulder Dam and the Henderson magnesium plant brought with them the racism of their origins, and local politicians soon adopted their own Nevadan Jim Crow. It was already harsh during World War II. "Japanese-Americans headed for internment camps," remembered Sarann Knight Preddy, a Las Vegas resident at the time, "received better accommodations than local blacks." This racism, along with the bigotry of the thugs who then took over, made modern Las Vegas the infamous "Mississippi of the West." By the early fifties—when the rest of the nation and even the Deep South were stirring with change—segregation of hotels and casinos was complete. Blacks could not get a room on the Strip or in Glitter Gulch. The few black servicemen or travelers who wandered into a joint were dealt with quickly, not noisily "thrown out," which might disturb white customers, as one reporter remembered, but "made to feel unwelcome" and quietly escorted to the door by house goons. Not even the black share of postwar prosperity afforded access to the attractions of "the most controlled society in the world," as one journalist described Las Vegas at the time. "For just under $25 you can fly round-trip from Los Angeles with free drinks enroute," noted a writer for *Holiday*, "but the champagne package flights are not available to Negroes." The small but growing black bourgeoisie of the era largely avoided the nation's new entertainment capital.

Then, in 1955, on a back street parallel to Glitter Gulch, a group of investors built the Moulin Rouge, "designed and planned to attract the Negro gambling crowd," as one visitor described it. It was a hotel at last where the casinos' growing number of black entertainers could stay the night, and a glittering array of stars from Harry Belafonte to Tallulah Bankhead made shows immediate sellouts. But just as suddenly as it opened, it was gone, its demise a "classic Las Vegas mystery," as one reporter wrote, though again insiders knew that the popularity of the Moulin Rouge, in addition to the racial implications, had also threatened the profits of the Strip, and "them guys," as one longtime casino manager euphemistically referred to the Syndicate, "put it out of business." At the end of the century, its decaying hulk remained a monument to the poisoned racial atmosphere of the city.

Meanwhile, working in the lowliest, least visible jobs, the town's slowly growing black population was cordoned off in the gritty Westside with no running water or sewage lines, living literally behind a barrier of blocks and mortar they called the "cement curtain." Almost none of the millions of visitors saw it. "The men who run Las Vegas," Wallace Turner concluded at the end of the decade, "are white supremacists as much as if they came from Johannesburg."

Greenspun's *Sun* covered the gradually gathering civil rights movement in the rest of America, and editorialized on what it called the "shameful" conditions in Las Vegas. But this ugliness went largely unreported, as did other daily outrages of the city. Contrary to glossy brochures or well-placed articles that advertised "an ideal year-round climate," the desert summer was always "hot as the hinges of hell," thought one visitor, and water now so precious in the bursting, ceaselessly irrigated town that sewage effluent was being used to keep the golf courses minimally green. In 1956, district engineers quietly called "an impending crisis in the water supply situation," and had begun in some desperation to pump a supplemental flow of water 1,000 feet up and twenty-five miles out from Lake Mead. But forces of nature were subject to civic censoring. "Negative news stories or unfavorable propaganda generally stopped at the city limits," wrote Mary Ellen Glass of the decade. "Discussion of the oppressive summer heat, occasional violence, or even minor unpleasantness failed to move over the newswires."

What could be learned in the city's relentless self-promotion was that Nevada was now the fastest-growing state in the Union, a lead it would rarely relinquish over the rest of the century. The population of Las Vegas tripled over the 1950s to more than 65,000, the metropolitan area exploding in the suburbs to 129,000, more than sixteen times the size of the town less than two decades before. Nevadans were now demographically the nation's youngest single state population, and as overall bank assets grew markedly and personal income rose steadily, boosters concluded Nevadans were surely some of the richest and happiest as well. The city's official handouts extolled its "broad streets, ranch-style homes, first-rate schools, eighty-one church groups, four hospitals, and no state income tax," as *Holiday* magazine repeated the claims. "Most Las Vegans felt satisfied with their city and its economy," as one writer summed it up for a college textbook. "If outsiders like U.S. senators did not agree, let them stay away from this amusing, colorful and interesting town."

Nearly half of the city's people were now dependent—"glaringly dependent," wrote Turner—on the 17,000 casino jobs. While ordinary citizens or migrants, more or less unaffiliated with organized crime, had some of the better-paying work, like the $16–$24-a-day dealers—most of whom were also paid handsomely under the table in tips and kickbacks that made their income higher than that of professionals in Nevada—many more were cruelly exploited. It was a captive economy where bare statistics reflected none of the realities of the caste system, income inequities, kickbacks and other extortion, drug and alcohol addiction, loan-sharking, and myriad other customs of the culture.

The houses brutally beat or killed employees caught or even suspected of cheating, and dealers were disciplined for the slightest infraction by having their hands crushed with leaded bats. Maimed men and women and hideously battered bodies in the desert were the unmistakable messages Las Vegas management sent its workforce. Owners replied no less summarily and grimly to protests about working conditions or labor's first feeble efforts to organize. With all the cash and power necessary, the owners conducted vicious warfare against any local not completely in their control, spending thousands of dollars publicly and tens of thousands secretly to support political bosses like Norman Biltz in his successful campaign during the fifties for a right-to-work, anti-organizing law.

Conditions were far worse for women. While dancers might make $150 a week—nude dancers made more—their "maximum combat life is seven years," as Arthur Steuer recorded in *Esquire*, "and few last more than two or three." Other casino positions were virtually out of reach. But even then, their abuse was more than occupational or economic. Within what *Life* called a "showgirl Shangri-La" was a harsh, sexist, sometimes barbaric world in which fresh, starry-eyed young women lured from around the country to the stages and payrolls of Las Vegas were treated "like meat hanging on a hook" or "slaves at some auction," one of them remembered. "They were really all Cecil B. De Milles," future governor Grant Sawyer would describe them, "all in the same search for the fabulous." Many of the women, already rejects from a savage Hollywood environment and not quite talented enough for the chorus lines, were destined to join the town's teeming hosts of prostitutes.

It was often said in Nevada—and would be frequently repeated over the decades to come—that if the legal casinos took a toll in gambling addiction, lost jobs, broken families, suicides, crimes to pay debts, and other misery, at least Las Vegas sent those agonies back out of state, home with the suckers who suffered them. But in fact the town shared in the plague. The sum of the oppression, violence, and abuse was for many a sad little society. "Las Vegas has many bitter people living in it," Turner wrote at the end of the decade. "This city has more trash peddlers per capita than any other city three times its size," wrote a former resident, "more broken homes, more prostitutes, and more so-called common law marriages than any city five times its size." According to FBI data that the state's newspapers often neglected to publish or buried on an inside page, Nevada now had the highest crime and suicide rates in the nation, with Las Vegas employing three times as many police as any other city its size, and dealing with record-breaking crime rates in bad checks and burglary, as well as liquor consumption more than 200 percent above the national average.

Like the casino tables, or the midday desert sun, the city was unforgiving. "To be a vagrant in Las Vegas," one visitor noted of a town crowded with the homeless decades before they were even recognized as a national social problem, "is to invite a jail sentence." But to be behind bars or even in a charity soup kitchen was hardly to escape the system. "The sheriff, the police, the preachers, the social workers—all are friends of the gamblers," wrote one author, concluding that in a Las Vegas that supposedly welcomed the world,

"Everything is against the stranger." Of the wave of new residents, some were wary if not contemptuous. "The voters, known as citizens in the other forty-nine states, are mostly indolent transients, temporary lodgers seated at the end of a rainbow stubbornly waiting for their pot of gold," noted two authors studying the city at the end of the decade. "Except for a few irascible natives, no one takes the state of Nevada seriously."

In the boomtown for the few, public services common to the rest of the nation would be nonexistent or stunted for years to come. The almost utter absence of state or county health and welfare programs forced the city to rely on federal funds "more heavily," said one wire service report at mid-decade, "than any other localities in the country." A compassionate local women's group called the Service League struggled valiantly to collect and distribute food and clothing for the needy, to gather private donations for indigent medical care, and even, against the opposition of local officials and business-men, to dig a well a few blocks east of the Strip to bring water to a desert plot they envisioned as the campus of a college in southern Nevada. Meanwhile, the tiny, underfunded state university in Reno, though respected for its train-ing in mining and agriculture, remained without a medical school or law school, and jealously fought any efforts to start rival institutions. No other higher education of any standing was offered anywhere else in Nevada until the fifties, and then it came only grudgingly. "If you wanted a decent educa-tion for your kids or up-to-date medical care for your family, or just a lot of the things that other folks had in even backward states, you had to go to Cal-ifornia or somewhere else to get it," said a parent who lived through it. "The gangsters and the bankers sent their kids out of state to private schools and for an operation if they needed it, and instead of baking here in the summer with the rest of us took their families to Newport Beach."

In its provincialism and want, Nevada might have been in many ways no different from neighbors Arizona, Utah, or Idaho—but for the billion-dollar parasite in its midst. Many who deplored what McCarran had called "the rotten bargain" with gambling still held fast to the faith and expectation that revenues would justify it all. But the return was, and would be, relative crumbs off the table. As the fraudulently reported profits grew, so did the pathetically low taxes paid on them, though much of those revenues went back to public works—access roads, water and power diversions, landscap-ing along the Strip, special zoning, and numerous other amenities—that supported and benefited the casinos far more than the residents of the city or state.

At that, the real measure of Nevada and its bargain was not what mas-sively corrupt gambling yielded, but what an uncorrupted industry should and could have brought to a people still "humbled by long neglect." In the arithmetic of growth and success, Nevada could never bring itself to measure the enormity of the theft from its treasury, its children, its future. The skim alone stole tens, then hundreds, of millions in revenues from the city and state, money that could have built schools, hospitals, parks, museums, public institutions, and services of every kind.

Instead, the money gushed out in ever more incredible amounts to vicelords, Swiss bank accounts, and eventually back into Las Vegas's own endless exploitation. "They harbor dire secrets in the realms of politics, graft, and racketeering," John Gunther wrote of what he called the "weird, wacky little city," at the end of the fifties. One of the best kept of those dire secrets was the real origin and course of much of the money that made it flourish.

10. "Character Loans"

It began on a deep-sea fishing trip in 1952. The wealthy Utah banker Walter Cosgriff was trolling off the coast of Mexico with his Los Angeles attorney, Sam Kurland, who handled legal matters for the banker's lucrative affiliates in California. Kurland told him about an unusual opportunity to expand his already impressive collection of western banks. There were contacts who could arrange for Cosgriff to receive a much-coveted charter to open in Las Vegas. In financial circles, Nevada was known as the closed preserve of a handful of dominant and conservative old bankers in Reno. There were only five banks in the state, and a single holding company controlled the two in Las Vegas. State officials had not chartered a new one in years. But, Kurland said, his brother happened to own shares of a Las Vegas casino called the Pioneer Club, and among his partners there was the lieutenant governor of Nevada, a figure they called "Big Juice," who had the right connections to gain a charter.

Cosgriff, a modern man who liked to seize the initiative, saw the possibilities right away. A new financial institution in booming Las Vegas could do on the spot what no other local bank had ever been bold enough to do: loan to the fastest-growing, most profitable industry in the West. It could discreetly funnel and screen money from other banks, companies, or interests that either had to or wanted to conceal their investment in Las Vegas, people who wanted the profit but not the publicity for financing the city and all it represented. There would be ready participants in that kind of cloaked underwriting, Cosgriff knew, including his own giant competitors back in Salt Lake City, and behind them, the even vaster and more aggressive business empire of the Mormon Church. It might mean substantial money for everyone. Free of stuffy old restraints, it was the kind of new banking mid-century America offered.

If you can get me a Nevada charter, go ahead, Cosgriff told Kurland. And having made a history neither could have imagined, they went on fishing.

The unfolding story was classically American.

James Cosgriff, Walter's father, settled in Salt Lake City in 1905, bringing a family inheritance from Connecticut as well as his own wool fortune acquired in Wyoming. A Roman Catholic, he arrived in the Mormon capital as an outsider. But five years later he founded Continental Bank and Trust Company and swiftly gained his place in the city's peculiar mingling of money and religion. It was a moment when the Mormon Church, after a long and costly battle with federal authority, was rebuilding its economic strength in alliance with Wall Street, and when Union Pacific, Kennecott, American Sugar, and other giant corporate monopolies of the age were combining with the Salt Lake business elite regardless of sect. In the resulting financial maneuvers, in a Utah ever more "dominated by oligopoly," as Thomas Alexander recorded in his history of Salt Lake City, *Mormons and Gentiles,* Continental became one of the area's leading banks despite its ownership by one of these "Gentiles," as Mormons called non-Mormons.

Between the wars, through the banking crisis of the Depression, Cosgriff's fortune grew. When the twenty-three-year-old son, Walter, succeeded his dying father in 1937, he presided over seven banks across Utah, Idaho, and Wyoming worth nearly $20 million. Walter was a tall, brawny young patrician, a "jut-jawed man," as one witness saw him, "who looks far tougher than he is." Raised in the country club society of provincial Salt Lake, he was educated not in the Ivy League but at the University of Utah, and worked part time in the family bank from the age of fifteen as a clerk. The community would know him as a philanthropist to Catholic schools, as well as a gifted athlete and sports enthusiast who won state championships in golf and tennis well into his forties, and bought the Salt Lake Bees minor league baseball team just to keep them in town.

"A determined man of strong beliefs," as one admirer called him, Walter also proved a shrewd, market-minded banker who prided himself on what he described as his "unorthodoxy" in modernizing his father's traditional methods and lending to a wider public. Soon after taking over, he promoted to executive jobs several young men who were lowly clerks with him, like fellow Catholic and onetime messenger boy K. J. Sullivan from Caliente, Nevada. He urged them to be more imaginative in assessing risks and making loans that conservative banks turned down. "We like to judge things for ourselves," Cosgriff told a reporter. "Extending credit to the little fellow" and "banking service on a mass basis" became his mottos. "They'll loan on anything that swims, creeps, runs, or flies," a competitor said ruefully. Continental soon acquired a reputation for more democratic practices, for offering higher interest rates on savings, for promoting women to management positions, and for other innovations. By the early fifties, it was flourishing. With 60,000 customers in an area with a population of a quarter million, the institution was remarkably strong despite competition with First Security, the commanding Mormon bank of the Eccles family combine. Cosgriff's own "family group," as it was now known, had grown to twenty banks in five states with more than $200 million in resources. The *Salt Lake Tribune* duly noted the "genius" of the group's young owner, "a liberal banker ready to finance new enterprise and small businesses seeking expansion."

Yet there was another side to the young Cosgriff's modern banking. Not all the unorthodox finance would be for "the little fellow." After the war, Cosgriff became an adherent of the buccaneering Walter Bimson of Valley National Bank of Phoenix. Like Cosgriff, Bimson emerged out of the musty world of thirties banking to claim a reputation as a champion of the common customer, pioneering installment loans, financing half the cars in Arizona, and lending seed capital for small business, often without collateral. But he had not built Valley National into a major force in the Southwest solely or even mainly on such plebeian borrowing. Beneath its populist image, Bimson's bank was also the principal bank of the mercantile and land development oligarchy of what came to be called "the Phoenix Forty," including construction magnate Del Webb and especially the politically prominent Goldwater family, who in turn had their own close ties to Gus Greenbaum and others in Las Vegas. It had been Bimson, typically, who loaned $900,000 to the Flamingo in 1946–47 so that his friend Webb could finish the casino. At the time Walter Cosgriff had joined them in financing the first major Syndicate casino, his headquarters bank quietly taking on some of the loan in the unprecedented financing of Bugsy Siegel and his silent partners by legitimate institutions. It was the first significant capitalizing of the Syndicate by prominent American banks, underwriting that would remain mostly hidden even in banking's inner circles for decades to come, revealed only by federal documents recently made public.

The visible freewheeling by bankers like Bimson and Cosgriff was controversial enough. The postwar "Bimson Plan," which Cosgriff promoted with characteristic ardor, proposed a scheme for packaging or syndicating capital in a fund under government auspices to provide major loans to borrowers who had been rejected through regular banking channels. With money from banks, thrifts, insurance companies, and other institutions, all backed by federal guarantees with public liability, the high-risk lending was intended to provide hundreds of millions for a new stratum of big business, and new, relatively unregulated power for big banking. Some, like Cosgriff, saw Bimson and what he seemed to represent as the expansive, progressive destiny of American capitalism. Others worried about a marauding concentration of wealth more like the nation's greedy past than an equitable future. Hotly debated at the time in banking circles, Bimson's design was never itself adopted as a government program, though his concept would have echoes decades later in the savings-and-loan crisis and other financial scandals.

If less known than Bimson or others, Cosgriff continued to push at the old constraints of conventional banking. By 1952, he had served a brief term as a Republican appointee of the Truman administration to the governing board of the Reconstruction Finance Corporation (RFC), where he was ostensibly brought in to help clean up the profligacy and cronyism of the scandal-ridden agency. But he resigned after only a few months, leaving behind a reputation less as a reformer than as what one reporter called a "zealous advocate" for even looser management of the RFC's $2 billion Korean War borrowing authority. Among the agency's controversial acts during Cosgriff's brief tenure on the board, a congressional inquiry would uncover later, was a $975,000 loan to Reno's Riverside Hotel and Casino, then controlled by Detroit hoodlums, the Wertheimer brothers, and other organized crime interests.

In Salt Lake, Cosgriff moved to expand his own lending. When the federal Comptroller of the Currency disagreed with his revaluation upward of Continental's capital funds—which would have allowed the bank to add substantially to the amount of any individual loan—Cosgriff audaciously renounced Continental's venerable standing as a national bank. He shifted instead to state bank status, freeing him under Utah law to escape the federal limit and increase individual loans. The dispute set off years of wrangling between Continental and the federal government, including formal—and eventually unsustained—charges of inadequate capitalization brought against the bank by the Federal Reserve.

Meanwhile, he continued what one account called "his free-handed way that gives his banking contemporaries the shudders." Before he was forty, Cosgriff had bought or sold an interest in some fifty financial institutions between the Rocky Mountains and the Pacific. "A veritable connoisseur of banks," *Newsweek* called him, noting that Continental's ratio of loans to total assets was "a whopping 43 percent," nearly twice the average of Federal Reserve system banks, though its losses from bad loans were at the same time less than half the national average. Many now admired Cosgriff's banking philosophy, "composed of equal parts liberality and a kind of easygoing neighborliness," as one journalist noted. "A bank is like a reservoir," Cosgriff would tell an interviewer. "The water does no good unless it is spread out over the land." It was all a matter of faith in people, "the way a fellow's face looks, the way he expresses himself, and his willingness to work." The future of banking, of America itself, he often said, could be summed up in a simple idea—"character loans."

Bill Kurland, Milton "Farmer" Page, and Tutor Sherer were Los Angeles vicelords, "gangsters . . . of the downtown gambling Syndicate," as one history of the period described them. Their smuggling and gaming boats off the California coast yielded such grand profits in the thirties that simply handling the hard cash became a transport problem. So immense were the deposits from one operation in a small Santa Monica bank that the manager threatened to close their account unless they provided an armored truck to handle their money. They did.

Squeezed out of Southern California at the end of the decade when their gang rivals endorsed the new successor to City Hall, the three shifted their operations to Las Vegas, opening a sawdust-floored joint in Glitter Gulch called the Pioneer Club. They had gotten their Fremont Street lease and state gambling license with the help of Cliff Jones, the ambitious Las Vegas politician and attorney, who extracted in return a small interest in the club. Yet neither Jones nor their old California cohorts and fellow exiles Guy McAfee and Tony Cornero were their real "juice" in Las Vegas. The role was performed by Kurland's brother Sam in Los Angeles, a low-profile, well-connected young lawyer.

From his one-man office on Spring Street, Sam Kurland represented both organized crime and Walter Cosgriff's lucrative California banks— First National Bank of Long Beach, Valley National Bank of Alhambra, and Bank of Encino. A graduate of the University of Southern California Law School in 1932, Kurland was ostensibly an expert in estates and trusts. But unlike most lawyers of his time in California and elsewhere, he never provided the customary listing of clients in the standard Martindale and Hubbell national directory of attorneys. It would never be clear whether Cosgriff—who hired lawyers all over the West to handle the legal affairs of his far-flung banks—knew that his upstanding family group had retained a full-fledged Mob lawyer. Whatever was known or intended on either side, when Kurland told Cosgriff on their fishing trip that they could get a Nevada charter, it was, as one Las Vegas lawyer looked back on it, "a marriage made in heaven and hell that got a lot of people gloriously rich."

The transaction was typical of Nevada's business politics. Presented with an application for a new charter, state banking superintendent Grant Robinson immediately came under "enormous pressure from the old bankers," as one witness put it, "not to open up the town, especially to outsiders." But Cliff Jones lobbied hard, as Kurland promised, and while Jones, who was on retainer to the only other bank in Las Vegas, could not represent them directly, his brother and law partner Herb served as the attorney of record, and everyone understood the forces behind him. As it was, Cosgriff's ownership, much less the Kurland connection, would also be masked by a handful of Las Vegans listed as founders of the new bank, including real estate promoter Nate Mack, Herb Jones, and Bruce Beckley, owner of the building that housed both the Jones law firm and the Kurland-Page-Sherer Pioneer Club. Beset by special pleading on every side, Robinson granted the charter. "It took a lot of guts to do it," said one state official.

Christened the Bank of Las Vegas, Cosgriff's bank opened on January 18, 1954, with a mere $250,000 in capital, a tiny amount in those days. Subterfuge no longer necessary, Cosgriff soon appeared in national directories as the institution's president, along with his old Nevada friend from Continental, K. J. Sullivan, as vice president. Usually, Cosgriff joined the board of his affiliates without taking an office or inserting his own men, sitting back and "trying not to interfere," as he once told an interviewer. From the outset, there was a sense that this bank would be different. Cosgriff began driving back and forth to Las Vegas to oversee the new acquisition, though he and Sullivan remained in residence in Salt Lake City. To run the small, meagerly capitalized bank day to day, he sent from Utah Edward Parry Thomas, one of Continental's young officers.

On his résumé, the handsome, polished thirty-four-year-old E. Parry Thomas, as he wanted to be known, hardly seemed typical of the Las Vegas scene. Raised in a family of means in Ogden, just north of Salt Lake City, he had been a varsity polo player at the University of Utah, and during World War II an officer in an elite mountain unit of ski paratroopers, working for a time in intelligence interrogating important German prisoners. With a bachelor's degree in banking and finance, Thomas joined Continental immediately after graduating in 1948. He would come to the little Bank of Las Vegas in 1955 as a vice president and cashier. Wearing a well-cultivated tan, with thick black eyebrows and what one person described as "Wedgwood-blue eyes," he would bring to his new assignment charm and intellect, an understated but undisguised ambition, a loan officer's discretion and reserve, as well as affability. "He was just a lot smoother than the average businessman in town in those days," said a rival Nevada banker.

But Thomas was no ordinary banker. What he really brought to Las Vegas was its future—much of it shaped by the enormous, often hidden money and power, the singular culture and society, of the church of his origins.

Mormonism was America's most controversial, secretive, and acquisitive religion. Propagated out of a rustic's epiphany and spread by singular passions of deliverance and persecution, it was unlike any other creed in the United States. Its course was peculiar, dramatic, more far-reaching and consequential, than most Americans knew—and like the ultimate power of the church in Las Vegas, obscured by layers of a shrouded history.

"A likable ne'er do well," as one biographer called him, Joseph Smith Jr. was a destitute twenty-four-year-old farmer and sometime necromancer, hauled into court on fraud charges three years before, when he began *The Book of Mormon* near Palmyra, New York, in 1829. He finished it in 1830. Typical of his time and place in a fascination with buried treasure, Smith was swept up as well in the evangelical ferment of the era, frequently given to supernatural visions. His text, he announced, derived from golden plates he had unearthed by angelic inspiration, deciphering their hieroglyphic etchings through two sacred spectacles, or "peepstones," he called the Urim and Thummim. Both plates and reading objects subsequently disappeared with the angel Moroni, who first disclosed them to Joseph.

Left behind on faith and in Smith's subsequent writings was a startling dogma: The charismatic farmboy was the chosen instrument for a divine revelation that all other religions were failed and false. Out of a new cosmology, neither Judaic, Christian, nor even monotheistic, the true church should now be "restored" in North America, its followers known as the Latter-day Saints. "Prophet, Seer, and Revelator," as Smith was titled, the leader of the order, and his successors, would "progress" to be as divine as the God of the Old Testament, who was revealed to be a corporeal being residing on a planet orbiting a star called Kolob and sexually active with a Heavenly Mother. Meanwhile, rank-and-file members of the church, or the "Saints," as they were called, would evolve in the hereafter into gods themselves, living forever in perfect physical bodies in a "Telestial Kingdom" of earthly delights.

"Chloroform in print," Mark Twain pronounced *The Book of Mormon.* Its theology would be widely denounced, ridiculed, scholastically discredited. But less than a decade after Smith emerged, he had attracted multitudes of adherents. Migrating to Ohio, he established a thriving communal settlement on the south shore of Lake Erie. It was clustered around the religion's first great temple, and a thickening doctrine that included secret sacraments, writhing ecstasies and divine visitations for selected church leaders, phallic fertility rites, energetic missionary work, and a ban on alcohol, coffee, tobacco, and red meat. Not least, there was a solemn stricture against any act or tolerance of gambling. In the church and in family households, a rigid, white male theocracy ruled the tightly knit sect—patriarchs eventually ordained to practice polygamy and govern with an infallible, sharply disciplined authority. It all drew fervid homage from the faithful, and often implacable hostility from the "Gentile" outside world.

From the beginning, too, the peculiar force of Mormonism lay in a devotion to material wealth. Industriousness and abundance were a measure of holy worth, initially expressed—in a frontier collectivism common in other sectarian communities of the era—by the church's expropriation of all but a remnant of members' property. When more well-to-do members of the church rebelled, communalism gave way to private ownership, though with a strict system of tithing 10 percent of personal wealth. Mormons were soon renowned for a clannish prosperity that invited still more converts, and more enemies. Founding their own bank, they grew rich in the Cleveland land bubble of the 1830s in which the city's real estate soared in value. "The dirt farmer's son," a historian wrote of Smith, "became a big-time banker as well as a prophet." But the bank soon went broke in the Panic of 1837, its owners fleeing angry depositors and a warrant for their leader's arrest on bank fraud charges.

In quick succession came what investigative reporter James Coates called a "pattern of colony building, prosperity, persecution, and collapse." The Mormons settled in Missouri, which they believed the true cradle of biblical civilization. But when Missouri's governor called for them to be "exterminated," they moved on to yet another Zion in Illinois. All the while—however uprooted by persecution, the main band of Mormons moving with Smith from refuge to refuge—their ardently tended farms and businesses flourished. As favorable publicity alternated with popular derision, the church claimed as many as 200,000 followers nationwide, who were often in violent clashes with non-Mormons. Advocating theocratic rule for the entire nation, Smith became a candidate for president in 1844. More discreetly, he was the "preening general," as one writer put it, of a 4,000-man private army, and also commanded the Avenging Angels or Danites, a consecrated, clandestine band of Mormon assassins who would murder dissenters in the church as well as Gentile enemies. The mutual fear and hatred erupted in June 1844 with the Mormon destruction of an Illinois newspaper deploring polygamy, Smith's arrest for the incident, and the gory death of the prophet and presidential candidate at the hands of a non-Mormon militia.

The ensuing martyrdom and the Mormons' exodus from the Midwest made for what Coates, in his respected history *In Mormon Circles,* called "the emigration feat of the age . . . a miracle of faith, organization, and sheer human fortitude, unmatched anywhere on the western frontier." The Mormon Moses was Smith's heir, an unschooled forty-six-year-old New England carpenter and logistical genius named Brigham Young. His hegira in 1847 led to an alternately torrid and icy valley on the shores of America's inland Dead Sea, the Great Salt Lake. In his wake, hundreds of men, women, and children, many of them immigrant converts who spoke little or no English, walked across a continent of prairie and mountains, doggedly pushing small handcarts Young had modeled after what he had once seen porters using in a New York railroad station. "Going Home to Zion," his followers scrawled hopefully on the little wagons.

Over the next half century in the place they called Deseret—the rest of the nation knew it as Utah—they waged a fitful struggle with the federal government over sovereignty, attempting to fulfill the church's dream of an "independent commonwealth," as one history put it, a "nation-state status" apart from the rest of America. In the process, the Mormons built tirelessly, procreated and colonized, defended and attacked, proselytized around the world like no other faith, and became one of the richest, fastest-growing, most powerful churches on earth.

The disciples' first decades in Utah had only continued the legacy of alienation, mistrust, and brutality that came to rival any other in the nation's annals, symbolized by Utah's almost total defiance of federal authority and most infamously by the Mountain Meadow Massacre in 1857. Amid reports of impending federal invasion and suppression of polygamy, an elite unit of Mormon troopers masquerading as Indians in warpaint set upon the wealthiest wagon train ever bound for California. After a brutal five-day siege, under guise of a flag of truce, they shot down or hacked to death some 130 innocents, mostly women and children, slitting the throats of the dead and dying so that the blood would be returned to the earth as part of the sect's doctrine of "Blood Atonement" for non-Mormons or apostates. They then plundered the livestock, gold, guns, and even the women's finery, stealing as well—by divine ordinance, some of the marauders claimed afterward—every child they deemed too young to testify to the event.

For generations the full horror of the massacre remained filed away in the National Archives, the culpability of Young and the church leadership never admitted, the shameful truth only whispered by the sect's growing number of defectors. Though a U.S. Army investigation of the atrocity left little doubt about where responsibility lay, any reckoning was cut short by an expedient agreement between Young and the hapless administration of James Buchanan, distracted by the onrushing prospect of civil war in the East. Twenty years later, pressured for some accounting of the massacre before Utah Territory could be given statehood, the Mormons offered up a single scapegoat, one of the attackers' leaders, John D. Lee, and with Lee's trial and execution by firing squad in 1877, the massacre passed into an official if uneasy obscurity. The politics of Mountain Meadow would begin a pattern of concealment of the church's emerging role, masking both the reality of its power and the enduring passion and prejudice, fear and ignorance, beneath.

By the early twentieth century, church leaders had made their accommodation with national authority by the requisite revelation reversing the Mormon doctrine ordaining polygamy in negotiating for statehood, at one point forfeiting or mortgaging under federal fiat much of the church's considerable property and business interests. Yet, as always, the Mormons recovered and prospered, making their own bargains with Wall Street and outside capital as well as with Washington. If they could not secede from the nation, they would be, as a still utterly distinct religious denomination and faction, uniquely successful and influential within it.

Announced by rows of Lombardy poplars and a groomed symmetry of land and life, the villages of what Wallace Stegner called "Mormon Country" dotted the modern West well beyond Utah, from Montana to the Rio Grande, western Canada to Baja California. The sect was particularly prevalent in neighboring Nevada, the home of fugitive dissidents as well as colonizing believers, many of them in Las Vegas, where in the postwar boom, despite the anathema on gambling, Mormons had become the "dominant local religious organization," as one of their leaders put it. And the Saints' success and ties to the larger economy of capitalism were strong indeed.

By the end of World War II, the church had discreetly become one of America's wealthiest institutions, commanding directly or indirectly a business kingdom that included agriculture, natural resources, manufacturing, and banking. Moreover, valued for their unquestioning loyalty to authority as well as general sobriety and diligence, Mormons were widely recruited—and thus began building their own sectarian cadres—among corporations and government agencies, including the CIA and national nuclear weapons laboratories, giving the regimented church a sphere of influence unlike that of any other American religion. With huge cash reserves and a new leadership intent on financial expansion, the Mormons were poised in the postwar period for unprecedented economic and political power—though still quietly fired by much the same old covert tribalism and separatist convictions.

Parry Thomas's ancestry lay in the great nineteenth-century Mormon proselytizing and migration of converts from England and Wales to the promised Zion. His parents, Thomas Edward Thomas and Olive Etta Parry, were second-generation Utahans descended from long lines of Mormon families. Both were devout, "sealed for time and eternity" and "endowed in special instructions, blessings, and covenants" by their marriage in the sect's traditional secret ceremony in the Salt Lake Temple in 1916.

Parry would be the third of their six children, growing up in an Ogden family wealthy from the father's plumbing and heating company. It was a major commercial contracting firm, engaged for schools and institutions throughout Utah, veterans' hospitals in California, South Dakota, and New Jersey, and other large-scale projects like a lavish Mormon temple outside Phoenix. A member of the ruling patriarchy of the Ogden Latter-day Saints Church, the elder Thomas was well connected in the widening regional and national network of Mormons in federal and state government as well as business, and many of his lucrative contracts far from Ogden he owed to those sectarian ties.

After the venerable, predominantly Mormon Ogden State Bank closed in 1931, Thomas as its largest commercial customer was appointed a special state liquidator. His son Parry was dispatched to collect defaulted loans for the collapsed institution as a child. "Very early in life, probably eleven or twelve, I decided I wanted to be a banker," he would tell a reporter more than a half century later. Taking over the remnant of the failed institution, his father went on to run in its wake his own Ogden State Investment Company. "He didn't start out in banking but it sort of ended up that way," Parry said later. But T. E. Thomas's eventual distinction lay less in his church seniority, public authority, or financial success than in an old, intimate, and mutually profitable friendship with a fellow Mormon who was among the richest bankers in the world.

George Stoddard Eccles was the handsome, gregarious heir of the single largest Mormon fortune, among the wealthiest lineages in twentieth-century America. He was one of the richest men in the Rocky Mountain West. His famous brother Marriner was chairman of the Federal Reserve for a dozen years and a New Deal architect of the nation's central banking system. They were the sons of a stern, unschooled, bearded Scottish polygamist who founded a timbering and mercantile dynasty—"so much money," *Newsweek* said of the inheritance in 1936, "there seemed nothing else to do but get into banking."

George presided over the family's great bank holding company, First Security Corporation, begun in 1927 and based in Ogden. By 1948, the family's aggregate of financial institutions controlled resources of more than $300 million, the biggest operation of its kind between Chicago and California. Behind the banking loomed the still more formidable Utah Corporation, the Eccleses' international conglomerate of mining, shipping, and construction. A builder of the Western Pacific Railroad, the Boulder Dam, the St. Lawrence Seaway, U.S. military installations, public works from Africa to Asia, and other mammoth projects, the company was also involved in strategic production of iron, coal, and uranium ore on three continents. Altogether it was a swelling but still relatively unnoticed giant of the era. "One of the most powerful, if least publicized," *Newsweek* described the Eccles colossus at the time. The close, ultimately historic relationship between the two Mormons, T. E. Thomas and George Eccles—a tie discreetly continued by Parry Thomas and pivotal in the continued rise of Las Vegas over the last half of the twentieth century—had been forged long before, and for relatively small stakes that were crucial to the eventual fortune.

On a hot Saturday in the summer of 1931, Eccles learned that Depression-battered Ogden State Bank, his only rival in the town of 40,000, might not open the following week, threatening a disastrous run on his own nearby headquarters bank. To stave that off—similar runs were destroying hundreds of banks around the country—the Eccles brothers took radical measures, including a scheme for an infusion of cash from the Salt Lake Federal Reserve. But also crucial was George Eccles's covert campaign to lure away that very weekend, while all the banks were shut, Ogden State's primary commercial depositors. Capitalizing on rumors that Ogden State might formally close down, he would offer those choice depositors instant currency and longer-term loans in return for the transfer of their lucrative business and payrolls, which would at once stem panic among his own First Security depositors and ensure it even higher long-term profits. Carried out in a flurry of phone calls to Ogden State customers and then to other business-men and bankers telling them of the defections, it was a ruthless raid. The defection of T. E. Thomas, Ogden State's largest commercial depositor and a leading figure in local church and business circles, was decisive.

By late Sunday, hours before the banks were to open, the stronger commercial customers had promised to desert the old pioneer bank. On Monday, Ogden State was shut, though it might still have survived if not for the wheedling away of its main depositors. But with those desertions it was destined in liquidation to repay its ordinary customers only cents on the dollar, if anything. By Tuesday, First Security had easily weathered a brief wave of withdrawals spurred by the rival bank's fall. When it was over, both Eccles and Thomas had made secure their own positions, and a friendship, at the expense of many in the rest of the community. The success of both was to be critical for Parry Thomas and the Las Vegas he would do so much to reshape.

"More than any other factor," the son would tell an interviewer years later, his admiration of his father's close friend Eccles had determined his decision to go into banking. "They were my *idols*," he would say of both the Eccles brothers, for what he called their "non-establishment views about banking." At the University of Utah after the war he had modeled himself on George, devising his own curriculum much as Eccles had done in college twenty-five years before. As the son of one of George's closest friends, young Parry might have naturally stepped onto a comfortable rung at First Security. Instead, he deliberately went with Continental. He chose it for independence from his father's circle. "It was the only non-Mormon bank of any size in Utah," Thomas said later. But then Cosgriff also seemed to offer even more leeway for the "non-establishment" finance he admired in the Eccleses, and in which he would make his own fortune. "I wanted to be my own person and start my own bank," he told the interviewer forty years later. "And I didn't want to start out with old loyalties and have to break them on down the line." Most important, he knew that Continental would be able to make openly the historic new loans in Las Vegas that a more clearly Mormon-dominated bank could never make directly without a worldwide scandal for the church.

The young banker, it turned out, knew Las Vegas and its masters well. He had often visited the city before Cosgriff assigned him to tend the new bank there in 1955. With some of his own money, he had invested substantially in real estate and done private lending around Las Vegas in the postwar years even when he was still a student and banking trainee. "When I came on the scene there wasn't a high-rise in town," he said. "There were only 16,000-

17,000 people then." By the mid-fifties, by one account at least, Parry Thomas "had been involved in Las Vegas for several years and grew to know several of the bigshots who ran the town."

There would be differing versions of how much Thomas as a junior officer in Salt Lake actually influenced Continental's decision to open in Las Vegas. "He convinced his boss . . . to help capitalize this new bank for gamblers," according to one Las Vegas banker. With his own liberality and early financing of the Flamingo, Cosgriff needed no prompting. In any case, Parry Thomas was the perfect agent on the scene. If Cosgriff was the financial and conceptual godfather of the Bank of Las Vegas, the smooth young Mormon from Ogden would be the man to maximize its possibilities beyond anyone's wildest expectations.

With Thomas's arrival in Las Vegas, the small bank was on the verge of a historic series of major loans to casinos. In the town's business and financial community, it was a revolutionary moment. Though local banks gladly took the growing deposits from gambling just as from Boulder Dam, the magnesium plant, or any other boon, there had been no question of legitimate lending or finance for the city's unsavory industry. Whatever might have been known of the Wingfield banks' collusion with Reno gangsters, or Bugsy Siegel's bank loans, commercial borrowing by casinos on the Strip or Glitter Gulch was for the most part unthinkable. No "self-respecting Nevada bankers," as one account put it, "dealt with casino operators."

Quite aside from the social or ethical barriers to financing gambling enterprises, the business seemed dubious to many bankers on purely pragmatic grounds. Casinos, after all, were notorious for the relative absence of traditionally bankable collateral. "These loans are supposed to be secured by *craps tables?*" one bank lawyer asked in dismay about the first wave of lending. And lack of conventional security for loans seemed to some only the beginning of the risks. In 1954–55, the Kefauver headlines still recent history, there were few illusions among Nevada businessmen about the casino owners of Las Vegas. Many thought that if loans were to be made to Moe Dalitz, Eddie Levinson, or any of a dozen like them, the hoodlums could refuse to repay with impunity. Though gamblers sought the respectability of legitimate financial ties and would have wanted to avoid unfavorable publicity about their practices, it was impossible in the regime of the skim to know the true state of their books if they were cited as a pretext for default. Still worse, under a thin veneer of civility, the casino overseers were known for settling financial disputes with reflexive violence.

"Gaming was still an infant industry . . . and looked like a risky one at that." But now Cosgriff, Thomas, and the forces behind them swept into the city with a radical new rationalization, treating gambling like any other western boom enterprise entitled to the expansive finance so long advocated by Cosgriff, Bimson, and others. In Nevada, Parry Thomas was soon an unabashed spokesman for their purpose. "How are you going to do banking in a state by ignoring its main industry?" he would ask. Yet many understood that loaning to the business on the Strip was no ordinary boosterism or community development.

Thomas and those he represented seemed "downright cocky about his ability to get things done," as one peer remembered. For years to come, in fact, several of the city's insiders assumed there was some extraordinary unseen authority behind the Bank of Las Vegas, something not even the most notorious criminal borrowers would flout, ultimately ensuring repayment of hundreds of millions of dollars. In what other bankers found an incredible symbiosis between the borrowers and lender, between supposedly competing casinos and the Bank of Las Vegas, the handful of owners would collude to cover each other's public and legal obligations as necessary, thus in effect collectively insuring Thomas's loans. It was another mark of how integral and interrelated the gambling interests had become. "The last thing anybody wanted was a dark joint on the Strip which created doubts about the solvency of the whole thing, and of course nobody wanted any single default to cause trouble for their golden goose Parry Thomas," said one Las Vegas lawyer of the era. "The gaming industry protected the bank against problems," Thomas's own son and successor would say decades later. "They didn't want their only bank to have a problem."

"Parry came to town with his own juice," said a contemporary, "and everyone on the Strip knew it." As it was, the new bank hardly needed to advertise its innovative loan policy. "The casinos knew what was coming the minute the charter was granted," one local lawyer recalled. Within months, and especially after Thomas took over, Bank of Las Vegas loans were becoming a momentous force in the further rise of the city. Thomas himself would have a memorable name for it, appropriating the term that few knew was Cosgriff's and not his. With no audible irony he called the new underwriting of Las Vegas "character loans." And what characters they went to.

One of the first loans would go to expand the Sahara, and thus to benefit the Lansky brothers, and later the Fischettis, Sam Giancana, and "the Chicago interests." Then, "in rapid fire order," as an observer put it, they financed over ensuing years the major expansion or remodeling of nearly a dozen more casinos, all Syndicate-controlled houses, including Dalitz's

Desert Inn with its twelve-way split among mobsters nationwide; the Fremont under Levinson with its Lansky and California ownership; the Sands in the grip of Adonis, Costello, and Lansky, and at the time of the loan paying a skim as well to the crime organizations in sixteen cities around the nation; the Dunes of New England's Patriarca crime family; the Stardust as it came under Dalitz and Lansky; the Riviera as another lucrative holding of the Chicago Outfit, which alone took more than $8 million a year in skim from its Las Vegas casinos; and with an aptness few appreciated, the Lansky-backed Thunderbird, where Cliff Jones's partners realized direct benefit from the Jones brothers' help with Cosgriff's charter. So large were additions and renovations funded through the bank that the existing casinos would accommodate the spurting growth of customers over much of the next decade, with no major new hotels added until Caesars Palace in 1966.

The rewards for those on the inside were huge. The Bank of Las Vegas's $250,000 capitalization grew into assets of more than $16 million less than two years later—one of the most phenomenal performances for a new bank in the history of American finance. Deposits totaled $11 million less than six months after the bank opened, principally gambling accounts and the behind-the-scenes "participation with correspondent banks who were interested in the Las Vegas area," according to a later banking report.

Legitimate money building up the Strip now enabled casino owners to fatten profits, including the constant skim and its state tax evasion. But they could also now reinvest more of that take, along with a greater share of the money from nationwide narcotics, prostitution, and other exploitation, back into still more drug trafficking and corruption, as well as penetration of energy and food resources, entertainment, medical care, insurance, real estate, and full circle back to Las Vegas itself.

The timing was historic. Those bank loans to the casinos became available at a particularly crucial moment in the mid- to late fifties when legitimate venture capital in the United States and abroad was still relatively hard to muster for high-risk operations about to mushroom, including oil exploration, corporate farming, technological manufacturing, and, above all, real estate development. The result was a vast expansion of the investors' economic and political power, most visible—though by no means confined there—in the building boom along America's southern tier. "It was Mob money," journalist Richard Hammer recorded afterward, "that bought the land and financed the hotels along the Miami Beach Gold Coast . . . that financed . . . the deserts of the Southwest, in Palm Springs and all across Southern California." In that landscape the growth of organized crime was of "incalculable proportions," as Kirkpatrick Sale summed it up. Cosgriff and

Bimson had been right. Lending to unorthodox customers yielded huge returns.

Parry Thomas rose rapidly and profited handsomely along with his clientele. Barely five years after moving to town as a nominal subordinate, at thirty-nine he became president of the Bank of Las Vegas, and was already known in the industry as "gambling's house banker." From the beginning, of course, he was only the middleman for the outside money channeled through the bank. With hardly enough capital to carry any one of the casino loans, the little institution could never have done it alone. It had lent more than $15 million in Thomas's first year, more than fifty times its capitalization and what Thomas himself proudly called "a new record from a banking standpoint." Compared to what was to follow, it was a pittance. The backing came from a neighboring state.

The fount of money, at least initially, was in Salt Lake City. "Thomas had begun funneling hundreds of millions of dollars from the Cosgriff and Eccles banking empires . . . ," noted one report based on Thomas's own admissions, "engineering the Bank of Las Vegas into the position of lead bank for countless loans with Eccles' and Cosgriff's as participating banks." At the time, this outside financing was largely secret, unknown to other Nevada bankers who commonly learned the provenance of local lending.

Cosgriff's Continental and family banks provided a portion of the proxy investment. But enormous, sometimes untraceable sums among the "hundreds of millions" came from the Eccles empire. "A lot of the real history of the city," said one of the institution's early shareholders, "was buried forever in the files of the Bank of Las Vegas." Directly or indirectly, the use of LDS (Latter-day Saints) church money or simply the funds of predominantly Mormon family and business depositors to finance Las Vegas gambling—to say nothing of aid and stimulation for an international criminal network—would have been a fateful revelation then and later.

Though "Mormons in name only," as one historian described them, the Eccles brothers had been crucial in the church's economic expansion. In 1932, they had taken over the struggling Deseret National, a bank founded by Brigham Young, when its vulnerability threatened a crisis for the church. With the LDS leadership's calculated decision to move out of direct ownership of banking or savings institutions after World War II, First Security became a principal depository for the huge and growing business of both Utah's Mormon majority and the commercial leviathan the church itself was becoming—its income by 1955 conservatively recorded as more than $1 million a day. Former officers and other bankers would later estimate that at least three-quarters of First Security Corporation's resources traced back to Mormon assets. If a single entity, beyond the Syndicate, financed the first great expansion of modern Las Vegas and all that carried with it around the nation and world, it was—wittingly and unwittingly—the Church of Jesus Christ of Latter-day Saints.

Publicly, especially in Las Vegas itself, Mormons would always be relatively fastidious about their proximity to gambling. In 1941, future LDS leader and prophet Spencer Kimball had driven to Las Vegas to look over property on the future Strip, but passed up the golden opportunity—deciding "that getting involved in a gambling town like Las Vegas was not a good idea for him," according to his family biography, "and that though there was money to be made, he did not want his two sons to grow up with that background."

Local Mormons proved less squeamish. The same year the Bank of Las Vegas opened, a delegation of the town's prominent Mormons—including civic boosters like future state senator James Gibson and banker Reed Whipple—were ordered to Salt Lake City to discuss with LDS leaders the proposed investment of church funds in a farm, chapel, and large meeting hall to accommodate the city's burgeoning population of the faithful, money that would signal unmistakably the sect's acceptance of the new "sin city." Mormon realtors and businessmen were also eager for the patriarchy's blessing on their own major new investments in the planned shopping center Vegas Village and other prospects. According to the Mormons' own later accounts, the LDS officials were at first "cautious and conservative," but became convinced by the Las Vegas Mormons that investments in once boom-and-bust southern Nevada would now be safe and profitable. "Things moved so fast," one Las Vegan recalled of the 1954 meeting, "that soon after, the General Authorities were encouraging us to buy more land, which we did, and to keep up with the growth, which we also did."

As for the spiritual difficulty posed by gambling, the sect adopted almost from the beginning a precept that allowed members to work not only around the casinos but in them as well. "They had a special relationship with the Mob bosses," one insider wrote of the Mormons' trusted role as the supervisors and middle managers. "The pit boss who watches you—when he finishes his shift he doesn't drink coffee," a Las Vegan quipped of the Mormon casino employees and their legendary large families. "He goes home to his wife and ninety-eight children." Others saw a common ethic shared by church and Syndicate—an unusual degree of comfort with an authoritarian system and an easy readiness to follow orders. ". . . the Mormon organization has a great deal in common with the Mafia," said Michael Ventura, a frequent visitor to the city. "Strictly hierarchical. Great rewards for loyalty. Great rewards for keeping your word. They take care of their own." It all placed the Mormons securely on the side of those who made money off the city, as apart from the rest of Gentile America giving it over. "We say in effect," an LDS leader once told a reporter, " 'Don't touch the dice.' "

For his part, Parry Thomas was soon loaning profitably as well to the projects in which his Mormon brethren were more openly acknowledged. In an image he encouraged, he would be known in the town as a "Jack Mormon," a less than fervent Saint who claimed to have left the church at the age of fourteen and who was reputed to take an occasional "highball," though his children and wife, who was also descended from an LDS family, were staunch adherents of the religion. In business, he would have it both ways—and again the result was measured in significant money and power. "Thomas, in effect, used his Mormonism as a means to establish himself in the community," wrote a team of journalists looking at the church's role in Las Vegas. As one of their own, he could "let the Mormon businessmen feel comfortable with him," as a church leader put it, "since they know that he knows them and who they are, and they can talk the same language to do business together." At the same time, what became millions in loans to local Mormon developers would still be only a fraction of the business the Bank of Las Vegas was doing much more discreetly with the Eccles banks. By any measure, the windfall for the Mormon Church was enormous. Not long after the bank opened, as a handful of insiders knew, a special private plane began leaving Las Vegas every Monday morning for Salt Lake City, carrying to LDS headquarters millions of dollars earned and tithed in the city.

By 1960, Thomas's "character loans" made him locally famous if not yet noticed nationally. Though he later disavowed the remark, the banker himself once summed up with rare candor his notable mix of clients from temple and counting room, church and criminal enterprise. "I work for the Mormons until noon," Thomas quipped, "and from noon on for my Jewish friends." Competing Nevada banks still held back from lending to the casinos while making their own fortunes from collateral real estate development, and much of the rest of the financial community continued to disdain the Thomas bank. "We were looked down upon by all the other states," Thomas would tell an interviewer years afterward, ". . . sinful business and so forth." But the loans to the casinos were repaid in due course, and the success of the Bank of Las Vegas was enormous.

"I'm in the banking business, and these people were good loans," Thomas would say to questioners. About the men who were his clients and later intimate associates, Dalitz and the others, he was typically blithe. "I never met a hoodlum," he later told a national reporter. And his impact on Las Vegas was duly noted. "The most important player in the city's history," one account would call him merely on the basis of his early years. "The real godfather of Las Vegas," said another. "Thomas has done more than any other man," *Business Week* later wrote of the nationwide rise of legal gambling in America, "to build up that industry." Other judgments were harsh. "A hoodlum banker," one report described him. "We called it the Mob's bank," said a senior FBI agent who served in Las Vegas.

As for the largely forgotten registered owner of the bank, Walter Cosgriff watched the meteoric rise of his Nevada institution and its Mormon manager with uncharacteristic silence. Earnings for the Cosgriff family group were major, and by 1960 its resources were nearly twenty times the fortune he inherited from his father two decades before.

In 1961, driving back home alone from a visit to Nevada, Cosgriff died instantly when his car apparently plunged off the road and over an embankment near Wells. He was forty-seven. The banker who had launched it all a few years before had lived to watch his upstart little institution become a grand success. Yet at his death, it was but a small preview of what was to come.

In the hands of Parry Thomas and others, Cosgriff's earnest "liberality," his lending as a "reservoir" to be "spread over the land," would be distorted and distended, knowingly or unknowingly, into a web of furtive international finance. The legacy he never lived to see was his bank's handling of hundreds of millions of dollars controlled by the corrupt leadership of the Teamsters, America's most substantial union, with the money from obscure Texas insurance companies and banks commingling with funds of the Syndicate, the Mormon Church, and clandestine fronts for U.S. intelligence— and beyond all that, with a Caribbean institution called Castle Bank, later infamous for laundering and hiding vast amounts of money for spies, bagmen, casino owners, and international drug traffickers alike. Ironically, Cosgriff's visionary, boomtime Bank of Las Vegas with its unprecedented "character loans" would become—consciously or not—a kind of nexus of American crime, finance, and government intelligence. As Cosgriff had hoped, his banking did foreshadow the nation's future, though in ways very different from the "easygoing neighborliness" and more democratic capitalism he stood for.

By 1960, the city Parry Thomas was helping build was still only on the threshold of its pervasive influence. A decade after Kefauver had flown so quickly in and out of what was now called McCarran Airport, Las Vegas was richer, and casino owners were more powerful, than ever. And Las Vegans were watching the election of a new president in which the masters of the Strip seemed to have all their bets covered.

Part Three

American Mecca

It has become a great city, a family town, as pristine as a Mormon picnic. It couldn't have turned out better. That's right, isn't it?

—Alan Richman, "Lost Vegas"

Today it is a corporate-run nightmare draped in the cotton candy of family values, a theme park where dead souls drift amid medication Muzak, believing, *knowing,* in their hearts that people who need people are the luckiest people in the world, and that no one should never, ever, double-down on a ten when the dealer shows a face card.

—Nick Tosches, "The Holy City"

Joe Kennedy loves Las Vegas, his kind of town, "with its high life, beautiful women, and easy access to political cash."

Kennedy also spends as much time as possible in northern Nevada at his favorite lodge on Lake Tahoe, where he has been such a regular guest since the 1920s that each year his friends who run the resort send him special Christmas trees cut from the shores of the great glacial lake. The ten-foot pines decorate the spacious living rooms of his imposing homes in New York and Massachusetts.

Among his sons are a future president of the United States who will share his father's relish for Las Vegas, and a younger brother, a future attorney general who will pose a mortal threat to the Strip. It will be historic irony, and haunting paradox. Together, they will form a national leadership deeply compromised by the multiple corruptions of Las Vegas. Together, they will also be in many ways the nation's last chance to challenge the rise of the city and all it embodies.

As small boys, though, they gather gleefully with the rest of the large Kennedy family around the Tahoe trees, opening their Christmas gifts under sweet-scented boughs of the High Sierra. It is a small, forgotten omen of how their destinies, and murders, will entwine with Nevada.

••

He is the polished, dapper envoy between worlds, and on occasion their shared executioner. "Smooth as fuckin' silk," a partner calls him. Wherever he goes, Johnny Rosselli belongs.

Golfing with his old friend Joe Kennedy in California before the war, doing favors later for Joe's son Jack, overseeing the Syndicate's interests in Hollywood in the thirties and forties and then in Strip casinos through the fifties, during the same era spying and acting as an enforcer for corporations and for the U.S. government in Central America and the Caribbean, even as "Colonel Rosselli" plotting assassination with the CIA and his own team of snipers based on a Florida key in the early sixties, he wears gracefully the clandestine but unmistakable authority he represents. His business card says simply: "John Rosselli, Strategist."

He, too, loves Las Vegas, runs it for years. As no other figure, he symbolizes its juncture of ethnic groups, of elites of crime, business, and government—and in the end the reckoning of those forces. His biographers call him the "All-American Mafioso," a description that fits as perfectly as his tailored clothes. Rosselli personifies the truth that it is really only one world after all.

In the late 1940s, in the hours after midnight, wearing "seersucker and sneakers," as one who was there remembers him, a heavily bearded, half-disguised Howard Hughes prowls Bugsy's Flamingo and other casinos, ordering his bodyguards or hotel employees to pick up young women for him. When they find one he likes, they require her to sign a legal disclaimer before she actually joins Hughes at a table or in his suite. With characteristic brashness, his new friend Hank Greenspun introduces Hughes to Flamingo showgirls, and once even hides him from a congressional investigator.

By the fifties, putative head of one of the country's largest military contractors and one of the wealthiest men in the world, Hughes is what a reporter calls "the most god-awful corporate creature you will ever encounter." Not in seersucker and sneakers but in pajamas on a stretcher, he will return in the middle of another night in 1966, and with a substantial part of his legendary fortune procure the town itself. In taking it, he is said to make an honest woman out of the harlot city—a showy Las Vegas wedding of casinos and corporate America. Like Hughes's own lurking in the lobbies decades before, however, Wall Street and the nation's great capitalists have been quietly cohabiting with the Syndicate for some time, and the celebrated buyout by the billionaire changes nothing of the essence of the city.

Though he nominally owns much of it, he never again cruises the Strip. Curtained off above the lights, imprisoned by his own mind and minions, the eccentric playboy-become-madman-wraith spends four years in his Desert Inn penthouse peering at old movies on television, recording in a diary enemas and bowel movements, hatching ever more imperious plans to suborn Nevada and the nation. But in the end, it is mostly he who is used. In a city of suckers, even Hughes is just one more mark.

Ronald Reagan's film career, never stellar, is sputtering to a close, and his new, second wife, an actress of even lesser talent, can hardly get a part herself. He has begun to make impassioned, well-received patriotic speeches around the country, and some California businessmen want him to run for the Senate. But he thinks the prospect of politics ludicrous. "I turned down the offer with thanks," he would later say, laughing with an easy candor about his public persona. "I'm a ham—always was and always will be." Others urge him to go into television, though he rejects that also. To him and to his wife, "the word had the scent of a terminal disease."

Almost desperate to pay his high living expenses, by the end of 1953 he asks his patrons and close friends at his booking agency, the powerful Music Corporation of America, or MCA—a company investigated by the Justice Department for monopolistic practices and dealings with organized crime—to find him what he calls "another source of loot." The "MCA troubleshooters," as he calls them, quickly arrange with their contacts a brief but lucrative engagement in Las Vegas. For $30,000, equal to his salary for his last motion picture, he will perform for only two weeks as master of ceremonies of a fifty-minute "review" at the Last Frontier. He quips lightheartedly about the job, but the press is unsparing about what one reporter calls "the fading film star fighting to survive."

In his new role as nightclub performer, he works earnestly in rehearsals, mastering the choreography and joke routines. At forty-two, he trains for his Strip opening like an athlete before a major event, never drinking or smoking, getting a daily massage, and even on the short trips back to Los Angeles stopping at Barstow to nap or sleep overnight to conserve his energy. His wife, Nancy, seems to match him in dedication and anxiety, silently sipping ice water during his four-hour rehearsals.

The show opens on February 15, 1954, the actor as emcee supported by a male quartet and one of the Strip's typical lines of "gorgeous showgirls," as one writer sees them, "dressed in South American costumes and two-foot-high plumed headdresses."

He tells jokes in an Irish accent, does a routine with the singers, advertises Pabst Blue Ribbon beer in incorrect German, and at one point races around the stage in baggy pants, hitting the other performers with a rolled-up newspaper. As a grand finale, he stands alone under the spotlight at center stage delivering a sentimental poem. The audience is unimpressed. Even the city's domesticated nightclub critics call the act "third rate." The casino doesn't offer to renew his contract. The morning after the last performance, he and his wife gloomily drive back to California. He had "hit rock bottom," a biographer wrote later. But leaving Las Vegas, he plans a new career in which he would take up politics after all and preside over policies that would make a national credo of the Las Vegas ethic of greed and exploitation. "Never again," Reagan would say after his embarrassing run on the Strip. "Never again will I sell myself so short."

Joe Yablonsky is a tough guy, a street cop in hard towns—Miami, Boston, Newark—an undercover agent known as the "King of Sting" for the cases he makes against the Lansky network. But he approaches the corruption he finds in the Nevada desert with fresh ardor, almost innocently, as if the rest of them here must feel the same way. He thinks he has seen it all before, but he's seen nothing like this. He is an idealist where ideals have been given up, a public servant where the public is resigned to its fate, a truth-teller where truth is a kind of cheating. He believes that right will win against the odds in a place where in the end nothing beats the odds.

For all that, Yablonsky is no simple martyr. He makes mistakes, overestimates the power behind him, underestimates the power of the enemy. In charge of the FBI in Las Vegas as the 1980s begin, a rare, random exception to the mediocrity and compromise of the bureau, he confronts the city's order, so ingrained and accepted that even the uncorrupted in its grip seem unable to recognize it as the outrage it has become. Still, Yablonsky cares for the place and the people, will not give up, believes he can somehow save them in spite of themselves even as he becomes one more casualty. He loses, is driven out. He is shocked, and lastingly angry.

Afterward, it might seem he never had a chance. When he is gone, the powerful ridicule him. Yet their sneers cloak the dread they once felt. If someone like Yablonsky had won, who knows where it might have led? Perhaps he was right to take it so hard, after all. His defeat was far more than his own.

The man who will be the figurehead for the city at the end of the century, for the forces that banish Yablonsky, first sees it as a ten-year-old boy. Steve Wynn visits Las Vegas in 1952 with his father, born Michael Weinberg, who lavishes gifts and outings on the little boy to make up for frequent absences and erratic fortunes.

Weinberg, the son of an obscure vaudeville performer, comes from a harsh childhood of foster homes, and changes his surname as a young man after encountering vicious anti-Semitism. Under his new identity he becomes a "ruthless force in the illegal bingo racket," as one journalist describes his "heavily skimmed operations" in backrooms in seven states on the East Coast. Given to fancy suits and flashing a wad of bills, Mike, as he is now known, is later driven out of his upstate New York headquarters amid what authorities call "wholesale abuses" of the law and another account describes as a "jumbled mess of scandal and corruption." He is a close associate of the Jacobs family of Buffalo, with their Emprise Corporation and its links to organized crime throughout professional sports from stadium concessions to team franchises.

Mike is a smaller-scale hoodlum, though his postwar racketeering, with sham licensing, fraudulent books, payoffs, kickbacks, and fronts, is a microcosm of the up and coming Las Vegas. In 1953, he applies for a gaming license in Nevada—"his dream of a score of a lifetime," as one reporter calls it. But his record is so blatant that even the notoriously lax state Tax Commission—the body that has licensed Binion, Dalitz, and so many like them, that now at the same session approves Frank Sinatra—rejects the ambitious bingo operator.

For now, however, he and his small son spend a memorable two-week vacation sightseeing and riding dude-ranch horses in the still empty desert just off the Strip. An inveterate gambler himself, Mike sneaks away in the evening to shoot craps after his child has fallen asleep. The little boy awakens and anxiously goes out to search for his dad, walking wide-eyed down the road from dazzling sign to dazzling sign in the garish Las Vegas night. They leave town broke. The child vows to return. At least that's the story he likes to tell.

Mike's boy will find another, more provident and discreet father in Las Vegas. As the figurative "adopted son" of Parry Thomas, though still very much his real father's heir as well, Wynn will become the city's most emblematic figure since Bugsy Siegel.

11. A Party in Carson City

It was a balmy evening, and the little state capital of Carson City sat quiet as usual. Designated the seat of government by the customary political connivance for private profit, the site south of Reno lies only fifteen miles from the Comstock Lode, at a junction of arching valleys that drain the great Sierra into the sprawling, unquenchable desert to the east. Mark Twain, otherwise caustic about Nevada society, thought the setting of the town had a kind of grandeur when he first saw it in 1861—"in the shadow of a grim range of mountains . . . whose summits seemed lifted clear out of companionship and consciousness of earthly things." A century later, its frontier rawness only slightly softened, Carson City was still a small, obscure, settlement. "A car backfiring at noon can be heard at the city limits," wrote a native, "and the sound would echo over empty sagebrush." But this was no ordinary night, if only a few knew it. Draped in the flaxen twilight of a mountain summer, the town was hosting an illustrious visitor.

With no enclosing wall or expanse of lawn, the Governor's Mansion sat unpretentiously near the street, like any other house in the modest old Victorian neighborhood a few blocks from the gold-domed Capitol. Still, it was an elegant home for the head of a poor, sparsely populated state whose mines were long since dying as the residence was built in 1908. Painted a creamy white, finished in an architect's flourish of Ionic columns and scalloped trim, the house had a long, inviting wraparound porch with graceful curving balconies above, all set off by towering native firs and northern Nevada's languid, sea green weeping willows. "Like something out of the Deep South," thought a writer who grew up a few blocks away. Two turn-of-the-century lampposts, only recently discharged from lighting nearby Main Street, now stood guard over the wide steps at the entrance. "It wasn't fancy inside as those things go," remembered a Nevadan and frequent visitor at the time, "but going in gave you a feeling of pride and dignity."

That evening, a steady stream of guests arrived under the yellowed porch light over the front door. The 1960 Democratic National Convention was opening a few days later in Los Angeles, and Governor Grant Sawyer had privately invited some of the delegates. Nevada's Democrats were still divided over the presidential nomination, a remnant hoping two-time nominee Adlai Stevenson would run again, others favoring the well-organized front-runner, Massachusetts senator John Fitzgerald Kennedy, or JFK, as he would soon be known. The state's senators, Alan Bible and Howard Cannon, backed Kennedy's ambitious archrival, the powerful majority leader Lyndon Johnson, whose chief Senate aide, Bobby Baker, a man with considerable Las Vegas connections, was "all over Nevada that spring," as one politico remembered.

The Kennedy camp had been courting Nevada avidly. "They seemed to understand the importance of this place long before most other national politicians," a prominent local Democrat at the time recalled, "as much for the money and power behind the scenes, I guess, as for our paltry number of delegates and electoral votes." In 1958, Kennedy intimate Hy Raskin had been sent to scout out the state, and ended up financing Sawyer's long-shot gubernatorial run. JFK himself once flew out briefly to stump for Sawyer, the thirty-nine-year-old, relatively unknown district attorney from Elko whose confident energy and crew-cut youthfulness seemed tailored to the Kennedy style. Not always comfortable in a candidate's obligatory appearances for local politicians, Kennedy had appeared to enjoy the Nevada trip more than most, somehow at home in this lunar landscape so far from the Georgetown drawing rooms or Cape Cod waters of his native East Coast.

At the beginning of 1960, Sawyer had invited Kennedy back to address the legislature in Carson City, a helpful forum for the candidate controversial for his Irish Catholicism, his youth, and his family wealth and background. The day before the speech, Kennedy had shown up unexpectedly on the porch of the mansion in Carson City hours early for a planned reception, catching the state's first lady in her curlers and her husband taking a shower. The senator had gone right upstairs and into the private quarters to sit casually on the toilet lid and talk politics while the governor finished showering.

Decades later Sawyer remembered it as a charmed moment, the future president chatting with him in the steamy bathroom as Kennedy's press secretary,
Pierre Salinger, played the piano downstairs. "They made themselves at
home," Sawyer would tell an interviewer wistfully.

Here, as elsewhere, the candidate radiated poise and intelligence. The
February 1 reception drew hundreds of ordinary people from around the
state. They stood patiently in a long line outside the mansion, waiting in
the icy chill of a Sierra Nevada winter to shake hands with the boyish-
looking, smiling Kennedy, who plainly enjoyed the succession of ranchers
and sheepherders, small-town lawyers and businessmen. He stayed an extra
hour, kept the press waiting, until the last Nevadan came through. "A whiz-
bang affair," thought Sawyer. "I was enchanted . . . we started a long and lasting friendship."

Typically, at the same moment, there was another, less public side to the
attractive young politician's delight in the place—another John Kennedy,
another Nevada. Only days after charming them all at the mansion, the presidential candidate was on the Strip, "ensconced at the Sands," as one account
put it, "drinking and schmoozing in the lounge . . . attending fund-raising
receptions . . . digging the scene." He had been there often—in the company
of his friend Frank Sinatra and "certain Mafiosi," noted an FBI report in
1959. As recently as a few months before addressing the legislature, Kennedy
had come to Las Vegas for one of the "Summit Meetings" of Sinatra's legendary "Rat Pack," a coterie that included singer Dean Martin, Sammy Davis,
Jr., and JFK's brother-in-law, the faded movie actor Peter Lawford, all of
them performing as a group at the Sands, impromptu and often drunk, in
the Strip's most popular show of the time. As Kennedy's own celebrity grew,
as he spent more and more nights at their raucous parties, Sinatra would call
them for a time the "Jack Pack."

"Did they make him feel at home there, or did he just feel that way?"
Michael Herr asked afterward about Kennedy's obvious delight in Las Vegas.
As late as the winter of 1960, running for the presidency, he could still be
almost anonymous on the Strip. "Half the people he met there thought that
'Senator' was just his nickname," said an onlooker. "He loved his brief visits
to Las Vegas," Herr reflected. "He was the most starstruck of stars . . . and his
Vegas friends arranged everything there for him, especially seeing to it that
his privacy would be respected, and he was always happy there."

Late on the night of February 8, 1960, during one of the Rat Pack's typical private parties for Kennedy, Lawford pulled Davis aside to point out a
closet with a brown leather satchel bulging with $1 million in cash. "It's a gift
from the hotel owners for Jack's campaign," the actor explained, adding with

a smile that in the next room they were also supplying "four wild girls scheduled to entertain him." Telling the story long afterward, Davis would say of the bag of money, "Some things you don't want to know." It was during this visit to Las Vegas, too, in Sinatra's "presidential suite" at the Sands, that Kennedy began an affair with a sensuous, dark-haired twenty-six-year-old divorcée named Judy Campbell, first introduced to him by Johnny Rosselli. Intimate as well with Sam Giancana and Rosselli both before and during her more than two-year relationship with Kennedy, Campbell was no ordinary Las Vegas pickup. The liaison would haunt a presidency.

Yet in the winter and summer of 1960 Kennedy's indiscretions on the Strip were still largely unknown, even among the better-placed Nevada politicians. Sawyer and Attorney General Roger Foley, a friend of Kennedy from World War II, were among the first western Democrats of their rank to endorse him for president. But on the eve of the convention Nevada delegates were still wavering, and Kennedy's nomination was still uncertain. To court the undecided, Sawyer put on an unusually extravagant reception at the mansion. "The party to end all parties," one delegate remembered the bar and buffet, lavish by Carson City standards. Moreover, as guest of honor the governor invited a famous figure already on hand nearby in the Sierra Nevada, John Kennedy's most ardent and powerful backer: his father.

With his own controversial past, the elder Kennedy had been and would remain carefully if uncharacteristically in the background of the presidential race, despite the decisive impact of his wealth and contacts. In Nevada, he was willing to appear more openly. Given his history with the state and the forces that ran it, he was in his element there as almost nowhere else. Still, the party at the Governor's Mansion was not publicized, and no reporters were present. Pointedly, some thought haughtily, the elder Kennedy stayed in the governor's private office on the second floor, "holding court," as a witness described it, talking with each delegate alone. "He refused to come down and mingle with the peasants," said a guest. "Up there in Grant's hideaway he did a little of everything with everybody," another recalled, "smiling as he twisted your arm or made offers." One by one the delegates went up to see him by the graceful old stairway that dominated the entry hall of the house. At the top of the steps was "the Ambassador," as he was known, once a challenger for the White House himself, now patriarch of a would-be political dynasty—and possessing, despite his fame, a tarnished history none of them really knew.

Well before the lively party ended, but with all the delegates cajoled or pressured, the seventy-two-year-old Kennedy thanked Sawyer and left abruptly in his limousine. A chauffeur drove him over the winding mountain pass to the Cal-Neva Lodge at Crystal Bay on Lake Tahoe, where he

LEFT: Meyer Lansky in the early 1940s, when he first drove across the desert to Las Vegas with Bugsy Siegel and conceived the city's transformation.
Courtesy of the authors

BELOW: Present-day casino owner Steve Wynn kneeling in front of gambling patriarch Benny Binion. "Give a gambler a good excuse," Binion once told Wynn. "They'll thank you for it."
Courtesy of the *Las Vegas Review-Journal*

BELOW: The original El Rancho Vegas just after World War II— one of the first Strip resorts.
Courtesy of the Davis Collection, University of Nevada, Las Vegas, Library

The outlaw as civic statuary—
Binion immortalized on horseback
in downtown Las Vegas.
Courtesy of the *Las Vegas Review-Journal*

ABOVE: The handsome Benjamin "Bugsy"
Siegel in the mid-1940s, as he began to
acquire interests in Las Vegas casinos for the
Syndicate. Courtesy of the Los Angeles Public Library

BELOW: Senator Pat McCarran in 1942,
at his desk in wartime Washington. His
bitter 1944 reelection race shaped his
postwar role in McCarthyism.
Courtesy of the Nevada Historical Society

Senator Estes Kefauver on the eve of his November 1950 hearing in Las Vegas, flanked on his left by committee counsel Rudolph Halley and on his right by the ubiquitous George White, whose role as an executive-branch spy on the panel fatefully truncated the investigation.

Courtesy of the Kefauver Collection, University of Tennessee

ABOVE: The lobby of the Flamingo Hotel not long after its 1947 opening, featuring Bugsy's extravagant chandeliers and the marble staircase he liked to descend with the beautiful Virginia Hill on his arm.

Courtesy of the Las Vegas News Bureau Collection, University of Nevada, Las Vegas, Library

RIGHT: Hank Greenspun, as so often in his colorful career, made news as well as publishing it. Here he is being interviewed in the early 1970s.

Courtesy of the *Las Vegas Review-Journal*

Glitter Gulch circa 1948, when the Las Vegas Strip was still largely in darkness, though the "players" were already in place running the sawdust-floored Pioneer Club. Those figures would be instrumental in the historic "character loans" of Walter Cosgriff and E. Parry Thomas that would soon build the modern city.

Courtesy of the Manis Collection, University of Nevada, Las Vegas, Library

Desert Inn front man Wilbur Clark shakes hands with then–Senate majority leader Lyndon Johnson, circa 1959. Johnson had more than the usual ties to the city so common among prominent American politicians. He enjoyed his own "juice" in Las Vegas through the Strip connections of aide Bobby Baker, Nevada senators Howard Cannon and Alan Bible, and, not least, his own Texas connections to organized crime.

Courtesy of the Wilbur Clark Collection, University of Nevada, Las Vegas, Library

A mushroom cloud from the Nevada atomic test site provides a backdrop to Glitter Gulch early on the morning of April 18, 1953.

Courtesy of the Las Vegas News Bureau Collection, University of Nevada, Las Vegas, Library

LEFT: Banker E. Parry Thomas at the height of his power in 1981. Only a few insiders knew the twisting paths taken by the hundreds of millions of dollars Thomas fed into Las Vegas.

Courtesy of the North Las Vegas Library Collection, University of Nevada, Las Vegas, Library

BELOW: Steve Wynn presents his mentor and benefactor E. Parry Thomas with one of the banker's many civic and industry awards. Courtesy of the *Las Vegas Review-Journal*

BELOW: Richard Nixon meeting with reporters under the watchful eye of a standing Bob Haldeman at Glitter Gulch's Fremont Hotel in 1961, not long after the theft of the 1960 presidential election, a theft largely financed and organized by Las Vegas interests. Nixon would find his political fate perennially linked to the city, from casino contributors in his earliest campaigns to the hidden role of Las Vegas in Watergate.

Courtesy of the Las Vegas News Bureau Collection, University of Nevada, Las Vegas, Library

A smiling Moe Dalitz stands in his Desert Inn next to (left to right) Elvis Presley, Juliette Prowse, casino figurehead Wilbur Clark and his wife, Tony, and Desert Inn stockholder Cecil Simmons. Courtesy of the Wilbur Clark Collection, University of Nevada, Las Vegas, Library

LEFT: Joseph P. Kennedy, Sr. (center), in June 1959, during one of his many visits to Nevada.
Courtesy of the Nevada State Archives

BELOW: The entrance to Cal-Neva Lodge on Lake Tahoe in the late 1940s, very much as it looked during the decades when Joseph P. Kennedy was a frequent guest, including his historic stay there in the days before the 1960 Democratic convention.
Courtesy of the Nevada Historical Society

ABOVE: The famous gaming room at Cal-Neva as it looked in the 1920s and 1930s, when the tables were pushed across the room from one state to another to thwart police raids.
Courtesy of the Nevada Historical Society

LEFT: From the near curbside, the Nevada Governor's Mansion in Carson City in the early 1960s.
Courtesy of the Nevada Historical Society

RIGHT: The tiny Nevada state capital, Carson City, as it appeared in the 1950s, its few blocks nestled at the foot of the majestic Sierra Nevada, with Lake Tahoe in the background. "In the shadow of a grim range of mountains," as Mark Twain wrote in the previous century, "whose summits seemed lifted clear out of companionship and consciousness of earthly things."
Photograph by James Griel, Sr., courtesy of Muffy Griel Vhay

The reception line for Senator John F. Kennedy at the Governor's Mansion on February 1, 1960. To Kennedy's left are Nevada first lady Bette Sawyer and a smiling, crew-cut Governor Grant Sawyer. Courtesy of the Nevada Historical Society

John F. Kennedy and brother-in-law Peter Lawford circa 1959, outside the Sands Hotel—a significant site in the Kennedy saga, where, early in the 1960 campaign, Lawford noticed a satchel containing a million dollars, and where JFK enjoyed fateful assignations with mistresses courtesy of organized crime figures until only weeks before his death. Courtesy of the Sands Hotel Collection, University of Nevada, Las Vegas, Library

Grant Sawyer with President John F. Kennedy in the Oval Office in the summer of 1961—their smiles belying the Nevada governor's angry clash the day before with Attorney General Robert Kennedy, who had ordered a large-scale raid by law-enforcement officials on Las Vegas casinos and organized crime figures. Courtesy of the authors

always stayed in northern Nevada—a drive that took him back as well into the lengthening shadows of his divided, emblematic life.

That summer of 1960 the plain pine frame entrance belied Cal-Neva's rustic luxury and resonant history. Built in 1926, ostensibly as the private preserve of wealthy San Francisco businessmen, the lodge from the beginning was a rendezvous of organized crime. Among its early owners was Reno vicelord Bill Graham, whose racketeering included the use of Cal-Neva to exchange marked or "hot" cash for famous bank robbers of the era like "Baby Face" Nelson and "Pretty Boy" Floyd, who took refuge at the resort and gambled at its still illegal—pre-1931—casino.

Nestled between the cobalt blue water and the dark emerald mountains ringing its edge, the summer-only resort was called Tahoe's "jewel of the North Shore." A massive log exterior opened onto a cathedral lobby with native stone floors and vestibules, set off by granite boulders and thick pine ceiling beams. Dominating the lodge was an imposing rock fireplace positioned, like the outdoor swimming pool, literally astride the state border that ran down the middle of the resort—accommodations and restaurant in California, casino in Nevada. "Card tables were pushed back and forth across the California-Nevada line," one reporter wrote of the late twenties, "depending on which state's police showed up to bust the place." But since Cal-Neva generally paid off officials on both sides of the boundary, raids were rare and seldom disturbed the clientele. Tucked away behind the main building were private chalets for celebrities and the wealthy offering the seclusion and immunity of what one guest called a "high class hideout."

Joe Kennedy began coming to Cal-Neva soon after it opened, staying for longer and longer periods, making it a kind of western headquarters. It was the scene of some of his notorious and constant machinations in business or politics as he became one of the richest, most influential men in America—and of his equally relentless trysts, the women ranging from ordinary Nevada prostitutes provided by the establishment to the world-famous actress Gloria Swanson.

From the resort he also hunted and fished the Sierras with wealthy associates like Errett L. Cord, the Checker Cab and automobile magnate whom Kennedy had known since the early twenties on Wall Street, and who had moved his fortune west and become a force in Carson City as an influential state legislator. Cord had been enticed to Nevada's tax haven by another of his friends, McCarran backer and local political boss Norman Biltz, who was also linked to the Kennedys by his marriage to Jacqueline Kennedy's aunt.

Millionaires like Bing Crosby, yeast heir Max Fleischmann, and broker Dean Witter were also part of Kennedy's Tahoe circle. Some were to be especially important in the rise of Las Vegas, and of the Kennedys. Cord's own tax legislation in the mid-fifties, a formula for a relatively generous apportionment of gambling revenues to the smaller counties, effectively bought the rest of the state's acquiescence in the swelling skim on the Strip. For his part, Biltz was to play a notable role as Nevada fund-raiser, if not Strip bagman, for the 1960 presidential campaign. Even more significant, however, the serene log chalets and cool stone halls of Cal-Neva were where Joe Kennedy consorted with some of his oldest, closest friends and partners—these were men from the domain of organized crime where he had begun to amass much of his own fortune decades before, and where he clandestinely maintained and unhesitatingly used his old contacts, for himself and his son's presidency, to the end of his active life. Even in a crowded lore and literature later surrounding the Kennedys, brimming with what one biographer called "the sins of the father" and another "the seeds of destruction," there was little about the telling role of Nevada, the gravity and meaning of the Cal-Neva connections.

It was a remarkable group in the annals of crime and corruption. Through the years it included Elmer M. "Bones" Remmer, a San Francisco gangster and drug dealer who conspired with Bugsy Siegel and McCarran to bribe officials in securing materials for the Flamingo, and whom the FBI called a "well-known local gambling boss." Remmer owned Cal-Neva for more than a decade, and belonged, as a team of writers put it, to the "highest echelons of the national Syndicate." Still closer to Joe was Remmer's successor at the lodge, one-armed Bert "Wingy" Grober. In 1960, guests found Grober presiding over Cal-Neva in white tie and tux, a distinguished man with silver hair combed back over an angular tanned face, fond of posing with resident celebrities like Marilyn Monroe. Tactfully disguised, like his missing arm, was Wingy's past as an accomplice of Meyer Lansky in Florida, Cuba, and Las Vegas, another of what were called "Miami hotel men," ubiquitous in Nevada. Joe's tie to Grober was so strong that a 1944 FBI report on Miami "mobsters" took note of their relationship through several "mutual associates" in liquor distribution and illegal gambling. "The Ambassador was very, very close to him," a Reno lawyer recalled. By the latter fifties, according to Las Vegas insiders, Grober was fronting in part for Kennedy's own secret interest in the Cal-Neva, the father of a future president one more hidden owner of a Nevada casino. "Wingy was old Joe's man there," one of them confided, "and he looked after his stake in the joint."

Joining Grober to manage Cal-Neva in the late fifties was Paul "Skinny" D'Amato, a onetime New Jersey gambler and pimp who had known Joe Kennedy since Prohibition, and from the 500 Club in Atlantic City had ties to the Syndicate's political and business adjuncts throughout the East and Appalachia. D'Amato in turn was close to Sinatra, another of Joe's old friends at Cal-Neva, and behind Sinatra at Tahoe and elsewhere was Chicago boss Sam Giancana, yet another gangster Joe knew from Kennedy holdings in Chicago. That summer of 1960, while working intently to secure his son the presidential nomination, and while Jack was telephoning him regularly at Tahoe to report on the campaign, Joe was acting as a broker and banker to negotiate a further division of shares in the Cal-Neva among some of Sinatra's Rat Pack as front men for both himself and the Syndicate. An FBI informant's report tersely described the gathering, which took place the same week, perhaps the same day, as Sawyer's party for the Nevada delegation in Carson City: "Joseph P. Kennedy (the father of President John Kennedy) had been visited by many gangsters with gambling interests and a deal was made which resulted in Peter Lawford, Frank Sinatra, Dean Martin and others obtaining a lucrative gambling establishment, the Cal-Neva Hotel, at Lake Tahoe. These gangsters reportedly met with Joseph Kennedy at the Cal-Neva, where Kennedy was staying at the time."

Joseph Patrick Kennedy lived one of America's fabled stories, though much of it was not told until after his death, and rarely then for what it all meant. Son of a saloon-keeper and petty politician become prosperous liquor dealer, he grew up in Brahmin-ruled Boston and at Harvard as an Irish outsider, burning to belong and rule, yet confronted by what historian Michael Knox Beran called "the patent-leather jack-boot of class thrust in his face." Lastingly embittered, convinced everything he wanted had a price, he spent his life pursuing the purchase. Through purloined information and speculative connivance, what a later generation outlawed as "insider trading," he took millions from Wall Street before the Crash, and made still more producing cut-rate movies in Hollywood. For helping to finance Franklin Roosevelt's presidential compaign in 1932, he was rewarded with the chairmanship of the new Securities and Exchange Commission, which began to police some of the same stock exchange abuses he had just practiced so profitably, "a crook to catch a crook," as Roosevelt once quipped to his adviser James Farley. In 1938, the president named Kennedy ambassador to the Court of St. James. Roosevelt was privately bemused at making a "red-haired

Irishman" his envoy to the English, as he told an aide, but happy as well to have a nakedly ambitious potential rival out of the country. All the while, as a liquor distributor and by more insider investments, Kennedy grew richer. By 1939, he was the wealthiest Irish-American in the world, and he planned the parvenu's supreme arrival, and revenge: the White House. But as Roosevelt ran for a third term, Kennedy became a target of slashing attacks. He accelerated his own ruin by urging that the United States pacify Hitler, and declaring that British democracy was too feeble to survive; and when his habitual private virulence became more public, his disloyalty to FDR and appeasement of the Nazis too plain, his chance was gone.

Then as later, men who were once his business or political partners, figures who had their own dubious connections, branded him with superlatives. "One of the most evil, disgusting men I've ever known," FDR, Jr., remarked. "As big a crook," Harry Truman said with authority, "as we've got anywhere in this country." The sheer force of the man created enmity. Kennedy's power was one of the obsessions of the far wealthier Howard Hughes. "A thorn . . . relentlessly shoved into my guts," Hughes would write of Joe's irrepressible maneuvering. How much any of them really knew of his reach and audacity would never be clear, though figures like Truman, politicians launched from their own alliance with big-city machines and organized crime, knew some of the stories firsthand. Old Joe, it was said, dealt with hoodlums; but the worst rumors were bare hints of the reality.

His "ties to the underworld," the son of a Syndicate friend wrote of Joe, "intersected at a hundred points." When he invested and made millions of dollars in the stock market, he was laundering profits made from Prohibition smuggling of scotch, gin, and Cuban rum, which he had done in concert with the organized-crime figures who controlled the world of big-time bootlegging. "In a lot of ways Joe was Meyer Lansky or Moe Dalitz with a Harvard pedigree," said someone who knew them all. When he went to Hollywood, it was in collusion with gangsters who held the studios hostage by "persuasive behind the scenes . . . muscle," as one of them described the extortion, blackmail, and physical violence against executives and workers alike. When Joe raised $100,000 for FDR in 1932, it was in part from criminal contacts in Chicago and Manhattan. When, at Repeal, he acquired the coveted franchise rights to Haig & Haig, Dewar's, and Gordon's, popular brands of liquor, it was by what organized-crime figures called their "national agreement" to concede the labels to his Somerset Imports, making him the nation's largest distributor of scotch. When he bought a controlling interest in Miami's Hialeah racetrack, it was in complicity with Lansky and other racketeers. When he gambled, which was often, it was at Lansky's Colonial Inn in

Florida as well as Grober's Cal-Neva, just as he pointedly frequented what one historian called New York's most notorious "gangster hangouts" like the Waldorf-Astoria barbershop and the Black Angus restaurant. When he shed Hialeah and Somerset to upgrade his political image, he sold both back to the Syndicate. When he bought the hulking Merchandise Mart in Chicago in 1945, he bargained with Syndicate leaders who controlled so much of local labor, politics, and business through bribery and extortion, and duly backed for mayor the Cook County clerk who was their creature, Richard J. Daley.

Through the decades he dealt with the same men who later lurked behind the lights of Las Vegas—the Patriarcas of New England, Costello in New York, Lansky, Giancana, D'Amato, and others. He was a fast friend of the colorful English killer Owney Madden, who went from Harlem's Cotton Club to run Hot Springs for Carlos Marcello. He often played golf with Rosselli, whom he had known since thirties Hollywood, and with Mike McLaney, a New Orleans mob figure and sports bettor long associated with Lansky in Havana and later in Las Vegas. "Match made in heaven," said a man who knew Joe and Mike, "both of 'em bigots, gamblers, golfers, Irish Catholics, and right-wingers."

The tie to Grober, the interlocking of Somerset and the Syndicate, his 1960 Cal-Neva meeting with "gangsters"—these shards turned up in FBI files or the Kefauver Hearings like traces of some entombed world, which they were, but went unassembled, unexamined. If no match for the incomparable political maneuvering of FDR, Joe could still navigate the system's inner politics. Obsequious with J. Edgar Hoover, in the forties he became a secret informer for the FBI, according to documents released years later, making sure to lard his trivial gossip with fawning praise of the director. He also cultivated Hoover's Cold War rivals, among them CIA director Allen Dulles, whom he knew from his days with the SEC, and who had shared Kennedy's prewar isolationism, if more discreetly. After the war, Dulles secretly schemed to give leading Nazi officers, businessmen, and scientists privileged asylum in the United States, an act surpassing anything Joe had advocated in London a few years before. But like others with whom Joe had much in common, Dulles and even Hoover would be more guarded in their compromises. "One rule always to remember," Joe once told union leader Harry Bridges, "is don't get caught."

Kennedy had been typical of those who seized American fortunes early in the century—no more rapacious, corrupt, or corrupting than most of the others. Figures like General Motors founder William Durant, Standard Oil's Rockefellers, and a host of others gained fortunes and the social register by trading in the stock market. But then in Durant's factories, the Rockefellers' oil empire, and in many other industries and businesses, they made their accommodations with Syndicate hoodlums who served both labor and management, paying kickbacks, joining the furtive de facto partnership of government, business, and crime that in Manhattan suites or Long Island estates was the privately understood while publicly unacknowledged shadow side of the American system. The deeply integrated, thoroughly national specter come upon by Kefauver arose not simply out of official corruption or public ignorance, or the appearance of the random pirate inevitable in human nature—as his nervous enemies liked to label Joe Kennedy—but with the knowledge, acceptance, and, often, complicity of the nation's wealthy. It was not how egregious this upstart Irishman had been, after all, but how representative; what a sharp reflection he threw back of the spreading collusion and compromise of his era. To do what Kennedy had done, from liquor to movies, racetracks to real estate, required connivance and collusion often more naked than the comparable machinations of his peers in the business and political worlds of the early decades of the century. He was more brazen, less classy, in the end less able to hide. He would be what one historian called an "upperworld gangster." But seen in terms of Las Vegas—where his methods were those of the ruling regime, where the distinction between upperworld and underworld hardly existed—he was no rogue at all.

There would be telling parallels between Joe and the Las Vegas that drew him. If he exemplified the two Americas, visible and hidden, so too did the city. Like Las Vegas, he craved respectability and set out to buy it. Like Las Vegas, he was in a sense expatriated for doing too openly what others did more stealthily. The meaning of his life, like the meaning of the city, was distorted by the myth of how aberrant, how unusual, their excesses were. In fact, many of his more respectable peers, men who governed much of the nation's economy and politics, practiced much the same methods and ethic, just as later evidence would show that Seattle, Miami, Los Angeles, Chicago, New York, Boston, and other cities would practice what William Chambliss called "the integral union" of the criminal and "legitimate" worlds epitomized by Las Vegas. Not least, both the town and Joe Kennedy thrust forward their next generation, and saw it gain the acceptance they could never buy for themselves.

The bootlegger, speculator, ambassador parlayed one asset above all: his large, photogenic family. Like a ghostly negative, every picture of the clan had its inverted image. Portraits of smiling Kennedys masked an impassive marriage, an emotionally vapid mother, and what an intimate called the father's "savage domination over those children." Indulgent and tyrannical, absent and invasive, loving and fearsome, ever the narcissist watching his own reflection in his issue, there would be no patriarch like him in twentieth-century America for the political legacy he left. In his four sons he instilled an unyielding competitiveness and sense of entitlement, as well as his own habits of sexual profligacy. "Kennedy might hope to protect his children from the world he knew . . . but he could not protect his children from himself," as Stephen Fox wrote in his history of organized crime, *Blood and Power.* "They perforce absorbed his amoral ways . . . [he] taught them about winning and appearances, at which he was adept, but not about ethics and values, of which he knew nothing." He would breed them not for the crude commerce he dominated, but for the public office he coveted—and far more for power than out of any notion of *noblesse oblige.* "The boys might as well work for the government," he remarked to his wife, "because politics will rule the business of the country in the future." Yet this imperious figure, who made deal after shady deal with few records, kept his sons strictly apart from his own business, cordoning off his world from theirs, even though one underwrote the other. "He built a literal wall between his family life and his outside life," Fox concluded. "He was careful to make sure we understood," his son Robert would say, "that his enemies were not to become our enemies."

When Joe's ascent ended in 1940, he shifted without pause to his heir apparent, his handsome but mediocre namesake. Then, when Joe Jr. died in a rash wartime mission, trying as usual to best his brother John, already decorated for heroism, the pursuit passed to that lissome, often sickly second son. He was no less competitive, but seemed to take himself less seriously, the family edge softened, disguised by a playfulness and skepticism, "graceful yet forceful yet diffident," wrote Michael Herr. "The most successful of his father's many enterprises, and by far the most attractive." In the end he would be just as possessed while more likable, more magnetic than the rest, tempering his often caustic arrogance and ambition with an ease and fatalism that grew into charisma. But he was also Joe's son, especially in Las Vegas, and his career paralleled the rise of the city. In the spring of 1947, as Bugsy Siegel was beginning to make a profit at the Flamingo, callow, thirty-year-old first-term congressman John Kennedy was penning a rake's note to the Plaza Hotel in Manhattan to retrieve his silver cocktail shaker, left behind after a wild weekend party with Fifth Avenue prostitutes. His reckless sexual hedonism would be incessant—some thought pathological. "A compulsive satyr," investigative journalist Jim Hougan called JFK accurately enough. Yet, constantly promoted and financed by his father, he was elected to the

Senate in 1952, narrowly missed the vice-presidential nomination four years later, and by 1958, barely forty, was poised for the presidency.

"He can't run my campaign sitting out in Nevada," Jack once complained of his father's drawn-out stays at the Cal-Neva. In the event, the presidential run would be the most richly financed, precisely organized, and altogether implacable in American history. Its most important figure, however, may have been less the candidate himself, or the deal-making father, than the campaign manager, the younger brother they called Bobby. Eight years Jack's junior, Joe Kennedy's third son was like his father in crucial ways. "When I hate some son-of-a-bitch, I hate him 'til I die," Joe would say, adding as a kind of vindication of his posterity, "Everybody in my family forgives—except Bobby."

Though Robert Kennedy was of average height, standing just over five feet nine inches tall, his aides remembered him as driven by an obsession with what he saw as his small stature, a "Napoleonic complex" for "no reason," one described it. Like much else, his exacting sense of self was forged out of the crucible of the Kennedy family, where he was "the runt," as one writer saw him among taller boys and men, and had to struggle ferociously at whatever he did to avoid the failure or just slacking that was the clan anathema. From childhood he wanted to be called the stronger, more adult-sounding "Bob." But even in fame and power, eventual public death and veneration, he could never escape the diminishing—for him—"Bobby." Combative and pensive, intrepid and morose, he would harden into a complex alloy of character. As a man, he was incorrigibly overbearing, and uncontainably tender. He appeared his father's "hard-eyed, hard-faced, hard-minded" heir, as biographer James W. Hilty wrote, yet softened and spurred by the moral absolutes and self-righteousness of a mother's retreat to an almost monastic Catholic piety—at once antagonist and acolyte. "A constellation of contradictions . . . a battleground," Hilty found him.

As a boy, he hoped to travel in space. At the end of his life, admirers and detractors alike thought he should have been "a revolutionary priest," as the acerbic Alice Roosevelt Longworth said of him, inspiriting and consoling a band of guerrillas in the hills however quixotic their mission. From a longer perspective, a more admiring biographer found him "the last patrician," an ambivalent conservative torn between ancient virtues and modern device. "The most interesting . . . imaginative . . . passionate . . . questioning," a thoughtful critic measured his true stature among the Kennedys. "An imperfect man, possessed of many grievous faults, and yet we may number him among the saints." Mostly he became what Hilty called "vizier and brother protector" to a president, an often haughty, heedless alter ego, a Mr.

Hyde and hatchetman who found his career in a brotherly love and loyalty unmatched in American politics. Then, suddenly, he would be his martyred brother's brooding inheritor, the shrill enforcer subdued by fate. It was a mark of the complexity of the man, of the fateful, ambiguous legacy he scattered behind him, that Bobby Kennedy fit each of these roles.

At Harvard, as a navy seaman, through a lesser law school at Virginia, he was scarcely noticed, always in the shadow of his shining brother, whom he called Johnny. An eager if undistinguished young attorney in the Washington of the early fifties, his first real job, typically, was one his father helped arrange. As a counsel to Senator Joe McCarthy's Red-baiting Subcommittee on Investigations, Bobby was obviously at home, whatever the venue impelled by the "idea of uncovering," as a reporter noted, "conspiracies and corruption." When he was passed over by McCarthy in favor of the scurrilous Roy Cohn, he thought about moving out West, making his name in the "open spaces and severe freedom" of the place he as well as his brother and father "genuinely loved," as one account put it. "Some hard work and a lot of handshaking," Bobby told a friend, "could get the Democratic nomination for Senator in a state like Nevada." As it happened, there was a promising new investigation in the offing on Capitol Hill, and he would never be a senator from Nevada, where "he might have learned earlier," Michael Knox Beran concluded in his piercing biography, *The Last Patrician*, "those lessons he was fated to learn only at the end of his life."

"Tempting targets" was how one writer described America's unions at midcentury. Strikes and violence, and then looming corruption exposed by Kefauver and in later news stories, all provoked public dismay—and predictable political opportunism. Congress made periodic forays into union racketeering. But union or Syndicate bribes—the origin of the money often indistinguishable—routinely fixed the inquiries, money given to the leadership to secure the appointment of docile committee members, or to those on the panel to ensure the impotence of the hearings themselves. Thus in 1954, Ohio GOP congressman George Bender dropped a House Government Operations Subcommittee investigation of labor racketeering in Detroit in return for Teamster political contributions to his forthcoming Senate campaign. Northern Democrats like the Kennedys traditionally hesitated to take on their labor constituency, justifying their tolerance of union corruption by management's even more blatant and longstanding abuses. Ironically, it was Kefauver's image as a racket-buster—the role that assured his loss of the presidential nomination in 1952—that eventually lured them to think investigating corruption would be a political asset. On the floor of the 1956 Democratic Convention, as Kefauver defeated Kennedy for the vice-presidential nomination under Stevenson, reporter Clark Mollenhoff taunted a weary Bobby smarting in defeat. "Well, goddammit do you believe me now?" he yelled above the din, mistaking second place on a doomed ticket as a mark of political power. "Got him enough clout to beat your brother's butt."

The Kennedy brothers were soon jockeying for positions on a new select committee being organized in the Senate to inquire into labor racketeering, JFK as a member, Bobby chief counsel—though not before an extraordinary shouting quarrel, vividly remembered by several onlookers, at the Kennedy compound in Hyannis Port around Christmas 1956. "The worst we ever witnessed," sister Jean Kennedy Smith recalled of the row between Bobby, the usually dutiful, pliant son, and the patriarch who dictated their lives, and who thought the inquiry a terrible idea. Joe was "deeply, emotionally opposed," she would tell a family historian, "and father and son had an unprecedentedly furious argument." An inquiry was bound to cost labor support in Jack's 1960 run, and Bobby was "frightfully naive about the physical and political risks," as one account described Joe's insistence. "The old man saw this as dangerous, not the sort of thing or sort of people to mess around with," said a friend who witnessed the altercation. "The father, of all people, knew how the underworld might flare back if provoked," wrote Stephen Fox. "His private, unspoken fears about where such an investigation might lead, what it might dredge up about his own past, may be inferred . . . only Joe Kennedy could fully gauge the ironies, the possibly tragic ironies, if one of his sons went after the mob." Yet Bobby was adamant that the probe was good politics, that it could be handled—a "first real defiance of his father's will," Fox described it. The brothers went ahead.

Formally it was the Senate Select Committee on Improper Activities in the Labor and Management Field; reporters named it the "Rackets Committee," though it would focus exclusively on union problems, and was better known by the name of its chairman, John McClellan, a three-term Democratic senator from Arkansas who was Washington hypocrisy personified. A devout Baptist, nativist bigot, anti-labor Dixiecrat, and defender of southern banking monopolies that discreetly financed his personal life as well as campaigns, McClellan was only too ready to take on unions and the predominantly northern, urban, ethnic caricature of crime—"to rid the country," as the onetime county prosecutor from Malvern drawled, "of characters who come here from other lands and take advantage." From the category of what he called "human parasites on society," the senator thoughtfully exempted his patron bankers as well as Madden and Marcello, the masters of Hot Springs' lucrative backroom gambling whose bribes—in "just plain old brown paper envelopes," said a woman who carried them—won the devotion of most Arkansas politicians. Otherwise, McClellan gave his aggressive counsel wide latitude.

Shrewdly starting with leads from labor and crime reporters around the nation, Bobby soon mounted an effort that matched and in part overtook Kefauver's. "The most thorough exposure of organized crime that Congress had yet undertaken," as a historian of the committee called it, the 30-month inquiry marshaled more than 1,000 witnesses and 500 open hearings to expose the underlying layers of labor corruption. Theft of union funds and the criminal ties of internationals led, as other trails took Kefauver before them, to the Syndicate itself. As the probe expanded, so did Bobby's authority, along with a self-revealing fervor for the cause and calling. He emerged a national figure on his own with a public persona of steeliness—though the authority and freedom allowed him to indulge, too, an emerging stridency and arrogance, seen from the inside as the sort of brash power and even abandon that alarmed and antagonized the larger Washington system, always threatened by authentic, unpriceable passion. His fateful choice of a particular adversary, a personalization again at odds with the political culture, traced to temperament—and chance. A reporter told him almost in passing to look into Dave Beck, a union official who had come out of the combine of crime, business, and politics that ran Seattle to head the country's largest, richest union and one of the most corrupt, the Brotherhood of Teamsters. Drawing his "moral dividing line between 'good unions' and 'bad,' " as biographer Hilty put it, Bobby struck at the monolithic Teamsters, and began a vendetta with Beck's successor, a pugnacious ex–Kroger Grocery dockloader named Jimmy Hoffa.

As the committee wound down in 1959, it had yet to establish clearly how long or how widely organized crime had infiltrated American labor, much less how integral management was to the systemic corruption, or how deep it ran into locals beyond a lightning-rod Beck or Hoffa at the top. Hearings drove out a few of the worst criminals, and left new standards for elections and finances. For Kennedy purposes, the publicity put them nearer the presidency. There were only obscure moments that dredged up Joe Kennedy's hovering complicities: Bobby with "audacious belligerence," as one biographer saw him, comparing Sam Giancana, smirking while he took the Fifth Amendment, to a giggly little girl; the usually avid chief counsel declining to question Irish hoodlum and local New York Teamster head Johnny O'Rourke after one of the Syndicate bosses of the New York waterfront installed by Lansky and the OSS in Operation Underworld, William J. McCormack, intervened with his old friend Joe Kennedy to have the sons go easy on O'Rourke; Abner "Longy" Zwillman—a New Jersey racketeer who had clashed violently with Joe Kennedy while they were both smuggling, and had later become Howard Hughes's personal bootlegger as well as a secret owner on the Strip—executed in the basement of his West Orange, New Jersey, mansion in a crudely staged "suicide" just before he was to testify under subpoena. But public attention fixed on the Teamsters, where Hoffa remained "out of jail and brazen as ever," a reporter noted, despite repeated indictments and trials. The unfinished business of bringing him down became Bobby's "fateful personal agenda," as one writer recorded. Whatever Kennedy's mix of motives, whatever he knew or avoided of his father's past, the dogged, deliberate targeting of Hoffa would take him toward a milieu of power where crime and government were firmly enmeshed, and where the Strip was already a nexus and symbol.

As he left to take over JFK's campaign, Bobby thought the Teamsters "prime villains" of labor racketeering. But beyond them he saw a larger, ultimate threat to the nation itself. In the hearings he had heard the term *Mafia* for the first time, and was skeptical that Italians alone could account for the scope of what the committee was discovering, always perceptive about the multiethnic, more ubiquitous reality disguised by bureaucratic clichés. His own vision of organized crime, of what he came to call "the Syndicate," was as sweeping as Kefauver's—and more sophisticated, more portentous than the stereotypes invoked by Hoover or Anslinger. At a moment when the political world was in thrall to the external threat of the Soviet Union, Bobby was in no doubt about the more serious peril. "Either we're going to be successful," he said to his staff about what the Syndicate represented, "or they're going to have the country."

He set out his grim conclusions in a book published in 1960. "An urgent and ominous tone permeated the pages," said one writer, "as Kennedy warned that within ten years unchecked organized crime activity could drastically alter the U.S. economy." Though he mentioned Las Vegas only in passing, the pages were an account of the pursuit and passion that would eventually draw him to Nevada. "The older brother's playground," Michael Herr wrote later of the Strip and the two Kennedys, "was the younger brother's nightmare." The title of Bobby's book sounded his foreboding for the country—and for more than he ever intended. He called it *The Enemy Within.*

"M ore than anything in the world I have always wanted people to accept and trust and respect me," Grant Sawyer told an interviewer near the end of his life. "But I was rejected in high school, and I believe it may be that

I went over the line, which I later learned is a risk . . . you arouse a lot of resentment and suddenly find yourself not a hero but an anti-hero . . . and you're discarded." It was the sad lament of a remorseful, chastened reformer, even maverick—to look back on criticism and defeat, and blame his own methods more than what he was up against. It was Sawyer's tragedy, both in his personal life and in the public role he played in Nevada's last genuine effort to curb the forces of Las Vegas.

He was the youngest son of itinerant osteopaths who argued incessantly, stole patients from each other, and went through a bitter divorce in 1921, when he was only three. He grew up divided between his unstable, politically volatile mother in Twin Falls, Idaho, and his stolid father in Fallon, Nevada, who had been convicted of practicing medicine without a license before he went on to become a state senator in Carson City and a friend of Pat McCarran. It was a bleak, scarring childhood—"right in the middle" of feuding parents and stepparents, as he recalled—of which the man he became spoke only in part, or in tears. He had a rich voice and a flair for drama he carried through life. His parents gave him elocution lessons and lent him seven dollars for a suit to wear while competing in a speech contest he lost to another theatrical youngster named Orson Welles. Mostly he was left with a mortifying sense of being "a poor farm kid," as he recalled painfully, with a deep, usually disappointed yearning to belong, and an equally gnawing fear of being left out. He would learn early to seal off his hurt, to hide much of what he was truly feeling physically as well as emotionally, and to keep his secrets.

From his mother's second husband he took an adolescent's discovery of old-fashioned American cheating and hypocrisy—the stern Baptist farmer presenting a "pillar-of-the-church facade," as Grant saw him, while weighting down his wheat for market. It was "the first time in my life," the boy recalled, "that I realized that people aren't always what they seemed." His impassioned but slovenly mother, a heavy, homely figure dressed in black, agitated to help the downtrodden—"a raving radical," he once called her, who provided an enduring if embarrassing example of small-town social conscience and courage. For his part, his father remained stony and impassive, "a proud man and quite guarded, and I find myself to be somewhat the same way," the son would say later with evident regret. But there were intervals, too, of some refinement with his stepmother in Fallon, a gentler, more cultivated spirit named Byrd who later wrote a popular history of Nevada.

None of it was what he wanted—a safe place with his peers. When he was not pledged in a high school fraternity, it was "one of the most traumatic experiences of my life," he confessed later. Despite his family's poverty, there was always the assumption that as an intelligent, hardworking young man he would go on to higher education. But when his mother divorced the wheat farmer in another vicious breakup, she grew despondent and insisted that young Grant give up school to take care of her. In a wrenching scene at their little apartment in Twin Falls, her sister and friends came to rescue him, literally pulling him away from a mother "pleading and crying," as he remembered, to take him down and put him on the bus for college.

On scholarship at Linfield College, a small Baptist school in Oregon, he was "the compulsive joiner and office seeker," but was soon expelled for organizing a school dance that mocked the administration, and went back to Nevada to finish at the university in Reno. He dreamed of being an actor, but thought himself "not good-looking . . . not very impressive physically," he said later, and chose the law to "do some of the same things I would if I were in the theater." Though his father had an angry falling-out with McCarran, the senator kept an earlier promise to take young Grant. Only months before Pearl Harbor, Sawyer began at George Washington Law School, working nights as a Capitol policeman under the patronage of the white-haired patriarch he called with fear and awe "the Holy Ghost." After four years in the army, Sawyer returned to finish at Georgetown. Soon he was back in Nevada with a wife from Reno and a 1939 Chevrolet. He was one of the most loyal of "McCarran's Boys," despite a strong distaste for the senator's Red-baiting, and quietly ablaze with his own political ambition.

After three years as district attorney of Elko in the northeastern corner of the state, where his phone number had been simply "2" in the tiny community of 6,000, he jockeyed to get the Democratic machine's endorsement for governor in 1954, though McCarran turned him down. That autumn, when the local political landscape quaked with the senior senator's sudden death, Sawyer began moving again toward higher office, losing a race to be a university regent but becoming state party chairman. Keen and pragmatic, he soon drew the attention of a small cluster of ardent, wealthy liberals around Reno who were looking for what one of them called an "educable" alternative to the usual machine candidate. Then, as later, the state's liberal rump preferred more traditional issues, "social and human needs of the state," as their leader Hazel Erskine called them. Ambivalent about gambling, many saw it as part of the frontier freedom prized in their own lives. Of what was happening "down south" in fulminating Las Vegas—the corruption that ultimately obliterated their social agenda—they were and would remain culturally disdainful, and lethally naive.

The last hours for filing in the 1958 Nevada election became one of those moments when impulse settled an era. Flouting convention, Sawyer left on the four-hour drive for the capital undecided about whether to file for U.S.

senator, governor, or attorney general. "Everyone wanted to know what Grant was going to do before they made their own decisions," a backer recalled. "But he wouldn't play their game." On the vacant highway from Elko to Carson City, Sawyer finally chose the governor's race rather than run, he said, against a friend who aspired to the Senate. His well-heeled liberal backers wanted him in the statehouse anyway. In the end, he was driven, as always, by the personal as much as the political, and by legacies of Twin Falls. "He was always insecure, very insecure about money and about practicing law on his own," a confidant recalled. "Grant would've done anything," said another colleague, "and I mean anything, to get out of Elko."

As it was, his friend lost in the primary, and Sawyer's scruple had the effect of opening the U.S. Senate seat to a Las Vegas city attorney, Howard W. Cannon, a transplanted Utah Mormon so intent on rising that he had given his insurance agent and crony his legal proxy—"for any of three declarations," as one witness remembered—to file for the highest office, whatever it was, that Sawyer passed up. Known by his crepe-soled shoes and loud sport jackets, Cannon would receive the support of powerbroker Norman Biltz and go on to twenty-four years in Washington as one of the Strip's servile, influential politicians. Meanwhile, Sawyer headed for the Governor's Mansion, and a different destiny.

The Kennedys singled out the young prosecutor soon after he filed. "They shrewdly recognized that political juice in Nevada would be in the hands of the governor more than the congressional delegation," said an insider, "that it was the state that dealt directly with gambling." Early in 1958, to scout out the right Democrat to back for the mansion, someone who would deliver for JFK two years later, Joe Kennedy sent one of his most trusted agents in the state, labor lawyer Hyman Raskin. Raskin had risen in the Arvey machine in Chicago and run Stevenson's 1952 and 1956 campaigns in the West. "A backroom man that he had to have if Jack was to be nominated and elected," one reporter described Raskin, "cashing in the chits he held for past favors." Characteristically hedging their bets, the Kennedys' "Irish Mafia," as one observer recalled, mustered at the same time Nevada kinsmen like the influential Foleys, who made overtures to the front-runner in the governor's race, Attorney General Harvey Dickerson, a machine Democrat fielded by Joe's Cal-Neva friends Cord and Biltz. "They were playing us all off against each other," said a man in the thick of the petty intrigue, "and they were masterful at keeping everybody in the dark."

Meanwhile, Raskin had talked to younger, more insurgent Democrats and came away recommending that the Kennedys support the underdog Sawyer as well as the favorite. The young prosecutor was running well in the two old centers of electoral power around Reno and in the outlying "cow counties." But he needed enough votes to hold his own in the burgeoning south, the new "blocking third" in the statewide calculus. "I convinced Raskin that we only had to have 1,600 votes from Vegas to win it all," a Sawyer manager would say. The day after their conversation, Raskin summoned Sawyer to the Riviera, where Syndicate front Ross Miller handed the candidate $1,300—"an astronomical amount at the time for a Nevada campaign," a Sawyer aide recalled. "It was the first big contribution we got," said another, "and on top of that, the money started pouring in from labor unions and others outside the state." Though Sawyer prided himself on winning with "small donations," the cash arranged by Raskin and the funds it released were decisive. He went on to an upset victory in the primary by the comfortable margin of more than 7,000 votes. "It made Grant governor, no question," a friend of Sawyer's said of the money handed over at the casino.

With an irony and näiveté few saw at the time, Sawyer's popular campaign theme was "Nevada Is Not For Sale." In the primary, the slogan hit at Cord and other oligarchs who had spurned the Elko newcomer when he asked them to back him four years before. In the general election, against the genial two-term Republican incumbent, Charles Russell, Sawyer soft-pedaled the motto, running on a more traditional platform, as he put it, that was "pro-labor, cheap water and power . . . no new taxes." Meanwhile, in a tepid campaign, both candidates paid ritual lip service to gambling control. "We had to project an image to the rest of the country that Nevada was not rolling over for . . . organized crime," Sawyer said typically. "Otherwise, legal gaming would never survive." The point, of course, was just that—to "project the image."

What McCarran had called prophetically the "rotten bargain"—overlooking gamblers' records elsewhere so long as the owners seemed "clean" in Nevada, where they brought economic salvation—had a sordid history. It was always a struggle, the state captive to the corruption it was supposed to police. Grappling began under Russell, a country teacher and publisher who went from the legislature to Congress in an upset victory, and then just as unexpectedly, amid interparty intrigues, to the statehouse, where the Republican's main adviser was Democrat Norman Biltz. In an office nearby in Carson City sat a former garage owner from Sparks, Robbins Cahill, whose power rivaled the governor's. Soft-spoken, with polish and learning that belied his origins, Cahill joined the small state government in 1940 when his business went under. Known for his rectitude, he rose to head the Tax Commission, rationalizing along the way that casino managers and owners need not be "bishops," as he said, just the "gamblers that they were."

Russell and Cahill had rendered the first regulation worth the name—though only in the glare of a bizarre scandal. It started in 1954 when a Clark County sheriff, attacked in the *Sun* for protecting petty vice, sued Hank Greenspun for libel. Greenspun hit back by hiring a con man named Pierre Lafitte to pose as a mobster moving onto the Strip, entrapping the sheriff in taped conversations about the usual bribes. Lafitte turned out to be an erstwhile drug dealer and double agent for the same George White of the FBN and CIA who subverted Kefauver. The tapes transcribed in the *Sun* ensnared the sheriff, Russell's Democratic opponent for governor (who had the support of the casino owners), and even Cliff Jones, forced to resign as Democratic National Committeeman. "I talk for the state . . . and believe me, I can deliver," Jones was heard boasting on the tapes to the impostor who wanted "to operate without no heat." The bugging also bared shady financing at the Thunderbird, where Jones fronted, and there was a resulting if reluctant Tax Commission inquiry, spurred by leaked IRS documents pointing to the Lanskys as secret owners.

The sensation offered a rare peek at the inner workings of the Strip, and more than anyone, including Greenspun, seemed to bargain for. Early in 1955, reelected but nationally embarrassed, Russell shut down the Thunderbird, put a ninety-day moratorium on licenses, and set up a new three-member Gaming Control Board. The state Supreme Court quickly allowed the Thunderbird to reopen, but Russell's board was to be proof that Nevada took the illegality seriously. The state also moved to close a remaining loophole from the 1931 legalization that some thought might allow corporate ownership of casinos. Now only individuals or partnerships were to be allowed, all operators duly licensed. It would be another semblance of control and regulation to be subverted by crafty lawyers and new front men.

The crisis met, Carson City relaxed into its usual torpor. "Partner rather than adversary," wrote Sergio Lalli of the capital's habitual view of gambling, Nevada a setting where "bacchanalia coexists with bureaucracy," as Robert Goodman saw it. Politicians were ever hostage. As Russell found in 1958, governors got scant flak from voters for laxity, and were punished by the gamblers for even minimal measures, like the board, to redeem the collective image. "Within the context of an economy built on vice," one history of regulation put it delicately, "the choice of how to maintain boundaries is a major task."

Meanwhile, the $250 million in casino profits reported to the state was a small fraction of the real count, and Nevada's picayune gambling tax—a graduated rate schedule from 3 percent to 5.5 percent of declared profits—a mockery. The revenue from that "official" income by 1960 would be less than the return to other states from horse and dog tracks alone, "just an *hors d'oeuvre* compared to [the] banquet from pari-mutuel racing," one reporter noted. Altogether, Carson City took in nearly $1 million less from supposed casino winnings than the federal government derived from its old flat tax of $250 for each slot machine. The fix had been simple. Joe Kennedy's friend Errett Cord shoved through a 1957 law to parcel the table tax equally to each county, giving Esmeralda's four hundred souls, like other empty cow counties, "money running out their ears," as one politico remarked, and so a permanent stake in the ransacked system. "The Esmeralda buy-off," Capitol lobbyists called it.

None of this, of course, was mentioned publicly in the campaign. Big Las Vegas money went to Sawyer only after the Kennedy-inspired bankrolling of his primary. In meetings along the Strip, in unmarked envelopes and wads of bills, as the candidate himself described the "distasteful" rite of Nevada political money-grubbing, the casinos deserted Russell and adopted the Democrat. "Suddenly I had a lot of friends on the Strip," Sawyer would say. He pledged to uphold the old states' rights resistance to "help from the outside," a euphemism for federal action. "Its destiny," he wrote of Nevada in a circular letter, "must remain in our hands." It was what the casinos expected from local politicians. Riding a Democratic wave in Clark County, Sawyer won in November with a record margin of 17,000.

On January 5, 1959, more than four hundred people jammed the old assembly chamber in Carson City to watch the swearing in of the youngest Nevada governor in four decades, the first of the postwar generation. To a standing ovation, he called in his inaugural address for "faith, trust and mutual understanding." That evening there was a gala party. In the reception line, in the lightheartedness of it all, the pretty young wife of a Sawyer adviser wore cat-eye sunglasses and a dental piece of buck teeth with a fake diamond set in gold. When she smiled, gleaming, some were taken aback for a second, as if she might be real, an Elko eccentric or some exiled heiress from Genoa—in Nevada you never knew. But then they saw, and laughed uproariously.

On that same day, 2,500 miles away, power was passing with a celebration of a different sort. Riding an American tank captured from the U.S.-backed dictatorship he had overthrown, Fidel Castro was making his way through cheering crowds toward a triumphal entry into Havana as the leader of the Cuban Revolution. Waiting nervously for him in the capital were more than a hundred of what Nevada newspapers headlined as "Vegans" or "Vegas gamblers," men like Jones with their lucrative casino interests on the Caribbean island.

The casino owners had been close to the old Batista regime, a major part of its repression, its lobbying in Washington, its financing. Their incessant bribes and kickbacks constituted much of that regime's revenue, a portion of the essential American support in money and arms. Politically, most of the "gamblers" were plain reactionaries who despised any popular revolt and saw Batista as a bulwark against instability or communism. But here as in the United States, their real politics were not a matter of party or ideology, but the simple cooptation and corruption of the government at hand. For years the Syndicate had dismissed Castro as "Fiddle," a former baseball hopeful and student agitator, a brash lawyer given to rambling speeches hours long. But as the rebellion grew, some gangsters had begun to slip money and weapons to the rebels in the mountains. Much of the contraband came from Havana casino owners Santo Trafficante and Norman "Roughhouse" Rothman, though the gunrunning to Castro also involved others with Las Vegas connections, including Hoffa and Dallas hoodlum Jack Ruby. In Cuba as in Nevada, they were always prepared for the next successful politician. When Batista fell, some of them joined the celebration in the streets, though crowds had vented their anger first on two hated, kindred symbols of exploitation—Havana's parking meters and the casino slot machines. Still, some of the bosses of the Strip were now among the throngs waving revolutionary flags along the graceful promenade of the Malecon. There, too, old connections linked men in unseen ways. Among the casino owners cheering for Castro was Joe Kennedy's pal Michael McLaney.

Rumored to have gone with Batista and his inner circle as they fled with loot of $300 million in a predawn panic on New Year's Day, Meyer Lansky had in fact stayed behind as the rebels marched on the city. He had been one of the suppliers of arms and cash to Castro over the several months just past, while dealing as usual with Batista. Protected from rioters at his plush Havana Riviera by his own henchmen manning sandbagged machine guns, Lansky now came down from his elegant penthouse atop the twenty-one-story casino resort to help feed hotel guests when chefs and waiters joined a general strike to prevent a countercoup. Usually loath to see the press, the man his Syndicate partners called "the Chairman" was now moved to grant a rare, exclusive interview to a paper with interested readers, the *Las Vegas Sun*. "I have no idea what Castro will have in mind," he told Greenspun's special correspondent. "No doubt they'll be around soon to talk with me."

Back in southern Nevada, the dispatches from Havana under banner headlines overshadowed apparently unrelated reports of the new governor's inaugural in Carson City. Yet the two beginnings so far apart were already linked, and so, too, would be the sequels: Cuba entwined with Nevada, Las Vegas bosses in a convoluted, murderous intrigue with the CIA against the new ruler in Havana, a conspiracy that consumed a new presidency in Washington as well, while leaving those on the Strip stronger than ever.

O ffshore Las Vegas," one writer called pre-Castro Havana, and the history of Cuba begat the one city as vividly as Nevada's past prefaced the other. Born out of the Spanish-American War to a sham sovereignty, the island nation ninety miles from Florida had long been a de facto U.S. colony. As a formidable group of scholars, including Thomas G. Paterson, Jane Franklin, and others later documented, successive administrations in Washington from Theodore Roosevelt to Harry Truman installed, braced, and bribed a half-century chain of repressive regimes in Havana. By 1950, American corporations controlled half of Cuba's sugar, and nearly all its oil, mines, minerals, ranches, and utilities, a billion-dollar monopoly unique in U.S. foreign investment. It was politics as possession and plunder, the same phenomenon Mark Twain found among the mining magnates of the Comstock and the other colonial masters of nineteenth-century Nevada. Asked how he had stolen $20 million from the national treasury in only weeks, a Cuban minister of the 1940s replied casually, "In suitcases."

Yet just as Nevada became more than another railroad or mining mandate in the American West, Cuba was no ordinary banana republic or commercial colony. For its sugar and molasses, and as a strategic transit point, the island constituted a crucial base for Prohibition-era bootleggers and rumrunners, including Joe Kennedy, Costello, Lansky, and others. American organized crime stayed on in Cuba after Repeal to cast a spreading shadow behind the American corporate presence—with which it coexisted, dominated, and flourished as easily and profitably as at home, serving as an enforcement arm, management, and eventually even a source of capital and investment for supposedly legitimate business. Lansky had come then, taking over the stately old Casino Nacional, crafting his alliance with Fulgencio Batista y Zaldivar—the burlesque but bloody-minded ex-sergeant fond of Hollywood monster movies and powder-white uniforms with high-heeled shoes—who strutted in and out of power for a quarter century after a military coup in 1933. With the nominal abrogation in 1934 of the Platt Amendment, which had "legalized" U.S. military interventions, the Syndicate increasingly functioned as agents and de facto private army of all American interests on the island. At the implicit and explicit behest of Washington officials and diplomats on the scene, as well as U.S. corporate agents from the sugar, mineral, and utilities monopolies, organized crime corrupted or strong-armed both governing politicians and the putative opposition, reducing Cuban leadership, as one historian summed it up, "to the role of docile feeders at the U.S. capitalistic trough." The regime was typified by United Fruit, a huge American corporation with a long tradition of interlocking ties to both the U.S. government and Syndicate barons, not only in Cuba but elsewhere in Central America. The company hired former U.S. government officials as well as gangsters, retained mob lawyers, and colluded blatantly with hoodlums, corrupt unions, and federal agents in ports like New Orleans, San Francisco, and New York.

On Cuba, which amounted to the Syndicate's own Caribbean possession, the gangsters established themselves in the decades before 1960 as nowhere else outside the continental United States, and their major stake would be as much drug trafficking as gambling. Beyond what one writer called "a vile commerce" in prostitution, white slavery, and other vice, by the late forties Cuba had become the principal processing point for raw opium from Latin America and Asia, and Havana's casinos "way-stations in the transfer of large heroin shipments from Europe to the United States." The price of sugar went up and down, shrewd investors knew, but Havana's drugs, casinos, and 270 brothels were a sure thing. "You could buy anything . . . ," a resident of the old city recalled, "*anything.*"

The parallels to Las Vegas were everywhere. As more than 300,000 American tourists streamed into Havana in the fifties, casino after casino went up, some built by venerable corporations like Hilton or Pan American, some financed by U.S. banks or from Cuban union pension funds under the auspices of the AFL-CIO. All of it came with special dispensations on taxes, duties, and fees from the captive Cuban regime that often matched the American investment in the resorts dollar for dollar, while fully conceding title and management. Regardless of the ostensible corporate owners, most casinos ran directly or indirectly as franchises of various factions of the Syndicate. It was a tacit arrangement accepted as readily in corporate boardrooms like those of Hilton or Pan American—where executives dealt directly and often by junket and phone with the management of their profitable holdings in Cuba—as in the mansions and barracks of the Batista regime. In their own version of the Nevada rationale, Cuban politicians eager for tourism and part of the take welcomed the gambling "professionalism" of gangsters. For his part, the U.S. ambassador in the fifties, Earl T. Smith, thought Syndicate control a service to customers otherwise bound to be cheated by the natives. "It's strange," Smith told a visitor, "but it seems to be the only way to get honest casinos."

So great was the migration of casino operators and floor men to Havana at one point in the decade that Nevada officials worried about the depletion of Las Vegas's own "professionals." There was talk in Carson City of prohibiting Nevada owners from operating in Cuba, though nothing would be done about it. In 1959, Sawyer would be instrumental in pushing through the Foreign Gaming Rule, prohibiting Nevada casino licensees from being involved in casinos anywhere else—legal or illegal. But that statute, like state regulation in general, was easily evaded by Syndicate front men in Cuba. Beyond Lansky's Riviera, where Las Vegas floor man Charlie Baron managed operations for a time, Dalitz and his Cleveland faction along with McLaney controlled the old Nacional; Lansky partner Charlie Tourine, the newer Capri; Las Vegas's Eddie Levinson and Cliff Jones, the $24 million Havana Hilton; Santo Trafficante and Lansky partner Norman Rothman, the ornate Sans Souci, which Strip overseer Johnny Rosselli managed for a time; and on and on.

For all the differences between a teeming tropical shore and the still largely empty desert valley, between the aging colonial capital and the spreading frontier crossroads, Havana and Las Vegas bore the resemblance of their common essence. Under marquees and on stages of similar design, Havana resorts offered the same entertainment as the Strip, from Sinatra to the inevitable chorus lines—and the rest of the city washed up around and through the garish glamour with the same unsettling contrasts. "Imposing and simple, graceful and tacky, elegant and tawdry, seductive and repellent, light and dark," a visitor said of the Cuban capital much as Noël Coward described Las Vegas at that very moment. "Havana both charmed and disappointed." At night there was the same surreal radiance against the blackness around them. Havana's "luminous halo of night life, the fatal phosphorescence that was so promising," Cuban writer Guillermo Cabrera Infante recorded; he could have been describing driving down from Tonopah and sighting the glow of Glitter Gulch in the starry desert sky.

Like Las Vegas, sinful, seductive Havana drew a throng of wealthy and famous Americans whose passages there, as in Nevada, later seemed jarring. John Kennedy first visited the Havana casinos at the end of 1957 and returned the next year, asking Lansky "if he could set him up with women," as Meyer's widow described it. At one point, JFK attracted the attention of Batista's secret police when his affair with the wife of the volatile Italian ambassador threatened a diplomatic incident. "Once they started looking after you, which they naturally would a senator, why it was just elegant," Kennedy's friend and fellow senator George Smathers recalled of their trips together. In the convolutions of their private world, the Kennedys were discreetly linked as well with U.S. Ambassador Smith, a "playboy extraordinary," as Acting Secretary of State Christian Herter called the Palm Beach socialite who had been the Kennedys' Palm Beach neighbor and Rose Kennedy's intimate before becoming Eisenhower's envoy. The social whirl apparently left little time for the future president to ponder the less savory politics and economics of the island. "I don't think I ever heard Kennedy express any feeling about Batista or Castro either way," Smathers would say.

Havana and Las Vegas shared serious and consequential secrets. Both were junctures of what a scholar later termed "the gray alliance" between organized crime and the U.S. government that in the name of national security and intelligence grew out of World War II on the New York docks, in Southern Europe, Mexico, and elsewhere. Postwar Cuba, like Nevada, was one of those tangled dark intersections where business, politics, foreign policy, and the Syndicate met with mounting frequency, ease, and complicity. As a dying Lansky later told the story with some pride, still discreetly keeping the names of his contacts secret, it had been at the specific request of White House emissaries and Naval Intelligence agents that the Syndicate leader had bribed Batista into a lush Miami exile in 1944 when the tyrant's concessions to Communists seemed ominous. When the dictator returned in a coup in 1952 (which ignited Castro's revolt)—now in overt partnership with Lansky, whom he hired as an official "consultant"—that, too, served equally the interests of organized crime and a Truman administration backing anti-Communist client regimes worldwide all but regardless of their criminality.

From Cuba the gangster-government collusion spread throughout the Caribbean and Central America in the fifties, with Las Vegas connections at every turn. In the wake of the CIA-sponsored anti-leftist coup overthrowing the Arbenz regime in Guatemala in 1954, Carlos Marcello had moved in to extend his holdings in the country, using some of the returns to build the Tropicana on the Strip three years later. Overseen by Rosselli, representatives of Trafficante, and other Syndicate figures—Rosselli and some of his associates working at the same time as sources for the CIA—drug trafficking became a major part of the new organized-crime presence in "liberated" Guatemala, with profits from the Syndicate-controlled enterprise duly laundered in Las Vegas and Havana. "A lot of funny money from down south came across the tables in those days, and got dealt into good greenbacks to go back to the outfits," a dealer and pit boss of the era remembered. The casino gambling that came to Guatemala City with the new U.S.-installed regime was operated by Ted Lewin, a Lansky associate and a future owner in Las Vegas who was already active in the Philippines, where he and other Lansky partners worked in similar close collaboration with the CIA and ambitious local politicians like future president Ferdinand Marcos.

Gliding easily between the Syndicate, government, and business, between the Strip and Havana, Rosselli openly consorted with U.S. agents in Cuba and Mexico through the mid-fifties, providing regular intelligence to the CIA while engaged in intrigues and even private wars in post-coup Guatemala for the behemoth Standard Fruit and Steamship Company, a New Orleans concern with long-standing ties to New York crime families as well as Marcello. Among Rosselli's close contacts during the Eisenhower years were Lewin; the legendary CIA operative David Sanchez Morales, known as "El Indio"; and still anonymous men who were liaisons to both the Syndicate and the CIA for Standard Fruit and United Fruit, and other big business—a fraternity that testified amply to what Rosselli's biographers called his "easy affinity with American intelligence agents."

As later testimony showed clearly, the ties of Rosselli's colleagues required no elaborate decision-making or coordination between corporations, government, and the confederated leadership of organized crime—though the contacts and work of full-time government operatives like Morales and rogue agents like Lewin were certainly known and approved at senior levels of the CIA, and Rosselli for one continued to work within the Syndicate under the auspices of his original Chicago patronage, specifically Sam Giancana by the fifties, as well as tending the stake of other factions in Las Vegas. The collaboration happened naturally, almost organically, out of the shared, mutual interests of the parties, their evolving interdependence on the scene, their longtime and increasing willingness to work with one another; the Syndicate found only added power and protection in the collusion. "The convergence of interests," two reporters described it later somewhat delicately, "between the mob and the U.S. government."

The paramilitary activity on behalf of corporations or client regimes, carried out with CIA knowledge and sanction, would have far-reaching effects. Among Rosselli's private army of thugs—not unlike enforcers in Chicago or Los Angeles, after all—would be the forerunners of later "death squads" in Guatemala and El Salvador as well as of the Contras in Nicaragua, another early example of the impact the Strip was already having on American foreign policy. Before the fifties ended, the triad of American business, government, and crime was locked around client regimes and their powerless societies as never before. In the Caribbean and Central America, as in Nevada, the interests of corrupt local governments, of U.S. banks, unions, exploitative corporations, of Cold War administrations in Washington, of the Syndicate, had become largely indistinguishable. If still shrouded in official or criminal secrecy and relatively invisible before 1960, that expanding, evolving alliance would be glimpsed eventually in Vietnam, in succeeding scandals of Watergate and Iran-Contra, and still later in an end-of-century America whose economy was dominated by a corporate oligarchy controlling much of government finance and business in the same way—in a sense, Strip foreign policy come home.

But now Fidel Castro defied them all. Sensualist, gourmand, and one-time CIA informer whose landed father made money from U.S. companies but was forced to bow to them, the gifted demagogue with Brylcreemed hair was not merely their next *caudillo*. His biographers would be impressed by how much Castro had in common, after all, with the Kennedys who would soon be his mortal rivals: rich, domineering political patriarchs from a family of recent immigrants; Catholicism and private schools; the drive for power. Castro was unimpressed by the clandestine arms aid and public flag-waving of his late converts out from the casinos. "We are not only disposed to deport the gangsters," he told a howling crowd, "but to shoot them." Havana's gambling houses reopened in February 1959, though with heavy taxes, a ban on slot machines, and the daunting requirement that the U.S. Embassy, like Nevada's Gaming Control Board, attest to the operators' "good reputation."

Lansky, it turned out, had not even waited to talk to the rebels, as he told the *Sun* so jauntily, but fled before Castro rode into Havana, leaving behind, by his own rueful account, nearly $20 million in cash. In April 1959, the new regime detained for a time some of Lansky's more notorious associates, including his brother Jake and the Cuban-American Trafficante, boss of Tampa and an emerging force in the drug trade who would be visited in his Havana internment camp by both Rosselli and Jack Ruby. Trafficante and Las Vegas's "Babe" Baron, the air force reserve general and once and future Strip greeter, even met privately with Fidel's deputy and brother Raul in a vain effort to reach some settlement on the casinos.

Meanwhile, the new regime in Havana, despite its rhetoric and distrust, quietly sought U.S. economic and humanitarian aid, but was rebuffed. The break with the old order on the island was too complete. During the fall and winter of 1958–59, the White House banned Cuban sugar imports and the Soviet Union moved in to buy the crop as Havana's new patron. The island was now a center of great-power rivalry, and with all the political animus of the anti-communism of the era, hostility between Washington and Castro was fixed. By the time of the party for Joe Kennedy in Carson City the following summer, American racketeers, like corporate overseers, were largely gone from the Cuba once theirs. For the moment at least, Castro razed the narcotics laboratories, shut down the smuggling, and nationalized Lansky's Riviera, along with the other casinos and many American companies. "As if the American auto industry lost Detroit to popular rebellion," a reporter wrote of the blow to the Syndicate's multibillion-dollar stake. Lansky now put out a million-dollar contract on Castro.

At the same moment, a separate conspiracy joining Las Vegas and the CIA was also underway to murder the Cuban leader. Two of the conspirators had met years before on the Strip on the floor of the old El Rancho. Partially revealed years later, the scheme seemed to many a shocking cabal of public servants and public enemies, at least as the public still understood the distinction. Yet in the prevailing but still furtive politics of government, business, and crime in 1960, a joint assassination plot was in a sense only natural, a fitting way to retake Cuba, where, as in Nevada, their interests coexisted so comfortably.

Helluva cast of characters," said one of the plotters. The CIA men were parodies of the agency's still-imposing mystique. J. C. King, head of the Western Hemisphere division, was a West Pointer and ex–pharmaceutical salesman in Argentina, his reactionary zeal and ties to companies like United Fruit so crude and blatant that in the Guatemalan coup even conservative cohorts shunted him aside as an extremist. Sheffield Edwards and his deputy James O'Connell, atop what one writer called the "glorified Pinkerton service" that was the CIA's Office of Security, were both ex–FBI agents. Fired or planted by Hoover—murky records suggest either—they were in any case disdained by their Ivy League betters at the agency. "You can see their lips move when they read," a CIA man from Yale noted. Joining them was another FBI castoff known as "the Pear," William Harvey, "short, fat, and hideous looking," as journalist Evan Thomas saw him, with "bulging eyes" and a "froglike voice," invariably packing a pistol from his private hoard of guns, and, like many ranking CIA men of the era, an acute alcoholic.

Their superior was Richard Bissell, one of what were called "Fifth Avenue cowboys," a patrician, square-faced economist of facile intelligence, whose glibness easily outshone the gumshoes, while his arrogance and insensibility matched their coarseness. "We should have been better about stepping in after a success like that to make the gains enduring," Bissell would say about post-coup Guatemala, not sufficiently pleased with the resulting tyranny and corruption, the pillage that followed in the wake of this and

other CIA interventions. With Bissell's blunders covered up and his sup-
posed successes—such as overseeing the U-2, which often took him to a top-
secret CIA area outside Las Vegas—he was largely, tragically, the epitome of
Washington's Cold War pretensions. He "personified American hubris in the
postwar era," concluded a biographer, and the careless ignorance of what his
Georgetown circle called smirkingly "the real world" beyond the Potomac.
"There will be no communist government in Latin America while I am
DD/P [Deputy Director of Plans]," he proclaimed on taking over covert-
action operations in 1959, at a time when many in Washington already
believed the Castro regime to be just that. He was a bureaucrat convinced
"that he could do things better than most people," as a reporter wrote,
though he seems to have had respect for at least one group beyond his own
office or circle. "Bissell," as a biographer noted, "attributed high standards of
efficiency to the Mafia."

It would never be clear how the collusion began, much less who was
using whom, only that it all grew far less as an aberration or from Bissell's
image of the Mob than as an extension of practices and trends already in
existence. In the winter of 1959–60, under pressure from United Fruit,
Hilton, sugar interests, and figures in the Cuban exile community, J. C. King
proposed the "elimination" of Castro. Approval for capital murder soon
came from Bissell and then from King's old friend and godfather of one of
his daughters, CIA director Allen Dulles. Dulles in turn was acting on the
authority of President Eisenhower, who, as archives and memoirs would
eventually reveal, readily used covert action as an instrument of foreign policy, including direct and indirect assassination in Iran, Guatemala, Indone-
sia, the Congo, and elsewhere, while carefully distancing himself from all but
the most inferential knowledge, and thus, he believed, ultimately from any
reputation-tarnishing culpability. Yet the lines of authority would be clear
enough. "This is money," Dulles assured a hesitant paymaster for the murder
plot, "approved by the president." Within weeks, CIA men were discussing
"assassination" with a federal narcotics official known to have extensive contacts in organized crime. At the same moment other agents were "in touch,"
as one of them related, with Lansky's man at the Sans Souci in Havana, Norman Rothman, a onetime gunrunner to the rebels. Having tried to have Castro killed in 1959, Rothman returned to Miami, bought a hotel with Batista's
relatives, and began backing a Cuban exile group under a former Castro
bodyguard, a defector named Frank Sturgis, better known later as a Watergate burglar. Meeting often with CIA agents, by the spring of 1960 Rothman
was supposed to recruit other Syndicate figures with Havana interests, and
apparently told his Sans Souci partner Trafficante and others about the plot.

The deal was patent. "The CIA obtained mobsters' aid," according to a *Time* magazine account based on secret documents, "by promising that they would be allowed to recover the booty left behind [in Havana]." As a summary of a later FBI report explained further, there was also agreement "to reestablish the pre-Castro Cuban drug traffic . . . securing the gambling, prostitution, and dope monopolies in Cuba." Afterward, some wondered why such a corrupt compact had been considered at all, why a great power's intelligence service, with its own assets for "wet work," as Jim Hougan used the term for murders of state, required "mobsters' aid" for killing Castro. The answer lay in part in the CIA's sense of its own limits—an internal history filled with many more failures than heralded successes even in the agency's heyday 1950s—and to some extent in the difficulty of the operation, given Castro's vigilant security informed by the Guatemala coup and other CIA activities. But most decisive was the very history that underlay their bargain, the mutual interest in killing the rebel and returning to power. The heart of the compromise, as few yet understood, was that the U.S. government was already deeply compromised. Organized crime had largely ruled Cuba as America's de facto colonial administration and had supplied intelligence and enforcement for all U.S. interests since the forties. From New York docks to the Cold War Third World, Washington had come to rely on and coexist with the same organized crime that covertly dominated so much of domestic politics.

But in the summer of 1960 the CIA grew impatient with Rothman and Bissell's ex–FBI men, Edwards and O'Connell, and began making contact with others it knew personally from the Las Vegas Strip. One of them was Bob Maheu.

For all the trust powerful men invested in him and despite his role in historic events, there was something relentlessly ordinary about this grocer's son from Maine. He had gone to Holy Cross University and on to the wartime FBI, where he claimed a shadowy success in counterespionage and was rumored to be involved in some of the bureau's more dubious wartime intrigues, including an intelligence operation that resulted in the murder of a dissident Indian nationalist. Then, after the war, he suddenly gave up his career, went bust in a business scheme to can fresh cream, and then to pay his debts became a Washington private investigator, opening Robert A. Maheu Associates in 1954. At least that was his story. "It is not at all clear if Maheu was a down-at-the-heels, feet-on-the-desk gumshoe trying to look big time," wrote journalist Michael Drosnin, "or a big-time front for the CIA trying to look like a sleazy bankrupt shamus."

From the outset his company was chiefly a CIA front, "a deniable proprietary," as they were known, and Maheu a "pimp for the cookie factory," as one of his employees said of him, whose control officer was his former FBI colleague O'Connell. A dour, doughy-faced man of no special intellect or talent, Maheu hired dozens of former CIA and FBI operatives, military officers, private detectives, and others to provide seamy services the intelligence agency wanted to use but deny, from wiretapping and blackmail with pornography to manipulations of shipping and oil markets, or even kidnapping of radicals annoying client dictators. In the growing postwar culture of secrecy and machination, of technological gadgets and intrigues, RAMA, as insiders knew Maheu's firm, became a singular cluster of James Bond–like private secret agents manipulating events for governments, corporations, and the rich. In the same orbit, Maheu worked with more public men of influence across the spectrum of politics, though they, too, did much of what they did under cover—Washington lawyer Edward Bennett Williams, Bobby Kennedy's close aide Carmine Bellino, Jimmy Hoffa, Greek shipping magnate Stavros Niarchos, Greenspun attorney Ed Morgan, Vice President Richard Nixon; corporations including the New York Central Railroad; political bodies such as the Senate Banking Committee.

With these men and his expanding business came "connections to the Mob," as one writer put it, including Hoffa and Williams, who represented Frank Costello. Beyond Maheu's own off-the-books "dirty tricks," much of his work involved "softening up parties" or "tawdry lobbying," as a reporter noted, pervasive payoffs and fixes, earning him the favor of clients but the contempt of law enforcement. "Some people call it political fix," Maheu once said, ". . . I call it conditioning the atmosphere." "Master Spook," Hougan termed Maheu. "A goniff, just a goniff," said a senior FBI agent familiar with the record, using the Yiddish word for "con man" or "thief."

Apropos of the petty detective he was, Maheu's first big case outside the government was snooping on sex. Photographing actress Jean Peters and her lover, who happened to be a CIA operative as well, he satisfied Howard Hughes's obsession with the movie star he eventually married. Maheu got more work from Hughes, becoming his "top bag man," as one said, and by the later fifties his "spook of choice." Shortly after RAMA was created, he had met Rosselli during a trip to Las Vegas, and the mobster, of obvious influence on the Strip, soon became his intimate, a friend his children called "Uncle Johnny," and someone who turned out to have as many important contacts—and some of the same friends.

"At the pinnacle of his criminal career, relaxed and confident," his biographers described Rosselli as he was in the fifties. He was as exceptional as Maheu was banal. Born on the Fourth of July in 1905 in a poor, rocky Italian village between Naples and Rome, he came to Boston at six crammed in steerage on a thirty-five-dollar ticket, only to see his family broken as his father died in the 1918 flu epidemic. By his early teens, having burned down his own family's house for the insurance, he was a numbers runner and bootlegger for Longy Zwillman, and then a hit man and drug dealer for Al Capone. In the mid-twenties, he was in California working for Tony Cornero on gambling boats, and was soon overseeing extortion of movie studios and political graft, his influence over Los Angeles City Hall driving out rivals Guy McAfee and Farmer Page to dusty Las Vegas.

"Socialite, labor boss and gangster," as Rappleye and Becker depicted him, Rosselli was a major Syndicate figure by the thirties, and on the West Coast the peer of Bugsy Siegel. Convicted of racketeering in an intra-gang battle, he emerged from prison as formidable as ever. His success sprang from more than the threat of violence, shrewd dealings, loyalty, and discretion. He was naturally charming, handsome, magnetic. But beyond any hoodlum of his era, he absorbed the lessons of the upperworld, shedding his accent and edge for tailored conversation and suits, impeccable manners and grooming. As he modeled his business practices on what he saw, and did, in the corporate world—"dealmaker's tact and the killer's will," one writer called it—he mimicked socially what a friend called "the right things to do," being seen in fashionable places. He did quiet favors and performed thoughtful gestures for the prominent, ingratiating himself with the audience at hand, from unknown starlets to Joe Kennedy or Howard Hughes. His ceaseless self-promotion was cloaked as earnestness or humor. He embodied the new politics of celebrity success in the culture, the triumph of appearance. "The Henry Kissinger of the Mob," a later partner aptly called him.

Rosselli went to Reno in 1948, fronting for hidden owners in the Bank Club. Three years later, he had points in a Las Vegas casino. At mid-decade, with the proxy of various Syndicate factions, he was in "constant travel" between Nevada, Cuba, and Guatemala. By 1957, he was Chicago's man at the Tropicana, living there or at the Desert Inn, making over $1 million a year, and though never mentioned in the occasional press exposés of the city, presiding "over every facet of business in the gambling capital," as one history recounted. "His power was universal." Like Lansky, friends said, Johnny envisaged the future of Las Vegas and the nation—"that element deep in the American consciousness drawn irresistibly to the towers of glass and neon pulsating above the Nevada desert," Rappleye and Becker wrote, ". . . a people beset by an unnamed hunger, ready to lay down their last dollar on a chance to break free . . . a shadow that haunted the American dream, and . . . the spring it welled from was bottomless."

Maheu and Rosselli had met in the mid-fifties through Edward Bennett Williams, at a time when all of them were embroiled with the CIA. RAMA had actually retained Rosselli's "advice and services" at least twice, and the two men became fast friends, Rosselli a frequent guest at Maheu's ranch-style home in suburban Falls Church, Virginia. It was there (well before most of them later acknowledged) at a 1959 clambake in honor of Scott McLeod, the notorious right-wing security official who had led the McCarthyite purges of the State Department under Eisenhower, that Rosselli met and talked intently with Maheu's CIA associates Edwards and O'Connell. At some point not long afterward, both the CIA and their Syndicate allies decided that the smooth and experienced Rosselli, the most dominant figure on the scene in Las Vegas, should replace Rothman as the main conduit for the Castro assassination, with Maheu the liaison.

The sequence of what followed would always be obscured by the twisting cover stories on all sides. While the CIA prepared a gruesome and ludicrous array of lethal devices for killing Castro—from cigars laced with botulism to disease-contaminated skin-diving suits and exploding seashells—Maheu and Rosselli met through the summer of 1960 to consummate the contract. Only days after the Democratic Convention in Los Angeles, they lunched across town at the Brown Derby as Maheu offered his friend the CIA's $150,000 bounty, which by all accounts Rosselli gallantly refused on grounds of patriotism—though both men were aware of the million-dollar Lansky contract, and Rosselli had already told Lansky, if not others, of the plot. "Let's just say they were eligible for Meyer's money, and the CIA offer was a joke," said one of Rosselli's Las Vegas bodyguards.

That September at the Plaza Hotel in New York, as Castro was speaking to a large crowd nearby at the United Nations, O'Connell met with Maheu and Rosselli to concoct a cover story artlessly approximate to the truth: that corporate and other "business interests" were "pooling money" to pay for the assassination, implying that the coalition was composed of anti-Communist right-wingers like Hughes and the powerful Murchison family of Texas. Having informed Edwards, Bissell, and Dulles the plot was proceeding—though without using any "bad words" like "Mafia," as one of them recalled—O'Connell flew later that month to Miami to meet again with Maheu and Rosselli. There they agreed to recruit other accomplices. In October, they gathered again at Miami's Fontainebleau Hotel, where O'Connell was introduced to two more conspirators he recognized immediately behind their flimsy pseudonyms, Sam Giancana and Santo Trafficante. It was the first of several sessions at what Maheu called their "headquarters," the notorious Syndicate-run hotel—Rosselli at one point buying O'Connell a "fancy silk shirt," as the bureaucrat remembered, to improve his drab wardrobe for the South Florida scene. Giancana ordered champagne and gray beluga caviar flown in every day from New York.

Their plotting, however, had been penetrated from the start by Cuban intelligence—possibly, as many thought, by Trafficante as a double agent—and their fitful efforts at assassination were swiftly and brutally crushed in Havana, agents butchered in their landing zones, teams taken at rendezvous points, radios flickering off to gunfire and screams. But the conspirators, and the caviar, kept coming to the Fontainebleau.

Meanwhile, on a winter night in Chicago, as Giancana and a group of Las Vegas owners ran into some FBI men they knew outside a nightclub, one of the drunken mobsters taunted the agents who seemed to be shadowing them. "What's wrong?" he shouted across the snow. "Why don't you guys stop this? We're all part of the same team."

That July at the convention, sequels to the currents swirling around the party in Carson City were played out in Los Angeles. Sinatra arrived from the Strip Sunday, before the opening, to put on a large fund-raiser for JFK at the Beverly Hilton, attended by several Las Vegas casino owners. The next night, as the convention began, JFK, after politicking effectively during the day, tried to involve the lover he had met at the Sands in February, Judy Campbell, in what she called "a threesome" with another woman. "I would think you had enough on your mind without cooking up something like this," she told him disgustedly as she left his private quarters.

The afternoon before the balloting, Joe Kennedy sat with his two older sons watching television in the mansion of an old Hollywood friend, where they received a stream of political bosses and Sinatra acted as "bartender and greeter," as a visitor saw him. When the Wyoming delegation later gave JFK the nomination, Sinatra "went wild, jumping up and down," slapping a Las Vegas friend on the back and shouting, "We're on our way to the White House, buddy boy. We're on our way to the White House." The next night JFK was at the Santa Monica home of Peter Lawford, where Kennedy ordered daiquiris by writing notes because he had lost his voice, and was soon "cozied up," as eyewitnesses saw it, with Marilyn Monroe, yet another lover with whom he had rendezvoused in Las Vegas and at the Cal-Neva over a period of years.

Meanwhile, in the little Nevada delegation Joe Kennedy had lobbied so hard in Carson City, the convention became a sour, divisive anticlimax. Bobby had personally intervened earlier to make sure the pro-JFK Sawyer faction led the state's caucus. As campaign manager Bobby already carried a reputation as a ferocious political infighter. "The Black Prince," Adlai Stevenson called him. For Lyndon Johnson, in whom he aroused jealousy, resentment, and fear, he was "that little shit-ass."

Bobby had been abrasive with the Nevadans during the race. "His arrogance and cavalier attitude turned me off," Sawyer would say. But he was gentle and imploring when he came by the governor's hotel room in Los Angeles, "pleading," as Sawyer heard it, "for the Nevada votes for his brother." JFK pointedly addressed the Nevada contingent first on an early round of appearances before the delegations. But old bonds held, especially Johnson's control over Nevada's senators, domination rooted not just in Washington but in LBJ's own backers, Marcello and others with huge holdings on the Strip. "We felt we had complete control of our people," said a Sawyer adviser. "Then after we arrived in L.A., it became clear we were not going to get the Reno liberals to give up Adlai after all, and of course LBJ had hold of [Nevada senators] Bible and Cannon. Grant felt real responsible for failing Jack."

In the Kennedy trailer command post adjacent to the floor, Hy Raskin tried to console the young governor whose career the Kennedys had helped launch with the Riviera money. They would not need Nevada after all, he assured him; JFK had the nomination on the first ballot. On the roll call Nevada gave a bare majority of delegates to Lyndon Johnson, the liberals splitting between Stevenson and Kennedy. Sawyer as titular leader was humiliated. When he heard LBJ was to be Kennedy's running mate—"The convention raised hell, loudly booing," a Nevadan remembered the spontaneous reaction to Johnson—it was a final blow. With his wife and close friends from Elko, Sawyer left Los Angeles even before the acceptance speeches.

Only decades later was it learned from a posthumous account by Raskin that Johnson had blackmailed his way into the vice presidency after Kennedy had dangled it in front of the Texan but before JFK made a final decision. "Those bastards were trying to frame me," a furious Kennedy had told Raskin, cursing LBJ and his patron, Speaker Sam Rayburn. Bobby, who returned Johnson's hatred—"That cornponed bastard . . . mean, bitter, vicious, an animal in many ways"—had already clashed with the majority leader's aide Bobby Baker over LBJ's closed-door remarks about Jack's hidden health problems and old Joe's appeasement, charges of special savagery because they were true. "You're gonna get yours when the time comes," Bobby had told Baker. But Johnson was on the ticket nonetheless.

"They threatened me with problems, and I don't need more problems,"

JFK confided to Raskin with unfeigned fury after the selection. An insider aware of many of Kennedy's potential scandals, Raskin would never be sure which one LBJ had threatened to expose—from sex to mob ties—any of which, given the still relative innocence of the 1960 electorate, would have destroyed Kennedy. But Raskin, who knew the Kennedys as well as anyone outside the family, had no doubt about the nominee's blackmail, and kept one of the sordid, seminal secrets of two presidencies for the next thirty-seven years, to be revealed for the first time in 1997 in Seymour Hersh's book *The Dark Side of Camelot.*

Sawyer, the proud, disconsolate young governor of Nevada, sensitive as ever to slights and rejection, knew none of this. His journey home was in many ways a passage from one era to another, though he didn't sense it at the time. Sawyer came to think his affront at the convention minor compared to the bitter events that followed. Within a year, Bobby Kennedy would pose an unexpected challenge to the governor's very authority and survival in office, what Sawyer would describe angrily as nothing less than "political treachery." Beyond that conflict would be the haunting murder of Jack Kennedy, the man and politician Sawyer still liked so much, who had sat there talking to him casually in the shower, who had charmed the Nevadans waiting to shake his hand. For Sawyer, there would be even more shocking revelations to come of unimagined intrigue and deception—a turmoil of the new decade that would soon make the party in Carson City a kind of poignant memory, as if nothing would ever again be what it was on that silky summer night in the placid little capital in the Sierras.

12. An Enemy Too Far Within

The night before the 1960 presidential election, the odds on the Strip were three to two, Kennedy over Nixon. Casino bookies ignored a 1919 Nevada law that made wagering on elections a misdemeanor. The candidate's youngest brother, Teddy, then campaign coordinator for the western states, excitedly telephoned a friend in Las Vegas to get down a $10,000 bet on Jack at the Riviera with casino boss Ross Miller, the Illinois hoodlum and onetime strip club operator now a front for Giancana and the Chicago outfit. A few hours later, as dawn broke on the East Coast and odds tightened, Kennedy brother-in-law Stephen Smith called still dark Tahoe from the Hyannis Port compound to have Wingy Grober put $25,000 on JFK at the Cal-Neva. The candidate's family seemed confident of victory even if professional gamblers were not so sure. The bookies on the Strip soon went to "six to five, take your pick." The race for president of the United States was too close to call, even in Las Vegas.

Across the nation, November 8, 1960, was a day like no other in the history of American politics. In Chicago, an election judge was so conscience-stricken by her own party's fraud in a polling place that she later slipped away, trembling, to confess it to her parish priest as a mortal sin. In Texas, while "the stuffing of ballot boxes reached a new high," as one account put it later, tens of thousands of votes were going uncounted, 100,000 more would be "disqualified," and still others would be clumsily altered. In New Mexico's northern counties, local sheriffs and *patrons* passed out cash within sight of the polls, and deputies and party cronies went into the booths with women and the old to stand at their side, in what a subsequent academic account called "informal and highly irregular voting procedures." In Hawaii, burly men were telling voters in Chinese and Japanese how to mark their ballots in order to avoid, as one witness later told the FBI, "unpleasantness for you and your family." In Nevada, in what one campaign aide delicately called "questionable practices," the tally of black votes from Las Vegas's squalid Westside was far heavier than expected, many more, some believed, than the actual number of voters who might reasonably have turned out from those precincts. In New Jersey, Pennsylvania, South Carolina, and Missouri, there were similar scenes.

That afternoon, one of the first calls Bobby Kennedy made from Hyannis Port was to a supporter in Las Vegas, anxious to know whether his brother was carrying the tiny ghost town of Goldfield in Esmeralda County, the obscure Nevada bellwether that had voted for the winner of the presidency in every race since 1868. He was. When it was over, John F. Kennedy won the popular vote by an official plurality of 114,000 votes out of nearly 69 million, the closest run for the White House in the twentieth century. There were eight states in which he won by less than 2 percent. In the West, he carried only Nevada, and that by less than 1,900 votes, a margin most notably achieved with the startling number of votes from the Las Vegas ghetto. But it was enough. An unknowing Graham Hollister—a wealthy Sierra foothills Democrat and future official in the Kennedy administration—brought Teddy his winnings in Los Angeles, guilelessly carrying the cash in a "brown paper package," as one witness remembered. Wingy Grober, it was said, sent the Kennedys their Cal-Neva winnings in similar wrapping.

On the Strip, and among its owners around the nation, it had been for many an election like any other. They knew that Norman Biltz, enlisting the Desert Inn's Wilbur Clark and others in Las Vegas, quietly raised what was at the time an astronomical $15 million for JFK. They knew that other Syndicate money—as usual in presidential runs over the previous three decades—had gone to both candidates, bags of cash from the Sands and other joints to Kennedy, the Tropicana's Carlos Marcello putting $500,000 into Nixon's coffers. Bets covered, most took the election in stride. But, as would be revealed later, a few had been smugly sure of JFK's victory. Some, like Giancana—one of the city's increasingly powerful overlords of skim from the Sahara, Sands, Riviera, Tropicana, and Mint, as well as the stake Joe Kennedy helped negotiate at the Cal-Neva—believed that they had made their own odds, that they had stolen the election for the new president, and that there would be a pay-off on that action as well.

T he night of the gnomes," chronicler of presidential races Theodore White called the 1960 election. Much of what happened was lost in delib-erate deception and self-serving evasion on all sides. Republicans lodged for-mal allegations in eleven states, the result of "a deluge of reports," as Edmund Kallina, a historian of the election, described the accusations around the nation that would be much more numerous than the customary partisan complaints of fraud in a presidential election. Even a brief and partial FBI field investigation in Chicago found massive evidence of what a thickening secret file captioned "Voting Irregularities": stuffing of ballot boxes, vote-buying, voting twice, falsification of absentee ballots, destruction of ballots and election documents, ghost voting, chain voting by premarked ballots, mechanical rigging of machines, pressuring and instructing of voters, smeared erasures. Meanwhile, a special prosecutor in Cook County, Illinois, Morris J. Wexler, appointed amid a public outcry, examined in detail returns in one-fifth of Chicago's precincts. A prominent Democrat staffed only with a handful of policemen from the Daley machine itself, Wexler still managed to uncover and document in those relatively few polling places the theft of more than 8,800 paper ballots (Kennedy carried Illinois by 4,400 votes). From all this and more, many observers—including the bitterly unforgiving loser in the race——concluded that Kennedy, or at least his backers, had stolen the election. "I don't suppose I would mind if it was just a matter of stealing the courthouse," said a local GOP candidate. "But when manipulations . . . take over the White House, it is a sad day."

Still, the election of 1960, like some national Pandora's Box, was to remain one of American history's tacitly forbidden chambers. While con-vinced of the theft himself, and despite Nixon's fury and maneuvering behind a public face of acceptance, outgoing President Eisenhower shut down the FBI field investigation after a few weeks for reasons of state, con-vinced that the nation could not afford a constitutional crisis and the possi-ble disruption of presidential succession at the height of the Cold War. A pragmatic Nixon, moreover, however unreconciled privately, knew that the nearly complete Democratic control over courts and legislatures in con-tested states would doom any procedural challenge, and leave him poten-tially even more damaged. "Charges of 'sore loser' would follow me through history," he later wrote, "and remove any possibility of a further political career." Democratic judges in Texas and elsewhere soon quashed any inquiries. Despite charging more than six hundred defendants, the special state's attorney in Chicago found himself thwarted by a partisan judge brought in from East St. Louis, John Marshall Carns, whose sweeping dismissal of the prosecutor's cases the Chicago Better Government Association called "carte blanche for future irregularities." Wexler's shocking inquiry would yield but three petty convictions—and those only because that trembling woman had gone so far as to release her priest to tell prosecutors about her confession.

The search for guilt was not a simple matter. A complete investigation of the vote nationwide, as studies later concluded, might well have exposed GOP fraud to parallel if not match the Democrats'. "No one will ever know precisely who carried the majority of 1960, for on that night political thieves and vote stealers were counterfeiting results all across the nation," as White concluded. "The three-o'clock-in-the-morning contest rested on whether the Democratic crooks or Republican crooks were more skillful."

The Kennedys were hardly unique in sinister allies and methods. Nixon's own relationship with organized crime traced back to the forties and Bugsy Siegel's drug trade and vice in Southern California, and would go on to include—as Robbyn Swan and Tony Summers would establish so authoritatively in their *Arrogance of Power*—contacts with Lansky ranging from prewar Havana to support by Lansky or his close associates in Nixon's 1968 election to the presidency. A decade before taking crime boss Marcello's half-million dollars in the presidential race, Nixon had run for the Senate from California in 1950 with the backing of Los Angeles gangster Mickey Cohen, who passed more than $75,000 to the candidate from Las Vegas hoodlums. In 1956, in danger of being dumped from the national ticket by a party revolt and Eisenhower's own habitual ambivalence about him, Nixon had been saved by a secret infusion of cash—first to purchase write-in votes in the New Hampshire primary, then for espionage, subversion, and trumped-up polls at the GOP convention itself. The money came by way of Maheu from government contractor and frequent Las Vegas player Hughes, who also "loaned" Nixon's brother Donald $205,000 in 1956, and who soon after Nixon's reelection as vice president received rulings by the IRS, SEC, Civil Aeronautics Board, and Justice Department worth untold millions to the Hughes conglomerate, favors fully expected to be continued in a Nixon presidency. Most significant at the time for Las Vegas, Nixon had been an avid supporter of the Eisenhower administration's covert operations to overthrow Castro, including the alliance with organized crime to assassinate the Cuban leader. As president in his own right, later documentation made plain, he would have continued with a vengeance the secret war to restore the Caribbean island to its old colonial-Syndicate rule.

In the 1960 election, the American system was now operating more brazenly as Las Vegas always had. In its aftermath, many came to believe, Nixon was convinced he had to match his ruthless opponents with extralegal measures of his own—1960 as the parent of Watergate. Yet embittering as the defeat was, the loser needed no instruction on the inner realities of the country's politics. Nixon's career-long patron Hughes, who embodied as much as anyone the juncture of crime, business, and government, was more blunt about the factional gang warfare presidential races had become. "You can see how cruel it was after my all-out support of Nixon," he scrawled, "to have Jack Kennedy achieve that very, *very* marginal so-called victory over my man." Never reconciled to "the Kennedy gang's 'theft' of the White House," biographer Drosnin wrote of Hughes, ". . . both he and Joe had set out to buy America. Kennedy had succeeded."

Whatever the ironies of Election Day, powerful men in Las Vegas believed they had made a president, just as Hughes believed he had been cheated out of making his own. The story slipped out over decades in memoirs, family reminiscences, footnotes to congressional probes, deathbed confessions, declassified FBI wiretaps, and physical surveillance, and the evidence documented beyond doubt that Las Vegas interests in particular were deeply involved in fixing JFK's nomination as well as the general election. The history was made in obscure, dramatic meetings. It was on a late-winter afternoon in 1959—as a man who brought them together remembered vividly, and as the writer Seymour Hersh revealed four decades later—that Joe Kennedy met with Sam Giancana in the office of a friendly Chicago judge, and began arrangements for the fix in the Chicago wards and elsewhere. They would soon confer again in an even more consequential meeting on February 29, 1960, at Felix Young's restaurant in New York, at a luncheon set up by Johnny Rosselli and attended by other Syndicate figures and a lawyer named Mario Brod, whose practice, according to the scholar Richard Mahoney, included representing the Teamsters and "combined top-secret work for the CIA's counterintelligence wing with legal troubleshooting for friends in the Syndicate." Joe had called on Sinatra and other Cal-Neva contacts as well. And, in perhaps the most important connection of all, revealed in print for the first time in 1997 by Gus Russo, Joe had gone to Florida to see Vincent "Jimmy Blue Eyes" Alo, Luciano's former liaison with politicians in the thirties, and now Lansky's closest friend and associate. Alo, to whom Mike McLaney and many others answered, not only shared ownership and skimming interests in Havana but oversaw as well for various factions their shares of the Las Vegas skim at the Sands and a half-dozen other Strip casinos. As "Blue Eyes" himself said thirty years after the fact, Joe came to solicit his and Lansky's help in electing John Kennedy—and like Giancana and his Chicago associates, they agreed.

Many of the intrigues, not surprisingly, had a Nevada connection. For the West Virginia primary in May, where victory in that Protestant state was seen as vital for JFK, "Skinny" D'Amato from the Cal-Neva had been sent to dispense as much as a half-million dollars of gambling money to Appalachian sheriffs and politicos whom D'Amato knew as gambling customers and debtors at his 500 Club in Atlantic City. Skinny's associate Sinatra played a similar role as political bagman in West Virginia, the payoffs going in large sums to some, to others in the traditional, cut-rate election day purchase. "Anywhere from $2 and a drink of whiskey to $6 and two pints of whiskey for a single vote," a local editor wrote of how the Sinatra and other mob money ended up. In either case, the Las Vegas infusion in the primary, as much as $2 million by some estimates, was overwhelming, unlike anything ever seen before in the impoverished state. Later in the fall, using a similar combination of bribery, influence peddling, and threats, Giancana mobilized Chicago unions and the local political machine for JFK not only in Cook County but also throughout the Midwest and in border states like Kentucky, Tennessee, and Missouri.

For all this and more, Norman Biltz had raised $15 million in Las Vegas, most of it disbursed to Kennedy representatives, where it was then pooled with other Syndicate-generated cash to fund the payoffs made by D'Amato, Sinatra, Giancana, and others. In Nevada itself, some of the money also paid for bribes and buses that brought in illegal black voters in 1960, much as Biltz had imported from Los Angeles the saving margin for McCarran in 1944. In New Mexico, the payoffs to county and town officials, often in sums of $20 or less, were neatly recorded in pencil in the tiny black address book of one of the Democratic bagmen. In Chicago, as Wexler could prosecute and establish only in microcosm, some of the cash was used to pay off the polling place judges, tally clerks, and other officials. And on it went. Added to the untold amount spent personally by Joe, Las Vegas helped make Jack Kennedy's war chest four or five times the total of any previous presidential candidate's. In the end, the Strip had bought the White House as if it were acquiring another casino.

That winter, the purchased power made a government. The president-elect joked about announcing the new head of his Justice Department. He would go to the door of his Georgetown townhouse at three in the morning, make sure no one was around, and whisper softly, "It's Bobby." When the president made his Nevada backer Roger Foley U.S. district judge, it was "the only federal appointment old Joe Kennedy ever asked for," as JFK told Foley. But Joe had also insisted on Bobby becoming attorney general. There will always be questions about why the old man forced it. When a visitor voiced Jack's own doubts, Joe shot back witheringly, "*Bobby is going to be attorney general.*" Was it the spoils of victory, grandiosity? "I'm going to see to it Bobby gets the same chance we gave Jack," Joe told a friend. Was it to control Justice, with its FBI secrets, its power to pursue or ignore? Or was it simply to bind a son? A "father's refusal to set him free," was how C. David Heymann described it. Both Joe and Jack had to push Bobby. "I'd been chasing bad men for three years," he said later of his role as McClellan Committee counsel, "and didn't want to spend my life doing that." But he now resumed that "chasing" of Hoffa with characteristic implacability, the most sustained effort of his life, setting the stage, a decade after Estes Kefauver, for another clash between Las Vegas and a haunted nemesis.

The appointment shocked Washington, but even more the Strip and its owners. "I know that certain people in the Chicago organization knew that they had to get John Kennedy in," gangster Mickey Cohen said later. "But nobody in my line of work had any idea that he was going to name Bobby Kennedy attorney general. That was the last thing anyone thought." One biographer concluded that Bobby did not know of "the family relationship with the mob world." Others would be just as certain that the second son and campaign manager, his father's son in resolve and rancor, must have known something of Joe's pervasive connections. In what was left of well-purged Kennedy campaign files decades later, there would be amazingly detailed sheets covering the nation precinct by precinct, with notes in Bobby's hand, though some states were unaccountably missing or incomplete—Illinois, Texas, New Mexico, Hawaii, Nevada.

The new attorney general soon learned officially of the fraud in the 1960 election. While the FBI investigation ended under Eisenhower, a report on the Illinois "irregularities" from the bureau's Chicago office found its way into Bobby's early briefing materials. "I can tell you that the fact that it was stolen was brought to Robert Kennedy's attention," former Justice official and Notre Dame law professor Robert Blakey told Seymour Hersh decades later. "Nothing happened," as Hersh recorded Bobby's response to the official documentation. At the same time, others believed the brothers knew none of it. "If the boys [the Kennedy brothers] would have known, things would have been different," said an old Kennedy retainer. But whatever Jack and Bobby understood, one outcome would be clear: They would fail to honor the marker as Las Vegas held it.

At the glittering Kennedy inaugural in January 1961, the victors and assorted camp followers celebrated together. Sinatra and other Strip entertainers put on a gala at the Washington Armory, but with the single black member of their Las Vegas "Rat Pack," Sammy Davis, Jr., quietly if pointedly excluded by the Kennedys in deference to southern Democrats, despite the fact that black votes had been decisive in JFK's victory, including, of course, in Las Vegas. In a further irony, a group of Las Vegas and Hollywood stars representing Howard Hughes sat in four inaugural boxes purchased by Hughes Aircraft at $10,000 each. Only weeks from his last meeting with organized-crime assassins and CIA figures to plot Castro's murder, Hughes's agent Maheu hobnobbed with the new regime.

The Kennedys flew in three hundred of the Strip's most alluring dancers to appear at various functions. Christened the "Golden Girls," the chorus line added "color, charm, and photographic appeal," an organizer explained. They were there on the sunny, frigid afternoon of the inaugural parade as John Kennedy made a richly symbolic and poignant gesture, rising out of the backseat of his open limousine to tip his top hat to his father in the reviewing stand. Late that night, a half dozen of the casino dancers were at the Georgetown home of Washington columnist Joe Alsop when the new president, leaving his pregnant wife at the White House after the balls, stopped by with Bobby for a nightcap, and both brothers enjoyed interludes with what one onlooker called the "beautiful young women" from Nevada.

Back on the Strip, the casinos took in record profits in the winter of 1960–61. At the Sands, guests entering the showroom found barrels full of silver dollars to be grabbed by the handful. Smartly uniformed ushers handed out Italian silk purses to the ladies, English leather wallets to the gentlemen, each enfolding a crackling new hundred-dollar bill courtesy of the house. At the Tropicana, Desert Inn, Stardust, and Dunes, there was similar largesse, floor captains happily thrusting chips or casino scrip on passing guests. The Hacienda Hotel's private airline junkets flew planeload after planeload at no charge from Chicago into McCarran Airport, stewardesses serving passengers what one of them remembered as "bubbly torrents of free champagne." The mood was more extravagant than ever. "Everything's nice and cool," Rosselli told a friend over dinner. "There's money pouring in like there's no tomorrow. I've never seen so much money."

Las Vegas, as every schoolboy knows, is composed entirely of money," *Newsweek* said in reporting the obvious. "Money brings nature to her knees, turning the desert green . . . and all things in Las Vegas proclaim and reflect money." Ten million customers a year, half of them return visitors, flooded into the valley at the beginning of the new decade, leaving behind a half-billion dollars along a thoroughfare now become a familiar scene of Americana. The "Ranch Rococo" or "Miami Baroque" look of the Strip might be "the dwelling place of the deity," of the "divinities of Lust and Greed," thought a symbol-conscious Arthur Steuer writing in *Esquire* in the summer of 1961, but "the flash and glitter has an ecstatic appeal . . . the utter frankness of the ostentation a certain vulgar charm."

"We have no gangsters here," a former state assemblyman instructed an out-of-town journalist. "We have qualified businessmen who are in a recognized industry—gaming." "Our business is no different from banking," said casino owner Allard Roen, now calling himself, along with other owners, a "managing director." Dean Martin drew howls of laughter at the Sands about his own points secretly negotiated for him by Joe Kennedy at the Cal-Neva when he quipped between numbers, "I'm the only entertainer who has ten percent of four gangsters." The *Saturday Evening Post* now judged Moe Dalitz, the owner of the Desert Inn, "a leading citizen of Las Vegas." Dalitz, who had stood up to Kefauver a decade before, was "as composed as ever" when interviewed in 1961. Given Nevada's official recognition of the legitimacy of Las Vegas, Moe was scarcely interested in local politics. "We don't have to ask ourselves like we used to in the old days," he answered with disarming candor, " 'Is this guy going to be a crusader?' " Naturally, they contributed to politicians regulating them. "They can't get it anywhere else," Dalitz laughed.

Visitors found the town more intriguing than ever at the beginning of the new decade, possessed of a "strange animus," wrote one journalist, making "the grotesque and the absurd appear to be quite normal." *Newsweek* marveled at the huge amounts of cash changing hands at the casino tables: "It is modern alchemy," the magazine marveled, "the turning of bodies and objects into pure gold." There seemed much to envy in the Las Vegas boom while the rest of the country bobbed up and down in periodic recessions. The population of the city had nearly doubled in five years to more than 70,000 by 1960; 200 families moved into southern Nevada every week for the seemingly inexhaustible jobs in and around the casinos. Those new "civic-minded inhabitants," a national magazine noted, made Las Vegas "a city like any other," and by standards any taxpayer or homeowner could appreciate. Supermarkets in Sin City were open twenty-four hours a day, with "slot machines lined up like cornflake cartons and more women in skimpier bikinis than may be seen at Cannes in high summer." But the town also boasted round-the-clock street cleaning covering nearly three hundred miles of newly paved avenues, and scouring the ever-expanding Strip five times a week. It was a daunting job, sweeping up the desert grit, the litter of the hordes who "tend to disregard trash receptacles," as a municipal official complained, and the inevitable dust from the city's constant, thrashing construction. "While we give top priority to the casino area as far as frequency is concerned," the director of street sanitation said reassuringly, "we by no means neglect the residential sections."

"Vast, opulent beyond imagination," a reviewer called the Dunes' "Casino de Paris," a cavalcade of bare-breasted showgirls wearing $69,000 in feathers in a lavish production costing $5 million—the investment in a single Las Vegas extravaganza more than the combined total of the ten most expensive musicals in Broadway history to that time. There was a similarly impressive and expensive show outside, in the glaring sun of the Strip: mile after mile of gray board and chain-link construction fence, a dramatic backdrop of cranes, scaffolding, and superstructure, diesels and jackhammers, swarms of laborers at site after site, busy at all hours.

Las Vegas was building as never before, pushing its already massive hotels up and out, as well as planning new casinos, transforming, reinventing the famous corridor. By 1963, $100 million in fresh investment had paid for 163 stories of new "high-rises," adding more than 5,000 rooms—the largest, fastest, most concentrated sustained expansion of its kind anywhere in the world. The names of all the well-known hotels were suddenly high above the old signs, visible miles away even in daylight without the glow of thousands of lights. "It was like coming on some mystery city in the wilderness," a man remembered of driving in from Railroad Pass to the south, "like some eighth wonder of the world you never expected to see out here. It just showed up."

The new skyline included the Desert Inn's nine-story "sky-rise" and the Top O' the Strip lounge in the Dunes twenty-two floors above the road with a nearly 200-foot marquee replete with its own elevator. The Sahara soon rose to twenty-four stories. Down the row, the Sands, Stardust, Flamingo, Thunderbird, and Aladdin were all soaring as well, along with additions to the downtown Four Queens. The skeleton of the gangling tower and dome of the Landmark, with twenty-nine stories (later to be thirty-one), bid to compete with downtown's Mint for tallest building in Nevada. With Teamsters' money and Bank of Las Vegas loans pouring in, construction went on ceaselessly through the decade, with majestic new establishments appearing beside the high-rise additions. Soon, investors would break ground in the empty desert across from the Flamingo for the city's most lavish hotel yet, the first of Las Vegas's great "destination resorts," a place they would call Caesars Palace, deliberately omitting the apostrophe for copyright protection. It would be a casino of imperial theme to match the city's rising and expanding power: its lobby of gold leaf and Brazilian rosewood set pretentiously back from the Strip, reached by a 135-foot entrance driveway adorned by eighteen sparkling fountains, imported Italian cypress, and a phalanx of classic Florentine statuary.

With "pastel skyscrapers jutting upward like the minarets of Mecca," as *Denver Post* reporter Bob Whearley found the Strip in 1963, there was already an intimation of the end-of-century city. The skyline was to change, thicken, crumple, burst, and spike upward again in unimagined silhouettes and pretense, size, and luxury. But the future was being formed now. Whatever came before or after, many thought this building orgy of the 1960s the true making of the city. And it was spurred and paid for with hundreds of millions by a historic manipulation of union pension funds. Ironically, it would be the life savings of truck drivers and warehousemen that were given over to create the criminal and corporate countinghouses of the Strip. "Without the Teamsters," concluded a *Wall Street Journal* reporter, "there might not even *be* a Las Vegas."

The story of the money traced to the old war between capitalists and workers, in which organized crime fought and won on both sides—and to government intrigue, corruption, and drug trafficking, and to a beautiful widow.

For years after James Riddle Hoffa was born in 1913, his family mockingly called him "The Tumor," because the doctor in their small Indiana town had insisted Hoffa's mother had a malignant growth until she collapsed in labor. The boy was seven when his father died of poisonous fumes in a coal mine; four years later the family moved in desperation to the west side of Detroit, where the mother and children worked in commercial washhouses, and where he first met a young thug named Dalitz whose family owned one of the biggest laundries and who was making a small fortune bootlegging on the side. "Tumor" was eighteen and an eighth-grade dropout unloading boxcars for thirty-two cents an hour when he helped form a union local and called his first strike. "A born organizer," said a laborer who knew him, ". . . stood right up close to you and looked right at you . . . the sincerest little guy I've ever seen." Within months he was working full-time for the Teamsters Union, in the early thirties still a small, stagnant organization in mortal battle with company goons.

As Hoffa rose, he made his own alliances with hoodlums to protect his strikes, just as companies used gangsters to break them. He and other organizers were brutally beaten, arrested, and tortured in jailhouse clubbings, their cars and offices bombed. They "bore all as a badge," wrote one historian. "Who didn't get in trouble with the police," Hoffa would say, "was either buying them off or he wasn't doing his job." On the eve of World War II, a burly, bull-necked man of twenty-seven with an engaging smile and a convulsive temper, speaking his mangled English yet spellbinding Teamster audiences, he had begun to understand how the system worked, and soon learned more.

He was an admiring protégé of radical union organizers in Minnesota. But when they tried to leave the Teamsters and AFL for a more militant CIO in 1941, he took "a hundred crack guys," he said proudly, into the streets of St. Paul to savage his former mentors. He did it to get ahead in the union; he was already ruthless in stamping out any dissent. Yet the suppression had another effect as well, and held a portent. Hoffa was not only serving his own ambition, but in that process, inseparably, the vested interests of some of his putative enemies—of corporations and their lackey police and politicians who had already coopted much of the AFL, of organized-crime elements dominating AFL locals in the upper Midwest, and of the FBI and conservative political forces in Washington who saw the leftist specter in authentically independent unions. As so often in American history, no outright conspiracy had been necessary to see everyone's stake. The radicals' grassroots labor movement had threatened them all, and they came together in a tacit, implicit alliance of power and profit—liberal-minded Minnesota and the Roosevelt administration standing by while Hoffa's toughs acted as the bloody enforcers of a status quo of which the Teamsters were becoming an accepted part.

It was much the same sort of collusion Lansky entered into in Havana and on the New York docks, or taken part in by others among Hoffa's early associates, like Detroit mobster Frank Coppola, the godfather of Jimmy's foster son. For his own organized-crime interests, Coppola participated as a U.S. government agent in the CIA-instigated suppression and murder of Italian leftists and any other Mafia opponents in Sicily after World War II, violence that also secured Southern Italy for the Syndicate drug trade, and eventually massively corrupted Italian national politics. Seen from the inside, the lessons of the alliance, its imperatives, were simple. "The mobsters have always been wedded to the political system. That's how they survive," was how Arthur Sloane, an old friend of Hoffa's and one of his biographers, would describe a central axiom of American politics as the Teamster leader saw it. "Without that wedding, they'd be terrorists—and we'd get rid of them."

The bloody purge in Minnesota "launched him toward national leadership," Peter Dale Scott wrote of Hoffa, and also into "closer ties with mob elements in Chicago and elsewhere." If more popular with, and more attentive to, the rank-and-file, seemingly more militant in style than the vapid Dave Beck, he also embodied what one writer called "a cynical, caustic opportunism." As he and the Teamsters solidified their positions, they became part of the wider system born of violence and venality. To gain and keep power, union bosses like Beck and Hoffa bought business support with labor stability and politicians with money, the latter a gallery of famous officeholders, including Kefauver and Nixon, quietly or openly backed by Teamster money. Accordingly, often at the expense of their rank-and-file, the bosses would be maintained by the economic and political establishment as alternatives to more radical union leadership. Beck had allied with Republicans, and Hoffa would do the same, most conspicuously with Nixon, though many saw Hoffa as a populist, especially in battle with the Kennedys. In the end, of course, the politics of both Teamster leaders were themselves, their power. If Teamster history held any moral, it was not that racketeering was some evil intrinsic and exclusive to unions. It was also the expedient that corporate America had in part utilized in the early repression of workers' rights, and then, when organized labor took hold, readily condoned and furthered in the implicit bargain to prevent the rise of a truly uncompromised, independent union power—"the symbiosis between business and corrupt labor practices," as two social historians called it.

No figure, no union, charted more tellingly that larger corruption enveloping the nation than Hoffa and the Teamsters. Entangled with organized crime at almost every level, locals in Detroit, Miami, New York, and elsewhere were deeply involved not merely in racketeering in goods and services, jukeboxes here or contract kickbacks there, but in the Syndicate's drug trafficking as well. In the southern United States in particular, the union would be blatantly complicitous with the networks of major traffickers like Trafficante and Lansky, Teamster locals often sharing offices with narcotics dealers and acting as a depository or drop for both drug shipments and cash profits. Yet neither the McClellan Hearings in the fifties nor subsequent and sensational Hoffa prosecutions in the sixties exposed the drug scandal, one of the secrets mutually beneficial to all sides in a political culture in which the drug trade was already by 1960 so enmeshed with government intelligence, and providing large amounts of money to politicians in both parties. The drug connections were added proof of the pervasiveness and integration of the Syndicate—of Las Vegas—and proved again the folly of an Italian-surnamed, simplistically "criminal" view of the system. "The postwar national Mafia became consolidated laterally, through kinship exploitation via the Teamsters of an intelligence-sanctioned drug traffic," Scott concluded, "rather than downward from a hypothetical ethnic 'national commission.' "

By 1957, springing to succeed Beck, Hoffa had a long-standing interdependence with notorious hoodlums, among them Paul "Red" Dorfman, whose sweetheart insurance monopoly with the union made millions in commissions for the Chicago outfit, and whose name and legacy, carried on by his stepson Allen, would be notable on the Strip. But one outgrowth of Teamster activities quickly overshadowed the rest—the pension funds instituted by Beck and now taken over by Hoffa. Like much else, the retirement booty was managed not by union or Syndicate crooks alone, but with the collusion of business leaders and other management figures, some of whom were actual trustees of the fund while dozens of others knew of the abuses and went along to protect their own contracts and profits. Collected from over 177,000 members, the Central States Pension Fund begun in 1955 soon had more than $200 million to lend, and was thickening by millions every year. The money was a prodigious new means of influence, giving the Teamsters what others in the system—big business, the banks, government, the Syndicate—already possessed. "To reward friends and make new ones," was how Hoffa unabashedly talked about the pension fund loans. "Business was business," Sloane said of his friend's attitude toward the money. "He made no apologies."

Dockloader and agitator suddenly become financier, Hoffa seemed conservative with the pensions in his first years in power, letting banks place most of the money, loaning to reputedly respectable companies. It was deemed preferable that Teamster money, similar to much of the Syndicate's cash from its various enterprises, go to what one analyst called "declining old wealth firms," investments in New York real estate and Wall Street brokerage houses. These joint ventures with the Rockefellers and others often lost heavily, sometimes in legal-political machinations and "legitimate" corporate exploitation and plunder, but the finance was another mark of the quiet comity between supposedly separate, hostile worlds.

By 1957–58, Hoffa was suddenly doing less orthodox lending: to Cleveland Raceways; to cronies and pension fund trustees; and to motels owned by Jay Sarno, the future owner of Caesars Palace, altogether loans that sometimes lost money or proved a public embarrassment and were swiftly paid back while nonetheless setting a precedent.

The first Teamster money went to Las Vegas in 1958—$475,000 to assume a loan already made through Parry Thomas's Bank of Las Vegas—for the golf course Hank Greenspun wanted in Paradise Valley. Hoffa and Greenspun knew one another from trips to the Middle East—they shared strong sympathy for Israel—as well as from mutual contacts like Washington lawyer Ed Morgan. Hoffa's organized-crime intimate "Red" Dorfman had gone to the signing of the Greenspun loan in Las Vegas—"the vilest man I ever met," said someone who saw Dorfman there—and seemed on familiar terms with Greenspun.

Hoffa and Las Vegas were not necessarily the perfect match they seemed later. The gaudy libertine city was at odds, one might think, with Hoffa's own "utter absence of show on any dimension," as a biographer described the union boss's "irreproachable" personal habits. He neither smoked nor drank, and despite the hundreds of millions of dollars he controlled, lived in an unpretentious home in Detroit, drove his own car, and followed what a friend called an "almost Victorian approach to sexual improprieties." It was part of the repugnance he felt toward his famous pursuers. "There were the Kennedys going from Palm Beach . . . to Las Vegas," Hoffa's namesake son and successor would say. "He watched them . . . photos of the touch football games . . . family gatherings, but he knew differently. He knew the Kennedy men were chasing every skirt and he was disgusted by it."

Yet there was never the same scruple with regard to Las Vegas. Late in 1959, Hoffa loaned $1 million to Sunrise Hospital of southern Nevada, owned by a group headed by his boyhood acquaintance in Detroit, Moe Dalitz, the familiar figure the press would soon find so relaxed at the Desert Inn. Hoffa had lost touch with the mobster since the twenties in Detroit. They came back together now, ironically, through a woman they both loved, Sylvia Pigano. She was a sultry, dark-eyed union clerk, "an outgoing brunette of ravishing beauty," by one account, when Hoffa had an affair with her in the early thirties before both of them went on to marry others. Sylvia's first husband, a chauffeur for Kansas City mobsters, died not long after they wed. Soon she lost a second husband, in Detroit. Then, in 1940, she and her six-year-old son moved in with Hoffa and his wife, who knew Sylvia from union work. It was a curious household, the two women "good company," as a Hoffa biographer put it, friends and family insisting that Hoffa was ever loyal to his wife while doting on Sylvia's boy, Chuckie, widely rumored to be his own and later legally declared his foster son. Whatever the domestic drama, it had historic consequences for Las Vegas.

Dalitz, who had known Sylvia's husbands, "had a thing for her, too," as an acquaintance put it, and began visiting her whenever he was in town, soon developing close ties as well to the rapidly rising Hoffa. In 1949, as informers later told McClellan Committee investigators, both Hoffa and

Dalitz had taken substantial payoffs to stop a Teamster strike against Detroit dry cleaners, and their collusion grew over the next decade.

Dalitz's Sunrise Hospital was a cornerstone of a business empire beyond gambling, and in a sense the start of modern Las Vegas outside the Strip and Glitter Gulch. For the mobster, the Teamster funding represented only the first of tens of millions in pension fund dollars that would flow to his real estate and other interests in Nevada and beyond, including in 1962 the luxurious Rancho La Costa near San Diego, a resort infamous over the next decade and more for its numerous organized crime guests and connections. Dalitz's partners in Sunrise, La Costa, and other ventures, Las Vegas developers Merv Adelson and Irwin Molasky, would be launched by Hoffa and Sunrise toward their own fortunes and domains, going on to found in 1970 Hollywood's huge Lorimar Productions. Shored up by the Teamster underwriting at Sunrise and eased by governmental concessions and favorable contracts at every turn, the trio's Paradise Development Company shaped the emerging commercial and residential map of the city.

In 1967 they built Boulevard Mall, the town's first modern shopping center, and soon sheathed Maryland Parkway, a narrow road paralleling the Strip to the east, into a major artery. Their developments would epitomize the sprawling, hackneyed, exhaust-polluted grid the rest of the town became. All of it spewed in a sense from the original Teamster loan, and almost none of it was by mere free enterprise. Hoffa ensured the success of Sunrise by imposing on the Teamsters and Culinary Workers unions in Las Vegas a health plan requiring treatment at either Sunrise or else the grim Clark County Hospital. In the early sixties, Dalitz's hundred-bed facility admitted what reporters called "thousands of 'captive' [Teamster] patients." But the city and the Teamsters had seen nothing yet.

"If Moe told them to make a loan," said one observer of the moment, "they made the loan." In 1960, Teamster money began pouring in to finance the next round of casino growth, even beyond what the Bank of Las Vegas was providing with its discreet "character loans." There were the expansions at the Fremont, Desert Inn, and Stardust, including the latter's own eighteen-hole course laid out with "golf bags full of pension funds," as a reporter described the $1.2 million financing. Of the first nine pension fund loans, Dalitz interests received four, though Hoffa soon diversified his portfolio. Major lending followed to the Dunes, Landmark, Four Queens, Aladdin, and for the first portion of what would be more than $20 million to Sarno's Caesars Palace (there were more funds later for Sarno's cavernous Circus Circus). The ever ready Bank of Las Vegas, now renamed and expanded as Valley

Bank, handled most of the Teamster loans on the scene, an amount climbing over the decade past $100 million. Typically, Parry Thomas was in close and lucrative relationships with Dalitz and Hoffa attorney Morris Shenker, a Syndicate lawyer from St. Louis with myriad political and business connections as well as his own casino interests then and later. The Teamster ties and corresponding bank loans began to take Walter Cosgriff's once modest bank into much wider, murkier terrain, though much of that world would not be exposed for decades to come.

Soon the power of the Teamsters, and of the organized crime around and behind Hoffa, seemed a new arbiter in the city. "Jimmy was *the* juice," one Las Vegan said of Hoffa in the early sixties. With the loans—"they all had unwritten strings attached," a lawyer for the casinos recalled—came still more claimants on the skim, Hoffa allies from the Midwest and elsewhere who added to the welter of gang holdings and levies along the Strip. But the predominant authority in the city remained Lansky and his closer associates. "A lot of guys were coming in then on the split," said a longtime manager, "but these were still mostly Lansky joints." The Hoffa millions did nothing in the end to change that reality in the backrooms, though outwardly the union presence was conspicuous. Represented in Nevada by U.S. senator Alan Bible's law firm in Reno, the Teamsters became one of Nevada's largest creditors and mortgage-holders, and of its kind, even in a place accustomed to absentee, colonial rule, a distant force to be reckoned with. "Any ambitious businessman in Las Vegas would eventually run across the Teamsters, the biggest lender in the state," a Cleveland journalist wrote of the period. "They have bankrolled the better part of Las Vegas," concluded a writer for the *Wall Street Journal*. Still, significant as it was, that corrupt union financing—from which Las Vegas was supposedly rescued later by more respectable millions—only tended to overshadow and distract attention from other money no less vital to the city.

As Hoffa was lavishing his pensions on the Strip, construction magnate Del Webb, whose huge corporation was already publicly traded, was doing some casino investing of his own. Webb's CEO in 1961, an ex-carpenter named L. C. "Jake" Jacobson, had known racketeer Al Winter in Oregon, where they were both connected in the Northwest's business-union-political nexus of Dave Beck and Seattle-Portland organized crime. Using what one account called "the substantial resources and good name" of the Webb Corporation, Jacobson had helped Winter and his mob partners finance the Sahara in the fifties. A decade later, Jacobson and Webb were brandishing their corporate stock to buy the Sahara along with the Winter faction's Mint in Glitter Gulch, and soon added the Thunderbird and the downtown Lucky, as well as building a massive new Sahara-Tahoe casino resort on the south shore of the lake not far from Cal-Neva.

By 1965, the deals amounted to a Webb investment in Nevada of more than $60 million, rivaling the Teamsters'. Like the mob, Webb had easily gotten around the Nevada restriction on licensing a public corporation by simply creating what Jacobson termed a "conduit"—an entity called Consolidated Casinos—with a handful of licensees that funneled profits back into the barely separate parent company. Snaking through Webb's construction firm and eventually into the purchase and expansion of the casinos were millions in loans brokered by Wall Street's venerable Lehman Brothers, discreetly shielding the actual lenders, which included trusts of Princeton University, the U.S. Steel Pension Fund, and Morgan Guaranty.

Webb and his prestigious investors were not the first of their sort along the Strip. Even before Webb bought the Sahara, a Manhattan investment consortium led by Lawrence Wien, who also headed a group that owned and operated the Empire State Building, had bought the Desert Inn and promptly begun leasing it back to Dalitz and its other original hoodlum owners—just as Webb turned the lucrative operations of his properties back over to Syndicate figures. "I mean it was a sweet deal for everybody," said someone who helped arrange it. "Baling up money like farmers bale hay," Jacobson would describe the cash to be shared all around by corporation, stockholders, and mob.

Further on the fringes of conventional finance there was other money as well for the massively skimmed, massively profitable casinos. By 1963, American National Insurance, a giant Galveston, Texas, concern owned by the politically powerful Moody family with old ties to Sam Maceo's organized crime regime in Galveston—and where Parry Thomas's mentor George Eccles now sat on the board—was embroiled with Shenker and his cohorts at the Dunes. Before mid-decade American National became what *Fortune* described as a "big" lender on the Strip. By 1964, financier Troy Post's Greatamerica Corporation, through its Gulf Life and American Life Insurance subsidiaries, held mortgage notes on Binion's Horseshoe, the Stardust, the Sands, and even the Wien-Dalitz Desert Inn. The rapid, massive expansion of the organized crime–controlled casinos was costing a fortune; but as so frequently after 1954, someone else was paying for it. Along with the Teamsters, those "outside sources," as Thomas said to a reporter the next year, accounted for "some $120 million in mortgage loans . . . to Las Vegas gambling houses." Much of that money, too, like the Teamsters' funds, coursed through Thomas's Valley Bank. The affable Mormon banker offered "favorable terms that include secrecy," as one business writer described it.

By the end of the sixties, though public attention was focused on the notorious Teamsters, the union's pension funds were scarcely the Strip's only major financing. From the Ivy League, Wall Street, and midtown Manhattan to the steamy Texas coast, the Arizona desert, and the Mormon temples in the Valley of the Great Salt Lake, it was American capitalism that was also building Las Vegas in quiet alliance with and support of its organized crime masters, long before and far more than myth would have it.

This was the immense power facing Grant Sawyer as he looked out at the casinos from Carson City in the early 1960s. But even while he was running for governor, events elsewhere would fuel his regulatory zeal—a slip of paper toting the Tropicana take was found in Frank Costello's pocket when he was shot in a bungled assassination attempt in 1957; the next year Gus Greenbaum, alcoholic and debt-ridden, was caught skimming the Riviera skim, and he and his wife had their throats slashed. Soon after Sawyer's inaugural, he pushed through the legislature a bill establishing an umbrella five-man citizens' commission, to be appointed by the governor, to license, regulate, and collect taxes from the gaming industry, and oversee enforcement by Charlie Russell's Control Board. To manage a handful of investigators assigned to the commission's staff, Sawyer hired a rough-hewn ex–FBI man, Ray Abbaticchio, pledging "to keep known hoodlums from discrediting the gaming industry." Portrayed as Nevada's most serious regulatory effort yet, the result was another symbol of the unequal struggle.

Ironically, especially in light of events to come, Bobby Kennedy had written Sawyer trying to place some of the McClellan Committee investigators in Nevada jobs when the Senate inquiry wound up in the summer of 1959. Whether suspecting some veiled federal interference or typically quick to take offense at what he may have considered an implication that he could not find his own men, the governor declined Bobby's offer. In the same mood, Sawyer regularly fired off letters defending Nevada against periodic allusions in the national press to the state's unsavory characters. "Nevada is not for sale, it never has been, and I am sure it never will be," he wrote *Time* magazine's publisher Henry Luce in 1960, adding captiously, "I might point out that there are more churches per capita in Nevada than in any state in the Union."

Meanwhile, on Sawyer's orders, Abbaticchio asked FBN chief Harry Anslinger and other Washington figures for any files federal agencies could provide on accusations of organized crime appearing in the press, stories usually afforded by self-serving federal leaks to begin with. "Nevada was always good for some career-making copy," Sawyer would reflect scornfully. But Anslinger, like Hoover, routinely refused to give local law enforcement any meaningful information on the grounds of protecting agency "sources." The pretext at once preserved the bureaucrats' petty if all-important prerogatives, masked national law enforcement's considerable ignorance and dereliction as well as the inherent corruption in dependence on double agents, and further stifled Nevada's parochial, outmanned efforts. It made for mutual contempt and impotence among state and federal officials for decades to come. "May I suggest," Anslinger, resorting to the Mafia cliché, brusquely answered a Carson City plea for help in 1960, "that you employ competent undercover agents of Sicilian extraction who should be able to develop sufficient information and evidence for your Board."

By June 1960, the Sawyer administration circulated the state's first official list of excluded persons. Known as the *Black Book*, the three-ring-binder notebook held looseleaf mimeographed mug shots and summary records of those who were to be barred entirely from the premises of Nevada casinos, much less permitted to own or operate any of them. The use of a child's school supply item was fitting. The eleven men snapped into the *Black Book* that June, the first of only thirty-eight to be listed over nearly four decades, turned out to be caricatures—petty hoodlums listed in the Kefauver Hearings and even older records, most with Italian surnames; few of the men were of consequence. The exception made the point: number eight, Chicago boss Sam Giancana, who went undisturbed as a secret owner of the Cal-Neva for the next three years, and even longer as a recipient of the skim at several Strip casinos. "I own Chicago. I own Miami. I own Las Vegas," the Chicago mobster was known to boast.

There was a flurry around the *Black Book* late in 1960 when state agents tried heavy-handedly to harass one of those named in it, a dapper, high-rolling murderer from Chicago named Marshall Caifano, known on the Strip as Johnny Marshall. Credited with "some of the mob's most grisly killings," as a reporter put it, Caifano had been an overseer in Las Vegas, and now taunted officials by staying at several Strip hotels after the *Black Book* appeared, "warmly greeted by owners and ranking executives," according to one report. Leaving town eventually, Caifano thereupon sued the state, and to the surprise of Sawyer, who doubted the constitutionality of the proscribed list, federal courts upheld Nevada's right to exclude customers from licensed casinos. But Caifano turned out to be a rare case. From the inception of the *Black Book,* the state omitted from it most of Nevada's better-known Syndicate powers, licensing again or anew what one analyst called "a considerable number of individuals . . . linked to Meyer Lansky."

In Carson City's growing files on gambling licenses—newspaper clips, perfunctory interviews, and rubber-stamp hearings—there would be no question of looking at the colossal finances of the casinos, much less the reality of the skim, topics that would have allowed the state at least to begin to get at the true ownership and operation of the business that dominated their economy. It was an unseen war for the soul and future of Nevada, between Sawyer, who had scarcely been to Las Vegas before he went there for campaign money in 1958, and the world of Parry Thomas, Hoffa, Shenker, Webb, Wall Street and the Empire State group, insurance boardrooms and mob counting rooms. It was no contest. With crude ethnic bias and fitful if showy enforcement, the *Black Book* only added to the illusion of "gaming control" which was perceived to be part of the city's gathering legitimacy. Still, Sawyer's three-hole binder represented a more serious effort than much of what followed him in Carson City.

As the Kennedys took office in the winter of 1961, a small, symbolic episode took place in Nevada. "A shudder ran through," a reporter noted of the reaction in the casinos as Governor Sawyer reportedly passed the word "that the new administration might crack down on hoodlums." Within days, the powers that be on the Strip sought and received reassurance. "A careful check of Kennedy circles here indicates that such a drive against syndicate criminals appears unlikely," wired the *Sun*'s Washington correspondent. The warning was only Sawyer's "latest move in his effort to persuade casino owners to banish gangsters," the old bogey of federal action "an empty threat." There was, after all, the reality of power. "The federal government can't war on big-time gangsters because they work with the politicians," including "early supporters of Kennedy," was how the reporter summed up talk in the nation's capital. "The influence of crime in politics, business and unions is growing steadily," the *Sun* concluded matter-of-factly, "and prospects for checking this growth are small, if, indeed, they exist at all."

As attorney general, Bobby Kennedy immediately began the attack on Hoffa and elements of organized crime left out in the McClellan Hearings—"the insidious rot," as one account described it, "he'd identified as infesting the nation's innermost core." On entering Justice, he asked advice from the retiring Anslinger, who had quietly aided and influenced the McClellan inquiry just as he had Kefauver's. While he had peremptorily dismissed Nevada's requests for similar help only months before, Anslinger now brought Bobby "a thick black book with data on eight hundred hoodlums," as one witness described it. The volume, like most of the agency's files, amounted to a genealogy of the FBN's old, deeply institutionalized construct of the "Mafia," generally obscuring with vulgar Italian stereotypes the multi-ethnic character of organized crime and the wider corruption around it, and not incidentally diverting attention from key narcotics traffickers used and protected by the government in covert operations. Kennedy's own, more sophisticated concept, what one scholar called his "syndicate model," would be much less ideologically or bureaucratically distorted. But for now, Anslinger's thicker black book was important. From its rogue's gallery, Bobby and his new staff—recruited from ambitious young lawyers around the country, noted for "loyalty to the Kennedys and, ultimately, to each other," as one of them recalled—quickly designated forty men as investigative priorities. The names included Giancana, Trafficante, Hoffa, and others linked to gambling, Las Vegas, and the Teamsters, though, from the vantage point of the Strip, notably missing was Lansky or any of his major associates. It would come to be known as the "hit list."

The substance as well as brash style collided head-on with J. Edgar Hoover, already threatened and flaring at a thirty-five-year-old superior at the Justice Department who was also the president's brother, campaign manager, and soon principal adviser on foreign as well as domestic issues. As the second most powerful man in the executive branch and arguably the most influential attorney general ever, Bobby posed a challenge to Hoover and his FBI like no other in the director's more than forty years as a federal bureaucrat. By 1961, some believed it hardly mattered whether Hoover had been blackmailed for homosexuality, transvestitism, or other personal proclivities. His ties to figures on the fringe and beyond were blatantly open, men like liquor tycoon Lewis Rosenstiel, Joe Kennedy, Del Webb, Rosselli, the Murchisons of Texas, Marcello associate Dub McClanahan, and Patriarca associate Irving "Ash" Resnick, many of them regular companions at San Diego's notorious mob hangout, the Hotel Del Charro. Added to Hoover's reactionary obsession with leftists, his abuses of bureaucratic power, and his ceaseless self-protection and -promotion, it all led to an institutional as well as personal intersection of interests between the FBI and the Syndicate. Like its ugly counterparts around the world, including most notably the Soviet KGB exposed in later revelations after the collapse of the USSR, the FBI was in fact a mediocre political police, intent on repression of dissent, allowing organized crime and public corruption to flourish. In the bureau's New York office, which was by the 1950s a parody of Hoover's multiple manias, he had assigned four hundred agents to communism, ten to organized crime.

When, suddenly, sixty-three Italian crime bosses were found gathered at Apalachin in western New York in 1957, the event made national headlines. Many suspected that Lansky, conveniently absent from the summit meeting, had leaked information about it to police in order to neutralize his competition, and the explosive arrests seemed proof of a "nationwide Mafia" that excluded Lansky from suspicion. Hoover responded to the publicity, typically, by establishing with fanfare a "Top Hoodlum Program," and even adopted essentially the same contorted Sicilian Mafia model propagated by his despised rival Anslinger, albeit christened with a name Hoover could call his own—"La Cosa Nostra," the "LCN" that entered the jargon of the bureau. But the FBI's subsequent illegal wiretaps and coarse surveillance precluded prosecution, and at the same juncture, Hoover suppressed an internal FBI report charting the rise of a multiethnic Syndicate spanning the very years when he had denied its existence. Still, he remained a politically fearsome force in Washington and the nation, cultivating a massive dossier on Jack Kennedy and Lyndon Johnson as on so many others, and there had been no question in the winter of 1960 that he would be one of the new president's first reappointments. Toward Hoover in all his power and pathology Bobby was outwardly, thinly respectful, while privately savage. "What was it," he asked an aide when Hoover's longtime companion and deputy Clyde Tolson entered the hospital for surgery, "a hysterectomy?"

Their tortuous relations and FBI bungling later played a major role in Las Vegas. But on the surface Kennedy seemed successful in spurring Hoover over the first two years of the new administration, at least up to a point, and with dramatic results. Within three months of the inauguration, the government was able to deport to Guatemala a forever embittered and vengeful Carlos Marcello. The secret owner of the Tropicana and ally of Hoffa, Marcello, called "Mafia Kingfish" by his biographer John Davis, had opposed the Kennedys by long financing Lyndon Johnson, and then Nixon in the 1960 general election. "If I don't make it," Marcello told a hireling during his exile, "tell my brothers when you get back what dat kid Bobby done to us. Tell 'em to do what dey have to do." Meanwhile, the object of his hatred was making history. In 1960, there had been 49 indictments in organized crime; in 1961, the number jumped to 121, the next year to 350, and in 1963 to 615, among them some of the ranking figures at Apalachin. As never before, the attorney general was leading publicly what he called his "war on crime" while pressing within government as well, authorizing some six hundred wiretaps, using singular influence at the White House and beyond to give the effort "first place," as one scholar wrote later, "in the Kennedy administration's domestic priorities."

There were shadows that few noticed. The targets seemed selective to people like Doc Stacher, Meyer Lansky, Moe Dalitz, and others who knew Joe Kennedy's background in bootlegging, Chicago, Lake Tahoe, and Hollywood. Much of Bobby's most concerted and sustained action struck at criminal-political strongholds like Marcello's New Orleans or others in the Midwest and border states that were current or potential rival centers of power to the new White House, not only in Democratic politics but as significant sources of money and influence for Kennedy opponents across the spectrum. Left comparatively untouched beyond the prosecution of minor figures were such regional and national combines as the far-flung Jacobs interests radiating from Buffalo, and, most strikingly, Lansky and his even more extensive labyrinth of associates and protégés around the nation and in the Caribbean, the Philippines, and elsewhere—men and networks that had in common intimate connections to Joe Kennedy and to the political fortunes of his sons, and were major forces in and around Las Vegas.

Hoover himself came to suspect Bobby's motives in reverting to an Eisenhower holdover, William Hundley, to head the burgeoning organized crime section in the department. Hundley was a Justice bureaucrat Bobby had earlier deplored and replaced, but he was now brought back when an initial appointee proved an indifferent manager. Hundley had prosecuted notorious, Red-baiting Smith Act cases, rose to preside over the comparatively passive approach to the Syndicate under Eisenhower, and was close to Edward Bennett Williams and other Washington fixers. "Hoover was certain," a historian would describe the director's suspicions about Hundley and his friends, that " 'the hoodlums of Las Vegas had a direct line' " into the command post of Bobby's "war." It was not a judgment, even in his notorious excesses, that Hoover made often about the generally indifferent career attorneys in Justice; and the suspicion gained credibility when Hundley left Justice and represented Washington clients with unmistakable ties to Las Vegas organized crime figures.

Before Hundley rejoined him, Kennedy had targeted what one of the attorney general's young aides would call the Syndicate's "huge financial bonanza . . . its federal reserve"—the casinos of the Strip. If Carson City was still imploring federal officials for bits of intelligence on "underworld influences," the new regime at Justice had no doubt about what it was facing, especially in the "rotten bargain" cooption of local authorities. "We knew that despite superficial proclamations by Nevada state officials that appropriate measures were in place to insure the legitimacy of gambling there," Kennedy prosecutor Ronald Goldfarb wrote in his memoir, "the mob had infiltrated." They also "knew," he went on, that "skimming . . . had been big business in Las Vegas for a long time." The government attorneys were focused on the Sahara, Thunderbird, and Tropicana, among other casinos. The city and its financial maneuvers were defensively protected by what the attorneys called Nevada's "core community of roughly 10,000," who "knew where and how their bread was buttered," a category that apparently included JFK supporters like Governor Sawyer and Attorney General Roger Foley. "Kennedy was virtually obsessed with allegations regarding the power of organized crime in the Nevada casino industry," Richard Spees wrote. "Kennedy was convinced that the State of Nevada regulation of the gaming industry was ineffectual at best, perhaps influenced or even controlled by the forces of organized crime."

Even to investigate the skim, Kennedy's investigators believed, required an extraordinary and devious approach. They could not "impose" or "sell" local officials on an independent field office. "And we certainly didn't trust any office that was under local control," Goldfarb wrote later. "The federal courthouse and prosecutor's office were firmly in the hands of that core community, which for all its civic and personal virtues, our sources explained, was very protective of the area's main industry." As it happened, though, the U.S. attorney in southern Nevada was looking for an experienced trial lawyer, and Kennedy would assign him just the man. The new lawyer would have a "dual mission," as Goldfarb put it, to "make himself indispensable" in routine Las Vegas prosecutions but work on the side with select FBI and IRS officers to "spin out" a skimming investigation—in effect to work alongside the FBI and other federal law enforcement in Las Vegas as an informant and virtual secret agent of Justice. Washington would treat Nevada as hostile territory, a foreign power, as the state in turn would properly see itself invaded or usurped by an alien force of furtive purpose.

As Kennedy prosecutors planned their drop behind enemy lines in Las Vegas, Hoover was in effect forced to crack down on casinos too, though he kept his operation secret not only from Nevadans but from the Justice lawyers as well. Early in 1961, FBI agents leased twenty-five private lines from the southern Nevada phone company, to be connected to the local bureau office and billed to something called the Henderson Novelty Company, located at the FBI address. Posing as telephone repairmen, the agents installed taps at the Fremont, Sands, Stardust, Desert Inn, and Riviera.

Hoover insisted afterward that Bobby had authorized the wiretaps, and though Bobby, like his prosecutors, denied knowing of the bugs, there would be new evidence decades later that Kennedy approved much more wiretapping than he admitted, and than even his close aides knew. What was indisputable was that the taps were installed, like most FBI bugs before and after

Kennedy's arrival at Justice, without a warrant or court order of any kind. Almost immediately, the yield was impressive. Skimming techniques were candidly discussed—"twenty-one holes in the bucket," one practitioner was heard to say in describing "fool-proof methods"—as was the distribution of the "dividends" around the country by couriers with satchels in planes, trains, and cars, including references to Swiss and Bahamian bank accounts. At the Desert Inn, ostensibly owned by Lawrence Wien's upstanding Manhattan investors and expanded with a Teamster loan, the microphones recorded an often shifting twelve-way split in 1961 and 1962, the skim divvied up between Dalitz, Giancana, Brooklyn's Joe Bonanno, Rosselli, Lansky, and others.

At the same time, there would be glaring discrepancies between the casinos targeted by Justice prosecutors and those tapped by the FBI over nearly three years, perhaps the result of bureaucratic politics, or something more. For Strip insiders, the FBI omissions, when they became known, were telling. While Kennedy lawyers had singled them out, there would be no wiretaps at the Sahara, where Hoover's friend Del Webb was the owner and operational front for a skim as blatant as anywhere in town, or at the Flamingo and Thunderbird, both built by Webb, and where the skim went primarily to Lansky. Though other bugs implicated Lansky and his associates, they were almost incidental. The ultimate effect of the choices the FBI made in targeting casinos minimized Lansky's role on the Strip, seeming to confirm the later suspicions of Hoover critics and biographers that Lansky had blackmailed Hoover. "Lansky appears to have been protected at the top of the FBI," one scholar concluded on the wiretap and other evidence. "That protector was Hoover himself," according to a Lansky biographer, basing his conclusion on IRS sources and documents. In the end, what the wiretaps of 1961 to 1963 confirmed or concealed seemed scarcely to matter. None of it could or would ever be used as evidence.

In Carson City, it was a languid Friday afternoon in the summer of 1961. Grant Sawyer was set to go home early when Roger Foley called, clearly upset, and said he needed to come see him right away. Once they were alone in the governor's office, Foley told Sawyer that the Justice Department had asked him to deputize sixty-five men as federal agents "to invade every major casino in Reno and Las Vegas . . . to carry out this big raid on Nevada gambling." Preparations were underway for a force of more than a hundred agents from Washington and Nevada to descend on the casinos from floor to counting room, finding what they might, closing down houses at their discretion. "I was stunned," Sawyer would say.

Bobby had suddenly decided to stage a dramatic attack on Las Vegas. Furious about the raid and the short notice, and frightened for his career, Sawyer telephoned Bobby's office for an emergency appointment the next day. Late on a Saturday afternoon, the nervous, still seething Sawyer was shown in to see Kennedy. Sawyer was dressed carefully and respectfully in a dark business suit; he found Bobby in tennis whites, barefoot and hair tousled, as if he had just come off the White House courts, "or something," Sawyer added caustically in telling the story. It was in its way a classic American political encounter: Twin Falls and Hyannis Port, Carson City and Washington, and two driven, deeply self-conscious men making history neither ever really fathomed.

Was he actually planning to raid Nevada, Sawyer asked Kennedy, "and if so, why?" It set off "a heated discussion," the governor remembered in a graphic account thirty years later. The last time they had met, Bobby was begging him for Nevada votes at the Democratic Convention. Now it was Sawyer who was pleading. The state had "tried desperately" to cooperate with federal authorities, he said, to "clean up anything" that was wrong—"if they would simply tell us, we would take care of it," Sawyer said he told Kennedy. "But here in the middle of what we thought was a cooperative effort to deal jointly with our problems, I discovered this secret plan." He was "shocked" that as governor, and a loyal Kennedy Democrat, he had not been "extended the courtesy of being informed." The media sensation around a raid, he said, "could do our state great damage," and by implication Sawyer too. But there was "no give or compromise" in his listener. As Sawyer would always see it, Bobby was openly contemptuous of the state, and of its earnest, sorely offended young governor. "You're a bunch of peasants out there; you're all sort of sleazy," was Sawyer's later paraphrase of what the attorney general had "projected" if not literally said. "Everybody who lived in or came to Nevada was corrupt, including me. Bobby looked on me as someone who had just stepped out from behind a crap table, and he seemed to imply that I was connected with the mob, which really burned me up." As the confrontation wore on, the governor began to pound the table and both men to shout, and the meeting eventually trailed off to an angry end.

As soon as he left Bobby Kennedy's office, Sawyer called the White House for an appointment with the president. The next day he saw Jack Kennedy in the Oval Office. He told him about the proposed raid, the meeting with Bobby. "I got the impression he knew nothing about his brother's plan," Sawyer said afterward. Nevada was making progress on gaming regulation, he assured the president, and this "precipitous move on the part of the attorney general . . . would be terribly damaging." Most of all—he now spoke to the man in the rocker as politician—it would be a "disaster" for Cannon, Bible, Sawyer, Foley, the Nevada Democrats. "If all of us combined did not command enough respect from the Democratic Administration to stop this cheap, sensational move . . . if we couldn't do that, we didn't amount to much," he remembered telling the president. In the end, this was politics, and would cost them all dearly, even Jack Kennedy. "He understood my point," Sawyer would say. Typically, the velvet glove to his brother's ax, JFK heard Sawyer out, was "very cordial, very nice," the governor remembered, but made no commitments.

The raid never took place.

Even so, Sawyer never got over the episode. "I felt personally betrayed," he would say. "To have this administration turn on us immediately after the election was a bit of political treachery." He detested Bobby as no one else in public life, or, for that matter, in the world of gambling and corruption they fought over. "I didn't trust him, and I didn't support him later," he told an interviewer long afterward. "I wouldn't have supported him under any conditions . . . the thought that Bobby might become president of the United States was frightening."

What the aborted raid of 1961 might have achieved remains one of the unanswered questions of Las Vegas history. A swarm of federal agents would have generated the kind of publicity that would undoubtedly have kept some visitors away. Sawyer and other politicians might have paid a price with the Nevada electorate for evident weakness. But a raid would have been unlikely to catch more than a random sample of the skim, which took place anywhere between the floor and the counting room at different times in every casino, and in any event the more telling evidence of theft and secret ownership discovered on the illegal wiretaps would have been unusable. Bobby's threatened raid bore the marks of a gesture, "a publicity stunt as much as anything else," Sawyer would say. "Bobby Kennedy wanted to show . . . that he was the guy to clean up all sin and corruption, and Nevada was a great place to start." Yet for all that, it would have been a gesture like no other in the annals of the city. For the discreet business investors, the banks, the insurance companies, even for Hoffa's Teamsters and some of the Syndicate, and not least for Carson City's proud but diffident regulators, its cowed or corrupted lawmakers, it would have been a display of power at a moment when contending forces were being measured and crucial decisions made.

As it was, Sawyer's personalization of the whole episode—seeing the issue of regulation as a matter of his own prerogative as well as the state's—drew him more and more into the role of fierce defender of, if not apologist for, the Strip. There was no question now of cooperation between Washington and Carson City, where Bobby and Hoover were seen as twin scourges manipulating their law enforcement authority to persecute Nevada; the two men were "in the same category," Sawyer would declare, unaware at the time of the critical distinctions. At the end of his life the former governor spoke with bitterness of the battle. "There may very well have been some mob influence during my years in office," he told an interviewer, "but if there was, I certainly didn't have any specifics, and I am confident that the people in charge of enforcement and control of gaming couldn't find any . . . and the federal agencies that were claiming mob influence would not give us any information that we could act on." It was a defense and justification he maintained until his death in 1996, undeterred and only reinforced by the revelations of the Kennedy and Hoover scandals, as well as of Las Vegas's Syndicate control, coming to light in the last decades of his life. Bobby was protecting his father's and brother's corruptions, and Hoover his own compromising, Sawyer would insist to friends; and Nevada, whatever its faults, was a convenient scapegoat for them all.

There are two people I'd like to get out," John Kennedy confided to an aide during the 1960 campaign, "Jimmy Hoffa and Castro." As a senator he had welcomed Castro's victorious rebellion. But in the presidential race—resorting to the requisite chauvinism to offset Nixon's hallmark demagoguery—he expressed belligerence toward a leftward-arching Cuba. Three decades later, thousands of newly released secret documents began to show the result. In what amounted to an international political tantrum, an American president and his brother acting as his closest adviser stalked a foreign head of state. Their purpose was to counter a revolution, but if they had achieved their ends, the expedient corruption of their means would have compelled a small nation to submit once again to the old American combine of colonial power and organized crime.

Early in 1961, Kennedy allowed to go forward a CIA invasion of Cuba never approved by a wary Eisenhower, and the rout of a proxy force of Cuban exiles at the Bay of Pigs shook the White House only weeks after the glamorous inaugural. JFK blamed his humiliation on CIA bungling, while the American right and the gathering of Batista-era Cuban expatriates in

Florida were furious at the new president's refusal to give the invaders U.S. air cover. Defeat made Cuba a White House fixation—"an obsessive, prideful, competitive hatred," Gus Russo, a scholar of the newly declassified documents, called it in a 1998 history. To avenge the shame, to satisfy the rage it unleashed, the president relied increasingly on his brother, and it was Bobby who typically took on the mania as his own, personally scheming to kill Castro, to return Cuba to U.S. control—and, whether wittingly or heedlessly, to the rule of the Syndicate. A biographer would describe his clashing roles as "*de jure* head of the Department of Justice, and *de facto* head of the CIA." After Bobby's murder in 1968, a naval officer who had worked with him on plots against Castro shocked onlookers with his glee. "It was like a millstone was removed from his neck," said the man's daughter. "He knew Bobby, and felt that if he was elected, we'd have a mobster president."

The Kennedys hotly pursued the Castro murder contract with the Syndicate, sometimes through Rosselli, sometimes through their own team of gangsters, though government agents at lower levels worried that their organized crime cohorts were not taking the effort seriously enough. "Maheu's conning the hell out of the CIA," Giancana told Rosselli at one point. "How you goin' to kill that guy over there?" he added of Castro. "He's an assassin. He knows all the tricks." As it was, Giancana was less involved in the intrigues after 1961, while his original co-conspirators, Maheu, Rosselli, and Trafficante, remained active. "There was never a time a halt was called," Rosselli would testify concerning his own activity.

How fully or precisely the new president and attorney general knew the details of the alliance between the CIA and organized crime was never clear, and never so telling as the wider reality. Rosselli's missions, like parallel CIA operations, failed again and again. The Cubans captured some of the would-be assassins alive, and under torture, Rosselli and others would claim, "turned" them back as double agents. By 1962, the FBI began to gather evidence that Trafficante was indeed a Castro "mole." The Tampa mobster had resumed a Havana numbers racket, with part of the skim going to the new regime's secret police, and was already reopening drug traffic through Cuba, a concession U.S. agents believed to be in return for informing on CIA-Syndicate plots.

With each debacle White House pressure mounted. For a time JFK vocally deplored the inept intelligence agency, threatening to "splinter the CIA into a thousand pieces and cast it to the winds." But he also pondered his own guilt, and would come to believe that "the blame for the Bay of Pigs," as Russo wrote of the presidential brooding, "was largely his and not the CIA's." Nonetheless, despite Kennedy's enduring contempt and distrust for the spies, the old reliance soon recommenced. Only weeks after the Bay of Pigs in 1961, JFK ordered the installation of a direct line from the Oval Office to the home of the CIA's ever-zealous corporate shill J. C. King, the red phone in the ex–drug salesman's private study ringing, his family recalled, "at all hours of the day and night." For his part, Bobby worked briefly with alcoholic, gun-toting Bill Harvey, though he had Harvey summarily reassigned to Rome when the latter grew skeptical of their quixotic attempts at official homicide. Rosselli, however, would be in contact with Harvey and other agents long after the Kennedys supposedly ousted them.

The attorney general soon had his own personal liaison to his organized crime confederates, a CIA operative whose pseudonym was "Rocky Fiscalini" and who spent much of his time in Las Vegas. As an agent, "Rocky" was run directly from the office of the attorney general, where at the same moment Bobby was acidly dismissing Grant Sawyer as compromised by ties to the Las Vegas mob. "The time, the place," a ranking CIA officer remembered of "Fiscalini's" frequent meetings on the Strip, "was all arranged by Bobby Kennedy and his Mafia contacts."

The "contacts" were Rosselli, Trafficante, and other Havana casino figures as well—and their prominence left unmistakable the Kennedys' reaffirmation of Washington's acquiescence, its implicit if not explicit agreement, to restoring at least a faction of the Syndicate in a post-Castro Cuba. Even Harold "Happy" Meltzer, Lansky and Siegel's ranking partner in the Mexican narcotics trade that had helped found Las Vegas two decades before, would be enlisted in the alliance to kill Castro, the old drug dealer richly symbolic of the forces at play. As a congressional inquiry revealed later, Norman "Roughhouse" Rothman, a Lansky man and Trafficante's partner at the Sans Souci, attended secret meetings at the White House and Justice in 1961 and 1962. "The White House Cubans," exile groups studded with veterans of the Batista drug trade and Lansky payroll, conferred with the Kennedy brothers in meetings memorialized by photos that later hung in Miami offices inscribed: "Los Amigos de Roberto," or: "To my good friends from John Kennedy."

In the fall of 1961, Joe Kennedy, John, and Bobby met with Joe's close friend and ex-Lansky operator in Havana Mike McLaney to discuss "getting rid" of Castro, as McLaney's lawyer, Steve Reynolds, an eyewitness, eventually disclosed. Months later, after a moving appearance with his wife, Jackie, before the repatriated Bay of Pigs veterans at the Orange Bowl, the president himself met at McLaney's nearby Miami villa with McLaney, along with Rosselli representing Giancana and Trafficante. At another face-to-face meeting on McLaney's houseboat in Florida, again witnessed by Reynolds,

Bobby angrily poked a finger in the chest of his father's old golfing partner, ordering him not to damage refineries or other corporate properties in Cuba, since the assets "would be needed," as Reynolds remembered his words, "in the post-Castro period." Not least, McLaney was implicated in July 1963 when the FBI on a tip raided an exile paramilitary camp and weapons cache on his brother Bill's property along Lake Ponchartrain near New Orleans. The White House quashed prosecutions in the raid. But accounts of the incident leaked out from both local law enforcement and Washington sources, and the preparations for another invasion became front-page news in New Orleans and elsewhere, agitating partisans on all sides, including a supposed Castro admirer named Lee Harvey Oswald.

Meanwhile, the anti-Castro plotting produced a comic, sordid shadow play in Las Vegas. Giancana was anguished at one time that his Strip mistress, singer Phyllis McGuire, was cavorting at the Riviera with Sinatra. To keep Sam appeased, Maheu offered to bug the lovers' suite, the CIA dutifully paying for the break-in and tapping. But when Maheu's operatives botched the operation—catching McGuire with television comedian Dan Rowan instead of Sinatra—and as a result Maheu faced criminal charges in Las Vegas, the CIA had to suppress the case. Its agent Sheffield Edwards told the FBI that the tap related to a covert operation involving Maheu and Giancana, and Hoover promptly passed that lurid tidbit on to the attorney general in May 1961. Officially, the memo was Bobby's first notification of the CIA-mob alliance, though many scholars later came to believe that he had known for some time of the original government conspiracy with organized crime, and in any case was already embarked on his own covert war against Castro with his own Syndicate allies.

The following February, drawing on FBI wiretaps on the Strip, Hoover happily reported to the president and Bobby that one of JFK's women, Judy Campbell, was intimate as well with Rosselli and Giancana. The implicit blackmail was less than secret. "J. Edgar Hoover has Jack Kennedy by the balls," Lyndon Johnson exulted to a friend. The FBI director, therefore, would reign as long as he wished, the rumor went, whatever Bobby's distaste. Yet Hoover's knowledge of the president's Syndicate mistress, as of other lovers, did not prevent the president from persisting in the affair, if a bit more furtively, for another eight months. Not long after gloating, Johnson himself was under investigation, his nemesis Bobby probing LBJ's all-too-real ties to Marcello, and corruption around aide Bobby Baker, including Baker's financial partnership with Las Vegas mobster Eddie Levinson of the Fremont and Horseshoe—all aimed at driving Johnson off the ticket in 1964.

Meanwhile, the obsession with Castro went on. As JFK was ending his romance with Campbell, the Pentagon was readying operational plans for an invasion of Cuba as early as the autumn of 1962. The countdown paused that October only when reconnaissance confirmed that Russian rockets were based on the island. Conventional history would interpret the missile crisis as the sum of relatively apparent geopolitical motives, the jockeying of giants in an evolving balance of power. Documents that came to light after the Cold War, however, made clear that the confrontation was also very much an outgrowth of the relentless U.S. onslaught against Castro, Moscow trying to protect a client. And as most of the American conspirators knew, the covert campaign provoking the Soviets had much to do with the lost plunder of American crime and business in Cuba. In that sense, the stakes in the "offshore Las Vegas" would be a shrouded but fateful factor in the most deadly crisis of the nuclear age.

In the settlement averting war, Washington pledged not to attack Cuba in return for the removal of Soviet missiles. By the fall of 1963, however, Pentagon officers were back at work under White House orders on OPLAN 380-63, charting an all-out U.S. invasion of Cuba in 1964, victory in Havana scheduled for just weeks before President Kennedy's reelection.

Earlier, during the winter of 1961, events had begun to move toward endings for the Kennedys. That December, before Joe's Christmas tree arrived from the Cal-Neva, he crumpled with a stroke that left him able to see, hear, and comprehend, but to communicate only with a long "NNNnnnooo!"

In Las Vegas, Teamster money flowed, the building boom hammered on, the illegal FBI wiretaps spooled miles of incriminating but legally inadmissible information. Working with the IRS in tedious analysis, Earl Johnson, the Kennedy prosecutor as agent-in-place in the local U.S. attorney's office, was "building," wrote one of his Justice colleagues, "toward a major series of prosecutions." Later, in the early fall of 1963, owing to a chance moving of phones, but also after Hoover leaks of wiretap material on the skim to a favorite reporter at the *Chicago Sun-Times* aroused Strip suspicions, an operator at the Sands discovered one of the FBI bugs. Soon taps were found at the Dunes, Stardust, Desert Inn, and Riviera. Carson City was disgraced, and duly outraged, not at the skim but at the federal impertinence in eavesdropping. "Nevada officials went ballistic," a Justice lawyer remembered. So, too, did many of his federal colleagues unaware of the tapping—some, like Johnson, their special assistant U.S. attorney on the scene, were routinely lied to by the FBI. As casino lawyers filed the inevitable lawsuits, even the non-wiretap cases collapsed, and Johnson and his IRS auditors in Las Vegas were "demoralized," as a colleague put it.

The bugging sensation only reinforced Nevada's indignant laxity. To the Hoover-inspired *Sun-Times* series earlier that summer about a Las Vegas skim "in the millions"—a fraction of the actual theft—Sawyer's gaming commission responded with bland denial. "Skimming," as one account summarized the state's conclusion, "was a media-created phenomenon started by Robert Francis Kennedy." Sawyer sent Bobby local news clippings curtly asking for "information on this matter," referring to the wiretap. Furious again that he was ignored, suffering what he took to be another personal assault, Sawyer angrily charged Kennedy and Hoover with "violating state and federal law."

In early September 1963, there was a brief flurry of Carson City ardor when the ubiquitous Giancana, now reunited with McGuire, was caught, again by accident, carousing and fighting with McGuire's manager at the Cal-Neva. The state Control Board's current head, a crusty former newswire reporter named Ed Olsen, promptly asked Giancana's licensed front, Frank Sinatra, to explain the presence at the Tahoe casino of one of the *Black Book*'s few star gangsters. In characteristic rage, Sinatra answered by telephoning Olsen to spew profanity and threats that shocked even the green-eyeshade journalist—several "fuckings" per minute of a prolonged harangue. Given weeks to reply to a formal complaint, Sinatra's lawyers did not bother to respond, in effect defaulting. In one of the rare acts of its kind, the state revoked Sinatra's license by the end of the month—though not before calls to the governor from prominent Las Vegas figures, among them Hank Greenspun, urging Sawyer to "ease up on Frank" in return for future campaign donations. It was pressure so naked, even for Nevada, that the bristling governor told the press about it, albeit declining to name most of the callers, some his major backers.

There had been one other memorable intervention for Sinatra that Sawyer did not disclose for years. On a western swing, John Kennedy visited Las Vegas on the weekend of September 28–29, 1963, speaking to an admiring crowd at the Convention Center near Glitter Gulch. Riding in from McCarran Airport, he had invited Sawyer as well as Senators Cannon and Bible to join him in the presidential limousine. Though Bobby had already warned JFK away from Sinatra for his visible mob ties, and though Sinatra had blown up when JFK canceled a long-planned trip to the singer's Palm Springs home, the president could not resist interceding.

"What are you guys doing to my friend Frank Sinatra?" Kennedy asked almost as soon as the limousine pulled away from the airport.

"Well, Mr. President," Sawyer spoke up typically as the senators sat silent. "I'll take care of things here in Nevada and I wish you luck on the national level."

That night, as insiders knew and FBI files eventually confirmed, the president of the United States stole away from his official party to stay in a private cottage, provided for him now as before by Rosselli, who supplied as well what one account called "several comely prostitutes" from the Strip. It was the last time Jack Kennedy enjoyed the city he loved, where he always felt at home.

W eeks later, on November 22, 1963, an era ended. The murder of a president in broad daylight on a city street—the trauma, cover-up, and slow but sure public disillusionment—marked the onset of a civic cynicism only compounded by other assassinations, official deceptions, political scandals to come, and a loss of public trust massive by the end of the century. In an unprecedented act, the Strip paid its respects to the dead president by stopping play. It was only fitting: The connections of Las Vegas to the death of John Kennedy were as telling as his links to the city in life.

Whatever else he was, Lee Harvey Oswald came out of a history molded by the Strip. As documents released in the nineties revealed, he was deeply involved in 1963 in the intrigues around Cuba. Historians have endlessly disputed whether the tortured Oswald, directly or indirectly, struck for Cuba, for organized crime, for a renegade CIA, for a larger political-bureaucratic-criminal coalition—or solely, characteristically, for himself. It was, in any case, a supremely political act, altering the course of government and society. In a maze of cover-up and suppression, there is still no definitive evidence of his motive, or of the identities of co-conspirators, if any, in the shooting, and there may never be, though the Kennedy scholar Richard Mahoney in his masterful 1999 study *Sons and Brothers* provided compelling documentation of the "turning" of anti-Castro Syndicate assassins and their Cuban exile cohorts against Kennedy during 1963, including Rosselli's highly suspect movements before Dallas. But whoever alone or in concert killed the president, the craze that surrounded that glaring noon in Texas traced back ultimately to the "other Havana" in the Nevada desert, to its masters eager to exploit a proud, arrogant politician's mania to reclaim their "offshore Las Vegas."

Jack Ruby, Oswald's assassin in turn, embodied Las Vegas's essence and its enveloping influence in Dallas as elsewhere. He was the quintessential petty hustler and hanger-on whom Las Vegas spawned and sustained. Though his seedy Carousel Club was in Dallas, Ruby had named one of his earlier "show-bars" there the "Vegas Club," and in many ways the Strip was the center of his universe. Of his thirteen long-distance calls in the days before the JFK murders, part of an extraordinary flurry of telephoning around the country in the weeks after the president's trip to Dallas was first announced, at least seven were to his old friend Louis McWillie in Las Vegas. McWillie, Benny Binion's casino manager in Fort Worth, had gone on to oversee Lansky's Tropicana in Havana, had worked in Cuba with Rothman and in both Havana and Miami for Trafficante, had recently been a pit boss at Giancana's Cal-Neva, and by that fall of 1963 had gone back to the Lanskys' Thunderbird. Along with McWillie's name, Ruby's address book also carried the name of another Las Vegas intimate, Johnny Drew, a Dalitz crony and Stardust front man later involved in an extortion case with the *Black Book*'s Marshall Caifano, and Ruby was suspected of being in close contact with his longtime Dallas associate, Russell B. Matthews, in the days before the assassination. Matthews would go on to work for his old friend Benny Binion in Las Vegas.

There would be convincing evidence, according to congressional investigators in the late seventies, that the weekend before the president's assassination Jack Ruby went to Las Vegas, where he tried to cash a check at the Stardust cage, though neither McWillie nor Drew admitted seeing him in Nevada. His purpose on the Strip—whether to get money to pay his heavy debts at the time or something more historic—remains among hundreds of unresolved questions about the assassination. Only weeks before, in October 1963, Ruby had met Rosselli twice in Miami, where Rosselli had the clear impression, as he would tell investigative reporter Scott Malone, that "Ruby was hooked up with Trafficante in the rackets in Havana." Yet like the Las Vegas weekend, there would be no explanation of the Miami trip in any public inquiry, or in 4 million still heavily censored, still "redacted" government documents on the assassination released by the late 1990s.

Fifty-two when he shot Oswald, Ruby had long consorted with figures in and around Las Vegas. As a child he had run errands for Al Capone, gotten his start in labor racketeering in Chicago in the forties with Hoffa's friend "Red" Dorfman and politico Jake Arvey, and knew well two of the local hoodlums involved in the Las Vegas contract murder of James Ragen. Voluble, with a violent temper, never a major player but on the knowing fringe of so much, Ruby had soon become a protected informer for the FBI and FBN, and even for the Kefauver Committee, where his secret testimony provided information about Illinois vice and confirmed him as a small-time hood-

lum, but also had the effect of diverting attention from Syndicate drug trafficking, and from Dallas and the Chicago mob's postwar move there. Aptly,
Binion's old payoff man in Texas, Bill Decker—a vassal surviving in the postwar Chicago regime, who had driven Benny from Fort Worth to Las Vegas in
1947—was Dallas County sheriff in 1963; and Decker and his men, some of
them Ruby's friends, were prominent in the initial arrest and interrogation
of Oswald and culpable in the chaotic handling of the case exposed in subsequent investigations.

Only days before the assassinations, two of Ruby's former associates had
visited and repeatedly called him in Dallas, both of them implicated with
Lansky, Siegel, and Meltzer in the Syndicate's Mexican drug traffic through
Southern California in the forties. They were men he had not dealt with for a
decade, contacts now suddenly reopened in November 1963 for reasons no
inquiry has explained. Ruby was even linked to Oswald through his relationships with the lawyers who came to represent Oswald's widow and brother,
though that too went largely unexplored in official investigations. Not long
after the killings, Oswald's wife, Marina, would be provided legal aid and
patronage from the Great Southwest Corporation of Dallas, a real estate
venture controlled by a close associate of Bobby Baker—and ties from all
that wound back to the Teamsters' pension fund, through Washington
lawyer Ed Morgan, and ultimately back to Las Vegas.

Skeptical authors were right that such connections in themselves could
not prove conspiracy behind Ruby or Oswald. In letters and notes, in a
deathbed interview with his rabbi in 1966, in a prison diary fully explored in
1998 by Gus Russo, Ruby consistently maintained he acted alone, gunning
down Oswald "because I was so emotionally upset." But the unanswered
questions have remained.

In what a ranking agent delicately called "a hurry-up job," the FBI's
investigation of the assassination was the most bungled and bureaucratically
corrupt in the bureau's sullied history. The FBI was content to see Oswald as
a lone madman, with no further action or accountability necessary. The day
after the murder of the president of the United States, much of the world in
shock and grief, Hoover and Clyde Tolson, as was their wont, went to the Saturday races at Pimlico.

Only miles away, the CIA at its new Virginia headquarters hurried not to
provide intelligence on the murder of its own chief of state—a momentous
act in world politics, after all—but to cover up its complicity in schemes
against Castro, and its own history with Oswald, surveillance and indirect
dealings in Minsk, Mexico City, New Orleans, and Havana, junctures implicating the widely corrupted agency by omission and commission in the

killing of a president. Only decades later, in the release of secret depositions taken by the House committee investigating the assassination, would there turn up shards of evidence of the CIA's even deeper corruption, and with a Las Vegas connection. "John Scelso," the pseudonym of the still-secret CIA officer who conducted the agency's own internal inquiry about the assassination at the time, would tell Congressional investigators under oath that it was "known" in the CIA that counter-intelligence chief James Angleton had ties to organized crime. Angleton, Scelso swore, was implicated in CIA dealings with Oswald, while also moving effectively in 1962–63 to quash CIA investigations of the Las Vegas skim in Panama and elsewhere abroad, as well as in the United States.

Not surprisingly, politics and predilection shrouded every official inquiry into the assassination: a Warren Commission hostage to the executive branch's restrictions on access to information; the Church Committee of the mid-seventies refusing to confront the culpability of John Kennedy in the assassination plots against Castro; the House Select Committee on Assassinations in 1978–79 ruled by its staff's preconceived finding of a "mob hit."

For his part, Lyndon Johnson repeatedly confided to friends and aides that JFK's murder had been some kind of "response and retaliation" for the cabal to murder Castro, "a damned Murder, Inc. in the Caribbean," he called what he claimed he found out after assuming the presidency. "Kennedy was trying to get Castro, but Castro got him first . . . ," he told a reporter off the record. "It will all come out one day." But "one day" was to be far away. To press home an investigation in 1963 or 1964 of the "damned Murder, Inc." and what it provoked—to blame Cuba—only risked public rage, and either war in indulging that rage or political oblivion in resisting it. Beyond all that was the new president's own corruption, involving Baker and others, liable to be revealed in any larger exposure, particularly a scandal that provoked the slain president's grimly silent brother, who was said to have had a thick file on Johnson's corruptions on his Justice Department desk the week John Kennedy was shot. At every turn, Johnson had compelling reasons for covering up, and common cause in others' suppression, whatever their motives or complicity. The new president promptly canceled plans for invading Cuba, ended the plotting against Castro—and moved on to his own disastrous foreign policy in Southeast Asia.

For his part, Bobby Kennedy never again met with his organized crime section, never again made a pronouncement of any significance on the subject of the Syndicate which he had so recently thought the most dire threat to the nation. He was strangely mute and passive on the question of his brother's death—silenced, it became clear over the years, by all their own complicities in Cuba and elsewhere. Whatever the extent of his knowledge or culpability, he had taken the favors of Las Vegas, become indebted to it, in the election of 1960, and even beyond that he had used its men and its power in the dark war against Castro, and at the same time challenged and threatened it—in Strip terms cheated the house, played it for a sucker—and for that they would all pay. In the larger view of the corruptions they shared, it hardly mattered in the end who killed John Kennedy. Las Vegas had won.

In 1968, on the verge of his own presidency that might have menaced the city again, it would be Bobby's turn. As investigative journalist William Klaber and scholar Philip Melanson documented three decades after Bobby's murder, that historic assassination as well remained shrouded in cover-up, judicial folly, and inconclusive evidence, with haunting questions about whether a once-more lone assassin, Sirhan Sirhan, acted alone, or whether his gun killed Kennedy. In Sirhan's bizarre mental distraction and tangled past, however, one fact became clear—like Oswald, he had earlier had contacts and even held a job in the same milieu of Southern California horse racing and gambling Rosselli and others in the Syndicate knew so well and ruled so long.

For Bobby, as for many after his assassination as well as his brother's, the reach of the forces behind Las Vegas was always hard to believe. Not even in his own paralyzing grief and guilt could Bobby Kennedy always contain the new, piercing dismay of the acolyte and antagonist who had been so resolved and haughty, thought himself so commanding and worldly. "I found out something I never knew," he said of Dallas not long before his own murder. "I found out my world was not the real world."

13. "Cleaning Out the Sucker"

After the shepherd came across the remains of the dead lambs, he walked into the Nevada mountain meadow, where he found the lion waiting for him. The animal crouched to attack, but the man walked forward, unwavering, raising his *makila,* his walking stick, high above his head as his only weapon. The great cat growled in warning, a deep ominous rumble from its chest. The man did not stop. They were only a few feet apart when the lion, eyes burning red, sprang toward him. For an instant, it seemed they would clash. Then the animal arched suddenly in the air, landed on the ground beside the man, and retreated, snarling in defeat and shame.

Later, the man's son, who became a distinguished author, wrote of his father's valor, and another son used the brother's book to help himself become governor of Nevada. Some saw in the shepherd's story a simple man of almost biblical virtues, the kind of example Nevadans eagerly embraced, sending the book to their friends as proof that the state was not all corruption and glitter. Later still there were those who came to see it as something else, something more, the brave old man confronting a predator as Nevada and his son, one of its leaders, never could.

Dominique Laxalt had been in the hills for so many years—sleeping under a panoply of stars in a tidy camp of firepit and canvas bags, perfect utensils and a burned tin coffeepot, sage in the summer and quaking aspen in the fall—that he found no comfort in the easy chairs of his Carson City home. "He preferred to relax on the floor," his son wrote of the man who had immigrated from the French Pyrenees to the Sierra Nevada, "and though he slept alone and on high in an attic room, the family could hear him tossing until late at night."

Theresa Alpetche had come to Reno at the end of World War I from the Basque village of St. Etienne de Baigorry, not far from where her husband had been born. She was a chef trained at the Cordon Bleu in Paris who fell in love with the promise of a new life. When she married Dominique, he was the proud and prosperous co-owner of Allied Land and Livestock, a band of sheep ranches that crisscrossed northern Nevada and California, and he put her in one of the graceful Reno mansions on Court Street on the bluff above the Truckee River. But when the Depression came, they would lose everything—except for a band of sheep he took again into the mountains—and Theresa's gourmet skills would be exercised cooking grub over leaping fires in the high country sheep camps that dotted the mountains around Lake Tahoe. Later, when the family's financial situation improved, they bought the Ormsby House, a small Carson City hotel across from the gold-domed Capitol, where "Mama Laxalt," as she was known throughout the village of 1,600, served sumptuous Basque meals and abundant booze while her husband roamed the wilderness. "A man like that should never get married," she told her sons, "because he didn't go with a house."

Paul Dominique Laxalt, the first of their six children, was born in the summer of 1922 and grew into a lanky, circumspect boy the close-knit clan called "Pablo." But he was soon known as "Chief" to his siblings, the surrogate for a father who was at home only a few days a year, with the mother running a demanding business and raising small children. "At a very tender age, he had a lot of responsibility thrust on him," one of his brothers would say later.

Though he spoke no English upon enrolling in elementary school and was relentlessly bullied and teased, Paul had a characteristic fierce pride in his Basque heritage, what his author brother Robert called their "flaming shield." Waiting tables at his mother's restaurant, serving the state's power-brokers who frequented the saloon during the legislative sessions, he absorbed the political talk, saw the importance and influence of their world, and already coveted a life beyond that of the priesthood his mother had chosen for him. When Pat McCarran, a fellow Catholic and regular at the establishment, tipped off Theresa to invest the family money in property—"those damned Republicans will close the banks yet," he told her—the Laxalt boys listened, one of them remembered, with awe and respect.

Paul excelled in tennis—something cowboys didn't play—which brought further wrath from the sons of the valley's ranchers. They saw tennis as effete, and made fun of Paul in his white shorts, calling him "sissy." His father built a makeshift dirt boxing ring for his sons, and Paul "developed a long reach, a good punch, and considerable style," as one brother put it. A well-rounded athlete, he fought his way into the semifinals of the Nevada Golden Gloves, became a nationally ranked junior tennis champion, and learned golf while working as a caddie for wealthy Reno and Tahoe visitors. He was a "tireless student" at Carson High, as one friend remembered, winning honors. For all his responsibilities at home—making financial decisions on leases and mortgages for the family while still in high school—many thought Paul a smiling, almost jaunty boy, destined for success as he left school to join the army during World War II.

The war changed all that. A medical corpsman, he saw brutal action, and was nearly killed following the invasion of Leyte in the Philippines, a scarring brush with death Laxalt and the rest of the family never talked about. "The most miserable and depressing 53 days of my life," he recalled of the battle, with little elaboration in his memoir more than fifty years later. He returned to Nevada a broken young man. "When he came home he seemed to have lost the decisiveness and confidence that had always been part of his makeup," his brother Robert wrote. "Like a wounded animal, he went to the mountains and lived with my father until he was healed again." He found his solace and renewal at his father's base camp near Marlette Lake, a breathtaking body of icy blue water cupped in the dark green mountains 2,000 feet above Lake Tahoe. It was his "compass," Paul called it, a place where he would go to find his "soul," he told friends, dozens of times over the years to come. The father's camp, though solitary, was never lonely. "He [his father] gave the appearance of being a quiet man," Robert wrote, "but he was not silent. He loved to talk, and his voice had a mountain softness to it that one never grew tired of hearing." The shepherd's spirited conversation in his softly accented English moved briskly from family dynamics to state politics to world affairs. Finally, from Marlette, the weak, hollowed-out boy emerged whole again, revitalized, and embarked on what would be a whirlwind career.

Ordered by Mama Laxalt before the war to attend the Jesuit Santa Clara College in California—the "strict and authoritarian" mother, as one historian called her, still hoping to turn out a man of the cloth—Paul had majored in history, and for a time after his service as a corpsman even thought about going to medical school. But he was too "impatient," he admitted later, to take the added scientific courses required, and after his discharge and recuperation at Marlette went back to Santa Clara for law school.

"My dad didn't think I had brains enough to be a sheepman," Laxalt once joked, "so he sent me to law school." After struggling through the first year, however, he transferred to the less demanding University of Denver, where he seemed to regain his boyhood luster, graduating at the top in his class and distinguished as a student leader and scholar.

It was 1949, a time when Siegel's Flamingo and Dalitz's Desert Inn were flourishing, and a defining moment in Paul's life and that of the state. As a boy and young man, he had been shaped by two worlds: Around his father's campfires he learned of a simpler, older Nevada "when bankers and businessmen in high white collars," Robert Laxalt wrote later, "talked big money with dusty men who smelled of leather and sagebrush, and money still had a soul in it, because these men had fought for it with sweat and blood and honest toil." But he had also seen the grasping, the crass politics, and the soulless money of the emerging regime in Carson City, the society from which his father had in part fled, but where his mother still sought financial success and the family's social vindication. When he returned from law school, he would make his choice about the world he intended to inhabit.

In 1946 he had met and married Jackalyn Ross, an aspiring writer who abandoned her own plans after "falling in love with the legs of a man named Paul," as she laughed later. Her father, John Ross, was a right-wing Republican lawyer who was appointed a federal judge, and he soon became Paul's political mentor. He joined his father-in-law's firm, then ran for district attorney in his home county of Ormsby, a move some saw as audacious for a man a year out of law school. He won. When he returned three years later to practice law with his venerable elder partner, he was now on an equal footing. During the fifties they built the firm, which now included his brother Peter and brother-in-law John Ross, into a profitable enterprise whose key clients were Harvey Gross and fellow Basque Johnny Ascuaga, owners of two of northern Nevada's most prominent casinos.

Under Nevada law, the governor and lieutenant governor could be from different parties, and when Democrat Grant Sawyer's Republican lieutenant governor, Rex Bell, decided to run against him for governor in 1962, and was looking for a running mate, he sought advice from his old friend Ross, Sr. Bell, a cowboy movie idol who was married to silent-screen star Clara Bow, assumed he had the southern part of the state covered thanks to his flamboyant celebrity, but needed a native northern Nevada family name to round out the ticket. Ross recommended his son-in-law—"a six-footer with close cropped, grey-black hair who fits into the old fashioned log cabin tradition with a Basque twist," as a Reno journalist described him at the time. "The GOP was nothing to speak of in those days," one Las Vegan remembered, "but with the bipartisan McCarran machine busted up, they set out to rebuild the party."

In accordance with Laxalt family protocol, the decision about whether Paul would run for office was made among the siblings around the family's lace-covered dining table, with the strong-willed matriarch serving platters of tripe, lamb, and potatoes, the dark-eyed brothers smoking cigarettes and drinking the stiff Basque cocktails called picon punches. Ever prodded by Mama Laxalt, who never forgot the slights she and her children had suffered in their adopted land, who knew that the immigrant family's stature, as well as her own social acceptance, was now dependent on her firstborn's rise, Paul himself was surprisingly reluctant. ("Bell practically roped and hog-tied him into running with him," recalled a friend.) With careers of their own in law and journalism, the three brothers were nonetheless expected to "drop whatever they were doing," as one insider remembered, "and focus their lives on furthering Paul's climb." By this time Paul "absolutely controlled the family," said one who knew them, "emotionally and financially," as the roving Dominique visited home ever less frequently. "Paul expected his brothers' loyalty and devotion, and he would get it from them in spades." Once the decision to run was made, it would be a family pursuit unlike any the state had seen, an us-against-them struggle that would bind the family fiercely, and, ultimately, decades later, divide the brothers and their own children even more savagely.

From the start, Sawyer would be pitted against not one but two macho cowboy images—whether real or confected—in a state where nearly every politician for a hundred years "had sprung from ranching roots," as one author described it. The crew-cut, bespectacled Sawyer—"a man on the move," as his campaign literature declared, whose photograph doing the risqué twist with a mobster's wife had been published in the Soviet Union's *Izvestia* as evidence of America's degeneracy—would have a hard time holding his own in the dozens of requisite parades throughout the hot summer stumping in which all candidates were expected to ride horseback. The first time Sawyer rode in Las Vegas's wildly popular "Helldorado Days," the governor entered the procession holding onto the saddle horn with one hand, a *faux pas* that set him instantly apart as a greenhorn in a state in which fifteen of the seventeen counties were still dominated by ranchers. As if that were not bad enough, he held on tightly to the spanking-new Stetson he had bought for the occasion—"so big on him it covered his ears and almost his eyes," according to one observer. Bell, on the other hand, was resplendent in his polished leather chaps, hand-tooled Garcia saddle, colorful Navajo blanket, silver-studded bridle with braided reins, and darted satin shirt from the western-wear store he owned. Fresh off his Searchlight, Nevada, ranch, his spirited stallion trotted along on the steaming asphalt of Fremont Street, as Bell stood in the stirrups and waved to the roaring crowds. "It was like riding next to frigging Gene Autry," a Sawyer intimate remembered.

Now Sawyer had not only Bell to contend with but Laxalt too, the offspring of what Laxalt's campaign rhetoric billed as a "longtime Nevada livestock family." And though in the future some would claim he actually had no riding expertise at all, having been frightened by a runaway mustang, in 1962 the tall, tanned lawyer in lizard-skin boots had his own movie star good looks. He also had what the local press was dubbing "the Kennedy charisma"—a pert brunette wife named Jackie, the Catholic overachieving siblings, conveniently named John and Robert; an essential nun in the family, Sister Mary; and six children of his own, three of whom were adopted.

But, in a turn of events bizarre even for Nevada politics, the showy Bell would have but sixteen days to live after filing for office. At a blistering Fourth of July rally at a Las Vegas park, he fell ill and died of a heart attack later that evening in the arms of his longtime mistress. "Grant was genuinely fond of old Rex, whom he thought a real gentleman," remembered a Sawyer aide, "but he had a hard time feeling sad about the death that assured his reelection."

Many on the Strip encouraged Laxalt to switch from the lieutenant governor's race to governor, feeling he could unseat Sawyer and his hated *Black Book*. Insecure and "feeling like a neophyte in the statewide process," as a friend remembered, Laxalt demurred, leaving the rare open slot to Hank Greenspun and Las Vegas mayor Oran Gragson, the latter trouncing the irascible, ambitious publisher in a runoff. Sawyer prevailed in the general election, Laxalt won his race handily, and for the second time Sawyer would be saddled with a Republican lieutenant governor. The enmity between them was to continue for decades.

For his part, Laxalt used his newfound status and strength to run two years later against the Democratic senator, Howard Cannon. Chairing the powerful Senate Rules Committee then investigating Bobby Baker, including Baker's ties to Las Vegas gamblers Eddie Levinson and Cliff Jones, Cannon was vulnerable, having acquired a reputation as a "puppet of the industry," as one observer described it. Laxalt enlisted the literary gifts of his brother Robert to attack Cannon with articulate and hard-hitting accusations. Robert's recently published memoir of their father called *Sweet Promised Land*—the title taken from a poem by Nevadan Walter Van Tilburg Clark— had received national attention, while also bringing the Laxalt family into statewide prominence. "Frenchie," as the well-liked younger brother was known, "ran the show for Paul," a friend said, "writing all speeches, press releases, and using his considerable talent and cachet with the reporters in the state."

A Reno newspaper described Paul Laxalt as a "stickler for honesty and integrity" after he gave up his biggest legal clients to avoid the appearance of a conflict of interest. Then he went after what he termed Cannon's "corruption" with a vengeance. He leaked to the press that the senator had flown on a plane sponsored by Bobby Baker to a fund-raiser in Las Vegas that toted an unprecedented $100,000 for Cannon's campaign, even producing a flight manifest that listed the names of several notorious capital fixers on board the flight. The Laxalt brothers blanketed the state with charges that Cannon had manipulated the Baker probe, not only as a favor to his longtime political ally Lyndon Johnson, but to hide his own vast compromises as well. "Cannon first crippled the investigation by setting the appropriation at $10,000 instead of the requested $100,000," Laxalt charged, claiming the senator then went on to block the appearance of key witnesses and effectively soft-pedal the inquiry of Baker. "For the first time in our history, a senator from Nevada has become suspect in the nation's eyes," he said, "and brought shame and embarrassment to the state."

Laxalt's name already being bandied about as a vice-presidential contender with his "good friend Barry Goldwater," who was seeking the presidency that year, he seemed to be "riding high," as an observer recalled the fall of 1964. But in what was seen by the media as "one of the closest, most contentious races in modern Nevada political history," Laxalt lost to Cannon by 48 votes out of 134,000 cast statewide. The defeat traced to what one insider called "shenanigans on the Westside," where the results in Las Vegas's ghetto were too one-sided to be credible, prompting rampant allegations of tampering with voting machines. A candidate for lower office who campaigned there said he knew "for certain" that "at least ten percent of the Negroes over there were too unhappy" to have possibly voted for an incumbent. "Look what we've got over here," one woman who lived in the ghetto told him. "I've got four children. Look at their soles coming out of the shoes. They got no clothes to wear." Cannon's Democrats had not only fixed the voting machines, Laxalt operatives would be told by their sources, but had spread the rumor in the black community that Basques had been some of the first slave traders.

The defeat, like his war trauma, drove him to a Marlette retreat. His loss was intensified by the recount he finally obtained, only to fall short again, by 84 votes. If the suspicion and rancor of Richard Nixon could be traced in part to the theft of the 1960 presidential election, so too would Paul Laxalt emerge a different man from the searing, suspicious defeat of 1964. He and his brothers would vow that such ignominy and humiliation would never stain the clan again. "What children we were," Robert Laxalt would write in his notes of those early political trials. "But even children learn fast."

I t was his first known walk on the edge," was how Dan Moldea described the thousands of dollars Laxalt would take in the 1966 campaign from major Syndicate figure Ruby Kolod in what many believed was perhaps the single most significant and decisive gubernatorial campaign in the state's history. Patronized by the Strip in his first run for governor in 1958 and continuing to get some of its contributions in 1962, Grant Sawyer was now the gamblers' target. "As an old man," a Sawyer intimate remembered, "Kolod had vowed to spend his every last dollar defeating Sawyer." Kolod and his Desert Inn mob partners were more than happy to throw their full support to Laxalt, giving him $200,000, according to author Gabe Vogliotti. Sawyer's men had revoked Kolod's gambling license pending the appeal of his extortion conviction, and "to add insult to injury his administration had prohibited Moe Dalitz from acquiring a second casino—the Riviera," as one Las Vegas politician put it. Between Kolod, Dalitz, who referred to Laxalt as "my man," and the disenfranchised Frank Sinatra still smarting from Sawyer's ejection of him from Cal-Neva, the Basque lieutenant governor was "rolling in dough," as a campaign insider recalled. Sawyer had further antagonized the gamblers by lobbying hard against efforts to allow the multiple licensing of casino owners, which meant that a licensed Nevada casino owner could own only one casino in the state. In addition, Nevada law prohibited license holders from investing in gambling operations anywhere else in the world, and Sawyer was firmly opposed to attempts to change that legislation, as well as to proposed corporate gaming laws that would have allowed publicly traded companies to be licensed casino owners. Sawyer "had been instrumental in killing corporate gaming bills in both the 1963 and 1965 legislatures," according to one historical account, fearing that corporations would "shield ownership by organized crime." The "whole Strip," a political observer summed up Sawyer's bid for a third term, "was pretty much lined up against him."

Despite all the casino money, Laxalt somehow portrayed himself "as a fresh, young Republican, the unfortunate victim of election chicanery who was taking on an aging Democratic political machine and entrenched governor," as Richard Spees, a onetime Laxalt aide, wrote. He found himself in the unusual position of building a political base on the Strip while "reassuring the FBI he would clean it up," journalists Peter Wiley and Robert Gottlieb later wrote. "He arrived in Las Vegas with his hand on his wallet," a Republican official recalled. Laxalt attacked Sawyer's battle with the FBI not only as unpatriotic—"if Sawyer wants to make irresponsible charges like this against one of the country's most honored men, he should not drag the rest of the state in with him," he would say—but as detrimental to the state's interest. With the skillful prose of his brother Robert, he vowed to work hand-in-hand with Hoover to "erase the image that we are in bed with hoodlums." Sawyer's challenge to Hoover to "give us your evidence or call off your dogs" only "intensified federal suspicion and surveillance," the casino owners believed, according to Spees.

Laxalt became one of the first of Nevada's modern politicians not just to defend the "rotten bargain" but to champion it openly, depicting gambling as an industry that had "lifted the state from economic backwardness to prosperity," as Robert's personal notes of the campaign put it. He refused to apologize for maligned Nevada making "above-board" what "existed . . . in crooked and dirty backrooms" throughout America. The state's economy is built on gambling, he argued, and "it is sheer hypocrisy to pretend anything different." In a tangled blend of Basque pride, self-righteousness, and a passion for sovereignty, Laxalt appealed to the earnest pioneer spirit of his constituency. "Just plain honesty about the facts of life is what is good about the state of Nevada," he said, "the most live-and-let-live state in the union." He attributed the natives' toughness to the harshness of the land itself. "All we have to do is take a good look at the deserts to remind us of this." He termed the specialness and independence of the place "a Nevada state of mind." Laxalt argued that the problem was not gambling, but Sawyer, for having "failed to protect the state's largest industry from corrupting influences." "Who owns Nevada?" Robert would pose the rhetorical question of the race. "The hoods, us, or the FBI?"

When Sawyer said in an interview aired on national television that he didn't know whether any skimming was going on in Las Vegas, Laxalt roundly attacked him. "After eight years in office, this is an appalling admission." "Sawyer's voice fell silent," as one journalist put it, when Sandy Smith of the *Chicago Sun-Times,* in the middle of the campaign, "armed with leaked Justice Department documents of the mob's skimming . . . made a mockery of the state's gaming licensing requirements and enforcement practices." Then later that summer, the FBI confiscated tons of crooked dice carrying the insignias of the Riviera, Stardust, and Dunes at a plant in Oklahoma. Also seized, according to press reports in other parts of the country, were "craps tables rigged with electromagnets to control the roll of the loaded dice, hundreds of decks of marked cards, electrical wiring of roulette tables so that a croupier could pick the winning number, and other gambling tables with electric wiring concealed in the legs." Now, Sawyer's contention that his officials' spot checks of casinos prevented the use of crooked equipment was also under fire.

It was a vicious campaign, with Hoover himself writing a letter harshly criticizing Sawyer—something Hoover had never done to a sitting governor before; Sawyer's longtime rival Greenspun highlighted it on the front page of his paper. "In those days, no one went against the almighty Hoover and came out alive," Sawyer reflected years later. "This was long before the evidence of his massive corruption became known."

Even with some celebrity endorsements—"a real swinging cat," Sammy Davis, Jr., would call Sawyer in a television spot, along with a favorable pitch from big Dan Blocker, who played Hoss Cartwright on *Bonanza*—the beleaguered Sawyer campaign fell into a slump. A staggering blow came when LBJ refused to visit the state for him, rekindling the old wounds of the 1960 Democratic Convention. Sawyer's Kennedy ties had alienated him from the Johnson forces, and his failed machinations to deliver Nevada for Kennedy, combined with his subsequent battle against Bobby, had distanced him from what was left of the Kennedy camp as well. Uncharacteristically, the White House hid behind states' rights, declining Sawyer's plea for help. "The election is a Nevada matter," the president's spokesman contended in a statement dripping with irony, considering how many times LBJ had stumped for his toadies Cannon and Bible, "and it is only proper that it be decided by Nevadans." But Sawyer knew the real reason for LBJ's punitive action was his close friendship with "that goddammed J. Edgar Hoover," whom Sawyer had likened to Hitler, and whose tactics had been called "Nazism" by Sawyer's chief aide. "When the election was over," Laxalt would later write, "the FBI people felt that it was as much a victory for J. Edgar Hoover as for Paul Laxalt."

What may have been the final blow to Sawyer, and a portent of the destiny of the Laxalt clan, was the decision to turn Robert Laxalt's gentle *Sweet Promised Land* into campaign propaganda. "That moment is when the family made its own Mephistophelian bargain," remembered a longtime political observer. Mass-distributed throughout the state, "the deep blue book," as Robert's daughter Monique would call it for the color of its original cover, was meant to equate the depth and integrity of Paul with that of his proud and honest shepherd father. "The day the deep blue book was given up," Monique wrote thirty years later in *The Deep Blue Memory*, her own moving *roman à clef* about the prostitution of her father's work of art and more, would mark the beginning of the haunting of the family.

While the "deep blue book" evoked passionate feelings in Nevadans even as its misuse cast a shadow on the clan, there would be a sinister specter of Nevada's future when Laxalt was elected. In the background of that pivotal 1966 gubernatorial campaign was a man secretly funneling untold thousands to Laxalt, someone who could not have been further from what the brave immigrant sheepherder symbolized. Yet Paul would welcome this phantom as absolution, salvation, and cleansing for the state. "Las Vegas as Lourdes," one journalist cynically called the city's next phase.

I t was a fine American story of money and redemption, something every-one wanted to believe, a tale men plundering Las Vegas needed to have people believe—one of the determining myths of the city, and the nation.

Howard Robard Hughes, Jr., was one of the richest people in the world, a businessman of legendary genius, a dashing, romantic celebrity. One night he came to the Las Vegas he loved for a private holiday, away from publicity he famously shunned. He overstayed his reservation in the hotel penthouse. When the owners asked him to make way for other important guests, to keep his rooms he bought the resort. He went on to purchase more casinos, a tele-vision station, much of Nevada. He decided to use his fantastic wealth to make Las Vegas into an even more impressive showplace in the desert.

In his grand gesture, it was to be believed, he bought out the disrep-utable elements that threatened the city's prosperity. Single-handedly, tycoon as hero, he ransomed Las Vegas from its unsavory past, staved off looming scandals, and made gambling at last a legitimate investment for reputable, corporate America. No Nevadan actually saw him behind the shuttered windows high above the Strip. But respected men, leaders of the community—a senator, a governor, a publisher, a banker, prominent lawyers—all vouched for the story, saying Hughes was Nevada's benefactor, its deliverer.

Almost none of it was true.

N o figure of his era was more reclusive yet invited more attention, retained such mystery and fascination despite the millions of words written about him from gossip columns to high court briefs. Yet what was most significant about Hughes was no enigma. The life he lived paralleled in many ways the course of the country over the same seventy years. From the sweaty wild-catting of turn-of-the-century Texas oil fields to clammy, closed-door intrigues of the Cold War and big-money politics, Hughes's progress was an allegory of the nation's passage.

He was born soon after the century, in an oil derrick–filled Houston pulsing with the country's reach for its treasure, and into a family, like many, divided between public striving and private torment. From a neurotic, possessive mother he took what became a pathological obsession with germs and bodily functions. From his sterner father he inherited one of the great, quintessentially American fortunes, built from the invention of a drill bit vital to a petroleum-ravenous world. He grew up a shy, suspicious boy, indifferent to education and with no evident talent. Then, orphaned at eighteen, he suddenly, unpredictably asserted himself on the death of his father, buying out relatives to assume sole control of Hughes Tool, the enduring, expanding basis of his legacy as he went into the movie business and other enterprises. Rake in the spree of the twenties, record-setting pilot in the escapism of the thirties, he became a celebrity tailored to the fashion and fantasy of his time, even given a ticker-tape parade down Broadway after an around-the-world flight. But it was 1938, and one of the last of those pageants for the country, and for the man.

Begun as a small machine shop servicing his personal plane, Hughes Aircraft became in World War II a major military contractor. Yet the company's Hercules flying boat, nicknamed the "Spruce Goose," the largest airplane ever built and flown only once, became what reporters called "a symbol of government waste." Losses on the plane were but the first of public millions squandered by Hughes's inefficiency and bungling. There was more folly: the crash of another amphibian plane into Lake Mead, the near-fatal crash of a prototype photo-reconnaissance spy plane in Beverly Hills in 1946 (into houses on the same block where his friend Bugsy Siegel would be murdered less than a year later). The latter crash left Hughes in grinding chronic pain, and dependent on ever stronger medication. But he survived, and indignantly parried congressional critics trying to expose his mismanagement. Besides being an industrialist, the seemingly apolitical magnate was, again in the temper of the postwar times, an ardent anti-Communist, lauded by politicians like Nixon for firing an alleged subversive from his movie studio even as others questioned his Pentagon waste. Failures, crashes, profligacy seemed only to magnify Hughes's aura, the prewar adventurer, again like the country, now turned to the serious, sacred business of national security, where price was no object.

By the mid-fifties he was "rich beyond imagination," as Canadian journalist Gerald Bellett described the old drill-bit wealth multiplied many times over by Cold War contracts. As always, money made him mythic. He could lose millions of dollars a year in this venture or that, and still be presumed a business marvel. He could cost the public millions in waste or failure, but the money hemorrhaged from unaccountable "black budgets," and so still the contracts kept coming. Once again he was an archetype, now of the military-industrial fashion in electronics and hardware for weaponry and the space race. By now, also, he controlled Trans World Airlines. When he sold TWA a decade later after years of legal machinations and a stockholders' revolt, the episode was a harbinger of the tortuous corporate intrigues and transactions that typified the last decades of the century; at the moment it was one of the largest stock sales in history, "for the biggest check," Michael Drosnin noted, "ever to go to one man at one time."

All that history and fortune came with Hughes to Las Vegas in 1966. Nearly sixty-one, he had grown up with and almost *as* part of the country, his own image changing with America's image. "The last of the great American robber barons," journalist Sergio Lalli called him. By 1958, he had "ceased virtually all contact with the outside world," according to his biographers. His seclusion only added mystery to legend, the stock photos of him part of an age—the tall, slim, unshaven young man in a fedora standing shyly by his silver Lockheed, the mustachioed playboy escorting lovely starlets, the somber defense industrialist in a double-breasted suit sparring with senators—his only slightly aging face frozen in time, "like Dorian Gray," wrote Drosnin, "a public image that remained forever young." Yet when he arrived in Las Vegas, he was another Hughes, of whom no photos were published, and part of a secretive history in which, once again, he was very much an embodiment of his country and times.

Behind the renown was a figure long and deeply compromised. His links to the Syndicate, like those of the city's other rulers, traced to Prohibition. His personal bootlegger, Longy Zwillman, remained a friend and contact as both Zwillman and Hughes became national powers. He knew Bugsy Siegel and Johnny Rosselli well, had socialized with them, dealt with them as Syndicate controllers of both studio labor and stars in the movie business in California. He bought RKO from organized crime associates, and when he sold it in 1952, it was to a longtime partner of Frank Costello. As he rose to new eminence in the forties, the FBI busily accumulated more than 250 files on his sordid connections. But his impunity, like Pentagon contracts, like what was happening in so much of the nation, was no accident or mere good fortune. Behind the scenes he deployed public relations men, lobbyists, lawyers, private secret agents—prototypes, too, of the postwar Washington and nation—to ply the press, Congress, and the executive branch with money,

sex, and career favors. "A man who distributed millions of dollars to p
cians of both major political parties at the local, state, and federal levels,"
biographers described Hughes, "who sought to manipulate office-holders
from state legislator to president . . . who attempted to influence the decisions of government agencies from city councils to the Internal Revenue Service." Like the U.S. government's pervasive secrecy, his relentless covert
manipulation of the political process hid his World War II profiteering, the
Cold War waste, and much more.

By the later fifties—Hughes Aircraft moving on from a near-monopoly
on air force electronic systems to even larger contracts in spy satellite technology—much of his empire was what a Pentagon official later called "a captive company of the CIA [with] their interests . . . completely merged,"
crowded with former intelligence operatives and government agents. From
the space work of the fifties to Hughes-leased islands as bases for CIA operations against Castro, to the suborning of TWA as a carrier and cover for
intelligence operations in the sixties, to the Hughes Tool *Glomar II* deep-sea
exploratory vessel, an incongruous, hugely expensive secret project in the
seventies to retrieve a sunken Soviet submarine, the use and bondage of
Hughes as a CIA contractor and front spanned the years before, during, and
after his strange Las Vegas sojourn.

He visited the city often, went there to gamble and find women during
the war, and more frequently afterward, when another favorite haunt, Benny
Binion's Top O'Hill Terrace in Fort Worth, closed in 1946. By the early fifties
he stayed regularly at the Desert Inn, El Rancho, and especially the Flamingo,
where he had come from the beginning as Bugsy's guest, and where Siegel's
eager publicity man Greenspun introduced him to showgirls. "He liked the
glamour and gaudiness of the town," wrote an observer, ". . . enjoyed prowl-
ing the city at night, cruising the casinos and hotels in search of attractive
young women."

Hughes talked then of moving his business empire to Nevada. During
the Korean War, he mysteriously acquired an immensely valuable piece of
property—nearly forty square miles around Las Vegas in Clark County—
which made him the county's largest private landowner. In a deal facilitated
by McCarran and by Hughes's longtime Washington lawyer Clark Clifford,
as well as his military and intelligence contacts, Hughes traded 73,000 acres
of worthless desert land he owned in five northern Nevada counties for the
smaller federal parcel down south. "Enormous pressure was applied by the
Pentagon to expedite the exchange, since it was claimed to be necessary to
the national defense effort," the local press reported at the time. Dubbed
"Husite" by its owner, the new possession took up more land than the entire

city of Las Vegas. When Nevada officials asked what Hughes planned for the site, the Defense Department intervened, maintaining that the details were "classified."

In 1953, he leased a small five-room home adjacent to the Desert Inn, a place called "the Green House" for its color, vivid against the desert. "Meeting hundreds of men with whom he does business," one news article proclaimed, Hughes summoned his associates from all over the world to what he called his "new small city." He lived in the Green House for nearly a year. When he left in 1954, he ordered the little bungalow he loved perfectly preserved just as it was for the moment he returned, though he never saw it again. The calamity overtaking the man was already visible at the Green House, in the special caulking and tape that sealed its doors and windows against the terrifying germs and radiation of the outside world.

He suffered a first breakdown in 1944, after bizarre behavior such as abandoning his Los Angeles headquarters for months as he flew aimlessly between Las Vegas and Reno, registering in hotels under false names. In 1957, he would marry the actress Jean Peters in a strange secret ceremony arranged by Las Vegas city attorney Howard Cannon and performed at the shabby old Mizpah Hotel in the ghost town of Tonopah, two hundred miles north of Las Vegas. Only a year later, he suffered another, final collapse which plunged him into the dementia that dominated the rest of his life. He reeled between lunacy and twilight rationality, babbling and a megalomania that passed for sanity, between urinating against a door or sitting blankly in his own excrement and a desperate, meticulous obsession with removing any contamination and contagion from his environment. From the few who saw him, biographers later formed a picture of an increasingly drug-addicted man imprisoned by his terrible, neurotic isolation, "in his white leather chair, naked, unwashed for months, his hair falling down his back, his beard unkempt, his toenails and fingernails grotesquely long," as one account portrayed him. That was eight years before he arrived back on the Strip, his condition only worsening in the interim.

Employees and associates, including senior government officials, exploited his illness. No one lifted a hand to give him obviously needed help. Even to acknowledge his suffering was to endanger the image of a "competent" Hughes, an image imperative to those around him with their own purposes, the managers and bureaucrats to retain their places in the far-reaching business empire he gave them, his lesser personal aides for mere perquisites.

In 1947, Hughes had hired as an administrative assistant a stolid, dependable young Mormon out of Salt Lake's Brigham Young University who predictably recruited other Mormons to the increasingly powerful inner circle of Hughes caretakers. "When a job opening occurred," said one account of Hughes's California office, "notices went up on Mormon church bulletin boards all over Los Angeles." Those who got the jobs were mostly ex–truck drivers, laborers, and clerks, happening onto a windfall in a rich man's madness. "By becoming willing participants in Hughes's fantasies," his biographers Donald Barlett and James Steele wrote of them, "they assured themselves of fabulous salaries, lavish expense accounts, the fringe benefits of a corporate executive, and secure financial futures far beyond what their talents would command in the ordinary business world." By going along with Hughes's aberrant behavior, they also made certain that he would never emerge from his asylum. By 1960, the caretakers had become de facto captors. But the Mormons and bureaucrats would not be alone. Waiting in Las Vegas were men who would make their exploitation seem petty.

In the predawn hours of Thanksgiving 1966, two private railroad cars pulled up to the desolate Carey Avenue crossing in North Las Vegas. Only sixteen days after the election, Governor-elect Laxalt's secret patron Howard Hughes was arriving on the same spur the city's original developer, Senator William Clark, had built fifty years earlier. Aptly, the Strip's "strategist," Johnny Rosselli, was there to meet the train. "Like an Oriental pasha—or a spoiled child," as a journalist described the disembarking passenger, the sixty-one-year-old Hughes was transported by litter from his Pullman car into what one account called a "make-shift ambulance," and whisked to the penthouse of the Desert Inn. "The Wizard of Oz had come to the Emerald City," was Hughes biographer Michael Drosnin's summing up.

His arrival was no accident. Secretly, he had been in "negotiations to buy the Desert Inn and the Sands before he ever came to Las Vegas," one insider revealed. Hughes's timing could not have been better for the Syndicate—especially the faction controlled by Dalitz and Lansky—or for Laxalt. The state had been "withering under a barrage of unfavorable publicity that profits were being funneled into organized crime," wrote Barlett and Steele. The city was still reverberating from the charges in the *Chicago Sun-Times,* prompted by yet another J. Edgar Hoover leak, that $6 million had vanished at the rate of $100,000 a month from the Strip's Desert Inn, Stardust, Flamingo, Sands, and downtown's Fremont and Horseshoe in one year—most of which went directly to Lansky in Miami, though the Hoover-planted story neglected to make that connection. Dalitz had been indicted on federal tax charges, and Hoffa would in the upcoming few months exhaust his legal appeals from his 1964 convictions for jury tampering and pension fund fraud, and be headed to jail himself. The Frontier's hidden owner, the Emprise Corporation in Buffalo, was under federal investigation for inter-state racketeering. A massive FBI wiretap operation had been publicly exposed, revealing that "prominent figures in both the Democratic and Republican parties," as one account put it, were receiving contributions from the gangsters, and that an unnamed former Nevada governor—presumably the FBI's erstwhile nemesis Sawyer—had received $200,000. Dalitz and the Detroit hoodlums, as well as Giancana and the Chicago outfit, were waging an awkward and violent gang war behind the scenes at the Riviera and Star-dust, according to the *Sun-Times*—factional disputes that were never fully obvious. The Chicago tabloid was also reporting the connections between a Bahamian bank run by Bobby Baker and Lansky associates in Las Vegas.

Las Vegas was portrayed nationally as "one gigantic beehive of crime . . . a vast metropolis of sin," according to Drosnin. Economically, the city was stagnating, at least in relative terms. Legitimate investors "shied away," as one historian put it, ". . . because of its unsavory reputation." There seemed more heat on the city and state than at any time since the Kefauver Hearings. Rumors of a federal crackdown, or even of casino closings, were rife. "Just when it looked like the jig was up, Hughes arrived," wrote Drosnin, "a mark with an unlimited bankroll." He was "greeted with messianic enthu-siasm," as journalist Gerald Bellett put it, "by Las Vegans desperately waiting to be redeemed from the stigma of Bugsy Siegel and his heirs."

Rosselli, working in tandem with his Washington attorney Edward P. Morgan, Hughes security chief Maheu, and Greenspun, had set the stage for the billionaire's arrival in Las Vegas. Together, with a handful of Morgan's other clients and associates—a roster that included Hoffa, Dalitz, and Parry Thomas—they would make a peculiar history in the next four years, as well as millions of dollars for some of them personally.

Greenspun was charged by Morgan with finding a suitable home for Hughes. First, he tried unsuccessfully to secure a suite at the Dunes, be-fore making arrangements for two entire floors of the Desert Inn, where it would take two weeks to install necessary electronic and medical equipment. When Morgan asked Greenspun to suppress any story that might spook the publicity-loathing Hughes, Greenspun "spilled over," as one account put it, to be of assistance, even agreeing to lobby the rest of the Nevada press to sit on the sensational story. So loyal was Greenspun to Morgan—whom he had once called his "greatest benefactor" following Morgan's pro bono representation of him, and to whom he had dedicated his memoir—that he put aside his civic duty as publisher and "camped on the story for over a month," he later bragged. The self-imposed blackout was "a curious stance for a news-man to take toward one of the world's most newsworthy individuals," J. Anthony Lukas noted afterward. But then in his relationship with his old acquaintance Hughes over the next four years, Greenspun would be "not so much a newsman," one reporter wrote, "as a fellow entrepreneur, and at times outright partner."

Once Hughes was comfortably installed, having escaped the hordes of media following him, Greenspun then scooped the entire state, his front page gushing over Hughes's choice of Las Vegas for his new home. His "self-effacement and humility," Greenspun wrote of the invisible man, "entitles him to a little private space here on his own earth. We hope he finds it in Nevada." Of all the spectacular places in the world, Greenspun told his read-ers, the shy mogul had chosen Las Vegas, recognizing its virtue and potential. It would be the first of dozens of *Sun* stories perpetuating the legend of Hughes in Las Vegas.

As the myth went, Dalitz threatened to evict Hughes and his entourage. Then, in a twisting tale of insider machinations, Maheu asked Rosselli to ask Hoffa to ask Dalitz for more time for Hughes, while Greenspun asked Morgan to ask Dalitz to sell the joint. "Johnny smoothed the way," Maheu later said of Rosselli, "while Morgan moved in to make the arrangements, repre-senting Dalitz and the Desert Inn." After what they all called protracted hag-gling, with Maheu and Morgan doing the bidding of both Hughes and Dalitz, the billionaire paid the recently indicted Dalitz and his convicted partner Ruby Kolod $6.2 million in cash, while assuming another $7 million in liabilities, principally due the Teamsters.

Morgan received a $150,000 "legal fee" from Dalitz, out of which he gave $50,000 to Rosselli. Thomas, who had business dealings with Dalitz and Hoffa, was paid a fee by Hughes for evaluating Dalitz's financial statements. Hoffa, whose pension fund loan to the Desert Inn was under federal scrutiny, would miraculously have his obligation suddenly paid in full. For his part Greenspun, through his new friend Maheu, immediately obtained a prepaid $500,000 advertising contract from the Hughes properties for his newspaper.

Maheu, who was paid a half-a-million-dollar annual salary by Hughes, profited from his boss's Nevada move in other ways. "The billionaire's top bagman . . . a glorified gumshoe," as Maheu was called by a journalist, set up his own front organization, an umbrella he called Hughes Nevada Opera-tions, with a string of subsidiaries that contracted various services at inflated prices back to Hughes. "Maheu's position afforded him the opportunity to create his own private empire in the desert," wrote Rappleye and Becker, "and he seized it."

"The odd man out," according to Barlett and Steele, "was Howard Hughes."

All that was left to do was obtain a gambling license from a Nevada governing body under intense federal pressure to be more stringent and thorough in keeping corrupt elements out of the business. That's where their well-groomed and -financed new governor came in, Maheu assured Hughes.

"The man who really made it rain in the desert was Laxalt," Maheu would later write.

Laxalt instantly recognized that substituting Hughes for Dalitz would "provide an improved national image over Teamster-financed property," as one historian put it. "The feds had suspicions about its [the Desert Inn's] ties to organized crime," Laxalt himself would later write. One of the first things Governor Laxalt did upon taking office in January 1967, along with his major contributors Thomas, Greenspun, and international hotelier Barron Hilton, was to lobby the state legislature successfully to change Nevada gambling laws so that corporate entities could hold licenses, because that would "clean up" Las Vegas. "I knew if we could get into corporate gaming with the SEC's full disclosure requirements," Thomas would say later, "it would gradually be the end of criminal involvement."

Laxalt also confronted the obstacle of licensing Hughes at the Desert Inn, even though, in defiance of Nevada law, the recluse had not been photographed or fingerprinted, and refused to fill out a financial background report or appear before the Gaming Control Board. "Any other applicant would have been summarily dismissed," wrote one journalist. At Laxalt's suggestion, Hughes hired Thomas Bell, a well-connected hometown lawyer, to help obtain the license. Bell, a protégé of Senator Alan Bible, was also recommended by the other Nevada senator, Howard Cannon. Conveniently, Bell's brother was the undersheriff; the sheriff himself, as chairman of the Clark County Liquor and Gaming Licensing Board, would be charged with approving the takeover of the Desert Inn.

A handful of skeptics in the legislature, as well as a few disgruntled applicants whose own licenses had been denied, raised awkward questions about favoritism being extended to Hughes. "So far as they know, that could be Bonzo the Chimp in there pulling the switches," as Omar Garrison wrote. To mollify the critics, and to sway public opinion, Maheu delivered a handwritten letter from Hughes offering to fund a desperately needed medical school at the University of Nevada in Las Vegas—promising "$200,000 to $300,000 per year for 20 years." Maheu allowed Laxalt to break the good news to his constituents at a hastily called news conference just forty-eight hours before the licensing body would meet. Two days later, the Gaming Control Board considered an application on which Hughes's eye and hair color, height and weight were listed, but all other requested information was deemed "not available." On March 30, they recommended to the Nevada Gaming Commission that Hughes be granted a license—a recommendation that was swiftly approved by the commission. Laxalt was lauded for bringing the "Good Housekeeping seal of approval," reporter James Phelan wrote, to a risky business of gambling that was suddenly transformed into what was now called gaming, no longer a vice, but an "industry," though it produced and manufactured nothing.

On April Fools' Day, the captive, mentally ill Hughes became the registered owner of the Desert Inn. "A gathering place for the statesmen of organized crime," as a historian described the resort, now belonged to a capitalist icon.

"No count was made the night of the changeover," one witness said of the thousands of dollars that went unrecorded through the Desert Inn's counting room on April 1, as Hughes's circle of senior aides, including Maheu and Raymond Holliday, the Hughes Tool executive who had flown in from Houston, sat upstairs wondering how to run a casino. "While the inexperienced Hughes executives wallowed in their big offices," wrote a journalist, "the casino employees who had been there from the early days may have helped themselves to what they could."

"None of us knew snake eyes from box cars," one of the Hughes men would later testify.

Maheu had the solution. "No matter what I thought about him," he would say, "Rosselli was like a key to the city, the ultimate mob fixer in the desert." Maheu installed Rosselli's representatives in the crucial positions of casino manager and entertainment director, and immediately hired back Dalitz as a "consultant."

"The mob went about its business as usual," wrote Sergio Lalli. In a classic Las Vegas shell game, all Hughes had really purchased for his $13 million was the right to operate the hotel and casino until the year 2022, while Dalitz and his three Cleveland partners maintained the powerful landlord position as owners of the physical grounds and property.

"The whole thing was a Syndicate scam," Rosselli would later confide. Rosselli knew the Hughes empire needed a place to invest their TWA profits, and that the "casino owners were seeking a new front organization that would shield them from the skimming investigations . . . and Rosselli's pal Maheu could be trusted not to meddle," as one account of the gambit put it later. "We roped Hughes into buying the Desert Inn," Rosselli would tell an associate. "He's just what we need, especially with Maheu running the show."

The licensing hurdle over, Hughes would begin "snatching up gaudy hotels and gambling casinos," as one of his biographers put it, "like some demonic demigod playing an outsized Monopoly game." In what would be described as "one of the genuinely incredible stories of the planet," Maheu, as overseer of the Hughes billions—one journalist called him "Hughes's Nevada gauleiter"—would purchase Syndicate-controlled casinos at dizzying speed. Strip insiders knew the casino purchases were far from random. "They were all Lansky joints," said one Las Vegan familiar with the deals. "There was another common denominator as well—most had outstanding notes due to the Teamsters." Accusations and investigations of hidden Lansky ownership swiftly came to an end. Just as immediately, the Teamsters were repaid in full, the substantial return on the union's investment in Las Vegas now overshadowing its unseemliness or impropriety.

The only real question was "who was calling the shots," one observer remarked, or, as Robert Laxalt told his brother, "whoever controls Hughes controls the empire." Weaving in and out of lucidity, now dictating orders, now drifting into a narcotic-induced trance, Hughes communicated with Maheu and other aides through thousands of pages of memoranda, handwritten in blue ballpoint ink on ruled yellow legal pads. Always behind the scenes, "conferring quietly with Maheu and orchestrating the casino acquisitions," as one account put it, "there was John Rosselli." At the heart of every deal, too, would be Morgan and Thomas—"Thomas, who now wore different hats at different times," as a Hughes biography put it, "one when he acted as Hughes's banker and personal agent, and another when he represented those doing business with Hughes." Thomas, "fronting for Hughes in other real estate transactions," according to Omar Garrison, purchased "parcel after parcel of real estate, worth millions of dollars, which dovetailed perfectly into acquisitions by Hughes Tool."

Almost immediately after closing the Desert Inn deal, "a group of thugs," as one journalist wrote, approached Maheu, using Laxalt as an intermediary, and said they wanted to sell the Sands. Dalitz recommended the purchase and "heartily endorsed" leaving in place the "array of talent," as he called the hoodlums already running the casino. Like the Desert Inn, the Sands desperately needed a new, improved image. Long Sinatra's playground and home base of the Rat Pack, it had recently been exposed as owned by Lansky and run by Jack Entratter, a onetime bouncer at New York's Stork Club. Entratter was involved in protracted litigation stemming from the death of a prominent New Yorker in a fatal collision a few years earlier. He was rumored to be "taking the rap for an Israeli diplomat who was really driving the car," according to an observer of the case, and the criminal charges and civil lawsuits hounding him were drawing unwanted attention to the casino.

The Sands purchase went smoothly and quickly for Maheu, who was aided by Morgan and Thomas on the other side of the negotiating table, and on August 1, 1967, Hughes became the owner of the famous Sands, having paid $14.6 million for the 777-room hotel and 183 acres on which it was situated. At the closing, huge finders' fees were once again divvied up among the close-knit network of participants. Thomas, who "collected fees for representing people dealing with Hughes in one transaction," as Barlett and Steele recorded, "while collecting fees from Hughes for representing him in another," received $275,000 for his role in the sale. Morgan received $225,000, promptly passing on the requisite $95,000 to Rosselli.

Next, at the suggestion of Rosselli, Hughes acquired the 571-room Frontier Hotel from Rosselli's longtime associate Maury Friedman, who had just been convicted of cheating at a card game at the Friar's Club in Los Angeles, and a newcomer to the Strip, twenty-five-year-old Steve Wynn, who had conveniently acquired an additional percentage in the hotel just days before Hughes purchased it. "Howard Hughes bought the hotel," Garrison wrote, "just after the sheriff and two investigators broke up a meeting between the Frontier's managing director and an alleged Detroit mobster," and Emprise Corporation had been indicted on charges of criminally conspiring to obtain secret ownership of the casino. Hughes paid $23 million for the Frontier, conveying a long-term lease to Rosselli to run the lucrative gift shop. He then moved on to acquire the smaller Castaways; the huge $17 million unfinished Landmark, with its outstanding $8.9 million Teamster loan; the Silver Slipper Casino; and an array of enterprises and raw land that included thirty-one acres across from the Sands, a hundred residential lots on the Desert Inn Country Club, Alamo Airways, the North Las Vegas Airport, "all of the land surrounding McCarran Airport," as Maheu put it, and gold and silver mining claims throughout the state that CBS's *60 Minutes* reported could "eventually be worth six hundred billion dollars."

He attempted to buy the Dunes, Stardust, and Caesars Palace as well— "basically the entire Strip," said one native. Before long, he would also buy "nearly every vacant lot along the Strip," as a historian put it, "in a 3-mile stretch from the Tropicana to the Sahara."

On the surface, and in the propaganda fed to and duly reported by the

local media, Hughes's selection of properties was haphazard and uncon-
nected. The stated reasons ranged from a personal distaste for a neighboring
property—which he would buy in order to renovate—to an egomaniacal
obsession to own all that he saw. At the heart of every choice, every decision,
existed a kind of catchall explanation that rebuffed all inquiry—the whim of
the eccentric, the entitlement of the mad genius. Not only was Las Vegas to
be a sanctuary from the harried life of a billionaire, Nevada citizens were
told, but the stranger was driven by a personal quest to "make Las Vegas as
trustworthy and respectable as the New York Stock Exchange—so that
Nevada gambling will have the kind of reputation that Lloyds of London
has, so that Nevada on a note will be like Sterling on silver," Hughes would
write in a memorandum to Maheu.

"No longer was Hughes just another Nevada curiosity, like bare breasts
and all-night wedding chapels," wrote Barlett and Steele. "He was now one of
the state's largest private landowners and employers." Considered the biggest
single economic developer in Nevada history—"bigger than the Comstock
Lode," one press account stated—he was spending more than $367,000 a day
in Las Vegas.

In November 1967, exactly a year after Hughes's arrival on the Strip, gaming
officials met in the middle of the night to discuss his purchase of the Frontier. "Gathered like a secret coven at the witching hour," as Drosnin described
the bizarre meeting, "they roused sleeping colleagues with a conference call,
and by 1:30 a.m. had formally approved the impatient billionaire's fourth
casino license." Hughes had been placed above the law and allowed to
assume control of $125 million in real estate and 27,000 acres of Nevada land.
A few legislators called for an investigation of the methods used to license
Hughes, according to one published account, "alarmed over the growing
concentration of ownership," but their complaints were ignored.

By now, Paul Laxalt had tied his entire career to Hughes—they had
never met—and observers wondered whether his ambition was financial or
political, or merely a banal quest for power. His family law firm received
$180,000 for legal work from Hughes while Laxalt was governor, and
throughout his tenure he was rumored to be angling for the six-figure position of general counsel to Hughes's Nevada empire, though Laxalt then and
later sharply denied any maneuvering of the kind. Hughes himself apparently had the loftiest ambition for Laxalt. "I'm ready to ride with this man to
the end of the line, which I am targeting as the White House," Hughes would
write. A regular passenger on the Hughes jet, a frequent tennis partner and

close confidant of Maheu, Laxalt was now receiving assurances from Hughes, via Maheu, of unprecedented financial support for some future presidential bid.

Privately, the governor was increasingly dubious, "haunted by a hidden fear," as one account put it, that he had allowed an "invisible man to control Nevada more completely than anyone has ever controlled a sovereign state." In secret talks with his advisers—"summoning his gambling czars to the state capitol," one observer wrote of the governor's gaming control officers— Laxalt and his inner circle decided to determine surreptitiously if Hughes in fact was "a live individual." First, it was decided, Laxalt would politely request a private audience with the magnate. Such presumption resulted in the inevitable threat that Hughes would abandon the state. "Hughes was too big of a sugar daddy to let slip away," one journalist wrote. "It was as if every state leader and businessman in Nevada instinctively understood that Hughes had to be kept here at all costs."

To pacify the governor, however, a Hughes lawyer provided a power of attorney purportedly signed by the billionaire. "Laxalt took this treasured scrap and nervously handed it over to the FBI for authentication," Drosnin wrote. The special agent in Las Vegas sent it along to Washington with a teletype to Hoover stating that "no one, including the Governor of the State of Nevada, has ever personally seen, talked with, or discussed licensing matters with Howard Hughes . . . there is grave concern it could all be a great hoax." Hoover, knowing of Hughes's ties to the CIA, and pleased to have Hughes "cleaning up" the gangster image of Las Vegas, scrawled across the internal memorandum: "We should have absolutely *nothing* to do with this." One Justice Department official wrote that he had heard "Mr. Hoover say that Del Webb and Hughes were far preferable" to other Las Vegas operators.

To calm the fearful governor, Hughes, or someone claiming to be Hughes, placed a phone call to the Governor's Mansion in Carson City—a call that the state's newspapers headlined as "something like the Second Coming," said one historian. Chatting about his future plans for the state, Hughes convinced Laxalt that he would shower Nevada citizens with good deeds and services. He was going to devote the rest of his life to making the city a paradigm for the nation. In "one of the most interesting conversations of my life," as Laxalt described the exchange that marked the first time Hughes was said to have spoken with anyone in Nevada outside his inner circle of aides, Laxalt's worries were laid to rest. "Anything this man does, from the gaming industry all the way down the line, will be good for Nevada." Laxalt later claimed that Hughes refused to meet personally because he was ill. "I look like a goddamn cadaver," Laxalt said Hughes told him.

After this "proof" that Hughes was indeed a living, breathing human being, Laxalt would proceed, now with even more fervor, to do the billionaire's bidding. "I think Laxalt can be brought to a point where he will just about entrust his entire political future to his relationship with us," Hughes would write. For his part, Laxalt would contend that Hughes called him repeatedly, usually awakening the governor in the middle of the night. "He phoned me day or night. Constantly alone, in bed, and in semidarkness." Finally, Laxalt claimed, he was forced to tell Hughes that he had a "hectic, exhausting schedule" as governor, and needed his sleep. The late night calls stopped.

Meanwhile, Hughes Nevada Byzantium continued to grow and lavish money following Laxalt's seal of approval, with Maheu always at the forefront playing "his new role as desert raja [sic] to the hilt," one biography stated. Claiming to be the billionaire's emissary—in reality he had never actually met the man, "though he never let that out," Robert Laxalt would write in his personal notes—Maheu described himself as the "Crown Regent" to Hughes's "King of Las Vegas." He had a security apparatus consisting of former IRS, CIA, and FBI agents, and was what Jim Hougan called "the most highly paid private intelligence operative in the U.S. . . . the spook of American capitalism."

Maheu benefited greatly from Hughes's secret state of dysfunction, using the billionaire's money to live a life of wealth himself, his loosely run Hughes Nevada Operations handling the millions of dollars a day that poured into the Hughes casinos. He built himself a $640,000 mansion on the grounds of the Desert Inn Country Club, known in Las Vegas as "little caesars palace," which one journalist called a "modified plantation house with a touch of Las Vegas style splendor," where he hosted lavish parties. He hired away Dean Elson, the head of the local FBI office, and put the vulgar and notorious Jimmy "The Greek" Snyder on his payroll for public relations. "While Hughes lay huddled in somber seclusion," wrote one journalist, "Maheu flashed through Las Vegas with flamboyant relish," hobnobbing with celebrities, politicians, and Syndicate kingpins.

The image of Hughes meticulously nurtured and cultivated by Maheu was that of "an archvillain in his hidden domain," as one biographer described it, "surrounded by war-room electronics and gleaming computer banks . . . sitting at the controls of a sophisticated array of advanced technology." In fact, Hughes spent all of his waking hours "naked in his bedroom, unwashed and disheveled, his hair halfway down his back." He watched Rock Hudson in *Ice Station Zebra* time and time again, interspersed with enemas and drug injections administered by his cadre of Mormon nursemaids—

"his little polygamous family, all the family Howard Hughes had left," wrote one journalist—and harangued state and federal officials about the bombs going off at the Nuclear Test Site.

Through Maheu, Nevadans learned of Hughes's fabulous plans for the state, all the while the aide promoting the image of the "powerful industrialist who had come to rescue the gaming industry from the clutches of the underworld," as one writer later put it. He would take the proletarian "Norman Rockwell vision of Americana" as expressed in the Strip's tacky excesses, and replace it with "the classiest resort in the world," Maheu quoted a Hughes memorandum. His master plan included high-speed trains on a micrometer laid track, and a vision that would change "Nevada's physical, economic, social, and educational landscape," as Barlett and Steele wrote. "A last opportunity to build a model city because of the sufficiency of raw land available in all directions," Hughes explained.

Maheu announced Hughes's plans "for the world's largest hotel, a $150-million, 4,000-room addition to the Sands," complete with a swimming pool second in size only to Lake Mead. He agreed to buy the Dunes, which was currently besieged with charges of corruption on the part of its St. Louis Syndicate owners. He then entered into negotiations with his own "gaming consultant," Dalitz, for the purchase of Dalitz's Stardust—the largest and most profitable Las Vegas hotel. The ubiquitous Morgan, who by now was on a $100,000 retainer from Hughes, handled the transaction and was paid an additional $500,000 fee by Dalitz.

It was the Stardust deal that set off alarm bells in Washington, if not in Nevada. Lyndon Johnson's Justice Department sought to block the sale, claiming that "it is contrary to our basic concept to permit one individual or one firm to control one-fifth of the economic activities of a city of 250,000." Justice officials summarily rejected what they called "the now familiar contention that Hughes was ridding Las Vegas of an undesirable element," pointing out that "most monopolists have used such an argument."

Once again Greenspun rushed to Hughes's defense, describing him as a "modest, self-effacing person . . . [who] has never throughout his career displayed any tendencies of control or of monopoly." Greenspun had publicly and passionately vouched for Hughes, even lobbying in Carson City for the billionaire's fifth and sixth gambling licenses. It was what Barlett and Steele called an "about face" for the newspaperman, who eight years earlier had argued vociferously against Dalitz acquiring a third license. "Hank Greenspun became the self-appointed protector of the man in the penthouse," wrote Ovid Demaris, "baring his teeth to all who dared invade his privacy." Along the way, "the financial future of Hank Greenspun . . . had brightened considerably," as one account put it. Not only had he received the prepaid Hughes advertising contract "to do with as he pleased," but he was paid an additional $488,000 for advertising without ever touching the "retainer." In September 1967, he received from Hughes a $4 million loan at a paltry 3 percent interest rate. Simultaneously, Greenspun sold his KLAS television station to Hughes for $3.6 million. Faced with the problem of Hughes obtaining the required license from the Federal Communications Commission without appearing in person, Maheu turned to Morgan, who now conveniently "specialized in communications law" and was able to arrange for the Washington licensing "with no inconvenience whatsoever to Hughes," as one of the participants described it.

When the "trust-busting" attorney general Ramsay Clark hardened his stance against the Stardust acquisition, Maheu called on the Nevada officials he had been cultivating. Laxalt had hardly been the only officeholder to milk the cash cow that was the Hughes empire. While Hughes jets ferried Laxalt back and forth between Las Vegas and Reno, and even to Washington to lobby prickly federal regulators, they also transported Senators Bible and Cannon upon request. From 1966 until 1969, nearly $900,000 passed from the Silver Slipper cashier's cage alone to Nevada politicians, dispensed by the omnipresent lawyer-turned-bagman Tom Bell. Bible got at least $50,000, according to later published reports, Cannon $70,000, and the up-and-coming Democratic politician Harry Reid picked up $10,000. Apart from campaign donations or other payments, however technically legal, politicians also enjoyed the usual perquisites of casino cage cash. An eyewitness, himself a state official, typically remembered one senior Washington official walking up to the Silver Slipper cage and holding his thumb and index finger "two inches apart to show the size stack of hundreds he needed." Now Cannon, Bible, and Laxalt were loyally there to pressure the attorney general. When Clark remained unmoved by the state officials' entreaties, Hughes brought a halt to the Stardust negotiations, focusing his attention instead on the upcoming 1968 presidential election that, he hoped, would bring in a new attorney general. Hughes merely did what he had been doing for decades: He shifted to the next stratum of politicians.

"I can buy any man in the world," he had once remarked, though he often bemoaned the fact that the wealthy Kennedy family eluded his influence. Called "the most powerful private political machine in the country" by one historian, Hughes's organization was essentially bipartisan. He would order Maheu to ensure that "his man" Nixon would become the next president. To that end, Maheu would pass $100,000 to Nixon, half through Laxalt and half through Morgan. Hedging his bets, as he had always done, Hughes sent another $100,000 to Democratic contender Hubert Humphrey, half through Maheu and another half through Grant Sawyer, now on retainer. Hughes even sent $25,000 to Robert Kennedy's presidential campaign—"the one candidate he did not want and could not control," wrote a journalist.

The June night of the senator's assassination, Hughes "was so excited he couldn't sleep," according to one account, staying awake for forty-eight hours and then demanding that Maheu move expeditiously to hire Kennedy's entire political organization. "I hate to be quick on the draw," Hughes wrote to Maheu in a memorandum, "but I see here an opportunity that may not happen again in a lifetime." Even as Bobby's body was being flown from Los Angeles to his New York funeral, Maheu was making overtures to the senator's inner circle. "I don't want an alliance with the Kennedy group," Hughes wrote to Maheu, "I want to put them on the payroll." His grandiose plan to coopt the Kennedy machine and make it his own "so that we would never have to worry about a jerky little thing like this antitrust problem" had a tertiary element as well: "The kind of set up that, if we wanted to, could put Gov. Laxalt in the White House in 1972 or 1976." Taking over the group was easier than he expected. As it turned out, many of the leaderless clan traumatized by the course of events begun on November 22, 1963, and culminating on June 5, 1968, were available for hire. Within days, in a bloodless coup of extravagant proportions, Maheu had hired top Kennedy loyalist Lawrence O'Brien, whom Hughes called the "leader of the Irish Mafia." The old friend of Joe Kennedy, the campaign manager for Jack, and an intimate of Bobby, now belonged to Hughes.

"With the inauguration of Richard Nixon," as Barlett and Steele put it, "harmony between Hughes and the federal government had returned." Nixon's new attorney general, John Mitchell, would relieve the antitrust pressure on the Las Vegas casino acquisitions. But by then Hughes had more immediate concerns.

The bubble burst in 1970," wrote one journalist. Incredibly, the Hughes casinos were suffering staggering losses—even the mammoth money-making Desert Inn. A victim of what James Phelan saw in the machinations of Maheu, Thomas, Greenspun, and others as "self-dealing schemes and conspiracies," Hughes was being relieved of millions of dollars. It was a version of what longtime Las Vegas observers called the "bust-out crew." In casino parlance, *bust-out* is the term used "when the joint's own people are sent in to clean out the sucker and stop the game," as one native explained it. "A mechanic *par excellence*," is how a journalist once described the bust-out man. "Posing as a player, he is called in when the going gets rough. His assignment is to win back for the house the money it has lost, and this he does with the aid of a fix." "Dalitz and other members of his Las Vegas clique saw Hughes' arrival for what it was," wrote one journalist, "an opportunity to take an unbelievably wealthy mark to the cleaners." A secret IRS report at the time estimated that "$50 million had been drained from the Hughes casino coffers under the Maheu regime."

"Close and ominous relationships have been established between May-hew [sic] and well known Mafia figures," a Nixon aide would write at the time to his boss, H. R. Haldeman, in a memorandum that would eventually end up in the hands of Watergate investigators. "Mayhew and these figures have been criminally skimming huge profits from casino operations for their own benefit . . . [O]nly now are the Hughes corporate officials becoming aware of the extent . . . it is feared that substantial millions are involved." In any case, a sophisticated, clandestine takeover orchestrated by Maheu's rivals now got underway to depose him. At the root of the planned overthrow was a mysterious entity called Intertel, known especially and remarkably for its composition of former organized crime strike force attorneys from Robert Kennedy's Justice Department. Even more interestingly, Intertel was a wholly-owned subsidiary of Resorts International—a company with a "predilection for funny-money often connected to organized crime associates," as one scholar described it. Formerly the Mary Carter Paint Company, which was widely considered to be a CIA front that laundered payments to the Cuban exile army in the early sixties, Resorts International now owned several Bahamian casinos and was thought to be dominated by Meyer Lansky. The IRS considered Intertel, originally incorporated in 1962 by Lansky associates, "an organized crime enterprise of some type aimed at the Bahamas," as one account summed up the agency's view. Robert Peloquin and William Hundley, Kennedy's top crime fighters, had joined the firm and recruited operatives from the CIA, FBI, IRS, Secret Service, and other intelligence agencies. Staffed exclusively by what one author called "Get Hoffa agents," it was likened to a corporate CIA. "With the murder of Robert Kennedy in 1968, the federal government's war on organized crime . . . was over," wrote Hoffa's biographer, Dan Moldea, ". . . and two of its best warriors—Bill Hundley and Bob Peloquin—were dressed for war but had no one to fight."

Summoned to Las Vegas in the summer of 1970 by longtime Hughes legal counsel and Maheu rival Chester Davis, Peloquin and the president of Resorts International heard Davis's proposal: "Intertel would replace Maheu as the fix-it expert in the Hughes organization. And Hughes would replace

Resorts in the Bahamas." Just as Hughes had provided a "perfect anti-Syndicate stance in Vegas," journalist Howard Kohn wrote, he would do the same for Lansky's interests in the Bahamas. Lansky, now as reclusive as Hughes, "hiding out in Israel, trying to avoid the lingering repercussions of Bobby Kennedy's Las Vegas investigation," according to one published account, was in desperate need of a front. But casino owners knew that Lansky's troubles in Las Vegas had begun not with Kennedy, but rather with the rise of Laxalt as governor, and had culminated with the 1968 presidential election of Nixon. "Lansky's established connections to the Democrats," as scholar William Chambliss saw it, "led Santo Trafficante, Jr. (and others such as Carlos Marcello of New Orleans) to forge political alliances with Republicans." As a result, Lansky had been frozen out of the "Teamsters-Republican coalition" and was "engaged in major conflict with Bebe Rebozo and other Nixon associates for control of casinos and banks in Miami and the Bahamas."

As the furnace heat of a Las Vegas midsummer day still hung over the evening, Rebozo, the Florida entrepreneur and intimate friend of President Nixon, and Richard G. Danner, the Hughes empire's liaison with the Nixon White House, joined the Hughes and Resorts representatives for dinner in a Strip casino showroom. Before the floor show was over, the two factions "reached a tentative agreement," as Kohn recorded.

Only a few months later, on Thanksgiving Eve 1970, Intertel agents descended on Las Vegas for the stated purpose of ridding the Hughes empire of the hoodlum elements that had infiltrated the organization under Maheu's reign. With the same mysteriousness and secrecy cloaking Hughes's arrival exactly four years earlier, he was now "placed on a stretcher, carried out of the Desert Inn to a waiting van and driven to Nellis Air Force Base," as Barlett and Steele described the event. A wasting wraith on a gurney, he was removed from Las Vegas by James Golden, a former Nixon Secret Service agent turned Intertel vice president, and whisked by private jet to Resorts International's Brittania Beach Hotel in the Bahamas.

As some Intertel agents carried Hughes down the back stairs of the Desert Inn, others "rushed cashier's cages and began stuffing money" and IOU markers into satchels. Kicking down doors of Maheu offices, they occupied all the Hughes casinos. In yet another ironic twist, Robert Kennedy's legendary organized crime team had suddenly taken charge of six major Las Vegas casinos, while Governor Laxalt and his gaming officials scrambled to figure out what was going on.

It took nearly a week for Maheu and Greenspun to learn what had happened, how Maheu's elaborate security systems were so thoroughly trespassed. "For all his power," wrote a journalist of Maheu, "he was still just the house dick." The first two days after Hughes's disappearance were marked by a "bitter corporate struggle," with Laxalt bringing in the full weight of the state of Nevada in support of his friend Maheu. Hughes aides produced a proxy claiming Hughes had fired Maheu. Panicked, refusing to acknowledge his dismissal, Maheu "gathered his war party at the Frontier," as Gerald Bellett put it. For the first time, he publicly questioned Hughes's competency, emotionally proclaiming that the billionaire had been kidnapped by competing forces in the empire—a theory avidly reported in both Greenspun's *Las Vegas Sun* and Jack Anderson's nationally syndicated column.

Maheu frantically sought to hold on to his power, even launching his own rescue mission. "Drinking huge amounts of brandy, he was getting an armed party to go to the Bahamas and take Hughes back," Robert Laxalt wrote in his personal notes, ". . . not unlike his gang attempting to assassinate Castro." Vice President Spiro Agnew called Laxalt to confirm that he had been informed by the CIA that Hughes indeed "wanted Maheu out," and then Hughes called Laxalt for the last time, Laxalt would write 25 years later, and confirm that he "wanted Maheu fired." Laxalt broke the unwanted news to Maheu at 3 a.m. at Maheu's house. "I've never seen a more crestfallen man," he would recall. The governor and state gaming officials then set out to determine who was controlling the casinos.

Las Vegans—not easily shocked and ready to believe almost anything by 1970—would watch what came to be known as the Thanksgiving Day Massacre with a blend of bewilderment and curiosity. The *Sun*, which had been assuring them that Hughes was Nevada's "fairy godfather," was now sounding alarm bells on its front page, reporting that the invalid billionaire had been spirited away against his will by Intertel. Greenspun personally went on the offensive against the company, warning that it was "the chosen instrument for the International Gambling Cartel . . . staffed by the very people who were in the law enforcement agencies designed to combat organized crime and using the knowledge and prestige gained in these agencies."

When Hughes, from his new Bahamas hideaway—or at least someone purporting to be the recluse—publicly called Maheu a "no-good dishonest son-of-a-bitch" who "stole me blind," Maheu slapped a $17.5 million slander suit on his former patron. The Hughes empire now suddenly called due Greenspun's low-interest loan. Stung by their sudden and unanticipated ousting from the Hughes cabal, Greenspun and Maheu would turn like spurned lovers against their onetime savior and object of devotion. "I prostituted my newspaper in Howard Hughes's interests," Greenspun later confessed. He now thought Hughes a "terrible menace to this country," and would be locked in his own protracted legal battle with the man he had done so much to bring to, and keep in, Las Vegas.

Hughes would never return to Las Vegas, and his legacy would be surrounded by intrigue long after his properties were sold and his corpse was buried. Intertel instigated an IRS probe of Maheu that "mushroomed into a full-scale audit of the entire Hughes empire, turning first against Hughes himself," as Drosnin described it, and "finally against Richard Nixon." Nixon's obsessive fear of Maheu, for his insider's knowledge as the keeper of secrets for the president's decades-long benefactor Hughes, would plant what one Nevada journalist called the "seeds of Watergate." Added to that already enormous paranoia was Maheu's close relationship with columnist Anderson and publisher Greenspun, both ready disseminators of anti-Nixon material. During this time White House operatives G. Gordon Liddy—"a gun fanatic who liked to watch old Nazi propaganda films," according to one account—and E. Howard Hunt would put Anderson under surveillance, and even discuss plots to kill or drug the muckraker. Shortly after Greenspun's leaks to the national media about Hughes, a plot to crack the *Sun*'s safe was spawned by Liddy and Hunt, in a joint venture with Hughes agents. Though that theft was aborted, a safe would be stolen from the office of one of Greenspun's Las Vegas lawyers, and found afterward in the desert, blown open and rifled.

For his part, Laxalt would retire as governor after one term—the only Nevada governor to do so since 1938—to spend more time with his wife, who had become an alcoholic, and his children, who were "rebellious and resentful," as one reporter described them. During his tenure as governor, not one individual was entered into Nevada's *Black Book*. He rejoined his old law firm, moving it to the historic Norcross mansion in the heart of Carson City, adjacent to the house where Mark Twain had lived. Within days of leaving office, he collected $72,000 in legal fees from Hughes, installing Tom Bell as a partner in the firm, though Laxalt in his 2000 memoir claimed he had refused to "join" the Hughes organization. His only other comparable client was Delbert Coleman, a Las Vegas gambler who paid Laxalt a $100,000 retainer, and whose business partner was Chicago labor consultant Sidney Korshak—once called by the Justice Department "one of the five most powerful members of the underworld . . . the most important link between organized crime and legitimate business," and with his own family ties through marriage to Nevada. One of Laxalt's first acts as a private attorney was a "Dear Dick letter," a request dated January 26, 1971, asking President

Nixon to pardon Jimmy Hoffa, whom he described as a "victim of Robert Kennedy's revenge." Teamster "loans to Nevada resort hotels represent by far the greatest investment in Nevada," Laxalt wrote Nixon. "Their activities here have been 'aboveboard' at all times and they have made a material contribution to our state."

By the following year Laxalt would be divorced and building the Ormsby House—the largest hotel and casino in Carson City—with unsecured notes arranged by Coleman from the First National Bank of Chicago. Built "as a monument to his mother," as one account said of the 237-room hotel on seven acres across from the picturesque state Capitol, the "gambling palace" opened in July 1972. "We had no family money at all," one of Laxalt's younger brothers told a reporter. But the Laxalts realized, according to investigative reporters Wiley and Gottlieb, that "in Nevada it was possible to make something out of nothing." "Paul learned you could finance these things without writing a check," a Reno lawyer told *The Nation*. "He learned these things as governor and he went out and did it." The two brothers invested a total of $1,851 of their own money. The rest would come from three Nevada banks, the Chicago institution, and private investors tied to Teamster financier Allen Dorfman.

The Ormsby House, and the ensuing scandal that would permeate it and all it symbolized, would have an impact not only in Nevada politics but in the national arena as well, and would irrevocably divide the Laxalt clan from their past, and, ultimately, from one another.

Over the next few years, Hughes would continue in and out of dementia, addicted to injections, with matted hair down his back and witchlike fingernails inches long. In name, he still owned most of Nevada's economy, officially its largest private employer and landlord. He, or rather the image of him, it was widely said, had cleansed the city, "bringing the best of American capitalism," as one version had it, "to what had been an underworld money laundry."

Much of the myth traced to Nevada's enduring sense of victimization, of being singled out, when other states were just as corrupt, for what they called "the diatribe." "There is no parallel for it, no state to compare it to," Sawyer's chief gaming regulator would later write,

> because no other state was ever blasted as a state. Our history shows attacks on individual men—Benedict Arnold, Al Capone, Huey Long, Joe McCarthy—the nation's individual bastards, but not states. For eighteen years, Nevada was raked in a continuing diatribe. The country's best reporters worked the dictionary of invec-

tive; they called it everything, gang-controlled, venal, corrupt, vile, immoral, whore-ridden, crime-ridden, rotten. It ran from Kefauver, who started it in 1950, and it stopped with Howard Hughes.

In the city of fronts, Hughes would be the greatest front man of all time. "Popular lore gives Hughes credit for chasing the mobsters out of town and ushering in the era of corporations," wrote one journalist long after he was gone. "None of this is true."

The state of Nevada and the nation at large were victims of the con, even as they played into the crooked hand that was dealt. What Hughes left behind was a modern city, but without any of the endowments he had promised. The $5 million medical school bequest he used to bribe the state in exchange for the Desert Inn gambling license would never see the light of day, Hughes going so far as to battle proposed legislation for the construction of the school. He would use his vast resources to lobby against sales, gasoline, and cigarette taxes in the state, fight school integration, and ban Communist bloc entertainers and rock concerts from his properties. The magnificent resort Hughes vowed to build on the Strip across the street from the Sands would never materialize, the invaluable real estate finding its way to the city's next famous deliverer, Steve Wynn, who would build the Mirage and Treasure Island hotels on the site. The 25,000-acre Husite parcel for which Hughes received national security clearance and special dispensation from the federal government for a guided missile base would instead become the city's largest, most upscale residential community—named for Hughes's grandmother Jean Amelia Summerlin, and partially developed by Greenspun's son-in-law and future mayoral candidate, Mark Fine.

"The only thing Hughes would actually ever build in Nevada," wrote one biographer, "was Maheu's new mansion, and indeed he would do his best to block *all* new hotels, *all* new industry, *all* 'competition.' "

When he died on an airplane flying between Acapulco and Houston in 1976, the once handsome rake and dashing pilot weighed 93 pounds, was covered with bedsores, had a bleeding tumor on his head, hypodermic needles broken off in his arms, and a lethal amount of codeine in his dehydrated body. At the time of his death he was earning $1.7 million a day from U.S. government contracts, mostly from the CIA, the majority of which were awarded without competitive bids, and this was only a fraction of the public money that in effect financed his many-faceted deliverance and patronage of organized crime and his other beneficiaries in Las Vegas. What would become clear over the next few years, according to one of his biographers, is that "certain government agencies, including the Central Intelligence

Agency, were well aware of Hughes's condition, that he had not been in control of his empire for some time, and that he was not responsible for many acts performed in his name."

Only twenty people attended the funeral of one of the most famous tycoons on earth. The sole eulogy came fittingly from one of the many who used him—the infamous, seamy Cold Warrior and CIA chief of counterespionage who was the Syndicate's highest-ranking ally in American intelligence, James Jesus Angleton. "Where his country's interests were concerned," Angleton said of Hughes with historic if unintended irony, "no man knew his target better. We were fortunate to have him. He was a great patriot."

14. High Rollers

R eckonings.

June 1972: A little after 2 a.m. on a humid night in Washington, D.C., five men in business suits and wearing blue surgical gloves enter a darkened office near the Potomac. They carry sophisticated cameras and telephone-bugging equipment. Their crime is mandated by the White House, and they are looking, in part at least, for material that could implicate a president of the United States in Las Vegas corruption. There will be evidence, in fact, that but for Las Vegas and the vortex of political forces it stirs, the epic scandal these men bring to the surface this night might never have happened. But now, as police and building guards suddenly appear at the door with guns drawn, the burglars huddle helplessly behind a small wood-and-frosted-glass partition. One of them whispers history's brief epitaph into a walkie-talkie. "They got us," he says in his Cuban accent.

July 1972: So powerful that it tears a gaping hole in the steel-reinforced concrete floor, a bomb blast shatters the quiet of a white-hot Las Vegas afternoon, and sets off secondary explosions in the gas tanks of five other cars on the third floor of the garage just off Glitter Gulch. Ex–FBI agent–become–casino landlord Bill Coulthard is literally blown to pieces when he turns the ignition key of his Cadillac, and can be identified only by dental charts.

June 1975: In his basement den in Chicago behind double-locked steel doors, Sam Giancana is cooking his usual midnight snack of escarole and sausage. He stands at the stove, trusting his back to an old friend, Tony "The Ant" Spilotro, who will soon be a dominant force in Las Vegas. One bullet, fired through a silencer at point-blank range, enters at the base of Giancana's angular skull, another through his mouth, five more in a methodical semi-circle beneath his chin. It is a message from the Strip—a verdict on the victim and, as always, a warning to the living.

July 1975: Jimmy Hoffa tells his sister he is going to the swanky Red Fox restaurant outside Detroit for a "sitdown" with labor and political leaders to talk about his return to power. Hoffa, the man who built so much of the Strip, drives away in his dark green year-old Pontiac, and vanishes from the face of the earth.

July 1976: "If they want to kill me they're going to kill me, but they're not going to scare me," Johnny Rosselli says to a friend that summer. On a Thursday afternoon, he heads off with golf clubs wearing a favorite pink shirt. A scrap of the bright fabric is the first thing a curious fisherman sees when he peers into a steel drum that has surfaced off the Florida coast. Stuffed inside is a decomposing body, the torso slit open from chest to navel, the legs cut off at the thigh with a hacksaw. As if a final indignity for the stylish Rosselli, he is gagged with an ordinary Cannon washcloth.

February 1977: Hikers find the remains of local union boss Al Bramlet in the desert near Mount Potosi, 50 feet off a dirt road along one of the old pioneer tracks west out of the Las Vegas Valley. Bramlet had been kidnapped from McCarran Airport two weeks earlier by men he had contracted to do his own bombings, but whom he refused to pay when some of the devices did not detonate. He was shot three times in the heart and once in each ear. His naked body is found under a thin layer of rocks, one arm deliberately left protruding above the shallow cairn.

December 1978: On days like this in West Texas, natives say, the air is so crisp you can hear it. Lee Chagra's wife has surprised her drug-dealer, criminal-lawyer husband with tickets to the Sun Bowl, but first he goes to check on something at his ornate, fortresslike El Paso office. An assassin's .22-caliber shell cascades perfectly through both of Chagra's lungs, severing his aorta, the body's main artery. The man they call the "Black Striker" on the Strip lies dying in a thickening plaster of blood for almost an hour, writhing on the plush carpet beneath his stained-glass window.

Like Watergate, the murders make history, and are a reminder of what always lies beneath the surface of Las Vegas—power, money, and secrets.

In a wider perspective, the 1970s are a decade of historic scandal, and of fitful, ultimately failed inquests. In congressional investigations of Watergate, of CIA assassination plots, of political murders at home, of the pandemic of drugs after Vietnam, there are glimpses of the underlying realities of power. The connections to Las Vegas are critical, the city a key to understanding the breadth and depth of what is happening in and to the country at large. Once more, to go behind the famous fronts of the Strip would be to see national events in a different light, and to find in the seeming sideshow of Las Vegas a foreshadow of the nation's future. The chance to confront Las Vegas is lost again. The city goes on to thrive as never before in the old alliance of gamblers, gangsters, and government that Estes Kefauver had warned of a quarter century before.

What came to be known as Watergate was etched in national headlines for more than two years. A burglary of the Democratic National Committee trailed slowly but inexorably back to the White House, where it turned out to be only one of many illegal acts by a rancorously suspicious president and his equally imperious men. Four of the burglars were Cuban exiles working for former CIA operative and Bay of Pigs veteran E. Howard Hunt, and the fifth a onetime CIA employee named James McCord. Scandal came oozing out by ambitious journalism and orchestrated leaks, dogged prosecution and sheer accident, by the cannibalism of White House aides informing on one another in a widening snare of incrimination, and by machinations deep inside government redolent of a furtive coup against a vulnerable, isolated, compromised president who had overstepped taboos of policy as well as political espionage. The abuses of power exposed in the process included bribery and hush money, other break-ins and obstructions of justice. The president and his co-conspirators, shockingly audible in the scratchy staccato of the infamous Oval Office tapes, were responsible for a spree of constitutional crime and cover-up that proved still more extreme as other presidential recordings became public over ensuing decades. When the crisis climaxed in August 1974 with the certain prospect of House impeachment and subsequent Senate conviction, Richard Nixon became the first president in U.S. history to resign. Lifting off in a marine helicopter from the South Lawn of the White House, he seemed to take the scandal with him, his banishment purging America of what appeared singular corruption.

Yet seen through the prism of Las Vegas, Watergate bared a governing system beyond the rule, or removal, of any single politician. Apart from the congressional articles impeaching Nixon for comparatively minor offenses such as obstruction of justice, dereliction of duty, or failure to produce subpoenaed evidence, apart from the crimes of bribery and tax evasion exposed on the edge of the scandal, there was a Medusa's head of entangled, intrinsic corruptions. The snakes all traced a lineage to the Strip: partisan warfare by covert gangs grown as decisive in American politics as any party or platform; payoffs far larger than any sums revealed by Watergate testimony; collusions with the Syndicate much older and more constant than any unsavory associations surfacing in the investigation; corporate alliance with crime and government intelligence more pervasive and powerful than the shadows thrown by any hearing. Much of this traced back to Las Vegas, from the pouring of casino skim into political campaigns, to ranking U.S. agents becoming private armies of spies and manipulators, to the old, enduring, haunting ties to Cuba.

Beyond the surface of Watergate revelations would be a deeper, secret world in which Nixon had operated for decades. But if the flawed, awkward figure who gave his defiant salute before leaving the White House that August day epitomized Strip politics, he was never alone. Both of his immediate predecessors had delved into this world as well—LBJ with his Marcello money and Jack Kennedy with his now historic Syndicate relationships and compromises. Nor would Nixon be the last president beholden to Las Vegas power and influence, such later chief executives as Ronald Reagan and Bill Clinton brazenly cultivating its powers and assimilating its money. But in that summer of 1974, Nixon seemed unique.

A series of sensational news stories strategically leaked, along with other burglaries in Las Vegas in the year preceding the DNC break-in, marked a high-stakes political game in which the Watergate episode was but one further volley. At the center of an astonishing series of events was that powerful nucleus responsible for bringing Howard Hughes to Las Vegas, now displaced from the billionaire's empire: Rosselli, Greenspun, Morgan, and Maheu. The pipeline for those forces would be journalist Jack Anderson, in a scenario described by Professor Peter Dale Scott as "a powerful Morgan-Maheu-Anderson team . . . able to exercise critical leverage upon a responsive White House."

On Nixon's side was a group of White House covert operatives officially called the Special Investigations Unit but informally known as "the Plumbers"—their assignment to "stop leaks," as one of their leaders said—and which included Hunt, McCord, former FBI agent G. Gordon Liddy, and a crew of miscreant "assets." The break-in for which they became infamous was but the last in a chain of lawlessness that came to be known as White House "dirty tricks."

Investigators and presidential aides eventually believed that the crux of Watergate revolved around Nixon's absolute fixation with what John Ehrlichman, head of the new White House Domestic Council, called "the Hughes connection." Historian Stanley Kutler would record the judgment of Chief of Staff H. R. Haldeman that in matters involving Hughes, "Nixon seemed to lose touch with reality." The "Hughes connection" became a catchall for a bevy of subjects ranging from a fear of Maheu's knowledge, to what Haldeman called an "obsession" with DNC chairman, onetime Hughes retainer, and longtime Kennedy insider Larry O'Brien, to what Ehrlichman called a "paranoia about Johnny Meier," referring to a shadowy Hughes "scientific adviser" in business with Nixon's brother, Donald.

Nixon's "almost irrational interest" in Greenspun, as Jim Hougan wrote in *Secret Agenda,* "clearly reflected Nixon's own worries about his family's past and present ties to industrialist Howard Hughes." Greenspun had been so "enmeshed in the reclusive billionaire's affairs" in Las Vegas, according to Hougan, that Nixon could not be certain how much Greenspun knew "about the President's own entanglements with Hughes." More threatening to Nixon than Greenspun and his relatively tiny and faraway *Sun,* of course, was the Las Vegas publisher's decades-long association with Drew Pearson, whose nationally syndicated "Washington Merry-Go-Round" political column was enormously popular. It had been Pearson, along with his heir apparent, Anderson, who had broken the "Hughes loan scandal" story on the eve of the 1960 presidential election. That story traced an inadequately secured $205,000 loan in 1956 from Hughes Tool to a company headed by Donald Nixon after Nixon had been elected to the vice presidency. Pearson had reported a blatant quid pro quo that resulted in improved Hughes relations with the Eisenhower-Nixon administration. Hughes's TWA received authorization for new world routes, Hughes Tool won massive defense contracts, and the Justice Department eased its antitrust oversight of the empire. Many political observers, including Nixon himself, thought this leaked story had cost him the 1960 election.

Whatever the motivation, however real or imagined the demons, it is clear that Nixon's long-smoldering fears about his Hughes and Las Vegas connections heated up with the 1970 Hughes ousting of the Rosselli-Greenspun-Morgan-Maheu combine. That Las Vegas faction ignited a battle with the White House, blackmailing and intimidating Nixon with meticulously crafted and planted news stories that were political time bombs. Their demands were both personal and collective. Rosselli was facing incarceration and deportation, his Friar's Club cheating conviction having been upheld by the Ninth Circuit Court of Appeals. He threatened to blow the whistle on that embarrassing caper of CIA-Syndicate partnership in the attempted assassination of Castro if the Nixon administration failed to intervene on his behalf. Maheu had been evicted from his Las Vegas mansion, and was now battling a massive IRS audit. He was also under investigation by the SEC for stock fraud, and was embroiled in multimillion-dollar litigation with Hughes. Like Rosselli, Maheu parlayed his incriminating knowledge of Nixon and the federal government into currency that might neutralize his personal crises. He knew far more about Hughes's relationships with the government and the president than relatively minor illegal political contributions. His knowledge extended to current covert CIA programs, including the use by the agency of Hughes's *Glomar II* vessel in a top-secret intelligence operation, as well as numerous untold agency machinations sure to embarrass the administration if revealed. "Maheu's tentacles touch many extremely sensitive areas of government," as one White House memo put it, "each of which is fraught with potential for Jack Anderson–type exposure." Greenspun, too, was under federal investigation by the IRS, and the SEC was probing his role in Hughes's manipulation of Air West stock as well. And even Anderson, grateful for the journalism scoops that were the envy of his colleagues, had personal motivations. Having acquired an interest in Greenspun's *Sun*, Anderson began to play an unprecedented, and increasingly active, role in Las Vegas politics. "I did hold a few shares of stock in the *Sun*— a token gift from Hank in appreciation for my help in saving him from a libel judgment," Anderson would claim in his 1999 memoir, but denied that it influenced his interest in Nevada elections and economics.

Beyond all their individual problems and claims, though, was their common interest in, and commitment to, that great Las Vegas benefactor, Jimmy Hoffa. The once infinite Teamsters and Hughes millions now lost to them, they each pressured the White House for a commutation of Hoffa's prison sentence. Once again, attorney for them all was Ed Morgan.

Rosselli, while he was awaiting sentencing in federal court in Los Angeles, appealed to Morgan to pull out all the stops. Three years earlier, Morgan had been Rosselli's "chosen conduit," as scholar Richard Mahoney put it, in a "disinformation campaign" orchestrated to protect the CIA from exposure of its partnership "in capital crime with Santos Trafficante." In that 1967 leak, Morgan had passed Rosselli's information to Pearson and Anderson, who reported it as expected in an explosive column that came to be known as the "political H-bomb" story, or the first "floating of the Castro-retaliation theory." This exposé of the alliance downplayed the role of both the CIA and the Syndicate, placing the blame on a personal vendetta between the Kennedys and Castro. "Senator Robert Kennedy may have approved an assassination plot," Pearson and Anderson reported, "which then possibly backfired against his late brother."

Anderson's column "sent tremors through official Washington," as one account put it. "Not only did it accuse Castro of plotting against Kennedy, but it revealed for the first time, albeit sketchily, the CIA plots against Castro." Left out of that first story were crucial details, resulting instead in a "very slanted attack against Bobby Kennedy," as one scholar described the article. Rosselli's reason and timing for this Castro retaliation story, according to his biographers and other historians, was to neutralize the flourishing investigation by New Orleans district attorney James Garrison into the role of the CIA in the Kennedy assassination. At the time, "there was an impressive national consensus that Kennedy had been killed by an orchestrated conspiracy, rather than by a scruffy little misfit with nothing but a cheap mail-order rifle," James Phelan wrote. "Garrison's lunacy," as Gus Russo called the southern prosecutor's probe, was gaining widespread public attention, and he had recently had a New Orleans businessman arrested on charges of conspiring to kill the president, as well as indicting fourteen CIA officials as co-conspirators. "It was the broadest and best-financed inquiry to be launched since the Warren Commission," Rosselli's biographers wrote of Garrison's inquest. "It fell to John Rosselli to limit the potential damage of the Garrison investigation." By deflecting attention onto Castro and away from the CIA, Rosselli was "seeking to influence the course of the Kennedy investigation," as one history put it. A "stand-up guy," his biographers claimed, Rosselli was merely following directives from his Syndicate and CIA handlers. His efforts, along with those of many others, were successful. Garrison's probe was marginalized, ridiculed, and disgraced, the man himself dismissed as a publicity-seeking madman. "Short of sparking another American invasion of Cuba, there was no other benefit to be obtained," wrote Rappleye and Becker.

Now, in November 1970, Rosselli, facing jail, decided to call in his marker from the CIA. First, Morgan and Maheu sent word directly to Director of Central Intelligence Richard Helms that if "the CIA did not intervene on Rosselli's behalf, he would spill the entire story of his work for the Agency," according to his biography. Helms replied to Maheu directly that the CIA would not assist in Rosselli's case. Rosselli had heard reports that the CIA was behind the effort to deport him, though government documents released decades later would reveal that the CIA had in fact been working behind the scenes with high-level officials of the Immigration and Naturalization Service to prevent the Italian native's deportation. Furious and somewhat desperate, Rosselli decided to "make good on his threat," as one account put it. The CIA had "broken the rules of conduct," and he would follow suit. Not surprisingly, the mouthpiece would be Anderson, Pearson having died the year before. "I kept a light in the window for him," Anderson would write decades later of

Rosselli, "and he began dropping by whenever he was in Washington." Opal Ginn, the columnist's assistant, plied him with aged scotch she kept in her desk drawer, and served him her signature cornmeal-dusted fried green tomatoes. Cultivating each other in the mutual symbiosis that was Washington journalism, Rosselli provided Anderson with further embellishments of the plots. On January 18, 1971, Anderson for the first time identified Rosselli as a player, though not as a source, breaking "the blockbuster story nationwide," as Rappleye and Becker put it. "Locked in the darkest recesses of the Central Intelligence Agency," Anderson wrote, "is the story of six attempts against Cuba's Fidel Castro." Steadfast, the CIA issued a denial and the Nixon White House refused to intervene on Rosselli's behalf.

Though Rosselli had told Anderson of the role of Trafficante and Giancana, the columnist intentionally left those details out of the story. "There was an etiquette to be followed in these matters," Anderson claimed nearly thirty years later in quoting Rosselli. "Santo Trafficante was the godfather-in-exile of Cuba . . . Rosselli couldn't even tiptoe through Trafficante's territory without permission, and he couldn't approach Trafficante without a proper introduction." But since Rosselli's boss Giancana had "godfather status," Rosselli told Anderson, "he [Giancana] could solicit Trafficante's help to eliminate Castro."

But Rosselli had withheld from Anderson the most significant information, or disinformation as some scholars believed, and it would be many years before Anderson would pierce the veil. During the operation there had been what Mahoney termed "supposedly . . . a disastrous reversal of fortune" of Trafficante's sniper team sent to kill Castro in 1963. "He selected three of the best, a trio of marksmen, and placed them on a rooftop in Havana," as one account put it. But the sharpshooters were "captured, tortured, and redeployed back into the United States to assassinate President Kennedy," as Mahoney described it. Rosselli would protect this "turnaround" information, his ace-in-the-hole, until his own death. "Castro, enraged by the attempts against his life," Anderson would conclude thirty years later, "struck back at Kennedy; the Mafia, enraged by Bobby Kennedy's unrelenting war on organized crime, became Castro's willing accomplice; thus the plot against Castro was transformed into a plot against Kennedy."

It would be this devastating inside knowledge about the Kennedy assassination, what the Washington Post called Rosselli's "monstrous interconnections," that would eventually get him killed, and which would not be published until the 1990s. But for now, a week after the Anderson splash, with no national newspapers following up on the story, and the CIA apparently refusing to come to his rescue, Rosselli quietly turned himself in to a county sheriff in Southern California. "I am just not able to conclude that Mr. Rosselli is entitled to brownie points for having tried to assassinate Fidel Castro," U.S. Judge William Gray tersely declared at Rosselli's July 1971 sentencing hearing, despite pleas to the judge by Anderson to go easy on his source from the underworld, a man whom Anderson described as a "patriot."

Meanwhile, the CIA issued a strong denial of Anderson's tale of a Castro assassination plot, and Maheu publicly discredited Rosselli's claims. "I will not dignify such a story by even commenting on it," he told the *Los Angeles Times*, distancing himself from his longtime friend and associate while hoping to ingratiate himself with the CIA. But he, Greenspun, Morgan, and Anderson would continue their coercion of the Nixon White House.

Alarmed at Rosselli's imprisonment, Maheu began his self-interested maneuvering within weeks. "Convinced that Nixon had joined forces with Hughes, that the president was conspiring against him, that the FBI and the CIA were also poised to attack," Michael Drosnin wrote in his book *Citizen Hughes*, "Maheu fired a warning shot at the Oval Office." Maheu leaked to Greenspun, who then leaked to Anderson, that he possessed documents showing a $100,000 payoff from Hughes to Nixon that had come from the skim—"siphoned like a sip of champagne from the Silver Slipper," Anderson wrote in 1999—and been passed through Rebozo. "Nixon waited in horror for the full story to explode," according to Drosnin, but nothing happened. Like Anderson's CIA-Syndicate assassination stories in the months before, they were ignored by the national press.

Just when the White House thought that might be the end of it, Greenspun himself approached Nixon's press aide, Herb Klein, at an Oregon convention of newspaper editors held on September 26, 1971. Greenspun told Klein he had a story that could "sink Nixon." When Klein reported the conversation to Ehrlichman, Ehrlichman immediately dispatched Nixon's personal attorney, Herb Kalmbach, to Las Vegas to meet with the publisher, determine what information he might have, and attempt to dissuade him from publication. It was neither Kalmbach's nor Ehrlichman's first foray into Las Vegas damage control. There had been great "gnashing of teeth," Ehrlichman said in an interview decades later, "over the relationship between Donald Nixon and Hughes aide Johnny Meier." The president's fifty-five-year-old brother had been spending a lot of time in Nevada with Meier, and Ehrlichman, Haldeman, and Rebozo were all watching the blossoming friendship warily, constantly warning Donald. "I just gave him the sermon," Ehrlichman later admitted. "He was to get off the gravy train at once, leave John Meier alone and lead a life of quiet rectitude." The fact that Meier was also a close friend of Greenspun and a suspected Anderson source heightened their anxiety.

Meeting at the Sahara Hotel on the Strip on October 12, Kalmbach and Greenspun conversed for several hours—"Kalmbach scribbling on yellow legal pads," according to Howard Kohn—Greenspun revealing that Nixon used $100,000 in Hughes money to furnish San Clemente, the western White House. Greenspun never reported the story, but the drumbeat of threatened scandal continued, and Greenspun's involvement never dissipated. He rarely published his own leaks, preferring to have them appear in the president's backyard and thus to keep the White House confused about the originating source of the stories and unable to trace them directly back to Las Vegas. Only days after the Kalmbach-Greenspun meeting, Hughes's public relations man in Washington, Robert F. Bennett, provided Charles Colson, the special counsel to the president, with a terrifying tidbit: The Las Vegas publisher had in his office safe hundreds of explosive memoranda that Maheu had secreted from his tenure with Hughes. Such knowledge quickened Nixon's fears and growing paranoia that some dark force was out to destroy his presidency, according to Ehrlichman. By December, the Plumbers were grasping for solutions to throttle the leaks to Anderson—they even went so far as to discuss assassinating "the columnist by coating his car's steering wheel with a poison," according to later published accounts.

Two months later, White House aides would be shocked to learn that what had begun as an IRS probe of Maheu had led to a multimillion-dollar mining swindle involving Donald Nixon and his Las Vegas friend Meier. A Long Island native, John Herbert Meier had been brought into the Hughes inner circle in 1968 as a computer expert who claimed to have two doctorates. "Dr. Meier," as the lumbering, gregarious man was known, immediately began "circulating throughout Washington and informing anyone who would listen that he was Howard's favorite," Maheu later wrote acerbically. "Meier had struck up a relationship with Donald soon after his brother moved into the White House."

With gold and silver prices surging throughout the world, Hughes had decided to buy up most of Nevada's once prolific mines—"the Hughes family had come full circle," as a team of reporters wrote, referring to the origin of the Hughes fortune in the mining drill bit. Hughes put Meier in charge of securing the gold and silver claims throughout Nevada, "an odd choice to head a multimillion-dollar mining program," said one account. One of the first Las Vegans to sell to Hughes was Nevada Gaming Commission member George Von Tobel. A former legislator from a pioneer Nevada family, Von Tobel sold his claim near the Comstock Lode to Hughes for $225,000—"a mere suggestion of what the future held," according to one observer. Von Tobel "saw no conflict of interest in selling mines to Hughes while regulating

Hughes's gambling operations," wrote Barlett and Steele, yet another kind of portent of the future. What followed was a spree as wild as Hughes's casino purchases. "Nevada had seen nothing like it in a hundred years," they reported. In a matter of months, Meier had acquired on behalf of Hughes 80 percent of the known silver reserves in Nye and Esmeralda counties.

Along the way, Meier became associated with Anthony G. "Tony" Hatsis, president of Salt Lake City's Toledo Mining Company. The two men first met at the Sands Hotel while Hatsis was vacationing in Las Vegas. Both were in the mining business, and embraced what the other had to offer: Hatsis's company owned a number of claims in Nevada and Utah, and Meier worked for a man who was willing to buy them. The two embarked on a scheme in which Hughes millions were deposited in Hatsis's escrow account, ironically at Walter Cosgriff's Continental Bank in Salt Lake City. When the con was over, Hughes had spent $20 million for virtually worthless gold and silver mines, the proceeds having been routed to numbered accounts in Switzerland, the Bahamas, and Liechtenstein.

Upon learning that Meier had brought Hatsis into Donald Nixon's circle, Ehrlichman looked at Hatsis's FBI file. He read that the Salt Lake man was "an unsavory character with organized crime connections." Secretly kept apprised of IRS developments by his friend the commissioner, Ehrlichman learned that "Donald's escapades with Meier were detailed . . . ," according to a Hughes biography, "not merely the bogus mining claims but land deals and stock deals with organized-crime figures. Hawaiian vacations paid for by Meier with Hughes ultimately picking up the tab, trips to the Dominican Republic for shady joint ventures with the island's top government leaders." Ehrlichman brought the disquieting news to the president. In response, Nixon personally ordered his brother surveilled and wiretapped, and dispatched his friend Rebozo to implore Donald once and for all to cut off contact with Meier. By December 1971, Meier was bragging of "secret meetings with the president himself," according to Drosnin—a claim corroborated by expense vouchers submitted to Hughes. A scandal loomed on the horizon, seemingly certain to implicate Donald Nixon and to engulf the White House. Distraught, the president "railed on and on about his 'stupid brother,' " according to one account.

The president was now dealt another harsh blow with Las Vegas overtones. On December 7, 1971, McGraw-Hill publishers in New York announced with great fanfare a publication coup—"a 230,000 word transcript of taped reminiscences of Howard R. Hughes." *Life* was scheduled to begin running excerpts from the book in March 1972. The revelation that Clifford Michael Irving, an American novelist living in Spain, had purportedly conducted one hundred taped interviews with the reclusive billionaire sent shock waves through the Nixon White House. Presidential assistant John Dean approached their Hughes "source," Robert Bennett, while Haldeman sought information about Irving's revelations directly from the FBI. Hoover personally reported the news to Haldeman: The book contained devastating information about Nixon's ties to Hughes and Las Vegas. Irving claimed to have evidence not only of a $400,000 bribe to Nixon in return for fixing the TWA case, and another $1 million for halting AEC testing in Nevada, but, most shocking of all to Nixon himself, that it had been Hughes who had leaked the 1960 loan scandal to Pearson. "The fallout from the Irving caper brought Nixon's paranoia to full boil," Drosnin wrote. Hughes spokesmen immediately dismissed the book as a hoax, stating unequivocally that the billionaire had never been interviewed by Irving. "I'll kiss your ass 130 times in the middle of the Vegas Strip if that book isn't a fake," Greenspun told journalist James Phelan only moments after its announcement came over newswires. "Hughes isn't in any shape to write a book." Both the Hughes people and the White House thought Maheu was behind the fraud. "It was . . . utter nonsense," Maheu later wrote. "I knew very well that Howard had never set foot outside the Desert Inn . . . if McGraw-Hill had been interested in verifying the facts, all it had to do was contact me."

It would be a long, grueling three months for the White House before Irving would plead guilty to criminal charges in New York for bilking the publisher out of $750,000. But by that time the president had been further damaged by Greenspun leaks that were coming faster than his Plumbers could stymie them. In January 1972, though the manuscript was officially on hold by the publisher, the *New York Times* headlined on the front page: "Hughes-Nixon Ties Described in the Book." That story was followed up a week later with a startling account of how Bobby Kennedy, while attorney general, had seriously considered prosecuting Nixon for the Hughes bribes. Still reeling from that story—Nixon calling the now-martyred Kennedy "a ruthless little bastard"—the White House was hit two weeks later with two more. First, Anderson re-reported the $100,000 Silver Slipper story, enhancing it with further details about the role of Nixon intimate Rebozo—"former filling-station attendant, chauffeur, airline flight attendant, owner of a tire-recapping business, operator of a self-service laundry chain, real-estate speculator, campaign worker for [George] Smathers, and now bank president, millionaire, and confidant of the president," as Barlett and Steele described Nixon's closest friend. Greenspun then told *Times* reporter Wallace Turner that he possessed two hundred of Maheu's most explosive memoranda in a Meilink safe in his Las Vegas newspaper office, located under a recently posed photograph of Greenspun with President Nixon. "Wally Turner was an old friend of mine," Greenspun would later say of his disclosure. On February 3, Turner reported the cache, identifying many as handwritten by Hughes himself, and indicating they were of a highly sensitive nature.

The very next day, Liddy was given a go-ahead by Attorney General Mitchell to break into Greenspun's *Sun* office to steal the contents of the safe. Liddy would refer the job to Hunt, who in turn would meet with Hughes security chief Ralph Winte to discuss what Hunt later described as their "commonality of interests." On February 19, Hunt, Liddy, and Winte met in Beverly Hills to prepare for the Las Vegas burglary. All three would later contend that the heist was aborted, although Greenspun claimed that his office actually was burglarized and a "steel plate was ripped off" his safe, according to *Rolling Stone*. A tape-recorded conversation later released also suggested the burglary had in fact taken place and been successful. "They flew out, broke [into] his safe, got something out," Ehrlichman told the president (possibly referring to the April 1972 robbery of the safe of one of Greenspun's Las Vegas lawyers).

Then, on Memorial Day weekend, a team led by Hunt and Liddy broke into the DNC headquarters at the Watergate. Though the details and motives of that break-in would be contradicted by participants and contested by historians for decades to come, the fact that O'Brien's telephone was bugged and documents were photographed was undisputed. The team returned on June 17. But on that night, a security guard notified police of a burglary in progress, and the unraveling of the presidency would be set in motion.

Eight months later, the U.S. Senate formed the Select Committee on Presidential Campaign Activities to investigate the myriad Watergate crimes, conspiracies, and cover-ups. Escaping direct implication in the intrigues at least throughout the summer and fall of 1972, Nixon was reelected by a landslide in November. But by the following February, the official probe underway, disturbing links between the president and Las Vegas were erupting.

Sam Dash, chief counsel to the committee, was "drawing a line from an aborted operation in Las Vegas [the escapade involving Greenspun's safe] to the most infamous burglary in the history of the United States," one journalist reported. "Almost from the beginning of the Watergate scandal," *Newsweek* noted, "rumors have swirled around Washington that billionaire recluse Howard Hughes was somehow linked to it." Senate aides were particularly interested in Hughes's 1970 attempted purchase of the Dunes. Rumors of bribes to Nixon's Justice Department to ease antitrust restrictions were rife, as well as reports of Governor Laxalt serving as a go-between for Hughes and Mitchell. Though Justice officials had reported to Mitchell that the

Dunes acquisition "would definitely violate antitrust guidelines," as one account made clear, one week later Mitchell gave Hughes a go-ahead. Such a decision likely had Nixon's support, according to Barlett and Steele, who reported Nixon's "rage" over the Justice handling of another monopoly case. "I want something clearly understood," the president ranted; ". . . I do not want [Justice] to run around prosecuting people, raising hell about conglomerates."

Watergate prosecutors focused on Mitchell's private meetings with Hughes aide Richard Danner. The two men had known each other since Nixon's 1968 presidential campaign. "Mitchell and Danner closeted together in three secret meetings over a period of seven weeks. Then Mitchell gave the green light," *Rolling Stone* reported. "We see no problem," Mitchell told Danner regarding the Dunes. "Why don't you go ahead with the negotiations." Danner, the former special agent in charge of the Miami FBI office, excitedly passed the approval along to his colleague Maheu. "It did not take long for the story to move along the Las Vegas Strip," according to one report, "that John Mitchell had told Howard Hughes he could buy the Dunes."

Terry Lenzner, the intense, square-jawed assistant chief counsel to what was simply being called the Watergate Committee, was also intrigued by the Nevada connections, especially as outlined to him by John Meier. Interviewed in October 1973, Meier was the first real Hughes "insider" to come forward. Meier provided Watergate investigators with more linkage of Nixon to Hughes, while simultaneously, and secretly, leaking to Anderson. He confirmed details of Hughes payoffs to Nixon through Rebozo. Meier also revealed what was perceived as devastating firsthand knowledge of the relationship between Donald Nixon and Hatsis. He disclosed the CIA's use of Cay Sal—the Bahamian island leased by Hughes since 1957—as a covert base for spying on Cuba. He claimed to possess "a list of dozens of politicians whose campaigns the CIA had asked Hughes to support financially," according to a Canadian journalist. Though flirting by providing details of the cozy association between the Hughes empire and the CIA, Meier withheld from the committee classified information about the ongoing multimillion-dollar *Glomar II* operation. Anderson now tipped off Lenzner that the $100,000 cash from the Silver Slipper came in wrappers imprinted with "Las Vegas," and was divided among Nixon's two brothers and the president's secretary, Rose Mary Woods.

Lenzner followed the leads to Nevada, dispatching his investigators to interview Paul Laxalt. They found him in "Laxalt's beautifully reconstructed turn-of-the-century office" in Carson City, according to a memorandum written to Lenzner by one of his aides. Questioned extensively on January

2, 1974, Laxalt was asked if he had passed $50,000 from Hughes to Nixon at a 1968 Palm Springs dinner. Laxalt adamantly denied giving any cash to the candidate, indignantly disavowing that he had ever served as a Hughes bag-man. Though he admitted speaking at length with Nixon at the party, Laxalt said they did not discuss political contributions of any kind. Coincidentally, Laxalt revealed, his brother Peter headed the Nixon campaign in Nevada and disbursed $50,000 of Hughes cash to various state GOP candidates—"cash was a common means of making contributions in Nevada at that time," he told them. Laxalt insisted "with a categorical statement" that he had never been contacted by "anyone" regarding Hughes's purchase of the Dunes, nor had he ever intervened with Washington officials on behalf of any Nevada gamblers. Grilled about his encounters with government agents, Laxalt acknowledged meeting personally with J. Edgar Hoover on two occasions, once accompanied by Del Webb, but said he was merely "paying his respects." He also recalled a meeting with John Mitchell, but could not remember discussing antitrust issues, and on a separate occasion accompa-nied Kirk Kerkorian, owner of the new $80 million, 1,500-room Interna-tional Hotel and Casino, to meet with the SEC, but denied he was exerting any political pressure on the enforcement agency that was scrutinizing Kerkorian. Laxalt told Lenzner's investigators he knew very little about the Dunes except that Las Vegas banker Parry Thomas played a pivotal role in financing the casino.

By the end of 1973, congressional investigators had settled on the Water-gate break-in theory that O'Brien's office was searched for information tying Nixon to Hughes and Las Vegas. Dash had arrived at this conclusion, he told the *Los Angeles Times* in December, after "privately" questioning Meier about a $100,000 campaign contribution from Hughes to Nixon. The Watergate prosecution force was looking at a "possible connection between the deliver-ies [of the cash] and the seeking of favorable consideration of matters which Hughes had before various agencies and two branches of the federal govern-ment during 1970," it reported to Special Prosecutor Leon Jaworski.

But the Hughes references were quickly passed over, due, in part, to the work of Hughes's Washington publicist Robert Bennett. A Utah Mormon and the son of Senator Wallace F. Bennett, he enjoyed "solid political con-nections," as well as an "uncanny ability to manipulate the news media," ac-cording to one historian. Intervening with Senate Watergate Committee chairman Sam Ervin, Bennett guided the committee's spotlight away from Hughes. Bennett's Mullen Company had been a CIA front since its inception in 1959, according to congressional testimony. Bennett himself was what one committee lawyer described as "sort of the mystery man of the whole Watergate thing." Following the break-in, Howard Kohn reported, "Bennett charted a course that protected the CIA and Hughes at the expense of Nixon." Included in that process would be the historic leaks to the *Washington Post*, the newspaper of course credited with breaking the Watergate story. "Bennett was feeding stories to Bob Woodward," a CIA memorandum reported, "who was 'suitably grateful.' " Although Bennett's name surfaced dozens of times, he was never called to testify. Instead, investigators interviewed him in executive session, sealing his testimony from public inspection in what would become a pattern of the committee inquiry where Las Vegas was concerned. "One Hughes executive after another was questioned in secret—when interviewed at all," Barlett and Steele said of the unusual proceedings that contrasted so starkly with the otherwise sensational televised hearings. "More than two dozen people with information relating to ties between the Hughes empire and Watergate were questioned in private, often informally, and not under oath." By early 1974, the Hughes–Las Vegas connections had disappeared from the public limelight altogether. "A lot of people are worried that by pushing the hearings into the realm of Howard Hughes a lot is going to be uncovered that involves more than Richard Nixon," one of Anderson's reporters told Meier.

Watergate investigators were intrigued from the beginning with Nixon's numerous references to "the whole Bay of Pigs thing" whenever he discussed the break-in. Shortly after the burglary, Nixon had warned CIA director Richard Helms that "this entire affair may be connected to the Bay of Pigs, and if it opens up, the Bay of Pigs may be blown," imploring the CIA to thwart the FBI's inquiry into Watergate on grounds of national security. Nixon's contemporaneous tape-recorded references to "the whole Bay of Pigs thing" seemed to some White House aides, including Ehrlichman, a euphemism for the CIA-Syndicate Castro assassination plots, since the decade-old Bay of Pigs invasion was hardly a secret. One theory Watergate prosecutors were exploring was that the president himself had ordered the burglaries of O'Brien and Greenspun in search of Maheu memos that might document Nixon's role in the CIA Cuba plots. Investigators had learned that the two 1971 Jack Anderson columns about the Castro plot backfiring against President Kennedy had "triggered a spate of memos inside the Nixon White House," according to one account, and led "directly to the White House's first ill-starred contacts with Robert Bennett." In pursuit of the hypothesis that Nixon might have culpability in the assassination scheme in his role as executive officer for the CIA's Cuban operations while vice president, the committee subpoenaed Johnny Rosselli.

Appearing in secret session in February, Rosselli was questioned extensively about then–Vice President Nixon's knowledge of CIA-Syndicate collusion. The Republicans believed that a "document existed showing Nixon was involved with or knew what was going on with the CIA and the assassination of Castro," according to Leslie Scherr, the Washington lawyer who appeared before the committee with Rosselli. "The explosive secret Nixon feared might come out," Rappleye and Becker concluded, "was his own direct involvement in the initial assassination plots against Fidel Castro," and, by extension, if indeed a captured hit team had been "turned," as Rosselli contended, then Nixon's own culpability in the assassination of his nemesis JFK.

But none of this was aired publicly, and by the time Nixon resigned on that muggy summer day in 1974, the odd and labyrinthine "Vegas connections"—which Rosselli's attorney described as "so convoluted you really had to be John Le Carré to follow it"—seemed to disappear with him.

Vice President Gerald Ford ascended to the presidency, and exactly one month after Nixon's resignation granted his predecessor a "full, free, and absolute pardon" for any crimes "which he, Richard Nixon, has committed or may have committed" during his presidency. Signing the proclamation, Ford brought the Watergate investigation to a standstill. But the American people had been rocked by the exposure of what scholar Kathryn Olmsted described as "previously unimaginable levels of corruption and conspiracy in the executive branch."

By the beginning of the following year, *New York Times* investigative reporter Seymour Hersh had further shocked the public with a series of articles dubbed "the son of Watergate," detailing an extensive CIA-sponsored domestic spying program. Hersh's exposé on the heels of the Nixon White House offenses "produced a dramatic response from the newly energized post-Watergate Congress and press," as one history put it, and ". . . both houses of Congress mounted extensive, year-long investigations of the intelligence community." The U.S. Senate created its Select Committee on Intelligence Activities, chaired by Idaho senator Frank Church, "charged with a broad mandate to probe both the CIA and the FBI," according to one report. Ford announced a "blue-ribbon panel formed to address allegations of domestic spying by the CIA," as one account described the Rockefeller Commission. "Ford knew that if everything was disclosed, the CIA would have been left helpless," Maheu later wrote. So the commission was designed to investigate CIA assassinations, "labeled internally as the 'family jewels,' "

Maheu wrote, ". . . while at the same time trying to protect the [CIA] from total disclosure." Then there was the House committee chaired by Otis Pike, a moderate New York Democrat, who promised to go deeper, to "examine the systemic problems of the intelligence community," as one author noted.

Almost immediately the press was provided with what Rappleye and Becker called "a steady supply of stunning new allegations—that the CIA had approved the assassination of . . . Castro . . . that Bobby Kennedy had known of the plots, and of the collaboration with the Mafia." The revelations of the massive abuses by both the CIA and FBI spawned widespread public mistrust of the federal government and renewed conspiracy theories, especially surrounding the assassination of Jack Kennedy. "After learning that Hoover's FBI had tried to convince Martin Luther King, Jr. to kill himself, that the White House Plumbers had plotted to kill Jack Anderson, and that the CIA had drugged unsuspecting citizens," wrote one historian, "some Americans began to question the official explanation of many recent events." Both Pike and Church expressed outrage at the secret government they were finding. "It took this investigation to convince me that I had always been told lies," Pike would tell a journalist, "to make me realize that I was tired of being told lies."

Once again, at the center of these lies and hidden history was Las Vegas and its inside players, and the summer of 1975 would be the final reckoning for many of them. "With CIA assassinations at the top of the agenda," according to one account of the Church Committee, "the spotlight of inquiry began to swing inexorably to the mobsters involved in the plots, to Rosselli, Santo Trafficante, and Sam Giancana." It would be the first time Trafficante's name was publicly mentioned in connection with the CIA and Syndicate plots, and the Florida crime boss fled to his Costa Rica estate to avoid congressional subpoenas, all the while staying in close contact with Rosselli.

Maheu honored his subpoena, finally deciding to abrogate his patriotic code of silence, according to his self-adulating autobiography, because "a top official at the CIA" told him the CIA had decided to "let the laundry hang out." Maheu pledged full cooperation in exchange for immunity from prosecution and gave most of his testimony in executive session. Still, Maheu only confirmed the scenario that had been well publicized in previous years by Anderson and Pearson, and therefore represented no real threat to either the CIA or the Syndicate. In an impassioned monologue against President Kennedy and the misdirection of the probe of CIA abuses, Maheu spewed out the reactionary vitriol that the true atrocities of the U.S. government "were the boys killed during the botched Bay of Pigs."

Giancana, in declining health, had no interest in appearing before the committee, but also had no intention of fleeing. Having recently been deported from Mexico and forced to testify before a federal grand jury in Chicago, the man still known as "the boss of bosses" was overseeing the transition of power of the Chicago outfit in Las Vegas as represented in the Stardust Hotel, and had "little taste for a grilling by a congressional committee," as one report put it. On June 19, Church Committee staffers arrived in Chicago to provide Giancana with safe transport back to Washington to testify on the Castro assassination attempts. But by the next morning the "juice" of Las Vegas was dead, the grotesque half-smile of bullet holes ringing his chin. "In the Mafia's argot of death," a team of journalists wrote, "the message was clear: Giancana had been silenced. Permanently."

Rosselli, released on parole two years earlier, was holed up in the Watergate apartment of his good friend Fred B. Black, Jr.—an erstwhile Las Vegan and "superlobbyist who drew a $300,000 salary," as one associate described him—when he got word of Giancana's death. Bobby Baker, a decades-long associate of Black, later revealed that Black too was "a direct leak to Jack Anderson" through a sexual liaison with one of Anderson's female employees. Black and Rosselli had been friends since the fifties, when Rosselli procured Las Vegas and Hollywood women, like Judith Campbell, for Black's suite at Washington's Sheraton-Carleton Hotel. It was to that suite, along with Baker's private Quorum Club located in the old Capitol Hill Carroll Arms Hotel, that lobbyists, congressmen, senators, and presidents came for "recreation"—what Maheu had coined "softening up parties." Black, one of "LBJ's dependent tribe of military industrial lobbyists," wielded behind-the-scenes political power in Washington long after his conviction on federal tax evasion charges.

Preparing to meet with a Church Committee investigator, Rosselli was already awake at 6 o'clock on the morning of June 20 when he got the call about Giancana's death. Donning his "finest smoking robe and his silk pajamas," his lawyer recalled, Rosselli calmly ordered room service. Those present found him strangely unaffected, though the "staff of the Church Committee were decidedly shaken," as one account described them. Convinced that Trafficante had ordered the hit on Giancana, and afraid that their only surviving Syndicate witness to the Castro assassination plots might be killed as well, committee staffers advanced Rosselli's testimony to that same day rather than risk losing him before his scheduled appearance four days later. Spirited into a congressional hearing room by Capitol police, he spoke to a standing-room-only crowd. In characteristic fashion, the impeccably tailored businessman blithely revealed details of the nefarious plot with a smooth, unruffled demeanor that one observer called "hypnotic."

In classically banal Capitol Hill questioning somewhat reminiscent of the Kefauver Hearings, Senator Barry Goldwater challenged Rosselli to back up his story with handwritten notes such as his CIA counterparts had provided the committee. In a line that would go down in Syndicate annals, Rosselli remained expressionless. "Senator," he responded, "in my business, we don't take notes." Though his testimony was astonishing even to the most cynical government insiders, it was little more than doublespeak for Rosselli. He had managed to shelter his CIA control agent in Miami, without revealing any more than Anderson had already reported in his columns, and even Rosselli's second appearance a few months later shed little new light. "He only told them what they already knew," an associate of Rosselli's said later. "He didn't divulge one iota more. No one had anything to fear from what Johnny said that time." Rosselli withdrew from the national scene into his role as adviser emeritus in Las Vegas—"an ambassador without portfolio," though with Giancana dead, his main allegiance now was to Trafficante—as the committees folded into their own failures. "The secret agencies clearly emerged the winners of their long battle with the investigators," one scholar commented. "The Pike committee collapsed in frustration and mutual recriminations. The Church committee issued a massive, detailed final report, but some of its sections on foreign intelligence struck many critics as vague and timid."

But Rosselli's slick performance had piqued rather than pacified at least two of the senators. Liberal Pennsylvania Republican Richard Schweiker and Colorado Democrat Gary Hart were deeply troubled by the ramifications of the Castro plots on the Warren Commission investigation into the assassination of JFK, specifically the role of the CIA and FBI in withholding crucial information about the Maheu-Rosselli-Giancana alliance. Forming a select committee to take up where the other committees had left off, they began their own carefully structured probe of the JFK assassination and the CIA and FBI follow-up, or cover-up. If Rosselli believed his evidentiary appearances were behind him, he was gravely mistaken. For in the next round he would no longer be able to talk his way through and around the momentous events.

Less than a year after his last appearance before the Church Committee, Rosselli stole into Washington on April 23, 1976, not even contacting his longtime friends in the capital. Under tight security and intensive grilling by Schweiker in the Carroll Arms Hotel, where Rosselli had spent many leisurely hours in the past, and which was now ironically owned by Congress, the gangster backtracked on earlier testimony, even contending that he possessed no "facts" about the Castro counterstrike theory. His forthright-

ABOVE: President Kennedy with Sands entertainment director Jack Entratter during JFK's last visit to Las Vegas in September 1963. He had just berated Nevada officials for lifting Frank Sinatra's Cal-Neva license, and that night would again stay at the Sands cottage provided by Johnny Rosselli.

Courtesy of the Sands Hotel Collection, University of Nevada, Las Vegas, Library

LEFT: An ever-charming, ever-dapper Rosselli at the height of his Las Vegas power in the early 1960s.

Courtesy of Ed Becker

Joe Kennedy's old friend and front man Wingy Grober leans in between Marilyn Monroe and Frank Sinatra at the Cal-Neva in 1959.

Courtesy of Don Dondero

The elaborate array of fountains and the cypress-lined entrance to the new Caesars Palace, circa 1970.

Courtesy of the Las Vegas News Bureau Collection, University of Nevada, Las Vegas, Library

LEFT: Sam Giancana, as he appeared in Nevada's first *Black Book,* which in the early 1960s listed people to be barred from involvement in the state's gaming industry. This was at a time when the Chicago gangster was sharing a mistress with the president of the United States, visiting frequently both the Strip and Cal-Neva, and taking millions a year in skim from several Las Vegas casinos.

Courtesy of the Nevada State Archives

Robert Kennedy at his brother's gravesite during the midnight re-interment of President Kennedy's casket in its permanent resting place on March 14, 1967. Until his own murder little more than a year later, RFK would continue to be haunted by the Kennedys' compromising ties to Las Vegas.

Photograph taken by the Department of the Army, courtesy of Gus Russo

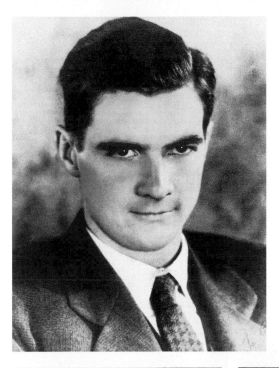

LEFT: A dashing young Howard Hughes when he first began to frequent Las Vegas casinos, and long before the ravages of drugs and dementia took hold.
Courtesy of the *Las Vegas Review-Journal*

BELOW: Hughes's security aide, and Las Vegas alter ego, Robert Maheu in a pensive pose in the 1970s, after his break with the billionaire.
Courtesy of the *Las Vegas Review-Journal*

LEFT: A smiling Governor Paul Laxalt and Republican presidential candidate Richard Nixon descend the stairs at the Governor's Mansion after meeting during the 1968 campaign; their conversation took place, ironically, in the same upstairs office where Joe Kennedy had met the Nevada delegation during the summer of 1960. Courtesy of the Nevada State Archives

Senator Paul Laxalt of Nevada greets his close friend President Ronald Reagan in Las Vegas in 1982. The powerful alliance of the two men was symbolic of the city's emergence as a shadow capital. Courtesy of the *Las Vegas Sun* Collection, University of Nevada, Las Vegas, Library

A billboard outside the unfinished Teamster-financed Landmark Hotel in the latter 1960s reflects the city's glee in welcoming Howard Hughes back to the Strip, where he purchased the Landmark as well as other casinos.

Courtesy of the Las Vegas News Bureau Collection, University of Nevada, Las Vegas, Library

RIGHT: Western movie star and Nevada lieutenant governor Rex Bell was in many ways an archetype of the state's postwar politics, the ceremonial cowboy as figurehead for powerful, more modern interests.

Courtesy of the Las Vegas News Bureau Collection, University of Nevada, Las Vegas, Library

ABOVE: Nancy and Ronald Reagan put on smiles for a respite on Lake Mead on the Last Frontier's yacht, during his ill-fated booking at the casino in the winter of 1954. There was no visible portent of the role the city would play in Reagan's transformation from fading actor to president.

Courtesy of the Las Vegas News Bureau Collection, University of Nevada, Las Vegas, Library

ABOVE: Kirk Kerkorian in Las Vegas in October 1968, fresh from his successes in Florida and California; his new, massive International Hotel rises behind him. Courtesy of the Las Vegas Review-Journal

LEFT: The print and television journalist Ned Day was the city's nearly lone conscience until his still suspicious death in 1987.

Courtesy of George Knapp at KLAS TV, Las Vegas

FBI Special-Agent-in-Charge Joe Yablonsky (right) with FBI Director William Webster. "Yobo"'s brief and stormy tenure in Las Vegas in the early 1980s was the last time federal authorities seriously challenged the established order. Courtesy of Joe Yablonsky

ABOVE: Labor leader Al Bramlet in one of his favorite leisure suits in the 1970s, when the Arkansas farm boy and ex-dishwasher was well into his quarter-century reign as leader of the Culinary Workers union in Las Vegas.
Courtesy of the *Las Vegas Review-Journal*

Attorney Oscar Goodman (left) with client and Mob hit man Tony "The Ant" Spilotro, circa 1980. Goodman would go on to City Hall as mayor, Spilotro to a shallow grave in a midwestern cornfield.
Courtesy of the North Las Vegas Library Collection, University of Nevada, Las Vegas, Library

Not far from the luxury and astronomical profits of the Strip, a father and daughter, two members of the homeless population of present-day Las Vegas, push their grocery cart full of belongings across a sweltering highway on the city's Westside. Courtesy of Kit Miller

ABOVE: The start of the Strip at the old Los Angeles highway in the year 2000. Courtesy of Darryl Martin

LEFT: Popular *Las Vegas Review-Journal* columnist John L. Smith, whose independent reporting on Steve Wynn and other Strip oligarchs was in a beleaguered but honored tradition of Nevada journalism. Courtesy of the *Las Vegas Review-Journal*

ness of the previous year had diminished. Most unbelievable to staffers and members who had heard his previous testimony, Rosselli recanted earlier claims, contending that he had never discussed the matter with his attorney Ed Morgan. That night, having stiffed the committee, the seventy-one-year-old Rosselli stole back to Miami, where he began maneuvering for a full-time return to Las Vegas. Meeting with a longtime friend, a Catholic priest, while on a trip to Los Angeles, "for the first time since childhood, Rosselli got down on his knees and made confession," according to his biographers. He then returned to Florida, and a few weeks later received a call from Fred Black warning him to leave Miami because Trafficante was going to have him killed. But Rosselli seemed to shrug off the threat, knowing full well that in his business there was nowhere to hide if Trafficante in fact wanted him dead.

The next day, July 28, 1976, Rosselli, the keeper of secrets, the man who dispensed some and withheld even more, disappeared. A week later, his mutilated body, crammed into a weighted steel drum, bobbed to the surface of Dumfoundling Bay off Miami, buoyed by gases of the decomposing corpse. His relatives hoped his murder was somehow linked to the CIA—"at least then Johnny, he would have died for a cause," one of them said—but the case would never be solved and investigators believed the grisly killing traceable to Trafficante. "Like Giancana, another message from the city," said a Las Vegas acquaintance of Rosselli. Senators on the Intelligence Committee implored the Justice Department to enter the homicide investigation since Rosselli had been a congressional witness. The FBI at first refused, only reluctantly joining the probe under pressure from congressmen and the *Washington Post*. Senator Hart especially was appalled at the gruesomeness of the death. "Never before had the murder of a hoodlum generated such a crisis of conscience in Washington," Rappleye and Becker wrote later.

Though Rosselli had seemingly violated *omertà,* the Mafia's code of silence, by voluntarily testifying before Congress, it was generally believed by the Syndicate and congressmen that his testimony had been nothing more than calculated disinformation. His admissions about the old Castro assassination plots revealed nothing new, and served instead to shroud both the "turnaround" theory and, especially, the ongoing relationship of the CIA and the Syndicate—specifically in the Southeast Asia opium trade that had flourished during the Vietnam War and the new cocaine pipeline from Colombia into Florida, both of which were controlled by Trafficante with CIA cooperation. "In southern Florida, beginning at least in 1960 and continuing well into the nineteen-seventies, the Mafia and the CIA were one and the same," as one history described the era, "indistinguishable in their objectives, in their personnel, in their methods." Certainly both the Syndicate and the CIA were concerned about Rosselli breaking his silence, a prospect that loomed increasingly with the gangster's advancing age, avowed patriotism, repeated meetings with the muckraking Anderson, and rekindled Catholicism. He was even boldly trying to get Hollywood interested in a movie on the Castro assassination plots.

Regardless of the motives of his killers, Rosselli's death signaled the end of an era and a world—the high-flying Ian Fleming days of sexual intrigue and political murder, of Cold War fanaticism and crusading reformers, of gabardine-clad hoodlums making foreign policy, all against the backdrop of the nation's only "open city," a Casablanca-like Las Vegas where anything goes. The town and its ruling class seemed to learn from those exposures and reckonings, limited though they were, and the next phase in the city's metamorphosis would be a calculated transformation. The heirs to the kingdoms of Rosselli, Giancana, and Hoffa—many the sons of gangsters themselves—graduated from their business schools and staked their claim in the Strip's palaces. Like them, the city too seemed to emerge from its adolescence with a more layered, complex identity, though with the old ethos of exploitation intact.

More sophisticated than ever, Las Vegas took its cues from the world at large, and under the sanitized facade of corporate America, it would continue its long-standing tradition of safe haven and bank for the proceeds of a commodity larger than anyone could have envisioned. The post-Vietnam drug market—first the Trafficante-controlled heroin and cocaine trade, then the Colombian cartel—was both unpredictable and incalculable to the average citizen. But not surprisingly, Las Vegas was prepared to handle the vast profits, unleashing billions of drug dollars into the nation's legitimate economy. As was always the case with the city, there would be many losers, and a handful of winners.

Only one major Strip hotel would be built during the 1970s, but a power struggle for control of those that already existed would dominate the decade, spawning a gangland war among the various Hughes, Syndicate, Teamster, and corporate factions, and fomenting a turnover of corporate shells and casino front men at a dizzying pace. Rife with stock scandals inspired by the state's new corporate gaming policies, flooded with illegal drug money, its frauds scrutinized by the SEC, its Teamsters millions investigated by the FBI, its casinos watched by the new DEA, its labor leaders slain, the city entered an era former FBI agent William Roemer called the "war of the godfathers."

Hit men from Kansas City and Chicago carried out their contracts in broad daylight—a point-blank murder in the Caesars Palace parking lot, the bombing of banker Parry Thomas's closest friend and neighbor in a down-town garage, the car explosion of the man in charge of the largest casino operation in the state—violence unthinkable a decade earlier. "The old order [has] changed and new rules now prevail," a *Sun* columnist wrote. "The code once held that even the lowliest gangster or other member of the underworld was untouchable in Nevada." The familiar names on the Strip were replaced with new "men of mystery," as one journalist described them. Gaming officials now conducted background checks on men named Meshulem Riklis, Ed Doumani, Lefty Rosenthal, Allen Glick, Tony Spilotro, Jay Sarno. State examiners analyzed companies for hidden owners, endlessly tracking mergers and name changes as one casino after another went on the block.

The sole casino built between 1969 and 1989 was a twenty-six-story structure that immediately became the largest hotel in the world. Inspired by the MGM film *Grand Hotel,* airline magnate Kerkor "Kirk" Kerkorian opened his own MGM Grand Hotel in 1973. It cost $106 million, drew Hollywood celebrities aplenty in keeping with its movie theme, and dominated the Strip.

Born in 1917, the son of an Armenian fruit peddler, Kerkorian dropped out of the eighth grade to cut logs for a Civilian Conservation Corps camp. He "hawked papers and ran with a gang called League of Nations," according to one account, and as a Golden Gloves boxer nicknamed "Rifle Right Kerkorian" was said to have been educated "at reform school, not high school." Though most of his earnings helped his Fresno family during the Depression, he saved whatever he could to pay for flying lessons. First a crop duster, then a flight instructor, he joined the Canadian Royal Air Force flying Mosquito bombers on dangerous missions out of Scotland. He bought a single-engine Cessna after World War II and began a tiny air carrier called Los Angeles Air Service to ferry gamblers from California to Nevada. Before long, Kerkorian was transporting air cargo, "aided by lucrative military contracts during the Korean War," one history recorded, and flying government loads from San Antonio's Travis Air Force Base to Guam.

Called the "Perry Como of the crap table" for his disconcerting quietude, Kerkorian first invested in Las Vegas in 1955, obtaining a small piece of the Dunes. Sporting a bizarre pompadour, he stealthily purchased the land across the Strip from the Flamingo in 1962 for $960,000, then sold it six years later to Caesars Palace for $5 million—a transaction *Forbes* described as "one of the most successful land speculations in Las Vegas history." By 1967, his fleet had grown into a worldwide air carrier called Trans International Airlines, the sale of which he parlayed into a $100 million personal fortune he then used to underwrite his casino purchases. That year he first bought the Flamingo to use as a training ground for his staff before beginning construction on his dream, the International. Opening the hotel in 1969 with Barbra Streisand in one showroom, the wildly popular *Hair* musical in another, and rock stars Ike and Tina Turner in the lounge, the International symbolized the new era of the psychedelic sixties. One journalist christened Kerkorian the "father of the Las Vegas megaresort."

"Intensely private," as one account portrayed him, with "balls of steel," as another described the new Las Vegas juice, he was simultaneously seizing control of an ailing MGM Studios in Hollywood. After intense pressure applied to both the SEC and Justice by Kerkorian's political water-carrier, Governor Paul Laxalt, Kerkorian was allowed by the SEC to take his International Leisure Corporation public, and sold 17 percent of the company. At the time, the Justice Department was probing the skim at the Flamingo, which had led investigators in turn to Kerkorian's fifties association with "Miami hotel men tied to Lansky," as one agent described the connections, as well as Lansky's continuing and current hidden ownership in the Las Vegas casino his old friend Bugsy had built. The stock quickly soared from $5 a share to $50, but when the SEC suddenly blocked Kerkorian from a second stock offering, claiming he had failed to disclose required information about hidden owners in the Flamingo, he had to sell both properties to Hilton Hotels in July 1970. Forced to sell for $16 million stock that had been worth $180 million six months earlier, Kerkorian accused the government of attempting to blackmail him into providing derogatory information about Lansky and others. But Kerkorian "was a stand-up guy, no snitch in him," as one of his peers put it, which meant in Strip parlance that he would be welcomed back in any new incarnation. He sold his Las Vegas mansion, his private jet, and his yacht, but less than a year later was back in town, new financing in place, and breaking ground in 1971 for "the world's largest resort hotel."

Meanwhile, concurrent with the Watergate investigation and the SEC inquiry into Kerkorian, numerous other probes had been underway in Las Vegas, though they received little local publicity. "Federal investigators . . . have been seeking clues to the disappearance of millions of dollars from Howard Hughes's seven casino-hotels and his other Nevada investments," *Business Week* reported in January 1973. Both a Los Angeles–based organized crime strike force and the SEC were scrutinizing the increasingly irascible Parry Thomas, himself deeply involved with most of the Hughes acquisitions. "When the Feds descended on Las Vegas," according to *Business Week,* "their first stop was the headquarters of Valley Bank of Nevada." By this time, Thomas had branched out from banking, amassing a personal fortune of $20 million, his holdings including an "$8.4 million chunk of the Riviera Hotel," stock in Continental Connector Corp.—the company that owned the Dunes—and a fleet of oil tankers flying Liberian flags that were directed from Thomas's "plush Manhattan offices."

Thomas's once minuscule bank, which had begun with $250,000 in start-up capital, had grown to resources of $270 million, earning more than any other bank in its Federal Reserve district. "I want an image and a name to be seen for many miles around," Las Vegas builder Irwin Molasky recalled Thomas telling him in 1975. "He wanted prestige and he wanted a modern branch downtown," Molasky said of Thomas's choice to retain Molasky's Paradise Development Company to build the tallest downtown Las Vegas building. From his new seventeen-story Valley Bank Plaza near Fremont Street, Thomas set out to "build Valley Bank into a Southwest banking powerhouse," Molasky said later. By then, Thomas and his family jetted between their luxury home in Las Vegas's Rancho Circle, their New York apartment, a Newport Beach vacation home, and a Sun Valley getaway. The man *Business Week* said had "made once rinky-dink Las Vegas into a major resort area," the financier whom the local Anti-Defamation League of B'nai Brith repeatedly named "Man of the Year," the figure one magazine said had done "more than any other one man to build up that [gambling] industry," was by the mid-seventies the figurehead for a clique of heavy hitters he had dubbed "the herd."

Thomas's coterie of trusted business partners included a notorious mix of national figures—Morris Shenker, Harvey Silbert, Sidney Korshak, Albert Parvin, Delbert Coleman, and Ed Torres—along with his longtime and ubiquitous bank officials, Jerome Mack and Kenneth Sullivan. The herd's land grab was rooted in the state's modified corporate gaming policies of a decade earlier, for which Thomas had so vigorously lobbied the state legislature and so blatantly guided the gubernatorial candidacy of Paul Laxalt. "After Laxalt had become governor and greased the wheels for corporate control of casinos," recalled a rival Las Vegas banker, "Thomas instantly began searching for a publicly traded corporation to take over. He and Valley Bank executive Jerry Mack bought controlling interest in Continental Connector, a New York electronics firm." Holding what one magazine called "a coveted listing on the American Stock Exchange," Continental Connector was "a strange acquisition for the Vegas crowd," as one journalist put it. But that small unknown entity would be the vehicle for what one report described as a "whirlwind of acquisitions and investments dozens of times the value of the original company."

"Continental immediately began acquiring companies in which Thomas and his friends had interests," *Business Week* reported in 1973. First it bought Western Transportation Co. of Chicago, a Teamsters-financed trucking firm owned by Syndicate figure Jake Gottlieb. Thomas had earlier financed Gottlieb's acquisition of the Dunes, including the valuable Strip real estate on which it was sited. The group's next big purchase was M & R Investment, the company that owned the Dunes. In one six-year period the Dunes had changed hands four times, with the same buyers in three of the four deals. "One big partnership selling something back and forth between themselves, except they kept marking up the price," reported an alarmed SEC attorney. Through the herd's machinations, the price of the Dunes Hotel and Country Club rose from $10 million to $59 million. "Thus, on paper," according to a financial reporter, "the value of the Dunes increased by 450% in six years."

Owning 40 percent of Continental stock, Shenker, "the brilliant lawyer and front man for the St. Louis Mob," as a colleague described Hoffa's attorney, "arrived in Las Vegas to take control of the Dunes." Though Shenker had long been steering major loans from various clients through Thomas's bank, his Las Vegas presence had been limited. Now he was the overt boss in a mob-dominated casino, just as many of his clients and ventures were coming under intensifying federal examination.

Shenker's controversial Galveston client, American National Insurance Company, or ANICO, had been quietly staking Thomas and the city for years, buying bank capital notes from Valley Bank as early as 1965. ANICO had funneled untold millions into Las Vegas gambling interests, including $13 million to Shenker himself; $5 million to the Liberian oil tanker venture owned by Thomas, Mack, and Silbert; and, most significantly, to Parvin-Dohrmann—the company that owned the Stardust, Aladdin, and Fremont, and on whose board of directors Thomas sat, along with fellow herd members Coleman, Torres, Korshak, and Silbert. Called by the FBI "possibly the highest paid lawyer in the world," and known in Las Vegas as the "Chicago Juice" who usually stayed in the Presidential Suite of the Riviera, Korshak was the personal fount of most of the Teamster money into Las Vegas in the sixties and seventies. At least once, according to Dan Moldea in his book *Dark Victory,* Hoffa vacated the suite to make room for Korshak. Torres was the Las Vegas gambling boss for all three Parvin-Dohrmann casinos. Coleman was a Chicago jukebox magnate and major stockholder of the Atlanta Braves. Silbert, one of Thomas's closest personal friends, was a Beverly Hills attorney known particularly for his intimate association with the fiduciary manager of the Teamsters Pension Fund, Allen Dorfman. And Dorfman, "with the possible exception of the late Meyer Lansky," wrote a Washington journalist, "was responsible for the massive organized crime infiltration of Las Vegas and its casinos."

In the late sixties, Parvin-Dohrmann had been at the heart of a national scandal involving U.S. Supreme Court justices Abe Fortas and William O. Douglas. The IRS had investigated Korshak's receipt of a half-million-dollar finder's fee for arranging the sale of the Stardust to Parvin-Dohrmann, while baseball commissioner Bowie Kuhn simultaneously opened an inquiry into stock holdings in the firm by top officials of the Atlanta Braves and the Oakland Athletics. "Weary of all the problems in Las Vegas," as one account put it, Albert Parvin, a reputed member of the Chicago mob and California furniture manufacturer who had contracts to provide furnishings to Syndicate casinos in Las Vegas, decided to sell out. "Waiting to buy the corporation was a Korshak business associate, Delbert Coleman, a Harvard man and attorney," who paid $35 each for 300,000 shares, with loans from the First National Bank of Chicago, "thereby acquiring all three coveted casinos in one fell swoop," an observer said of the transaction. In a stock scheme that was becoming pro forma for Las Vegas, "a bizarre and complex series of financial manipulations sent the stock skyrocketing to $141," according to one history, before its collapse just as suddenly to $12.50 a share; the SEC was forced to suspend trading and open an investigation of the company and its three Las Vegas casinos. Governor Laxalt had "attacked the probe," according to one published source, and accompanied his "good friend" Coleman to Washington. Laxalt would also accept a free round trip to Switzerland from Coleman even as Nevada gaming officials were forcing Coleman out of the Stardust because of the pending stock fraud charges—a conflict of interest becoming increasingly routine and open behavior for Nevada public officials. In a blatant quid pro quo, Coleman would repay the governor by arranging for Laxalt to obtain the interest-free, collateral-free loan from the First National Bank of Chicago that built Laxalt's dream Ormsby House.

When the various probes ended, Coleman was forced to resign as head of Parvin-Dohrmann, and was replaced by Parvin. Parvin quickly changed the name of the disreputable company to Recrion, and sent a clean-shaven, mild-mannered San Diego real estate developer named Allen Glick to serve as the new front man. Glick would later emerge with his own corporate shell, Allen R. Glick Enterprises, or Argent. Several key employees of Continental Connectors' Dunes Hotel were indicted for skimming, and the SEC brought action against the company and its major stockholder Shenker; Thomas himself became the subject of federal scrutiny. Like Kerkorian, Thomas blamed the uncomfortable government probe on its attempts to pressure him into becoming a snitch and informing on his fellow Las Vegans.

His own casino acquisition vehicles tarnished, Thomas would now shift his considerable resources and contacts to the making of a surrogate mogul, creating the casino boss to rival all Las Vegas casino bosses in what John L. Smith described as "a series of stepladder business deals . . . carefully planned" by the powerful banker. "Volatile, vindictive, charismatic, and smart as a whip," as one author described the young man, Stephen Alan Wynn would become what Smith, in his biography of Wynn, *Running Scared,* called "a legend as carefully sculpted as the man."

"He's like a son to me," Thomas said of Wynn as the banker orchestrated his young protégé's remarkable rise, a sentiment echoed by the adoptee. "He had four sons and one daughter," Wynn said of Thomas, "and I became the sixth kid."

Though accounts vary as to how, and through whom, the two now legendary Las Vegas figures initially met, most observers of the blossoming relationship identify Korshak as the go-between. What is indisputable is that the twenty-five-year-old Wynn appeared on the scene suddenly in 1967 with juice, the source of which was never clear.

Born in New Haven on New Year's Day 1942, he was raised the son of a gambler. "A kid no mother could control," as Smith described the young Wynn, he spent high school at a West Point preparatory school called Manlius Academy in upstate New York. He enrolled at the University of Pennsylvania, where he studied English literature while taking courses at the Wharton School of Business, returning on weekends to help run his parents' bingo hall in Wayson's Corner, Maryland. He frequented Miami, where Wynn claimed to have been inspired to "own his own joint" by the trendsetting Fontainebleau Hotel. That inspiration, along with his father's gambling debts, convinced the young man that "if you wanted to make money in a casino, the answer was to own one."

Following an arranged date with the visiting daughter of one of his father's Florida cronies, a teenage Wynn was smitten with Elaine Pascal. Outclassed but cocky, he pursued the blonde beauty with a fervor that would be characteristic of his future entrepreneurship. The former Miss Miami was studying political science at UCLA, but soon transferred to George Washington University in Washington, D.C., to be nearer her suitor. She later attributed his surprisingly successful courtship to his brazenness—"he flim-flammed me," she would say—and the two married in New York in 1963, shortly after the death of his father. The newlyweds moved to Wayson's Corner, where his mother and wife "ran things," according to one account. Wynn called numbers in a bingo parlor. The couple was quickly bored—"not enough action for either one of them," an acquaintance said—and shifted their gambling expertise to Las Vegas.

In 1967, they took the Strip by storm, he with his Ivy League education, impeccably tailored suits, and whispered-about bona fides from his father's connections, she with her own glamorous designer wardrobe and svelte figure. His first purchase was 3 percent of the Frontier, for which he paid $45,000 and became slots manager. Wynn got his stake in the casino from Rosselli's partner Maury Friedman, Thomas told Timothy O'Brien in 1997, a fact denied by Wynn—"Thomas wasn't recollecting that detail properly." At any rate, his Frontier venture coincided nicely with the Friar's Club conviction of his father's old benefactor Friedman—"an obese fast-buck artist, casino operator, and mob conduit," as one history described the aging gangster. Shortly afterward three Detroit La Cosa Nostra figures were indicted on racketeering charges, and Wynn was able to acquire two more percentage points in the Frontier, borrowing the money from Thomas's Valley Bank. Days later billionaire Howard Hughes paid what many thought an inflated price of $24 million for the troubled casino, in a deal brokered by Wynn's mentor Thomas.

Having survived his first high-stakes round on the Strip, the new golden boy had dealt himself into the big time, and insiders already knew that Thomas was "orchestrating young Steve Wynn's ascent in Las Vegas." Wynn himself would later say that Thomas's "sponsorship was the equivalent of having Bernard Baruch guiding you on Wall Street." Thomas "is to casino industry entrepreneurs what the Big Bang was to the Universe," the city's revered columnist Ned Day aptly described the relationship many years later.

The newly prominent Wynn attracted unwanted publicity in August 1967 by his presence at a ghastly accident that left a Las Vegas woman dead. It started innocently enough—Wynn socializing with mobsters Friedman and Lansky courier Irving "Niggy" Devine, cruising Lake Mead on the Caesars Palace yacht with a bevy of party girls. But when one of the guests, a dark-haired, bikini-clad prostitute and, according to contemporaneous news stories, an undercover FBI informant, dove into the water for a swim, the 45-foot cabin cruiser backed over her—its propeller cutting her in half. No one saw her jump, according to the witnesses' statements. Wynn and Friedman both claimed to have been asleep.

The tragedy would dog Wynn for decades, surfacing whenever he was subjected to background investigations. With no autopsy or probe into the cause of death, and nothing beyond the boating party's vague, terse state-ments, the event remained a mystery—including exactly what Steve Wynn himself was doing that day aboard the Caesars Galley yacht.

Apparently unfazed by the incident, the handsome, glib young promoter bounced around Las Vegas, producing lounge shows and becoming increas-ingly prominent socially. When he was ready for his next venture, he went to his mentor. "Pop, I gotta get something to do," Wynn reportedly told Thomas in 1969. "I gotta go to work." Thomas responded with his usual alacrity, introducing Wynn to yet another of the bank's remarkable customers, the colorful, immensely wealthy magnate Meshulem Riklis. The connection would be of almost incalculable importance in the future of Las Vegas. Just as Thomas guided Wynn, so too did Riklis tutor a shrewdly unorthodox and ambitious young broker named Michael Milken. Riklis launched a tumul-tuous turn in the history of American business by becoming what one author later called a "likely mentor to Milken in the uses and abuses of junk debt." And out of the links Milken and Wynn would form their own far-reaching kinship as veritable brothers.

Riklis—variously described as a native Hungarian raised in Turkey by parents who were diplomats in the British Foreign Service, or from Palestine working "as a secret operative for the Haganah," or as a soldier with Mont-gomery's Eighth Army "fighting against Rommel in North Africa"—had a past shrouded in mystery. Whatever the truth of the intervening years, he was born in Istanbul in 1923, and arrived in Minneapolis via Israel in 1947, where he was quickly known as a boy wonder of finance. Upon his arrival in the late sixties in Las Vegas, Riklis already owned Playtex, RKO theaters, and several other companies. He had recently taken control of Schenley Indus-tries from the notorious Lewis Rosenstiel, and would soon buy the Riviera. "What Riklis had done was acquire one company and then use its assets to acquire the next . . . in ever larger circles," as Connie Bruck put it in her book *Predator's Ball.* "Considered the godfather of the form of high-interest, high-risk funding that later became commonly known as junk bonds," as one writer described Riklis, it would be his model that defined the next two decades of Las Vegas expansion, with Thomas and Wynn avid devotees of the method.

Bankrolled by Thomas, by 1969 Wynn became the exclusive Nevada dis-tributor for Schenley—a coveted contract in Nevada that allowed Wynn to sell Boodle's Gin and Dewar's Scotch to all the major hotels and restaurants in Las Vegas and Reno. Wynn would get his wholesale liquor license at a time when "such licenses were so restrictive and there was such a monopoly in the city," according to a Las Vegas casino owner who knew Wynn well, "that they

were virtually impossible to obtain." But Wynn did just that. Off and running, Wynn would now parlay his liquor cash cow into a series of staggering
financial maneuvers. The next year he bought ten acres on the Strip for
$154,000, borrowing $600,000 from Thomas's bank to build a liquor warehouse on the site. Then he sold his liquor franchise, and on the surface, at
least, acquired a financial portfolio. Now he was ready for one of the most
legendary deals in Las Vegas history, what John L. Smith called "the Caesars
shuffle—as choreographed by Parry Thomas."

In 1972, with a loan from Thomas co-signed by J&B Scotch magnate
Abraham Rosenberg, Wynn bought a sliver of land on the busiest corner in
the city for $1.1 million—Wynn would commonly describe it, with under-
statement, as a "one in a million deal." The narrow strip was sandwiched on
the corner of Flamingo Road and the Strip, and was being used as a Caesars
Palace parking lot. Originally owned by Chicago trucking executive Jake
Gottlieb, Thomas had acquired it in 1968 and then apparently sold it to
Hughes in 1969. Hughes had been leasing the land to Caesars, which
"assumed it would be given the right of first refusal on it," according to a
Caesars executive. The valuable slice fronted the Strip, and bordered Caesars
for 1,500 feet. Thomas intervened with Maheu for Hughes to sell it to Wynn.

First threatening to erect what a Las Vegas architect called "the world's
narrowest casino" on the property, thereby making the land all the more
valuable to Caesars, Wynn sold his "acre of pure gold" to Caesars less than a
year later for $2.25 million. Wynn repaid his loan to Valley Bank, and divided
a cool million with Rosenberg. Strategically leaked details of the sale to the
Sun portrayed Wynn now as a brilliant businessman with a clean bankroll
and with no questions raised about the financing or associations that had
launched him. Greenspun gushed that the real estate transaction proved that
Strip frontage was now worth "$18,000 a foot," though most Las Vegans knew
that the land in question washed away with every major rainstorm, situated
as it was in a floodplain.

Wynn long attributed his meteoric Las Vegas rise to this deal, and there
was no doubt of its seminal importance. With his windfall he could now buy
out gangster Jerome Zarowitz of the Golden Nugget, who was about to be
blacklisted by gaming officials. "Caesars bought it at an inflated price, which
gave Wynn the money needed to buy the Golden Nugget, where he had been
acquiring stock for several years," said one Strip casino owner. "All of Wynn's
public announcements about building the tallest, skinniest casino in history
on the 25-foot-wide tract was a charade to make the inflated price appear
reasonable."

Whether by calculation or coincidence, two months after the Caesars deal, Wynn offered to buy Zarowitz out of the Golden Nugget in what would go down in the city's annals as a famous business coup. The historic downtown casino once owned by Bugsy had been thriving unfettered since 1949, consistently one of the most successful gambling operations in the city. Thomas's Continental Connectors had been trying to acquire the casino for the past few years, but had been blocked by the SEC. At the same time, the Gaming Control Board had made it clear that Zarowitz, an organized crime associate in partnership with the Genovese and Patriarca crime families, would not be licensed. But by March 1973, Thomas's protégé Wynn had bought Zarowitz's 92,000 shares, and by summer, age thirty, he had completed the Golden Nugget takeover.

The state's licensing of Wynn would have far-reaching ramifications in American gambling, and would in effect nullify the last of Grant Sawyer's naive 1959 attempts at regulation. At his hearing before the Gaming Control Board, Wynn claimed he needed to maintain his interest in Wayson's Corner bingo in order to finance his investment in the Golden Nugget. Insiders knew such a contention was laughable with Valley Bank financing his every move. Shannon Bybee lobbied his colleagues on Wynn's behalf, contending that Wynn shouldn't have to surrender his interest in out-of-state gaming. "He's not an outsider," Bybee said of Wynn. "He's been a resident of some six years." The board agreed to let him maintain his other gambling interests, ironically setting a precedent that would open the way to the nationwide expansion of casino gambling. With Steve Wynn's Golden Nugget license, Nevada gambling was subjecting itself to more widespread competition than it had had since the heyday of Havana.

For now, Wynn kept his sights on Las Vegas, focusing first on remodeling the old casino and adding a hotel. "With the help of the bank of the Mormon Church, the First Security of Utah, and my Mormon Las Vegas banker Parry Thomas, who got me $12 million," Wynn would boast to an interviewer in 1996, "I built a new garage and a 600-room hotel."

That was only the beginning, as author Tim O'Brien would write, of "the rise and rise of Steve Wynn."

J ust when Laxalt was facing the most serious financial crisis of his career," Dan Moldea said in referring to the fledgling and much-skimmed Ormsby House casino, "Nevada Democratic Senator Alan Bible conveniently announced that he was not going to seek reelection. Laxalt—who had previously given 1,000-to-1 odds against his ever returning to politics—immediately made his bid for the vacant Senate seat."

Pitted against Lieutenant Governor Harry Reid, Laxalt faced an uphill battle. Reid had been weakened by his unseemly and chauvinistic primary confrontation with the respected conscience of the state's Democratic Party, Maya Miller, a Carson City philanthropist and feminist. National political activist and journalist Ken Bode came to Nevada to run Miller's campaign, but she was doomed to be abandoned by the Las Vegas powers-that-be. "They called it the battle between the titans," Miller recalled, referring to Grant Sawyer, who had become a Democratic National Committeeman and titular head of the party, and the increasingly powerful Democratic governor Donal "Mike" O'Callaghan. Sawyer and O'Callaghan went head to head in their own power struggle as they sought to anoint Senator Bible's successor. By now, Las Vegas had so overtaken northern Nevada, more than doubling in population and commerce the Reno area, that the once important liberal voices of the north were relegated to quaint idealism by the southern Nevada "titans." Sawyer had forsaken all personal ambition of political office, reportedly after seeing his smear-ridden, Hoover-inspired FBI dossier, and was earning millions as a senior partner in one of the state's most powerful law firms representing Strip casinos. O'Callaghan had been a dark horse gubernatorial candidate in 1970, Greenspun's handpicked emissary to Carson City, who had quickly become one of the most popular governors in the state. O'Callaghan prevailed and the more malleable Reid won out over Miller in an act that alienated women voters, further divided north from south, and sent the liberal wing of the party into permanent remission.

Despite the rifts in the opposing party, Laxalt had all he could handle. "We thought we knew politics, but that was for Governor," brother Robert would write, having been enlisted once again to help in the campaign. "There was a whole new set of rules to go by."

In the wake of Nixon's resignation, Republican candidates throughout the country were facing landslide defeats. "Paul was upset when he saw Nixon on television," Robert Laxalt wrote. "What bothered him was not that he looked nervous, but that he looked guilty." Distancing himself from the scandalized White House, Laxalt "almost singlehandedly built up a Republican party in Nevada," as one account described his efforts, which eventually paid off. Laxalt and Utah's Jake Garn were the only Republican senators elected in 1974. The first Basque-American ever elected to the Senate, Laxalt won by only 624 votes, following a recount. Laxalt was now known as "a rugged individualist with a neoconservative, Western-populist vision of the world," a man who dressed "like a French banker," said Moldea, the Washington journalist. Laxalt quickly emerged as a powerful and outspoken proponent in Washington for Nevada's gambling interests. "What may be a proper standard of morality in Nevada may well not be a proper standard elsewhere, and we know that," Laxalt testified before a national commission. Championing the Sagebrush Rebellion, which began in Nevada as a grassroots protest against the federal control of land, but expanded in Laxalt's jargon to embody federal law enforcement as well, Laxalt gained national notoriety as a passionate states' rights advocate.

He married his longtime secretary Carol Wilson and became a "leading conservative critic" of President Jimmy Carter, "thrust into the Senate spotlight" by the Panama Canal issue. A close friend of neighboring California governor Ronald Reagan, Laxalt was an early and avid supporter of a Reagan candidacy, urging him to challenge President Gerald Ford, even forming the first Citizens for Reagan Committee. "They both loved the outdoors. They both liked horses and wore cowboy boots," an intimate wrote of the affinity between the two men. They also both had in common powerful benefactors, including Sidney Korshak, Moe Dalitz, Allen Dorfman, and the Teamsters.

As Reagan's popularity broadened and deepened, so too would Laxalt's, his name first bandied about as a vice-presidential contender, and eventually as a presidential hopeful himself. But his accommodations from earlier in his political career—his Syndicate money in the 1966 gubernatorial race, his unsecured loans from Chicago, his pressure on the Nixon administration on behalf of Hoffa, Coleman, and Kerkorian, his close friendship with Ed Doumani, his quid pro quos from Howard Hughes, his association with Hoffa's pension fund heir Dorfman—all would eventually preclude him from higher office. Perhaps Senator McCarran's admonition to Sawyer decades earlier had been true: A Nevada public official should never aspire to the presidency.

What Laxalt didn't know as he charted his political elevation was that the FBI had initiated "its largest investigation since the Lindbergh Kidnapping case against Allen Dorfman." Called Operation Pendorf, that probe would result in the political demise of longtime Democratic senator Howard Cannon. "Once you're tied into the hoods, you spend the rest of your life trying to break away from them," Laxalt once confided to a brother, determined to avoid that pitfall. "Poor Howard," he said of his Democratic counterpart. "I'm not going to make his mistake. He let three of them give him most of his money, and he hasn't been able to call himself his own man since."

Cannon's real problems began when Jackie Presser, an international vice president of the Teamsters, became an FBI informant, providing details of Syndicate control of Las Vegas. Presser's father, Bill, had been a powerful Cleveland Teamster boss who in 1974 "put together a Teamster-financed scheme that put two major Las Vegas casinos into the hands of the Mafia and netted him as much as $600,000 in kickbacks," according to journalist James Neff, "—a masterful conspiracy that involved the cooperation of Kansas City, Chicago, Milwaukee, and Cleveland crime families, and helped the Mafia coil its grip on the Strip even tighter." At the heart of all of the Las Vegas deals about which the younger Presser knew was Dorfman, the insurance executive and "pension-fund kickback artist." Presser gave agents details of how Dorfman wrote overpriced insurance policies for the casinos, all countersigned by the Harley E. Harmon Insurance Agency for many years. Then he switched to former Las Vegas mayor Bill Briar's insurance company when Briar became a member of the powerful Clark County Commission. "They wrote policies for everything," recalled a Las Vegas attorney, "—fire, liability, equipment. And did it for practically everyone—Caesars, Circus Circus, the Stardust, Riviera, Desert Inn, Dunes, Aladdin, and Sands." The massive profits were then "channeled back through the Dunes," Presser told the FBI, and "split up by Korshak, [labor leader Al] Bramlet and Dorfman." Dorfman himself was a secret owner with Chicago gangster Ross Miller of the Bingo Palace, while Miller's district attorney son held stock in a blind trust in the casino, according to Presser. When the FBI opened its investigation of Dorfman's hidden ownership in Las Vegas casinos to which he steered Teamster millions, their probe led immediately to Senator Cannon's office.

Called by Neff the "FBI's most valuable snitch," Presser claimed to have enough information to "close down Las Vegas," and dangled the opportunity to nab a U.S. senator in the process. An intercepted telephone conversation between Cannon and Dorfman "revealed a labyrinth of powerful and influential individuals stretching across the industrial midwest to the west coast and back to D.C." But perhaps most surprisingly, "it was discovered that Jackie [Presser] and the Teamsters' Executive Board were planning to bankroll Ronald Reagan's campaign for the White House."

Agents homed in on Presser's contention that Cannon had agreed to tie up legislation pending before the Commerce Committee he chaired in exchange for a valuable piece of Las Vegas real estate. Senator Ted Kennedy introduced the Trucking Deregulation Bill into Congress in January 1979—a bill that threatened the trucking industry and the Teamsters Union—and indeed it died from inactivity. Less than two weeks earlier, Cannon had met with Dorfman at his Las Vegas Senate office to discuss the purchase of a 5.8-acre parcel on Las Vegas Country Club Estates that was owned by the Teamsters.

Cannon long denied that he had agreed to sabotage the bill as a quid pro quo for the real estate. He had been approached, he claimed, by neighbors in his subdivision who were alarmed at the proposed development on the property of three nine-story buildings that would obstruct their view—a claim that was substantiated by his neighbors. Cannon contended he had agreed to act as an intermediary with Dorfman, whose father, "Red" Dorfman, he had known since the fifties. The senator admitted meeting with Dorfman, and said they agreed that the neighbors could buy the land for $1.4 million, or $200,000 less than the current high bidder. But he adamantly and steadfastly denied that deregulation factored into the negotiation.

By the end of 1979, the Chicago Strike Force had subpoenaed all of Cannon's travel records and was calling witnesses to a grand jury there. Cannon and his neighbors never bought the property, and he maintained his innocence throughout the ordeal, but his three-decades-long political career would be finished when he was defeated in the subsequent election by a virtual unknown.

Other federal investigations in Kansas City and Chicago would dovetail into Las Vegas as well—from skim at the Tropicana to hidden owners at the Stardust to drug money laundering at Caesars Palace and the Golden Nugget—sending many Nevada gangsters and politicians for cover at the end of the seventies. If Nevada's senators Cannon and Laxalt endeavored to present to Washington an elevated, cleaned-up portrait of their home state, it was pure mythology. Las Vegas casinos were fast becoming the depot of a multibillion-dollar drug network and underground economy far surpassing anything the country had ever seen.

By the late seventies, the Drug Enforcement Agency (DEA), Washington's latest successor bureaucracy to the old FBN, in Las Vegas had focused on Caesars Palace as the headquarters of a multimillion-dollar, international drug-smuggling organization that called itself "The Company." Whether a renegade offshoot of the CIA, which was commonly called "the company" in intelligence circles, or not, it was a highly sophisticated, impenetrable enterprise. The DEA was forced, with some embarrassment, to admit that "The Company" surpassed the federal government's crime-fighting abilities. Code-naming the Caesars Palace drug trafficking and money-laundering probe Operation Jaeger, the DEA admitted in a highly confidential internal memorandum to Washington superiors that "the magnitude, scope, and complexity of the operations" exceeded its field capabilities. At the heart of the Las Vegas investigation was a Texas high roller named Jamiel "Jimmy" Chagra, an American drug kingpin tied to both the Patriarca crime family in New England and the Chicago Syndicate.

"Our intelligence told us they were bringing heroin and hashish from the Middle East, and cocaine through Mexico," wrote a ranking DEA agent from the Las Vegas office. "They would land at a private airstrip, be met by a Caesars Palace limousine and casino security. It was way beyond our reach at the time."

O n a mid-June morning in 1977, a Lear jet eased in over the Caribbean to land at Santa Marta on the northern coast of Colombia. As it taxied to a stop near the small terminal, an ambulance carrying a hideously burned man pulled out on the runway, and two paramedics rushed from the plane to attend to the patient. They were with him only seconds, though long enough to see that he was dying, when Colombian federal police surrounded the jet and ambulance, arrested everyone, and impounded the aircraft.

When the first sketchy news of the incident reached Nevada, there was shock and outrage. The chartered Lear, flying for a Las Vegas air ambulance service called Jet Avia Ltd., had been on what the company described as a "mission of mercy" to evacuate a critically injured American to San Antonio for treatment. One of the victim's friends, whom the local press identified simply as a "Texas businessman," commissioned the flight, came as a passenger, and was now detained in Santa Marta along with the crew and paramedics from Las Vegas. There were vague reports that the Colombians suspected the plane of being involved in narcotics smuggling. But Jet Avia dismissed those rumors, insisting that the only drugs on board had been painkillers and burn cream for the patient, and a search of the plane by police at Santa Marta reportedly found no contraband. The seizure was "nothing more than a kidnapping," a Jet Avia spokesman would say indignantly.

As many Nevadans knew from the favorable publicity it received since its founding in 1974, Jet Avia had become an air ambulance as well as a charter for casinos to ferry high rollers and celebrities of all kinds, from the governor to Strip entertainers. The firm's three owners were among the city's most prominent citizens. Elias Ghanem, "physician to the stars," had been a casino house doctor, regularly treated Elvis Presley in a room specially built for the singer atop Ghanem's luxurious Las Vegas home, and in 1977 was starting a chain of private clinics that would make him one of the wealthiest medical contractors in the West. Dr. Harold Feikes, the first cardiovascular specialist in Las Vegas, had been Howard Hughes's personal physician, one of the few to see Hughes in the last decades of his life. By Feikes's own testimony he was giving the wasting recluse life-saving transfusions at the Desert Inn, and thus he was a key to settling the question of Hughes's condition on leaving Las Vegas. The third partner, Christ "Chris" Karamanos, was in some ways an even more conspicuous figure. A helicopter pilot in Vietnam and a Newport Beach, California, policeman with only a junior college education and no business experience, he had come to Las Vegas at twenty-seven, had joined the largest casino-hotel in the city, and had quickly become its vice president, after which he was named to important state boards and became a regent of the University of Nevada.

Naturally enough, Jet Avia's influential owners promptly enlisted powerful political help in pursuing the release of their plane and those aboard. Senators Cannon and Laxalt, as well as Nevada congressman James Santini and Governor Mike O'Callaghan, all pressed the Carter administration to intervene with Colombia. It was a matter of concern throughout the community. Jet Avia did millions in business with Valley Bank, and other Las Vegas institutions had a stake in the airline. Little Rock businessmen had leased the plane to Jet Avia, so Arkansas politicians were urging its return as well. Within weeks, Colombia freed the passengers and crew. In spite of political pressure, it would be nearly a year and a half before they let the Lear return to Las Vegas. But by then, Jet Avia was out of business, and the incident all but forgotten. For the city, it was just as well—and typical. There was far more to the story than the public version.

The patient on the runway was no ordinary accident victim, but the fatally burned copilot of a transport so overloaded with narcotics that it crashed on takeoff from a remote jungle airstrip. The "Texas businessman" who was on board, and whose men were smuggling the load that had exploded in flames, was Jimmy Chagra. Not incidentally, Chagra was also one of the Strip's most flamboyant gamblers and men-about-town, laundering tens of millions of drug money at Las Vegas tables, a figure with an eight-million-dollar line of credit at Caesars Palace alone, where the casino provided him with armed guards, a penthouse suite, aliases for his transactions, and other chartered Lears. So conspicuous was Chagra in Las Vegas through the seventies that he was called "the number one high-roller in a city that sprinkles high-rollers on its Wheaties." But the real kingpin of the operation was Jimmy's brother, Lee, renowned on the Strip as "the Black Striker"—"Black" for the gambling wardrobe he took two hours to don, "Striker" for betting enough to break the house. An El Paso criminal defense attorney, "the best narcotics lawyer in the world," one reporter called him, Lee Chagra was also known for his defiance of what he saw as the corruption of American drug enforcement, an officialdom deeply implicated in the vast trafficking of the era. With his murder, brother Jimmy would rise to take over the family's drug empire.

As for Jet Avia, Chris Karamanos was no random business prodigy. The jovial, portly ex-cop had his own ties to organized crime and drug trafficking, and was also, as he would later testify secretly to Nevada officials, a sometime CIA operative, whose meteoric rise and political patronage in Las Vegas were hardly accidental. Whether the air service's other owners, Ghanem and Feikes, knew it or not, federal law enforcement officials as well as Karamanos's closest associates were aware that Jet Avia had been used by the CIA since the company's inception, if not a full-fledged Agency proprietary, at least one of its many business assets on call. "Chris spent hours talking about flying for the CIA, bragging about having Jet Avia take stuff like infra-red spy maps to Central and South America," said an intimate friend.

Then, too, the Lear flying Jimmy Chagra to Colombia was hardly one more leased aircraft. The plane's owner was fast-food millionaire Danny Ray Lasater, himself a Las Vegas high roller who was soon to be under investigation for ties to organized crime and eventually convicted for cocaine distribution. Moving back to his native Arkansas not long after the Santa Marta incident, Lasater would also become an intimate personal friend and major backer of that state's ambitious young governor, Bill Clinton. Nor was Lasater a future president's only link to Jet Avia. Ghanem was a man with his own impressive connections. Born to an Arab oil executive in Haifa, Israel, Ghanem had come to Las Vegas in the early seventies, worked at Dalitz's Sunrise Hospital before starting his lucrative clinics, and was said to slip hundred-dollar bills to security officials at Strip hotels to have them send their emergency cases to his facility. Around the time of the Santa Marta incident, Ghanem would be embroiled in the drug controversy over the death of his onetime patient Elvis Presley, and later came under FBI investigation for alleged collusion in funneling both union members and state employees to his clinics, an inquiry eventually dropped by the Bureau. Along the way, through mutual friends on the Strip, the doctor developed a close relationship with the future president's mother, gambling enthusiast and Las Vegas habitué Virginia Clinton. Ghanem would go on to become a major fund-raiser and contributor for Clinton, as well as one of his closest personal friends with whom the president stayed on visits to Las Vegas.

As if to span it all from the seventies to the end of the century, there was Jimmy Chagra's lawyer, Oscar Goodman. Drug and other mob money paid Goodman's fees, and his reputation was made when Jimmy Chagra was acquitted in the murder of a federal judge. Goodman would go on to become mayor of Las Vegas on the eve of the twenty-first century, with his own ambitions for Carson City or Washington beyond.

In a larger sense, Jet Avia's flight to Santa Marta was far more than an ill-fated "mission of mercy." It symbolized another stage in the rise of Las Vegas—its preeminent role as an international nexus of drug trafficking, gunrunning, and money laundering, the grim, high-stakes reality behind the post–Howard Hughes corporate facade, and a corruption deeper and wider than ever.

15. One Last Cruise

At FBI headquarters in Washington, they called the Las Vegas field office "the black hole, a dumping ground for mediocre agents." All but the most trivial cases at the small branch seemed to go unsolved. Its agents often went through a revolving door into the highly paid ranks of casino security, taking early retirement or even sacrificing pensions to earn lavish salaries from those they might have investigated. One agent looking into Benny Binion's bombing of Las Vegas attorney William Coulthard ended up working at Binion's Horseshoe himself. Another had gone to Caesars Palace and taken much of the FBI staff with him, at a time when skimming and the laundering of drug money at the ornate statue-laden casino were at their height.

In the late seventies, the FBI was struggling to regain a measure of self-respect and public trust as the first revelations of historic abuses came seeping out after Hoover's death in 1972. Even then, Las Vegas was hardly seen as an assignment for agents serious about their job. Since the collapse of Bobby Kennedy's war on organized crime, the corridors of Justice had echoed with rumors that it was the Strip and its considerable Washington juice that dictated the choice of the Special-Agent-in-Charge, or SAC, in southern Nevada. On the scene, casino insiders knew the routine. "They had a dossier on every new head agent before sundown the day they got to town," said a native Las Vegan, "and they'd been doing that for years."

So there was an unaccustomed sense of surprise and unease in both Nevada and Washington late in 1979 when the FBI's reform-minded director, a stern, thin-lipped St. Louis judge named William Webster, handpicked his Las Vegas SAC. Despite the widely accepted fiction of a corporate cleansing of Las Vegas by Hughes, Webster still referred to the city as "the crossroads of organized crime," exercising a candor increasingly rare in the political dialogue. The judge's choice was Joseph Yablonsky, a twenty-seven-year veteran of the bureau, twenty-one of them "on the street." He was remarkable not only for pioneering the bureau's modern sting operations, and for his subsequent undercover work from New England to Florida, but also for his original enlistment and subsequent rise through the ranks in an agency encumbered with what Robert Friedman called "Hoover's truculent anti-Semitism." In the FBI's fitful, largely unsuccessful contest with organized crime—a fight compromised by Hoover during his lifetime and afterward by the persisting legacy of bureaucracy and incompetence—Yablonsky was a breed apart, distinguished by his enduring idealism and clear-eyed insight into the makeup, dynamic, and wider implications of the Syndicate. He was a devoutly religious Jew, who had effectively infiltrated and come to understand the significant but relatively overlooked Jewish elements of organized crime. He gauged not only their preeminent criminal success in the United States but also their ties to Israel, which carried with them far-reaching international ramifications. But he had also rolled up his share of Italian and Irish gangsters. Like Bobby Kennedy—who had often come to talk with the organized crime squad in the New York office where Yablonsky was posted in the early sixties (Kennedy was, as Yablonsky remembered, "well tuned-in to Vegas, with an all-encompassing knowledge of the mob and their widespread controls and influences")—Yablonsky recognized the existence of an all-American Syndicate that much of the FBI and public, generally conditioned to "Mafia" stereotypes, seldom acknowledged.

Fifty-one when he was assigned to Las Vegas, Yablonsky was a tall, bespectacled man, with a pleasant oval face, big sensitive eyes, and a keen sense of humor that belied an inner toughness and drive. He was easily distinguishable from what one observer called "the ruddy All-American-Boy-Next-Door types" who still tended to dominate the ranks of the bureau. Even after coming into the open from undercover work, Yablonsky retained in his wardrobe and manner "the traits and tastes of the culture he had moved in"—the broad-lapeled, dark striped suits; gleaming gold chains, rings, and cuff links; chomped Cuban cigars; and the raw, caricaturish profanity of the underworld. Well before he was assigned to Las Vegas, because of his dealings with the Lansky operations in Miami, he already knew by sight and reputation most of the major players on the Strip and in Glitter Gulch. "I think he saw them as symbols and in some cases the bosses of the guys he had been chasing most of his life as a street agent," one of his colleagues recalled. "He landed right in the middle of the higher-ups here in Vegas, and I think he really saw being SAC as a mission to finish his job." The files awaiting Yablonsky in the desultory Las Vegas field office in January 1980 showed that at least five major casinos were being skimmed by the New York, Chicago, and Kansas City branches of the Syndicate; fencing of stolen art and jewelry, as well as drug money laundering, was rampant; Chicago overseer Tony Spilotro, represented as needs be by the mob's resident mouthpiece Goodman, was rampaging with his own burglary, arson, and assassination-for-hire operation known as the "Hole in the Wall Gang"; and the bureau had identified from extensive murder records no fewer than what an agent's report called "sixteen other made members of the mob residing in Las Vegas."

Not long after he arrived in Las Vegas, Yablonsky strolled into the Riviera coffeeshop and was taken aback to find a tableful of nationally notorious racketeers, men whose presence and obvious authority his colleagues in the FBI, local police, and Nevada gaming control, as well as the city's business and banking leaders, seemed to find unremarkable. In Miami, for all that city's corruption, the bosses were more discreet, agents only catching glimpses of them from time to time in known hangouts like the Forge restaurant. But in Las Vegas there was no need for discretion. "Everyone was there," he remembered of that day, "but Lansky." The group included Dalitz, Moe's Mayfield Gang partner at the Desert Inn; Morry Kleinman; and Stardust manager Herb Tobman, who "swaggered over to" Yablonsky's table and "hissed" at Yablonsky's companion, "I guess you don't mind who you're seen with." They had obviously intended to intimidate the new SAC. Soon after the Riviera episode, however, Yablonsky ordered an investigation into Tobman and his partner Al Sachs, including their skimming at both the Fremont and the Stardust—the first sustained probe of its kind since the abortive Kennedy effort of 1961 to 1963, and one that would eventually lead to the revocation of the licenses of both men. It was the start of a full-scale war, covert and open, that was to rage across Nevada and into Washington and other locales over more than four years.

Tobman's venom notwithstanding, in the first weeks and months—before the conflict broke into the open with shocking, unprecedented subpoenas of the prominent, and rumors of a specially impaneled federal grand jury—the community seemed to embrace Yablonsky like any other impor-

tant newcomer. Greenspun and others entertained him. Local papers published fulsome, lighthearted articles about the agent they called the "man of
many faces" in his undercover career, some accompanied by photos of
Yablonsky and his pretty wife, Wilma, dressed as "mobster and moll" for a
Halloween party. Leading Jewish citizens like political activist Edyth Katz
welcomed the Yablonskys into the local Temple Beth Shalom—Dalitz, Tobman, and several of their associates were members of the same congrega-
tion—and Wilma began an active role in community affairs. But when Joe
was duly invited to address the usual round of civic clubs, he began to
unnerve his audiences by referring, as if it were self-evident, to the continuing power and presence of organized crime in the city, and going so far as to
give an actual figure—as much as $170 billion—for what the Syndicate was
taking from the national economy each year. "Just imagine if taxes were collected on that kind of income," he said to a stunned Rotary Club audience,
"how much it might affect each and every one of you." Some among his lis-
teners knew only too well the accuracy or even underestimation of his portrayal. But in a Nevada thoroughly invested in its post-Hughes image, the
speeches seemed to many incredible, then dismaying, then infuriating. "It
was like a cancer patient who was first assured by some quack that he was
cured now being told his malignancy was massive and maybe terminal," a
local physician recalled of one of Yablonsky's luncheon-meeting bombshells.
"The city went through being numb, and then in denial, and eventually
blamed Joe for the real diagnosis."

The *Sun* and *Review-Journal* continued for a while to reflect a kind of
polite, clichéed indulgence of Yablonsky's grim picture. As so often in the rise
of the city, Las Vegans like everyone else would officially deplore organized
crime and criminals in the generality. But to take those forces out of the
abstract, to give them a specific identity, to see how much particular men
and their pillage of the state were woven into political and civil society, was
unallowable. As if calling out the Syndicate were not enough, Yablonsky went
still further to blame its scourge on Nevada's own hireling politicians, and on
the deity of money the city worshipped so reverently. "Without the compromise and corruption of public officials, many of the activities of organized
crime would be frustrated," he said in stating the obvious, which for many in
the city was outrageous. "So long as Las Vegas's vaults are filled with ready
cash," he said in equal heresy, "the city will be a magnet for gangsters and
weak politicians."

To Yablonsky's surprise, the Las Vegas he found in 1980 was more than
ever in the grip of Nevada's traditional anti-federalism, its modern version

dating back to Kefauver and whipped to a kind of frenzy by Sawyer's twenty-year-old clash with the Kennedys and Hoover, still fresh in public memory. In the desert and mountain expanse beginning not far from Yablonsky's office in the federal building on 4th Street, U.S. government agencies still controlled more than 86 percent of Nevada's land. While Nevadans might have greeted powerful individuals like Wingfield or Hughes as deliverers, their frontier pride never seemed reconciled to Washington as their ultimate colonial master. Yablonsky miscalculated, moreover, the sheer economic force of gambling. "Las Vegas," he was fond of saying, "was a strong contributor to the coffers of organized crime through . . . narcotics, stolen property, and casino skimming." But in addition, in 1980 the Syndicate and its fronts provided some 30 percent of the state's 424,000 jobs. Even with the thievery of the skim and the scandalously low gaming tax on admitted profits, barely increased by a quarter percent over thirty years to 5.75 percent, public revenue from casinos still constituted nearly half of Nevada's income. The consequence was a society held hostage if not utterly manipulated or corrupted, and in any case readily hostile to an FBI SAC who would not meld into the common compromise, who turned out to be one more "outsider" passing judgment.

His entire life, Yablonsky would reflect, he had always thought of himself as "one of the good guys." Now, suddenly, in Las Vegas he was one of the bad. "I was in a subculture that was totally different from anything I had ever experienced," he told a writer later. "In a community that worships the almighty buck, where Moe Dalitz was a patron saint," he would say on another occasion, "there's a strange assimilation that takes place and your values get distorted—or else." By the latter months of 1980 the town's ritual welcome of a ranking official had already begun to turn to social shunning and political backstabbing, including the increasingly vocal opposition of Greenspun and other city fathers.

As with Tobman's first insult, the venom galvanized Yablonsky's sense of purpose, if not self-righteousness, and he struck back even harder. Over the ensuing period, he began to bring in a sizable contingent of the bureau's most expert and experienced men in organized crime to constitute a Las Vegas strike force. Having once thought he was coming to a middle-sized city of some cosmopolitanism, Yablonsky soon discovered the small-town incestuousness and insularity of Las Vegas at its core, particularly on matters of politics, money, and public integrity. It was never merely a matter of the sloth or compromise of the FBI field office. Facing him was a refined, thoroughly interlaced system of complicity that had been operating for

decades—judges obstructing investigations, politicians publicly stigmatiz-
ing and quietly hemming in the FBI and IRS, wiretaps leaked, grand jury
minutes unsealed. An FBI wiretap elsewhere caught Tropicana mobster
Joseph Vincent Agosto bragging about his influence with the ranking state
gaming regulator he called "Mr. Clean," or "Cleanface," an official widely
believed by law enforcement to be the former Gaming Commission chairman and future congressman and senator Harry Reid, who of course loudly
denied it.

Whatever Yablonsky knew about the place, some federal prosecutors
were well aware of Las Vegas's pervasive culture of complicity. "Until the late
nineteen-seventies, there had been a hiatus in law enforcement in Las Vegas,"
Justice Department official Mike DeFeo would say later. "There was corruption . . . we were beating our heads against the wall." Yablonsky responded by
tightening security around a fortresslike field office, and by cutting off any
potentially compromising collaboration with federal and state judges as well
as state and local law enforcement, all commonly party to the bureau's past
perfunctory cases. He moved without pause outside Nevada to get federal
court approval for extensive wiretaps, again the first of their kind since the
illegal bugs of the early sixties, and aggressively instituted other surveillance.
"The streets were filled with unmarked vans," one reporter noted later.
Yablonsky's visible acts of preparation set off alarms from the wide halls of
the federal building through Glitter Gulch and the Strip to Carson City and
beyond. But the rumors and leaks about the actual targets of the unprecedented FBI mobilization were the most sensational in the city's history.

In some cases, even before the first subpoena or documentary evidence
was announced, Yablonsky was reported in the local press to be going after,
among others, such current untouchables as Benny Binion for the Coulthard
bombing, U.S. District Judge Harry Claiborne for tax evasion, and state senator Floyd Lamb for bribery. Tension grew with the telltale arrival of new
government attorneys from the Justice Department's Public Integrity section
and Office of Professional Responsibility—prosecutors brought into states
only in political corruption cases. With the initial indictment of Lamb in an
undercover operation reminiscent of the recent ABSCAM congressional
scandal on the national level, it was clear that the "King of Sting" had indeed
come to town. Yablonsky's attack on the city, code-named Operation YOBO,
could not be allowed to succeed.

To kill the investigation, to destroy Yablonsky, Dalitz and his cohorts
would enlist, as they had done so many other times, their ranking political
proxy, "turning on the Washington juice like never before," as a casino boss
remembered. Their champion, Paul Laxalt, close friend of President Reagan,

had become one of the most powerful men in the nation's capital. They were as certain of his loyalty as of his decisive connections.

"My boy," Dalitz once called him. "I put him there."

Laxalt, Nevada's silver-haired, suntanned handsome junior senator, had risen to heights no one imagined only a few years before. The ex-governor and casino owner, who survived business failure and scandal at his Carson City Ormsby House to win his Senate seat by a razor-thin margin after a recount in 1974, won reelection in 1980 by a landslide. "Nothing less than a Laxalt lovefest," one politician called it. As Yablonsky was incurring the wrath of the Strip, Laxalt was taking from the same people much of a record-breaking $1.1 million in recorded campaign contributions, outspending his Democratic opponent, Reno liberal Mary Gojack, by more than four to one. His donors were a who's who of Las Vegas and all it represented. In addition to his longtime underwriters Dalitz and the Syndicate's Doumani brothers, there were Operation YOBO targets Binion, Tobman, and Sachs, mob lawyer Morris Shenker, Syndicate front Jay Sarno, casino owner Frank Fertitta, Las Vegas entertainment fixture Wayne Newton, the ever present Parry Thomas, and a host of other notable Strip figures.

Never audibly embarrassed by the character or interests of his backers, Laxalt, who in past races had viciously attacked Cannon and Sawyer for being tools of the gamblers, was now insouciant, often arrogant, about his own patronage. "For a Nevada politician to refuse a contribution from Moe Dalitz would be like running for office in Michigan and turning down a contribution from General Motors," he quipped with unintended irony about how much the two worlds had come to resemble each other. "A friend of mine," he would call Dalitz on another occasion when questioned about his ties to the Desert Inn hoodlum who had funded him so decisively in the 1966 race for governor. "I'm not going to say to him 'get lost, you're too hot.'" Gojack had tried to make an issue of the Syndicate contributions—money one political insider called "obscene even by Nevada standards." She emphasized that Laxalt had missed most of a year of votes on the Senate floor while out campaigning for both Reagan and himself. But Laxalt's appeal, and access to the likely next president, seemed to render him impervious. "The only people who really cared," Gojack would say of the unanswered roll calls, "were a minority of intellectuals and more thoughtful newspaper editors." Some in Nevada considered his absences fortuitous. As he moved up in GOP circles Laxalt had become increasingly right-wing, one of only six senators to vote against the meals-on-wheels program for the indigent, elderly, and crippled. Gojack repeatedly told voters around the state about the dubious Chicago loans to the Ormsby House casino. "If you're beholden to those people, it's for life. You make a pact with the devil and that's it." But Laxalt's potential political vulnerabilities hurt him no more than his reactionary views.

Laxalt emerged a singular force in the Reagan administration, the new president appointing an unprecedented number of Nevadans to key jobs. As a longtime friend and neighboring governor, Laxalt had been one of Reagan's earliest supporters, and in 1980 his most trusted adviser through the Republican primaries and then the general election against Jimmy Carter. Laxalt was especially close to the sharply opinionated, powerful Nancy Reagan. The new first lady preferred the courtly, solicitous Nevadan to most of the rest of her husband's circle, particularly Vice President George Bush, whom many saw as Laxalt's future rival in the party, but a man Nancy regarded as weak and vacillating, privately nicknaming him "Whiney." With the 1981 inauguration, Laxalt became what the Washington media called "first friend" to the president and his wife. He socialized frequently with the Reagans, watching movies and riding horses, Nancy calling her husband and Laxalt "my two favorite fellas."

Laxalt would maintain those bonds, with all the attendant access and cachet, over the next eight years. The relationship was in many ways unique in the annals of the presidency, and conferred a power in and over the White House Nevada had never come close to enjoying. It was in part the fruit of the temperament and ideology the two western politicians had in common, but they also shared patrons in Las Vegas and Hollywood. In some respects, Washington insiders came to feel, Laxalt would be a kind of shadow president in the Reagan years, speaking with authority not only for the chief executive but for the forces that put him there. It was no ordinary politician that Dalitz and his friends had chosen to rid them of Yablonsky.

Laxalt wasted no time bringing his weight to bear, and conducted his lobbying with a brazenness that defied the traditional discretion thought obligatory to the Washington fixer, as if national politics were already no different from Nevada's. He seemed jaunty not only in his own new power, but in the presumed respectability and thus immunity of Las Vegas. He would use his "ties with the Reagan administration to curtail organized crime investigations in Nevada," he baldly told one journalist.

Laxalt raised the subject with Reagan, who cautiously sent him to Attorney General William French Smith, formerly the president's personal lawyer and leader of his California "kitchen cabinet." Three times during 1981, Laxalt met with Smith to discuss what was described as "minimizing the role of the Justice Strike Force in Vegas"; on one occasion, Laxalt asked that FBI director Webster join them, but Webster pointedly refused to attend. The senator was "rankled by having federal people in here all the time," said one Las Vegan, "hassling and harassing the people in this community." Yablonsky's aggressive agents were persecuting the legitimate gaming industry, "trampling on people's private rights," Laxalt repeatedly told the attorney general, demanding that the SAC be reassigned, if not cashiered. If Smith did not act, Laxalt would call for Senate hearings on the Justice Department abuses in Las Vegas. The pressure shocked even hardened veterans in the capital, the president's close friend and campaign manager muscling one of Reagan's cabinet officers and another of his intimates.

In October 1982, Laxalt brought in the formidable Greenspun to remonstrate with Justice officials to stop the investigation of their mutually close friend Judge Harry Claiborne, who was under investigation before a grand jury in Las Vegas for accepting an $85,000 bribe from Mustang Ranch owner Joe Conforte. Greenspun later claimed to have brandished some eight hundred "secret documents" to prove Yablonsky's abuse of power. But assistant attorneys general found Greenspun's claims "preposterous," as one of them later leaked to the press. He then returned to Las Vegas to launch increasingly bitter attacks on both Yablonsky and Justice, calling for a corruption investigation of the SAC.

Washington politicians were loath to be seen infringing on bipartisan pledges of Webster's independence. Nonetheless, he was "besieged by calls about Joe Yablonsky from the White House and everywhere else," as one of Webster's aides remembered. "They really want your head out there," Webster told Yablonsky at one point during the onslaught in 1981. But the director would stand firm behind the Las Vegas investigations. As remarkable as the push to oust him, Yablonsky's survival sent the unmistakable signal to the capital of rising stakes. Many could see that the gauntlet had been thrown down for Laxalt, French, and Webster, that something would have to give sooner or later among powerful men.

Only a few at Justice and in law enforcement around the nation saw something deeper behind the usual elbowing in the present administration. Since the first construction graft at the Flamingo in 1946, regional or local FBI agents had been stopped whenever and wherever they got too close to Las Vegas. "A pattern was established that this town didn't want any heat, and they always got their way," Yablonsky himself would say later. "Agents early on looking at Bugsy, or Lansky, or Costello, or the Flamingo were all called off." Threats from Kefauver and Kennedy had been dispensed with. Individual mobsters or scandals might come and go, but the base power of the city remained intact and only grew. Laxalt's flexing in Washington in the early eighties was another display of that might, though also perhaps a test of it, and a few casino owners thought the future of Las Vegas might be in the balance.

For now, emboldened by Webster's support, intrigued as well as appalled by the exceptionally fierce opposition of a U.S. senator, Yablonsky not only pressed on with his probes but began to look at Laxalt as well. "I guess none of us knew very much about Paul Laxalt except that he was Reagan's buddy and you sure couldn't read anything critical about him in the Nevada papers," said a Justice prosecutor who worked in Las Vegas during the period. "But we had to wonder why this guy put so much on the line to protect a bunch of sleaze in Vegas." What Yablonsky and his investigators soon found was the lengthening shadow of the Ormsby House financing, connections that had already appeared in a 1981 *Miami Herald* story. "It was astonishing," Yablonsky would say later. "But while governor, Laxalt had a meeting with Dorfman, Korshak, and Coleman, and then wrote a letter to President Nixon extolling the virtues of Jimmy Hoffa, and Korshak arranges his Chicago loan right after that. It was pretty blatant." The more Yablonsky dug up about the senator, the more he started questioning Laxalt's "commitment to law and order," as one account put it later. "Laxalt began to emerge in my mind as a tool of organized crime," Yablonsky told a reporter. When Yablonsky subpoenaed the business records of Laxalt's political consultant Sig Rogich—a Las Vegas ad man turned political imagemaker who would go on to prominence working for both the Reagan and Bush White Houses, and as an eventual power in end-of-century Las Vegas—Yablonsky looked to be striking at the heart of the Nevada political establishment.

The visible tip of Yablonsky's investigation in press reports and other accounts set off still more rumors: that an undercover sting was underway to net both Laxalt and Governor List, that the senator would retaliate by having Reagan install a U.S. attorney to get a grand jury indictment of Yablonsky. Fact and fiction drove Greenspun to still more florid attacks on Yablonsky on the front page of his newspaper. Branding Yablonsky "an enemy of the *Sun*," the publisher was purportedly defending old friends—Binion, who had been the only holdout in the casino boycott of the paper decades before, and the Texan's old crony and Horseshoe lawyer Claiborne, whose elevation to the federal bench Benny was said to have bought with substantial bribes. But the effect was to smear Yablonsky and discredit the efforts of the field office in general. Laxalt and his staff gladly fed material to the publisher, whose choler alternated on apparent whim between fury and dismay. "The FBI chief came to Las Vegas with a preconceived notion that everyone in

Nevada is evil," Greenspun huffed, as if Operation YOBO were some totalitarian dragnet rather than the targeting of a relative few of the state's worst marauders.

Inside the FBI outpost on 4th Street, Yablonsky's own view of his antagonists grew increasingly personal. "Greenspun always wanted a piece of the action and he was an extortionist, fashioned himself a lord of a fiefdom," Yablonsky would say later. "He saw me as a threat to all the finagling deals he had made to make himself a rich man." Social ostracism and political malice were cascading down on Yablonsky and his family. He had been unanimously elected to the board of his temple, Beth Shalom, soon after joining. With that, Dalitz pledged $400,000 to build a new synagogue, vowing to take most of the membership with him, including the Greenspuns. As Yablonsky brought more cases, Beth Shalom board meetings and services he attended grew thick with sneers and snubs. "The Jews treated me worse than anyone else," he would say of a city where the small but affluent Jewish community was a potent force in society, business, and politics.

There seemed no finish to the drumbeat. When a Reno paper printed murmurs that Yablonsky's strike force had a "rogue's gallery" of photos of prominent Nevada figures "with creative captions underneath," federal judge Roger Foley, who was close to Binion and Claiborne, ordered a raid on the offices. The unique court-sanctioned invasion of federal law enforcement quarters—the only one quite of its kind in U.S. history—turned up some of the photos, confirming several of the rumored targets as well as whimsical, demeaning captions beneath mug shots, and stoked the animus on both sides. "Joe and his agents and prosecutors were mostly tough men and professionals," said one of their colleagues, "but you had to be there to know what that kind of hostility does to you, when it's every time you open a newspaper and everywhere you go to work or shop or even pray." As if to underscore the point, Wilma Yablonsky walked outside their Las Vegas home one day and found a single bullet lying inexplicably and ominously in their driveway.

Yablonsky always had his champions in the city, some who saw his mettle as heroic, a means by which at last to strike at the thugs and their fronts who ran Las Vegas and the state. "Will the lynch mob get Joe Yablonsky?" asked the upstart *Valley Times,* since the late seventies a rising daily rival to the *Sun.* The *Times*'s publisher and editor was Bob Brown, who brought decades of experience around the country as well as a stint as editor of the *Review-Journal* before resigning in protest at editorial interference by the paper's crudely partisan and baronial chain owner from Arkansas, Don Reynolds. Bright and proudly professional, a short balding man with sparkling eyes and quick wit who passionately believed, as he told a friend, that "Las Vegas is the greatest news town in America," Brown was a lively contrast to his staid colleagues at the *Review-Journal* as well as to Greenspun's selected raving. With fearless zest he had taken on Governors O'Callaghan and List, the latter for his accepting the kind of complimentary meals, room, and other favors, or "comps," by which the Strip routinely suborned Nevada politicians. He would back Yablonsky as part of training his small paper's coverage, as never before or after in the city, on the central issue of gambling and political corruption. But the *Times*'s circulation was rarely over 15,000, only a fraction of his larger competitors, and Brown himself soon fell prey to the seductions of the city.

At the same time, at a local television station and then as a columnist at the *Review-Journal*, Ned Day, Jr., an investigative reporter only a few years out of the University of Wisconsin who had worked briefly as Brown's star reporter at the *Times*, wrote regularly about the "get Yablonsky" conspiracy. A boyishly handsome, Runyonesque rake with a poetic empathy for the casino workers and ordinary people of the city—men and women of "gumption and courage," as he once described them—the streetwise Day loved the Strip but deplored its masters. Namesake of a professional bowler, Ned Jr. had grown up in Wisconsin in what he later described as "sleazy pool halls," where he "learned all the cons," lessons he applied when his father went broke in the early sixties. The teenage son had "bounced from a loading dock in New York City to the racetracks of Florida, to the murkiest bars of Chicago," before beginning college in earnest at twenty-eight, and eventually pursuing a career in journalism, along with a brief marriage to a Miss Nude America. Arriving in Las Vegas in the autumn of 1976, he saw the gambling capital as the biggest con of all—"a pool hall to the four-hundredth power."

Day's coverage now of Yablonsky's investigation took on Greenspun directly, exposing what he aptly called the *Sun*'s "singularly vicious, monthslong campaign . . . intent on discrediting and humiliating" the FBI agent. "Why is there no journalistic outrage at the malodorous campaign of vilification aimed at Yablonsky?" he asked in one of his columns, shaming most of his colleagues. "The hypocrisy, unbridled silliness, and self-aggrandizing power plays . . . could break the heart of a ten-dollar hooker who thought she'd seen everything."

Still, the barrage on Yablonsky, private and public, pounded on in Nevada. In Washington, Laxalt persisted in his attempts to have Yablonsky removed by fiat. In time-honored Washington fashion, however, the senator's early bravado and then the increasingly virulent and strident public attacks on Yablonsky in Las Vegas made it all the more difficult for the administration to dispose of him without a potentially nasty little embarrassment to the president himself. By 1983, with the Reagan regime intent on preserving its own law-and-order image, Yablonsky stood to become the kind of martyr that opponents of any administration seized on with cries of cover-up or political interference. By Laxalt's very ardor, by invoking his importance as he did, he had drawn attention to Las Vegas as perhaps never before. Dalitz and his "boy" had violated Lansky's cardinal rule, picking too public a fight, drawing attention to the place and its hooded power.

The Las Vegas old-timers understood the overreaching in their own idiom. "Moe started believing he really was Man of the Year like they kept callin' him," remembered a pit boss who had worked for Dalitz in northern Kentucky and then at the Desert Inn. "He forgot he was just a bootlegger and killer." The Strip had long since ceased being a local story alone; now its connections were leading to a far wider field of political and economic vision. By 1983, two years after the first *Miami Herald* story, reporters at the *Wall Street Journal, Village Voice, The Nation, Mother Jones,* and most notably the *Sacramento Bee* were drawn to look at Laxalt's past, not only because of his prominence or intimacy with the Reagans but also because of his eyebrow-raising exertions to call off Yablonsky. A few reporters had begun to think, irresistibly, that to look at Laxalt might be to find Reagan as well—perhaps to bare long-suspected corrupt roots of the president himself.

If the White House and Justice could not do Laxalt's bidding by yanking Yablonsky outright, they would adopt the next best expedient, the tactic already rumored for some time in Las Vegas. Attorney General Smith and his aides began casting about for a new U.S. attorney for the southern district of Nevada who could be counted on to thwart Yablonsky, if not impeach him legally. The man presently in that post, native Nevadan Mahlon Brown, had been, much to the consternation of his patron, Senator Cannon, steadfast in his support of Yablonsky, bravely jeopardizing his own promising political future. But by the summer of 1983, the administration was finally able to install their man, Lamond R. Mills, a local Mormon handpicked by Laxalt and state Republican chairman Frank Fahrenkopf. As the chief federal prosecutor on the scene, Mills had the power effectively to shut down Yablonsky in the name of curbing investigative abuses and in the tradition of Nevada's anti-federalism, masking the looming issue of the mob. "After promising to do what he could to reduce the FBI's role in Nevada," as one account put it, the new U.S. attorney was sworn in in June 1983, and immediately launched an investigation of Yablonsky for eating a complimentary meal at the MGM Grand and other minor violations of civil service ethics.

Though now only six months away from mandatory retirement, Yablonsky was undeterred as always. He promptly installed a hot line for public support of his office as well as for tipsters on political corruption, a move approved by Webster, who had already slapped Yablonsky on the wrist administratively for the comped meal—which even Yablonsky's admirers would remember as one of many of his lunches or dinners on the Strip, the agent's only real indiscretion in the city. In any case, the phone line predictably infuriated Laxalt, who was still excoriating Yablonsky to battle-weary Justice officials who had heard it all before.

The seedy melodrama ended mercifully at the close of 1983 with the pensioning off of Yablonsky. Unlike most of his peers, the hated and feared SAC ended his career all but officially proscribed, as Greenspun insisted in repeated editorials, from ever getting a job in Nevada, his foes vowing to oppose any effort on his part to obtain even a private investigator's license. Not surprisingly, on a Strip soon to be crowded with former federal prosecutors and agents working for casinos, no house offered him the usual post-FBI sinecure.

Despite the powers arrayed against him in Washington and Las Vegas, despite the fact that the millions skimmed from Nevada casinos during the period continued to provide organized crime and its growing number of legitimate outlets more cash than from any other criminal source, including the vast drug traffic, Yablonsky's record would be impressive. Of dozens of cases brought, all but two resulted in conviction, under the circumstances one of the most remarkable rates in the annals of FBI field offices, and by far the highest for the Las Vegas branch. Crucially reinforcing and merging with other cases to sustain federal prosecutions in Chicago, Kansas City, and elsewhere, far-reaching skimming convictions at the Tropicana, Stardust, and Sundance led to still other convictions, giving Yablonsky much of the credit for a substantial expulsion of Chicago organized crime from Las Vegas for the first time since its arrival on the Strip nearly three decades before. FBI agents caught many of Spilotro's "Hole in the Wall Gang" in the act and put them away. Undercover operations recovered more than $6 million in stolen art, drugs, and other contraband, with nearly fifty convictions. Waves of evidence rolled outward to wash over Laxalt's friends and Thomas's customers, the Doumani brothers and others, whose old immunity to operate would never be the same.

There were other Las Vegas reckonings and omens across the country. In January 1983, sixty-year-old Allen Dorfman, just convicted of using Teamster funds to try to bribe Senator Cannon, and facing a fifty-five-year sentence if he didn't cooperate with the government, was shot in the head at close range by Spilotro and friends as he left a suburban Chicago restaurant. "Dorfman," said a ranking federal agent, "could have put away everybody in Vegas."

Four months later, also in part the result of Yablonsky's relentless pursuit, the already convicted Joe Agosto turned government informant, sending a shudder through Nevada, and especially politicians like his "Cleanface." "No one proved conclusively that Harry Reid was 'Cleanface,' " Yablonsky recalled of the allegations against the rising Mormon politician and future U.S. senator, "but when Agosto became a federal witness, Reid freaked." Agosto was now promising prosecutors to incriminate numerous Nevada officials said to be "on the take," and to implicate other figures. Among other admissions, Agosto told agents that Syndicate leaders had asked him and Dorfman to obtain explosives to kill Argent Corporation's Allen Glick, the San Diego real estate hustler who fronted for mobsters at the Stardust and Fremont and was duly voted Las Vegas "man of the year," but who seemed a weak link in the skimming probe. Though planning for the murder had begun, Glick attracted new publicity and the contract murder never took place. For his part, the newly confessional Agosto begged to go into the witness protection program so that he "wouldn't end up," as he put it, "another statistic like Allen Dorfman." Yet soon after making the request and before he could complete his testimony, he died of an apparent heart attack.

Spilotro, having escaped several charges thanks to Goodman's maneuvering, in 1986 was still facing three pending indictments that had evolved partly out of Yablonsky's work. But the ever cocky, ever ruthless executioner of Giancana, Dorfman, and some two dozen others would himself be bludgeoned to death that same year, his pulped body dumped in a midwestern cornfield.

There were casualties on the other side as well. At the Valley Times, Brown was squeezed relentlessly in public and private by his rivals at the Sun and Review-Journal, and by his creditors, part of an establishment threatened by the Times's uncompromised journalism. "A newsman's newsman," as television reporter Liz Vlaming described him, "Bob would have done almost anything to save his newspaper." Struggling to keep the Valley Times afloat, he became embroiled with one of his Strip advertisers, and was eventually caught in an indictment for kickbacks that was partly his own folly, partly a set-up. Broken by the episode, the fifty-three-year-old crusading editor died of a heart attack in 1984, and his beloved Valley Times, Las Vegas's only authentically independent paper in the last half of the century, folded two weeks later.

His equally courageous and outspoken protégé, Ned Day, died in 1987 at forty-two while on a Hawaiian vacation. After an inquiry, the cause of death was officially declared as heart failure; there had in fact been cardiac disease in the lineage of the high-living young journalist. But Day, whose sources on the Strip were unprecedented, and who had recently completed a devastating, informed portrait of Dalitz, Spilotro, and others in a television documentary on the city called perhaps too optimistically *Mob on the Run*, had been increasingly threatened, including by two car bombings only months before his death. "Ned was becoming a real danger to the Syndicate," said another colleague. "And he was relentless when it came to Spilotro. There was said to be bad blood between the two men from Ned's days on the streets of Milwaukee or Chicago."

Around the same time, Day had gone to California and "purposely sought out the hangouts of Spilotro cronies," as a colleague put it, and had called home to Las Vegas in the middle of the night after being drugged and left for dead in a San Diego alley. On this trip and others, Day had learned that there was a veritable "wanted poster" of him, complete with a blowup picture and urgings to "take him out," being circulated among underworld figures.

Despite the intimidations, Day refused to back down, sometimes seeming to flaunt his invulnerability, convinced that he had become too public a figure to be killed. "If something happens to me, then 'Sixty Minutes' and ABC's '20/20'—Geraldo Rivera and all those jerks—are going to be all over here like they were in Arizona where reporter Don Bolles was murdered," Day said defiantly in a 1981 interview with the *Las Vegan City Magazine*. "I'm like a mosquito on the back of a money-making elephant. You don't throw the elephant off a cliff to kill the mosquito." But outside reporters did not swarm the city to investigate his death.

"In an eerie twist," as the *Review-Journal* described it, he mailed his final column from Hawaii—"a vintage Day offering"—which he urged the newspaper to save "as a potential historical record in the event that . . . I sleep with the fishes tonight." The next day he was dead. "I know Agosto, Brown, and Day all officially died of heart attacks," said longtime Las Vegas reporter A. D. Hopkins, who knew the three men. "But they all pissed off the same people and their deaths were mighty convenient."

Together, spanning less than a decade, Brown and Day had been a fleeting golden age of Las Vegas journalism—like Yablonsky's example in law enforcement—never matched before or after. Their instinctive sense of the importance and centrality of the casino corruption story—much less their fearless portrayal of so much of what the city they both loved actually was— left them martyred exceptions to a Las Vegas media so often a de facto accomplice to the Syndicate. In a poignant symbolic moment, one of the pallbearers at Day's funeral had asked the chauffeur of the hearse to take the reporter's casket for "one last cruise" down the Strip in jaunty, defiant farewell to the street Day knew so honestly. The driver refused.

For years afterward, Day's close friend and investigative reporting colleague George Knapp would receive anonymous phone calls warning him off some potential or ongoing story, "tough guys," as Knapp would describe the calls, "telling me that what happened to Ned could happen to me." But Day's memory and example endured. Every year on his birthday, Knapp went to the cemetery with a bottle of Jack Daniels and one of Diet 7-Up, the martyred reporter's favorite combination, and the two old friends had a drink together before Knapp walked away, leaving the bottle of whisky behind.

As he left, Yablonsky's prize trophy had been federal judge Harry Claiborne, a senior if often farcical figurehead of the state's confederacy of gamblers, gangsters, and government. Though represented by Syndicate attorney Oscar Goodman, Claiborne was convicted in 1984 of filing a false income tax return. Two years later, the hearing evidence having overwhelmed Goodman's blustery claims of FBI abuses, the U.S. Senate impeached Claiborne. He was the first federal judge to be so dishonored in modern history, though the Nevada Supreme Court, ruling that Binion's crony had suffered enough and was the victim of "questionable investigative motivations," soon restored Claiborne to the state bar.

There would be a tolling as well for Yablonsky's principal pursuer. When Yablonsky left Las Vegas and the bureau at the end of 1983, there was the impression that Laxalt had finally won a personal as well as political victory. But that November, as Yablonsky was packing, the *Sacramento Bee* ran a story by Pulitzer Prize–winning reporter Denny Walsh on alleged skimming at the Laxalt family's Ormsby House. Based on IRS sources, on what many suspected as the cooperation of dissident Nevada gaming investigators alleging a cover-up in their own agency, and not least on suspected leaks from Yablonsky's strike force, the *Bee* exposé would be a kind of final straw in a series of articles about Laxalt's dubious ties. Though Walsh never reported that Laxalt himself was involved in the skim, the story hit agonizingly close to home. Unlike other, national publications, and beyond Walsh's or the *Bee*'s journalistic authority, the paper was read by many who had known Dominique and Theresa Laxalt and their boys.

For nearly a year, the *Bee* story seemed to have come and gone like the rest. Riding high as ever in 1984, Laxalt was managing Reagan's reelection campaign, and being mentioned as a U.S. Supreme Court appointee with Greenspun's son Brian said to be waiting in the wings to fill his Senate seat. But that autumn it became known that both CBS's *60 Minutes* and ABC News were planning major exposés of Laxalt, with shocking interviews of his old FBI nemesis Joe Yablonsky. Laxalt's retinue pounced on the networks, letting it be known that the senator would soon file a $250 million libel suit against the *Bee,* and against them too, if they broadcast the story. Greenspun called CBS, telling Mike Wallace of *60 Minutes* that putting Yablonsky on the air "would be an injustice to Israel," since "anything that hurts Paul Laxalt and Ronald Reagan will hurt Israel." The two networks then fell into competition over exclusive rights to Yablonsky, who had ingenuously promised to appear on both. In pique, both networks canceled their pieces. The effect was to bury the Laxalt story, and with it a rare glimpse in the mass media of Las Vegas's national reach.

Laxalt's libel action against the *Sacramento Bee* filed in September 1983 dragged on for three and a half years, with law firms and private investigators from coast to coast, including the retired Yablonsky, poring over every aspect of Laxalt's life. For many, the nadir of the case, an event haunting both sides and what many thought responsible for its dismissal, was the breaking and tragic suicide of Laxalt's former sister-in-law, Katherine. Under oath in a deposition, the ex-wife of Laxalt's brother and Ormsby House partner, Peter, had denied knowing anything about a pivotal 1970s Palm Springs meeting of the two Laxalt brothers with Dorfman and Korshak to secure financing for the Carson City casino. But then in a guileless, secretly tape-recorded reminiscence with an old intimate who turned out to be an undercover investigator, she readily admitted that she knew "damn well" that the Teamsters were financing the casino, and that when her husband returned from Palm Springs, he had told her, as she quoted him, that "every hood in the nation" was there. It was a devastating turn in the lawsuit, scheduled for trial in Reno just three weeks later, in June 1987. Threatened with perjury, now become the single most important witness against the senator, Katherine formally recanted her earlier testimony, and four days later was found dead on the banks of the Napa River in Northern California, having taken an overdose of barbiturates. Though he would claim in his memoirs that the death had nothing to do with the ending of the litigation, Laxalt promptly dropped the suit with no retraction or damages from the *Bee.*

Shortly before that climax, Laxalt had retired from the Senate in 1986, one of the most powerful and popular figures on Capitol Hill. Despite the events of 1987, and with much the same hubris that marked his vendetta against Yablonsky, he was already running for president in 1988. Because both Reagans preferred Laxalt to Vice President Bush as a successor, the president was profuse in his praise of Laxalt, coming just short of an endorsement. "Look to the son of the high mountains and peasant herders, to the son of the Sierra and the immigrant Basque family," the president said with audible emotion at a $1,000-a-plate dinner for Laxalt in 1986. "Look to a man, to a friend, to an American who gave himself so that others might live in freedom." With no more modesty, Laxalt would say he had spent so much time in the White House that he felt like a full-time resident. "In Western parlance, this hired hand is ready to take over as foreman," he told the National Press Club.

It grew clear, however, that Laxalt's candidacy would never survive some of the controversies from his past. He eventually dropped out of the race and never returned to Nevada to live, becoming a wealthy Washington lobbyist for the casino industry. (He was said to have sold off much of his father's original property around the family's beloved retreat on Marlette Lake, where he had once recovered from his own shattering war wounds, high in the Sierra above Tahoe. "No place on earth is as important to me," he wrote in his 2000 memoir.) Yet as Robert Laxalt's daughter Monique made clear in her gently elliptical but unmistakable novel-as-memoir, *Deep Blue Memory,* for much of the Laxalt clan there was no easy escape from pain and dishonor. In the end, even the good name of the shepherd who had faced down the mountain lion would be one more Nevada sacrifice.

None of these dramatic sequels was envisioned in 1983 when Yablonsky's friends and colleagues gave him a going-away party. They invited some two hundred guests, but calls flooded the FBI switchboard from common citizens asking to attend. The overflow crowd at the Jubilation, Paul Anka's fashionable disco, was a kind of social and moral demarcation for the city. As with a gathering of dissidents in the old Soviet Union—with Hank Greenspun's private detectives taking down license plate numbers in the parking lot, and Greenspun personally haranguing some of the guests the next day—many came at professional or personal risk. They were saying good-bye to a valiant enemy of the company in this ultimate company town and state.

Though many had been silent through his ordeal, they now pressed Yablonsky's hand and thanked him, their presence a reminder of how much the cowed people of the place needed a champion, how widespread good and decency still were in a community so deeply exploited and compromised. The evening was gay, if poignant. There was still no sense that Yablonsky would prove the last real challenge to the rulers of the city, that they were about to flourish and expand until they were mightier than anything Operation YOBO ever faced.

As the Yablonsky episode played out in Las Vegas, a furtive revolution—what one historian called a "slow motion *coup d'état*"—was overtaking Washington and the nation. No tanks crouched along shaded streets of Capitol Hill. No troops prowled thoroughfares. The seizure of power took place instead more discreetly, in legislative committee rooms and paneled executive suites, with no sudden sharp report but the impact of new authority and old compromise. Yet it was a coup nonetheless. By the close of the eighties, America would be a different country, in which Las Vegas was to have a legitimacy, a massive infusion of capital, and the opening to its own national empire beyond the wildest dreams of Lansky or Thomas. In Strip terms, the emcee of the revolution, in the most historic comeback in the annals of show business, turned out to be Ronald Reagan, the faded movie actor who had bombed in his two-week stand at the Last Frontier a quarter century before.

Reagan's presidency transformed the nation as had no other governance in modern American history. A convergence of newly minted right-wing ideology and conservative capture of the GOP with the long-building dominance of special interests, the revolution that bore his name was charted in a series of decisive, bipartisan measures. In 1981, tax cuts drastically reduced rates for the rich while giving corporations and wealthy individuals still more subsidies and windfalls. In 1982, sweeping financial deregulation unleashed and rewarded a speculative fever in financial markets, setting loose a plague of business seizures and sackings at a cost of hundreds of thousands of jobs, billions of dollars in productivity, and plundered pension funds and public revenues. In 1983, a $200 billion Social Security tax fell overwhelmingly on the middle class and working poor.

Over the next three years, more tax manipulation made what one account called "spectacular beneficiaries" of those with incomes of $200,000 or more, while budget acts enshrined the regressive system and shifted the burden of deficit reduction to people making less than $50,000. "The hogs were really feeding," Reagan's own budget director would say in looking back. The toll was further ravage of corporations and institutions; stagnation of real wages; lost jobs, benefits, and security for millions; and a spree of lending by savings-and-loans at the cost of hundreds of billions of dollars to depositors and taxpayers—altogether a climactic change. One study called it "the largest transfer of wealth in the nation's history," as billions of dollars moved by de facto political expropriation from middle-class and poor Americans to the already affluent and powerful, for some, a frightening form of free market prosperity. "America traveled," wrote *Washington Post* journalist Haynes Johnson, "from the New Patriotism to the New Greed all within a mere decade."

Swept into office with heavy contributions from Las Vegas as from increasingly similar precincts of corporate and private wealth, the Reagan administration was obviously friendly to Las Vegas in traditional political terms. For the Strip, even beyond the unprecedented number of patronage Nevadans Laxalt took with him to Washington, many in the new regime were kindred figures from California and the throbbing new Republican southern tier of the nation, figures of the booms in tourism and entertainment, real estate development, oil, corporate farming, technology, banking, insurance, the law, and much else so widely seeded by Syndicate economic and political investment since the fifties. Not since the early months of Kennedy's presidency had the casinos enjoyed such a presence in body and spirit along the Potomac. Like some twentieth-century presidents before and after, Reagan came with his own suspect associations with the Syndicate and its corporate allies, most notably Music Corporation of America. Before the first term was over, more than a hundred administration officials "involved in instances of criminal wrongdoing, abuse of power and privilege, and improper behavior," as one congressional inquiry put it in 1984, embodied the "Sleaze Factor" that came to be synonymous with the Reagan years.

There were the ritual White House pronouncements, timed to the election cycle, against crime and corruption. "I've always believed that government can break up the networks of tightly organized regional and national syndicates that make up organized crime," Reagan said in 1983, in one of his repeated promises to "get rid of the Mob." All the while, his men quietly slashed the budgets of the FBI, SEC, DEA, and other agencies, and in other ways choked off the investigative scope of federal law enforcement. Not least, there was the president's own political consorting with the still blatantly Syndicate-installed leaders of the Teamsters, Reagan on one memorable occasion addressing by closed-circuit television the union convention in a Las Vegas it had funded so lavishly, telling the cheering crowd that "I want to be a team with the Teamsters."

In Reagan's second term, his own presidential Commission on Organized Crime would criticize the administration for what it called the "appearance of impropriety" in ties to the notorious union. In a final report in 1986, the body would also deplore the "money laundering and the mob's entrenchment" in Las Vegas casinos, as one account put it. But the findings were duly ignored and the commission proved more political window-

dressing, "leaving important issues unexamined . . . a saga of missed opportunity," as one of its dissenting members charged afterward. For many who
knew the shrouded history on all sides, the record left a pall over the most
popular presidency of the time, moving Dan Moldea to call Reagan's elections a "dark victory."

Yet none of that evident compromise, banal or extraordinary, would be
as important to the forces of Las Vegas as the changes the Reagan era
wrought in the political economy. Whatever the hoary compromises of the
Washington regime, the face of the Syndicate was changing in the eighties as
so much else in the country. By the natural attrition of aging feudal barons,
by the periodic prosecutions of crime lords in New York and elsewhere, the
previously recognizable mob was fading. A new, educated, more refined,
carefully groomed, and legalized postmodern Syndicate was already emerging. Financed and reinforced by the political economy created by the Reagan
revolution, Las Vegas was no longer to be its outpost colony or clearinghouse, but its sparkling capital. And alongside, out of the ethos and easy
money of the decade, came a new brand of capitalists and capitalism, intent,
like the Strip, only on making money, no longer constrained like their Wall
Street or corporate predecessors of the decades before to disguise or conceal
the obscenity of either their investments or their profits. When these postmodern speculators and predators met the postmodern Syndicate, it would
be the most spectacular Las Vegas wedding of all.

B enny Binion was having lunch at the Horseshoe with a friend from the
Strip on November 3, 1976, when a call came from his old partner, Meyer
Lansky, and a phone was brought to his table. Binion took the receiver
almost cautiously, and listened for a few seconds to the open line before he
finally spoke. "Hello, Meyer. How you feelin'? Won your election, I see." Lansky offered Binion his own license and casino in Atlantic City in a New Jersey
that had voted in legalized gambling by referendum the day before. But the
aging Binion decided to stay in Glitter Gulch.

When casinos came to Atlantic City it was the Syndicate's, and thus the
Strip's, first major colony since the loss of Havana eighteen years before.
Untold millions had been put into lobbying and public relations; before the
1976 referendum, gamblers outspent their opponents as much as sixty to
one. Their victory was the capstone of what one writer described as decades
of political agitation and pressure by organized crime families in New York,
New Jersey, and Pennsylvania, who expected, as in Las Vegas, not only
a take from the casinos, but to dominate all the collateral business from

construction, transportation, food, liquor, entertainment, and every other service.

The first company to be granted a temporary license by supposedly vigilant New Jersey gaming officials would be Resorts International, the company notorious for its sixties association with Lansky, but which had gone to extraordinary lengths to present a Syndicate- and Lansky-free image by hiring Bobby Kennedy's top crime fighters. As Resorts awaited final licensing, an explosive tape-recorded conversation in the infamous ABSCAM undercover sting operation made it clear Lansky was the man with "influence" in Atlantic City. "Resorts is originally his, through the Mary Carter Paint Company," a New Jersey public official was overheard declaring. Gaming officials were briefly taken aback, even the state's attorney general publicly announcing the company should be denied a permanent license. Resorts stock plummeted. But a few weeks later, officials unanimously granted the license, and the shares skyrocketed. At seventy-six, Lansky was off and running in yet another rendition of his old carpet joints.

In May 1978, only weeks after the Resorts casino on the boardwalk opened, it hosted a historic visitor from Las Vegas. "Well-acquainted with Resorts president Jack Davis," as John L. Smith described it, Steve Wynn had come to Atlantic City to explore the new market for himself. Customers were lined up three-deep at the slot machines and craps tables, "like alcoholics at the only bar in town," Smith recounted in his Wynn biography. But the admittedly grandiose owner of the Golden Nugget needed no inaugural crowds to remind him that with casinos legal in Atlantic City, as *Philadelphia Inquirer* reporter David Johnston wrote later, "suddenly one in four Americans live within a six-hour drive of a blackjack table." Wynn had been there a year earlier with Parry Thomas, prompting rumors that he had been planning for some time to move into Atlantic City, despite the ostensible Nevada prohibition against such expansion, and at the same time apparently not sharing his plans with all his fellow stockholders at the Golden Nugget. But now, with the urging and introductions from his Resorts contacts, he quickly moved to buy the old Strand Motel and adjacent property at the end of the boardwalk for $8.5 million. Writing a check for $1 million as a down payment on the spot, he acquired in a matter of minutes some of the most coveted real estate in gambling's latest satellite. It struck many as the same stupendous if implausible good fortune the thirty-six-year-old former slots manager had enjoyed in Las Vegas.

Two and a half years later, the 506-room Atlantic City Golden Nugget staged its grand opening, and "set the East Coast ablaze," as Smith put it, "with its opulence and success." But the extravagance and audacity of Wynn's new casino was nothing compared to the brazen means of its finance. If the throngs at Lansky's Resorts casino had inspired Wynn to a piece of the Atlantic City action, it would be the Reagan era's speculative orgy that ultimately provided the money, in the person of a toupeed, outwardly unprepossessing but arrogantly intense young Wall Street broker named Michael Milken.

Whatever the precise origins of Wynn's relationship with Milken, whether Wynn bought into Atlantic City before or after his capital was assured, their connection traced unmistakably to their mentors, Thomas and Riklis, and the history-making collaboration of the younger men would be very much in the tradition of their older patrons. In the later seventies, Milken was already a budding legend on Wall Street, the most impatiently fervent, almost messianic purveyor of what came to be known as junk bonds—the once shunned, low-rated, high-risk debt and securities that would provide $160 million of ready cash to build Wynn's New Jersey Golden Nugget.

As Drexel Burnham Lambert's wily pitchman and inside operator, and like the junk bonds he dealt in, Milken would be in many ways the epitome of the freebooting Reagan eighties. Like so much else in the period, his daring, often heedless maneuvers made himself and others—mostly the already wealthy and well-positioned—fabulously rich, though at a larger social and economic price for the vast majority of Americans still to be reckoned decades after his fall. He was funding risky new industries like cable television and cell telephones. At the same time, his junk bonds were also feeding corporate raiders for some of the most predatory and disastrous takeovers of the times, as well as bringing the collapse of more than fifty-five savings-and-loans nationwide with enormous social and personal cost.

Both windfall and ruin would be achieved not only by Milken's boldness and creativity but also by one of capitalism's oldest practices, getting rich by breaking the law. By the end of the decade, convicted of six felonies, fined $1 billion, and sentenced to twenty-two months in a white-collar minimum security prison, Milken would be known in one account as "the biggest Wall Street criminal in the United States." None of that affected the matches made between the bond broker and the casino tycoon, junk bonds and Las Vegas. "Milken was the new sugardaddy," *New York Times* reporter Timothy O'Brien wrote, "the purse that replaced the former largesse of the Teamsters Pension Fund." In Las Vegas itself, in May 1989, even as the charges against Milken were moving toward conviction, Greenspun typically lauded the buccaneering broker as a "twentieth century phenomenon" and "wizard of Wall Street," more the victim of jealous competitors than indicted "for any real wrongdoing." The felon who had given billions of dollars in loans to the Strip, Greenspun urged, should be "placed in charge of the nation's credit" as President Bush's "director of the Office of Management and Budget."

Milken had used Wynn to help sell investors in Las Vegas casinos on the first $160 million. Junk bonds would soon go on to provide some $2.5 billion to Las Vegas interests overall, and hundreds of millions in capital to Wynn as he sold his Atlantic City casino in 1987 to begin to build his Las Vegas dominion.

The fantastic fortunes that now began to pour in and out of casino gambling, several times the money made by owners and chief executives of manufacturing concerns or other traditional industries, made the Strip seem like any other Wall Street commodity. Still, rude ghosts intruded from time to time. It had taken Wynn until 1981 to be licensed by New Jersey, well after the November 1980 opening of the Boardwalk Golden Nugget—in part because he had been questioned more extensively by New Jersey authorities about his Las Vegas operation than he had ever been by officials in Nevada. In Las Vegas at the time, a federal grand jury was said to be looking into allegations of cocaine trafficking and other offenses by Glitter Gulch Golden Nugget employees.

Two years later, Wynn sought to acquire a property zoned for gambling in London. Though results were never formally filed and much of the substance would be fraught with controversy, the routine Scotland Yard investigation triggered by Wynn's application raised rumors and allegations that would plague him for years to come. For the moment, however, details from the Scotland Yard inquiry remained secret, and when Wynn suddenly withdrew his application for the British license, the issue seemed to vanish.

By 1987, when Wynn had sold his New Jersey Nugget in a Drexel maneuver with Bally's—the money along with more Milken junk bonds to be used to build his majestic new Mirage on the Strip—such unpleasantness seemed in the distant past, and like so much in Las Vegas, easily disregarded. Financed largely by Milken's junk bonds the way Teamster loans had once poured in, places like Caesars led the city in a boom greater than any before. In the roaring eighties, the number of hotel rooms on the Strip and in Glitter Gulch had doubled in a constant expansion of the existing resorts, surpassing even the splurge of the sixties. Despite another round of periodic moaning by hotel managers and city publicists about "downturns" and even "losses" during the national recessions of the era, the crowded gambling floors flourished. By the end of the decade, twice as many visitors as the hordes of 1980 were pouring into the casinos, nearly 25 million, with the inevitable plans to draw millions more than that in a few years.

The city publicists, ever attuned to the national mood now so skillfully fostered by a reactionary but singularly theatrical and popular president, had a new lure. "During the Reagan years," David Johnston wrote, "Las Vegas shamelessly wrapped itself in the flag, selling itself through national television commercials as 'The American Way to Play.' " It was another ironic juxtaposition of the inner reality and outer image, themes of Americana and patriotism at a moment when the Strip was more cosmopolitan than ever, awash in international drug money, increasingly a playground and laundering center for foreign organized crime.

There was also something beyond Reagan-era bunting and good feeling. Las Vegas was painting itself more and more as a place for the whole family to vacation—Mom and Dad and the kids to enjoy new amusement parks and other collateral attractions, though at the end of the eighties with all the millions of dollars spent for promotion there was only the barest hint of what was to come. The city was on its way to having more hotel rooms than any other place in America, outdistancing the Orlando of Disneyworld in ordinary tourists, hosting more national conventions than New York or Chicago. Las Vegas would soon have twelve of the fifteen largest hotels in the world, and then fifteen of the largest twenty.

The grand vision was no longer bounded by the jagged mountains surrounding the increasingly inhabited and expanding Las Vegas Valley. For more than half the decade, in a stark and historic compliment to the city's slick and conspicuous national advertising, Las Vegas interests had been lobbying around the country. They worked patiently and shrewdly to persuade state, county, and city officials in dozens of locales that lifting their once unchallengeable bans on gambling, allowing casinos in like any other business, would be the instant high-revenue answer to the bust and bleakness of so many communities left behind during the Reagan years. In Iowa, South Dakota, Mississippi, Illinois, Missouri, Louisiana, and Colorado, only the beginning of the roll call, Las Vegas would be ready to bring in its landlocked gambling "boats" and gamblers, free-flowing capital and freewheeling ethic, to rescue the nation—to do for America what it had done for Nevada. When the U.S. Supreme Court opened the way for gambling on Indian reservations in 1987 and Congress passed the Indian Gaming Act in 1988, the same Strip missionaries were ready to help scores of impoverished tribes, soon establishing casinos Indian-owned and -run in name only in Connecticut, California, Michigan, Minnesota, Nebraska, and Wisconsin, with dozens of casinos in twenty more states swiftly to follow.

Here and there, as in New Jersey a decade earlier, there were ominous signs of how some of it had been accomplished, and by whom—in Arizona, six state legislators pleaded guilty in 1990 to accepting bribes and illegal campaign contributions in return for their support for legalizing casino gambling; in Kentucky, seven lawmakers were found guilty of taking bribes from what would be delicately described as "gambling interests"; in West Virginia, where Las Vegas money had made history in the presidential primary and election thirty years before, one governor, Arch Moore, Jr., pleaded guilty to accepting a bribe from the same vaguely identified "gaming interests"; and on reservations throughout the country, Native Americans speaking out against casinos were threatened, beaten, blackmailed, and murdered. But that too, like Wynn's Scotland Yard embarrassment, Las Vegas would ignore, denying any responsibility. The last decade of the twentieth century was going to be like no other in the history of Las Vegas, the era when the Strip crowned its new wealth and power with a huge new national dominion. At the end of the eighties it was clear that that would be accomplished, whenever necessary, by the old Vegas methods.

In 1989, within a few months, the city would suitably mourn the passing of three of its founding fathers—Binion, its redoubtable symbol of the old West; Dalitz, its seeming philanthropist; and Greenspun, its wheeler-dealer guardian of civic virtue. Each died a multimillionaire, with rich, dizzying histories; like the history of the city, only a fraction of what they had actually done, or affected, was known. To a friend who once suggested he write his autobiography, Binion, in effect speaking for all of them, was adamant. "No books, no nuthin'. What I know, I know, and it's goin' . . . with me."

Six years earlier an era had ended with the death of Lansky, the man whose vision and organizational genius built and sustained the city that made them all rich, a man who understood as well the necessity of secrets. Not long before his death in a Miami hospital bed, Lansky had been asked by an Israeli journalist if he would have changed anything, led his life another way. He fell silent for a while and then replied, "I have nothing on my conscience. I would not change anything."

There would be no evidence that any of them saw exactly what was coming, or knew much about the sophisticated new machinery of advertising, lobbying, and the national and international political manipulation that the city of the next decade was already assembling. But it probably wouldn't have surprised them much. They, of all people, knew that the essence of their fabulous, ever-changing Las Vegas was always in the changeless power and purpose of its past.

16. "A Joint's a Joint"

It is the last night of the twentieth century. In extravagant worldwide programming to befit the occasion, television networks from the United States and several other countries beam their live satellite coverage back and forth among the major cities of the world. Most of the focus is on the great centers of Western civilization and commerce, Paris, London, New York—and Las Vegas.

As the day and evening wear on, it is striking: In a half-dozen languages broadcast to an audience of hundreds of millions, no metropolis, no locale on the planet, receives more attention, has more of its entertainment, color, and imagery portrayed to the world, than the city in the southern Nevada desert that scarcely existed when the century began. The extraordinary television coverage reflects a consensus of producers, and a careful demographic survey of what the universal viewers want and expect. The cameras register a reality of power. On the eve of the millennium, Las Vegas is a global capital.

The backdrop of the city's mammoth, towering resorts tends to dwarf the special New Year's Eve correspondents standing in front of them to deliver their reports. Television's latest digital cameras swivel, zoom, and then retreat in vain efforts to encompass the famous Strip. Las Vegas has changed so much so rapidly over the last decade, says commentator after commentator, that the city would be unrecognizable to those who had not been there recently. Yet so many millions of people have visited the city over the last half century that reporters seem to take for granted the audience's fascination with the place, their easy familiarity with the most famous street on earth.

Straining to picture the panorama, one network positions a crew atop the 1,149-foot-tall Stratosphere Tower casino, only 200 feet short of New York's World Trade Center and the tallest building west of the Mississippi. Another camera hovers nearby in the cabin of a blimp 1,500 feet above the Las Vegas Valley floor. No lens, no single vantage point seems able to take it all in. But then the sweep of the city has never been easy to discern, whatever its scope.

What the cameras are trying to convey is the result of a transformation so complete that the familiar phrase "building boom" seems a trivializing description. The Las Vegas of the later eighties, though an impressive national showcase and already the country's major tourist attraction, seems shabby in comparison to what stands here now.

In 1989, Steve Wynn builds on a South Seas theme the Strip's first wholly new resort in sixteen years, the luxurious $610 million Mirage, with more than 3,000 guestrooms in three thirty-story towers, atop grand ballrooms larger than any tsar's. In 1990, Circus Circus Enterprises, under its president, Bill Bennett, opens the $300 million "medieval" Excalibur, the first theme park concept resort casting Las Vegas as a family playground, though beneath its castle turrets is a casino the size of four football fields.

In 1993, Bennett expands on an Egyptian theme to open the $375 million Luxor, with more than 2,500 rooms and the world's largest atrium in a thirty-story bronze and glass pyramid, entered through a sphinx of matching magnitude. That same year, Wynn and his associates open the $430 million Treasure Island, a 2,900-room resort on a Caribbean theme with three thirty-six-story towers and a 100,000-foot casino designed on the model of a pirate city. By now, too, Kirk Kerkorian has built his new $1 billion MGM Grand Hotel, Casino, and Theme Park, the world's second-largest hotel, with more than 5,000 rooms, and the biggest casino on the planet, featuring 3,500 slot machines and 170 tables around the motif of *The Wizard of Oz* and Hollywood.

In 1996, Bob Stupak builds Las Vegas's own space needle, the towering $550 million Stratosphere with its 100,000-square-foot casino, and amusement thrill rides as high above the street as the top floors of the Empire State Building. That year, too, Wynn and other partners build the $344 million Monte Carlo as an expression of what they call the "popular elegance" of Monaco; its 3,000 rooms make it the seventh largest hotel in the world.

In 1997, a consortium of Kerkorian and other associates who own

Nevada casinos outside Las Vegas build New York New York, a $2 billion replica of what they call the "Best of the Big Apple," complete with copies of famous skyscrapers, street mimes, a Statue of Liberty, a Brooklyn Bridge, a Coney Island roller coaster, and a casino cashier's cage designed after the Manhattan financial district. In 1998, Wynn opens the $1.8 billion luxury Bellagio, with its thirty-five stories and 3,000 rooms. The same year, Circus Circus Enterprises inaugurates the $1 billion, 4,000-room Mandalay Bay, set in a "rainforest," and featuring at the entrance to its Red Square restaurant and vodka bar a larger-than-life statue of Lenin imported as a trophy from the former Soviet Union.

In the last year of the century, computer trade show promoter Sheldon Adelson brings on his $2 billion Venetian Hotel Resort and Casino, with two ornate thirty-five-floor towers and 6,000 accommodations—all suites. Also in 1999, Arthur Goldberg, formerly of Bally's and now the head of Park Place Entertainment (merging Bally's and Hilton), opens the $750 million, fifty-story Paris with 3,000 rooms and a two-acre swimming pool.

To make way for it all, monuments of the past are erased, a grand publicity stunt made of the destruction. Two hundred thousand people gather on an October night in 1993 as Wynn throws the switch to implode floor by floor the old Dunes, with the Sands, Hacienda, and Landmark soon to follow, more hotel rooms demolished in a few years than most cities have come to possess over the century. Off the Strip, hundreds of millions of dollars in public as well as private funds have gone to rebuild and modernize, and the result is the "Fremont Street Experience," a five-block-long pedestrian mall (enclosed by 2 million lights), the city's old Glitter Gulch, including the Horseshoe, California, El Cortez, Four Queens, Fremont, Golden Nugget, and Las Vegas Club. And beyond the Strip and downtown are a string of showy new satellite casinos set about the valley—among them the Rio, the Boulder, the Sunset, and the Palace Stations.

Opulent beyond anything Las Vegas has ever known, the new Strip mega-resorts, with their $400-a-night accommodations, house world-famous gourmet cafés, and fashionable international boutiques with such tenants as Armani, Chanel, Lagerfeld, Hermès, and Gucci. The new casino complexes, self-contained bazaars of luxury, mark Las Vegas's appeal to the richest and increasingly prosperous top 5 percent of America's population. Though the city still draws and depends upon the general populace—striving "to sell its elitism to the masses," as one local journalist puts it—it has always been a place where ordinary people come to feel extraordinary. But now that the preponderance of visitors cannot afford the sumptuous new rooms and restaurants, they troop through the new resorts and their enclosed malls with Paris street names or Italian marble walkways, peering at the window displays and ornate lobbies as if they were passersby in the exclusive blocks of some Gilded Age city.

Yet beyond the glamour and massiveness of the once again reinvented city, its essence never changes. The new corridors of affluence and pretension still lead to the gigantic casinos that are the heart of the matter, the reason for all the rest. However discreetly lit or adorned, electronically encased or programmed, the racket works now as it always has, with the single ultimate purpose of taking the public's money in a manner no other industry in the world can match. Those who see that reality most clearly, the few who knew the old Las Vegas, are unfazed by the new facade. "A joint's a joint," says a casino manager who came to the city with Meyer Lansky.

As the millennial midnight approaches, ABC's Connie Chung appears outside the Bellagio to interview longtime Las Vegas entertainer Wayne Newton, now a jowly, heavily made-up intimation of the plump teen star of Glitter Gulch, under contract to play the Stardust for the entire first decade of the new century. They chat for a while, Chung visibly searching for something amusing and interesting to say. What will Las Vegas be like in the new millennium, she finally asks the singer, adding in jest one of the city's forbidden questions: Will the mob come back to run it? she asks him with a smile. But instead of dismissing the question as the banter it was meant to be, Newton flares in nervous alarm, revealing how close beneath the surface the elaborately masked reality still is. For those who understand the city, Chung's question is no lighthearted joke. "Oh, I wouldn't know anything about that," Newton says too quickly in utter seriousness, looking at the camera as if at an audience he can see in the flesh. "I just want everyone to know that I don't have anything to do with that kind of thing."

But the unease of the performer is soon forgotten in the extravaganza of the evening's climax. As the clock strikes midnight Pacific time, the grand finale of the continent's millennium celebration shows the dancing waters of Steve Wynn's 1,000 carefully lighted fountains in front of the Bellagio, sending choreographed streams as high as 240 feet in the air to the accompaniment of Handel's *Messiah*. It is a moment of the sensational and the sacred, fittingly broadcast from the American Mecca.

Ten days after the millennium-eve spectacle, headlines blared the largest corporate merger in history, a $350 billion deal between U.S. communications giants Time Warner and America Online. The looming media-Internet conglomerate, determining so much of what the public might see, hear, and read in a seductive new computer technology, seemed to many a stunning sign of the trend toward corporate monopolies of unprecedented reach and force. "In our lust for profits," wrote columnist Jill Nelson, "we have forgotten democratic principles." Yet viewed from the Strip, the new behemoth seemed only another version of the kind of concentrated power Las Vegas had seen over the past decade and before. Once again, the city had been an augury for the nation.

By any measure economic or political, the oligarchy that ruled Las Vegas at the millennium was—as it had been in essence for fifty years—an exclusive regime. As always in the city, the juice belonged to a handful of prominent men, representing larger, less conspicuous interests behind them, and with their own power inseparable from their emblematic pasts. The umbrella companies of end-of-century Las Vegas were with few exceptions traded on Wall Street. "America, Inc. buys out Murder, Inc.," was how David Johnston summed up the apparent advent of corporate chain ownership of casinos and what Las Vegas would officially celebrate as yet another cleansing crossing of casinos into "mainstream American business." Yet, as in the city's earlier passages with Del Webb, Hughes, Parvin-Dohrmann, Continental Connectors, Recrion, Argent, and dozens more publicly chartered entities, the corporate veil remained in many ways as thin and deceptive as it had always been. The operational decisions still remained in the hands of a few. Seventeen of the twenty largest, most consequential casinos on the Strip, and thus most of its jobs and the bulk of its profits, were effectively controlled during the nineties by five men—MGM's Kerkorian, Bennett leading Circus Circus Enterprises, Wynn atop his Mirage, Inc., Adelson with his Las Vegas Sands, Inc., and Arthur Goldberg presiding over the Park Place Entertainment combine. The rest of the city's casinos of any note were divided among less than a dozen other owners, including hotel chains like Hilton and a few inheritors of venerable local names and companies—Jack Binion, Michael Gaughan, and Bill Boyd, the sons of families who had been in Las Vegas since the forties. But it was the five mega-resort giants who clearly dominated.

In the fashion and ritual of the times, like Milken's lavish meetings with his bond buyers that they called the Predators' Ball, the Strip CEOs at the statutory intervals would parade their profits and plans before shareholders. In that venue, they might be subject to the predictable power plays—not unlike their Syndicate forerunners, after all—as when a falling out with big investors eventually drove Bennett from the chairmanship of Circus Circus in the mid-nineties. But behind the brand-name logos, portfolios, and casting of ballots, the men at the top were resonant of the order they ostensibly replaced.

They were mostly creatures of the city's culture, or at least of its ethic practiced elsewhere. Shadows of early Miami connections and securities schemes had hung over Kerkorian as he moved, without challenge, in and out of a Las Vegas in which the Syndicate was arbiter over nearly four decades. Bennett rose in the same milieu over the same span, from host and night manager to boardroom baron. He had been an intimate of the infamous Allen Dorfman, his career entangled with Teamster-financed and Syndicate-controlled Jay Sarno. Wynn's provenance was clear enough. Adelson, the billionaire promoter and right-wing Zionist with business and political ties to Israel, had the same mentality as the Strip's former overseers. He had gotten his start distributing vending machines in the fifties on the streets of Brockton, Massachusetts, where the Patriarca branch of the Syndicate rarely allowed competitors in the field, and his reactionary anti-unionism echoed the animus of the old mob toward independent organized labor. A crass new mogul who behaved with the arrogance and impudence of an old boss, he went about the city in the nineties, even into the editorial offices of the *Review-Journal*, with ex-Mossad bodyguards brazenly carrying semi-automatic weapons.

Goldberg had made a fortune as an executive in the rarefied world of New Jersey trucking. He had moved on to Bally's with that company's heritage of organized crime ties, and then engineered its merger with a casino-hungry Hilton, conditioning the agreement on his own enrichment by tens of millions in a questionable stock swap, and provoking a shareholder suit alleging kickbacks. His deal created the world's largest single casino operator, although conglomerate scale was no bar to hoary Strip methods. At the end of 1999, New Jersey regulators scathingly censured Bally's for political payoffs in Florida in a scheme in which Goldberg's chief aide was a former head of the Newark FBI office.

Genealogies and corporate customs aside, what was most revealing about the latest Las Vegas monopolists—what placed them in a lineage with their predecessors—was how they ran gambling's ever-growing tyranny over the city and state. By the nineties, the industry's economic weight alone was crushing. The eleven largest companies in Nevada were all casinos, eight of them bigger than state government. Of the twenty-five largest employers statewide, seventeen were Las Vegas resorts. The Strip's security guards were a legion four times the size of the Clark County police force. It left gambling

more than ever "the sacred cow that all Nevada politicians treat with deference," a historian of company power in communities wrote in 1999. "Company towns only grow beyond their roots when the politicians stop giving
the company everything it wants."

In Nevada, that had long since been political suicide, and by century's
end the casinos were not simply resting on their massive, preemptive presence but commanding the political process as never before. As a 1999 study
recorded, in almost every political campaign of any import in Las Vegas or
statewide for decades, half and often more of the campaign funds of winning
candidates had come from the casinos and their masters. The permanent
axiom of Nevada politics was that no one could win without them. The rare
exceptions were, as always, effectively isolated and neutralized. In cities and
towns the de facto dictatorship ensured any public easement or added infra-
structure helpful to the casinos. In Carson City, it maintained the sanctity of
the meager gambling tax, barely raised in 1991, again by a fraction, to only
6.25 percent on gambling profits, a rate lower than any other state's. While its
comparatively meager declared revenues paid for more than one-third of
Nevada's public expenses, what the industry continued to abscond from the
state held the society hostage. The new business culture and managerial
regimes of the resorts imposed a pervasive conformity with even more
impact than the crude violence of the past. "The heavy hand of the industry
controlled virtually every area of life in the Las Vegas valley," a team of out-
of-state reporters concluded at the end of the century. "The concept of plu-
ralism that is crucial to the stabilization of democratic systems is foreign to
Las Vegas," wrote Chuck Gardner, a lawyer and editor, of the respected
Nevada Index in 1998. "A culture of influence and corruption has permeated
all walks of political life." The resulting bleakness of the human landscape
was more stark than anything recorded by writers since the fifties.

Over the last decades of the century Clark County had grown by more
than twenty times—"a record no other large U.S. county even comes close
to matching," as one account described the incessant boom. All along the
way there were warning signs of unmet crises, and of an underlying social
dysfunction as constant as the city's phenomenal growth—overcrowded
schools, a depleted and polluted water supply, an alarmingly high rate of
violent crime, unrelieved traffic congestion despite new roads, and runaway
construction described by one writer as "an unreadable chaos of non-
planning."

In 1974, the Twentieth Century Fund had conducted an extensive independent survey of what it called "this remarkable community" in southern
Nevada, duly noting the explosion of jobs and population and the relative

overall if skewed prosperity of Las Vegas, which gave it the thirty-seventh highest household median income in the nation. But the study's authors were astonished at what they also found to be "the social disorganization" behind the apparent progress and wealth. In the early seventies, as in the postwar decades before and those after, the city's crime rate was far higher than the national average or that of comparable metropolitan areas, with twice the rates of murder and rape. There were a third again as many alcoholics in Clark County as the national average, making tiny Nevada second only to New York in deaths from cirrhosis of the liver. The study's extensive interviews pointed to the same inordinate rates of child neglect and abuse, local divorce and domestic violence, lung cancer and other serious or terminal illnesses, and a veritable plague of untreated psychiatric disorders. Beneath the surface impression of abundant, well-paid jobs and employment security, there was a high turnover rate among a labor force evidently far more alienated than anyone—unions, casinos, or the workers themselves—admitted. The suicide rate in Las Vegas was "far in excess of both the national average and the average for all . . . metropolitan areas," as the study found, data that included the suicides of scores of nonresidents over a brief period—customers the casinos never talked about—while the number of local suicides alone would have still led the nation. "Many of the area's residents display high rates of pathology," the Twentieth Century Fund concluded tersely, though adding that it could find no simple statistical evidence or interview data that necessarily identified gambling as an industry, or Las Vegans' own gambling habits, to account for this misery.

Twenty-five years later, the gambling industry in Las Vegas and Nevada had become one of the most profitable in human history. Nevada's senators over the years were among the most powerful in the nation. Metropolitan Las Vegas was five times again larger. In the late nineties, a team of journalists from the University of California at Berkeley led by former *Wall Street Journal* correspondent David Littlejohn took much the same measure of the city as the earlier academic survey of the Fund. Their findings coincided with the research of a handful of local scholars and writers around the same period. If Las Vegas still led the nation in growth, it was also the highest in total crime, automobile accidents, alcohol consumption, teen pregnancies, and births to unwed mothers; the city also had one of the higher percentages of citizens lacking health insurance. Suicide rates were still double the national number. Las Vegas had one of the highest air pollution indexes in North America, fed by a profit-driven grid of sprawl, thrown across the valley with scant public transportation. There were less cultural and recreational facilities relative to its population than in any other comparable metropolitan area in the nation.

Outside the casinos' increasingly expensive entertainment, it had no accredited civic symphony, opera, or major art museum. Its school district was the ninth-largest in the United States, and one of the most overcrowded and outmoded. It welcomed its tens of millions of visitors to America's twelfth-busiest airport, which many pilots and air traffic controllers thought dangerously strained by laggard funding.

As always, the lights of the Strip—and now its well-paid corporate publicists—seemed to dazzle the rest of the country, many visiting journalists oblivious to the reality behind the neon. In 1994, in a cover story typical of much of the coverage of the moment, *Time* declared Las Vegas "an All-American city," what it called "the new American hometown."

The toll hardly stopped at the edge of the valley. The Nevada that Las Vegas casinos now dominated and cheated still had one of the highest per capita and median incomes in the nation, statistics that reflected the vast wealth of Las Vegas but said nothing about the actual distribution of income, much less power. Thus it also had one of the highest proportions of bankruptcy in the United States, as well as one of the worst high school dropout rates. Despite graduate schools, buildings, and other monuments named after some of the city's most infamous predators, its system of higher education remained relatively starved and neglected, as always by the ruling megaresorts, which drew the preponderance of employees from the ranks of those with a high school education or less, and most of their top executives from out of state.

Even beyond gambling's stranglehold, there might have been other sources of revenue to address the state's needs. By the nineties, in an ironic reprise of the Comstock boom, Nevada led all states in gold and silver production, though with the same piracy and colonial exploitation in public policy. A "sort of informal agreement since 1989" had existed "between the casino and mining industries to respect each other's interests regarding tax policy," as Nevada historian Eugene Moehring recorded in 1999. "Nevada has once again served as a bank where mining companies have used their undertaxed profits . . . to fund mining operations in other states and nations."

Not surprisingly, the governor presiding over the mining-gambling collusion and much else was Bob Miller, the son of the Riviera mobster. With the rise of the former Clark County district attorney to the Governor's Mansion in 1988, the last figment of any ostensible separation between politicians and gamblers was erased. The man who had been in a blind-trust casino partnership with Allen Dorfman and others, who had been less than zealous to prosecute the depredations at Binion's Horseshoe, was the Strip's own—enjoying "political support from nearly every major casino owner in the state," as Moehring noted, and on any issue of importance doing their bidding.

Amid the monopolization of economic and political power and the accumulating social cost, there was always the anomaly, the tragedy, and the remnant potential, of organized labor.

Bugsy Siegel was still building the marbled lobby and curving stairway of the Flamingo in 1946 when a twenty-nine-year-old Arkansas farmboy and ex-dishwasher named Elmer Alton Bramlet came to town as the business agent of the bartenders' union. Seven years later, he had taken control of the growing Culinary Workers as their secretary-treasurer, and would dominate union politics in the city for the next quarter century. Fond of leisure suits and long Macanudo cigars, riding in a union-supplied silver Lincoln Continental, the wooly, bulbous-nosed Bramlet was a caricature of the autocratic and corrupt union boss. From the beginning of his dominance he had given the Syndicate casinos almost unbroken labor stability, while steadily adding to the ranks of his local, and at the same time joining in the plunder of kickbacks and inside dealing, owning on the side operations that did business with casinos, some in services that competed with his own members.

His first real clash with owners began in the sixties in a series of short but fierce strikes against Hughes casinos and others in their new corporate garb. Over most of his reign, though, Las Vegas remained the paradox of a widely unionized, strife-free town in a right-to-work Nevada whose oligarchs were traditionally anti-labor. He would make his large union, and himself, an integral, mostly congenial part of the system. In 1976, as B'nai Brith named Bramlet Man-of-the-Year, he was loaning cronies millions from the local's pension fund, taking kickbacks from Dorfman and Korshak, bombing any business that hesitated to collude, and battling over various spoils with the Chicago outfit, casino kingpins, and his own mob-dominated international. Tipped off that Spilotro had a contract on him, he was frantically expatriating money in preparation for fleeing the country when three of his own bombers and arsonists whom he owed money hustled him into the back of a van in a McCarran parking lot. They stopped at a pay phone to let him call a friend at the Dunes and ask that $10,000 be delivered to Benny Binion. Unappeased, they took him into the desert and slaughtered him anyway, leaving under a shallow pile of rocks his stripped body and the many secrets he knew about the juice of the city and state.

Bramlet's murder was part of the opening of the city to the takeover by the Spilotro faction from Chicago that Yablonsky found rampant in the early eighties. The next several years in Las Vegas labor history were equally scandalous. After Bramlet's death, the Las Vegas Culinary Workers local—the nation's second largest affiliate of the Hotel Employees and Restaurant Employees International, and dominated from Chicago by the union's president, Ed Hanley—remained as compromised as ever. "The classic example," the Justice Department would later call Hanley, "of an organized crime takeover of a major labor union." The fraud and fixes of Hanley, Korshak, and Bramlet's successor Ben Schmoutey were so egregious that the three were called to testify in 1983 before a Senate subcommittee—the last accompanied by Oscar Goodman, who won his client immunity for little in return, while, as ever, ritually claiming persecution of the city. Though the hearings silhouetted an interlaced national corruption around the union's health and welfare funds, Hanley's presidency and its own pillage of the Las Vegas spoils continued for another dozen years. The tentacles from the era curled forward to the end of the century and reached the heights of American politics. A major beneficiary of Hanley's regime, the recipient of an exclusive multimillion-dollar contract to provide health care to 30,000 union members and their families in Las Vegas, was the well-connected Strip physician Elias Ghanem, the close friend, major donor, and fund-raiser of Bill Clinton.

Meanwhile, as the casinos reveled in junk bonds and the latest corporatization, Las Vegas labor began a series of bitter, prolonged battles to win a modicum of gambling's gushing profits. A two-month-long strike taking on some of the giants in 1984 ended in a mixed settlement for the Culinary Workers. The union lost four resorts altogether, dealing it an almost crushing blow, from which it struggled to recover for more than a decade. Over the next few years, including a stormy strike at Binion's Horseshoe in 1990, the local continued a slow comeback, though not from any industry largesse. There opened a widening wedge between the big, heavily leveraged casinos, whose Wall Street standing, despite their vast reported profits, remained sensitive to labor unrest, and local, family-owned joints more venomously anti-union than ever. But if the newer monoliths were sometimes quicker to settle, their very size and corporate structure also made for much more impersonal, cost-conscious relations with their growing labor force. However savage its rule, the Syndicate's old paternalism was in some ways an easier, more predictable regime for some of its workers. "I think the old Mob always figured that there was plenty to go around and they didn't want any trouble. So they kind of took care of people," said a longtime union member. "But this new Mob only cared about the bottom line and you were just another number." The split produced poignant scenes on the streets of the city—at one of the Boyd family casinos, son and CEO Bill refusing to recognize the union while his retired father, Sam, an old California gambling boat dealer who had clawed his way to some independence in the mobster-dominated city, joined his former employees picketing outside.

Though few saw it at the time, a small but symbolic test of the union came in 1991 in a strike against the now comparatively shabby Frontier. While the big casinos never broke openly with the Frontier's reactionary owners, they were visibly concerned by what many thought an "eyesore" of pickets on the Strip year after year. Once remarking to reporters that Las Vegas had "enough problems without this thing," Bennett at Circus Circus even instructed his kitchen to help feed the Frontier protesters. While that conflict dragged on, the Culinary Workers won a dramatic victory at Kerkorian's MGM Grand in 1995, after putting 5,000 pickets onto the Strip at the casino's grand opening, moving many Nevada politicians to honor the line despite their abiding subservience to the casinos. Two years later, the union won the Frontier boycott as well, climaxing the longest strike in American history.

By the later nineties, the Department of Justice had finally ousted Hanley, installing new leadership at the international under former Las Vegas organizer John Wilhelm, and the Culinary Workers seemed as uncorrupted and powerful as at any moment in their turbulent run with the rise of the city. More than 50,000 waitresses, maids, slot attendants, bellmen, kitchen workers, and others in Las Vegas casinos large and small, they had won health care, a measure of job security, and on the average 30 percent higher wages than workers in non-union casinos, still the rule in the rest of Nevada and most of the nation outside Atlantic City. "Las Vegas, whatever else anybody says about it," boasted Hattie Canty, the widowed mother of ten who was now president of Las Vegas Local 226, "has become a city where maids can own their own homes and raise their families." At the same time, in Washington, after ferocious backroom maneuvering, the leadership of the AFL-CIO passed surprisingly to the head of the Service Employees International Union, a feisty Irishman named John Sweeney, who promptly declared the Culinary Workers' success in Las Vegas "the heartbeat of the American labor movement." In an impassioned speech, he named the city the symbolic and substantive "ground zero" for the revival of labor after its near-eclipse in the Reagan-Bush era.

Typical of the city, however, the apparent new counterbalance, if not challenge, to casino power, was not all it seemed. At century's end, Adelson's stridently anti-union Venetian, opening despite pickets, threatened to turn the clock back—the longer it operated without negotiating, the more compelling its example to the other casino giants. Despite its recovery, the

Culinary Workers Union looked out on a ruthless, cost-cutting corporate landscape only a little less bleak than the rest of America. Its members were still vulnerable, as one account at the millennium put it, to "being down-sized, split-shifted, part-timed, seasonally employed, and subcontracted," like workers across the nation. And the union that Sweeney held up as a national example had yet to organize the flourishing neighborhood casinos off the Strip. Also, while most casino construction was done by union labor, the city's laggard, racism-ridden building trades unions had scarcely begun to organize the city's huge non-Strip commercial sector or its massive residential construction. "It may look like we're home, but if you look closely, it's really a house of cards," one local labor leader confessed.

That precariousness hardly allowed labor to back even the smallest spark of political reform. When a lonely Las Vegas African-American state senator, Joe Neal, quixotically proposed a gambling tax increase in 1999 from the old 6.75 percent to 8.25 percent—a rate still far lower than many states with legalized gambling—the labor movement held back. They would argue that other whole sectors of the booming economy, from retailing to service industries to many elements of real estate development, paid relatively little or nothing, and they knew well that the gamblers would eventually recoup from their employees any levy on the Strip. "You must always remember," one casino manager said, looking back on a half century in the city, "these bastards [corporate managers] are even greedier than the outfits."

In the last presidential election of the twentieth century, the national political power of the city—long wielded for the most part discreetly, if not covertly—came dramatically into the open. Unlike the millions of gamblers who went to Las Vegas seeking a windfall, the 1996 candidates, Clinton and Bob Dole, seemed to beat the proverbial Las Vegas odds. Both parties, in equal measure, raked in gambling money as never before, gratefully taking official record contributions of more than $5 million and millions more generated from its collateral businesses and influence. But much of the real game remained hidden, and the house would be the only winner in the end.

If the Strip had once quietly given Jack Kennedy a valise with a million dollars at one of the Rat Pack parties at the Sands, if Marcello had made his secret payoffs to Lyndon Johnson and Hughes to Richard Nixon through poker-faced middlemen, if Reagan had taken their campaign backing by way of Sunbelt and Teamster proxies, if Laxalt only a few years before had given up a run for the White House because of the city's taint, now the passing of the cash was one more public show.

In June 1995, with some fanfare, Senator Dole went to Shadow Creek—Wynn's 320-acre, $48 million private golf course, a guarded preserve where the staff was sworn to secrecy and the few guest players, required to have a minimum credit line of $100,000 at one of the Wynn casinos, were served caviar on the fairway. But Dole had no trouble getting in. At a $5,000-a-plate luncheon, where the guests included Frank Fertitta and Blake Sartini of the Station Casinos, Binion's son Jack, and other wealthy Las Vegans, Dole raised a half-million dollars. In 1994, Wynn had hosted a breakfast that gave the GOP another $540,000 at one sitting, though the cash from both events was only a fraction of the more than $7 million Las Vegas interests put into local races throughout the country, as well as "soft money" coffers of both parties over the early nineties. After the Shadow Creek golf outing, Wynn personally would go on to raise more than another $1 million for Dole, including some $90,000 from his family and Mirage, Inc., employees, and Wynn's close friend and associate John A. Moran became Dole's finance chairman. There was not simply an extension of gambling's political investment—there was an explosion. By the first weeks of 1996, the Strip had contributed eight times more cash to the presidential race than in 1992.

Republicans had been ahead at first in what one candidly called "Vegas winnings," but the Democrats soon hit their jackpot. In June 1996, President Clinton had lunch at the home of *Sun* publisher Brian Greenspun, a long-time friend and sometime Shadow Creek golfer whose wife, Myra, had recently given $35,000 to the Democratic National Committee. Dark-windowed limousines jammed the streets of an exclusive subdivision of Green Valley—the now lush suburb built on desert Hank Greenspun had bought decades earlier—as the city's wealthy ate salmon catered by Spago at $25,000 a couple, and executives of the Sands, Bally's, and Circus Circus, as well as the peripatetic Wynn, gave some $650,000 to the Democrats. It was only the beginning of Las Vegas cash for Clinton's reelection, with still more money generated by his good friend Ghanem.

In a long-standing tradition going back to the Syndicate's support of Nixon as well as Kennedy in 1960, and of both presidential candidates in almost every subsequent race, Wynn's presence and money in support of the Democrat as well as his earlier backing of the Republican surprised no Strip insiders. Within weeks of addressing Nevada Republicans and extolling Dole as a "good, solid-thinking man," Wynn was also promising to raise six-figure donations for Clinton. The bipartisanship coincided not simply with Clinton's early lead in the polls, but apparently with a golf game in May 1996 when Governor Miller arranged for the president and Wynn to play together at the Congressional Country Club in Washington. "I'm just one of those fence-jumpers," the owner of the Mirage joked with a local reporter after-ward. "I just see which way the wind's blowing." True to form, within days of the Green Valley luncheon there were reports from Wynn's corporate spokesman that the casino executive was still supporting Dole as well.

Tracking Clinton and Dole, the national media now began to discover in earnest, if not in some shock, that behind all the highly publicized and bipar-tisan good fortune there were enormous stakes. The Las Vegas interests now inserting unprecedented amounts of money into the political process had expanded throughout the nation. More and more localities fiscally ravaged in the eighties had turned for revenue to the apparent rescue of casino gam-bling, from riverboats to Indian reservations to huge new carpet joints coast to coast. The industry now commanded the attendant political influence not only in Nevada, but in governors' offices, legislatures, county commissions, and city councils in forty-seven other states, where it spent more than $100 million in lobbying and contributions in the nineties. Corporate casinos boasted heavily staffed "government relations" departments, conducting sophisticated polls on issues and candidates on all sides. While Laxalt himself served as a senior consultant to Dole, his old crony, the elaborately coiffed Fahrenkopf who had succeeded him as GOP chairman, was now the $750,000-a-year head of the industry's American Gaming Association in its ceaseless Washington lobbying.

Moreover, Americans were gambling their money as never before—and losing more than $40 billion a year. Uncertain of the present and future, suf-fering "a collapse of confidence in the utility of work," as A. Alvarez wrote in *The New York Review of Books,* the nation was now spending six times more on gambling than all other forms of entertainment combined, more on slot machines, cards, and numbers rackets than on movies, theme parks, cruise ships, and recorded music altogether.

"We're not U.S. Steel," a colleague of Wynn's was quoted as saying about the industry's still shady image. Only a few noticed the unintended mockery. In the popular 1974 movie *The Godfather,* the Meyer Lansky character had turned to his younger Italian partner at one point to characterize their inter-national gambling empire. "Michael," he breathed in words borrowed from an actual FBI wiretap of Lansky, "we're bigger than U.S. Steel." It had been true enough during the time depicted in the movie—the late fifties—but now even more salient as gambling surpassed not only the money generated by the nation's decaying manufacturing base but also the profits of the thriv-ing new sectors of high technology and service. With 30–50 percent profits, double the average of most businesses, the trillion-dollar gambling industry had become a force like few others in the nation's history. From Las Vegas as

its global headquarters, the gambling industry unabashedly and conspicuously dictated the politics of much of the nation as it had long dictated to
Nevada. "In the old days, casino owners just gave money to politicians and
stayed in the background," *Review-Journal* columnist Smith would say in a
passage quoted by the *New York Times.* "Now it's an open orgy of power. If
politicians don't give back what they want, they run them out."

There would be two unmistakable displays of their power during the
Clinton years. In 1994, the White House had floated a 4 percent federal gaming tax as a possible component of welfare reform, or even as a source of
potential billions of dollars to slash the budget deficit without further cutting social programs. But casino owners characterized even the first vague
reports of the proposal as a "reign of terror," the Culinary Workers through
Hanley joined in the opposition, MGM reportedly paid Laxalt a handsome
retainer to lobby against the legislation, and Dole as well as other Republicans and Democrats promptly condemned the concept. Not long after,
because of what the *Los Angeles Times* described as a "fierce lobbying effort,"
including several senators and congressmen besieging the White House, the
president quickly abandoned what had only been a trial balloon to begin
with. By the time he got to Las Vegas for his $650,000 lunch at the Green-
spuns in June 1996, Clinton was openly apologetic, disowning the gambling
tax as the ill-conceived idea of "someone well down" in the Treasury Department. "That was never a recommendation of my Cabinet," he assured the *Las
Vegas Sun,* "much less of anyone in the White House."

As Clinton spoke, the casinos were already being threatened elsewhere.
Their national expansion had provoked a grassroots backlash in many communities, embodied in an unusual alliance that included the right-wing
Christian Coalition, racetrack owners, and liberal activists. By mid-decade,
working with little money, local anti-gambling movements had managed to
defeat the industry around the country in more than twenty referendums on
the expansion of casinos, and were seizing on what seemed a growing public
concern over issues of addiction, increased crime, and a general corrupting
influence associated with the spread of the industry. While the new, more
corporate, but perennially monopolized Strip was financing both sides in the
1996 election, Congress in time-honored fashion was appeasing the widening popular opposition by legislating a Gambling Impact Study Commission
to examine the industry's social effects. Many of its backers welcomed the
inquiry as the nation's first chance to expose what they called a "scavenger
casino economy" that took billions, addicted thousands at great physical and
human cost, and siphoned spending from local businesses to the point of
ruin, all while giving back nothing of social or economic value.

A federal commission's expected subpoena power might afford for the first time since Kefauver or the Kennedys a comprehensive probe into what law enforcement officers and others suspected to be the continuing regime of hidden casino ownership, profit-skimming, money laundering, casino corporations' exploitative cooperative agreements with Indian gambling, and the unrelenting ties to organized crime. It was a prospect Las Vegas casino owners would never allow. Over the past decade, Las Vegas had spent millions to change its public mien from "rackets" to "industry," "gambling" to "gaming," "joints" to "mega-resorts," "nude revues" to "family entertainment," "mob" to "mainstream corporate America." Faced with the first potential challenge in more than thirty years to its enduring order as well as a benign new image, it reacted with a might and decisiveness eloquent of its power.

The morning after dining with Wynn in Las Vegas in April 1996, Speaker of the House Newt Gingrich told a Republican fund-raiser at the Mirage that the bill on the study "should be modified," as the *Washington Post* recorded his remarks, "so that the commission does not have the power to issue subpoenas." As promised, Gingrich would eliminate effective subpoena power in the final House-Senate conference committee version of the bill creating the commission. For his part, Dole had quietly supported a matching Senate bill in which subpoena power, as one Democratic senator described it, was "completely gutted." Predictably, Clinton would also pledge during his June 1996 visit to Las Vegas that he would never allow a "witch hunt" of gambling, telling casino owners at the gathering that the commission would emerge only as the emasculated version in the Gingrich-Dole legislation.

What followed was another caricature of politics toyed with by private interests. Even before Congress created the weakened commission in the summer of 1996, the casinos were moving to control its makeup—Clinton, Gingrich, and Senate GOP majority leader Trent Lott were to make three selections each. Reminiscent of the Kefauver Committee forty-seven years before, the commission would be the sum of political maneuvering and accommodations to Las Vegas. When the choices were made, Las Vegas gambling industry figures and pliable, uninformed "neutral" members, including a Native American with no serious knowledge of Indian casinos, far outnumbered two token critics. As the commission then began a perfunctory series of hearings over the next three years, unable to subpoena any individual witness, the industry poured another $6 million into the coffers of both parties as insurance.

As it was, the commission's 300-page report in June 1999 dealt primarily and all but irrelevantly with adjustments in state lotteries, a raising of the gambling age to twenty-one, and foredoomed suggestions to prohibit betting on college sports, to exercise more oversight of Native American casinos generating nearly $7 billion a year, and to limit the industry's political contributions that had made the commission what it was. Altogether, the recommendations were "so general or watered down," as the *Los Angeles Times* summarized the results, "that they pose little threat to the industry." There had been no serious investigation or discussion of casino ownership and financing, of money laundering and drug trafficking, of the role of organized crime, of insider trading or executive plundering that marked gambling's latest corporate era, of the astronomical odds in the slots more weighted against the player than ever, of electronic poker and other popular rackets, of the Mob ethic become a national business creed and political standard. Casinos would continue to lavish millions of dollars on congressional and senatorial campaign funds over the last months of the century to guarantee that none of the commission's bland proposals became law—just as their forerunners had used Senator McCarran and others to kill bills born of the Kefauver inquiry.

Beyond the ceremonial mockery of the commission lay still deeper issues never broached in the national political dialogue, questions only a few commentators raised about the influence of the Strip and the future it represented, what one author called "the Las Vegasing of America." The heedless rise of the city presented a dark picture, part of what Michael Ventura called "the appalling cost we pay for the dominance of money." But if a handful were worried about a ruling industry that consumed a national fortune, it was not evident in Washington.

Once again in the 2000 election, the casinos, planning heavy contributions to both presidential nominees, would have their bets covered. That cash and the power it bought made Las Vegas a kind of shadow capital, in political as well as socioeconomic terms, and the masters of the Strip and Glitter Gulch knew a good thing when they saw it. No matter what happened in the first elections of the twenty-first century, the Vegas connections would win. As the founders of the city always understood, parties and personalities were minor compared to the stakes now shared among an ever-expanding group of profiteers. Corporate veils and Wall Street brokering had made thousands of stock-owning individuals and institutions, from the Harvard University endowment to the California State Employees Pension Fund, the successors to Costello, Luciano, Siegel, Giancana, and the others as the capital funders of the gambling empire. More than Lansky could ever have known, it was a form of the grand alliance of upperworld and underworld that he had founded and developed over half a century—not simply a city but a nation in which gambling was openly and unashamedly an integral part of a political economy that had always been in the shadows, where the only real winners were the few who owned the house and controlled the game, and the losers were all the rest. It was an ultimate corrupt capitalism in which the Polish immigrant boy's place of angels, "somewhat like heaven," had become so largely his "paradise of suckers."

President Clinton—raised in Hot Springs, his family deeply involved in the backroom gambling there in the fifties when it rivaled Las Vegas, his own political career launched by the backing of his uncle Raymond, who ran slot machines in the town for the Marcello family—seemed to understand the city's bipartisan politics as clearly as any politician of the century. He spoke a kind of jovial epitaph on the system when he attended a $10,000-a-person luncheon in October 1999, held in the gourmet restaurant of the new Paris Casino's Eiffel Tower, with its dramatic view of the Strip. "One of the things that I like about Arthur Goldberg and a lot of the others of you who have been my longtime friends here, is that you have a sense of enlightened self-interest," he told a select group of backers, including Elias Ghanem. "You're intelligent enough to support Democrats so that you can continue to live like Republicans."

It was still business as usual in Las Vegas. In 1995, publisher Lyle Stuart's Barricade Books had included among its new titles *Running Scared: The Life and Treacherous Times of Las Vegas Casino King Steve Wynn*. Written by John L. Smith, a fourth-generation Nevadan and a popular award-winning *Review-Journal* columnist, the biography was the first critical book-length look at the city by a local journalist since *The Green Felt Jungle* by Ed Reid and Ovid Demaris more than three decades before. Though Smith never called Wynn a creature of the Syndicate, he made clear his skepticism about the casino owner's adamant denials of any questionable associations, and that he believed the old Las Vegas differentiation between "gangsters" and "friends of gangsters" was a distinction without meaning. The young journalist was also among the first to report some of the controversial Scotland Yard material from Wynn's aborted application for a London gambling license more than a decade earlier.

Well before Smith's *Running Scared* was published, Wynn filed a multi-million-dollar libel suit against Stuart in Nevada for the publisher's catalogue copy, and subsequently brought a separate lawsuit against the book in Kentucky. As Smith's book appeared, legal battles raged over reliance on Scotland Yard information that Wynn angrily denounced and attacked as untrue and unsubstantiated, but which now gained unprecedented notoriety and dissemination—including a quoted passage from British investigators: "The strong inference which can be drawn from the new intelligence is that Stephen Wynn, the president of GNI [Golden Nugget, Inc.] has been operating under the aegis of the Genovese family since he first went to Las Vegas in the 1960s to become a stockholder in the New Frontier Casino." It was this assertion in the British intelligence files that Stuart paraphrased in his catalogue copy, though substituting the term *front man* to describe Wynn because the publisher assumed that bookstore owners in Nevada and elsewhere would not understand the meaning of the word "aegis," and it was that catalogue summary of the book that Wynn contended was libelous.

The message of the Wynn litigation was plain along the Strip. "He wants to bust you out," Stuart, himself a frequent high roller, told Smith in an all-too-accurate gambling metaphor. In addition to a battery of lawyers who filed suits in Nevada and Kentucky, Wynn would have his own figurative bust-out crew at the Las Vegas trial. Nevada governor Ross Miller and former car salesman become Las Vegas mayor Jan Jones appeared as fulsome character witnesses for the plaintiff, depicting him as a "gee-whiz guy." Hearing the Las Vegas case was one of Miller's appointees, Judge Sally Loehrer, who narrowed the defendant's discovery from a requested 10,000 items to eventual receipt of only 6 pieces of paper. Loehrer would go on to be elected to the bench and lead a judicial effort to defeat a term-initiative for judges in a campaign financed heavily by Mirage Resorts. When the trial was over, more than two years after the book appeared, Smith himself had been dropped from the Nevada suit, and Wynn would withdraw his Kentucky action as well. But eight Las Vegas jurors ordered the publisher, Stuart, to pay the casino mogul $500,000 for emotional distress suffered from the catalogue copy, as well as more than $1.5 million for damage to reputation and professional standing, and another $1 million in punitive damages. "We live in a town with no standard of obscenity, but criticizing a casino boss is a sin," Smith would tell reporters at one point. The victor was not in the courtroom when the verdict came in. Wynn was back at the Mirage with President Clinton, hosting a meeting of the nation's governors.

As a result of the jury award, Stuart's Barricade Books filed for bankruptcy, and as the publisher's appeal of the verdict wound through higher courts in Nevada, Wynn's lawyers would threaten to drag Smith back into the lawsuit. In the summer of 2000, the case was heard before the Nevada Supreme Court.

For his part, Smith continued to write his "On the Boulevard" column—chronicling the Strip's colorful characters with the toughest, most insightful reporting since Ned Day. Yet Wynn's retribution left a palpable chill. "In the old days the casinos sent their hit men. Now the corporations send their lawyers after you," said a retired newsman. "The point is never how they do it, but that they just do it over and over one way or another. The town gets the message. Everybody accepts the silencing and censoring just like always." Though the object of intimidation in the form of thuggish slurs in public places as well as the posturing of attorneys, Smith emerged from his libel ordeal still loving his city without illusion. "This is a frontier town peopled by a lot of good souls," he told an interviewer in December 1999. "But never forget that the evil is ten feet deep."

At the same moment, Wynn was drawing more unwanted notice. In November 1999, he had shocked a group of Wall Street investment analysts with his presentation at a conference on the future of the "hospitality industry." Rather than the usual recital of cash flow, depreciation, and projected profit, Wynn strode on stage to warble number after number from the original score of a song-and-dance revue called *Miss Spectacular* that was about to play his 1,500-seat Mirage Theater. This bizarre performance, which a rival industry figure called "an abortion," prompted the *New York Observer*'s respected financial columnist, Christopher Byron, to question Wynn's fitness for corporate command in general, including taking nearly $4 million from his company in rent for the paintings at the Bellagio. "Does that seem right or proper to you—to assemble a personal art collection of some of the most famous and expensive artists of all time, then have a publicly traded company, of which you own a controlling 12 percent stake, finance the whole thing?" Byron asked in his January 10, 2000, column. "It sure doesn't to me." Moreover, as the *Observer* noted, Wynn was also realizing $3.8 million a year in salary and bonuses, keeping his wife Elaine on Mirage's board, and gathering more than $100 million in exercisable stock options. "We're shocked that firms like J. P. Morgan & Company, the TCW Group, Capital Research and Management Company, and State Street Research & Management Company, which collectively own 26.9 percent of the company, would put up with this," Byron concluded. "Why haven't they thrown the bum out?"

The question was answered only weeks later, by the $6.7-billion takeover of Wynn's Mirage Resorts, Inc. on March 7, 2000, by MGM Grand mogul Kirk Kerkorian. Headlines around the world heralded the seizure, which left fourteen of the fifteen largest hotels on the Strip under just two companies, the new MGM-Mirage colossus and Park Place, giving Kerkorian almost half of gambling's global empire, and creating an even more powerful oligopoly in the trillion-dollar international casino industry. Meanwhile, typically, in

Las Vegas itself the single most important business transaction in the annals of the Strip went largely unexplored in local journalism. The minimal coverage was one more sign of how much America's most prosperous, fastest-growing city had become captive to the corporate lords of gaming.

Even on the surface, the takeover was a resounding business story. There was the buccaneering Wynn, once gambling's prodigal son become reigning king, now seen by many as one more petulant, profligate, overpaid CEO besieged by discontented shareholders. His nemesis was billionaire octogenarian Kerkorian—hailed as the "Lion of Las Vegas" by the local media while known in the taxonomic system of the national press simply as the "old jackal," or what the *New York Observer* called "one of the most thoroughly detested men on Wall Street." Behind the familiar profiles of Wynn and Kerkorian, there were richer, relatively untold stories about the provenance of both men. But in a city with a constantly reinvented reality, burying its history and throwing up glitzy new facades, Las Vegans found little of the authentic past or present in the local news coverage of the deal.

On February 23, MGM Grand had signaled an interest in buying Mirage for $17 a share. Though posturing to fight, Wynn maneuvered, amid orchestrated leaks of another buyer in the wings, to raise the bid to $21. The gambit drove up the price of the company from $5.4 billion to $6.7 billion. Wynn came out with more than $500 million for his 12 percent stake, Kerkorian with the new MGM-Mirage behemoth amounting to the greatest concentration of power since Bugsy had moved in on Las Vegas's stuttering neon a half century before. Readers of the *New York Times, Business Week,* the *Wall Street Journal,* the *New York Observer,* and other business journals would have known months earlier that Wynn's Mirage was ripe for takeover. Between the lines it was also clear that Kerkorian was jockeying to acquire it, having first bought Mirage stock "to take the pulse of the company," as one reporter said, then unloading his shares after a rift with Wynn. From a high of $26.38 in May 1999 to $10.88 the day before the takeover was announced, Mirage stock had plummeted, and various national reports tolled the reasons. Wynn was given to cavorting in company jets, lucrative personal stock options, sweetheart corporate leases of his paintings, and the seating of his wife on the Mirage board. His $2.5 million salary, annual $1.25 million bonus, and $5.2 million for renting the art made him one of the most lavishly paid executives in the country. Moreover, there were increasing reports of his volatile outbursts and of sometimes bizarre public behavior, including the already cited, incongruous "warbling" of show tunes at an investors' gathering the previous winter. Seen as a sacrifice of solid return to old Strip extravagance at a moment when casino management was judged more than ever by cost-cutting and portfolio performance, Wynn's actions all served to stoke share-holder unrest.

Meanwhile, however, in the customarily polite Las Vegas press, there seemed not a cloud on Wynn's horizon. Nevada officials had just given him a tax break on his $400 million art collection—a concession crafted for Wynn by legislators in Carson City he had backed with bipartisan contributions, and where he was reputed to be the most powerful man in the state. He was also thought to have neutralized the Nevada journalist most knowledgeable about him, John L. Smith.. In the late winter of 2000, just as Wynn was tee-tering on the edge of his corporate summit, he was still riding high in his hometown papers. *The Independent* of London summed up his writ in a March story with a directness and candor all but unknown in the Las Vegas press. "Politicians jumped at his command, candidates prostrated them-selves to seek his endorsement and his campaign contributions. City plan-ners re-routed roads and sewers at his behest, water authorities allowed him to siphon off millions of precious gallons to feed his private golf course."

Despite national or foreign accounts of Mirage's vulnerability, Kerko-rian's takeover struck southern Nevada like a thunderbolt out of a clear desert sky. Neither the *Review-Journal* nor the *Las Vegas Sun* had delved into how shaky Wynn's hold had become, and many readers were stunned by the purchase. "Las Vegans would have had to go to a library to find out what was happening in an industry that totally dominates their state," said one retired journalist. "I am still in shock," *Sun* editor Brian Greenspun wrote days after the takeover. "We barely had time to figure out who was on what side."

In fact, the deal evoked a classic example of what much of Las Vegas journalism had become at the millennium, beginning with the labeling of the story as a "merger," or "unsolicited offer," when in fact it was nothing less than a hostile takeover of a company and the corporate humiliation of a tycoon who had been off limits to critical reporting. In local stories the decline in value of the Mirage stock was attributed variously to casino com-petition in Las Vegas, Wynn's "frustration with Wall Street," and financial problems of his Mississippi casino. When it was over, the *Sun* portrayed Wynn "reveling in 'delicious' choices he has for the future," while the *Review-Journal* blandly editorialized that Wynn was exiting "a winner."

In contrast, the *New York Times* reported the deal as less the result of Wynn's dissatisfaction with Wall Street than of Wall Street's skepticism about Wynn. *Time* similarly reported on March 6 that "hours after Kerkorian launched his offer, five Mirage shareholders brought class actions in Las Vegas demanding that Wynn and his board seriously consider all bids."

Among the more intriguing collateral stories after the deal was an April 10 piece in the *New York Observer* describing "a cozy agreement . . . for Mr. Wynn to purchase these masterworks at below-market-prices—and sell them again to interested parties." One buyer was media magnate S. I. Newhouse, a longtime friend of Wynn's, who boarded his corporate jet the night before Wynn's exit from Mirage to dine with the casino kingpin as part of Newhouse's effort to acquire a 1942 Picasso. But little of this colorful byplay was reported in Las Vegas.

"I long ago learned that if I wanted to know what was happening in Las Vegas I had to read the *Los Angeles Times*," a local historian says in reflecting on the local coverage of the buyout.

Conspicuously missing from local press accounts of the MGM-Mirage deal was Smith. "It's awkward," Smith said, "because I can't write anything about Wynn without a disclaimer." While the columnist himself continued to produce his enormously popular column, he now rarely mentioned Wynn. What happened to him as a reporter, what he called "the big chill," was broadly illustrative of the fate of Las Vegas journalism in general. By the time of the MGM-Mirage deal, Stuart's appeal of the Las Vegas verdict was on the docket of the Nevada Supreme Court, where Wynn's lawyers were trying to reinstate Smith as a defendant in the case against Smith's publisher. At a June 16, 2000, hearing, one of the judges pointed out that all seven justices on the state's highest court had received campaign contributions from Wynn's companies, though none felt this should disqualify them from hearing the case. In an unrelated appeal before the court that same day, a Las Vegas attorney claimed that "every lawyer believes it is impossible for the court to rule against Steve Wynn. We know [he] is a powerful man, much more powerful than the governor. He makes kings and breaks kings."

By the autumn of 2000, Wynn seemed on his way back again as a player. Within days of exiting the Mirage, he had bought Moe Dalitz's legendary Desert Inn, where he gave ninety-day notice to its 1,500 workers, many of them twenty-year veterans, and announced plans to tear down the elegant landmark to make way for yet another extravagantly moated casino.

While the chilling of critics was relatively public, there were equally telling suppressions beneath the surface in law enforcement.

Outwardly, Ken Mizuno had been one of the more notorious Asian high rollers along the Strip in the 1980s. When the former baseball star moved to open a gourmet Japanese restaurant and health spa in the Tropicana and applied for a liquor license, even the usual desultory investigation uncovered his long-standing associations with the Yakuza, Japanese organized crime. Initially, the Clark County commission had denied Mizuno the license; but in a subsequent session a few weeks later—a distant echo of Bugsy's experience with the same body—the commissioners promptly reversed themselves. For nearly a decade Mizuno would be one of the city's leading international citizens, attended by his own personal hostess at the Mirage, where he gambled hundreds of millions.

Then, in the 1990s, wealthy Tokyo investors pressured Japanese police to implicate Mizuno in a $853 million golf club pyramid scheme. His fall was mourned by casinos where he had been known as a "whale" for his $100,000-a-hand bets at baccarat, and Mizuno eventually ended up in a Japanese jail. His fall was long in coming.

In 1991, the small U.S. Customs office in Las Vegas received warnings about Mizuno from the Customs attaché at the U.S. Embassy in Tokyo. Las Vegas agents began to trace not the gambler's links to the Yakuza, or the massive expatriation of funds to foreign organized crime—one of the city's thriving industries, and to law enforcement a more familiar pattern—but rather the pouring into Las Vegas of hundreds of millions through foreign criminal combines. At one point following a path from the Federal Reserve Bank in San Francisco to the Las Vegas Strip with bills bound in casino wrappers, the Customs agents traced an enormous traffic. While Mizuno had a locker at Shadow Creek next to Wynn's, and was a popular high-tipping man-about-town, he was bringing in as much as $220 million through bank channels, wire transfers, and other means that escaped currency reports. There were additional indicators that he transferred to southern Nevada as well much of the remainder of his $800 million take from the Tokyo fraud—altogether hundreds of millions more than even he wagered at Las Vegas tables.

As the investigation continued, many of the trails led to the luxury Mirage. Mizuno's girlfriend turned out to be working in the "international department" of the casino. The high roller himself was "said to have . . . dropped upwards of $75 million in two years" at the Mirage tables. Often met by a Mirage limousine at a private landing strip when he returned from trips abroad, and then whisked to the casino behind darkened windows, arrangements that defeated Customs surveillance, Mizuno went on to buy from his close friend Wynn a personal DC-9 jet later seized by Customs authorities and implicated in the massive financial crimes they suspected. Agents as well as at least one prosecutor familiar with the accumulating evidence came to believe that looming behind Mizuno was the shape of a vast new criminal investment in, and thus control of, the new mega-resorts going up on the

Strip, casinos like Treasure Island and others supposedly funded entirely by Wall Street investment in their new corporate proprietors. Even the sums visible in Mizuno's "gambling"—a minimum of $150 million by one account at a time when Kerkorian had purchased both the Desert Inn and Sands for $167 million—made the Customs calculus only too plausible.

Early in the investigation, the small five-man Customs office in Las Vegas had been overwhelmed by the magnitude of the traffic, the intricacy and sophistication of the means, the network of legitimate institutions around and behind the crimes, and not least by the obdurate secrecy and refusal of casinos to share more than the minimally required information. As agents told their stories later, they could not even enter a casino to observe Mizuno, much less interview employees, without encountering the house's heavily armed force of security retainers. "It is a world unto itself," said one investigator, echoing Yablonsky and others. "I've been in enemy territory as a soldier in battle and felt more at home." But when the beleaguered Las Vegas agents asked their superiors for the obvious support a major investigation required—more personnel, undercover money, and authority to go to the top of what they termed under the federal racketeering statute "the continuing criminal enterprise" they saw in and behind Mizuno—their requests were effectively denied, buried or put off in organizational delays, never openly rejected with any individual liability or record but quietly stifled by bureaucratic device. Eventually Customs would seize more than $60 million in Mizuno's assets, including golf courses in the Las Vegas Valley and Palm Springs, real estate and other assets in Clark County. By most measures it might have seemed a success—the largest single non-narcotics money-laundering case in American history. But agents on the inside knew, as one described it, that it was only "the tip of an iceberg here in the middle of the desert." The agents never knew why they had been called off before following the case to its conclusion.

On the heels of the truncated Mizuno case, there would emerge the silhouette of the even larger, more dramatic, more sweeping national system that at once was central to Las Vegas and by now far transcended it. Beginning in 1996, and for the next two and a half years, Customs agents based in Los Angeles had conceived and carried out a unique investigation of the money-laundering at the core of the drug trade: Operation Casablanca, a sting of Mexican bankers, organized crime figures, and others. By the late nineties, Mexico accounted for 70 percent of the cocaine sold in the United States, far more than the notorious Colombian cartels or any other channel. The traffic yielded much of what the United Nations had carefully documented as the $25-million-an-hour, $600-million-a-day laundering of drug profits at the end of the century, the surge of a criminal fortune far larger than the wealth of many countries. Organized crime, long in control of the presidency and government of Mexico, effectively headquartered in the National Palace in Mexico City, had also captured Mexico's financial system. By converting drug cash into bank drafts, highly liquid currency difficult to trace, Mexican banks legitimized billions in illegal income and official graft, taking out their own huge fees.

To penetrate the system, U.S. Customs operatives had set up their own illicit enterprise, a sham import-export firm named the Emerald Empire Corporation with an office and warehouse in Santa Fe Springs, fifteen minutes outside Los Angeles and a short drive from the frontier. The innocuous storefront offered crucial services in the laundering; its undercover agents picked up drug proceeds from couriers or warehouses in New York, Chicago, Houston, Miami, and a dozen other American cities, and then returned the cash to Los Angeles, where it was either taken across the border or deposited in designated accounts to be wire-transferred directly to Mexican banks. From there, in turn, "clean," untraceable bank drafts payable in American dollars were drawn on financial institutions in both the United States and Mexico, for final distribution to the traffickers and their facilitators. Throughout the process, just as in Mizuno's operation, transactions in the millions of dollars evaded tax or Customs reports ostensibly required for deposits of $10,000 or more. Channeling smoothly into the fraud, Emerald Empire quickly established its credibility. "We are not criminals," an undercover man in Santa Fe Springs assured a wary Mexican banker, pointing to a plaque on the wall. "We are accepted by the Chamber of Commerce." The clients were grateful. "May God bless you," one drug dealer said to an agent after a lucrative transaction. The operation lured them on with more laundered profits—and with visits to Las Vegas, where they often met to discuss business and celebrate their successes during the two-and-a-half-year collusion.

From a series of midnight arrests by Customs officers in May 1998 on a highway outside Las Vegas and elsewhere across three continents, unprecedented indictments of drug traffickers and their attorneys, and especially thirty-one Mexican bankers from the largest financial houses in that country, charges against three Mexican banks, and the seizure of $35 million along with two tons of cocaine, followed. Evidence filed in court, congressional testimony, internal Customs reports, and other intelligence documents began to chart the magnitude of what Operation Casablanca had glimpsed from its storefront. Laundering only a small fraction of the traffic, undercover agents had handled more than $180 million. "We were so conservative," one reflected. "We could have done not millions of dollars, but hundreds of millions." At a safe house for dealers in Illinois, agents found a ledger of $200 million in profits over a few weeks by a minor part of the network.

Operation Casablanca incriminated some of the highest officials of the Mexican regime. Undercover Customs agents in the nineties joined the drug trade, like Meyer Lansky and Bugsy Siegel fifty years before, by making payoffs to Mexican federal police and intelligence officials. On four different occasions, Casablanca records would show, they delivered money in bulging suitcases in the lobby or suites of a luxury hotel along the fashionable Reforma in Mexico City. "Bags of cash for Mexican intel," a U.S. agent would describe it matter-of-factly. Outsized luggage crammed with bills was commonplace in the operation. At one videotaped rendezvous, an undercover agent would be seen straining and staggering as he tried to heave a suitcase of bribe money onto a hotel bed, almost falling backward under its weight.

The cash emptied into a well of corruption. Testimony would implicate the offices of Mexico's president and attorney general in the drug trade. Casablanca operatives dealt repeatedly with emissaries of the Mexican minister of defense, General Enrique Cervantes, seeking to launder $1.15 billion in graft. Fifteen audio- and videotapes of exchanges with two drug traffickers and at least four bankers left the role of Cervantes and others "indisputable," as a U.S. agent would testify to Congress. In April 1998, one of the men representing the minister warned undercover U.S. contacts about caring for the billion plus. "He said it could be very dangerous if it got screwed up," a Customs agent recalled, "because the money belonged to 'all of them, including the President.' " Moreover, Washington's codebreakers, the National Security Agency, had intercepted communications incriminating Cervantes, texts seen by the chairman of a congressional committee, Customs agents, and other high-ranking government officials.

But then, as Casablanca records would also show, Cervantes and his Mexican cohorts were hardly alone. Of the $180 million handled by U.S. undercover agents, every transfer had been arranged with the cooperation if not criminal complicity of an American bank. "Not a dollar was laundered by a Mexican bank," an undercover agent would recall, "that wasn't in a U.S. account under American scrutiny at one time or another." Operation Casablanca would document over a hundred money-laundering accounts in the case tracing to more than seventy U.S. banks, including many of the nation's most powerful and respected—among them, Chase Manhattan, Bankers Trust, Bank of New York, Chemical Bank, Citibank, Great Western, Nationsbank, Norwest, American Express Bank, and scores of others. In Florida alone, some twenty banks were implicated, along with several South

Florida trading companies, part of what agents discovered to be a parallel laundering conduit in fraudulent trade transactions costing the public an added $50 billion a year in tax revenue.

For the enormity of money laundering in the nineties, many Customs agents would blame the North American Free Trade Agreement (NAFTA) of 1993, which had made the crime easier in the United States as well as Mexico. Provisions heavily lobbied by businessmen and politicians in both countries had left banks and other concerns exempt from earlier safeguards. "The North American free trafficking agreement," one agent called it bitterly. Whatever the treaty's effect, the sequel was stark. The money-laundering collusion uncovered inside the United States in 1996–98 during the operation matched if not surpassed the mythic Mexican corruption. In the first days and weeks after the midnight arrests near Las Vegas in the spring of 1998, it seemed Casablanca would erupt into one of the great international scandals of the century. But only a year later—after the guilty pleas of two Mexico City banks, along with the conviction of a handful of Mexican bank employees and the acquittal of others—the episode was all but forgotten. What had happened, much as in the Mizuno investigation, was a case called off short of its connections in Las Vegas, Washington, the nation, and the world.

The forces and impulses killing the investigation were much the same confluence of interests that had come together to serve the power of Las Vegas. Confronted with the unwanted findings, politicians, bureaucrats, and bankers had all behaved predictably. When the Mexican government and the anxious American creditors of its financial system angrily protested the one-sided blame of Mexico as well as the fingering of General Cervantes and others, the State Department and White House had quickly and characteristically moved to contain the diplomatic and political damage, including the staving off of any Mexican counterexposé of American complicity. At the time of the arrests in 1998, Treasury Secretary Robert Rubin had called the money-laundering revealed by Casablanca "the lifeblood of organized crime," yet most other Washington leaders, including the president, the secretary of state, the attorney general, and not least a Congress beholden to the Strip, would not even acknowledge the existence of "American organized crime," so long after the death of the "Mafia" in Las Vegas and elsewhere, let alone its "life" or "blood."

Meanwhile, in the bureaucracy, ranking officials jealous of or compromised by an operation run, like the Mizuno investigation, against the odds of civil service lethargy, found their own reason to discredit and inter the investigation. Finally, an American business and banking community, itself so widely compromised like its Mexican counterparts, gave no voice or impetus to pursue what Casablanca had only begun. "We were at the edge of unraveling Las Vegas," a Customs agent in Nevada would say of the Mizuno case. "We were about to get at the whole damned system," a Casablanca agent would say in grimly identical terms. But in both cases, yet again, the house had won.

In June 1999, Las Vegas elected its last mayor of the twentieth century and its first of the new millennium. Richly symbolic of what the city was and had become, the landslide winner would be the lawyer Oscar Goodman. Apologist for the worst of the Strip's past and present, the fifty-nine-year-old Philadelphian had been "juiced in" since his arrival in 1964. Since then, as lawyer, spokesman, and social friend of a retinue of some of the vilest clients in organized crime, he had won local fame and fortune not simply as a constitutional defense lawyer but as the Syndicate's on-call publicist and legal manipulator.

Soon after Goodman's election, and even during the campaign, at startling moments in interviews with British television, *The New Yorker, 60 Minutes,* and others, Goodman could descend suddenly into a gritty cold venom that lay just beneath his exterior of bravado and banter—lapses he lamely dismissed afterward as jokes no one understood. In one documentary broadcast not long before his political debut, he had been caught in an unexpected confrontation with an old adversary from the FBI. "The former agent gets the better of him in their shouting match, saying that Goodman turned the world upside down to suit his ends, making evil good and good evil," *The New Yorker's* Connie Bruck would write in describing the scene. "Goodman starts to leave, and then, turning—with a look and a tone that bespeak the company he has kept for nearly thirty-five years—says 'Drive Safely.'" But the too obvious public snarling was no barrier to his election in Las Vegas. Goodman's mania and reputation would make it possible once again for many not to take the city seriously.

The summer Goodman took office, crowds along the Strip were bigger than ever, building toward the turn of the millennium when, despite the threat of terrorism and national uncertainties about computer failures, hundreds of thousands would throng the surreal corridor where sirocco winds across the empty desert once whipped Bugsy Siegel's gabardine topcoat. Las Vegas expected more than 50 million visitors in the year 2000.

Las Vegas would continue to offer them, as it had for decades, a kind of controlled nostalgia. There would be souvenirs, posters, and other memorabilia of the already legendary performers in this long unrivaled capital of entertainment: carefully posed portraits of the first Copa Girls; candid shots of Sinatra and his Rat Pack cavorting at the Sands; a bloated, perspiring Elvis stuffed into one of the sequined leisure suits that became his last costumes; a pompadoured Liberace smiling across his own Las Vegas–scale white grand piano, and a long troop of sentimental lounge favorites. There are pictures and memorials, too, in tribute to the vanished casinos, some of their famous neon signs and symbols restored like precious artifacts and displayed in the canopied "Fremont Experience" downtown. In curio shops and bookstores off the Strip, in a place where both tourists and residents seem ravenous for the city's raucous and bloody history, there are the inevitable grainy depictions of Bugsy. The long-dead gangster stares out harmlessly from a past officially as bygone and ancient as the prehistoric bones still turned up at Tule Springs, the crumbling adobe of the old Mormon Fort in North Las Vegas, the first crude safety helmets, hard-boiled in tar, worn by the muckers, high-scalers, and powder monkeys at Boulder Dam. In the cumulative effect of this commercialized, often kitsch, history there are memories for generations of Americans, the tens of millions of losing gamblers—one statistic the number-spewing city never evokes—and the equally impressive hordes who come for all the Las Vegas reasons, and despite the odds will remember it fondly, will come back again.

Still, for all the commemoratives, the new millennium's crowds along the Strip will be accompanied by other ghosts as well, whose heritage is too complex, and often too ominous, for tourist consumption. Casino to casino, from the old Horseshoe and Golden Nugget downtown to the new Mandalay Bay at the far end of the Strip, through the fresh luxury and aged seediness, across the lots traded in dizzying land deals and the new corporate facades built over the rubble of the old joints, Las Vegas's indomitable customers will walk wide-eyed, if unseeing, with them all: politicians naive and corrupt; moneymen visionary and venal; hoodlums banal and vicious; hustlers charming and maniacal; journalists courageous and compromised; unions plundered and persevering; police heroic and hireling. Not least, the visitors will see the spectral reflection of the rest of America whose underworld Las Vegas only copied in the open, and whose upperworld came to adopt the city as its own. The apparitions will all be there, many as faceless to the public and the people of the town as the real owners of the city over the years, as the banks and groups of investors behind the Strip at the millennium, as invisible to history as to gaming control authorities.

But one ghost above all carries the question that still haunts the living. The bespectacled owl-like Senator from Tennessee had known from the beginning that it was never a matter of the freedom of vice, of any old-fashioned morality curbing what one scholar called "a people of chance," the irrepressible American penchant to bet, to take a risk, to believe in winning. A civilized society, he knew, might still allow gambling, though with the odds better, the winnings spread more fairly, the profit reasonable but far less, the ownership in the hands of its workers as much as its bosses, the profit taxed fairly, the political influence curbed and social costs compensated. That day in March 1951 when Lansky met Kefauver privately after a closed hearing, the two men had both understood the essence—not a matter of principle, but of the oldest political issue on earth, of the fateful challenge posed by the rise and reign of Las Vegas, ultimately a question of power.

"What's so bad about gambling?" Lansky had asked the senator. "You like it yourself. I know you've gambled a lot."

"That's right," Kefauver had replied. "But I don't want *you* people to control it."

Epilogue

Shadow Capital

The terrible ifs accumulate," Winston Churchill wrote of the moments when history turns so fatefully on choice or chance. So it was—and is—with Las Vegas.

There was nothing predetermined or inevitable about the outcome of the city, the rise and reach of its corrupting influence. If the state of Nevada had come to grips with the Strip in the 1940s before it became too powerful; if Estes Kefauver's exposure of the alliance of gamblers, gangsters, and government had been followed by authentic national reform in the 1950s; if U.S. intelligence and law enforcement agencies had not been so compromised for more than a half century by the forces behind the city; if John Kennedy had not been assassinated and if Bobby Kennedy had continued and won his declared war on organized crime; if Wall Street, American banks, the Mormon Church, and other powerful institutions had not financed the casinos from the 1950s onward and thus the growing empire of their owners beyond Nevada; if Howard Hughes had not lent himself as one more front for the city's incessant manipulations and self-enrichment; if the Justice Department antitrust division, from the 1970s to the takeover of Steve Wynn's Mirage, Inc., by Kirk Kerkorian in the spring of 2000, had ever addressed casino gambling as the historic monopoly it was; if any president before or after the Kennedys' interlude had publicly acknowledged and confronted the formidable Vegas connections in Washington and the insidious enormity of the drug trade and money laundering in American politics—the story of the city, and the nation, might have been very different. If another direction had been taken at any of these turning points, the city might not have continued in the unbroken grip of a criminal and then corporate tyranny, might not have become the staging ground and financial fount of the same forces as they came to dominate national politics. As it was, each successive failure, every act of collusion, heedlessness, or default, perpetuated and extended the city's malignant power.

Other "ifs" accumulate about the people of Las Vegas. Over the turbulent half century of the city's rise, most of them lived out ordinary, decent lives in a setting marked so often by the extraordinary and the indecent. Ned Day was right about the pluck of those who worked in and around the casinos. It took spirit to leave their homes elsewhere and come to this desert to wait on tables or deal cards, to try out for the chorus line or simply try to make a better living any way they could for themselves and their children. It took spirit to stick, like the town's early pioneers, when for many the promise of the place turned hard and cold. Las Vegans were part of the city's dynamism and charm, much of its magnetism for native Nevadans as for new immigrants. But beyond the neighborhoods and shopping centers, the sprawling developments and freeways that gave the metropolis the look of any other American city, there remained the underlying reality of what Las Vegas was, of how and by whom, and to what ends, it was really run. "This is a great town and I love it," native son John L. Smith would say. Yet he and others would know that there was also no denying that, as he once put it, the city had a dark heart.

Whatever happened beyond the jagged mountains enclosing that valley in southern Nevada, whatever others did or did not do in Carson City or Washington or New York, the people of Las Vegas obviously bore responsibility for their city as well. If they had ever refused the commercial blandishments and Faustian bargain of the casinos, if they had ever truly attacked the corruption instead of so largely joining or acquiescing in it, that, too, even out of the martyrdom of defeat, might have rescued them from their fate.

But then there is the most important and decisive "if": if Las Vegas had not been such an outgrowth of the rest of America. The city was not only a reflection of culture and values and the near-complete rule of money in American life. From the beginning with the Flamingo in 1947, Las Vegas was the more open reflection of an economic and political corruption that was still furtive though already pervasive in the rest of the nation. What the city would do so raucously and visibly after World War II—from the gambling itself to the Syndicate's naked dominance of government and society—

dozens of other cities and towns in the country had been experiencing in secret for decades, their business and politics held hostage to shadow regimes whose Nevada replica could now be seen more plainly in the glaring desert light. What Las Vegas continued to do beneath the surface—from money laundering of drug profits and other criminal proceeds to contract murder—derived no less from that national hinterland. The city was never, in truth, some perverse Atlantis apart from the main. The nation at large populated the ranks of the Strip's criminal and corporate overseers, under-wrote and owned the casinos, took in the skim as well as admitted earnings, trafficked with the place in every way legal and illegal—America the city's roots and mentor.

When Las Vegas became the greatest business success story of the twentieth century, it was because the rest of America made it so with capital as well as customers. When Las Vegas grew into a kind of shadow capital in the last decades of the century—the city a Mecca for politicians as for tourists, not a state or locale beyond the reach of the gambling industry, money and power begetting still greater wealth and influence—it was because the rest of America made it so by embracing the ethic of greed and exploitation.

By the millennium, the national surrender of democracy to oligarchy in the United States—the submission to house rules, as they might put it on the Strip—had simply come into the open, where it had long been in Las Vegas. It has been difficult, of course, to see the city honestly in that context. What a sad, grim reflection Las Vegas gives back to us. America has yet to come to terms with its own hidden history, let alone the city's—a trap from which there was, and has been, no escape.

Notes

Abbreviations

CL	*Las Vegas City Life*
DTD	Robert Gottlieb and Peter Wiley, "Just Don't Touch the Dice" (September 1980)
EKP	Estes Kefauver Papers
FBI	Federal Bureau of Investigation Documents (Individual Files by Name)
FBIVI	FBI Voting Irregularities Field Investigation, 1960–61
GJ	*Reno Gazette-Journal*
HSCA	House Select Committee on Assassinations
JFKAA	John Fitzgerald Kennedy Assassination Archives
LAT	*Los Angeles Times*
LVL	*Las Vegas Life*
LVPL	Las Vegas Public Library Special Collections
NHS	Nevada Historical Society, Reno and Las Vegas
NSLA	Nevada State Library and Archives, Carson City
NYT	*New York Times*
OH	University of Nevada Oral History Program
RJ	*Las Vegas Review-Journal*
SUN	*Las Vegas Sun*
UNLV	University of Nevada Las Vegas, Special Collections
UNM	University of New Mexico, Clinton P. Anderson Special Collections
UNR	University of Nevada Reno, Special Collections
WP	*Washington Post*
WSJ	*Wall Street Journal*

Prologue: First City of the Twenty-first Century

The account of Operation Casablanca here and in Chapter Sixteen draws on extensive interviews with Customs agents and prosecutors in Nevada, California, and Washington, D.C. Sources also include 1998 unpublished testimony before the U.S. Congressional Subcommittee on Criminal Justice, Drug Policy, and Human Resources, interviews with staff investigators of the subcommittee as well as with officials of the Central Intelligence Agency (CIA) and National Security Agency (NSA), and the relatively few contemporaneous press reports, especially in California and Florida. Background on the Mexican drug trade 1940 *et seq.* derives most notably from McCoy's *The Politics of Heroin;* Scott's *Deep Politics;* the FBI file of Benjamin "Bugs" Siegel, FBI #62-2837; the 1964 Senate Hearings on Organized Crime and Illicit Traffic in Narcotics; Noyes's *Legacy of Doubt;* Block's *Perspectives on Organizing Crime;* Eisenberg *et al.;* and Turkus and Feder's *Murder, Inc.*

The overview of the financing of Las Vegas by criminal and other capital summarizes material elaborated and documented extensively in subsequent chapters. Figures on the city's commerce and demography in 1999 are from files and papers of The Center for Business and Economic Research at the University of Nevada, Las Vegas; the Nevada Development Authority; and the 1997 and 1999 editions of *Las Vegas Perspective*, produced by the city's Metropolitan Research Association under the aegis of the Nevada Power Company, Wells Fargo, and other corporations.

PAGE

3   **scene in Mesquite:** Confidential interviews.

"Last Supper": The term was used by William F. Gately, Assistant Special Agent in Charge of the Financial and Drug Smuggling Investigations Division of Customs Los Angeles Office, and the ranking field agent who conceived and directed Casablanca.

3-4   **cheering and shouting; "Sorry, I guess I was speeding":** *San Diego Union-Tribune*, September 29, 1998.

4   **"takedown":** Confidential interviews; NYT, June 11, 1998; RJ, May 20, 1998; LAT, June 3, 1998.

"The largest, most comprehensive": *Washington Times*, May 19, 1998.

crimes in the hundreds of billions: *Financial Times* (London), May 30, 1998.

"All of them felt comfortable"; stay at Mirage; casinos treat well: Confidential interviews.

far-flung financial conspiracy: Confidential interviews with U.S. Customs agents and others participating in the investigation, which was generally known as the Mizuno case. As with Casablanca, further details and the fate of the investigation are traced in Chapter Sixteen below.

5   **"Play it again":** *San Diego Union-Tribune*, September 29, 1998. (The line spoken by Ingrid Bergman in *Casablanca* is actually "Play it, Sam.")

"In Vegas everybody's watching" . . . "The casinos . . . and tipped them off": Confidential interviews.

"The key to being": Confidential interview.

"Why wouldn't they want Vegas? . . . These people know their history": Confidential interview.

Meltzer as formidable if less known: Scott, *Deep Politics*, 141–45, 343–44; Noyes, 57. The 1964 Senate Narcotics Hearings, 781, describe him as "a major figure in the organized underworld . . . known to all the important narcotics traffickers throughout the United States." See also Reid's *The Grim Reapers*, 292, citing FBI File #113017, with accounts of Meltzer's bookmaking and prostitution operations in California, and noting his role as "a world traveler for the organization, having visited Canada, Cuba, Hong Kong, Japan, Hawaii, and the Philippines in recent years" with "associates in Oklahoma, Texas, Baltimore, Miami, Las Vegas, and Boston." On the basis of Meltzer's voluminous law enforcement files, Reid concluded by 1968 that he "ranks with gaming chieftain Meyer Lansky in the Syndicate hierarchy." For Meltzer's subsequently documented role as a CIA-enlisted assassin in plots to murder Fidel Castro during the Kennedy administration, see Mahoney, 269, 412; "Mason Cargill Memorandum to the File," 30 April 1975, HSCA; and Chapter Twelve below.

Siegel's trafficking and black Chrysler convertible: FBI Memo, "Vice Conditions Las Vegas," June 24, 1946, Benjamin Siegel File. See also *Los Angeles Daily Reporter*, June 24, 1947; *Los Angeles Examiner*, June 29, 1947; *Los Angeles Mirror*, June 16, 1949; FBI Memo, "Re: Benjamin 'Bugs' Siegel," November 29,

1946, with extensive marginal references to the files of the Federal Bureau of Narcotics detailing Siegel's drug smuggling.

corrupt officials in both Mexico and the United States: Scott, *Deep Politics*, 104–05, 123–24, 141–49, 301; Scott and Marshall, 33–43, 85–86. See also Walker, 162–67, 178. The long-standing collusion between the CIA and its Mexican counterpart and offspring, the Dirección Federal de Seguridad (DFS) and its successor agencies, was also confirmed repeatedly by confidential interviews with U.S. Customs agents, officials of the U.S. Drug Enforcement Agency, state police or Highway Patrol investigators of New Mexico, Arizona, and other jurisdictions, as well as past and present officials of the CIA and NSA.

6   **constant outpouring of cash:** See especially Chambliss, 156 ff., on the nation-wide collection of weekly and monthly criminal profits, and the convergence of cash through and for Las Vegas casinos.

national underwriting: For this overview, see especially Sale, 84–88, and Kwitny's *Vicious Circles*, 159–72, as well as the extensive literature on the Teamsters cited for Chapter Eleven ff. Like the money from drug proceeds and money laundering, the capital finance of Las Vegas is elaborated and documented extensively in subsequent chapters.

8   **the might of a single business:** See especially the authors' "Easy Money in Vegas," NYT, July 19, 1996.

"Las Vegas now melds . . . first city of the twenty-first century": Rothman and Davis, "First City of the Twenty-first Century."

9   **"pathology of hope":** Goodman, 137–38.

"catering cynically": John H. Findlay, "Gambling, Las Vegas, and American Culture: Chance and Change in the Mid-20th Century." Paper delivered before the Organization of American Historians, Reno, March 25, 1988.

10   **"deliciously deranged":** NYT, September 5, 1999.

"An overpowering cultural artifact": Davis's "Las Vegas Versus Nature," in Rothman, ed., *Reopening the American West*, 54.

12   **"How much still remains":** Daniel Boorstin, *Hidden History* (New York: HarperCollins, 1988), 17 ff.

Part One: The Juice

19   **"The First One Hundred":** See the series by Hopkins *et al.* in RJ.

1. Meyer Lansky

Any interpretation of Meyer Lansky owes a primary debt to Hank Messick's pioneering 1971 biography, and to the virtual oral history by Israeli journalists Eisenberg, Dan, and Landau eight years later, works which together brought Lansky out of the relative obscurity secured by the gangster's own profound discretion and by his protectors and disciples in the political and business worlds. Lacey's *Little Man* more than a decade afterward was a finely drawn portrait, giving its subject a human face, pathos, and complexity. But the ironic sum of that affecting portrayal may cloud further the depth and breadth of Lansky's influence in national politics, his impact in what amounted to a systemic adoption of his ethic by much of the American corporate world, and not least his decades-long interplay with Las Vegas. Dozens of interviews with those who knew him and his legacy, and an impressive array of scholarship beyond Messick and Eisenberg *et al.*—

including Turkus and Feder, Chambliss, Scott, Moldea, Gentry, Summers's *Official and Confidential* and *Arrogance of Power*, Hersh, Block and Chambliss, and Balboni's essay on Dalitz in Davies's *The Maverick Spirit*—leave no doubt that Meyer Lansky was the founding father of Las Vegas, his power enormous and his legacy still to be reckoned in the twenty-first century.

21   "somewhat like heaven": Eisenberg *et al.*, 32.
      "overpowering memory": *Ibid.*, 33.

22   "There's no such thing . . . the boss": Lacey, 33.
      "crazy as a bedbug": *Ibid.*, 35. Messick's *Lansky*, 19–20, attributes the nickname, perhaps apocryphally, to a judge's comment—"You boys have bugs in your heads. Go and sin no more"—after Lansky and Siegel had been arrested in 1918 following their chance meeting when both intervened to stop a back-alley rape.
      "the most efficient arm in the business": Turkus and Feder, 81.
      "gave their hoodlums . . . crippled for life": Eisenberg *et al.*, 64.
      "no choice": Messick, *Lansky*, 153.
      "the most important people in the country": Eisenberg *et al.*, 79.

23   cost Joe Kennedy "a fortune": *Ibid.*, 108–09.
      "They were more than . . . was thinking": Fox, 42.

24   paid "handsomely": Chambliss, 162. Chambliss's chapter "The Higher Circles," *On the Take*, 150–81, written in 1978 and revised a decade later, remains one of the most succinct and powerful perspectives on the elemental, indivisible corruption of American politics—along with Michael Dorman's *Payoff* and Scott's *Deep Politics*. See also Eisenberg *et al.*, 153–55, Messick, *Lansky*, 117.

25   "You can't help liking Mr. Dewey": Woodiwiss, 72. See also Benjamin Stolberg, "Thomas E. Dewey, Self-Made Myth," *American Mercury*, June 1940.

26   "Lansky and the Bureau": Scott, *Deep Politics*, 145; see also 100, 146, 165, 169, 345. And see Summers, *Official and Confidential*, 6–13, 22, 242–45, 258, 446.
      "dirty little secret": Confidential interview. On Operation Underworld, see Chambliss, 161–65; Messick, *Lansky*; and Rodney Campbell, *The Luciano Project: The Secret Wartime Collaboration of the Mafia and the U.S. Navy* (New York: McGraw-Hill, 1974), though Campbell, who also edited a first volume of Tom Dewey's memoirs, did not do justice to Lansky's role or its subsequent significance in American politics. The episode ostensibly began with the navy approaching Joseph "Socks" Lanza, rackets boss of the Fulton Fish Market, to enlist fishermen on a watch for German submarines. In a dispatch on Campbell's book on October 9, 1977, the *New York Times* reported the Syndicate-government alliance, albeit only obliquely and on page 40, with scant reference to Lansky. See also Scott, *Deep Politics*, 100, 145, 165–69, 175–78; Alan A. Block and John McWilliams, "On the Origins of American Counterintelligence: Building a Clandestine Network," *Journal of Policy History* (1989); R. Harris Smith, *OSS* (Berkeley: University of California Press, 1972); Block, *Perspectives on Organizing Crime*; Henrik Krueger, *The Great Heroin Coup* (Boston: South End Press, 1981); Marshall, 44–53; McCoy, 31–34; and Lacey, 114–27, 163, 176, 197.

27   small handkerchiefs with "L": In addition to the sources cited immediately above, see especially Peter Robb, *Midnight in Sicily* (New York: Vintage Books, 1999), 51 ff., noting Gore Vidal's apt remark that "Sicily had been liberated by Lucky Luciano, Vito Genovese, *and the American Army*," and that Syndicate leaders enjoyed close relationships—"a good friend," as Luciano referred to

one of his contacts—with the U.S. high command. Robb's is a stunning history of the U.S.-instigated and -supported political sequel in Sicily and the rest of Italy, in some ways as much a story of American foreign policy as of Italian politics. See also Nash, 251–56; Sifakis, 200–02; Messick, *Lansky,* 138 ff.; and others cited above for how the commutation of Luciano's sentence by Dewey and his immediate deportation in 1946, as a reward for the collaboration on the New York docks and in Sicily, left the Syndicate, and thus its nascent Las Vegas colony, largely in Lansky's hands.

Lansky and Batista bribe: See especially Eisenberg *et al.,* 227, though Lansky's relationship with the Cuban dictator is dealt with extensively as well in Messick and Lacey. From the perspective of U.S. and Latin scholarship on Cuba, Franklin, 21, notes that the election of Batista's successor in 1944, Ramon Grau San Martin, in no way diminished the influence of the American underworld and "coincides with . . . a subsequent increase in the impact of organized crime in Cuba."

by a "prominent American Jew": Eisenberg *et al.,* 295.

"What's the problem?": *Ibid.*

"There were times": *Ibid.,* 225.

28   **"What I had in mind" . . . "Once you got tourists":** *Ibid.,* 226.

"Meyer owns more in Vegas"; "No matter where": FBI wiretaps quoted in Scott, *Deep Politics,* 146. See also Messick, *Hoover,* 198–201; Eisenberg *et al.,* 261 ff.; Demaris, *The Last Mafioso,* 63–70, 85–86, 104–07; Giancanas, 144, 178, 194, 211, 263–64; and Fox, 283–84.

2. Benny Binion

The Binion story offers a somber reflection on the sociology of knowledge in American history—that crude and illiterate thugs, however decisive their role, seldom get the serious attention (as apart from celebrity) given more culturally preferable villains, tyrants seen as worthy of their subjects. It is no mere nuance; the omission can conceal an essence of national experience. Only a handful of authors have seen the embarrassing reflection and importance in Binion's life as an archetype—Cartwright's "Benny and the Boys"; Steven Reed's revealing series in the *Houston Chronicle* a few months before Binion's death; A. D. Hopkins's profile in Sheehan's *The Players;* and David Johnston's colorful chapter "I'm Still Able to Do My Own Killings" in his *Temples of Chance,* 29–37.

Still, there are fascinating shards of relatively new information from a wide variety of sources. For the intriguing relationships between Binion and organized crime figures in Texas and elsewhere, including men who appear repeatedly in various investigations of the Kennedy assassination, see Scott, *Deep Politics;* Reid and Demaris; and Scheim. Binion's long-standing but long-hidden ties to Lansky were revealed in interviews with Bobby Baker, and several confidential sources, as well as in passing by O'Dessky, 154. Scott, *Deep Politics,* 206 ff., and HSCA Vol. 5, 1970–71, describe Binion's equally interesting relations with Texas moguls H. L. Hunt, Sid Richardson, and Clint Murchison, Sr. The Chagra drug organization and assassination of Texas federal judge John Wood is detailed in Denton, and in Cartwright, *Dirty Dealing.* See, too, A. Alvarez's "The Biggest Game in Town" in Tronnes. Hundreds of newly released FBI documents on Binion, in addition to the bureau file on former agent William Coulthard, make clear Binion's contracting for the Coulthard murder as well as for several others. Binion's claim of compromising U.S. senator Howard Cannon to secure the appointment of Harry Claiborne as federal judge comes from several confidential interviews, as well as FBI files and interviews with former Las Vegas FBI SAC Joe Yablonsky (though numerous other reliable sources argue just as persuasively that Cannon had owed the favor to Claiborne for the latter's instrumental role in fixing the notorious 1964 Senate election against Paul Laxalt). Scarcely a decade after Benny Binion's death, his son Ted, having lost his gambling license because of his blatant links to organized crime, was murdered amid a family quarrel over control of the now national Binion empire. Even among hardened veterans of Las Vegas history, the Binion name still evokes fear. "The juice didn't die with Benny," said one source.

30   "interrupted by bad roads": FBI interview with Binion (undated), File #92-3241.

   "hip-pocket bootlegger": Alvarez, "The Biggest Game in Town," in Tronnes, ed., *Literary Las Vegas*, 65.

31   "especially the odds that he could handle the people": Interview with Professor Michael Green, Community College of Southern Nevada.

   "square craps fader": Cartwright, "Benny and the Boys."

   "Do your enemies before they do you": *Ibid.*

   "king of the racketeers": *Ibid.*

   "a cross between Paul Bunyan and the Dalton Gang": O'Dessky, 154.

   "to join the action": *Ibid.*

32   "in very high places": Pearson, 470.

   "the narcotics racket": Scott, *Deep Politics*, 154–60.

   "Solly, you didn't finish the job": Berman, 58.

   "shoved bichloride-of-mercury": *Ibid.*

   "Ragen's dead": *Ibid.*

33   "black chefs with high white hats": *Ibid.*

   "My sheriff got beat in the election": Alvarez, "The Biggest Game in Town," 66.

   "a million dollars' worth of property": FBI File #92-3241.

   Binion's appearance before Nevada Tax Commission: OH, Robbins Cahill.

   "Shot him three times . . . very bad man": Johnston, 31.

   "Yeah, but he was just a nigger": *Ibid.*

34   "The state of Nevada . . . benefits": Reid and Demaris, 186.

   "If you want to get rich": A. D. Hopkins in Sheehan, 63–64.

   "where the action is": Alvarez, "The Biggest Game in Town," 65.

   "cocked like a gunfighter": Hopkins in Sheehan, ed., 48.

35   "If I marry Benny Binion": Cartwright, "Benny and the Boys."

   "the wily sage": Smith, *No Limit*, 95.

   "I would almost certainly": Hopkins in Sheehan, ed., 51.

36   "trimble trigger with a guitar pic": Confidential interview.

   "as black as pitch": Alvarez, "The Biggest Game in Town," 82.

37   "even smarter than his father": Convicted Judge Harry Claiborne told the *RJ*.

3. Pat McCarran

In the sheer color and sweep of his life, Pat McCarran is obviously the stuff of major biography. Thus far, he has been given only a 200-page academic monograph, Jerome E. Edwards's *Political Boss of Nevada*. Elizabeth Raymond's admirable portrait of George Wingfield fills a few of the gaps in the Nevada story. McCarran's wider and deeper origins are largely unexplored, however, to say nothing of his Washington power, his international and District of Columbia corruptions, his furtive as well as public impact as a Red-baiter, his thwarting of Kefauver, and his sometimes hidden intercessions on behalf of Las Vegas. Only intriguing traces of the senator's machinations and influence turn up in FBI files like Bugsy Siegel's. Interviews with the dwindling number of "McCarran's Boys" or others who knew him in his later years must be approached with caution because of understandably enduring loyalties and the sense of awe Nevadans felt toward their last patriarch. More reliable pieces of the puzzle lie in the history of his powerful committees, in collateral characters like Jay Sourwine, in archival papers and letters, oral histories, and contemporary national press accounts, as well as Hank Greenspun's inimitable columns. McCarran and his Nevada, his America, cry out for a serious portrait.

The account in this chapter, *inter alia*, of Nevada's colonial past draws chiefly on Bancroft's flawed but colorful history, on Ostrander's brilliant work, and on Findlay, Hulse, Laxalt, and the still incomparable Mark Twain.

39   "The plaything of San Francisco nabobs . . . Nob Hill": Ostrander, 132.
"In Nevada the lawyer, editor, banker . . . to be illustrious": Mark Twain, *Roughing It*, in WPA, 42.
"They all had the same agenda": Green, "Understanding Nevada Today," *Halcyon*, 1994.
"capitalistic authoritarianism": Ostrander, 66.
40   "consisting of the leading professional men, bankers, and brokers": *Ibid.*, 67.
"hundreds of thousands": Bancroft, 175.
"State history reads like a novel": Lillard, 11.
"Poor, empty, used up Nevada": Ostrander, 82.
"plutocratic populism": *Ibid.*, 97.
politicians only a "shadow" of authentic radicalism: Richard Hofstadter, *The American Politician Tradition and the Men Who Made It* (New York: Vintage Books, 1958), 186 ff.
41   "more money in the bank": For his trenchant criticism of the Silver Party as "doctrinaire, parochial, and childishly self-interested," see Ostrander, 97–131.
"humbled by long neglect": WPA, 3.
"His heart was with the sinner": Jerome Edwards, 8.
labeled a "dangerous radical": *Ibid.*, 12.
"owner and operator of Nevada": Raymond, 1.
42   "desperation and embarrassment": Jerome Edwards, 24.
"compulsive electioneering": *Ibid.*, 25.
"a natural part of the human beast": *Ibid.*, 15.
"whirlpool of vice": See Raymond, 199. The apt phrase originated with *New York Evening Graphic* writer Laura Vitray, one of the more eloquent journalistic critics of Nevada gambling in the thirties. See, for example, her colorful dispatches on the Reno scene in the *Graphic*, July 3 and 18, 1931.
"Can liberty . . . in the state": *Nevada State Journal*, September 11, 1927; *Reno Evening Gazette*, September 12, 1927. See also Raymond, 175–79.
"to no faction" "toilers and . . . men in the mediocre walks of life": Letter to Sister Margaret P. McCarran, February 12, 1933, McCarran Collection, NHS. See also Jerome Edwards, 47–48.
43   "unpredictable mustang": *Life* magazine, November 29, 1937.
"for the masses rather than the classes": George Creel, "Under the Underdog," *Colliers*, April 6, 1935.
"Dear dear . . . from the diadem of God": Letter to Sister Margaret P. McCarran, August 4, 1946, McCarran Collection, NHS. See also Jerome Edwards, 44.
"There was nothing in this world": Interview with Chet Smith.

44   "heartbroken": Confidential interview.
"Nothing is too good": Alfred Steinberg, "McCarran: Lone Wolf of the Senate," *Harper's* magazine, November 1950.
"patronage pigsty": See Robert Allen and William V. Shannon, *The Truman Merry-Go-Round* (New York: Vanguard Press, 1950), 225.
"the finest intelligence service on Capitol Hill": Steinberg, "McCarran: Lone Wolf of the Senate."
stockpiling of silver: *Ibid.*
"made it their primary ... inordinately cheap": See *U.S. News & World Report*, August 31, 1951, and *The Reporter*, September 13, 1949.
45   "Jew money": Jerome Edwards, 139.
"I have just doomed myself to Purgatory": Confidential interview.
"an instrument of communist global conquest": Donner, *Age of Surveillance*, 409.
"terrified witnesses" "a scorn for legal niceties": *Ibid.*
"the ninety-seventh Senator": *Ibid.*
47   "very wealthy and influential in politics": From extracts of a "master list" of 800 names of figures in organized crime submitted to the Kefauver Committee by FBN commissioner Harry Anslinger in June 1950, cited in Lait and Mortimer, 303. See also Reid, 178, 184, 219.
Moody's "history of dealings with criminal types": Sale, 82.
"as far as the English language": Moore, 52–53.
"that stretches on for pages": SUN, July 12, 1954.
"not unduly shocked": Jerome Edwards, 123.
"one of the most difficult" ... "the state has builded its economy"
"woven ... in its various forms": Letter to Joseph F. McDonald, July 3, 1951, McCarran Collection, NHS.
"Virginia Street would be in mourning": *Ibid.*
"tinhorns" ... "like a Nevada whore": Confidential interview.
"listening or laughing, condemning or ridiculing": Letter to Joseph F. McDonald, July 3, 1951, McCarran Collection, NHS.
48   "You say you don't ... very often": *Ibid.*
"The smell of mothballs": Laxalt, *Nevada*, 72.

4. Bugsy Siegel

The Las Vegas version of a mythic founder suckled by a wolf, Siegel is the subject of a widespread, almost ritual literature that invariably, and not always by accident, misses the point. As the designated and caricatured gangster scapegoat of Strip and national lore, he absorbed much of the stain and obscured most of the reality of the city's origins. Historically, Bugsy was far more than a killer with an explosive temper or extravagant tastes. His commonly ignored business empire beyond the Flamingo gives an ominous glimpse of the enormity of the Syndicate in the thirties and forties. His role in the narcotics trade points to a city founded and built by drug money, Las Vegas, Nevada, not Medellín, Colombia, as the true narcotics capital of the Western Hemisphere. His seminal financing by institutions of American capitalism exposes a collusion of underworld and upperworld that would be a dominant and unacknowledged reality of American history over the last half of the twentieth century.

Primary sources for Siegel, those less mythological than most, include his remarkably revealing FBI File #62-2837 *et seq.*, and James F. Smith's 1992 article in the *Journal of Popular Culture*. Useful biographies include Jennings, Edmonds, Hanna, and Lacey, as well as

John L. Smith's "The Ghost of Ben Siegel," in Sheehan's *The Players;* Messick; and Eisenberg *et al*. Pearl supplies colorful details. Sources for Siegel's role in the Mexican drug trade, including principally Scott and Bugsy's FBI file, are enumerated in notes for the Prologue above. For his early contact and connections with Nixon, see Eisenberg *et al.,* 258–316, and also Cohen, 153 ff., and Summers, *Arrogance of Power,* 54.

49–50   "He had gotten . . . done by him": Laxalt, *Nevada,* 102.

50   "insane along certain lines": FBI Memo, August 7, 1946, L.A. 62-2837, "Background of Benjamin 'Bugs' Siegel."

"business interests" "hand in glove": *Ibid.* especially pp. 22, 45–46, 89–91.

"His rages were so pure . . . at least": Lacey, 157.

"a beachhead of organized crime": Turkus and Feder, 273.

51   "Stream-lined upholstered chairs": RJ, October 28, 1942.

"The people of Las Vegas": RJ, March 4, 1943.

52   "enmeshed in the drug intrigues": Scott, *Deep Politics,* 142.

"one of the world's biggest . . . smuggling and distribution": FBI Memo, June 23, 1947. See also *Los Angeles Daily Reporter,* June 24, 1947.

"abysmally ignorant": Laxalt, *Nevada,* 104.

"To the local gentry": *Ibid.,* 104.

53   "A casino ambiance": Lacey, 153.

"The goddamn biggest, fanciest": Pearl, 26.

"Pipe, palms, perfume": Odessky, 10.

54   "The public will tolerate": *Las Vegas Tribune* (weekly), July 25–August 1, 1946.

"Siegel's hook-up": FBI Memo, August 7, 1946. See also FBI Memo, August 21, 1946.

McCarran "already cooperating . . . SIEGEL, et al.": FBI Memo, August 21, 1946.

"an open and thorough investigation": FBI Memo, August 1, 1946. Memo for the file from Los Angeles SAC A. E. Ostholthoff.

"immediately discontinue": FBI Memo relating the bureau's instructions, January 30, 1947.

"We don't run for office": Turkus and Feder, 272.

"His guiding principle was *class*": James F. Smith, "Ben Siegel," *Journal of Popular Culture,* Spring 1992.

"When he started building": Lewis, 198.

"From this day forward": Smith, "Ben Siegel." See also Kaufman, 178.

55   "fabulous woman of mystery": FBI Memo, June 24, 1946, #62-1125.

"turned some tricks": Roemer, *Man Against the Mob,* 45.

"They're like children": Messick, *Lansky,* 146.

"playing like a horse put out to stud": *Ibid.,* 145.

"a Utah corporation": FBI Memo, August 1, 1946, detailing information derived from a wiretap as well as other confidential sources in Las Vegas.

the Havana meeting: There are many accounts of this meeting, but for the most reliable eyewitness testimony, see especially Eisenberg *et al.,* 235 ff.

56   "I can't do a thing with him": *Ibid.*

"the gaudy opulence": Pearl, 29.

"A lonely giant": Messick, *Lansky,* 148–49.

"Siegel's most desperate days": Smith, "Ben Siegel."

a "gyp joint": See *ibid.;* Jennings, 182–83; and FBI Memo, May 1, 1947, #62-81518.

57   "white slave trade": See especially FBI Memo, June 16, 1947, summarizing

informants' reports of the Flamingo as a major depot of a nationwide prostitution ring and white slave trade, implicating casting directors and others at the Metro-Goldwyn-Mayer studios in Hollywood as recruiting and supplying young women for Siegel's new Las Vegas casino.

57   "an inevitable outgrowth": Chambliss, 101, adding tellingly: "The ruling elite from every sphere benefits economically and socially from the presence of a smoothly running association. Law enforcement and government bureaucracies function best when the network is part of the governmental structure. And the general public is satisfied when control of the vices gives an appearance of respectability without curbing availability."

"The killer almost had to shoot": FBI Memo, June 23, 1947, apparently from L.A. Assistant Special Agent in Charge J. C. Ellsworth.

"When this thing . . . in corners": OH, Robbins Cahill.

58   "Blood isa gonna run": *Ibid.*

"wickedly enticing": Lacey, 158.

"A couple of gaming gents": Pearl, 30.

men with "grifter sense": Smith, "Ben Siegel."

"like generals mopping up after a coup": Lacey, 158.

5. Hank Greenspun

The author and publisher of literally millions of words, Greenspun himself was the subject of relatively few, though his national and international escapades were as fascinating and significant as any topic his *Sun* ever addressed. The first four decades of his life—the period before Las Vegas and the obvious origins of his relations with powerful contacts in the United States as well as Israeli intelligence, all crucial to his subsequent career and power—have been shrouded in mystery, written about, if at all, only by Greenspun himself. In addition to *Where I Stand,* an autobiography the author's *hauteur* rendered more revealing than intended, early portraits are limited to Donovan and Cater in 1953 in *The Reporter;* Lukas in *More* (Pollak); Dalton; and, most entertainingly, Joe Liebling's "Out Among the Lamisters" in *The New Yorker* (1954). More serious and recent profiles belong to Las Vegas professor and sometime journalist Michael S. Green, whose insightful "Where He Stood" for Davies and "The Las Vegas Newspaper War of the 1950s" are major sources for this profile.

The target of the FBI "Top Hoodlum" investigation 92-3244 during the fifties, as well as other federal inquiries related to his arms smuggling and application for a pardon, as well as his several proximities to Jimmy Hoffa, Red Dorfman, and Teamster money, Greenspun accumulated a sizable FBI file spanning the era from Bugsy Siegel and the Flamingo to Watergate, and that too is a rich new source. Kitty Kelley's *His Way* is particularly revealing about Greenspun's business partnership in the Del Webb Corporation with Frank Sinatra, and both Barlett and Steele and Drosnin provide valuable perspective on the publisher's self-enriching machinations with Howard Hughes.

The historic interplay between Greenspun, Ed Morgan, Bob Maheu, Drew Pearson, and Jack Anderson, introduced here and elaborated further in chapters Twelve, Thirteen, and Fourteen, emerges from an array of primary and secondary sources as disparate and intriguing as the relationships themselves—including Pearson's diary, Anderson's 1999 memoir, and *Where I Stand,* tellingly dedicated to Morgan and tracing the root of the life-long friendship. Barlett and Steele, Scott in his *Crime and Cover-up,* and especially the incomparable biography of Johnny Rosselli by Rappleye and Becker add to the story.

Not surprisingly, Greenspun's Israeli connections, including his posthumously recognized service to the Mossad, are the most shadowy aspects of an already obscure saga.

The Cockburns' *Dangerous Liaison* and Teddy Kollek's memoir *For Jerusalem* (New York: Random House, 1978) detailed the "huge Mossad operation" in Eastern Europe and the United States in the late forties involving Schwimmer, Greenspun, and others, although the Cockburns concluded inaccurately that "Greenspun, a Jewish Army veteran, had had no previous contact with organized Zionism of any sort." Kollek was more candid in acknowledging the bribery of Latin American presidents and the collaboration of American organized crime in moving illegal arms shipments on the New York waterfront and elsewhere. Ironically, on Greenspun's death, the *Jerusalem Post* was more accurate about his life than any Las Vegas obituary.

59   "The episode taught me a lesson": Greenspun, 5–6.
60   "deep sense of its Jewish identity": Green, "Where He Stood."
     "I knew every wrinkle": Greenspun, 4–5.
     "lamisters" known for "making a fast buck": *Ibid.*, 12.
     "A lawyer who liked": *Ibid.*, 19.
61   "Fast-talking Joe Smoot": *Ibid.*, 64.
     "It was love at first sight": *Ibid.*, 68.
     "a perfect paradise": *Ibid.*
61–2 "The whole town": Greenspun, 68.
62   "He quickly found people": Dalton, "The Legend of Hank Greenspun," *Harper's*, June 1982.
     "well paid position": Green, "Where He Stood."
     "Greenspun's pen": John L. Smith, in Sheehan's *The Players*.
     "a man I soon came to love": Greenspun, 5.
63   "anything that shoots": *Ibid.*, 167, quoting Israeli army colonel Netanel Lorch's *The Edge of the Sword* (Hartford: Hartmore House, 1968).
     "other covert operations": Green, "Where He Stood."
     "key operative": NYT, May 13, 1990.
     "Two million dollars": Cockburns, 27.
     "to keep Greenspun from going to jail": Author's interview with Chet Smith.
     "Innocent people?": Greenspun, 192.
64   "friends of Israel": *Ibid.*, 179.
     "man sometimes has to bend the law": *Ibid.*, 191.
     Cleveland "investors": *Ibid.*, 168.
     "draining $282,331 of pension funds": See RJ, August 21, 1955, and August 23, 1955.
     Greenspun's credo: Greenspun, 186.
     "two rows of square": Liebling in *The New Yorker*, March 27, 1954.
     "primitive, pungent": *Ibid.*, 9.
65   "had the rival": See Green, "The Las Vegas Newspaper War."
     "A large high-floating balloon": Liebling in *The New Yorker*, March 27, 1954.
     "Let's face it": *Ibid.*
     the "Israelite": Green, "The Las Vegas Newspaper War."
     "old buzzard" "snorting" style: See Jerome Edwards, 157–64, for an account of the McCarran/Greenspun rivalry.
     "The president might . . . senator from Nevada": SUN, July 12, 1954.
     "bent on throttling all opposition": *The Reporter*, June 9, 1953; also Green, "Where He Stood."
     1952 boycott of the *Sun*: Told many times, the story is best recounted in *The Reporter*, June 9, 1953, and Green, "Where He Stood."
     "It was decided to clip his wings": Green, "Where He Stood."

65   "You know as well": *Ibid.*
"He was harder than ever to handle": *Ibid.*
66   "Greenscum": *International News Service,* March 3, 1957.
"the scabrous, slimy, loathsome thing": Green, "Where He Stood."
a "nasty report": *Ibid.*
FBI "Top Hoodlum investigation": Hilty, 202.
"Chewing an expensive cigar": Green, "Where He Stood."
the "*Sun* That Wouldn't Set": *The Reporter,* June 9, 1953.
"fine, free-rolling frontier invective": Liebling in *The New Yorker,* March 27, 1954.
"Greenspunism must be defeated": See the *Nevada State Journal,* September 29, 1954, and the *Reno Evening Gazette,* September 29, 1954. See also *Time,* June 6, 1975.
67   "Paid in Full": Greenspun, 264.
"my greatest benefactor": Confidential source.
"widely heralded": Green, "Where He Stood."
"watch for the next demagogue": *Newsweek,* May 2, 1955.
"unhorsing several corrupt leaders": Green, "Where He Stood."
"I prefer the sweet smell": Green, "The Las Vegas Newspaper War."
"a powerful force for civil rights": Green, "Where He Stood."
"He deplores discrimination": RJ, May 30, 1960.
"More feared than liked": *Newsweek,* May 2, 1955.
68   "I saw him do wonderful things"; "If he liked you": Authors' interview with John Squire Drendel.
"Greenspun by comparison": Green, "Where He Stood."
"Nevada is not ready": *Nevada Appeal,* September 1962.
69   to "ease up" on Hoffa: Pearson, 383.
"that the *Sun* was riding": Westbrook Pegler, King Features Syndicate, 1960.
"which of his several accountants": RJ, November 23, 1955.
"ticked off numerous ventures . . . Market Town": *Ibid.*
now a financial "player": Green, "Where He Stood."
70   "two guys" "exchanged a few cryptic words": Lukas in Pollak, ed., 231.
traveled the world with "his buddy" . . . "many, many times": See Turner, 166; Dalton; and Lukas in Pollak.
"free of criminal domination": Lukas in Pollak, ed., 217.
"Hank isn't a liberal crusader": *Ibid.*
70-1   "His crusades . . . a way of settling scores": See *ibid.*
71   Maheu's agency: See especially Hougan's *Spooks,* 259-306, and Maheu, 40.
"The debate over Greenspun's motives": Green, "Where He Stood."
72   "He's like God in Israel": Authors' interview with Seymour Hersh.
For Hank Greenspun's Israeli connections, including the ties to Khashoggi and other intrigues, see Kessler, the Cockburns, and *Jerusalem Post,* ca. July 1989, December 1993.
73   "Greenspun's substantial holdings": *Time,* June 6, 1975.
"hobnobbing with the bigshots": Authors' interview with Ed Becker.
"putting out his legendary": Dalton, "The Legend of Hank Greenspun."
"Barron Hilton, a good friend": *Time,* June 6, 1975.
"He used the Italian definition": Authors' interview with Ed Becker.
"That's the goddamnedest, most fabricated lie!": *Time,* June 6, 1975.
"When you live in this town": *Ibid.*

74   "A blackjack to advance": Green, "Where He Stood."

"never turned . . . a very mediocre newspaper": Dalton, "The Legend of Hank Greenspun."

"Hank knew it had to be done": Green, "Where He Stood."

6. Estes Kefauver

One of the most interesting, complex, and consequential American politicians of the twentieth century, Kefauver, like McCarran, awaits his biographer. Charles Fontenay, a Tennessee reporter and longtime Kefauver friend, wrote the most admirable profile to date in 1980, and added to it tellingly in his remarks fifteen years later as recorded in Kenneth Thompson, ed., *Statesmen Who Were Never President*, pp. 73–89. Other biographies included Gorman's equally laudatory 1971 *Kefauver*, and, still lighter, *The Kefauver Story*, taken by Jack Anderson and Fred Blumenthal from a 1952 campaign biography written by Fontenay himself. None of these accounts went to the depths of the man or his national experience, much less the world of organized crime and bipartisan national corruption that he confronted. The committee, arguably one of the most important in the history of the Congress, has fared in its historiography little better, the best accounts still being Moore's 1974 *The Kefauver Committee* and Theodore Wilson's 1975 essay in Vol. 5 of *Congress Investigates*. No political life—and by its omissions and absence no political literature—reflects more starkly than Kefauver's the inability or unwillingness of conventional history to come to grips with the dark side of American politics. Ironically, even Kefauver's rather burlesque colleagues Tobey and Wiley, who were irresistible fodder for lampoons for reporters and later authors, proved more honest and courageous than many who wrote their story. The most revealing portraits of Kefauver, of his foibles and of the valor of his ambition, come only indirectly from other authors who touch or imply his experience from the larger picture—principally Fox, Scott, Chambliss, Messick, Jack Anderson in his columns, and even in the disdained but accurate crime reporting of Lait and Mortimer.

75   "The smartest child that ever lived": Fontenay, 15.

Robert's drowning: *Ibid.*, 22–23.

75–76   "a salty-tongued sense of humor": *Ibid.*, 15.

76   "the experience I best remember": Undated Kefauver letter to Thomas N. Schroth of the *Brooklyn Eagle*, EKP, Special Collections Library, University of Tennessee.

"Panama hat and four-in-hand" "round hats and flowing bow ties": Fontenay, 21.

"a personal triumph": *Ibid.*, 22.

"dreams of the old South": *Ibid.*, 17.

"a concept of family worth": *Ibid.*, 15.

ever "a Southern lady": *Ibid.*

"tempering ambition with kindness": *Ibid.*, 21.

effect of the death: *Ibid.*, 23–24.

77   "like resting fireflies": The scene and recollections as recounted by Fontenay, 25.

"a good average student": *Nashville Tennessean*, December 13, 1951.

"Ambition: To Be President": "Friendship Book" of Mrs. Ed Hicks, EKP.

Kefauver at Tennessee: See *Reader's Digest*, August 1954; *Newsweek*, October 15, 1956; *Nashville Tennessean*, December 15, 1951; Kefauver "Scrapbook," EKP; Anderson and Blumenthal, 33–34; and *Quick* magazine, April 7, 1952.

78   "you name it, and you could buy it here": *Maclean's* magazine (Canada), July 20, 1992.

"Kef was a very fine poker player": Fontenay, 38.

the "kissing cousin": *Ibid.*

79   "constantly, vulnerably broke": For Kefauver's finances in Chattanooga, see Fontenay, 83–87, and Fox, 305. See also checkbooks and canceled checks in Box 9:6, EKP.

"join everything in town": Moore, 45.

"Shaymmme on youuu": Fontenay, 116–17.

"too Southern for the liberals": See *The Progressive*, March 1956, and Fontenay, 119.

"Reminds me of the pet coon": Fontenay, 137.

"I may be a pet coon": *Ibid.*, 148.

"a normal life": *Ibid.*, 133.

"incredible stamina": *Nashville Tennessean*, October 10, 1948.

80   "Jesus, Estes, don't you want": Fontenay, 164.

"receive the public credit" . . . "talent and luck" . . . Kefauver's decision to pursue the committee: See Graham, 184–86; Fox, 293–97; Moore 44–49; and Fontenay, 164–67.

81   "lumbered off": Moore, 49.

"both in and out of government": *Ibid.*, 135. For the opposition to the committee, see especially Moore, 49 ff., and Fox, 295–97.

"in cahoots": Lait and Mortimer, 201.

"a busy Babbitt from Chippewa Falls": Moore, 68.

82   "ex-cops, disappointed lawyers": Lait and Mortimer, 138.

"the most searching study of crime": Messick, *Lansky*, 171.

"the old American proclivity": Moore, 41. See also Moore, 237 ff.

"American underworld and upperworld": Fox, 304.

"like a countryboy": Woodiwiss, 123.

"People had suddenly gone": Quoted in Gorman, 92.

83   "nervously writhing hands": Fontenay, 183.

"An oversize owl": *Ibid.*, 170.

"plough through the shrubbery": Fontenay, 185.

a "political whitewash": Fox, 294 and 304–05.

"Organized crime had so": *Ibid.*, 304.

84   "boldfaced political treason": Anderson and Blumenthal, 168.

"everything short of tossing away": Moore, 171.

"six-figure" bribes: Gorman, 97.

"making bets and expecting free passes": Fox, 304–05. See also EKP, especially Letters 1942–50, Box 4C:5.

meeting with Meyer Lansky; "What's so bad about gambling?": Eisenberg *et al.*, 306 ff., Fox 305, and EKP as cited immediately above.

85   Kefauver's revelation: Fox, 292 ff.

"had lightning bolts in both hands": Lait and Mortimer, 194.

Part Two: City of Fronts

89   "casino kingpins" "prominent local citizens": RJ, November 15, 1950. See also *Christian Science Monitor*, November 18, 1950.

"Reporters pelted them with questions": SUN, August 17, 1963; see also

Greenspun's recollections of his encounters with Kefauver, SUN, May 1, 1951, August 19, 1961, and August 17, 1963.

7. "Beyond This Place There Be Dragons"

To match the color, and poignancy, of its history, one of the richest in the annals of America if not the world, Nevada has attracted a small but gifted group of chroniclers, beginning with Mark Twain, whose youthful genius gives us both the physical and the human texture of the place at its nineteenth century birth. Richard Lillard's *Desert Challenge* is a graceful and insightful portrait of the state on the threshold of the casino era, as insightful an interpretation of its beleaguered but indomitable people as any American state has ever been given. Ostrander's *Great Rotten Borough* is a classic of political history that foreshadows much of what would happen after the early period it covered, and stands as a model for the kind of history that ought to be written for the other forty-nine states. Of the Nevada historians who have confronted the dilemmas of writing about their beloved home, historian James Hulse has written a solid and thorough series of books to educate his fellow citizens, and journalist become novelist Robert Laxalt has brought literary artistry and sometimes pure poetry to a forbidding landscape in every way. Finally, and not least, investigative journalists Ed Reid and Ovid Demaris in their legendary *Green Felt Jungle,* so sensational and so viciously attacked at the time, provided not only a rare and invaluable scorecard for the 1960s, but also what proved to be some of the most serious and authoritative history ever written on an American city and industry.

91 "living rivers of ice": Harrington, 4.
"nature played violent games": *Ibid.*
"bold and brazen-faced sun": Bancroft, 4.
"light, elastic, and porous": *Ibid,* 5.
"a collection of desert shrubs": Kasindorf, 7.
92 "rivers to nowhere": *Ibid.*
"the Diamond of the Desert": Findlay, 111.
"They were nearly fearless": Quoted in Hulse, 35.
"the long pig": Reid, 214.
"In starving times": *Ibid.*
"The quietude of death": Bancroft, 3.
93 "Turn back!" Koenig, 11.
"Beyond this place": *Ibid.*
"scattered remnants of Israel": WPA, 185.
"rolling bones and colored sticks": Reid and Demaris, 15.
the "Lord had forgotten": Paher, 257, 261.
"It is easy to foresee": Findlay, 111.
94 "I guess we had more sheep": Greenspun, 67.
95 "relaxed and wild": Findlay, 113.
"They were proud of an exciting": Confidential interview.
"Nevada made a deliberate choice": Confidential interview.
96 "should not seek the riffraff of the world": Turner, 33.
Las Vegas as "seductive": See McBride, as well as Stevens, 118–20, 222–26, 260–61.
"Nevada was eighteen bumpy": Lacey, 150.
96–7 "The people were not here yesterday": Priestley cited in Findlay, 175.
97 "as empty as could be found": Lewis, 190.

97   "free of racketeers": WPA, 4.
      "knew the business": OH, Robbins Cahill.
      "Every town had its outfit": Confidential interview.
      "the fat boy that every gang needs": Lacey, 35.
98   "king of the western rumrunners": Rappleye and Becker, 39.
      "more socially prominent hoodlums": Reid and Demaris, 184.
99   "A sunny place for shady people": Berman, 49.
      "turned their real estate agents loose": O'Dessky, 45.
      "peach-colored cardboard": Noël Coward in the *New York Times Magazine*,
      June 26, 1955.
100   "patchwork of gambling clubs": *The New Yorker,* May 13, 1950.
      "working without a script": Sheehan, ed., viii.
      on the Carrier Air Conditioning company: Confidential interview.
      "add a gallon of water": O'Dessky, 12.
101   "If you can't do it": Laxalt, *Nevada,* 89.
      "That's the promise of Vegas": Michael Ventura's brilliant "Las Vegas—The
      Odds on Anything," in Tronnes, ed., 177.
      "grizzled prospectors": *Ibid.,* 117.
      "alligator shoes": *Ibid.*
      "modern amalgamation of Sodom . . .": Laxalt, *Nevada,* 89.
      "Believe nothing of what you hear": O'Dessky, 28.
      "the classiest resort for a generation": McCracken, 69.
      "the toughest Jewish mobster in Vegas": For Dalitz's background, see Mes-
      sick, 32 ff.; Porrello, 123–27, 141, 205; John L. Smith's profile in the RJ on May 2,
      1999; as well as in Sheehan's *The Players,* and especially Allen Balboni's por-
      trait of Dalitz in Davies's *Maverick Spirit,* 25–43.
      "ruthless beatings, unsolved murders": Turner, 70.
      "the big fix": Reid and Demaris, 67.
102   "extensive mob ties": Turner, 294.
      "the second toughest Jewish mobster": Sifakis, 145.
      "during period of stress": Berman, "Memoirs of a Gangster's Daughter," in
      Tronnes, ed., 111.
      "Three for us": Berman, 93.
      "Sin and Sun Pay Off": *Business Week,* June 17, 1950.
      "the biggest boom that has ever hit": *Life,* June 7, 1949.

8. "This Alliance of Gamblers, Gangsters, and Government"

As often in the bibliography of the city, important clues to its history are found outside Nevada in seemingly unrelated stories and books. This is particularly true of Porrello, Lait and Mortimer, Woodiwiss, Chambliss, Messick, and others, and, more predictably, Lacey. The findings of the Kefauver committee at the time attracted front-page attention nationwide, as well as in Las Vegas, but with the exception of Moore and Fontenay, almost no one reported the crucial aftermath on Capitol Hill and around the country in which legislation inspired by the inquiry was uniformly killed. Fewer still, with the exceptions of Reid and Demaris, noted the centrality of Las Vegas in the larger picture the committee discovered. There remains no penetrating history of the fateful 1952 Democratic convention, though Robert H. Ferrell's *Choosing Truman* (University of Missouri, 2000) traces some of the antecedents to the Kefauver "throat cutting" to the 1944 convention in which Syndicate-backed political bosses installed Truman as FDR's imminent successor.

105 " 'skunk" . . . "may have hurt": For the Democratic reaction to Kefauver after the election, see Fontenay, 177 ff.; Gorman, 82–84; Moore, 171; *New York Times*, November 13, 1950.

106 "the heat in a usually cool November": SUN, August 19, 1961, and August 17, 1963.
"the top brass of Las Vegas": SUN, August 19, 1961.
"You might own 'em": Confidential interview.
"You just got to the point": Confidential interview.
"It was always part of their greed": Confidential interview.
"Privately my father": Berman, 104.
"The mobsters behind the casinos": Levy, 93.

107 "The crime committee knew . . . on friendly terms": SUN, May 2, 1951.
"We are here to find out": Committee's initial statements covered in the local press. RJ, November 15 and 16, 1950.
"in possession of information" . . . "But if there is any": RJ, November 15, 1950.
Bill Moore: For these and further exchanges in the committee's Las Vegas hearing, see Kefauver Hearings, Part 10, Nevada-California, November 15, 1951.

109 "Big Juice": Reid and Demaris, 153.

112 "We were perfectly happy": OH, John Cahlan.
"The United States senate's crime": RJ, November 16, 1950.
"like the black plague": SUN, May 1, 1951.
"the complete corruption": Porrello, 18.

113 "clearly a man": Balboni in Davies, ed., 6.
"Big Jewish Navy": Porrello, 126.
"Now, to get your investments": Kefauver Hearings, February 28, 1951.
"Well, I didn't inherit any money": *Ibid.*
"If you people wouldn't have drunk it": *Ibid.*

114 "How was I to know": *Ibid.*
"the largest single accumulation of data": Lacey, 193.
"As a case history": Reid and Demaris, 96.
"Whenever witnesses or informers": Lait and Mortimer, 198.

114–115 "The profits which have been taken" "The availability of huge sums": For the Kefauver findings relating to Las Vegas, see especially the second interim, third interim, and final reports, dated February 28, May 1, and August 31, 1951, respectively.

115 "alliance of gamblers, gangsters": Reid and Demaris, 154.
"It was the sword": Confidential interview.

116 "make a beeline for Nevada": O'Dessky, 16.
"Kefauver, one would think": *The Nation*, October 22, 1960.
"The fact that it was": Moore, 241.

117 "hysterical country" in the fifties: Woodiwiss, 107 ff. See also Theodore White, *In Search of History* (New York: Harper & Row, 1978), as cited in Roger Morris, *Haig: The General's Progress* (New York: G. P. Putnam's Sons, 1982), 43.
"Organized crime": Chambliss, 6.
"Without political and economic corruption": Messick, 171.
"There is a sinister criminal organization": Kefauver findings in final report.
"the binder": Lacey, 201.

118 "In the country's underlying racism" "Moreover . . . apple pie": Authors' interview with Professor Michael Green.

118   **"The spirit of graft and lawlessness":** Lincoln Steffens, *Shame of the Cities* (New York: Harcourt Brace, 1931), 8. See also Chambliss, 2–3.

119   **"deep politics":** Scott's title. *Deep Politics and the Death of JFK.*
George White and his impact: Authors' interviews with investigative journalist Douglas Valentine and author Jim Hougan; Woodiwiss, 139–42; Scott, *Deep Politics,* 141–46, 164–69, 171–75.

120   **"Where else could a red-blooded American boy":** quoted Woodiwiss, p. 140. See also John Marks, *The Search for the "Manchurian Candidate": The CIA and Mind Control* (London: Allen Lane, 1979), 20, 88–89, 101, 199, 220. See also A. W. Scheflin and E. N. Optom, *The Mind Manipulators* (London: Paddington Press, 1978), 134–41.

121   **"The boy has struck a wave":** Fontenay, 188.
"The road behind him": Anderson and Blumenthal, 231.

122   **"young Democrats":** Fontenay, 190.
"Truman at that time": *New York Post,* October 30, 1955.
"Cowfever": David McCullough, *Truman* (New York: Simon & Schuster, 1992), 889.
"a man Truman instinctively disliked": *Ibid.*
"We must first clean our own house": *Nashville Tennessean,* January 24, 1952.
"eyewash": Fontenay, 193.
"poured on the coal": *Ibid.,* 195.

123   **"on pennies":** *Nashville Banner,* May 17, 1952.
"I guess some" . . . **"That's about it":** *Nashville Tennessean,* July 10, 1952, in a dispatch by reporter Victor Riesel.
"few meals of black-eyed peas": *Nashville Tennessean,* June 6, 1952.
"Scores of bushel baskets": Fontenay, 222.
"We love him because": Gorman, 153. For Johnson's gathering record of corruption and ties to organized crime, see especially Mahoney, 39, 44, 276–7, 304–5, and 384, as well as William Roemer's *Man Against the Mob,* Russell's *The Man Who Knew Too Much,* and Dorman's *Payoff.*

124   **"But my mind *isn't* open":** *Nashville Tennessean,* October 27, 1955; *The Reporter,* November 3, 1955; *New York Post,* May 11, 1956; Fontenay, 225.
"I think the Stevenson strength": *Nashville Tennessean,* July 26, 1952; Fontenay, 225.
"sitting there with a drink": Fontenay, 225.

125   **Humphrey's compromises and corrupt ties:** See especially Fox, 273–80, 334, 475–77, citing extensively the Hubert Humphrey Papers at the University of Minnesota; Solberg's *Hubert Humphrey;* and Humphrey's autobiography, *The Education of a Public Man* (New York, 1976). "He moved quickly from a callow idealism," Fox concludes of Humphrey, "to the real-life compromises of an ambitious politician."
"Exhausted and disconsolate": Anderson and Blumenthal, 191; Fontenay, 227.
"as far as I'm concerned": Fontenay, 227.
"Had I not come to Chicago": Dunar, 143.
"Cowfever could not have": For Truman's reaction, see Fontenay, 231; Anderson and Blumenthal, 193 ff.; Gorman, 152–55, 243.
"firmly and calmly" "Ladies and gentlemen": Fontenay, 229.
"without looking back": *Ibid.*
"smiling happily": Anderson and Blumenthal, 194.

9. "Temple Town of the American Dream"

The 1950s were a genuine golden age of American magazine writing about Las Vegas, and some of the best journalists of the century described the city. Led by A. J. Liebling and Daniel Lang of *The New Yorker*; John Gunther; Lucius Beebe; Sean O'Faolain; *The Nation*'s Fred Cook; and the *New York Times*'s exceptional western correspondents of the era, Wallace Turner and Gladwyn Hill, they and others make the *Reader's Guide to Periodical Literature* perhaps the best single listing of sources on the historic explosion of the Strip. For those other detonations of the period out on Frenchman's Flat, Rosenberg, Pringle and Spigelman, and Udall are grim, authoritative portraits of how America's nuclear weapons establishment joined the spectacle of the city. One of the best of Nevada's own historians, Mary Ellen Glass fortunately turned her talents to these otherwise neglected years. More recent scholars and writers, including Findlay, O'Dessky, and Tronnes's remarkable compendium in *Literary Las Vegas*, provide wonderful perspectives on this decade as well.

127   "A river of wealth": Turner, 29.

"classiest women in Vegas": McCracken, 73.

128   "A disease, a nightmare": Nick Tosches, "The Holy City," in Tronnes, ed., xv.

"a kind of mobster metropolis": Sheehan, ed., 207.

"represents the ultimate": *Holiday*, December 1952.

"When the town was exploding": Confidential interview.

"to keep the women busy": Liebling in *The New Yorker*, May 13, 1950.

129   "unrestricted vistas": *Holiday*, December 1952.

130   "people of chance": John M. Findlay's title.

"beset by an unnamed hunger": Rappleye and Becker, 168.

"The satisfactions sold" "Las Vegas deals": Halevy, "Disneyland and Las Vegas," *The Nation*, June 7, 1958.

"all the sad-faced people having fun": *Saturday Evening Post*, May 26, 1956.

131   "a temple town": Tosches, "The Holy City," xvi.

"victims to be plucked": Turner, 151.

"personal take": Giancana and Giancana, 264.

"Miami hotel men": Balboni in Davies, ed., 30.

"They all trusted Meyer": Confidential interview.

"When we borrowed money": Eisenberg *et al.*, 251.

132   "controlled by more mobs": Reid and Demaris, 91.

"the mob's amateur operation": Reid, 218.

"ever to go broke": *Ibid.*

"a short man": Turner, 84.

"unspoken secrets": *Ibid.*

133   "Godfather of Sports": *Sports Illustrated*, May 29, 1972.

133-4   "What occurred to me": Laxalt, *Nevada*, 104.

134   "The reverse proved": Sheehan, ed., 198.

"sought respectability passionately": Confidential interview.

"They knew their place": John L. Smith quoted in *New York Times*, July 9, 1996.

"They didn't push": Confidential interview.

"mostly older Jewish men": Berman, 49 ff.

"Former outlaws could show up": *Ibid.*

134-5   "This is a fabulous, extraordinary madhouse" "The gangsters who run . . .

devoid of scruples": Noël Coward, "The Noël Coward Diaries: Nescafé Society," in Tronnes, ed., 211.

135   "some of the most notorious gangland": O'Dessky, 14–15.
"Vegas is supposed to be clean": *Ibid.*, 15.
"monopoly export economy": Goodman, 17.

136   a "purity code": Laxalt, *Nevada*, 108.
"You'll get your money": Rappleye and Becker, 139. For Binion's contracts on Russian Louis and the aftermath of his death, see also Laxalt, *Nevada*, 108, and Demaris, *Last Mafioso*, 66.
"obligingly faded": Fred Cook, "Gambling, Inc.," *The Nation*, October 22, 1960.
"the big guessing game in Las Vegas": Reid and Demaris, 60.

137   "a steady stream of ex-Communists": Rosenberg, 42.
"safe for the people": *Ibid.*
"gardens of leukemia": Michael Ventura, "Las Vegas: The Odds on Anything," in Tronnes, ed., 176.
"The people of the United States": Truman, 312.

138   "a second-rate scientist": Udall, 219.
"The population problem": *Ibid.*
"Can this be done" "Every precaution": Truman, 312.
"marked the beginning": Udall, 219.
"statements of reassurance": Glass, 46.
"Tests snowfall Rochester": Pringle and Spigelman, 182.

139   "went through the streets": Glass, 45.
"the uncrowned king of Las Vegas publicists": O'Dessky, 85.
"The angle was to get": *The New Yorker*, March 20, 1952.
"I saw the big guy": RJ, February 6, 1951.

140   Las Vegas's reaction to the tests: See Daniel Lang's remarkable dispatch in *The New Yorker*, "Blackjack and Flashes," September 20, 1952, and also Gladwyn Hill's "Atomic Boom Town in the Desert," *New York Times Magazine*, February 11, 1951; Glass 43–47; and Pringle and Spigelman, 181 ff.

141   Teller and Graves: Pringle and Spigelman, 181–82, 500; Udall, 243–48.

142   keep Nevadans and others "confused": Glass, 46.
"Since all the atomic tests": *Ibid.*
"Residents of Nevada": *Ibid.*, 43–47.
"Judging by the effects": Ventura, "Las Vegas," 176.
"We're in the throes": *The New Yorker*, September 20, 1952.
"A study of which group": Glass, 47.

143   "The subterranean spook culture": Ned Day in *Valley Times*, May 15, 1979.
"Japanese-Americans headed": Sarann Knight Preddy, as quoted by Faith Fancher and William J. Drummond, "Jim Crow for Black Performers," in Tronnes, ed., 307.
"Mississippi of the West": *Ibid.*, 306.

144   "made to feel unwelcome": Turner, 95.
"the most controlled society in the world": Berman, 113.
"For just under $25": *Holiday*, July 1961.
"designed and planned to attract": Turner, 95.
"classic Las Vegas mystery": *Ebony*, June 1965.
"them guys": Confidential interview.
"cement curtain": Berman, in Tronnes, ed., 117. "Memoirs of a Gangster's Daughter."

"The men who run": Turner, 5.

"shameful" conditions: See Berman, 115 ff.

"hot as the hinges of hell": Turner, 12.

"an impending crisis in the water supply": *The American City*, June 1956.

145   "Negative news stories": Glass, 27.

"broad streets, ranch-style homes": *Holiday*, July 1961.

"Most Las Vegans feel": Glass, 27.

"glaringly dependent": Turner, 153.

146   "maximum combat life": Steuer.

"showgirl Shangri-La": *Life*, June 21, 1954.

"like meat hanging on a hook": Confidential interview.

"Cecil B. De Milles": Vogliotti, 178.

"Las Vegas has many bitter people": Turner, 20.

146-7   "To be a vagrant in Las Vegas" "The sheriff, the police" "Everything is against": *Ibid.*, 14.

147   "The voters, known as" "Except for a few": Reid and Demaris, 149.

rely "more heavily": Associated Press dispatch in SUN, May 25, 1955.

"If you wanted" "The gangsters and the bankers": Confidential interview.

"The rotten bargain": Jerome Edwards, 152-55.

148   "humbled by long neglect": WPA, 3.

"They harbor dire secrets": Gunther, "Inside Las Vegas."

10. "Character Loans"

Apart from the deepest and darkest classified secrets of national security—and often even more so—there seems no task of American history more difficult than following the money through the often convoluted and hidden recesses of American banking and finance. Added to those obstacles in the case of Las Vegas is the comparable blanketing secrecy of organized crime that conceals its records *ipso facto*, and the Mormon Church that buries much of its real history literally in a mountain vault. This account of the finance of Las Vegas would not have been possible without some very remarkable journalism and scholarship that penetrated those sanctums. Walter Cosgriff and his freewheeling banking, like the history of the Eccles's business empire, were the subjects not only of the *Salt Lake Tribune*, but also of some fine dispatches in both *Newsweek* and *Business Week*. Coates's *In Mormon Circles*, Brodie's biography of Joseph Smith, the Ostlings's *Mormon America*, and especially Wiley and Gottlieb's "Don't Touch the Dice," as well as their *America's Saints*, were indispensable in piecing together the background of the sect and the historic importance of its business power—and the latter were unique in tracing the impact of that history on Las Vegas. Kent Fielding's *The Unsolicited Chronicler* and other works, and especially William Wise's *Massacre at Mountain Meadow* on that emblematic tragedy, were also crucial sources. Sidney Hyman's bank-commissioned paean to First Security Corp., *Challenge and Response*, provided unintended clues to the Eccles and Thomas history. Ironically, Parry Thomas's ancestry, which remained obscure despite several reports about the increasingly prominent Las Vegas banker, was plain in the Ancestral File, Pedigree Chart, and Family Group Record publicly available at the Mormon Church's Internet Web site and at church computer libraries throughout the world. Thomas's national reach soon grew much larger than ever covered or indicated in the local Las Vegas press, but was fortunately reported by a number of insightful national dispatches in *Business Week*, and other publications, especially Ida Picker's reporting in *Institutional Investor*.

150   If you can get me a Nevada charter: Confidential interview.
"dominated by oligopoly": Thomas Alexander, 134.
"jut-jawed man": *Newsweek*, February 20, 1956.
"A determined man of strong beliefs": *Salt Lake Tribune*, December 28, 1952.

151   "We like to judge things": *Ibid*. See also *Fortune*, November 1956; *Newsweek*,
February 20, 1956.
"They'll loan on anything": *Newsweek*, February 20, 1956.
"a liberal banker ready to finance": *Salt Lake Tribune*, September 28, 1961.

152   "zealous advocate": *Business Week*, August 19, 1950. See also NYT, August 10,
1950.

153   "his free-handed way": *Newsweek*, February 20, 1956.
"A veritable connoisseur of banks": *Ibid*.
"composed of equal parts liberality": *Ibid*.
"A bank is like a reservoir": *Ibid*.
"character loans": *Ibid*.
"gangsters . . . of the downtown gambling Syndicate": Rappleye and Becker,
50–51.
Sam Kurland: Though the influential lawyer never received publicity during
his life, there were ironic tributes to him at his death in 1976. See "In Memoriam: Tribute to the Honorable Samuel L. Kurland," *Southern California Law
Review*, 49:212 (1976), 211–19.

154   "a marriage made in heaven": Confidential interview.
"enormous pressure": Authors' interview with Parry Thomas.
"trying not to interfere": *Newsweek*, February 20, 1956.

155   "Wedgwood-blue eyes": *The Nevadan*, July 17, 1988.
"He was just a lot smoother": Confidential interview.
Mormonism: The origins and course of Mormonism, including details surrounding the Mountain Meadow Massacre, are drawn from Fawn Brodie's
courageous, unmatched biography of Joseph Smith, *No Man Knows My History*; Coates, *In Mormon Circles*; Gottlieb and Wiley, *America's Saints*, and
Wiley and Gottlieb, *Empires in the Sun*.

159   "sealed for time and eternity": Ancestral File, Pedigree Chart, Family Group
Record for Thomas and Parry families, 1793–1999.
"Very early in life": *AMP* magazine, October 1987.
"He didn't start out in banking": Authors' interview with Parry Thomas.

160   "so much money": *Newsweek*, February 1, 1936.
"One of the most powerful": *Newsweek*, October 3, 1960.
Ogden State Bank episode: The official Eccles–First Security version of the
story is told in Hyman, 112–16, though scarcely concealing the fact of the raid,
or George Eccles's role. "The responsibility for handling these incoming
emergency accounts was assigned to George," Hyman, 115.

161   "More than any other factor"; "They were my *idols*": Authors' interview with
Parry Thomas.
"It was the only non-Mormon bank": *Ibid*.
"I wanted to be my own person": *Ibid*.
"When I came on the scene": *Ibid*.

162   "had been involved": DTD.
"He convinced his boss": Confidential interview.
Banks avoid casinos: Wiley and Gottlieb, 198–99. See also Picker, "The Great
Gambling Crapshoot," *Institutional Investor*, November 1993; Art Smith,

81–93; *Business Week*, January 20, 1973; *AMP*, October 1987; *Business Week*, April 2, 1969; *The Nevadan*, July 17, 1988; and *Forbes*, November 14, 1988.

163   "downright cocky": Confidential interview.

"The last thing anybody wanted": Confidential interview.

"Parry came to town" "The casinos knew": Confidential interview.

"in rapid fire order": DTD.

164   "participation with correspondent banks": Picker, and DTD.

"It was Mob money": Sale, 86.

"incalculable proportions": *Ibid.*, 87.

165   "gambling's house banker": Picker.

"Thomas had begun funneling": *AMP*, October 1987.

"A lot of the real history": Confidential interview.

165–6   Eccles family background and Mormon Church: See Hyman, especially 122–26.

166   "that getting involved": DTD.

"cautious and conservative": *Ibid.*

"Things moved so fast": *Ibid.*

"They had a special relationship" "The pit boss . . . ninety-eight children": Berman, 106.

167   " 'Don't touch the dice' ": DTD.

occasional "highball": *Ibid.*

"Thomas, in effect, used his Mormonism": *Ibid.*

"let the Mormon businessmen": *Ibid.*

"I work for the Mormons": *Ibid.*

"We were looked down upon": Picker.

168   "I'm in the banking business": Confidential interview.

"I never met a hoodlum": *Business Week*, January 20, 1973.

"The most important player": Smith, *No Limit*, 61.

"The real godfather of Las Vegas": DTD.

"Thomas has done more": *Business Week*, January 20, 1973.

"A hoodlum banker": RJ, December 31, 1964. See also Smith, *Running Scared*, 63.

"the Mob's bank": Authors' interview with Joe Yablonsky.

Part Three: American Mecca

173   "with its high life, beautiful women": Hersh, 55.

174   "Smooth as fuckin' silk": Munn, 219, quoting Sam Giancana's description of his friend and partner.

"John Rosselli, Strategist": Rosselli's calling card, published on the back cover of Rappleye and Becker.

"All-American Mafioso": Rappleye and Becker, i.

"seersucker and sneakers": Pollak, 222.

"the most god-awful corporate creature": From a blurb by Robert Sherrill from *The Nation* on the back cover of Barlett and Steele Norton paperback edition.

175   Reagan in Las Vegas: "the fading film star" . . . "gorgeous showgirls"; "hit rock bottom" . . . "Never again": Anne Edwards, 445–47.

"the word had the scent": *Ibid.*

177   "ruthless force in the illegal": Smith, *Running Scared,* 34.

177   "wholesale abuses" of the law: *Ibid.*
"jumbled mess of scandal and corruption": *Ibid.*, 35.
"his dream of a score of a lifetime": *Ibid.*

11. A Party in Carson City

In the bulky but largely pedestrian corpus of work on the Kennedys, Beran and Mahoney are gracefully written as well as recent exceptions, based on the most up-to-date documentation, and viewing Robert Kennedy as in many respects the most interesting of the clan, the combination of crude striver and symbolic figure that his life encompasses. Heymann is more scatological than the scholarly Hilty, but the profiles are comparably documented and impressively complementary. Joseph P. Kennedy is well drawn by Fox and Hersh as well as by Hamilton and his own biographers; the challenge, as Beran begins to suggest, has been to see Joe as something much more than the exceptional "sinister capitalist," and instead as widely representative of his era *and* posterity, an embarrassing while common reflection of the ethic and practice that was the nation's, and, by extension, Las Vegas's. For his part, particularly after Nigel Hamilton's multivolume work was thwarted by the Kennedy family, John Kennedy still awaits the biography of his mature years, particularly the fifties and his late but incipient evolution in the presidency.

The poignant, telling story of Grant Sawyer is reconstructed here principally from confidential sources who knew him over much of his life as well as from his own revealing oral history, *Hang Tough*, ironically the only interview of such intimacy he ever gave. The seedy, sordid history of U.S. involvement in Cuba, including the colorful chapter it supplied to the ongoing saga of the "gray alliance" of government and organized crime, is now thoroughly documented, most recently by Russo (1998) and Mahoney (1999), though Rappleye and Becker, Scott, especially in *Crime and Cover-up*, and even Maheu provide vivid pictures. One of the most impressive and important American biographies, revealing its subject and so much more, Rappleye and Becker's Rosselli is, as Mahoney noted, "magisterial." It supplies much of the background for this and the following chapter.

179   "in the shadow of a grim range": Mark Twain, "Roughing It." *The Works of Mark Twain*, Vol. 2 (Berkeley: University of California Press, 1972), 155.
"A car backfiring": Vogliotti, 16.

180   "Like something out of the Deep South"; lampposts and other descriptions: Laxalt, *The Governor's Mansion*, 3–4.
"It wasn't fancy": Confidential interview.
Bobby Baker "all over Nevada": *Ibid.*
"They seemed to understand the importance": *Ibid.*

181   "They made themselves at home": OH, Grant Sawyer, 191.
"A whiz-bang affair": *Ibid.*
"ensconced at the Sands": Levy, 109–10. See also Michael Herr, "The Big Room," in Tronnes, ed., 144–47.
"certain Mafiosi": Mahoney, 39. See also Summers, *Official and Confidential*, 269. The contacts were recorded in part by the small Las Vegas office of the FBI.
"Summit Meetings" . . . "feel at home there" . . . "Half the people he met" . . . "most starstruck of stars" . . . "loved his brief visits there": This evocative description of John Kennedy in Las Vegas is from Herr, "The Big Room," 145 ff.

181–2   million-dollar "gift from the hotel owners" and "Some things you don't want to know": Levy, 110.

182   "The party to end all parties": Confidential interview.
      "holding court": Confidential interview.
      "He refused to come down": Confidential interview.
      "Up there in Grant's hideaway": Confidential interview.

183   "jewel of the North Shore": Levy, 243.
      "Card tables were pushed back and forth": *Reno Gazette-Journal,* June 23, 1991.
      "high class hideout": For descriptions of the Cal-Neva, including photographs of its entrance and interior in the fifties, see *Reno Gazette-Journal,* June 23, 1991. See also RJ, June 17, 1964, November 23, 1976, and April 2, 1977. 1992. Also see especially the oral histories of Warren Nelson, *Always Bet on the Butcher;* Jack Douglas, *Tap Dancing on Ice;* Robbins Cahill, *Recollections of Work in State Politics;* and Ed Olsen's *My Careers as a Journalist.*

184   "the sins of the father": The title term of Ronald Kessler's book on Joseph P. Kennedy.
      "the seeds of destruction": Similarly from the title of Ralph G. Martin's book, *Joe Kennedy and His Sons.*
      "well-known local gambling boss": See Hoover letter to White House counsel John D. Ehrlichman, April 25, 1969, subsuming Sinatra's voluminous FBI File #62-83219-61. The reference to Remmer is at p. 52, taken from a San Francisco teletype dated August 13, 1946, and drawing on wiretap surveillance of Bugsy Siegel.
      "highest echelons of the national Syndicate": Rappleye and Becker, 128.
      "mutual associates" in liquor distribution: 1944 FBI Report.
      "The Ambassador was very, very close": Confidential interview.
      "Wingy was old Joe's man": Confidential interview.

185   "Joseph P. Kennedy had been visited": FBI Memo from SAC-Tampa to Director, August 9, 1962, File #122-3323-3. The memorandum is substantially redacted but quotes "numerous sources not named." These sources refer to FBI informants as well as wiretap and other surveillance information. There is no evidence of bureau surveillance of the senior Kennedy himself in the relatively shallow and fragmentary FBI file on Joseph P. Kennedy that survived the Kennedy administration and Hoover's subsequent death, including the extensive burning and other destruction of the director's personal files. But there is ample evidence of bureau surveillance both physical and electronic in 1962 covering Giancana, Marilyn Monroe, Sinatra, and others who would have been present at the Cal-Neva meeting. In sum, even in the murky world of self-censored and purged FBI records, this meeting is one of the more reliably documented.
      "the patent-leather jack-boot": Beran, 7.
      "a crook to catch a crook": Martin, *Seeds of Destruction,* 44.

186   "One of the most evil, disgusting men": Summers, *Official and Confidential,* 261.
      "As big a crook": *Ibid.*
      "A thorn": Drosnin, 255, describing what Howard Hughes thought of what he called "the old bastard."
      "ties to the underworld": Giancana and Giancana, 227.
      "In a lot of ways Joe" "persuasive behind the scenes": Confidential interview.
      "national agreement": See Fox, 315 ff., who concluded of Joseph P. Kennedy that "mobsters recognized him as one of their own."

187   "Match made in heaven": Confidential interview.
       "One rule always to remember": Fox, 318.
188   an "upperworld gangster": See Fox, 308 ff., and especially Beran's portrait of
       JPK as the "Sinister Capitalist" and "traitor to his class," Beran, 23–28.
       "the integral union": See Chambliss, 61 ff.
189   "savage domination": Martin, *Seeds of Destruction*, 13.
       "Kennedy might hope" "They perforce": Fox, 318.
       "The boys might as well": Beran, 25.
       "He built a literal wall" "He was careful": Fox, 317–18.
       "graceful yet forceful": Herr, "The Big Room," 145.
       "A compulsive satyr": Hougan, *Spooks*, 118.
190   "He can't run my campaign": Martin, *Seeds of Destruction*, 238.
       "When I hate": Hilty, 167.
       a "Napoleonic complex": Russo, 28.
       he was "the runt": William V. Shannon, *The Heir Apparent: Robert Kennedy
       and the Struggle for Power* (New York: Macmillan, 1967), 44.
       "hard-eyed, hard-faced": Hilty, 96.
       "A constellation of contradictions": *Ibid.*, 4.
       "a revolutionary priest": Jean Stein and George Plimpton, *American Journey:
       The Times of Robert Kennedy* (New York: Harcourt Brace, 1970), 193.
       "the last patrician": The title of Beran's thoughtful book about Robert
       Kennedy.
       "The most interesting": Beran, 34.
       "An imperfect man": *Ibid.*, 215.
       "vizier and brother protector": Hilty, 5.
191   "idea of uncovering": Bly, 98.
       "open spaces and severe freedom," and Kennedy's thoughts about moving to
       Nevada: Beran, 55–56.
       "Tempting targets": Hilty, 100.
192   "Well, goddammit" "Got him enough": *Ibid.*
       "The worst we ever witnessed": Fox, 321 ff.
       scene at Hyannis, "deeply, emotionally opposed" *et seq.*: Hilty, 97.
       "The father, of all people" "His private, unspoken fears": Fox, 321.
       "first real defiance": *Ibid.*
       "to rid the country": Hilty, 104.
       "human parasites on society": *Ibid.*
       "just plain old brown": Roger Morris, *Partners in Power: The Clintons and
       Their America* (New York: Henry Holt & Co., 1996), 38.
193   "The most thorough exposure": Fox, 321.
       drawing a "moral dividing line": Hilty, 105.
       "audacious belligerence": *Ibid.*, 125.
194   "out of jail and brazen": Fox, 329.
       "fateful personal agenda": *Ibid.*
       "prime villains": See Heymann, 125 ff., for Bobby's animus toward the union.
       "Either we're going to be": Kennedy, x.
       "An urgent and ominous tone": Hilty, 132.
       "The older brother's playground": Herr, "The Big Room," 146.
194-6 "More than anything in the world" and the description that follows: OH,
       Grant Sawyer.
196   "the compulsive joiner and office seeker": What his oral history interviewer
       and profiler called Sawyer. *Ibid.*

Support of Sawyer by northern Nevada liberals: Reno resident Hazel Erskine was one of the early members of Columbia University's Bureau of Applied Social Research and was "instrumental in making possible Grant Sawyer's successful campaign for governor," as Nevada historian Gary Elliott wrote in his Introduction to *Hang Tough,* Sawyer's published oral history. In a tribute to Erskine published in the *Public Opinion Quarterly* (1975–76), the authors wrote that she "spotted in Grant Sawyer . . . an astute and pragmatic politician who was at the same time a man of principle" and "educable—as Hazel put it—in the social and human needs of the state."

197   "Everyone wanted to know": Confidential interview.
"He was always insecure": Confidential interview.
"Grant would've done anything": Confidential interview.
"for any of three declarations": Confidential interview.
"They shrewdly recognized": Confidential interview.
"A backroom man": O'Connor, 154.
the Kennedys' "Irish Mafia": Confidential interview.
"They were playing us all off": Confidential interview.

198   "I convinced Raskin": Confidential interview.
"an astronomical amount": Confidential interview.
"It was the first big": Confidential interview.
"small donations": Sawyer, 59 ff.
"It made Grant governor": Confidential interview.
"Nevada Is Not For Sale": OH, Grant Sawyer.
"pro-labor, cheap water": *Ibid.*
"We had to project": *Ibid.*
owners need not be "bishops": OH, Robbins Cahill.

199   "I talk for the state" and text that follows: Reid and Demaris, 128 ff.
"Partner rather than adversary": Sheehan, 9.
"bacchanalia coexists with bureaucracy": Goodman, 1.
"Within the context of an economy": Farrell and Case, 11.

200   "just an *hors d'oeuvre*": *The Nation,* October 22, 1960.
"money running out their ears": Jerome Edwards, "Gambling and Politics in Nevada," in Lowitt, ed., 157, quoting Norman Biltz.
"The Esmeralda buy-off": Confidential interview.
"Suddenly I had a lot of friends": OH, Grant Sawyer.
"Its destiny": Campaign letter addressed to "Fellow Democrat," July 31, 1958, Sawyer Papers, NSLA.
"faith, trust and mutual understanding": RJ, January 6, 1959.

201   "I have no idea what Castro": SUN, January 5, 1959.

202   "Offshore Las Vegas": Russo, 5.
"In suitcases": Hinckle and Turner, lx.

202–3 Pre-Castro Cuba: See Paterson, 52–56; Russo, 3–9; Scott, 111–17, 140, 157, 173–80, 198–204, 240; Hinckle and Turner, lx–lxiii. For the traditional Cuban narcotics connection, see especially McCoy, 39–45, though Scott, Paterson, and a number of other historians have amply documented the reality as well.

203   "a vile commerce": Paterson, 52.
"way-stations in the transfer": Russo, 5, and also Franklin, 21 ff.
"You could buy . . . *anything*": *Ibid.*

204   "It's strange": Earl T. Smith quoted in *ibid.,* 55.
"Imposing and simple": Paterson, 53.
"luminous halo of night life": Guillermo Cabrera Infante quoted in *ibid.*

204   "if he could set him up": Russo, 10, as well as Paterson, 52.

204-5 "Once they started looking after you": George Smathers quoted in Paterson, 52.

205   a "playboy extraordinary": Christian Herter, quoted in Paterson, 235.
       "I don't think I ever heard": Smathers quoted in Michael Beschloss, *The Crisis Years: Kennedy and Khrushchev, 1960-1963* (New York: HarperCollins, 1991), 99.
       "the gray alliance": Scott, *Deep Politics and the Death of JFK*, 80, 87, 102–05, 203.
       "A lot of funny money": Confidential interview.

206   "easy affinity": See Rappleye and Becker, 146 ff.
       "The convergence of interests": *Ibid.*, 187.

207   "We are not only disposed": Paterson, 235; Lacey, 252.

208   "As if the American auto": Rappleye and Becker, 175.
       "Helluva cast of characters"; "short, fat, and hideous looking"; "Fifth Avenue cowboys" *et seq.*: For descriptions of the plotters, their mentality, remarks, etc., see in particular Evan Thomas, 204–26; Russo, 31–37, 50–67; Rappleye and Becker, 175–88.

210   "The CIA obtained mobsters' aid"; "securing the gambling, prostitution, and dope monopolies": *Time,* June 9, 1975; Russo, 51.
       "It is not at all clear": Drosnin, 66.

210-11 Maheu's background; "a deniable proprietary"; "connections to the Mob": See foremost Hougan's brilliant chapters in *Spooks,* 259–375, along with Drosnin's insightful portrait. Maheu's own selective version is in his *Next to Hughes,* 17–150.

211   "softening up parties": Anderson and Boyd, 51–55.
       "A goniff": Authors' interview with Joe Yablonsky.
       "top bag man": Drosnin, 70.
       "spook of choice": Hougan, *Spooks,* 331.

211-12 Rosselli: "At the pinnacle of his criminal career"; "Socialite, labor boss and gangster"; "Henry Kissinger of the Mob" *et seq.*: The portrait here is drawn from Rappleye and Becker, as well as Mahoney's compelling mosaic of Rosselli's appearances in the Kennedy story, much of it from new sources, in *Sons and Brothers.*

213   "Let's just say": Confidential interview.

214   "What's wrong?": Rappleye and Becker, 190.
       "I would think you had": Levy, 164.
       "bartender and greeter": *Ibid.*, 165.
       "went wild"; "We're on our way": *Ibid.*
       "cozied up": *Ibid.*

215   "The Black Prince": Hilty, 149.
       "that little shit-ass": Heymann, 169.
       "His arrogance and cavalier attitude" . . . "pleading": OH, Grant Sawyer.
       "We felt we had complete control": Confidential interview.
       "The convention raised hell": *Ibid.*
       "Those bastards were trying": Hersh, 126.
       "That cornponed bastard": Shesol, 3; Heymann, 164 ff.
       "You're gonna get yours": Heymann, 164.
       "They threatened me with problems": Hersh, 126.

216   Sawyer's journey home: Confidential interviews.
       "political treachery": OH, Grant Sawyer.

12. An Enemy Too Far Within

Widely doubted, resisted, or cautiously ignored by scholars and journalists (and just as widely known or credited by political insiders as well as members of the Syndicate), the decisive fraud of the 1960 presidential election now seems beyond dispute. The recently released FOIAs of the FBI field investigation in Cook County, Illinois, and the report and files of Special Prosecutor Morris J. Wexler are unique archives in the annals of constitutional crime, establishing the thievery in Chicago and elsewhere with overwhelming evidence and precision worthy of any courtroom. For the rest of the country as well, Hersh's *Dark Side of Camelot* is the definitive investigative journalism on the thefts, confirming what Earl Mazo reported at the time in the *New York Herald Tribune,* and Victor Lasky later amplified in the seventies, albeit from nakedly partisan perspectives. Fleming and Kallina provide scholarly substantiation of the West Virginia and Chicago frauds, while Fox and Mahoney document the national scene. Still further confirmation of the general election thefts in Nevada, New Mexico, and Hawaii, and in the West Virginia primary, comes from the authors' confidential interviews. The story of Sawyer's dramatic confrontation with Bobby Kennedy is told in *Hang Tough,* with much of the background and sequel provided by Goldfarb, Hilty, and confidential sources from both the Kennedy and Nevada camps. Scott, among so much else, meticulously records Jack Ruby's myriad connections that would lead to Las Vegas.

217 **bets on JFK; Vegas odds:** Confidential interviews; Stephen Smith's $25,000 bet is also recorded by Fox, 334; tightening odds were noted by the RJ and SUN, November 7 and 8, 1960.
election day scenes: Kallina, 80–95, 220 ff.; Fox, 335; Lasky, 56–64; confidential interviews.
conscience-stricken polling judge: Kallina, 220 ff.
"the stuffing of ballot boxes": Lasky, 58.

218 **"informal and highly irregular":** Kallina, 98.
"unpleasantness for you and your family": Confidential interviews.
"questionable practices": Confidential interviews.
"brown paper package": Confidential interview.

219 **"The night of the gnomes":** Theodore H. White, *Breach of Faith: The Fall of Richard Nixon* (New York: Dell, 1975), 96–97; see also Hilty, 179.
"a deluge of reports": Kallina, 97.
"Voting Irregularities": FBI File 52-2854-9 *et seq.,* including voluminous press reports and other law enforcement documents. In a memorandum of December 1, 1960, Justice Department officials ordered the investigation in Illinois concluded "within ten days," a timetable Hoover promptly cut further by scrawling across the document in his inimitable handwriting, "Set deadline of 1 week"—in either case, an interval that was no match for the magnitude of the evidence.
"I don't suppose": Quoted in Kallina, 96.
"Charges of 'sore loser' ": Richard Nixon, *RN: The Memoirs of Richard Nixon* (New York: Grossett & Dunlap, 1978), 224.

220 **"carte blanche for future irregularities":** Kallina, 214. A scholar concluded from examining the files almost three decades after the event that Democrat Wexler's inquiry had proceeded "with rare conscientiousness and thoroughness." Kallina, 171.
"No one will ever know": White in *Breach of Faith,* 70.
Nixon's corruption: The definitive account is Summers and Swan, establishing Nixon's ties to organized crime and other corrupt influences literally throughout his political career.

221   "You can see how cruel": Drosnin, 255.
       never reconciled to "the Kennedy gang's": *Ibid.*, 257.
       Joe Kennedy's meetings: See Mahoney, 43–44 and 384, and Hersh, 135–36.

222   "Anywhere from $2": John H. Davis, *The Kennedys: Dynasty and Disaster* (New York: McGraw-Hill, 1984), 234, quoting Charles D. Hylton, Jr., editor of the *Logan Banner*.
       appointment as attorney general; "It's Bobby," *et seq.:* Heymann, 184–200; see also Fox, 335–36, Hilty, 186–91.

223   "the only federal appointment": Heymann, 144.
       "I'd been chasing bad men": Martin, *A Hero for Our Times*, 236.
       "I know that certain people": Cohen, 153–54.
       "the family relationship with the mob world": Martin, *Seeds of Destruction*, 250.
       "I can tell you that": Hersh, 153.
       "Nothing happened": *Ibid.*
       "If the boys would have known": Confidential interview with a source who also had no doubt that the theft took place in a number of states—"much more than anybody's ever come across."

224   "color, charm, and photographic appeal": Heymann, 200.
       the "beautiful young women": *Ibid.*
       "Everything's nice and cool": Rappleye and Becker, 173.
       "Las Vegas, as every schoolboy": *Newsweek*, November 28, 1964.

225   "The dwelling place of the deity" . . . "the flash and glitter": *Esquire*, August 1961.
       "We have no gangsters here": *Saturday Evening Post*, November 11, 1961.
       "Our business is no different": *Ibid.*
       "I'm the only entertainer": *Ibid.*
       "a leading citizen of Las Vegas": *Ibid.*, in a story, ironically, by Peter Wyden, author of the later book on the Bay of Pigs.
       "We don't have to ask": *Ibid.*
       a "strange animus": *Esquire*, August 1961.
       "It is modern alchemy": *Newsweek*, November 28, 1964.
       "civic-minded inhabitants": *Ibid.*

226   "tend to disregard trash receptacles": *The American City*, July 1961.
       "It was like coming on": Confidential interview.

227   "pastel skyscrapers": *Denver Post*, August 13, 1963.
       "Without the Teamsters": Kwitny, *Vicious Circles*, 142.

227–8 On Hoffa: The description of his background and career is drawn principally from Sloane's intimate portrait, and from Moldea; Brill; Kwitny, *Vicious Circles;* Block and Chambliss; James and James; Mollenhoff; and Sheridan.

228   Italian corruption: See especially Peter Robb's *Midnight in Sicily*.

229   "launched him toward national leadership": Scott, *Deep Politics*, 173.
       "a cynical, caustic opportunism": See Chambliss, 163–64, and Scott, 174–75.
       "The symbiosis between business": Block and Chambliss, 80.

229–30 "The postwar national Mafia became": Scott, 174–75.

230   "To reward friends and make new ones": "Business was business": Sloane, 272 ff.
       "declining old wealth firms": Scott, *Deep Politics*, 288.

231   "the vilest man I ever met": Confidential interview.
       "utter absence of show": Sloane, 47.

"almost Victorian approach": Sloane, 46.

"There were the Kennedys . . . disgusted by it": Heymann, 126.

"an outgoing brunette": Sloane, 47.

"had a thing for her, too": See Friedman and Schwarz, 86; Sloane, 47 ff.

232   "thousands of 'captive' patients": Reid and Demaris, 104.

"If Moe told them": Sheehan, ed., 45.

233   "Jimmy was *the* juice": Reid and Demaris, 99.

"A lot of guys": Confidential interview.

"Any ambitious businessman": Neff, 201.

"They have bankrolled the better": Kwitny, *Vicious Circles,* 143.

234   "I mean it was a sweet deal": Confidential interview.

"Baling up money": Jacobson, Alexander, "What Webb Is Up To in Nevada," *Fortune,* May 1965.

those "outside sources": *Ibid.*

235   "favorable terms that include secrecy": *Ibid.*

"to keep known hoodlums from discrediting": *Nevada State Journal,* September 18, 1960.

"Nevada is not for sale": Grant Sawyer letter to Henry Luce, January 25, 1960, Sawyer Papers, Nevada State Archives. See also Sawyer campaign letter "Fellow Democrat," July 31, 1958, Sawyer Papers, Nevada State Archives.

236   "Nevada was always good": OH, Grant Sawyer.

"May I suggest": Anslinger letter to Ray Abbaticchio, February 4, 1960, Sawyer Papers, Nevada State Archives.

"I own Chicago": Hilty, 206.

"some of the mob's most grisly killings": Farrell and Case, 41 ff.

"warmly greeted by owners": *Ibid.*

237   "a considerable number of individuals": Confidential interview.

"A shudder ran through" *et seq.:* SUN, December 30, 1960.

"A careful check": *Ibid.*

"the insidious rot": Heymann, 201.

238   "a thick black book": Hilty, 205.

"loyalty to the Kennedys": Hilty, 195.

239   "What was it": Hilty, 231.

"If I don't make it": Hilty, 205.

give the effort "first place": Hilty, 197.

240   "Hoover was certain": Hilty, 201.

"huge financial bonanza": Goldfarb, 77.

"We knew that despite superficial": Goldfarb, 78 ff.

240–1   "skimming . . . had been big business": *Ibid.*

241   "core community: *Ibid.,* 80.

"Kennedy was virtually obsessed": Spees in Davies, 172.

"And we certainly didn't trust": Goldfarb, 80.

a "dual mission": *Ibid.,* 81.

242   "twenty-one holes"; "fool-proof methods": *Ibid.*

"Lansky appears to have been protected": Summers, *Official and Confidential,* 244 ff.

"That protector was Hoover himself": Hoover and Lansky biographer Hank Messick, as reported in Scott, 145; see also Hank Messick, *John Edgar Hoover* (New York: David Mackay, 1972).

242–3   "to invade every major casino" *et seq.:* Sawyer, OH 89 ff.

245   "There are two people I'd like to get out": Russo, 37.
246   "an obsessive, prideful, competitive hatred": Russo, 449.
       "*de jure* head": Heymann, 257 ff. See also Russo, 47 ff.
       "It was like a millstone": "He's an assassin": Russo, 59.
       "Maheu's conning the hell": Hogan, 308 ff., 119–20.
       "There was never a time a halt": Russo, 242 and 393 ff.
       "splinter the CIA": Russo, 33.
       "the blame for the Bay of Pigs": *Ibid.*
247   "at all hours of the day and night": Russo, 44.
       "The time, the place": Russo, 65.
       "getting rid" of Castro: Russo, 69.
248   assets "would be needed": *Ibid.*
       "J. Edgar Hoover has Jack Kennedy": Russo, 72. See also Hilty, 208 ff.
249   "building toward a major series": Goldfarb, 130.
       "Nevada officials went ballistic": Goldfarb, 309.
250   Johnson . . . "demoralized": *Ibid.*
       "was a media-created phenomenon," "violating state and federal law": Sawyer, OH.
       "ease up on Frank": Kelley, *His Way,* 323.
251   "What are you guys doing": Sawyer, OH.
       "several comely prostitutes": Heymann, 264.
252   Ruby relationship with R. B. Matthews: See Scheim, 130ff.
       "Ruby was hooked up with Trafficante": Scott Malone, quoted in Scott, 180. See also Scheim, 225, and Scott Malone, "The Secret Life of Jack Ruby," *New Times,* January 23, 1978.
253   "because I was so emotionally upset": Russo, 501.
       "a hurry-up job": Confidential interview.
254   Scelso deposition: JFK Assassination Records Collection, National Archives, RIF number 180-10131-10330, especially pp. 168–69, which contains this remarkable passage: *Question:* "Do you have any reason to believe that Angleton might have had ties to organized crime? *Answer:* Yes." According to Scelso's testimony, when he told the well-connected J. C. King that Angleton had quashed a CIA inquiry into Las Vegas skim proceeds in Panama on grounds that the money was an FBI matter, "King . . . smiled a foxy smile and said, 'Well,' he said, 'that's Angleton's excuse. The real reason is that Angleton himself has ties to the Mafia and he would not want to double-cross them.' . . ."
       "a damned Murder, Inc.": Russo, 377. Johnson speaking on background to the new CBS anchor, Walter Cronkite.
       "Kennedy was trying to get": *New York Times,* June 25, 1976.
255   "I found out something": Russo, 381. See also Lester David and Irene David, *Bobby Kennedy: The Making of a Folk Hero* (New York, 1986), pp. 3ff.

13. "Cleaning Out the Sucker"

Among their many singular contributions to American investigative journalism, and of all the millions of words written about Howard Hughes, *Empire* by Donald Barlett and James Steele is by far not only the best biography of Hughes but also the most revealing account of Hughes's involvement in Las Vegas. Likewise, Jim Hougan's earlier reporting on Robert Maheu in *Spooks* and Michael Drosnin's later *Citizen Hughes* probed and explored the wider Nevada and national political implications. For this often bizarre period in Nevada history, archival material at the University of Nevada at Reno is remarkably useful, including the papers of both Paul Laxalt and his brother Robert, whose notes for his reality-based novel *The Governor's Mansion* and other ostensibly fictional works, are candid, tragic, and fascinating. In this chapter as in previous sections, the Oral History collection of the University of Nevada was invaluable, especially Grant Sawyer's *Hang Tough*. And once more, the authors are deeply indebted in this chapter as in others to the masterful Rosselli biography by Rappleye and Becker.

257   "He preferred to relax": Laxalt, *Sweet Promised Land*, 15.
"A man like that": *Ibid.*, 1.
"At a very tender age": Waas in *City Paper*, May 28, 1994.
"their flaming shield": Roberts, "Reagan's First Friend."
"those damned Republicans": UNR, Laxalt notes. See also *Denver Post Magazine*, April 1, 1984.

258   "developed a long reach": Roberts, "Reagan's First Friend."
a "tireless student": Confidential interview.
"The most miserable and depressing": Laxalt, Paul, 36.
"When he came home": *Denver Post Magazine*, April 1, 1984.
his "compass": Condon, in *Washington Dossier*.
"He gave the appearance": Laxalt, *Sweet Promised Land*, 20.
"strict and authoritarian": Spees in Davies, ed., 168.

259   "My dad didn't think I had brains": *RJ*, October 16, 1966.
"star athlete, student leader": UNR, Laxalt files.
"when bankers and businessmen": Laxalt, *Sweet Promised Land*, 46.
"a six-footer with close cropped": *Reno Evening Gazette*, November 9, 1966.
"The GOP was nothing": Confidential interview.

260   "Bell practically roped and hog-tied him": Confidential interview.
"drop whatever they were doing": Confidential interview.
"absolutely controlled the family": *Ibid.*
"had sprung from": Laxalt, *The Governor's Mansion*, 38.
"so big on him it covered": Confidential interview.

261   "It was like riding": *Ibid.*
"Grant was genuinely fond of old Rex": Confidential interview.
"feeling like a neophyte": *Ibid.*
"puppet of the industry": UNR, Laxalt notes.

261–2 "Frenchie ran the show": Confidential interview.

262   "Cannon first crippled" . . . "shame and embarrassment to the state": UNR, Laxalt notes.
"good friend Barry Goldwater": *Ibid.*
"riding high": Confidential interview.
"shenanigans on the Westside": For accounts of the 1964 Cannon and Laxalt Senate race, and charges of vote fraud, see Spees in Davies, ed., 171.
"at least ten percent" . . . "Look what we've got" . . . "They got no clothes to wear": OH, Peter B. Merialdo.

263   "What children we were": UNR, Laxalt notes.
"It was his first known walk": Moldea, *Crime Control Digest.*
"As an old man": Confidential interview.
"to add insult to injury": *Ibid.*
"rolling in dough": *Ibid.*
"had been instrumental in killing": Spees in Davies, ed., 178.
"whole Strip was pretty much": Confidential interview.
"as a fresh, young Republican": Spees in Davies, ed., 178.

263   "reassuring the FBI": Gottlieb and Wiley, "The Senator and the Gamblers."
264   "He arrived in Las Vegas": *Ibid.*, as quoted by Las Vegas lawyer Alvin Wartman.
       "if Sawyer wants to make": UNR, Laxalt notes.
       "erase the image that we are in bed": Spees in Davies, ed., 174.
       "intensified federal suspicion": *Ibid.*
       "lifted the state from economic backwardness" . . . "existed in crooked": UNR, Laxalt notes.
       "sheer hypocrisy": UNR, Laxalt notes.
       "Just plain honesty": Condon in *Washington Dossier.*
       "All we have to do": UNR, Laxalt notes.
       "failed to protect the state's": UNR, Paul Laxalt 1966 press release.
       "Who owns Nevada?": UNR, Laxalt notes.
       "After eight years in office": UNR, Paul Laxalt press release.
       "Sawyer's voice fell silent" . . . "armed with leaked Justice Department": Moldea, *Crime Control Digest.*
265   "In those days, no one went": OH, Grant Sawyer.
       "a real swinging cat": UNR, Paul Laxalt 1966 press release.
       "The election is a Nevada matter": UNR, Laxalt notes.
       "When the election was over": Laxalt, 124.
       "That moment is when": Confidential interview.
       "the deep blue book": Urza, 14.
266   "Las Vegas as Lourdes": Interview with John L. Smith.
267   "a symbol of government waste": Barlett and Steele, 118.
268   "for the biggest check": Drosnin, 49.
       "The last of the great American robber barons": Lalli in Sheehan, 144.
       "ceased virtually all contact": Barlett and Steele, 232.
       "like Dorian Gray": Drosnin, 47.
269   "A man who distributed": See Barlett and Steele, 339–40, 345–46.
       "a captive company of the CIA": Scott, *Crime and Cover-up,* 30–31.
       "He liked the glamour": Barlett and Steele, 187. For Hughes's early days in Las Vegas, see also Drosnin, and Lalli in Sheehan.
       "Enormous pressure was applied": Ed Oncken in *Scene,* 1967.
270   "Meeting hundreds of men" . . . "new small city": RJ, January 25, 1954.
       "in his white leather chair": Barlett and Steele, 240.
271   "When a job opening occurred": *Ibid.*, 212.
       "By becoming willing participants" "By going along": *Ibid.*, 240.
       "Like an Oriental pasha": Drosnin, 51.
       "make-shift ambulance": RJ, December 1, 1966.
       "The Wizard of Oz": Drosnin, 51.
       "negotiations to buy": Confidential interview.
       "withering under a barrage": Barlett and Steele, 291.
272   "prominent figures in both": *Chicago Sun Times,* July 10, 1966 series on Las Vegas.
       "one gigantic beehive of crime": Drosnin, 121.
       "Just when it looked like": Drosnin, 120.
       "greeted with messianic enthusiasm": Bellett, 26.
       Greenspun "spilled over": *Ibid.*
       "camped on the story": Barlett and Steele, 279.
273   "a curious stance for a newsman": Lukas in Pollak, ed., 223.

"self-effacement and humility": Barlett and Steele, 279.

"Johnny smoothed the way": Maheu, 160.

"The billionaire's top bagman": Drosnin, 70.

274   "Maheu's position afforded him": Rappleye and Becker, 282.

"The odd man out": Barlett and Steele, 289.

"The man who really made it rain": Maheu, 167–68.

"provide an improved national image": Barlett and Steele, 292.

"The feds had suspicions": Laxalt, 132.

"I knew if we could get": Picker.

"Any other applicant": Lalli in Sheehan, 142.

"So far as they know": Garrison, 52.

275   promising "$200,000 to $300,000": Maheu, 169. See also RJ, March 23, 1967.

the "Good Housekeeping seal of approval": Lalli in Sheehan, 142.

"A gathering place": Drosnin, 107.

"No count was made": Garrison, 54.

"While the inexperienced Hughes": Sheehan, 150.

"None of us knew snake eyes": Sheehan, 147.

"No matter what I thought": Maheu, 159.

"The mob went about its business": Lalli in Sheehan, 133–58.

"The whole thing was a Syndicate scam": Jimmy "The Weasel" Fratianno, quoting Roselli in Drosnin, 120.

276   that the "casino owners were seeking": Rappleye and Becker, 280.

"We roped Hughes": Drosnin, 120.

"snatching up gaudy hotels": Drosnin, 106.

"Hughes's Nevada gauleiter": Lukas in Pollak, 214.

"They were all Lansky joints": Confidential interview.

"who was calling the shots" "whoever controls Hughes": UNR, Laxalt notes.

"conferring quietly with Maheu": Rappleye and Becker, 283.

"Thomas, who now wore different hats": Barlett and Steele, 298.

"fronting for Hughes": Garrison, 120.

"heartily endorsed" . . . "array of talent": Barlett and Steele, 297.

277   "taking the rap for an Israeli diplomat": Confidential interview.

"collected fees": Barlett and Steele, 298.

"Howard Hughes bought": Garrison, 78.

"all of the land": Maheu, 172.

"eventually be worth six hundred billion dollars":

"basically the entire Strip": Confidential interview.

"nearly every vacant lot": Rothman.

278   to "make Las Vegas as trustworthy": Drosnin, 108. See also Lalli in Sheehan.

"No longer was Hughes": Barlett and Steele, 303.

"bigger than the Comstock Lode": Russell Nielsen for UPI, September 26, 1967.

"Gathered like a secret coven": Drosnin, 104.

"I'm ready to ride with this man": Ibid.

279   "haunted by a hidden fear": Ibid., 103.

"summoning his gambling czars": Ibid., 105.

"Hughes was too big of a sugar daddy": Lalli in Sheehan, 142.

"Laxalt took this treasured scrap": Drosnin, 105.

"no one, including the Governor": Ibid.

279   "We should have absolutely *nothing*": Drosnin, 105.
"something like the Second Coming": *Ibid.,* 110.
"one of the most interesting conversations": Barlett and Steele, 305.
"Anything this man does": *Ibid.*
"I look like a goddamn cadaver": Laxalt, 134.

280   "I think Laxalt can be brought": Drosnin, 104.
"He phoned me day or night": Laxalt, 135.
"his new role as desert raja": Rappleye and Becker, 283.
"though he never let that out": UNR, Laxalt notes.
"King of Las Vegas": Maheu, 178.
"the most highly paid": Hougan, *Spooks,* 261.
a "modified plantation house": Drosnin, 86.
"While Hughes lay huddled": *Ibid.,* 88.
"an archvillain in his hidden domain": *Ibid.,* 52.
"naked in his bedroom": *Ibid.,* 53.

281   "his little polygamous family": *Ibid.,* 62.
"powerful industrialist who had come": *Ibid.*
"Norman Rockwell vision": Drosnin, 119.
"the classiest resort in the world": Barlett and Steele, 306.
Hughes's master plan and hotel: *Ibid.*
"it is contrary to our basic concept": *Ibid.,* 321.
"modest, self-effacing person": *Ibid.,* 312.
"Hank Greenspun became": Demaris, *The Last Mafioso,* 185.
"the financial future": Barlett and Steele, 299.

282   "to do with as he pleased": *Ibid.*
"specialized in communications law": *Ibid.,* 302.
"two inches apart": Confidential interview. Details of cash contributions to Nevada political figures can also be found in Drosin, 123.
"I can buy any man": Barlett and Steele, 451.
"the most powerful private political machine": Drosnin, 257.

283   "the one candidate he did not want": *Ibid.*
"was so excited he couldn't sleep": Drosnin, 262.
"I hate to be quick on the draw": *Ibid.,* 38.
"I don't want an alliance": *Ibid.*
"The kind of set-up": *Ibid.,* 112.
"leader of the Irish Mafia": *Ibid.,* 265.
"The bubble burst": Rappleye and Becker, 285.
"self-dealing schemes and conspiracies": Phelan, 208.
"A mechanic *par excellence*": Whearley, "The Truth About Las Vegas."

284   "Dalitz and other members": Timothy O'Brien, 33.
"Close and ominous relationships": White House Memorandum to H. R. Haldeman. See also Senate 1974 Watergate hearings.
"only now are the Hughes": *Ibid.*
"predilection for funny-money": Block, *Masters of Paradise,* 100.
"an organized crime enterprise": *Ibid.*
"Get Hoffa agents": Moldea, *Interference,* 177.
"With the murder of Robert Kennedy": *Ibid.*
"Intertel would replace Maheu": Kohn, "The Hughes-Nixon-Lansky Connection."

285   "perfect anti-Syndicate stance": *Ibid.*
Lansky "hiding out in Israel": *Ibid.*

"Lansky's established connections": Chambliss, 178 ff.

frozen out of the "Teamsters-Republican coalition": *Ibid.*

"reached a tentative agreement": Kohn, "The Hughes-Nixon-Lansky Connection."

"rushed cashier's cages": Bellett, 83.

286   "For all his power": Drosnin, 70.

a "bitter corporate struggle": Barlett and Steele, 442.

"gathered his war party": Bellett, 83.

"Drinking huge amounts of brandy": UNR, Laxalt notes.

"wanted Maheu out": *Ibid.*

"wanted Maheu fired"; "I've never seen a more crestfallen man": Laxalt, 141.

"fairy godfather": Drosnin, 122.

"The chosen instrument": Greenspun column in *Sun,* 1970.

"no-good dishonest son-of-a-bitch": Smith, *No Limit,* 175. See also Maheu, 245 and Rappley and Becker, 285.

"I prostituted my newspaper": Greenspun, quoted by Lukas in Pollak, 226.

287   "mushroomed into a full-scale": Drosnin, 419.

"seeds of Watergate": Lalli in Sheehan, 152.

"a gun fanatic": Drosnin, 424.

"rebellious and resentful": Roberts in the *New York Times Magazine.*

refused to "join": Laxalt, 143.

"one of the five most powerful": Gottlieb and Wiley, "The Senator and the Gamblers."

"Dear Dick letter": Moldea in *Crime Control Digest.* See also Barlett and Steele, and Drosnin.

288   Ormsby House: For background and details surrounding the construction of the Ormsby House, as well as portraits of Paul Laxalt, see especially Denny Walsh's groundbreaking, consequential, and historic pieces of investigative journalism in the *Sacramento Bee,* November 1, 1983. See also *New Republic,* August 25, 1986; Waas in *City Paper;* Roberts in the *New York Times Magazine;* Friedman in *Mother Jones;* Gottlieb and Wiley in "The Senator and the Gamblers"; Moldea in *Crime Control Digest;* George Condon, Jr., in "The Power Gamble: Paul Laxalt and the Nevada Gang," *Washington Dossier,* September 1983; and Stephen Singular in *Denver Post Magazine,* April 1, 1984.

"We had no family money": Gottlieb and Wiley, "The Senator and the Gamblers."

"in Nevada it was possible to make something": *Ibid.*

"Paul learned": *Ibid.*

"bringing the best of American capitalism": Drosnin, 122.

"because no other state was ever blasted": Vogliotti, 200.

289   "Popular lore gives": Lalli in Sheehan, 143.

"The only thing Hughes": Drosnin, 116.

290   "Where his country's interests": Drosnin, 458.

14. High Rollers

Howard Kohn's groundbreaking piece, "The Hughes-Nixon-Lansky Connection," in *Rolling Stone* remains a primary source to explain the 1970s in Las Vegas and in much of America. Colodny and Gettlin, Hougan in *Secret Agenda,* Scott in his *Crime and Cover-up,* and Bellett's biography of the shadowy Johnny Meier are essential to any deeper understanding of Watergate, and especially its Las Vegas connections. Not least, the authors were extremely fortunate to have enjoyed several lengthy and very candid conversations with the late John Ehrlichman before his untimely death during the writing of this book. Dan Moldea's reporting in general on organized crime and American politics in this period is in a class by itself, as is the reporting of Gary Cartwright on the Chagras in Texas. Finally, this interpretation owes much to the work of an old friend and a true giant of American journalism, Jack Anderson, whose recent memoir, *Peace, War, and Politics,* is a rare model of a public man's candor and honesty.

291   "They got us": Colodny and Gettlin, 158.
292   "If they want to kill me": Rappleye and Becker, 310.
294   "a powerful Morgan-Maheu-Anderson": Scott, *Crime and Cover-up*, 34.
295   "the Hughes connection": Authors' interview with John Ehrlichman. See also Kutler.
"Nixon seemed to lose touch": Kutler, 203.
"paranoia about Johnny Meier": Authors' interview with John Ehrlichman.
Nixon's "almost irrational interest": Hougan, *Secret Agenda*, 107.
"enmeshed in the reclusive billionaire's affairs": *Ibid.*
296   "Maheu's tentacles": White House Memo, reprinted in Watergate hearings.
Jack Anderson's stock in the *Las Vegas Sun:* Anderson, *Peace, War, and Politics*, 145.
Rosselli's "chosen conduit": Mahoney, 336.
"political H-bomb" story": Drosnin, 259. See also Scott, *Crime and Cover-up*, 24.
the plot that may have "backfired against his late brother": *Ibid.* Drew Pearson and Jack Anderson column, March 3, 1967.
297   "sent tremors through official Washington": Rappleye and Becker, 272.
a "very slanted attack": Scott, *Crime and Cover-up*, 26.
"there was an impressive": Phelan, 140.
"It was the broadest and best-financed" "It fell to John Rosselli": Rappleye and Becker, 268.
"seeking to influence": *Ibid.*
Rosselli as a "stand-up guy":
"Short of sparking": *Ibid.*, 274.
if "the CIA did not intervene": *Ibid.*, 296.
to "make good on his threat": *Ibid.*
"I kept a light in the window": Anderson, *Peace, War, and Politics*, 110.
298   breaking "the blockbuster story nationwide": Rappleye and Becker, 297.
"Locked in the darkest recesses": *Ibid.*
"There was an etiquette to be followed" . . . "solicit Trafficante's help to eliminate Castro": Anderson, *Peace, War, and Politics*, 108.
"a disastrous reversal of fortune": Mahoney, 336.
"He selected three": Anderson, *Peace, War, and Politics*, 109.
"Castro, enraged": Anderson, *Peace, War, and Politics*, 113.
299   "I am just not able": Rappleye and Becker, 300.
"I will not dignify such a story": Maheu, *Ibid.*
"Convinced that Nixon had joined": Drosnin, 418.
"siphoned like a sip of champagne": Anderson, *Peace, War, and Politics*, 218.
"Nixon waited in horror": Drosnin, 419.
a story that could "sink Nixon": *Ibid.*, 420.
great "gnashing of teeth": Authors' interview with John Ehrlichman.
"I just gave him the sermon": Bellett, 53.

300　"Kalmbach scribbling on yellow legal pads": Kohn, "The Hughes-Nixon-Lansky Connection."

"assassination "by coating his car's steering wheel": Anderson, *Peace, War, and Politics,* 230.

"circulating throughout Washington": Maheu, 215.

"odd choice to head": Barlett and Steele, 400.

Von Tobel "saw no conflict of interest": Barlett and Steele, 399. See also Gottlieb and Wiley, "The Senator and the Gamblers."

301　"Donald's escapades with Meier": Drosnin, 420.

"secret meetings with the president himself": *Ibid.,* 421.

"railed on and on about his 'stupid brother' ": *Ibid.*

"a 230,000 word transcript": Barlett and Steele, 467.

302　"The fallout from the Irving caper": Drosnin, 431.

"I'll kiss your ass 130 times" "Hughes isn't in any shape": Phelan, 4.

"It was . . . utter nonsense": Maheu, 245.

"Hughes-Nixon Ties Described in the Book": Drosnin, 425.

"a ruthless little bastard": *Ibid.*

"former filling-station attendant": Barlett and Steele, 451.

303　"steel plate was ripped off": Kohn, "The Hughes-Nixon-Lansky Connection."

"drawing a line from an aborted operation": Bellett, 132.

"Almost from the beginning": *Newsweek,* October 22, 1973.

304　"would definitely violate antitrust": Barlett and Steele, 449.

"I want something clearly": *Ibid., 450.*

"Mitchell and Danner closeted together": Kohn, "The Hughes-Nixon-Lansky Connection."

"We see no problem": Barlett and Steele, 450.

"It did not take long": *Ibid.*

the first real Hughes "insider": Authors' interview with Terry Leuzner.

"a list of dozens of politicians": Bellett, 130.

"Laxalt's beautifully reconstructed turn-of-the-century": Interview of Paul Laxalt by Watergate investigators Jim Moore and Bob Muse on December 19, 1973. Memorandum dated January 2, 1974, from Moore to Watergate Prosecutor, 1974.

305　"cash was a common means": *Ibid.*

"with a categorical statement": *Ibid.*

"paying his respects": *Ibid.*

"possible connection between the deliveries": 1974 Senate Watergate Hearings.

"solid political connections" . . . "uncanny ability to manipulate": Barlett and Steele, 459.

"sort of the mystery man": *Ibid.,* 514. See also Drosnin, 416–18.

306　"Bennett charted a course": Kohn, "The Hughes-Nixon-Lansky Connection."

"Bennett was feeding stories": Barlett and Steele, 513.

"One Hughes executive after another was questioned": Barlett and Steele, 515.

"A lot of people are worried": Bellett, 132.

"the whole Bay of Pigs thing": Rappleye and Becker, 306.

"this entire affair may be connected": *Ibid.*

"triggered a spate of memos": Scott, *Crime and Cover-up,* 26.

307　"document existed showing Nixon": Rappleye and Becker, 307.

307   "the explosive secret Nixon feared": *Ibid.*, 306.
     "so convoluted you really had to be": *Ibid.*, 307.
     "previously unimaginable levels of corruption": Olmsted, 49.
     "the son of Watergate": *Ibid.*, quoting Hersh in the NYT.
     "produced a dramatic response": *Ibid.*
     a "blue-ribbon panel formed": Rappleye and Becker, 308.
     "Ford knew that if everything": Maheu, 127.
     "labeled internally as the 'family jewels' ": *Ibid.*
308   "examine the systemic problems": Olmsted, 111.
     "a steady supply of stunning": Rappleye and Becker, 308.
     "After learning that Hoover's": Olmsted, 49.
     "It took this investigation": *Ibid.*, 111.
     "With CIA assassinations": *Ibid.*, 49.
     "a top official at the CIA": Maheu, 127.
     "were the boys killed during the botched": Maheu, 130.
309   "In the Mafia's argot of death": Rappleye and Becker, 310.
     "superlobbyist who drew a $300,000 salary": Baker, 169.
     "a direct leak to Jack Anderson": Author's interview with Bobby Baker.
     "LBJ's dependent tribe": Scott, *Deep Politics*, 223.
     "finest smoking robe and his silk pajamas": Rappleye and Becker, 310.
     "staff of the Church Committee": *Ibid.*
310   "in my business, we don't take notes": *Ibid.*, 313.
     "He only told them": Confidential interview.
     "an ambassador without portfolio": Rappleye and Becker, 317.
     "The secret agencies clearly emerged": Olmsted, 49.
311   "for the first time since childhood": Rappleye and Becker, 319.
     "at least then Johnny": *Ibid.*, 323.
     "Like Giancana, another message": Confidential interview.
     "Never before had the murder": Rappleye and Becker, 322.
     "In southern Florida, beginning":
313   "war of the godfathers": Roemer.
     "The old order changed": SUN columnist Paul Price.
     "hawked papers and ran with a gang": Sheehan, 162.
     "aided by lucrative": Barlett and Steele, 317.
     "Perry Como of the crap table": *Ibid.*
314   "one of the most successful land speculations": *Forbes,*
     "father of the Las Vegas megaresort": K. J. Evans, in RJ, "First 100," Part 3.
     "Intensely private" "balls of steel": Sheehan, 159.
     "Miami hotel men tied to Lansky": Confidential interview.
     Kerkorian "was a stand-up guy": Confidential interview.
     "Federal investigators . . . have been seeking": *Business Week,* January 20, 1973. See also DTD.
315   "When the Feds descended": *Business Week,* January 20, 1973.
     "plush Manhattan offices": *Ibid.*
     "I want an image and a name": RJ, "First 100," May 2, 1999.
     "build Valley Bank into a Southwest": *Ibid.*
     "made once rinky-dink Las Vegas": *Business Week,* January 20, 1973.
     Thomas did "more than any other one man": *Ibid.*
     "After Laxalt had become governor": Confidential interview.
     "a coveted listing": *Business Week,* January 20, 1973.
316   "whirlwind of acquisitions and investments": *Ibid.*

"Continental immediately began acquiring companies": *Ibid.*

"Thus, on paper": *Ibid.*

"The brilliant lawyer and front man": Confidential interview.

317   "with the possible exception of the late": Authors' interview with Dan Moldea.

"Weary of all the problems": Moldea, *Dark Victory*, 248.

"Waiting to buy the corporation": *Ibid.*

"a bizarre and complex series": *Ibid.*

Laxalt had "attacked the probe" . . . accompanied his "good friend": Gottlieb and Wiley, "The Senator and the Gamblers."

318   "a series of stepladder business deals": Smith, *Running Scared*, 22.

"Volatile, vindictive, charismatic": Timothy O'Brien, 45.

"a legend as carefully sculpted": Smith, *Running Scared*, 21.

"He's like a son to me": RJ, May 2, 1999.

"He had four sons": SUN, December 5, 1996.

"A kid no mother could control": Smith, *Running Scared*, 37.

"if you wanted to make money": *Ibid.*, 44.

318–19   "he flim-flammed me": *Ibid.*, 40.

319   "not enough action": Confidential interview.

"Thomas wasn't recollecting that detail": Timothy O'Brien, 47.

"an obese fast-buck artist": Smith, *Running Scared*, 47.

"orchestrating young Steve Wynn's ascent": Timothy O'Brien, 48.

"sponsorship was the equivalent": Wynn, quoted in Smith, *Running Scared*, 66.

"is to casino industry entrepreneurs": *Ibid.*, 65.

320   "Pop, I gotta get something": Smith, *Running Scared*, 66.

"likely mentor to Milken": *Ibid.*, 68.

"as a secret operative for the Haganah" "fighting against Rommel in North Africa": Stein, 44.

"What Riklis had done": Bruck, 37.

"Considered the godfather": Smith, *Running Scared*, 68.

"such licenses were so restrictive": Confidential interview.

321   "the Caesars shuffle": *Ibid.*, 73.

"assumed it would be given the right": Confidential interview.

"the world's narrowest casino": Confidential interview. See also *Sun*, April 4, 1982.

"acre of pure gold": Smith, *Running Scared*, 73.

"He was depicted as": *Ibid.*

"$18,000 a foot": *Sun*, October 26, 1972.

"Caesars bought it at an inflated price": Confidential interview.

322   "He's not an outsider": Gaming Control Board member Shannon Bybee as quoted in Smith, *Running Scared*, 84.

"With the help of the bank": Berman, 163.

"The rise and rise": See Timothy O'Brien, 47.

"Just when Laxalt was facing": Moldea in *Crime Control Digest.*

323   "They called it the battle between the titans": Author's interview with Maya Miller.

"We thought we knew politics": UNR, Laxalt notes.

"Paul was upset when he saw Nixon": *Ibid.*

"almost singlehandedly built up": *Ibid.*

"a rugged individualist": Moldea in *Crime Control Digest.*

323–4   "What may be a proper standard of morality": Laxalt testimony before the commission on the Review of the National Policy Toward Gambling, August 19, 1975.

324   "leading conservative critic": Moldea in *Crime Control Digest.*
"They both loved the outdoors": *Ibid.*
"its largest investigation since the Lindbergh Kidnapping": Robert James, 417.
"Once you're tied into the hoods"; "Poor Howard": UNR, Laxalt notes.

324–5   "put together a Teamster-financed scheme": Neff, 194–211.

325   "pension-fund kickback artist": Brill,
"They wrote policies for everything": Confidential interview.
"channeled back through the Dunes": Robert James, 235.
the "FBI's most valuable snitch": Neff, 266.
"revealed a labyrinth of powerful": *Ibid.,* 266 ff.
"it was discovered that Jackie": Robert James, 232.

327   "Our intelligence told us": Confidential interview. See also Denton, 68.
accounts of Jet Avia/Chagra episode in Colombia: *Sun,* March 1, 1979; Associated Press, February 27–28, 1979, March 7, 1979. See also Cartwright, *Dirty Dealing;* and Denton, RJ, June 22, 1977, August 7, 1977, August 17, 1977, August 25, 1977, September 14, 1978, October 5, 1978.
"physician to the stars": RJ, August 17, 1990.

328   "the number one high-roller": *Las Vegan,* June 1986.

329   "Chris spent hours talking": Confidential interview.

15. One Last Cruise

Though common knowledge in Las Vegas, much of the inside history of the city in the 1980s made its way into the local press only in bits and pieces, and in even lesser fragments into the national media. But the later Laxalt career and especially his libel suit against the *Sacramento Bee* were widely reported throughout the country, and often along with it the city's feud with Yablonsky, and the impeachment of U.S. judge Harry Claiborne. Again, Dan Moldea's work in *Dark Victory* was seminal. O'Dessky's small memoir was colorful and useful. *Las Vegas City Magazine* did revealing portrayals of Ned Day. Dorman's "The Mob Wades Ashore in Atlantic City" was similarly important, as was Johnston's *Temples of Chance* and O'Brien's *Bad Bet.*

331   "the black hole, a dumping ground": Authors' interview with Joe Yablonsky.
"They had a dossier": Confidential interview.

332   "the crossroads of organized crime": Robert I. Friedman, "Senator Paul Laxalt," *Mother Jones,* August–September 1984.
"Hoover's truculent anti-Semitism": *Ibid.*
"well tuned-in to Vegas": Author's interview.
"the ruddy All-American-Boy-Next-Door types": *Ibid.*
"the traits and tastes of the culture": *Ibid.*

333   "I think he saw them as symbols": Confidential interview.
"He landed right in the middle": *Ibid.*
"Everyone was there": Friedman, "Senator Paul Laxalt."
"I guess you don't mind who": *Ibid.*

334   the "man of many faces": RJ, April 27, 1980.
"Just imagine if taxes were collected": RJ, September 3, 1981.
"It was like a cancer patient": Confidential interview.
"Without the compromise" "So long as Las Vegas's": RJ, May 22, 1981.

335   "Las Vegas . . . a strong contributor to the coffers": *Ibid.*
"I was in a subculture": Authors' interview with Joe Yablonsky.

336   "Mr. Clean": *Valley Times,* April 5, 1983.
"Until the late nineteen-seventies, there had been a hiatus": See Michael Defeo, quoted in Nick Pileggi's *Casino,* 257.
"The streets were filled with unmarked vans": Ned Day interview with *60 Minutes,* August 27, 1984.
"turning on the Washington juice": Confidential interview.

337   "My boy . . . I put him there": Friedman, "Senator Paul Laxalt."
"Nothing less than a Laxalt lovefest": Moldea in *Crime Control Digest.*
"For a Nevada politician": Condon in *Washington Dossier.*
"A friend of mine": Moldea in *Crime Control Digest.*
"obscene even by Nevada standards": *Ibid.*
"The only people who really cared": *Ibid.*

338   "If you're beholden": *Denver Post Magazine,* April 1, 1984.
Nancy Reagan nicknaming Bush "Whiney": Kelley, *Nancy Reagan,* 506.
"my two favorite fellas": *Denver Post Magazine,* April 1, 1984.
"ties with the Reagan administration": Moldea in *Crime Control Digest* and *Dark Victory.*

338–9   "minimizing the role of the Justice Strike Force": *Ibid.*

339   "trampling on people's private rights": Confidential interview.
found Greenspun's claims "preposterous": Friedman, "Senator Paul Laxalt."
"besieged by calls about Joe Yablonsky": Confidential interview.
"They really want your head": Friedman, "Senator Paul Laxalt."
"A pattern was established": Authors' interview with Joe Yablonsky.

340   "I guess none of us knew": Confidential interview.
"It was astonishing": Authors' interview with Joe Yablonsky.
"Laxalt began to emerge": *Ibid.*
"an enemy of the *Sun*": *Ibid.*
"The FBI chief came to Las Vegas": *Ibid.*

341   "Greenspun always wanted a piece": *Ibid.*
"The Jews treated me worse": *Ibid.*
a "rogue's gallery": *Ibid.*
"Joe and his agents": Confidential interview.
"Will the lynch mob get Joe Yablonsky?": Ned Day in RJ, December 15, 1982.

342   "Las Vegas is the greatest news town": *Las Vegan City Magazine,* October 1981.
"sleazy pool halls" . . . "learned all the cons": *Ibid.*
"bounced from a loading dock": *Ibid.*
"a pool hall to the four-hundredth power": *Ibid.*
"singularly vicious, months-long campaign": Ned Day in RJ, December 15, 1982.
"Why is there no journalistic outrage?" *Ibid.*

343   "Moe started believing he really was": Confidential interview.
"After promising to do what he could": Friedman.

345   "Dorfman could have put away": Confidential interview.
"No one proved conclusively": Authors' interview with Joe Yablonsky.
"wouldn't end up another statistic": *Ibid.* See also Pileggi. Moldea, *Dark Victory.*
"A newsman's newsman": Authors' interview with Liz Wilson Vlaming.

346   "Ned was becoming a real danger": Confidential interview.

346   "If something happened to me" "I'm like a mosquito": *Las Vegan City Magazine*, October 1981.

"In an eerie twist": RJ, September 4, 1987.

"I know Agosto": Authors' interview with A. D. Hopkins.

347   "one last cruise": *Las Vegan City Magazine*, October 1987, tribute to Ned Day from friend and colleague George Knapp.

"questionable investigative motivations": LAT, May 19, 1988.

348   "would be an injustice to Israel": Ken Cummins in *City Paper*, October 5, 1984.

she knew "damn well" that the Teamsters . . . "every hood in the nation": For accounts about the death of Katherine Laxalt, and Laxalt's dropping of the libel suit against the *Sacramento Bee*, see *San Francisco Examiner*, June 5, 1987; WSJ, June 3, 1987; WSJ, June 5, 1987; and *San Francisco Chronicle*, July 1, 1987. For Laxalt's own account of the settlement, see his memoir, *Nevada's Paul Laxalt*, in which he blames the death of his "beloved" former sister-in-law on the "bastards" who worked for the *Sacramento Bee*, 366–67.

349   "Look to the son of the high mountains": Moldea, *Dark Victory*, 349.

"No place on earth": Laxalt, Paul, 391.

350   "slow motion *coup d'état*": See Morris, *Partners in Power: The Clintons and Their America*, 251.

"the largest transfer of wealth": *Ibid.*, 254.

350-1 "America traveled from the New Patriotism": Cited in *ibid.*

351   "involved in instances of criminal wrongdoing": Moldea, *Dark Victory*, 333, drawing on a report from the House Subcommittee on Civil Service.

"I've always believed": Quoted by Moldea in *Dark Victory*, 330.

"I want to be a team": *Ibid.*, 321.

"appearance of impropriety": *Ibid.*, 348.

352   "leaving important issues": *Ibid.*

a "dark victory": The title of Dan Moldea's book.

"Hello, Meyer": O'Dessky, 158.

353   "Resorts is originally his": O'Brien, 69. See also Dorman, "The Mob Wades Ashore in Atlantic City," and O'Dessky, 159.

"Well-acquainted with Resorts president Jack Davis" . . . "like alcoholics": Smith, *Running Scared*, 111.

"suddenly one in four Americans": Johnston, 22; see also pp. 9–22.

"set the East Coast ablaze": Smith, *Running Scared*, 115.

354   "the biggest Wall Street criminal": *Ibid.*, 192.

"Milken was the new sugardaddy": Timothy O'Brien, 86.

"twentieth century phenomenon" . . . "wizard of Wall Street": Sun, May 19, 1989.

356   "During the Reagan years": Johnston, 20.

357   "No books, no nuthin'": O'Dessky, 158.

"I have nothing on my conscience": Eisenberg, 324.

16. "A Joint's a Joint"

The Grit Beneath The Glitter, a remarkable collection of essays on the contemporary city gathered by University of Nevada at Las Vegas historian Hal Rothman and his coeditor Mike Davis, was generously supplied to us by Professor Rothman in manuscript prior to its publication by the University of California at Berkeley, and was indispensable in capturing Las Vegas at the close of the century. Though Professor Rothman and others of his contributors may disagree with some of our interpretation of the city's past and present, scholars and journalists should gratefully welcome their contribution. Similarly, David Littlejohn's *The Real Las Vegas*, the perspectives of a team of young journalists from the University of California at Berkeley, and in many ways a rival view to Rothman's, was also quite valuable in composing the seeming chaos of the end-of-the-century city. Day to day journalism about the city and its worldwide imperial industry has always been a mixed affair, and never more so than in the national and local reporting of the Kerkorian takeover of Wynn's Mirage, Inc. For a perspective on that reporting beyond this book itself, see the author's article, "Las Vegas's Big Deal," in the special business journalism edition of the *Columbia Journalism Review*, November/December 2000. Connie Bruck's perceptive *New Yorker* piece on Oscar Goodman in August 1999 was a fitting way to climax more than a century of writing about Nevada, beginning with Mark Twain's reflections on stick-pinned bartenders and ending with a portrait of a mob lawyer in City Hall.

361   "A joint's a joint": Confidential interview.
       "Oh, I wouldn't know": Connie Chung's television interview with Wayne Newton, December 31, 1999, ABC News.

362   "America, Inc. buys out Murder, Inc." . . . "mainstream American business": Johnston, 9.

364   "the sacred cow that all Nevada politicians": William Fulton quoted in Littlejohn, 17.
       "The heavy hand of the industry": Littlejohn, 11.
       "The concept of pluralism": Chuck Gardner, "The Town That Bugsy Built," from *Casino II. Las Vegas in the 90s,* Nevadaindex.com
       "a record no other large U.S. county": Littlejohn, 5.
       "an unreadable chaos of non-planning": *Ibid.*, 11.
       "this remarkable community": Richardson, *Project Report.*

365   "far in excess": *Ibid.*
       "Many of the area's residents": *Ibid.*

366   A "sort of informal agreement": Moehring, in *Grit Beneath the Glitter*, 72.
       "political support from nearly every major": *Ibid.*

368   "The classic example of an organized crime": Senate Hearings on Hotel and Restaurant Employees Union.
       "I think the old Mob always figured": Confidential interview.

369   "the heartbeat of the American labor movement": *Minneapolis Star Tribune,* July 13, 1997.

370   "being downsized, split-shifted, part-timed": Miller, 17.
       "It may look like": Confidential interview.
       "You must always remember": Confidential interview.

371   "Vegas winnings": Denton and Morris, in the *New York Times*, July 9, 1996.
       "good, solid-thinking man": *Ibid.*

371-2 "I'm just one of those fence-jumpers": *Ibid.*

372   "a collapse of confidence": *Ibid.*
       "We're not U.S. Steel": *Ibid.*

373   "In the old days": *Ibid.*
       "fierce lobbying effort": *Ibid.*
       "someone well down": *Ibid.*
       "scavenger casino economy": *Ibid.*

374   the bill on the study "should be modified": *Ibid.*
       would never allow a "witch hunt": *Ibid.*

375   "so general or watered down": *Los Angeles Times*, June 18, 1999.

"the Las Vegasing of America": A. Alvarez in *The New York Review*.

"the appalling cost we pay": Michael Ventura, "The Psychology of Money," *Psychology Today*, March–April 1995.

376   "One of the things that I like": Clinton in RJ, October 2, 1999.

377   Wynn "has been operating under the aegis": Scotland Yard report as quoted in Smith, *Running Scared*, 181ff.

a "gee-whiz guy": Confidential interview.

"We live in a town with no standard": Author's interview with John L. Smith.

378   "In the old days the casinos": Confidential interview.

"This is a frontier town": Authors' interview with John L. Smith.

"hospitality industry": *New York Observer*, January 1, 2000.

"an abortion": *Ibid.*

"Does that seem right or proper to you": *Ibid.*

"We're shocked": *Ibid.*

379   "one of the most thoroughly": *New York Observer*, August 31, 1998.

"take the pulse of the company": Confidential interview.

380   "Politicians jumped at his command": *The Independent* (London), March 9, 2000.

"Las Vegans would have had to": Confidential interview.

"I am still in shock": *Sun*, March 12, 2000.

"reveling in 'delicious' choices": *Sun*, March 24, 2000.

Wynn exiting "a winner": RJ, May 30, 2000.

"hours after Kerkorian launched his offer": *Time*, March 6, 2000.

381   "a cozy agreement": *New York Observer*, April 10, 2000.

"I long ago learned": Confidential interview.

"It's awkward" . . . "the big chill": Authors' interview with John L. Smith.

"every lawyer believes it is impossible": RJ, June 15, 2000.

382   "said to have . . . dropped upwards": For details about Ken Mizuno's background, his many years as a Las Vegas high roller, his connections to Steve Wynn's Mirage and Treasure Island, and the federal criminal case against him, see LAT, March 16, 1993; *Daily Yomiuri*, September 14–16, 1991, October 8, 1991, March 1–2, 1992, May 14, 1992, June 11, 1992, June 24–25, 1992, July 2, 1992, July 4, 1992, and April 15, 1993; *San Francisco Chronicle*, June 20, 1992; *Business Week*, April 4, 1994; and RJ, February 6, 1998. For further information about the collection of gambling debts and money laundering in Asia, see news accounts about the fascinating Laura Choi case. The Mirage employee, a Korean-born American, was held in a South Korean jail for collecting $630,000 in gambling debts. RJ, September 24, 1997, August 20, 1998, July 28 and 30, 1999.

383   "It is a world unto itself": Confidential interview.

"the tip of an iceberg": Confidential interview.

383–6   Accounts of Casablanca: Authors' interviews with Bill Gately and further confidential interviews with other Customs agents and U.S. prosecutors. See also *Los Angeles Times*, May 29, 1998, *Broward Daily Business Review*, July 15 and July 31, 1998, *Financial Times* (London), May 30, 1998, *The New York Times*, June 11, 1998, July 15, 1998, March 16, 1999, June 11, 1999, *Washington Times*, March 18, 1999.

384   "We were so conservative": Authors' interview with Bill Gately.

387   "We were about to get": Confidential interview.

"The former agent" . . . "Drive Safely": Bruck, "They Love Me," *The New Yorker,* August 1999.

389   "a people of chance": Findlay's title, *People of Chance.*

Epilogue: Shadow Capital

390   "The terrible ifs accumulate": From Winston Churchill, *The World Crisis,* Vol. One, chap. XI, as quoted by Barbara Tuchman in *The Guns of August* (New York: Bantam Books, 1980), 9.

391   "This is a great town": Authors' interview with John L. Smith.

Bibliography

Books

Abt, Vicki, James F. Smith, and Eugene Martin Christiansen. *The Business of Risk: Commercial Gambling in Mainstream America*. Lawrence, Kansas: University Press of Kansas, 1985.

Adams, James Ring, and Douglas Frantz. *A Full Service Bank: How BCCI Stole Billions Around the World*. New York: Simon & Schuster, 1992.

Alexander, Shana. *The Pizza Connection: Lawyers, Money, Drugs, Mafia*. New York: Weidenfeld & Nicolson, 1988.

Alexander, Thomas G. *Mormons and Gentiles: A History of Salt Lake City*. Boulder, Colorado: Pruett Publishing, 1984.

Anderson, Jack, and Fred Blumenthal. *The Kefauver Story*. New York: Dial Press, 1956.

Anderson, Jack, with James Boyd. *Confessions of a Muckraker: The Inside Story of Life in Washington During the Truman, Eisenhower, Kennedy and Johnson Years*. New York: Random House, 1979.

Anderson, Jack, with George Clifford. *The Anderson Papers*. New York: Random House, 1973.

Anderson, Jack, with Daryl Gibson. *Peace, War, and Politics: An Eyewitness Account*. New York: Forge Books, 1999.

Anderson, Jon Lee. *Che Guevara: A Revolutionary Life*. New York: Grove Press, 1997.

Ashby, LeRoy, and Rod Gramer. *Fighting the Odds: The Life of Senator Frank Church*. Pullman, Washington: Washington State University Press, 1994.

Baker, Bobby. *Wheeling and Dealing: Confessions of a Capitol Hill Operator*. New York: W. W. Norton, 1978.

Baker, Jean. H. *The Stevensons: A Biography of an American Family*. New York: W. W. Norton, 1996.

Bancroft, Hubert Howe, and Frances Fuller Victor. *History of Nevada, 1540–1888*. Reno: University of Nevada Press, 1981 (originally published as a portion of *The Works of Hubert Howe Bancroft*, Vol. XXV, 1890).

Barlett, Donald L., and James B. Steele *Empire: The Life, Legend, and Madness of Howard Hughes*. New York and London: W. W. Norton, 1979.

Baum, Dan. *Smoke and Mirrors: The War on Drugs and the Politics of Failure*. Boston and New York: Little, Brown, 1996.

Behr, Edward. *Prohibition: Thirteen Years That Changed America*. New York: Arcade Publishing, 1996.

Bellett, Gerald. *Age of Secrets: The Conspiracy That Toppled Richard Nixon and the Hidden Death of Howard Hughes*. Ontario, Canada, and New York: Voyageur North America, 1995.

Beran, Michael Knox. *The Last Patrician: Bobby Kennedy and the End of American Aristocracy*. New York: St. Martin's Press, 1998.

Berman, Susan. *Lady Las Vegas: The Inside Story Behind America's Neon Oasis.* New York: A&E Network and TV Books, 1996.

Bertram, Eva, Kenneth Sharpe Blachman, and Peter Andreas. *Drug War Politics: The Price of Denial.* Berkeley: University of California Press, 1996.

Bigler, David L. *Forgotten Kingdom: The Mormon Theocracy in the American West, 1847–1896.* Logan, Utah: Utah State University Press, 1998.

Blakey, G. Robert, and Richard N. Billings. *Fatal Hour: The Assassination of President Kennedy by Organized Crime.* New York: Berkley Books, 1981.

Block, Alan A. *The Business of Crime: A Documentary Study of Organized Crime in the American Economy.* Boulder, Colorado: Westview Press, 1991.

———. *Masters of Paradise: Organized Crime and the Internal Revenue Service in the Bahamas.* New Brunswick, New Jersey, and London: Transaction Publishers, 1991.

———. *Perspectives on Organizing Crime: Essays in Opposition.* Boston: Kluwer Academic Publishers, 1991.

———, and William J. Chambliss. *Organizing Crime.* New York: Elsevier, 1981.

Bly, Nellie. *The Kennedy Men: Three Generations of Sex, Scandal and Secrets.* New York: Kensington Publishing Corp., 1996.

Bouza, Tony. *The Decline and Fall of the American Empire: Corruption, Decadence, and the American Dream.* New York and London: Plenum Press, 1996.

Brady, Frank. *Onassis: An Extravagant Life.* Englewood Cliffs, New Jersey: Prentice-Hall, 1977.

Brewton, Pete. *The Mafia, CIA and George Bush.* New York: SPI Books, 1992.

Brill, Steven. *The Teamsters.* New York: Simon & Schuster, 1978.

Brodie, Fawn M. *Richard Nixon: The Shaping of His Character.* Cambridge, Massachusetts: Harvard University Press, 1983.

———. *No Man Knows My History.* New York: Alfred A. Knopf, 1971.

Brooks, Juanita. *The Mountain Meadows Massacre.* Norman: University of Oklahoma Press, 1991.

Brown, Peter Harry, and Pat H. Broeske. *Howard Hughes: The Untold Story.* New York: Penguin, 1997.

Brownstein, Ronald. *The Power and the Glitter: The Hollywood-Washington Connection.* New York: Pantheon, 1990.

Bruck, Connie. *The Predators' Ball: The Inside Story of Drexel Burnham and the Rise of the Junk Bond Raiders.* New York: Simon & Schuster, 1988.

Burdick, Thomas, and Charlene Mitchell. *Blue Thunder: How the Mafia Owned and Finally Murdered Cigarette Boat King Donald Aranow.* New York: Simon & Schuster, 1990.

Burleigh, Nina. *A Very Private Woman and the Life and Unsolved Murder of Presidential Mistress Mary Meyer.* New York: Bantam Books, 1998.

Burrough, Bryan. *Vendetta: American Express and the Smearing of Edmond Safra.* New York: HarperCollins, 1992.

Cartwright, Gary. *Dirty Dealing: Drug Smuggling on the Mexican Border and the Assassination of a Federal Judge—An American Parable.* El Paso, Texas: Cinco Punto Press, 1998.

Cashman, Sean Dennis. *Prohibition: The Lie of the Land.* New York: The Free Press, 1981.

Center for Business and Economic Research. *Historical Perspective of Southern Nevada.* Las Vegas: University of Nevada, Spring 1997.

———. *Economic Outlook 1998.* Las Vegas: University of Nevada, December 1997.

Chafin, Raymond, and Topper Sherwood. *Just Good Politics: The Life of Raymond Chapin, Appalachian Boss.* Pittsburgh: University of Pittsburgh Press, 1994.

Chambliss, William J. *On the Take: From Petty Crooks to Presidents.* Bloomington and Indianapolis: Indiana University Press, 1978.

Coates, James. *In Mormon Circles: Gentiles, Jack Mormons, and Latter-Day Saints.* Reading, Massachusetts: Addison-Wesley, 1991.

Cockburn, Leslie. *Out of Control: The Story of the Reagan Administration's Secret War in Nicaragua, the Illegal Arms Pipeline, and the Contra Drug Connection.* New York: Atlantic Monthly Press, 1987.

————, and Andrew Cockburn. *Dangerous Liaison: The Inside Story of the U.S.-Israeli Covert Relationship.* New York: HarperCollins, 1991.

Cohen, Mickey. *Mickey Cohen: In My Own Words.* Englewood Cliffs, New Jersey: Prentice-Hall, 1975.

Cohn, Art. *The Joker Is Wild: The Story of Joe E. Lewis.* New York: Random House, 1955.

Collier, Peter, and David Horowitz. *The Kennedys: An American Drama.* New York: Summit Books, 1984.

Colodny, Len, and Robert Gettlin. *Silent Coup: The Removal of a President.* New York: St. Martin's Press, 1991.

Committee for a Courageous Congress. *Wake Up to Tomorrow: A Book of Facts Too Startling to Be Fiction—Too Shocking to Be Ignored.* Hartford, Connecticut: Heritage, Hall, 1961.

Conover, Ted. *White Out: Lost in Aspen.* New York: Random House, 1991.

Cook, Fred J. *The Secret Rulers: Criminal Syndicates and How They Control the U.S. Underworld.* New York: Duell, Sloan & Pearce, 1966.

————. *A Two-Dollar Bet Means Murder.* New York: Dial Press, 1961.

Corn, David. *Blond Ghost: Ted Shackley and the CIA's Crusades.* New York: Simon & Schuster, 1994.

Cressey, Donald. *Theft of the Nation: The Structure and Operations of Organized Crime in America.* New York: Harper & Row, 1969.

Dannen, Fredric. *Hit Men: Power Brokers and Fast Money Inside the Music Business.* New York: Times Books, 1990.

Davies, Richard O., ed. *The Maverick Spirit: Building the New Nevada.* Reno and Las Vegas: University of Nevada Press, 1999.

Davis, John H. *Mafia Dynasty: The Rise and Fall of the Gambino Crime Family.* New York: HarperCollins, 1993.

————. *Mafia Kingfish: Carlos Marcello and the Assassination of John F. Kennedy.* New York: McGraw-Hill, 1989.

————. *The Kennedys: Dynasty and Disaster, 1848–1984.* New York: McGraw-Hill, 1985.

Davis, Kenneth S. *The Politics of Honor: A Biography of Adlai E. Stevenson.* New York: G. P. Putnam's Sons, 1967.

De Leon, Peter. Thinking About Political Corruption. Armonk, New York, and London: M. E. Sharpe, 1993.

Demaris, Ovid. *Captive City.* New York: Lyle Stuart, 1969.

————. *The Director. An Oral Biography of J. Edgar Hoover.* New York: Harper's Magazine Press, 1975.

————. *Dirty Business: The Corporate-Political Money-Power Game.* New York: Harper's Magazine Press, 1974.

————. *The Last Mafioso: The Treacherous World of Jimmy Fratianno.* New York: Times Books, 1981.

Denton, Sally. *The Bluegrass Conspiracy: An Inside Story of Power, Greed, Drugs, and Murder.* New York: Doubleday, 1990.

Dietrich, Noah, and Bob Thomas. *Howard: The Amazing Mr. Hughes.* Greenwich, Connecticut: Fawcett, 1972.

Dombrink, John, and William N. Thompson. *The Last Resort: Success and Failure in Campaigns for Casinos.* Reno and Las Vegas: University of Nevada Press, 1990.

Donner, Frank. *Protectors of Privilege: Red Squads and Police Repression in Urban America.* Berkeley: University of California Press, 1990.

————. *The Age of Surveillance: The Aims and Methods of America's Political Intelligence System.* New York: Alfred A. Knopf, 1980.

Dorman, Michael. *Payoff: The Role of Organized Crime in American Politics.* New York: David McKay, 1972.

Dowd, Robert H. *The Enemy Is Us: How to Defeat Drug Abuse and End the War on Drugs.* Miami: The Hefty Press, 1996.

Drosnin, Michael. *Citizen Hughes.* New York: Holt, Rinehart & Winston, 1985.

Dugger, Ronnie. *The Politician: The Life and Times of Lyndon Johnson. The Drive for Power from the Frontier to Master of the Senate.* New York: W. W. Norton, 1982.

Dunar, Andrew J. *The Truman Scandals and the Politics of Morality.* Columbia: University of Missouri Press, 1984.

Early, Pete. *Super Casino: Inside the "New" Las Vegas.* New York: Bantam Books, 2000.

Edmonds, Andy. *Bugsy's Baby: The Secret Life of Mob Queen Virginia Hill.* Secaucus, New Jersey: Carol Publishing, 1993.

Edwards, Anne. *Early Reagan: The Rise to Power.* New York: William Morrow, 1987.

Edwards, Jerome. *Pat McCarran: Political Boss of Nevada.* Reno: University of Nevada Press, 1982.

Ehrenfeld, Rachel. *Evil Money: Encounters Along the Money Trail.* New York: HarperBusiness, 1992.

Eisenberg, Dennis, Uri Dan, and Eli Landau. *Lansky: Mogul to the Mob.* New York and London: Paddington Press, 1979.

Elliott, Gary E. *Senator Alan Bible and the Politics of the New West.* Reno: University of Nevada Press, 1994.

Epstein, Jay Edward. *Agency of Fear.* New York: G. P. Putnam's Sons, 1977.

Escalante, Fabian. *The Secret War: CIA Covert Operations Against Cuba 1959–62.* Melbourne, Australia: Ocean Press, 1995.

Evans, Peter. *Ari: The Life and Times of Aristotle Socrates Onassis.* New York: Summit Books, 1986.

Fabian, Ann. *Card Sharps, Dream Books, and Bucket Shops: Gambling in 19th Century America.* Ithaca, New York, and London: Cornell University Press, 1990.

Farrell, Ronald A., and Carole Case. *The Black Book and the Mob: The Untold Story of the Control of Nevada's Casinos.* Madison: University of Wisconsin Press, 1995.

Fay, Stephen, Lewis Chester, and Magnus Linklater. *Hoax: The Whole Truth About the Clifford Irving Affair.* New York: The Viking Press, 1972.

Feinberg, Barbara Silberdick. *American Political Scandals: Past and Present.* New York: Franklin Watts, 1994.

Felknor, Bruce L. *Political Mischief: Smear, Sabotage, and Reform in U.S. Elections.* New York, Westport, Connecticut, and London: Praeger, 1992.

Fielding, R. Kent. *The Unsolicited Chronicler: An Account of the Gunnison Massacre.* Brookline, MA: Paradigm Publishers, 1993.

————, with Dorothy S. Fielding. *The Tribune Reports of the Trials of John D. Lee.* Higganum, CT: Kent's Books, 2000.

Findlay, John M. *People of Chance: Gambling in American Society from Jamestown to Las Vegas.* New York and Oxford: Oxford University Press, 1986.

Fite, Gilbert C. *Richard B. Russell, Jr.: Senator from Georgia.* Chapel Hill: University of North Carolina Press, 1991.

Fleming, Dan B., Jr. *Kennedy vs. Humphrey, West Virginia, 1960: The Pivotal Battle for the Democratic Presidential Nomination.* Jefferson, North Carolina: McFarland & Company, 1992.

Fontenay, Charles. *Estes Kefauver.* Knoxville: University of Tennessee Press, 1980.

Fox, Stephen. *Blood and Power: Organized Crime in Twentieth Century America.* New York: Penguin, 1989.

Franklin, Jane. *The Cuban Revolution and U.S.* Melbourne, Australia: Talman Co., 1992.

Fraser, Nicholas, Philip Jacobson, Mark Ottaway, and Lewis Chester. *Aristotle Onassis.* Philadelphia: J. B. Lippincott, 1977.

Friedman, Allen, and Ted Schwarz. *Power and Greed: Inside the Teamsters Empire of Corruption.* New York and Toronto: Franklin Watts, 1989.

Friedman, Robert I. *The False Prophet: Rabbi Meir Kahane—From FBI Informant to Knesset Member.* London and Boston: Faber & Faber, 1990.

Frischauer, Willi. *Onassis.* London: The Bodley Head, 1968.

Garrison, Omar V. *Howard Hughes in Las Vegas.* New York: Lyle Stuart, 1970.

Gentry, Curt. *J. Edgar Hoover: The Man and the Secrets.* New York: W. W. Norton, 1991.

Gerber, Albert B. *Bashful Billionaire: The Story of Howard Hughes.* New York: Lyle Stuart, 1967.

Giancana, Antoinette. *Mafia Princess: Growing Up in Sam Giancana's Family.* New York: William Morrow, 1984.

Giancana, Sam and Chuck. *Double Cross: The Explosive Inside Story of the Mobster Who Controlled America.* New York: Warner Books, 1992.

Gilmore, Mikal. *Shot in the Heart.* New York: Doubleday, 1994.

Glass, Mary Ellen. *Nevada's Turbulent 50s: Decade of Political and Economic Change.* Reno: University of Nevada Press, 1981.

Goldberg, Robert Alan. *Barry Goldwater.* New Haven: Yale University Press, 1995.

Goldfarb, Ronald. *Perfect Villains, Imperfect Heroes: Robert F. Kennedy's War Against Organized Crime.* New York: Random House, 1995.

Goldwater, Barry M. *With No Apologies: The Personal and Political Memoirs.* New York: William Morrow, 1979.

Goodman, Robert. *The Luck Business: The Devastating Consequences and Broken Promises of America's Gambling Explosion.* New York: The Free Press, paperback, 1995.

Gorman, Joseph Bruce. *Kefauver: A Political Biography.* New York: Oxford University Press, 1971.

Gottdiener, M., Claudia C. Collins, and David R. Dickens. *Las Vegas: The Social Production of an All-American City.* Oxford: Blackwell Publishers, 1999.

Gottlieb, Robert, and Peter Wiley. *America's Saints: The Rise of Mormon Power.* New York and London: Harcourt Brace Jovanovich, 1986.

Goulden, Joseph C. *Death Merchant: The Brutal True Story of Edwin P. Wilson.* New York: Simon & Schuster, 1984.

Graham, Katharine. *Personal History.* New York: Alfred A. Knopf, 1997.

Greider, William. *One World, Ready or Not: The Manic Logic of Global Capitalism.* New York: Touchstone, 1997.

Green, Michael S., and Gary E. Elliott, eds. *Nevada: Readings and Perspectives.* Reno: Nevada Historical Society, 1997.

Greenspun, Hank, with Alex Pelle. *Where I Stand: The Record of a Reckless Man.* New York: David McKay, 1966.

Groden, Robert J. *The Search for Lee Harvey Oswald.* New York: Penguin, 1995.

Gugliotta, Guy, and Jeff Leen. *Kings of Cocaine: Inside the Medellin Cartel—An Astonish-

ing True Story of Murder, Money, and International Corruption. New York: Simon & Schuster, 1989.

Haldeman, H. R. *The Haldeman Diaries: Inside the Nixon White House.* New York: G. P. Putnam's Sons, 1994.

Hammer, Richard. *Gangland U.S.A.: The Making of the Mob.* Chicago: Playboy Press, 1975.

Hamilton, Nigel. *JFK: Reckless Youth.* New York: Random House, 1992.

Hanna, David. *Bugsy Siegel: The Man Who Invented Murder, Inc.* New York: Belmont Tower Books, 1974.

———. *Virginia Hill: Queen of the Underworld.* New York: Belmont Tower Books, 1975.

Hardeman, D. B., and Donald C. Bacon. *Rayburn: A Biography.* Austin: Texas Monthly Press, 1987.

Harrington, M. R. *Ancient Tribes of the Boulder Dam Country.* Los Angeles: Southwest Museum Leaflets, 1937.

Harris, Patricia. *Adlai: The Springfield Years.* Nashville, Tennessee: Aurora Publishers, 1975.

Hersh, Seymour M. *The Dark Side of Camelot.* Boston and London: Little, Brown, 1997.

Heymann, C. David. *RFK: A Candid Biography of Robert F. Kennedy.* New York: E. P. Dutton, 1998.

Hilty, James W. *Robert Kennedy: Brother Protector.* Philadelphia: Temple University Press, 1997.

Hinckle, Warren, and William Turner. *Deadly Secrets: The CIA-Mafia War Against Castro and the Assassination of JFK* (rev. edn. of *The Fish Is Red*, New York: Harper & Row, 1981).

Homer, Frederic D. *Guns and Garlic: Myths and Realities of Organized Crime.* West Lafayette, Indiana: Purdue University Studies, 1974.

Hougan, Jim. *Secret Agenda: Watergate, Deep Throat and the CIA.* New York: Random House, 1984.

———. *Spooks: The Haunting of America.* New York: William Morrow, 1978.

Hulse, James W. *The Silver State: Nevada's Heritage Reinterpreted.* Reno: University of Nevada Press, 1991.

Hyman, Sidney. *Challenge and Response: The First Security Corporation—The First Fifty Years, 1928–1978.* Salt Lake City: First Security Foundation, 1978.

James, Ralph C., and Estelle Dinerstein James. *Hoffa and the Teamsters: A Study of Union Power.* Princeton, New Jersey: D. Van Nostrand, 1965.

James, Robert. *The Informant Files: The FBI's Most Valuable Snitch.* Las Vegas: Electronic Media, 1992.

Jennings, Dean. *We Only Kill Each Other: The Life and Bad Times of Bugsy Siegel.* Englewood Cliffs, New Jersey: Prentice-Hall, 1967.

Johnston, David. *Temples of Chance: How America Inc. Bought Out Murder Inc. to Win Control of the Casino Business.* New York: Doubleday, 1992.

Jones, Maxine Temple. *Maxine: "Call Me Madam."* Hot Springs, Arkansas: Pioneer Press, 1987.

Jonnes, Jill. *Hep-Cats, Narcs, and Pipe Dreams: A History of America's Romance with Illegal Drugs.* New York: Scribner, 1996.

Kallina, Edmund F., Jr. *Courthouse Over White House: Chicago and the Presidential Election of 1960.* Orlando: University Presses of Florida, 1988.

Kasindorf, Jeanne. *Nye County Brothel Wars.* New York: Linden Press, 1985.

Katz, Jack. *Seduction of Crime: Moral and Sensual Attractions in Doing Evil.* New York: Basic Books, 1988.

Kaufman, Perry Bruce. "The Best City of Them All: A History of Las Vegas, 1930–1960." Unpublished dissertation, University of California, Santa Barbara, August 1974.

Keats, John. *Howard Hughes.* New York: Random House, 1966.

Kefauver, Estes, with Irene Till. *In a Few Hands: Monopoly Power in America.* New York: Pantheon, 1965.

Kelley, Kitty. *His Way: The Unauthorized Biography of Frank Sinatra.* New York: Bantam Books, 1986.

———. *Nancy Reagan: The Unauthorized Biography.* New York: Simon & Schuster, 1991.

Kelly, Robert J., Ko-Lin Chin, and Rufus Schatzberg, eds. *Handbook of Organized Crime in the United States.* Westport, Connecticut: Greenwood Press, 1994.

Kennedy, Robert F. *The Enemy Within: The McClellan Committee's Crusade Against Jimmy Hoffa and the Corrupt Labor Unions.* New York: Harper & Row, 1960.

Kennon, Patrick. *The Twilight of Democracy.* New York: Doubleday, 1995.

Kessler, Ronald. *The Richest Man in the World.* New York: Warner Books, 1986.

———. *Sins of the Father: Joseph P. Kennedy and the Dynasty He Founded.* New York: Warner Books, 1996.

King, Rufus. *Gambling and Organized Crime.* Washington, D.C.: Public Affairs Press, 1969.

Klaber, William F., and Philip H. Melanson. *Shadow Play: The Murder of Robert F. Kennedy, the Trial of Sirhan Sirhan, and the Failure of American Justice.* New York: St. Martin's Press, 1997.

Knoedelseder, William. *Stiffed: A True Story of MCA, the Music Business, and the Mafia.* New York: HarperCollins, 1993.

Koenig, George. *Beyond This Place There Be Dragons: The Routes of the Tragic Trek of the Death Valley 1849ers through Nevada, Death Valley, and on to Southern California.* Glendale, California: Arthur H. Clark Co., 1984.

Koskoff, David E. *Joseph P. Kennedy: A Life and Times.* Englewood Cliffs, New Jersey: Prentice-Hall, 1974.

Kutler, Stanley I. *The Wars of Watergate: The Last Crisis of Richard Nixon.* New York: Alfred A. Knopf, 1990.

Kwitny, Jonathan. *The Crimes of Patriots: A True Tale of Dope, Dirty Money, and the CIA.* New York: W. W. Norton, 1987.

———. *Vicious Circles: The Mafia in the Marketplace.* New York: W. W. Norton, 1979.

Kyvig, David E. *Repealing National Prohibition.* Chicago and London: University of Chicago Press, 1979.

Laake, Deborah. *Secret Ceremonies: A Mormon Woman's Intimate Diary of Marriage and Beyond.* New York: William Morrow, 1993.

Lacey, Robert. *Little Man: Meyer Lansky and the Gangster Life.* Boston: Little, Brown, 1991.

Lait, Jack, and Lee Mortimer. *Washington Confidential: The Low-Down on the Big Town.* New York: Crown, 1951.

Lasky, Victor. *It Didn't Start with Watergate.* New York: Dial Press, 1977.

Laxalt, Paul. *Nevada's Paul Laxalt: A Memoir.* Reno: Jack Bacon & Company, 2000.

Laxalt, Robert. *The Governor's Mansion.* Reno, Las Vegas, and London: University of Nevada Press, 1994.

———. *Nevada: A History.* Reno, Las Vegas, and London: University of Nevada Press, 1977.

———. *Sweet Promised Land.* Reno and Las Vegas: University of Nevada Press, 1957.

Levine, Gary. *Jack "Legs" Diamond: Anatomy of a Gangster.* Fleischmanns, New York: Purple Mountain Press, 1995.

Levine, Michael. *The Big White Lie: The Deep Cover Operation That Exposed the CIA Sabotage of the Drug War.* New York: Thunder's Mouth Press, 1993.

Levy, Shawn. *Rat Pack Confidential: Frank, Dean, Sammy, Peter, Joey, and the Last Great Showbiz Party.* New York: Doubleday, 1998.

Lewis, Oscar. *Sagebrush Casinos: The Story of Legal Gambling in Nevada.* New York: Doubleday, 1953.

Lillard, Richard Gordon. *Desert Challenge: An Interpretation of Nevada.* New York: Alfred A. Knopf, 1942.

Lilly, Doris. *Those Fabulous Greeks: Onassis, Niarchos, and Livanos.* New York: Cowles Book Co., 1969.

Lindsey, Robert. *A Gathering of Saints: A True Story of Money, Murder, and Deceit.* New York: Simon & Schuster, 1988.

Littlejohn, David, ed. *The Real Las Vegas.* New York: Oxford University Press, 2000.

Lowitt, Richard, ed. *Politics in the Postwar American West.* Norman: University of Oklahoma Press, 1995.

Lukas, J. Anthony. *Nightmare: The Underside of the Nixon Years.* New York: The Viking Press, 1973.

Maas, Peter. *The Valachi Papers.* New York: Bantam Books, 1969.

Maclean, Don. *Pictorial History of the Mafia.* New York: Pyramid Books, 1974.

Mahan, Sue, with Katherine O'Neil, eds. *Beyond the Mafia: Organized Crime in the Americas.* Thousand Oaks, California, and London: Sage Publications, 1998.

Maheu, Robert, and Richard Hack. *Next to Hughes: Behind the Power and Tragic Downfall of Howard Hughes by His Closest Advisor.* New York: HarperCollins, 1992.

Mahon, Gigi. *The Company That Bought the Boardwalk: A Reporter's Story of How Resorts International Came to Atlantic City.* New York: Random House, 1980.

Mahoney, Richard D. *Sons and Brothers: The Days of Jack and Bobby Kennedy.* New York: Arcade, 1999.

Mangold, Tom. *Cold Warrior: James Jesus Angleton, The CIA's Master Spy Hunter.* New York: Simon & Schuster, 1991.

Marshall, Jonathan. *Drug Wars: Corruption, Counterinsurgency, and Covert Operations in the Third World.* Forestville, California: Cohan & Cohen, 1991.

Martin, Ralph G. *A Hero for Our Time: An Intimate Story of the Kennedy Years.* New York: Fawcett Crest, 1983.

———. *Seeds of Destruction: Joe Kennedy and His Sons.* New York: G. P. Putnam's Sons, 1995.

McBride, Dennis. *Hard Work and Far from Home: The Civilian Conservation Corps at Lake Mead.* Boulder City, Nevada: Boulder City Images, 1995.

———. *Midnight on Arizona Street: The Secret Life of the Boulder Dam Hotel.* Boulder City, Nevada: Hoover Dam Museum, 1993.

McClellan, John L. *Crime Without Punishment.* New York: Duell, Sloan & Pearce, 1962.

McClintick, David. *Swordfish: The True Story of Ambition, Savagery, and Betrayal.* New York: Pantheon, 1993.

McCoy, Alfred W. *The Politics of Heroin: CIA Complicity in the Global Drug Trade.* New York: Lawrence Hill Books, 1991.

McCracken, Robert D. *Las Vegas: The Great American Playground.* Reno and Las Vegas: University of Nevada Press, 1996.

McDougal, Dennis. *The Last Mogul: Lew Wasserman, MCA, and the Hidden History of Hollywood.* New York: Crown, 1998.

McKeever, Porter. *Adlai Stevenson: His Life and Legacy.* New York: William Morrow, 1989.

McMillen, Jan, ed. *Gambling Cultures: Studies in History and Interpretation*. London and New York: Routledge, 1996.

Messick, Hank. *John Edgar Hoover: An Inquiry Into the Life and Times of John Edgar Hoover and His Relationship to the Continuing Partnership of Crime, Business, and Politics*. New York: David McKay, 1972.

———. *Lansky*. New York: G. P. Putnam's Sons, 1971.

———. *Of Grass and Snow: The Secret Criminal Elite*. Englewood Cliffs, New Jersey: Prentice-Hall, 1979.

Miller, Kit. *Inside the Glitter: Lives of Casino Workers*. Carson City, Nevada: Great Basin Publishing, 2000.

Miller, Nathan. *Stealing from America: A History of Corruption from Jamestown to Reagan*. New York: Paragon House.

Mills, James. *The Underground Empire: Where Crime and Governments Embrace*. Garden City, New York: Doubleday, 1986.

Moehring, Eugene. *Resort City in the Sunbelt: Las Vegas 1930–1970*. Reno: University of Nevada Press, 1989.

Mokhiber, Russell, and Robert Weissman. *Corporate Predators: The Hunt for Mega-Profits and the Attack on Democracy*. Monroe, Maine: Common Courage Press, 1999.

Moldea, Dan E. *Interference: How Organized Crime Influences Professional Football*. New York: William Morrow, 1989.

———. *Dark Victory: Ronald Reagan, MCA, and the Mob*. New York: Viking Penguin, 1986.

———. *The Hoffa Wars*. New York: Paddington Press, 1978.

Mollenhoff, Clark. *Tentacles of Power: The Story of Jimmy Hoffa*. Cleveland: World Publishing Co., 1965.

Moore, William Howard. *The Kefauver Committee and the Politics of Crime, 1950–1952*. Columbia: University of Missouri Press, 1974.

Morrison, Robert S. *High Stakes to High Risk: The Strange Story of Resorts International and the Taj Mahal*. Ashtabula, Ohio: Lake Erie Press, 1994.

Muller, Herbert J. *Adlai Stevenson: A Study in Values*. New York: Harper & Row, 1967.

Munn, Michael. *The Hollywood Connection: The True Story of Organized Crime in Hollywood*. New York: Robson Books/Parkwest, 1997.

Nash, Jay Robert. *The World Encyclopedia of Organized Crime*. New York: Da Capo, 1989.

———. *Citizen Hoover: A Critical Study of the Life and Times of J. Edgar Hoover and His FBI*. Chicago: Nelson-Hall, 1972.

Neff, James. *Mobbed Up*. New York: Atlantic Monthly Press, 1989.

Newman, John. *Oswald and the CIA*. New York: Carroll & Graf, 1995.

Nown, Graham. *The English Godfather: Born in Leeds, Raised in Wigan, Duke of the West Side*. London: Ward Lock, 1987.

Noyes, Peter. *Legacy of Doubt*. New York: Pinnacle Books, 1973.

O'Brien, Joseph. *Boss of Bosses: The FBI and Paul Castellano*. New York: Island Books, 1991.

O'Brien, Timothy L. *Bad Bet: The Inside Story of the Glamour, Glitz, and Danger of America's Gambling Industry*. New York: Random House, 1998.

O'Connor, Len. *Clout: Mayor Daley and His City*. New York: Avon, 1975.

Odessky, Dick. *Fly on the Wall: Recollections of Las Vegas' Good Old, Bad Old Days*. Las Vegas: Huntington Press Publishing, 1999.

Olmsted, Kathryn S. *Challenging the Secret Government: The Post-Watergate Investiga-*

tions of the CIA and FBI. Chapel Hill and London: University of North Carolina Press, 1996.

O'Neill, Tip, with William Novak. *Man of the House: The Life and Political Memoirs of Speaker Tip O'Neill.* New York: Random House, 1987.

Ostling, Richard N. and Joan K. *Mormon America: The Power and the Promise.* New York: HarperSanFrancisco, 2000.

Ostrander, Gilman Marston. *Nevada: The Great Rotten Borough 1859–1964.* New York: Alfred A. Knopf, 1966.

Paher, Stanley W. *Nevada: Official Bicentennial Book.* Las Vegas: Nevada Publications, 1976.

Paterson, Thomas. *Contesting Castro: The United States and the Triumph of the Cuban Revolution.* New York: Oxford University Press, 1994.

Pearl, Ralph. *Las Vegas Is My Beat.* New York: Lyle Stuart, 1973.

Pearson, Drew. *Diaries: 1949–1959,* ed. Tyler Abell. New York: Holt, Rinehart & Winston, 1974.

Petrakis, Gregory J. *The New Face of Organized Crime.* Dubuque, Iowa: Kendall/Hunt Publishing Co., 1991.

Phelan, James. *Scandals, Scamps, and Scoundrels: The Casebook of an Investigative Reporter.* New York: Random House, 1982.

Pileggi, Nick. *Casino.* New York: Simon & Schuster, 1995.

Pollak, Richard, ed. *Stop the Presses, I Want to Get Off: Inside Stories of the News Business from the Pages of MORE.* New York: Random House, 1975.

Popper, Frank. *The President's Commissions.* New York: Twentieth Century Fund, 1970.

Porrello, Rick. *The Rise and Fall of the Cleveland Mafia.* New York: Barricade Books, 1995.

Porter, Bruce. *Blow: How a Small-Town Boy Made $100 Million with the Medellín Cocaine Cartel and Lost It All.* New York: HarperCollins, 1993.

Powers, Thomas. *The Man Who Kept the Secrets: Richard Helms and the CIA.* New York: Alfred A. Knopf, 1979.

Pringle, Peter, and James Spigelman. *The Nuclear Barons.* New York: Henry Holt, 1981.

Rappleye, Charles, and Ed Becker. *All American Mafioso: The Johnny Rosselli Story.* New York: Barricade Books, 1995.

Raymond, C. Elizabeth. *George Wingfield: Owner and Operator of Nevada.* Reno: University of Nevada Press, 1992.

Reeves, Thomas C. *A Question of Character: A Life of John F. Kennedy.* New York: Free Press, 1991.

Reich, Cary. *Financier: The Biography of Andre Meyer: A Story of Money, Power, and the Reshaping of American Business.* New York: William Morrow, 1983.

Reid, Ed. *The Grim Reapers: The Anatomy of Organized Crime in America.* Chicago: Henry Regnery, 1969.

———, and Ovid Demaris. *The Green Felt Jungle.* New York: Trident Press, 1963.

Reuter, Peter. *Disorganized Crime: The Economics of the Visible Hand.* Cambridge, Massachusetts, and London: MIT Press, 1983.

Robb, Peter. *Midnight in Sicily.* New York: Vintage, 1999.

Robbins, Christopher. *Air America.* New York: Avon, 1979.

Robinson, Jeffrey. *The Laundrymen: Inside Money Laundering, the World's Third-Largest Business.* New York: Arcade, 1996.

Roemer, William F., Jr. *Man Against the Mob.* New York: Donald I. Fine, 1989.

———. *War of the Godfathers: The Bloody Confrontation Between the Chicago and New York Families for Control of Las Vegas.* New York: Donald I. Fine, 1990.

Rosenberg, Howard L. *Atomic Soldiers: American Victims of Nuclear Experiments.* Boston: Beacon Press, 1980.

Ross, Shelley. *Fall from Grace: Sex, Scandal, and Corruption in American Politics from 1702 to the Present.* New York: Ballantine, 1988.

Rothman, Hal. *Devil's Bargain: Tourism in the Twentieth Century American West.* Lawrence: University Press of Kansas, 1998.

———, ed. *Reopening the American West.* Tucson: University of Arizona Press, 1998.

Rothman, Hal K., and Mike Davis, eds. *The Grit Beneath the Glitter.* Berkeley: University of California Press, forthcoming.

Rumbarger, John J. *Profits, Power, and Prohibition: Alcohol Reform and the Industrializing of America, 1800-1930.* Albany: State University of New York Press, 1989.

Russell, Elliott R. *History of Nevada.* Lincoln and London: University of Nebraska Press, 1973.

Russo, Gus. *Live by the Sword: The Secret War Against Castro and the Death of JFK.* Baltimore: Bancroft Press, 1998.

Sadowsky, Sandy. *Wedded to Crime: My Life in the Jewish Mafia.* New York: G. P. Putnam's Sons, 1992.

Sale, Kirkpatrick. *Power Shift: The Rise of the Southern Rim and Its Challenge to the Eastern Establishment.* New York: Vintage Books, 1976.

Scheim, David. *Contract on America: The Mafia Murder of President John F. Kennedy.* New York: Shapolsky Publishers, 1988.

Schlesinger, Arthur M., Jr., ed. *Congress Investigates: A Documented History 1792–1974.* New York: Chelsea House, 1975.

Schlesinger, James. *Robert Kennedy and His Times.* Boston: Houghton Mifflin, 1978.

Schrecker, Ellen W. *No Ivory Tower: McCarthyism and the Universities.* New York and Oxford: Oxford University Press, 1986.

Scott, Peter Dale. *Crime and Cover-up: The CIA, the Mafia, and the Dallas-Watergate Connection.* Palo Alto, California: Ramparts Press, 1977.

———. *Deep Politics and the Death of JFK.* Berkeley, Los Angeles, and London: University of California Press, 1993.

———, and Jonathan Marshall. *Cocaine Politics: Drugs, Armies, and the CIA in Central America.* Berkeley and Los Angeles: University of California Press, 1991.

Severn, Bill. *The End of the Roaring Twenties: Prohibition and Repeal.* New York: Julian Messner, 1969.

Sheehan, Jack E., ed. *The Players: The Men Who Made Las Vegas.* Reno and Las Vegas: University of Nevada Press, 1997.

Sheridan, Walter. *The Fall and Rise of Jimmy Hoffa.* New York: Saturday Review Press, 1972.

Shesol, Jeff. *Mutual Contempt: Lyndon Johnson, Robert Kennedy and the Feud That Defined a Decade.* New York: W. W. Norton, 1997.

Shields, Jerry. *Daniel Ludwig: The Invisible Billionaire.* Boston: Houghton Mifflin, 1986.

Sifakis, Carl. *The Mafia Encyclopedia: From Accardo to Zwillman.* New York: Facts on File, 1987.

Sklar, Holly. *Chaos or Community: Seeking Solutions, Not Scapegoats for Bad Economics.* Boston: South End Press, 1995.

Skolnick, Jerome H. *House of Cards: The Legalization and Control of Casino Gambling.* Boston: Little, Brown, 1978.

Sloane, Arthur A. *Hoffa.* Cambridge, Massachusetts, and London: MIT Press, 1991.

Smith, John L. *No Limit: The Rise and Fall of Bob Stupak and Las Vegas' Stratosphere Tower.* Las Vegas: Huntington Press, 1997.

———. *On the Boulevard.* Las Vegas: Huntington Press Publishing, 1999.

———. *Running Scared: The Life and Treacherous Times of Las Vegas Casino King.* New York: Barricade Books, 1995.

Smith, Sam. *Mob Politics*. Washington, D.C.: Progressive Review, 1997.

Solberg, Carl. *Hubert Humphrey: A Biography*. New York: W. W. Norton, 1984.

Spada, James. *Peter Lawford: The Man Who Kept the Secrets*. New York: Bantam Books, 1991.

Steel, Ronald. *In Love with Night: The American Romance with Robert Kennedy*. New York: Simon & Schuster, 2000.

Stegner, Wallace. *Mormon Country*. New York: Duell, Sloan, & Pearce, 1942.

Stein, Benjamin J. *A License to Steal: The Untold Story of Michael Milken and the Conspiracy to Bilk the Nation*. New York: Simon & Schuster, 1992.

Sterling, Claire. *Octopus: How the Long Reach of the Sicilian Mafia Controls the Global Narcotics Trade*. New York: Simon & Schuster, 1990.

Stevens, Joseph E. *Hoover Dam: An American Adventure*. Norman: University of Oklahoma Press, 1988.

Strange, Susan. *Casino Capitalism*. Oxford: B. Blackwell, 1986.

Sullivan, William, with Bill Brown. *The Bureau*. New York: Pinnacle Books, 1982.

Summers, Anthony. *Conspiracy*. London: Fontana, 1980.

———. *Official and Confidential: The Secret Life of J. Edgar Hoover*. New York: G. P. Putnam's Sons, 1993.

Summers, Anthony, with Robbyn Swan. *The Arrogance of Power: The Secret World of Richard Nixon*. New York: Viking, 2000.

Terrell, Jack, with Ron Martz. *Disposable Patriot: Revelations of a Soldier in America's Secret Wars*. Washington, D.C.: National Press Books, 1992.

Theoharis, Athan. *J. Edgar Hoover: An Historical Antidote*. Chicago: Ivan R. Dee, 1995.

———, ed. *From the Secret Files of J. Edgar Hoover*. Chicago: Ivan R. Dee, 1991.

Thomas, Evan. *The Very Best Men. Four Who Dared: The Early Years of the CIA*. New York: Simon & Schuster, 1995.

Thomas, Gordon. *Gideon's Spies: The Secret History of the Mossad*. New York: St. Martin's Press, 1999.

Thompson, Charles C. II. *The Death of Elvis: What Really Happened*. New York: Delacorte, 1991.

Thompson, Kenneth W., ed. *Statesmen Who Were Never President*. Vol. II. New York: University Press of America, 1996.

Thomson, David. *In Nevada: The Land, the People, God, and Chance*. New York: Alfred A. Knopf, 1999.

Tinnin, David B. *Just About Everybody vs. Howard Hughes*. Garden City, New York: Doubleday, 1973.

Tronnes, Mike, ed. *Literary Las Vegas: The Best Writing About America's Most Fabulous City*. New York: Henry Holt, 1995.

Truman, Harry S. *Memoirs by Harry S. Truman*. Vol. II: *Years of Trial and Hope*. Garden City, New York: Doubleday, 1956.

Turkus, Burton B., and Sid Feder. *Murder, Inc.: The Story of the Syndicate*. London: Victor Gollancz, 1952.

Turner, Wallace. *Gamblers Money: The New Force in American Life*. Boston: Houghton Mifflin, 1965.

Udall, Stewart. *The Myths of August: A Personal Exploration of Our Tragic Cold War Affair with the Atom*. New Brunswick, New Jersey: Rutgers University Press, 1998.

Urza, Monique. *The Deep Blue Memory*. Reno, Las Vegas, and London: University of Nevada Press, 1993.

Venturi, Robert, Denise Scott Brown, and Steven Izenour. *Learning from Las Vegas*. Cambridge, Massachusetts, and London: MIT Press, 1977.

Valentine, Douglas. *The Phoenix Program: A Shattering True Account of the CIA's Bloodiest Reign of Terror—The Most Shocking Covert Operation of the Vietnam War.* New York: William Morrow, 1990.

Vlachos, Helen. *House Arrest.* Boston: Gambit Inc., 1970.

Vogel, Jennifer, ed. *Crapped Out: How Gambling Ruins the Economy and Destroys Lives.* Monroe, Maine: Common Courage Press, 1997.

Vogliotti, Gabriel R. *The Girls of Nevada: Prostitution in Nevada, from the Roadside Brothels to the Beauties of Vegas, Told Against a Background of Gambling and Glamour.* Secaucus, New Jersey: Citadel Press, 1975.

Von Hoffman, Nicholas. *Citizen Cohn.* New York: Doubleday, 1988.

Wadsworth, Ginger, and Jimmy Snyder. *Farewell Jimmy the Greek, The Wizard of Odds.* Austin, Texas: Eakin Press, 1996.

Walker, William O. III. *Drug Control in the Americas.* Albuquerque: University of New Mexico Press, 1989.

Weberman, Alan J., and Michael Canfield. *Coup d'Etat in America: The CIA and the Assassination of John F. Kennedy.* New York: The Third Press, 1975.

Weissman, Steve, ed. *Big Brother and the Holding Company: The World Behind Watergate.* Palo Alto, California: Ramparts Press, 1974.

Wendland, Michael F. *The Arizona Project: How a Team of Investigative Reporters Got Revenge on Deadline.* Kansas City: Sheed Andrews & McMeel, 1977.

White, Theodore H. *The Making of the President 1960.* New York: Atheneum, 1961.

Wills, Garry. *Reagan's America: Innocence at Home.* New York: Doubleday, 1987.

Wiley, Peter, and Robert Gottlieb. *Empires in the Sun: The Rise of the New American West.* Tucson: University of Arizona Press, 1985.

Wilkerson, W. R. III. *The Man Who Invented Las Vegas.* Beverly Hills: Ciro's Books, 2000.

Winter-Berger, Robert N. *The Washington Pay-off: An Insider's View of Corruption in Government.* Secaucus, New Jersey: Lyle Stuart, 1972.

Wise, William. *Massacre at Mountain Meadows: An American Legend and a Monumental Crime.* New York: Thomas Crowell, 1976.

Wolfe, Tom. *The Kandy-Kolored Tangerine-Flake Streamline Baby.* New York: Farrar, Straus & Giroux, 1965.

Woodiwiss, Michael. *Crime, Crusades and Corruption: Prohibitions in the United States, 1900–1987.* Totowa, New Jersey: Barnes and Noble Books, 1988.

Woolner, Ann. *Washed in Gold: The Story Behind the Biggest Money Laundering Investigation in U.S. History.* New York: Simon & Schuster, 1994.

Woon, Basil. *When It's Cocktail Time in Cuba.* New York: Horace Liveright, 1928.

Work Projects Administration Writers' Program. *The WPA Guide to 1930s Nevada.* New York: Hastings House, 1948.

Wyden, Peter. *Bay of Pigs: The Untold Story.* New York: Simon & Schuster, 1979.

Zendzian, Craig. *Who Pays? Casino Gambling, Hidden Interests, and Organized Crime.* New York: Harrow & Heston, 1993.

Zinn, Howard. *A People's History of the U.S: 1492–Present.* New York: Harper Perennial, 1995.

——— *The Zinn Reader: Writings on Disobedience and Democracy.* New York: Seven Stories Press, 1977.

Government Documents

U.S. Senate, Special Committee to Investigate Organized Crime in Interstate Commerce, *Hearings, Part 10, Nevada–California,* 81st Congress, 2nd sess., 1950.

U.S. Senate, Special Committee to Investigate Organized Crime in Interstate Commerce, *Second and Third Interim Reports,* 82nd Congress, 1st sess., 1951.

U.S. Senate, Committee on Government Operations, *Organized Crime and Illicit Traffic in Narcotics, Hearings,* 88th Congress, 2nd sess., 1964.

U.S. Senate, Committee on Government Operations, Permanent Subcommittee on Investigations, *Organized Crime: Securities, Thefts and Frauds,* 93rd Congress, 1st sess., 1973.

U.S. House of Representatives, Select Committee on Crime, *Organized Crime in Sports (Racing),* 92nd Congress, 2nd sess., 1973.

U.S. Senate, Select Committee on Presidential Campaign Activities, Executive Session Hearings, *Presidential Campaign Activities of 1972, Senate Resolution 60; Watergate and Related Activities,* 93rd Congress, 2nd sess., 1974.

U.S. Senate, Committee on Governmental Affairs, Permanent Subcommittee on Investigations, *The Robert Vesco Investigation,* 93rd Congress, 2nd sess., 1974. *Report to the President by the Commission on CIA Activities Within the United States,* June 1975.

U.S. Senate, Select Committee to Study Governmental Operations with Respect to Intelligence Activities, *Intelligence Activities, Senate Resolution 21,* 94th Congress, 1st sess., 1976.

U.S. Senate, Committee on Government Operations, Permanent Subcommittee on Investigations, *Federal Drug Enforcement,* 94th Congress, 2nd sess., 1976.

U.S. Senate, Select Committee to Study Governmental Operations with Respect to Intelligence Activities, Final Report, *The Investigation of the Assassination of President John F. Kennedy: Performance of the Intelligence Agencies, Book V,* 94th Congress, 2nd sess., 1976.

U.S. Senate, Committee on Governmental Affairs, Permanent Subcommittee on Investigations, *Illegal Narcotics Profits,* 96th Congress, 1st sess., 1980.

U.S. Senate, Committee on Governmental Affairs, Permanent Subcommittee on Investigations, *Hotel Employees and Restaurant Employees International Union,* 98th Congress, 1st sess., 1983.

U.S. Senate, Joint Hearing, Subcommittee on Security and Terrorism, Subcommittee on Western Hemisphere Affairs, and Senate Drug Enforcement Caucus, *The Cuban Government's Involvement in Facilitating International Drug Traffic,* 98th Congress, 1st sess., 1983.

U.S. Senate, Committee on Governmental Affairs, Permanent Subcommittee on Investigations, *Organized Crime: 25 Years After Valachi,* 100th Congress, 2nd sess., 1988.

Select Newspapers and Periodicals

Albanese, Jay S. "What Lockheed and La Cosa Nostra Have in Common: The Effect of Ideology on Criminal Justice Policy." *Crime and Delinquency,* April 1982.

Alexander, Tom. "What Del Webb Is Up To in Nevada." *Fortune,* May 1965.

Alvarez, A. "Learning from Las Vegas." *New York Review,* January 11, 1996.

Arrington, Leonard J. "The Mormons in Nevada." *Las Vegas Sun* series, 1979.

Bastone, William. "The Last Jewish Gangster." *Village Voice,* April 23, 1996.

Beebe, Lucius. "Las Vegas." *Holiday,* December 1952.

Bergman, Lowell, and Jeff Gerth. "La Costa: The Hundred-Million-Dollar Resort with Criminal Clientele." *Penthouse,* March 1975.

Betsky, Aaron. "Wizardry of Odds: Decoding the New Las Vegas Style." *Los Angeles Times Magazine,* December 12, 1993.

Bruck, Connie. "They Love Me." *The New Yorker,* August 1999.

Cartwright, Gary. "Benny and the Boys." *Texas Monthly,* October 1991.

Clark, Neil M. "The Brash Banker of Arizona." *Saturday Evening Post,* April 10, 1954.

"Come and Get It." *Newsweek,* February 20, 1956.

Condon, George, Jr. "The Power Gamble: Paul Laxalt and the Nevada Gang." *Washington Dossier,* September 1983.

Cook, Fred J. "Gambling, Inc." *The Nation,* October 1960.

Cook, James, and Jane Carmichael. "Casino Gambling: Changing Character or Changing Fronts." *Forbes,* October 27, 1980.

Dalton, Joseph. "The Legend of Hank Greenspun." *Harper's,* June 1982.

Danforth, Richard C. "The Cult of Mormonism: The Religion That Runs Utah." *Harper's,* May 1980.

Danto, Arthur C. "Degas in Vegas." *The Nation,* March 1, 1999.

Davis, Mike. "House of Cards. Las Vegas: Too Many People in the Wrong Place, Celebrating Waste as a Way of Life." *Sierra,* November–December 1995.

"Desert Hotel." *Architectural Forum,* 85:5 (1945).

Denton, Sally, and Roger Morris. "Easy Money in Vegas." *The New York Times,* July 9, 1996.

Donovan, Richard, and Douglass Cater. "Of Gamblers, a Senator, and a *SUN* That Wouldn't Set." *The Reporter,* June 9, 1953.

Dorman, Michael. "The Mob Wades Ashore in Atlantic City." *New York* magazine, January 30, 1978.

Eadington, William R. "The Evolution of Corporate Gambling in Nevada." *Nevada Review of Business and Economics,* 6:1 (1982).

Fairfield, William S. "Las Vegas: The Sucker and the Almost Even Break." *The Reporter,* June 9, 1953.

French, William F. "Don't Say Las Vegas Is Short of Suckers." *Saturday Evening Post,* November 5, 1955.

Friedman, Robert I. "Senator Paul Laxalt, the Man Who Runs the Reagan Campaign." *Mother Jones,* August–September 1984.

———, and Dan Moldea. "Networks Knuckle Under to Laxalt: The Story That Never Aired." *Village Voice,* March 5, 1985.

Gabriel, Tripp. "From Vice to Nice." *New York Times Magazine,* December 1, 1991.

"Gambling Town Pushes Its Luck." *Life* magazine, June 20, 1955.

Gottlieb, Bob, and Peter Wiley. "Just Don't Touch the Dice: The Las Vegas/Utah Connection." *Utah Holiday.* September 1980.

———. "The Senator and the Gamblers." *The Nation,* July 24–31, 1982.

Gottschalk, Simon. "Ethnographic Fragments in Postmodern Spaces." *Journal of Contemporary Ethnography,* July 1995.

Green, Michael S. "The Las Vegas Newspaper War of the 1950s." *Nevada Historical Society Quarterly,* Fall 1988.

———. "Where He Stood: Hank Greenspun and the Making of Modern Nevada." Unpublished MS; later published in Richard O. Davies's *Maverick Spirit,* pp. 75–95.

———. "Understanding Nevada Today: The Southward Shift." *Halcyon,* 1994.

———. "Politics, the Press, and the 1978 Election: The Valley Times and the Governor." Unpublished MS.

Gunther, John. "Inside Las Vegas." 1959.

Halevy, Julian. "Disneyland and Las Vegas." *The Nation,* June 7, 1958.

Hayden-Guest, Anthony. "The Young and the Riklis." *New York* magazine, January 2, 1982.

Hill, Gladwin. "Atomic Boom Town in the Desert." *New York Times Magazine,* February 11, 1951.

———. "Las Vegas Is More than the 'Strip.' " *New York Times Magazine,* March 16, 1958.

Hiltzik, Michael A. "A Borrowed Empire." *Los Angeles Times Magazine,* August 17, 1986.

Hochman, Sandra. "Alice in Vegas." *Holiday,* May 1966.

Hopkins, A. D. *et al.* "The First One Hundred. Parts I, II, III." February 7, May 2, and September 12, 1999. *Las Vegas Review-Journal.*

"In Memoriam, Samuel L. Kurland." *Southern California Law Review,* vol. 49, 1976.

"It Makes Money." *Newsweek,* November 28, 1964.

Knebel, Fletcher. "It Wins, It Worries, It Weeps." *Look,* December 27, 1966.

Kohn, Howard. "The Hughes-Nixon-Lansky Connection: Secret Alliances of the CIA from World War II to Watergate." *Rolling Stone,* May 20, 1976.

Labich, Kenneth. "Gambling's Kings." *Fortune,* July 22, 1996.

Lang, Daniel. "Blackjack and Flashes." *The New Yorker,* March 20, 1952.

"Las Vegas: Nice People Live on Divorce, Gambling." *Newsweek,* April 20, 1953.

"Las Vegas: Sin and Sun Pay Off." *Business Week,* June 17, 1950.

"Las Vegas Strikes It Rich." *Life* magazine, May 26, 1947.

"Las Vegas's Industrial Hope." *Business Week,* October 25, 1947.

Liebling, A. J. "Action in the Desert." *The New Yorker,* May 13, 1950.

———. "Out Among the Lamisters." *The New Yorker,* March 27, 1954.

———. "Dressed in Dynamite." *The New Yorker,* January 12, 1963.

Loehwing, David A. "Future Blue Chips? Some Smart Money Is Betting Heavily on Las Vegas." *Barron's,* September 16, 1968.

McDonald, John. "Dig Marriner Eccles's Company. It Digs." *Fortune,* January 1961.

McInnes, Neil. "The Other Las Vegas." *Barron's,* August 1, 1966.

Mechling, Tom. "I Battled McCarran's Machine." *The Reporter,* June 9, 1953.

Millstein, Gilbert. "Mr. Coward Dissects Las Vegas." *New York Times Magazine,* June 26, 1955.

Moldea, Dan E. "Nevada's Senior Senator: Little Attention Has Been Focused on His 'Connections.' " *Crime Control Digest,* May 28, June 4, and June 11, 1984.

Mulkey, Tyrus R., Jr. "Howard R. Hughes, Jr. and His Influence on the Transition from Gambling to Gaming." *University of Nevada, Las Vegas,* December 6, 1994.

Mulligan, John E., and Dean Starkman. "An F.O.B. and the Mob." *Washington Monthly,* May 1996.

O'Brien, Meredith. "Place Your Bets: The Gambling Industry and the 1996 Presidential Elections." *Center for Public Integrity,* 1996.

O'Faolain, Sean. "Las Vegas." *Holiday,* September 1956.

"Organized Crime in Washington: If We Don't Have a Godfather, Then What Do We Have?" *Washingtonian,* April 1976.

Picker, Ida. "Raising the Stakes for the Great Gambling Crapshoot." *Institutional Investor,* November 1993.

"Pleasure Palaces" ("After Hours" unsigned column). *Harper's,* February 1955.

Reed, Steven R. "The High Stakes Life of Benny Binion." *Houston Chronicle,* March 13, 14, and 15, 1989.

Renshaw, W. C. "1000 Feet Up and 25 Miles Away." *The American City,* June 1956.

"Resort Hotel for Postwar Travelers," *Architectural Record,* 96:2 (1944).

Richard, Joseph. "Las Vegas Is the Place Where the Action Is Not Governed by the Clock." *Esquire,* October 1962.

Richardson, Philip. "Project Report: Effects of Legalized Gambling on Community Stability in the Las Vegas Area." March 18, 1974, a paper prepared for the Task Force on Legalized Gambling sponsored by the Fund for the City of New York and the Twentieth Century Fund.

Roberts, Steven V. "Reagan's First Friend." *New York Times Magazine,* March 21, 1982.

Sauer, R. P. "The City of Bright Futures." *The American City,* December 1960.

———. "Street Cleaning in a 24-Hour-A-Day City." *The American City,* July 1961.

Shawhan, Casey, and James Bassett. "Las Vegas Lowdown." *Los Angeles Times Magazine,* July 26, 1953.

"Showgirl Shangri-La." *Life* magazine, June 21, 1954.

Skolnick, Jerome H., and John Dombrink. "The Limits of Gaming Control." *Connecticut Law Review,* Summer 1980.

Smith, James F. "The Premium-Grind: Atlantic City Casino Hybrid." *Nevada Review of Business and Economics,* 6:1 (1982).

———. "Ben Siegel: Father of Las Vegas and the Modern Casino-Hotel." *Journal of Popular Culture,* Spring 1992.

Smith, Sam. "Mob Politics." *Progressive Review,* 1997.

Smith, Sandy. "The Mob." *Life* magazine, September 1 and 8, 1967.

Stamos, George, Jr. "The Great Resorts of Las Vegas—How They Began." *Las Vegas Sun Magazine,* April 1, 8, and 22, 1979.

Stein, M. L. "Shootout in the Desert." *Editor & Publisher,* April 19, 1986.

Steuer, Arthur. "Playground for Adults Only." *Esquire,* August 1961.

Taney, Thomas E. "Reactions from Nevada." *The Reporter,* July 7, 1953.

"The Desert Song." *Newsweek,* August 24, 1953.

"The Heat on Mr. Las Vegas." *Business Week,* January 20, 1973.

"The Mob: Hard Hit But 'Still a Force.' " *U.S. News & World Report,* March 25, 1996.

"The Players." *Saturday Evening Post,* May 26, 1956.

Thompson, William N. "Gambling as a Growth Industry in Tourism: A Nevada Perspective." *American Travel Writers' Editors Council,* March 1992.

"Trouble in Paradise." *The Economist,* October 15, 1966.

Underwood, John, and Morton Sharnik. "Look What Louie Wrought." *Sports Illustrated,* May 29, 1972.

"Unseen Saviour of Vegas." *The Economist,* September 21, 1968.

"Vacation in Las Vegas." *Ebony,* June 1965.

Velie, Lester. "Las Vegas: The Underworld's Secret Jackpot." *Reader's Digest,* October 1959.

Ventura, Michael. "The Psychology of Money." *Psychology Today,* March–April 1995.

———. "Soul in the Raw." *Psychology Today,* May–June 1997.

Waas, Murray. "Paul Laxalt's Debt to the Mafia." *The Rebel,* January 30 and February 6, 1984.

———. "The Senator and the Mob." *City Paper* (Washington, D.C.), May 25–31, 1984.

Weaver, John D. "A Lightning Guide to Las Vegas." *Holiday,* July 1961.

Whearley, Bob. "The Truth About Las Vegas." *Denver Post* series, August 1963.

"Wherever You Look There's Danger in Las Vegas." *Life* magazine, November 12, 1951.

Wolfe, Thomas K. "Las Vegas!!!!" *Esquire,* February 1964.

Wyden, Peter. "How Wicked Is Vegas?" *Saturday Evening Post,* November 11, 1961.

University of Nevada Oral History Program

Adams, Eva B. *Windows of Washington: Nevada Education, the U.S. Senate, the U.S. Mint.*

Anderson, Frederick M. *Surgeon, Regent, and Dabbler in Politics.*

Bible, Alan. *Recollections of a Nevada Native Son: The Law, Politics, the Nevada Attorney General's Office, and the United States Senate.*

Biltz, Norman H. *Memoirs of the "Duke of Nevada": Developments of Lake Tahoe, California, and Nevada; Reminiscences of Nevada Political and Financial Life.*

Boyd, Sam.

Cahill, Robbins. *Recollections of Work in State Politics, Government, Taxation, Gaming Control, Clark County Administration, and the Nevada Resort Association.*

Cahlan, John F. *Reminiscences of a Reno and Las Vegas, Nevada, Newspaperman, University Regent, and Public-Spirited Citizen.*

———. *Fifty Years In Journalism and Community Development: An Oral History.*

Dixon, Mead. *Playing the Cards That Are Dealt: Mead Dixon, the Law, and Casino Gambling.*

Douglas, Jack. *Tap Dancing on Ice.*

Kofoed, Leslie S.

McCloskey, John R. *Seventy Years of Griping: Newspapers, Politics, Government.*

McDonald, Joseph F. *The Life of a Newsboy in Nevada.*

Merialdo, Peter B. *Memoirs of a Son of Italian Immigrants, Recorder and Auditor of Eureka County, Nevada State Controller, and Republican Party Worker.*

Miller, Thomas Woodnutt. *A Public-Spirited Citizen of Delaware and Nevada.*

Moore, William J.

Nelson, Warren. *Always Bet on the Butcher.*

Olsen, Edward A. *My Careers as a Journalist in Oregon, Idaho, and Nevada; in Nevada Gaming Control; and at the University of Nevada.*

Ray, Clarence. *Black Politics and Gaming in Las Vegas, 1920s–1980s.*

Russell, Charles H. *Reminiscences of a Nevada Congressman, Governor, and Legislator.*

Sampson, Gordon A. *Memoirs of a Canadian Army Officer and Business Analyst.*

Sanford, John. *Printer's Ink in My Blood.*

Sawyer, Grant, ed. Gary Elliott. *Hang Tough. Grant Sawyer: An Activist in the Governor's Mansion.*

Shamberger, Hugh A. *Memoirs of a Nevada Engineer and Conservationist.*

Slattery, James M. *Recollections of a Nevada Politician and Sportsman.*

Smith, Art. *Let's Get Going.*

Wilson, Thomas Cave. *Reminiscences of a Nevada Advertising Man, 1930–1980, or Half a Century of Very Hot Air, or I Wouldn't Believe It If I Hadn't Been There.*

Wilson, Woodrow. *Race, Community and Politics in Las Vegas, 1940s–1980s.*

FBI Files Obtained Through Freedom of Information Act

Binion, Benny

Coulthard, William G.

Giancana, Sam

Greenspun, Herman Milton

Hoover, J. Edgar (Official and Confidential Files)

Hughes, Howard Robard

Kennedy, John F.

Kennedy, Joseph P.

Kennedy, Robert F.

Onassis, Aristotle

Rosselli, Johnny

Sawyer, Frank Grant

Seigel, Benjamin ("Bugsy")

Sinatra, Frank

Zwillman, Abner ("Longy")

Acknowledgments

This book owes a seminal debt to our publisher at Alfred Knopf, Sonny Mehta, and our editor, Jonathan Segal, both of whom shared from the beginning our often lonely conviction that this was a story worth telling, however grim some of the implications. Jonathan Segal has been everything his distinguished reputation promised—intellectually challenging, stylistically demanding, ever faithful to the integrity of the substance and process. Also at Knopf, Ida Giragossian was ever thoughtful in helping to shepherd the manuscript and photographs to publication; Melvin Rosenthal was wonderfully sensitive to every nuance in checking the text; and Amelia Zalcman managed to be both brilliant and cheerful in her own demanding contribution. And in addition to Gloria Loomis's incomparable support and inspiration Katherine Fausett at the Watkins-Loomis Literary Agency was always a champion of the authors and the book.

Of the literally hundreds of people in Las Vegas and elsewhere who helped us so significantly through five years of research, interviews, and writing, there are several who deserve particular thanks: Bobby Baker for his invaluable candor about his own connections and others in Las Vegas, Texas, and Washington; Ed Becker for giving us his matchless insight and experience; the late John Ehrlichman, who contributed his singular insider's knowledge and bold questioning about the maelstrom of Watergate, Howard Hughes, Richard Nixon, and so much more; Professor Michael Green for his painstaking and encyclopedic scholarship in treating this book from the beginning as if it were his own; our much-admired friend Jim Hougan, whose characteristic, selfless sharing of knowledge and sources added so much to his own earlier books that are standards in the field; Dan Moldea, who generously lent us archives from his own courageous and groundbreaking work on the Teamsters, Laxalt, Reagan, and organized crime; Gus Russo, who steered us toward important documents and sources in the story of the Kennedys' covert war against Cuba; Professor Peter Dale Scott, who not only gave us important guidance at crucial points, but whose historic book, *Deep Politics,* has revolutionized the writing of recent American history for us and others; John L. Smith for the brilliance of so many responses, the valor of so much journalism, the inspiration of his example; George Knapp for his unflinching reminiscences of his best friend, Ned Day; and finally, Joe Yablonsky, for his indomitable honesty about the city that touched and scarred him so deeply. Like Yablonsky, former U.S. Customs agents William Gately and William Hengler were singularly helpful in unraveling the complicated Casablanca and Mizuno cases in which their individual bravery and integrity were so conspicuous.

This book would not have been possible without the extraordinary financial support of private foundations devoted to new perspectives on the American past. At pivotal and sometimes desperate moments, we were fortunate to have the aid of the Schumann Foundation under the leadership of Bill and John Moyers, and with the assistance of Sam Hitt of the Forest Guardians; the Lannan Foundation led by Patrick Lannan; and the Fund for Constitutional Government directed by Conrad Martin, with special assistance in the case of our project from fellow writers Sam Smith and Christopher Hitchens.

Archivists, librarians, owners of private collections, and government officials from Nevada to Washington sustained us again and again with sometimes obscure documents and facts, including Mason Alinger of the House Subcommittee on Criminal Justice, Drug Policy, and Resources; Bruce Alverson in lending his personal collection of Nevada oral histories; Bob Coffin and his incomparable store of rare books and documents; Ruthe Deskin and Brian Greenspun, for graciously opening the Greenspun archives at the *Sun;* Christopher G. Driggs of the Nevada State Library and Archives; the Gambler's Bookshop in Las Vegas for its unique resources and assistance; Susan Jarvis and Kathy War at the University of Nevada, Las Vegas Library, for so many courtesies, large and small; Eric Moody, the chief of the Nevada Historical Society, for both his aid and fine scholarship, and his archivist John Gomes; Padmini Pai and her assistant Pamela Busse at the *Review-Journal* library; and Frank Wright of the Las Vegas Historical Museum.

In addition we should also acknowledge with appreciation the contributions of: Glen Arnodo, Mahlon Brown, the late Joe Catelli, Frank Cremen, John Squire Drendel, George Foley, Doug Frazier, Dorothy Gallagher, Billy Gallinaro, A. D. Hopkins, David Johnston, W. Scott Malone, Phil Manuel, Jonathan Marshall, Darryl Martin, Bob McDonald, Bryan McKay, Kit Miller, Jim Mintz, Tom Mitchell, Mike O'Callaghan, Nick Pileggi, Karen Rogers, Professor Hal K. Rothman, Jack Sheehan, Chet Smith, Bob Stoldal, E. Parry Thomas, Charlie Thompson, Al Tobin, Harriet Trudell, Dale Van Atta, Gary Webb, Mike Ybarro, and Charles Zobel.

Of all those who have given of themselves to this book, however, no group is more important than the literally dozens of sources in Las Vegas, throughout Nevada, and elsewhere in the nation, who agreed to speak with us only under a pledge of anonymity. With this acknowledgment we thank you all for your trust and the often startling truths you told, even at your own expense.

Several friends have extended warm personal help in everything from child-sitting to lodging and transportation, and in many cases thoughtful listening and exchanges on subjects they sometimes found, no doubt, depressing if not bizarre. For all that we are deeply grateful to Janeal Arison and Herbie Mann; Shaune Bazner and her husband, Peter Miller; Kathy Bond; Rosvita Botkin; Maxine Champion; Jeff Della Penna; Mark and Alice Denton, along with Leslie, Marianne, Jacqueline, and Patrick; Scott and Ruth Denton, along with Sara, Jeff, and Kris; Felice Gonzales and Gene Gallegos; Muffy Griel and David Vhay; Hank and Erika Holzer; Ethan Morris; Ellen Reiben; Karl Seitz; Sam and Luke Van Orden; and the inimitable colleagues of Santa Fe "Speakeasy," coconspirators all.

Among the many sources for this book, real and potential, there is one that requires special note. Sally Denton's father, Ralph L. Denton, was one of "McCarran's Boys," and has practiced law in Las Vegas for over half a century, during which he was one of Grant Sawyer's closest personal friends and political associates, himself twice a candidate for the U.S. Congress, and represented a number of prominent clients, including Hank Greenspun, Mike McClaney, and others whose names may appear in this book. Similarly, Sally's mother, Sara Denton, worked for many years as an administrative assistant to U.S. senator Howard Cannon. The authors would have liked nothing more than the confidences that might have flowed from those relationships. But attorney-client privilege, personal loyalties, and other restraints of principle precluded either of them from being sources for this book in any respect, and they bear no responsibility for its content. The nagging necessity to get so many good stories elsewhere, rather than simply calling home, made a daughter's sense of independent accomplishment all the more rewarding.

Finally, there are three unsung heroes of this book—our sons Carson, seven, Grant, nine, and Ralph, thirteen—who constantly inquired about our progress, wearied of our incessant discussions of ancient conspiracies over dinner, worried about our relative poverty and the enemies we must be making, and most of all wanted to get on the computers for their own adventures. Gentlemen, the Strip is yours.

Sally Denton and Roger Morris
April 17, 2000

Index